3580
p. 10/98

# Fodor's Portugal

KU-176-016

PRAISE FOR FODOR'S GUIDES

*"Fodor's guides . . . are an admirable blend of the
cultural and the practical."*
—The Washington Post

*"Researched by people chosen because they live or have
lived in the country, well-written, and with good
historical sections . . . Obligatory reading for millions
of tourists."*
—The Independent, *London*

*"Usable, sophisticated restaurant coverage, with an
emphasis on good value."*
—Andy Birsh, Gourmet *restaurant columnist,
quoted by Gannett News Service*

*"Packed with dependable information."*
—Atlanta Journal Constitution

*"Fodor's always delivers high quality . . . thoughtfully
presented . . . thorough."*
—Houston Post

*"Valuable because of their comprehensiveness."*
—Minneapolis Star-Tribune

Fodor's Travel Publications, Inc.
New York • Toronto • London • Sydney • Auckland

Second Edition

ISBN 0–679–02829–3

"Family Affairs" is excerpted from *The Portuguese*, by Marion Kaplan, © Marion Kaplan 1991. Reproduced by permission of Penguin Books, Ltd.

## Fodor's Portugal

**Editor:** Conrad Little Paulus
**Contributors:** Robert Blake, Jules Brown, Echo Garrett, Dennis Jaffe, Laura Kidder, Deborah Luhrman, Bevin McLaughlin, Mary Ellen Schultz, Nancy van Itallie
**Creative Director:** Fabrizio La Rocca
**Cartographer:** David Lindroth
**Illustrator:** Karl Tanner
**Cover Photograph:** Bob Krist

Design: Vignelli Associates

## Special Sales

# Contents

**Maps**

# Foreword

While every care has been taken to ensure the accuracy of the information in this guide, the passage of time will always bring change, and consequently, the publisher cannot accept responsibility for errors that may occur.

All prices and opening times quoted here are based on information supplied to us at press time. Hours and admission fees may change, however, and the prudent traveler will avoid inconvenience by calling ahead.

Fodor's wants to hear about your travel experiences, both pleasant and unpleasant. When a hotel or restaurant fails to live up to its billing, let us know and we will investigate the complaint and revise our entries where the facts warrant it.

Send your letters to the editors of Fodor's Travel Publications, 201 E. 50th Street, New York, NY 10022.

Special thanks to Jorge Felner da Costa and María João Ramires with the Portuguese National Tourist Office in New York; Gloria Melo at TAP Air Portugal; António Alonso at Marketing Ahead; Pilar Pereira at the Portuguese Trade and Tourism Office in London; Candida Gonzalez in Sintra; Manuel Duarte Fernandes of Hotel Lisboa Plaza, Lisbon; John Pare; and the ubiquitous Captain I. Little; and Dr. Pinto de Silva in Covilhã.

# Highlights
# and
# Fodor's Choice

# Highlights

Portugal is a rapidly changing country. Since its entry into the European Community (EC), in 1986, it's seen a deluge of high-rise office buildings and apartment complexes, twisting super-highways where men with oxcarts used to dominate brick-paved lanes, and an influx of scantily clad sunbathers who frolic with their blaring boom boxes along once-secluded stretches of beach.

However, this is not to suggest that Portugal has become one huge shopping mall surrounded by asphalt. The Portuguese are proud and respectful of its history, and they understand the necessity of preserving the past. A walk through almost any town or village here reveals Portugal's tradition: *Fado* (traditional Portuguese music, with a soulful blues sound) drifts into the alleys from neighborhood cafés, and smells of fresh grilled sardines permeate the air.

The Portuguese Office of Tourism has earmarked considerable amounts of money to promote its country around the world. Hence, tourism has increased tenfold between 1976 and 1993 to 20 million visitors from 2 million. This is good and bad news for the overseas traveler. No longer is Portugal the inexpensive destination it once was, both because of its increasing popularity and because the dollar has been weak throughout Europe. On the up side, however, Portuguese tourist offices inside and outside the country have become genuinely enthusiastic and are well stocked with literature, itineraries, and maps.

The exhibits, concerts, and cultural events celebrating the **"Discoveries,"** are continuing all over the country, though at a lower level than during the anniversary year, and visitors in 1995 can expect to reap the full benefit of Lisbon's being 1994 European City of Culture. After a face-lift, some of the country's best-loved monuments—including the **Torre de Belém** in Lisbon—should be looking as good as new. Also by 1995 several of the capital's museums will have reopened after lengthy closures for restoration. Look out particularly for the **Museu Etnografico** and the **Museu Escola de Artes Decorativas.**

No one can say, however, that Portugal lives in the past: With an eye toward the future, Lisbon, as the site of **EXPO '98** (the last EXPO of the century) will host multimillion-dollar exhibits that are expected to attract at least 9 million visitors over a three-month period. The theme of EXPO '98 will be "The Oceans, A Legacy for the Future," which will spotlight the key role the seas have played in world history and their vital importance in the coming century.

Hotel construction and renovations continue apace, especially in the capital. A rolling program of refurbishment is now complete at the smart **Lisboa Plaza,** while the same family owners are responsible also for the relaunch of one of the capital's most intimate lodgings. The former annex of **York House,** next to the Museu de Arte Antiga, has reopened as **As Janelas Verdes,** an 18th-century mansion turned comfortable, historic inn.

Work also continues on improving Portugal's roads and upgrading Lisbon's transportation systems. For visitors, the principal effect of this is some unsightly (and noisy) construction work on main avenues and streets. If your hotel room overlooks such a road, request a room on a higher floor or at the back. The major road overhaul will continue for some time.

Portugal recently celebrated the 50th anniversary of the opening of its first *pousada,* the government-run inns, mostly in rural areas, whose name means "resting place." Presently there are 37 of these small, elegant hostelries in converted castles, convents, and national monuments throughout the country, and a visit to at least one should be on every itinerary.

The important thing to remember when visiting Portugal is that no matter how much time you have to explore, the country is both small enough to cover a lot of territory in a few days and large enough to hold out the promise of more to discover the next time.

# Fodor's Choice

No two people will agree on what makes a perfect vacation, but it can be fun and helpful to know what others think. We hope you'll have a chance to experience some of Fodor's choices yourself while visiting Portugal. For detailed information of individual entries, see the relevant sections of this guidebook.

## Castles and Palaces

Castelo de Bragança (Bragança)

Castelo de São Felipe (Setúbal)

Castelo de São Jorge (Lisbon)

Fortaleza de Sagres (Sagres)

Palácio dos Biscainhos (Braga)

Palácio Nacional de Pena (Sintra)

Palácio Nacional de Queluz (Queluz)

## Towns and Villages

Arraiolas

Batalha

Câmara de Lobos (Madeira)

Cascais

Coimbra

Évora

Funchal (Madeira)

Guimarães

Lisbon

Loulé

Óbidos

Oporto

Sagres

Santana (Madeira)

Setúbal

Silves

Sintra

Viana do Castelo

Vila do Conde

## Churches and Monasteries

Basilica de Santa Luzia (Viana do Castelo)

Convento de São Gonçalo (Amarante)

Convento do Carmo (Lisbon)

Igreja de Sao Domingos (Guimarães)

Igreja do Carmo (Faro)

Mosteiro de Alcobaça (Alcobaça)

Mosteiro de Batalha (Batalha)

Mosteiro de Mafra (Mafra)

Mosteiro dos Jerónimos (Lisbon)

Sé (Lisbon)

Sé Velha (Coimbra)

Sinagoga de Tomar (Tomar)

Templo de Diana (Évora)

## Museums

Museu Calouste Gulbenkian (Lisbon)

Museu de Arte Antiga (Lisbon)

Museu de Grão Vasco (Viseu)

Museu de Machado de Castro (Coimbra)

Museu de Rafael Bordalo Pinheiro (Caldas da Rainha)

Museu do Convento de Jesus (Aveiro)

Museu Municipal de Viana (Viana do Castelo)

Ruinas de Conímbriga (Conímbriga)

## Squares and Parks

Jardim de Monserrate (Seteais)

Jardim do Antigo Paço Episcopal (Castelo Branco)

Parque Nacional de Peneda-Gerês (Braga)

Parque Nacional de Serra de Aire e Candeeiros (between Lisbon/Coimbra)

Praça da República (Viana do Castelo)

Praça do Comércio (Lisbon)

Praça de Dom Dûarte (Viseu)

Praça do Geraldo (Évora)

Rossío (Lisbon)

Serra d'Arrábida (near Setúbal)

## Hotels

Buçaco Palace, Buçaco (*$$$$*)

Hotel Palácio, Estoril (*$$$$*)

Hotel Ritz, Lisbon (*$$$$*)

Pousada dos Lóios, Évora (*$$$$*)

Reids, Funchal (*$$$$*)

Hotel Dom Luís, Coimbra (*$$$*)

Pousada da Ria, Aveiro (*$$$*)

Pousada de Santa Marinha, Guimarães (*$$$*)

Pousada de São Felipe, Setúbal (*$$$*)

Pousada de São Pedro, Tomar (*$$$*)

Quinta do Bela Vista, Funchal (*$$$*) Quinta das Sequóias, Sintra (*$$–$$$*)

Albergaria Senhora do Monte, Lisbon (*$$*)

Arcada, Aveiro (*$$*)

Grande Hotel do Porto, Oporto (*$$*)

Hotel Grão Vasco, Viseu (*$$*)

Hotel Praia, Nazaré (*$$*)

Casa de Lumena, Faro (*$*)

Hotel Flamingo, Lisbon (*$*)

## Restaurants

Aviz, Lisbon (*$$$$*)

Tavares Rico, Lisbon (*$$$$*)

Buçaco Palace, Buçaco (*$$$–$$$$*)

Cidade Velha, Faro (*$$$*)

A Ruina, Albufeira *$$–$$$*

A Veranda da Sé, Viseu (*$$–$$$*)

O Alambique, Viana do Castelo (*$$*)

Pedro dos Letões, Curia (*$$*)

Rio Azul, Setúbal (*$$*)

Bom Jardim, Lisbon (*$*)

O Peleiro, Figueira da Foz (*$*)

# Regional Borders of Portugal

0       50 miles

0       50 km

N

*Minho*

Valença

**MINHO**

Viana
do Castelo

*Lima*

Barcelos

N101

Serra do Gerês   N103

Bragança

Chaves

Póvoa de Varzim

Braga

Guimarães

*Tâmega*

Mirandela

**TRAS-OS-MONTES**

N15

Vila do Conde

**DOURO**

Amarante

Vila Real

*Douro*

*Sabor*

Mogadouro

Oporto

Penafiel

*Duoro*

Espinho

*Douro*

Oliveira
dos Azeméis

Lamego

Moimenta
da Beira

**ATLANTIC
OCEAN**

Albergaria-a-Velha

S. Pedro
do Sul

*Vouga*

Viseu

**UPPER
BEIRA**

Aveiro

Pinhel

Mealhada

Sta. Comba
Dão

Mira

Cantanhede

*Mondego*

Guarda

**COASTAL BEIRA**

Coimbra

*Serra da Estrêla*

Figueira
da Foz

E1/A1

Arganil

Covilhã

Fundão

N109

*Zêzere*

Pombal

N110

Serra da
Gardunha

Penamacor

**ESTREMADURA**

Leiria

N233

**LOWER
BEIRA**

Batalha

Ourém

Proença-
a-Nova

Nazaré

*Sra.
da Aire*

Tomar

Castelo
Branco

Alcobaça
Caldas
da Rainha

Fátima

Abrantes

Nisa

*Tagus*

Óbidos

N118

Aveiras de Cima

Torres
Novas

Torres Vedras

Santarém

Ponte
de Sor

Portalegre

**S P A I N**

Mafra

*Tejo*

**RIBATEJO**

Sintra

Vila Franca
de Xira

**U P P E R**

N8

*Sorraia*

Avis

**A L E N T E J O**

Cascais
Estoril

★ Lisbon

*Tejo*

Arraiolos

Estremoz

Elvas

A2

Montemor-
o-Novo

Sra. de Ossa

Seixal

Vila
Viçosa

*Guadiana*

Setúbal

*Cabo
Espichel*

*Sado*

Évora

Reguengos

**ESTREMADURA**

Alcácer
do Sal

N2

Ferreira do
Alentejo

Vilaverde
de Ficalho

Sines

Santiago
do Cacem

Beja

Moura

*Cabo de
Sines*

E1

**L O W E R**

Serpa

**A L E N T E J O**

N123

Odemira

Ourique

Castro
Verde

*Chança*

Mértola

*Guadiana*

N120

*Mira*

Monchique

Almodovar

**A L G A R V E**

Vila do Bispo

Portimão

N125

Albufeira

S. Brás

Lagos

*Cabo de
S. Vicente*

Faro

Tavira

Vila Real de
S. António

Olhão

# Europe

**Reykjavik**
ICELAND

NORWAY
**Bergen**○

SCOTLAND
○**Edinburgh**

*North Sea*

Skagerra

NORTHERN IRELAND

✪**Belfast**

IRELAND    *Irish Sea*

✪**Dublin**

U N I T E D
K I N G D O M

WALES

DENMARK

**Hamburg**
○

ENGLAND    NETHERLANDS

**Cardiff**✪

**London**✪    **The Hague**○    ✪**Amsterdam**

○**Rotterdam**

G E R M

*ATLANTIC OCEAN*

*English Channel*

**Brussels**✪    **Bonn**
○

BELGIUM

**Frankfurt**○

**Paris**✪

LUXEMBOURG

F R A N C E    **Zürich**○

**Muni**

**Bern**✪

SWITZERLAND

**Lyon**○

LIECHTENSTEI

**Milan** ○    **Ven**

PORTUGAL    ANDORRA

**Monte**
**Marseille**○    **Nice**○**Carlo**

MONACO

✪ **Madrid**    **Florence**○

✪**Lisbon**    **Barcelona**○    *Corsica*

S P A I N

**Seville**○    ○**Granada**    *Sardinia*

*Balearic Islands*    *Tyrrhenia*

○**Gibraltar**    *Mediterranean Sea*

MOROCCO    ALGERIA

0 ————————— 400 miles

0 ————————— 600 km

TUNISIA

# World Time Zones

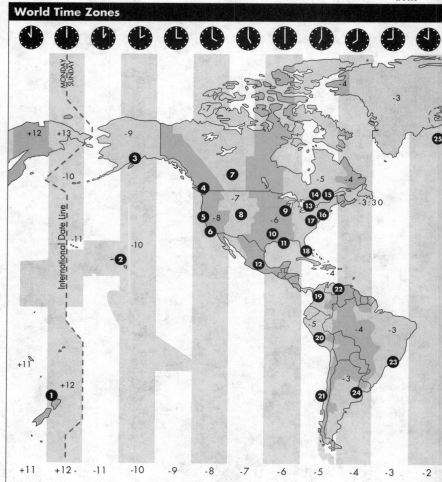

Numbers below vertical bands relate each zone to Greenwich Mean Time (0 hrs.).
Local times frequently differ from these general indications,
as indicated by light-face numbers on map.

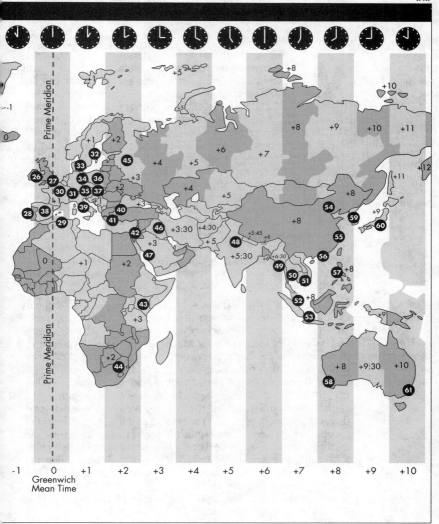

| Mecca, **47** | Ottawa, **14** | San Francisco, **5** | Toronto, **13** |
|---|---|---|---|
| Mexico City, **12** | Paris, **30** | Santiago, **21** | Vancouver, **4** |
| Miami, **18** | Perth, **58** | Seoul, **59** | Vienna, **35** |
| Montréal, **15** | Reykjavík, **25** | Shanghai, **55** | Warsaw, **36** |
| Moscow, **45** | Rio de Janeiro, **23** | Singapore, **52** | Washington, D.C., **17** |
| Nairobi, **43** | Rome, **39** | Stockholm, **32** | Yangon, **49** |
| New Orleans, **11** | Saigon (Ho Chi Minh City), **51** | Sydney, **61** | Zürich, **31** |
| New York City, **16** | | Tokyo, **60** | |

# Introduction

By Jules
Brown

Jules Brown,
who was
born in
Africa,
hasn't
stopped
traveling
since. An
editor and
freelance
writer based
in London,
he has
covered the
world, from
the Utah
desert and
England's
Lake District
to Hong
Kong by way
of the
Bahamas.

**W**est across the Iberian peninsula from Spain's arid plains and burning sun, Portugal springs on the unwary traveler perhaps Europe's greatest surprise. Its landscape unfolds in astonishing variety to reveal a mountainous, green interior and a sweeping coastline. Portugal provides many things you might expect if you're familiar with Spain, including fine food and wine, spectacularly sited castles, medieval hilltop villages, and excellent beaches. But the similarities are far outweighed by the myriad differences, by the country's delightful distinctions. Portugal seems to revel in its often contrary identity. Despite its proximity, the language is a world apart from Spanish; and though, like Spain, Portugal has a Mediterranean air, it is firmly Atlantic-facing. Even the people seem undecided as to their origins, looking markedly Celtic in the north and rather Moorish in the south. But most important for the visitor, Portugal sees far less tourism than Spain, and it's still possible to travel into the heart of the provinces and be among few, if any visitors.

High economic growth (in excess of that of most of its European partners) and heavy foreign investment have benefited large sectors of the population. Many people are employed in the tourism industry, which now accounts for about 10% of the country's gross national product. Accordingly, the resort areas and cities are now anything but undiscovered: The Algarve coast, for example, is one of Europe's most visited regions. Lisbon, too, has rapidly acquired the trappings of a forward-looking commercial capital. Many of its turn-of-the-century buildings are being replaced by skyscrapers, and renovation and modernization have touched every part of the capital. Much of the architecture and culture that once made Portugal unique now stand side by side with contemporary styles and lifestyles, an all-too-familiar development in late-20th-century Europe. Away from Lisbon and the busy Algarve, however, there are still country villages, isolated beaches, crumbling historic towns, and hidden valleys that have barely changed over the past few hundred years.

**Geography** The major surprise for most visitors to Portugal is its topography: It's a far greener land than Spain, with a riot of flowers, trees, and shrubs that provide color and shade throughout the country. There's also an enormous variety of landscapes in this relatively small European nation. A long rectangle slightly larger than the state of Indiana, it's just 560 kilometers (350 miles) from north to south and 220 kilometers (138 miles) at its widest east–west point. It's bordered on the north and east by Spain and on the south and west by the Atlantic Ocean, and is temperate year-round, especially along the coasts. Portugal rarely suffers the extreme heat of other southern European countries.

The mountainous northeast provides the greatest contrast for travelers who have just left the central plains of Spain. This seldom-visited region with the Shangri-la name of Trás-os-Montes (Beyond the Mountains) is an unspoiled area of rugged beauty, with tumbling rivers, expansive forests, hilltop castles, and sparsely populated villages. Extremes of temperature dictate custom and the local economy: the northern part of region often has long, harsh, winters, but June, July, and August are dry and hot, turning the land tawny. In the milder, more fertile, southern part lie the vineyards of the Upper Douro valley. Grapes from this area contribute to the country's most famous export, port wine. The vineyards, like all the land of Trás-os-Montes, depend upon the Rio Douro (River Douro), whose tributaries (the Tamega, Corgo, and Tua) lace the area.

To the west, beyond Vila Real, lies the region known as the Minho. Touching the Atlantic and stretching from the northern border south to Oporto (the country's second largest city), the Minho displays a gentler character. It contains the lush hinterland of the Rio Minho, the Lima, and the Douro. In this mass of predominantly green landscape are the Costa Verde (Green Coast), the beautiful pine-tree- lined coast north of Oporto, and the inland hills and valleys where the slightly sparkling *vinho verde* (green wine) is produced. Winters are mild here, with plenty of rain, and the Minho is heavily cultivated. Summers are short and temperate—a climate akin to that of Galicia, in northwest Spain, which the Minho resembles at several points.

Moving southeast, the central Beira region contains Portugal's highest mountains, the Serra da Estrela (Estrela Mountains), which reach a height of 1,991 meters (6,530 feet) and offer the country's best hiking and skiing. In the Beira Alta (Upper Beira)—between Viseu, Guarda, and Covilha—the winter frost is fierce, and the wind whistles through a string of hill towns that, while little known to foreigners, are at the heart of Portugal's history. As in the very north of the country, there's a distinct geographical and climatic shift as you move west toward the coast, leaving the mountains behind for the fertile expanses of the Beira Litoral (Coastal Beira) plain. It's a temperate, low-lying country, threatened by flooding from the mountains, though at Aveiro in the north of the region the water has been tamed by an extensive network of canals and drainage channels. The coast itself, the pine-forested Costa da Prata, is one of the finest sandy stretches in the country, and inland from its main resort of Figuera da Foz, the famous university town of Coimbra stands on the banks of the Rio Mondego.

The mountains finally peter out on the southern edge of the Beira. The provinces of the Estremadura and the Ribatejo extend south and west to Lisbon, following a line drawn by the wide valley of the Rio Tejo (River Tagus). The populous Estremadura's rolling hills and glorious coastline contain some of the country's most famous towns and monuments. Summers are long, hot, and bright, particularly in the seaside resorts, which stretch south as far as the Estoril Coast, west of Lisbon. There's a unique microclimate at work here, which ensures that the winters are milder than in the capital; in summer, the resorts of

Estoril and Cascais enjoy a permanent breeze that offsets the high temperatures that plague Lisbon itself. Out of the capital, and across the Rio Tejo, you're soon in the Ribatejo (literally translated as the "banks-of-the- River Tagus"), famous as a bull-breeding district, whose mainly flat lands fade into the vast plains of the southern Alentejo region.

Once known as the granary of Portugal, the Alentejo is a thinly populated, largely agricultural region of grain fields, cork, and olive trees, and is as remote in its way as Trás-os-Montes, though with none of the compensating grandeur. That said, there are some impressive Atlantic beaches (whipped year-round by a strong wind), and a pretty eastern section, where the Rio Guadiana forms the frontier with Spain. In the Alentejo summer starts early (March), and there's little shade from the sun. There's also very little rainfall, except perhaps in early spring and autumn.

Dividing the Alentejo from Portugal's southernmost coastal province, the Algarve is a continuous range of mountains—the Serra de Monchique (Monchique Mountains) and the Serra de Caldeirão (Caldeirão Mountains). The Algarve boasts some 3,000 hours of sunshine annually, and its low-lying plains, rocky coastline (in the west), sand-bar islands (in the east), and sweeping beaches comprise Portugal's busiest tourist region. In August, when the sun is hottest, this is probably the Portuguese province where the midday heat is most unbearable, though it's easy to cool off in a pool or in the sea. The Algarve is also the only real year-round destination in Portugal, despite the general clemency of the climate elsewhere. The region feels semi- tropical: Coastal winter days are warm and bright, the wildflowers strung across the low hills start to bloom early in February, and temperatures stay high until late October.

Off the coast of Morocco 900 kilometers (560 miles) southwest of Lisbon lies subtropical Madeira and a tiny group of mostly uninhabited islets. These islands, autonomous possessions of Portugal, have an equable subtropical climate tempered by the Gulf Stream, with warm summers and mild winters, a healthy wine industry, and great numbers of British residents and visitors. Also belonging to Portugal, lying 1,220 kilometers (760 miles) west of Lisbon, nearly halfway to New York, are the volcanic islands of the Azores (not covered in this book), whose remoteness and relative poverty keep them somewhat unvisited despite their temperate weather year-round.

A result of Portugal's varied geography and climate has been that the country has become a fascinating target for nature lovers. Many regions have been turned into nature reserves, which are excellent places to see the country's flora and fauna. The oldest reserve is Peneda-Gerês, in the extreme north of the country, reaching up to the Spanish border, where wild boar and horses roam the mountains. Lesser northern reserves are those of Alvão, near Vila Real, and the Serra da Malcata on the Spanish frontier, east of the peaks of the Serra da Estrela. Interesting wildlife areas farther south include the mountainous regions around Sintra, near Lisbon, and the Serra da Arrábida (Arrábida Mountains), near Setúbal, while water-based reserves include the estuary of the Rio Sado, south of Lisbon, and the Algarve coast, from Faro east to Vila Real de Santo Antónío. This last region is a stopover for waders and seabirds on their migration south.

**History** Blessed with this salubrious climate and abundant game and fish, this part of the Iberian peninsula once supported a flourishing prehistoric population. Few traces of the culture remain, however, save the ancient sculpted stone boar fertility symbols found in Trás-os-Montes, and the huge Colossus of Pedralva, a mysterious seated figure in granite, on display in the Museu Martins Sarmento in Guimarães. The later arrival of the Celtic peoples in northern Portugal (700 BC–600 BC) is recorded in a series of *citânias* (fortified hill settlements), which appear throughout the Minho; the most impressive example is at Briteiros, between Braga and Guimarães. Phoenicians traded at the site of present-day Lisbon, and the Carthaginians and Greeks set up trading posts on Portugal's southern shore, but it wasn't until the Roman annexation of the peninsula after the Second Punic War (218–202 BC) that the region came under any kind of unified control. There was resistance to the Roman advance, particularly in central Portugal, where the heroic chieftain Viriatus of the Lusitani tribe held the legions at bay for several decades, until his eventual defeat in 139 BC. Despite the subsequent colonization of much of the country, little of the Roman period survives in modern Portugal. Roads, aqueducts, and elegant bridges (like those at Chaves and Ponte de Lima) were built, and cities founded, though the only substantial remains are at Évora, where there's a fine temple from the 2nd century, and at the preserved Roman town of Conimbriga, near Coimbra. A less obvious Roman relic is the system of vast agricultural estates—*latifundia*—established in the Alentejo. Here the Romans introduced to Portugal new crops that have become mainstays of the domestic economy: wheat, barley, olives, and grapes.

The Moorish invasion of the Iberian peninsula in 711 had a lasting effect on the country, particularly in the south, where place names and peoples' features still reflect those times. The Moors established a capital at Silves in the Algarve (derived from the Moorish, *al-Gharb*, meaning "west of the land beyond"); allowed freedom of worship; planted great orchards on irrigated land; and spread a Moorish-Arab culture of great significance. Arab rule stood firm until the 12th century, when Christian forces under Dom (King) Afonso Henriques moved south from their stronghold at Guimarães in the Minho to take successive Moorish towns and castles at Leiria, Santarém, and Sintra. The ramparts and battlements of these fortresses are all visible today, a reminder of both the Moorish genius for siting defenses and of the Christian effort involved in overcoming them. The most significant victory was at Lisbon in 1147, with the storming of the Moorish fortress on the site of the present–day Castelo de São Jorge. A Burgundian by descent, Afonso Henriques was by now being called the first king of all Portugal, and he ordered the building of Lisbon's proud Sé (Cathedral) in celebration of the victory. Many other churches in Portugal mark the path of the reconquest (as the Moors were pushed south), particularly the numerous Romanesque chapels that cover the landscape between the Rio Minho and Rio Douro.

Southern Alentejo and the Algarve remained in Arab hands until the mid-13th century, by which time the fledgling kingdom of Portugal extended to its current borders. The country reached its final shape in 1260 when Afonso III—who re-took Faro and the western Algarve from the Moors—moved the capital from Coimbra to Lisbon.

The early kings of Portugal, from the dynastic House of Burgundy, moved quickly to establish their independent country. Recognition was gained from the neighboring Castilian rulers, although fortresses were built along the Spanish frontier as a precaution. Those at Beja and Estremoz are evocative examples. A *Cortes* (parliament) was assembled, and a university founded, initially in Lisbon in 1290 but transferred to Coimbra in 1308. The grand university buildings that you see there today date from the 16th century, when the scholastic foundation was declared permanent, but the evident sense of pride in the city goes back to the university's origins; it remained the only university in Portugal until this century. The transitional Gothic style of building was superseded by a more typically Portuguese style, and some handsome cloisters in particular survive from this period, at Guimarães, Coimbra, Lisbon, and Évora.

The House of Burgundy was succeeded by the House of Aviz, whose first king, Dom João I, roundly defeated the Castilian army at the Battle of Aljubarrota (1385) to end any lingering Castilian thoughts of dominion over Portugal. It was a significant victory that secured the independence of Portugal for nearly two centuries, and allowed Portuguese kings to turn their attention to the maritime ventures that were to guarantee them fabulous colonial wealth. João I marked the victory by building the extraordinarily beautiful abbey of Santa Maria da Vitoria at Batalha in Estremadura, not far from the battlefield. It's one of the finest expressions of Portuguese nationalism. Triumphant in tone, the abbey celebrates not only the Portuguese release from Castilian interference, but also the important historic link with England. The Treaty of Windsor, signed a year after the battle, confirmed the Anglo-Portuguese alliance, and in 1387 João I married Philippa of Lancaster, daughter of John of Gaunt. Philippa and João are buried side by side in the abbey's chapel, as are their children, one of whom was Prince Henry the Navigator, the man who did the most to influence Portugal's rapid 15th-century expansion.

Based at Sagres, on the western tip of the Algarve, Prince Henry surrounded himself with seamen, mapmakers, and astrologers. Under the protection of the mighty *fortaleza* (fortress), which still stands, these men were the first to establish the principles of navigation on the high seas. The caravelle, a ship capable of navigating in a crosswind, was developed and the famous maritime discoveries were soon under way: Madeira and the Azores were discovered in 1419 and 1427 respectively, and by 1460 (when Henry died) the west coast of Africa was known to Portuguese seamen. There were no limits to the inquisitiveness, or to the bravery of the Portuguese sailors. Bartolomeu Dias rounded the southern tip of Africa in 1487, naming it the Cape of Good Hope; 10 years later, Vasco da Gama reached Calcutta; and in 1500 Pedro Alvares Cabral sailed to Brazil. By the mid-16th century, the Portuguese empire had spread over four continents, with trading posts in the Far East and a Portuguese monopoly in force throughout the Indian Ocean.

The wealth gained from this aggressive expansionism knew no bounds. Portugal was at the height of her influence, with Lisbon the richest city in Europe, and under Dom Manuel I (1495–1521), the Crown intervened to take a fifth of the maritime trading profits. With the proceeds, Manuel began to adorn Portugal with buildings and monuments worthy of an Imperial power, and the late-Gothic architecture that evolved has since come to be called Manueline style. If there's any doubt about the brimming confidence of that era, one look at the Manueline buildings of Portugal will dispel it immediately. The elaborate decoration that is the hallmark of Manueline architecture is at once inspiring in its sheer novelty and instructive in that it could only have been the outpouring of a great maritime power. Buildings and monuments are supported by twisted stone columns and covered with sculpted emblems of Portugal's conquests on the high seas and in distant lands: Representations of anchors, seaweed, and rigging mingle with exotic animals and strange, occasionally pagan, symbols, a fusion of diverse cultures and civilizations brought together under the umbrella of a Christian Portuguese empire. The interior decoration of the Igreja de Jesus (Church of Jesus), begun in 1494 in Setúbal, near Lisbon, is generally considered to be the earliest appearance of the Manueline style in Portugal. It was soon overshadowed by exuberant works in the capital itself, at Belém, where the Mosteiro dos Jerónimos (Jerónimos Monastery) and the Torre de Belém (Belém Tower) are two of the most visited surviving examples in the country. The abbey of Batalha was transformed by its Manueline renovations, in particular the portal of the Capelas Imperfeitas (Unfinished Chapels), which is among the most impressive of all Manueline works. A tour of any of these buildings is a requisite to understanding the untrammeled power and influence of 16th-century Portugal, but also perhaps to recognizing the strong national identity that the Portuguese retain today. The pride in these buildings, which goes beyond mere architectural prowess, is most evident in Tomar's Convento de Cristo, whose supreme Manueline ornamentation (windows of the Chapter House) stands as the most eloquent reminder of the Portuguese age of discovery.

The buildings have survived, but the glories of the Portuguese empire were relatively short-lived. Arts and literature flourished for a while with the emergence of the 16th-century dramatist Gil Vicente and the publication in 1572 of the great poet Luís de Camões' epic "Lusiads," which told of the proud era of discovery. But the disastrous crusade in Morocco by the young Dom Sebastião in 1578, where the king perished alongside most of the country's nobility, allowed Phillip II of Spain to renew his claim to Portugal. Camões died in the same year that Portugal fell to Spain, and it's said his last words were, "I am dying at the same time as my country."

Spanish rule lasted 60 years (1580–1640), during which time many of Portugal's overseas possessions were lost, but in 1640 the Portuguese took back their throne when a nobleman from the powerful Portuguese House of Bragança was installed as Dom João IV. The Bragança dynasty was to last until the first years of the 20th century, but for the most part there was a hollow ring to its pretensions as a power. Fueled by the gold and diamonds extracted from Brazil, there was extravagant spending on irrationally grand projects, like the massive monastery at Mafra (which employed 50,000 workmen), the university library at Coimbra, and the excessive decoration of the Capela de São João Baptista (Chapel of St. John the Baptist) in Lisbon. However, with the domestic economy still weak, and society strictly feudal, it took the appalling devastation of the 1755 earthquake, which destroyed Lisbon, to breathe new life into commerce and industry.

The king's chief minister at the time, the Marquês de Pombal, ordered that the capital's dead be buried and the living fed. He then immediately set about creating a new, planned Lisbon that took heed of the most advanced architectural and social ideas of the age, resulting in an elegant but restrained style of building later known as "Pombaline." To walk through downtown Lisbon today is to walk through shades of the 18th century, starting in the elegant colonnaded riverside square, the Praça do Comércio, and through the gridded Baixa (Lower) district, expressly designed by Pombal to house the trades and commercial concerns he was keen to promote. Lisbon's glory is its 18th-century buildings, and its sense of measured space, an early example of town planning that's repeated elsewhere in Portugal, most notably in the gridded streets of Vila Real de Santo António, the easternmost town of the Algarve.

These developments proved to be mere diversions from the economic, social, and moral poverty of the Portuguese crown. Napoleon's invasions during the Peninsular War left the country devastated, and the monarchy was finally overthrown in 1910. A republic was proclaimed, but the rot of instability had set in and during the next 16 years 44 different governments attempted to rescue Portugal from its malaise. A coup d'état followed in 1926, and from 1928 onward the country was governed by the right-wing dictatorship of António Salazar, who—first as Minister of Finance, then as Prime Minister—was strongly influenced by the contemporary Italian and Spanish Fascist movements led by Mussolini and Franco, respectively. The dictatorship was to last until 1974.

**Art and Architecture** The four-and-a-half decades of introverted Portuguese dictatorship were a chastening experience for a people whose ancestors had joyfully announced their political independence and superiority in innovative architecture, daring decorative arts, and challenging painting and literature. The Manueline style is perhaps the most obvious manifestation of the Portuguese national character, but other developments proved to be of similar significance. Following the discovery of gold in Brazil at the end of the 17th century, churches, particularly, began to be embellished in an extraordinary rococo style, which employed *talha dourada* (polychrome and gilded carved wood) to stupendous, pictorial effect. Sadly, the great golden interior of the Cistercian abbey at Alcobaça was removed at the beginning of this century, leaving its structure evocative but bare. Nevertheless, there are superb surviving examples at the churches of São Francisco in Oporto and Santo António in Lagos, and at the Convento de Jesus at Aveiro. As a contrast, for rococo at its most restrained, you must visit the lovely royal palace at Queluz, near Lisbon.

Aside from the baroque and rococo work in buildings and churches all over the country, one of the most notable images of Portugal that visitors take away with them is the abundance of *azulejos* (painted ceramic tiles) originally introduced by the Moors. Throughout the country, in nearly every town and village—adorning churches, palaces, fountains, public buildings, and private homes—you can see a veritable open-air art display of the tiles, reflecting the Portuguese love of decoration and ostentation. They featured geometrical designs and a wide variety of colors, and the best example of them is at the Paço Real (Royal Palace) in Sintra. By the 17th century the early styles were being replaced by whole panels that depicted religious or secular motifs, often based on engravings and colored blue and white. These are the most enduring of all Portugal's azulejos, with fine examples throughout the country, especially at the Fronteira palace on the outskirts of Lisbon. Anyone particularly interested in the development of the tile work should visit at least one of the museums that exhibit well-preserved examples: Lisbon's Museu do Azulejo and Museu de Arte Antiga, and Coimbra's Museu Machado de Castro. Also, Portugal's Baroque country residences (called *quintas* or *solares*) often display the most delightful combinations: for instance, an elegant pastel-colored house whose outside walls and landscaped gardens are lavishly adorned with grandiose panels of azulejos. The most interesting examples are found in the Minho region in the north though there are also attractive quintas on the Setúbal Peninsula.

Sculpture and painting styles in Portugal evolved in a similar way, inspired first by the excitement of the newly emerging Portuguese nation and subsequently by the baroque experimentation allowed by the wealth available from the colonies. The earlier, rarer works still speak volumes about the confidence of those caught up in the Imperial age. A Portuguese tradition in sculpture found its first outlet in grand royal and noble funerary monuments, as witnessed by the realism on display on the Gothic tombs in the cathedrals of Lisbon, Guarda, and Braga. These were precursors of the masterpiece of their kind, the 14th-century tombs of Pedro and Inês at Alcobaça, while similarly eloquent are the hand-clasped figures of Dom João I and his queen, Philippa, in the chapel at Batalha. Portuguese painting came into its own in the 15th century, with the completion of Nuno Gonçalves' Flemish-inspired polyptych of São Vicente (St. Vincent), which portrayed the princes and knights, monks and fishermen, court figures and ordinary people of Imperial Portugal in six remarkable painted panels. It's on display in Lisbon's Museu de Arte Antiga. The next great Portuguese painter, the 16th-century Vasco Fernandes (known as *Grão Vasco*, "The Great Vasco"), was also influenced by the Flemish tradition, but his work has an expressive, realistic vigor. Grão Vasco's masterpieces are on show in Viseu, at the Museu Grão Vasco.

By way of contrast, the later baroque styles in art and sculpture said less about the country, and more about the indiscriminate use of wealth. There were flamboyant creations, to be sure, including the unsurpassed granite-and- plaster staircases, pilgrimage shrines, and sculptures at Bom Jesus and Lamego, in the Minho, but these were built at a time when the monarchy had lost the vision and moral will that had sustained it during earlier, greater periods. Nevertheless, there were always sculptors and artists ready to work in styles that drew on the strengths of the Portuguese character and not the weaknesses. The 18th century saw the emergence of the sculptor Machado de Castro, who produced perhaps the greatest equestrian statue of his time, that of Dom José I in Lisbon's Praça do Comércio. Domingos António Sequeira (1768–1837) painted historic and religious subjects of international renown, while portrait and landscape painting became popular in the 19th century; the works of José Malhoã and Miguel Angelo Lupi can be seen in the Museu de José Malhoã in Caldas da Rainha. Other museums throughout the country display the works of talented contemporaries. The Museu Soares dos Reis in Oporto—named after the 19th–century sculptor António Soares dos Reis (1847–1889)—was the first national museum in the country. His pupil was António Teixeira Lopes (1866–1942), who achieved great popular success, and who also has a museum named after him in Oporto, in the suburb of Vila Nova de Gaia.

**Literature** In literature, there was a long, barren period after the time of Camões, only briefly illuminated in the 18th century by the lyric poet, Bocage. Revival came in the 19th century with the Romantic Movement, whose most brilliant exponent was Almeida Garrett, a novelist, dramatist, and poet, who died in 1854. Garrett influenced a whole generation of remarkable writers, including novelists Camilo Castelo Branco and Julio Dinis; the historians Alexandre Herculano and Oliveira Martins; and the poets Antero de Quental and António de Castilho. The latter half of the 19th century almost exactly covered the life of the great Portuguese novelist Eça de Queiroz, an early realist, while the first half of the 20th century only produced one outstanding figure, the poet Fernando Pessoa, who died in 1935.

**Contemporary Politics, Culture, and Economy** In the 20th century, industrialization passed Portugal by, the economy remained agricultural, the political system was unreformed, and the lot of the people did not improve. The country preserved its age-old traditions and customs within an almost feudal social structure, causing it to fall behind developing nations. Portugal was ready for change. In 1968 its government appointed Dr. Marcelo Caetano to replace then-dictator António de Oliveira Salazar, who had just suffered a severe stroke. Long-brewing discontent in the African colonies of Angola and Mozambique led to the revolution that occurred six years later, on April 25, 1974, in which Caetano was ousted in a virtually bloodless coup (fewer than 20 people were killed) led by General António de Spinola. It was the move that the Portuguese people had long awaited, and huge demonstrations in support of the left-wing, officer-led *Movimento das Forças Armadas* (Armed Forces Movement) left no doubt that Portugal had entered a new era. The remaining colonies were granted independence: Initially it was a relatively peaceful operation in Mozambique and Guinea-Bissau, but in Angola and East Timor it was fraught with conflict. Land on the huge estates of the Alentejo was redistributed, and in the name of democracy, free elections produced a popular Socialist government.

Today Portugal is a stable country, its people keen to share in the prosperity offered by the developments within the European Union of which it held the presidency in 1992. In 1994 the capital came of age when Lisbon was selected as European City of Culture. The government has shifted steadily to the right since the heady days of revolution; the Social Democrats have been the largest party in government since 1985. Visitors may find the obvious stability surprising, given the relatively short time since the revolution, and indeed it speaks well for the inherent qualities of the Portuguese people. Moreover, since 1975 more than 700,000 refugees from the former Portuguese colonies in Africa and Timor have been absorbed into the country, and there has been remarkable integration in that short period, especially if one considers that the number of refugees represents more than 7% of the total population.

The refugees have bestowed a welcome new face on Portugal: in Lisbon, for example, African music and dance is extremely popular, and dozens of places serve authentic Brazilian, Mozambican, Angolan, and Goan food. And in the final chapter of Portugal's colonial adventures, because the country has agreed to take in as many citizens of Macau as wish to leave before the handover of that territory to China in 1999, there are sure to be more Chinese and Macanese restaurants opening up. There's a buoyancy in other cultural matters, too, with Lisbon, Oporto, Coimbra, and other major towns providing visitors with plenty of opportunity to see the best in contemporary Portuguese art, music, and dance. Excellent modern art museums in both Oporto and Lisbon are high on many itineraries: the painter Maria-Helena Vieira da Silva is the most famous name Portugal has produced this century, though others have also been influential, including pioneer modernist Almada Negreiros, and Amadeu de Sousa Cardoso (who has a separate gallery for his works in Amarante). Contemporary writers whose works are translated into English include José Cardoso Pires, António Lobo Antunes, and José Saramago, and architects strive to recreate that Imperial Portuguese sense of confidence in their buildings—Lisbon's vast, colorful Amoreiras shopping and residential complex and the new Cultural Center in Belém are as bold as such projects come.

And there is also that perennial art form, best encountered in cities, that is the essence of Portugal and the Portuguese. In bars and clubs, especially in Lisbon and Coimbra, you will hear performed *fado*, or "fate," a mournful, soulful singing tradition thought to have originated in African slave songs, and imported from the colonies by way of the slave trade. There are two distinct strands of fado: in Lisbon, emotive feeling is the dominant force in the lyrics, while Coimbra's fado (said to date to the age of the troubadours), has a more intellectual edge. But both are timeless—the lament of the past, the acceptance of the future.

Political stability and artistic confidence couldn't have been maintained without improvements in the economy, and there have been great strides forward since 1974. Membership in the European Union has undoubtedly helped in reviving the economy, with grants and subsidies paying for the modernization of agriculture; massive aid and loans from the United States have also played a part. One effect of this regeneration that regular visitors will notice is that Portugal has become a more expensive place over the last few years, though you're unlikely to find costs pro hibitive. The government, of course, faces its own problems, not least a marked disparity in economic development between the north and south of the country. In addition, there are relatively high illiteracy and infant mortality rates; inflation causes concern; and agriculture is stubbornly inefficient, despite modernization.

The challenges to the government and people of Portugal during the remainder of the 1990s are clear, and there are few countries in Europe better equipped to deal with them, since a young democracy often has an uncommon will to succeed. But there's a challenge to the visitor, too. Take time to get off the beaten track, and you'll be rewarded—more than anywhere else in western Europe—with glimpses of a traditional life and culture that has been shaped by the memories of empire and tempered by the experience of revolution.

# 1 Essential Information

# Before You Go

## Government Tourist Offices

By Mary Ellen Schultz
Contact the Portuguese government tourist offices for information on all aspects of travel to and in Portugal.

**United States** 590 5th Ave., New York, NY 10036–4704, tel. 212/354–4403, fax 212/764–6137.

**In Canada** 60 Bloor St. W, Suite 1005, Toronto, Ont., M4W 3G8, tel. 416/921–7376, fax 416/921–1353.

**United Kingdom** 22 Sackville St., London W1X 1DE, tel. 0171/494–1441, fax 0171/494–1865.

**Travel Briefings** The U.S. Department of State's **Overseas Citizens Emergency Center** (Room 4811, Washington, DC 20520; enclose SASE) issues Consular Information Sheets, which cover crime, security, political climate, and health risks as well as embassy locations, entry requirements, currency regulations, and other routine matters. For the latest information, stop in at any U.S. passport office, consulate, or embassy; call the interactive hot line (tel. 202/647–5225; fax 202/647–3000); or, with your PC's modem, tap into the Bureau of Consular Affairs' computer bulletin board (tel. 202/647–9225).

## Tours and Packages

When considering a tour group, read the fine print in the brochure and expect only what it specifies. Be sure to find out exactly what expenses are included (particularly tips, taxes and service charges, side trips, additional meals, and entertainment); and their ratings of all hotels; and, if you are traveling alone, the cost of a single supplement. Note whether any of the arrangements offered are subject to change, and check out the operator's policy regarding cancellations, complaints, and trip-interruption insurance. Most tour operators request that bookings be made through a travel agent; there is no additional charge for doing so. Below is a sampling of the operators and packages available (note that tours change from year to year, and at press time operators had not yet worked out final details of their 1995 schedules). For additional resources, contact your travel agent or a Portuguese National Tourist Office (*see* Government Tourist Offices, *above*).

**Fully Escorted Tours**
**United States**
**Certified Vacations** (Box 1525, Ft. Lauderdale, FL 33302, tel. 305/522–1414 or 800/233–7260) arranges escorted and freelance tours to Lisbon and Madeira in addition to tours combining highlights of both Spain and Portugal. Tours last one to three weeks. **TWA Getaway Vacations** (100 S. Bedford Rd., Mt. Kisco, NY 10549, tel. 800/439–2929) offers similar packages. **TAP Air Portugal** (399 Market St., Newark, NJ 07105, tel. 800/336–6690; in NY, 800/324–3520) offers a variety of escorted and fly-and-drive itineraries. **Travcoa** (Box 2630, Newport Beach, CA 92658, tel. 714/476–2800 or 800/992–2003; in CA, 800/992–2004) offers an 18-day tour of "Unusual Spain and Portugal." The tour begins in Madrid and goes to Segovia, Toledo, Oviedo, Leon, Salamanca, and several other Spanish cities before heading to Oporto, Coimbra, Fátima, Nazaré, and Lisbon. Travcoa's tours are small, usually 25 or fewer participants. **Maupintour** (1515 St. Andrews Dr., Lawrence, KS 66047, tel. 919/843–1211 or 800/255–6162) offers "Pousadas and Paradors," a 16-day tour of the western Iberian peninsula, with stops in Lisbon, Buçaco, Vila

Nova de Cerveira, Estremoz, and several other Portuguese cities, as well as Benavente, Segovia, Madrid, and Salamanca in Spain. If you wish to tour Portugal without visiting Spain, **Abreu Tours, Inc.** (317 E. 34th St., New York, NY 10016, tel. 212/532–6550 or 800/223–1580) has several tours, including "North of Portugal," which begins and ends in Lisbon and passes through Nazaré, Fátima, Coimbra, Oporto, Viana do Castelo, Braga, Portalegre, Évora, and several other cities. Accommodations and most meals are included. **Sun Pleasure Tours** (383 Rockdale Ave., New Bedford, MA 02740, tel. 508/997–9361 or 800/431–8810) and **Portuguese Tours** (Box 729, Elizabeth, NJ 07207, tel. 201/352–6112 or 800/526–4047) offer similar packages. **Cultural Heritage Alliance** (107–115 S. 2nd St., Philadelphia, PA 19160, tel. 215/923–7288) takes student and adult groups to Lisbon and the north of Portugal.

Other operators offering tours that range from one or two cities to one or two regions to the entire country include **Brendan Tours** (15137 Califa St., Van Nuys, CA 91411, tel. 818/785–9696 or 800/421–8446), **Caravan** (401 N. Michigan Ave., Chicago, IL 60611, tel. 800/227–2862), **Collette Tours** (162 Middle St., Pawtucket, RI 02860, tel. 401/728–3805 or 800/832–4656), **E C Tours** (10153½ Riverside Dr., Toluca Lake, CA 91602, tel. 213/874–3848 or 800/777–7246), **Globus** (5301 S. Federal Cir., Littleton, CO 80123, tel. 303/797–2800 or 800/221–0090) and its more budget-minded sister company, **Cosmos Tourama, Marsans International** (2121 Ponce de León Blvd., Suite 715, Coral Gables, FL 33143, tel. 305/441–1555, 212/239–3880, or 800/777–9110), **Petrabax Tours** (97-45 Queens Blvd., Suite 600, Rego Park, NY 11374, tel. 718/897–7272 or 800/367–6611), **Pinto Basto Tours** (40 Prince St., New York, NY 10012, tel. 212/226–9056), and **Trafalgar Tours** (11 East 26th St., Suite 1300, New York, NY 10010, tel. 212/689–8977 or 800/626–6603).

For cruises from Lisbon to the island of Madeira, contact **Cunard Line Ltd.** (555 5th Ave., New York, NY 10017, tel. 212/880–7500 or 800/221–4770) and from New York to Southampton with a stopover in Madeira, contact **Princess Cruises** (2029 Century Park E, Los Angeles, CA 90067, tel. 213/553–7000 or 800/421–0522). **Royal Cruise Line** (1 Maritime Plaza, San Francisco, CA 94111, tel. 415/956–7200 or 800/227–4534) also offers a cruise up the Portuguese coast, stopping at Oporto before heading out to the Atlantic Ocean and Madeira.

*United Kingdom* **Abreu Travel Agency Ltd.** (109 Westbourne Grove, London W2 4UL, tel. 0171/229–9905), **Caravela Tours** (38–44 Gillingham St., London SW1V 1JW, tel. 0171/630–9223), and **Club Mediterranee** (106–108 Brompton Rd., London SW3 1JJ, tel. 0171/581–1161).

## Independent Packages

Independent packages, or FITs (foreign independent travel), are offered by airlines, tour operators who may also do escorted programs (*see above*), and any number of other companies, from large, established firms to small, new entrepreneurs.

**Extra Value Travel** (683 S. Collier Blvd., Marco Island, FL 33937, tel. 813/394–3384 or 800/255–2847) arranges self-drive programs of a week or more that provide a rental car, unlimited mileage, accommodations, and a daily Continental breakfast.

**TWA Getaway Tours** (tel. 800/438–2929), **Delta Dream Vacations** (tel. 800/872–7786), and **TAP Air Portugal** (tel. 800/221–7370) will send you brochures of many tour packages (golf, bicycling, gourmet, *pousadas*, manor houses, castles, etc.) offered in conjunction with leading tour operators in the United States; **Abreu Tours** (317 E. 34th St., New York, NY 10016, tel. 212/661–0555 or 800/223–1580) offers escorted motor-coach tours of varying lengths that allow plenty of time to do your own exploring. Also try **Jet Vacations** (1775 Broadway, 24th Floor, New York, NY 10019, tel. 212/474–8773), **Skyline** (376 New York Ave., Huntington, NY 11743, tel. 516/423–9090 or 800/645–6198), and **Sun Travel** (3545 Midway Dr., San Diego, CA, tel. 619/222–2786).

**Special-Interest Art and Architecture** **Prospect Art Tours** (454 Chiswick High Rd., London W4 5TT, tel. 0181/995–2163) has several tours of Portugal, all staffed with expert guides and focusing on Iberian culture. **Serenissima Travel** (21 Dorset Sq., London NW1 6QG, tel 0171/730–9841) has similar tours, and **Swan-Hellenic** (77 New Oxford St., London WC1A 1PP, tel. 0171/831–1616) has art tours of Lisbon and the northern part of the country. In the United States, contact **Esplanade Tours** (581 Boylston St., Boston, MA 02116, tel. 617/266–7465 or 800/426–5492) for information and reservations.

**The Texas Connection** (217 Arden Grove, San Antonio, TX 78215, tel. 210/225–6294) has a "Handicraft Tour" of Portugal. The "Village Weavers Tour" in 1991 was the first of what promises to be a fascinating series of expeditions to Portugal's myriad folk-art and handicrafts centers.

**Bicycling** **Cycling Through the Centuries** (2279 Lake Tahoe Blvd., Suite 3, South Lake Tahoe, CA 96150, tel. 916/541–4713 or 800/245–4226) offers eight–10-night bicycle tours through many quaint and out-of-the-way parts of the country—from the lush, green Minho to the wine regions to the strikingly different Algarve in the south, with the pace as relaxed or as strenuous as you prefer. Bring your own bike or rent one of theirs. Offering similar wanderings are **Backroads** (1516 5th St., Suite L101, Berkeley, CA 94710, tel. 510/527–1555 or 800/462–2848) and **Easy Ryder Tours** (63 Everett St., Arlington, MA 02174, tel. 617/643–8332 or 800/488–8332). **Tip Tours** (Av. Costa Pinto 91-A, 2750 Cascais, tel. 01/483–3821) rents bicycles and runs bicycle tours throughout the country, with accommodations. Cyclists are accompanied by a guide, a mechanic, and a luggage van. During summer a "Volta de Portugal" (similar to the Tour de France) tests bicycle racers' endurance. Check with the tourist office for dates and more details.

**Cruises** For cruises up the coast from Lisbon to Oporto, or up the Douro from Oporto, or from Lisbon to Madeira contact **Classical Cruises** (132 E. 70th St., New York, NY, tel. 212/794–3200 or 800/252–7745), **Crystal Cruises** (2121 Ave. of the Stars, Los Angeles, CA 90067, tel. 310/785–9300), **Elegant Cruises and Tours** (158A Main St., Port Washington, NY 11050, tel. 516/767–9302 or 800/683–6767), **EuroCruises** (3030 W. 13th St., New York, NY 10014, tel. 212/691–2099 or 800/688–3876), or **Sea Air Holidays** (733 Summer St., Stamford, CT 06901, tel. 203/356–9033 or 800/732–6247).

**Gastronomy and Wines** **Altamira Tours** (860 Detroit St., Denver, CO 80206, tel. 303/399–3660 or 800/747–2869) offers a 15-day food-and-wine tour of Portugal and Madeira. Both the host and the lodgings are first class. **Thomson Holidays** (Greater London House, Hampstead Rd., London NW1 7SD, tel. 0181/200–8733) has a "Wine Routes of Portugal" tour, which includes excursions to Lisbon and Oporto, the Sandeman Port cellars, the Mateus estate, and the Dão wine cellars; it can be combined with seven nights in Estoril.

Golf **Adventure Golf Holidays** (815 North Rd., Westfield, MA 01805, tel. 413/568–2855 or 800/628–9655), **Golf International** (275 Madison Ave., New York, NY 10016, tel. 212/986–9176 or 800/833–1389), **ITC Golf Tours** (4134 Atlantic Ave., Suite 205, Long Beach, CA 90807, tel. 310/595–6905 or 800/257–4981), and **Perry Golf** (8302 Dunwoody Pl., Suite 305, Atlanta, GA 30350, tel. 404/641–9696 or 800/344–5257) offer land packages to the best courses in the Algarve and Madeira. Also, contact the **Portuguese National Tourist Office** for a list of courses throughout the mainland, Madeira, and the Azores.

History **Alta Tours** (870 Market St., Suite 784, San Francisco, CA 94102, tel. 415/777–1312 or 800/338–4191) and **Marsans International** (2121 Ponce de Leon Blvd., Suite 715, Coral Gables, FL 33134, tel. 305/441–1555 or 800/777–9110) offer tours that concentrate on history, sweetening the education with spectacular scenery and visits to beaches. **Odysseys and Adventures** (535 Chestnut St., Box 305, Cedarhurst, NY 11516, tel. 516/569–2812 or 800/344–0013) focuses on Jewish history with 10-day tours. There is no traveling on the Sabbath, but these tours are not kosher. **Kesher Tours** (370 Lexington Ave., New York, NY 10017, tel. 212/949–9580 or 800/582–8330) specializes in Jewish heritage and kosher tours.

Horseback **FITS Equestrian** (685 Lateen Rd., Solvang, CA 93463, tel. 805/688–
Riding 9494 or 800/666–3487) provides native Lusitano horses for scenic rides through national parks, picturesque villages, and along beaches and lagoons.

Pilgrimages **Pilgrimage Tours and Travel** (39 Beechwood Ave., Manhasset, NY 11030, tel. 516/627–2636 or 800/669–0757), **Regina Travel** (401 South St., 4-B, Chardon, OH 44024, tel. 216/286–9141 or 800/228–4654), and **Select International** (525 Boulevard, Kenilworth, NJ 07033, tel. 908/276–2000 or 800/842–4842) run tours to Christian landmarks and the cities of Batalha, Fátima, and Tomar.

Spas Portugal has 44 hot springs on the mainland and the islands; contact the Portuguese National Tourist Office nearest you for a complete list of spas, or get in touch with the **Associação Nacional dos Industriais de Aguas Minero-Medicinais e de Mesa** (Rua de S. Jose, 93,1–1100 Lisbon, tel. 01/347–5623). **Custom Spa Vacations** (1318 Beacon St., Suite 5, Brookline, MA 02146, tel. 617/566–5144 or 800/443–7727), organizes tours of varying lengths in different parts of the country, combining American- and European-style treatments. **Marketing Ahead** (433 5th Ave., 6th Floor, New York, NY 10016, tel. 212/686–9213 or 800/223–1356 outside NY) custom designs luxury spa tours.

## When to Go

The tourist season begins in spring and lasts through the autumn. In midsummer it is never unbearably hot (except in parts of the Algarve and on the mainland plains), and it is especially pleasant along the coast, where a cool breeze springs up in the evening. Winter is mild and frequently rainy, except in Madeira, where winter has long been popular; off-season travelers have the advantage of reduced hotel rates. In the Algarve, springtime begins in February with a marvelous range of wildflowers. Late September and early October herald Indian summer, ensuring warm sunshine through November.

Climate The following are average daily maximum and minimum temperatures for major cities in Portugal.

| Faro | Jan. | 59F | 15C | May | 72F | 22C | Sept. | 79F | 26C |
|---|---|---|---|---|---|---|---|---|---|
| | | 48 | 9 | | 57 | 14 | | 66 | 19 |
| | Feb. | 61F | 16C | June | 77F | 25C | Oct. | 72F | 22C |
| | | 50 | 10 | | 64 | 18 | | 61 | 16 |
| | Mar. | 64F | 18C | July | 82F | 28C | Nov. | 66F | 19C |
| | | 52 | 11 | | 68 | 20 | | 55 | 13 |
| | Apr. | 68F | 20C | Aug. | 82F | 28C | Dec. | 61F | 16C |
| | | 55 | 13 | | 68 | 20 | | 60 | 10 |

| Lisbon | Jan. | 57F | 14C | May | 71F | 21C | Sept. | 79F | 26C |
|---|---|---|---|---|---|---|---|---|---|
| | | 46 | 8 | | 55 | 13 | | 62 | 17 |
| | Feb. | 59F | 15C | June | 77F | 25C | Oct. | 72F | 22C |
| | | 47 | 8 | | 60 | 15 | | 58 | 14 |
| | Mar. | 63F | 17C | July | 81F | 27C | Nov. | 63F | 17C |
| | | 50 | 10 | | 63 | 17 | | 52 | 11 |
| | Apr. | 67F | 20C | Aug. | 82F | 28C | Dec. | 58F | 15C |
| | | 53 | 12 | | 63 | 17 | | 47 | 9 |

| Oporto | Jan. | 55F | 13C | May | 68F | 20C | Sept. | 75F | 24C |
|---|---|---|---|---|---|---|---|---|---|
| | | 41 | 5 | | 52 | 11 | | 57 | 14 |
| | Feb. | 57F | 14C | June | 73F | 23C | Oct. | 70F | 21C |
| | | 41 | 5 | | 55 | 13 | | 52 | 11 |
| | Mar. | 61F | 16C | July | 77F | 25C | Nov. | 63F | 17C |
| | | 46 | 8 | | 59 | 15 | | 46 | 8 |
| | Apr. | 64F | 18C | Aug. | 77F | 25C | Dec. | 57F | 14C |
| | | 48 | 9 | | 59 | 15 | | 41 | 5 |

*Information Sources* For current weather conditions and forecasts for cities in the United States and abroad, plus the local time and helpful travel tips, call the **Weather Channel Connection** (tel. 900/932–8437; 95¢ per minute) from a touch-tone phone.

## Public Holidays

January 1 (New Year's Day), March 7 (Mardi Gras—a holiday in Lisbon and other towns), April 14 (Good Friday), April 25 (Liberty Day), May 1 (Labor Day), June 10 (Portugal's and Camões Day; also Corpus Christi), June 13 (St. Anthony's Day—Lisbon), August 15 (Assumption), October 5 (Republic Day), November 1 (All Saints' Day), December 1 (Independence Day), December 8 (The Feast of the Immaculate Conception), December 24 (Christmas Eve), and December 25 (Christmas Day).

If a national holiday falls on a Tuesday or Thursday, many businesses also close on the Monday or Friday in between, for a long weekend called a *ponte* (bridge).

## Festivals and Seasonal Events

It is said that there is a different market day or festival every day of the year in Portugal. Market days, whether in big cities or small towns, are an irresistible attraction. In **Lisbon:** the Thieves Market, Tuesday and Saturday behind the Church of São Vicente de Fora. Near Lisbon: every Wednesday and Saturday in **Cascais;** the second and fourth Sunday of the month in **São Pedro de Sintra** (known for the antiques and handicrafts); every Thursday at **Malveira,** near Mafra, and **Carcavelos** on the Cascais train line; every first Sunday at **Azeitão** south of the Rio Tejo (Tagus). In the north: every Thursday at **Barcelos;** Monday through Friday and Saturday morning in **Oporto** (look for *palmitos,* sprays of flowers made of golden foil paper), at the Bolhão Market on Rua Sá da Bandeira. In the Algarve: every third Sunday at **Albufeira;** every first Saturday at **Lagos;** every first Monday at **Portimão;** every third Monday at **Silves;** every third Monday at **Tavira;** and every Saturday at **Loule** and at **São Braz de Alportel.**

**Religious festivals** called *romarias* are held throughout the year. Some of the leading annual festivals, fairs, and folk pilgrimages are listed below. Verify the dates with the Portuguese tourism office, which can also send you its complete listing of the numerous events, plus advice on when to book hotel reservations (well in advance).

**Mid-January: St. Gonçalo** and **St. Cristovão Festivities** in Vila Nova de Gaia, Oporto; **St. Gonçalinho Festivities** in Aveiro.

**Mid–late January: St. Sebastião or Fogaceiras Festivities** in Santa Maria da Feira in Aveiro.

**Early February: Our Lady of Candeias Festivities,** Mourão (in Évora).

**Early March: Festivities of Carnival (Mardi Gras),** the final festival before Lent, are held throughout the country, with processions of masked participants, parades of vehicles decked out with satirical motifs, and exuberant flowers.

**Mid-April: Holy Week Festivities** are held in Braga, Ovar, Póvoa de Varzim, and other major cities, with the most important events taking place on Monday, Thursday, and Good Friday, when the faithful march in parades.

**Early May: Festival of the Crosses (Festas das Cruzes)** in Barcelos includes a large fair with handicrafts, concerts, an affecting Procession of the Holy Cross, and a spectacular display of fireworks on the Rio Cavado.

**Early–mid-May: First Annual Pilgrimage to Fátima.** Hundreds of thousands from all over the world travel to Fátima for the commemoration of the first apparition of the Virgin to the little shepherd children on May 13, 1917.

**Late May:** Three days of **Festivities honoring "Senhor Santo Cristo"** in Ponta Delgada, S. Miguel Island, Azores, climax when the 16th-century image of Christ of the Miracles, accompanied by its legendary treasure, parades for hours through the town.

**May–June: Algarve Music Festival** in the larger towns of the Algarve features more than 40 concerts by leading Portuguese and foreign artists.

**Early June:** The **National Fair of Agriculture** in Santarém is the most important agricultural fair in Portugal, with a colorful program of bullfighting, folk songs and dancing, and typical fair amusements.

**Late June: Festivities in honor of St. Anthony** in Lisbon honor the city's patron saint with an impressive show of *marchas* (walking groups of singers and musicians) parading along the Avenida da Liberdade while the various city districts carry on their own music, dances, and bonfires. **Festivities in honor of St. John** are held in many towns, but the festivities in Oporto are the most colorful. Every corner has its own *cascatas* (arrangements of religious motifs), bonfires, and all-night groups of singing and dancing merrymakers.

**Early July: The Red Waistcoat Festival (Coletes Encarnado)** in Vila Franca de Xira honors the *campinos,* Portuguese cowboys who guard the brave bulls in the pasturelands of the Ribatejo.

**July–August: Estoril Music Festival** features leading Portuguese and foreign artists in Estoril, Cascais, and other towns of the Estoril coast.

**Early August: St. Walter's Festival (Festas Gualterianas)** in

Guimarães is a fascinating show of music bands, folk-dance groups, and the spectacular Procession of St. Walter.

**Mid-August:** Festival in honor of **Our Lady of the Monte** is held near Funchal, Madeira Island, with an evening fair, group dancing and singing, and a procession.

**Mid–late August:** **Our Lady of Agony Festivities** in Viana do Castelo are extremely colorful, with the Lady paraded throughout the town over lush carpets of flowers, and spectacular fireworks.

**Late August–late September:** **Saint Matthew's Fair** in Viseu is an important agricultural and livestock fair with folk dancing and singing, held since the Middle Ages.

**Early September:** The **Wine Harvest Festival** in Palmela has a colorful parade of harvesters, wine tastings, the election of the "Queen of the Wine," and a spectacular fireworks display.

**Early–mid-September:** **Our Lady of Nazaré Festivities** has bullfights, folk dancing and singing, and three festive processions of Nazaré fishermen carrying the Lady's image on their shoulders.

**Mid-September:** In the **Annual Folk Music and Dance Festival,** singing and dancing in all the Algarve's larger towns culminate at Praia da Rocha with performances by groups from all over the country.

**Our Lady of Good Voyage Festivities** take place in the ancient town of Moita (near Setúbal), bathed by the waters of the Rio Tejo, and center on the blessing of the fishing boats.

**Early October:** **October Fair** in Vila Franca de Xira, a short distance from Lisbon, has farming and agricultural activities, handicraft displays, bullfights, and the traditional running of bulls in the streets.

**October 12–13:** **Last Pilgrimage to Fátima** brings thousands of pilgrims from all over the world to Fátima to honor the last apparition of the virgin on October 12, 1917.

**Late October–early November:** **The National Gastronomy Festival** in Santerém presents traditional regional dishes, cooking contests, and lectures.

**Early November:** **St. Martin's Fair** and the **National Horse Show** in Golega combine parades of saddle horses and bullfight horses with riding competitions, handicrafts exhibitions, and wine tasting.

**December 31:** **St. Sylvester's Festival** for New Year's Eve transforms Funchal, Madeira Island, into a vast fairground, with a breathtaking fireworks display over the city's beautiful bay.

## What to Pack

**Clothing** The Portuguese, like the Spanish, tend to dress up more than do Americans or the British. Summer can be brutally hot, spring and fall mild to chilly, and winter cold and rainy. Sight-seeing calls for casual, comfortable clothing (well-broken-in, low-heel shoes, for example), but in the cities, dressier outfits are needed for restaurants and nightclubs. American tourists can be spotted easily in Portugal because they wear sneakers; if you want to blend in, wear leather shoes instead. Jeans are another story: nowadays they blend in anywhere. For the most part, there is no dress code, but people still frown on shorts in churches, and bathing suits on the street or in restaurants and shops is not considered good taste.

**Miscellaneous** Sunscreen and sunglasses are a good idea any time of the year, since the sun in Portugal is particularly bright. Bring an extra pair of eyeglasses or contact lenses in your carry-on luggage. If you have a health problem that requires a prescription drug, pack enough to last the duration of the trip or have your doctor write a prescription using the drug's generic name, because brand names vary from country to country. Always carry prescription drugs in their original packaging to avoid problems with customs officials. Don't pack them in luggage that you plan to check in case your bags go astray. Pack a list of the offices that supply refunds for lost or stolen traveler's checks.

**Electricity** The electrical current in Portugal is 220 volts, 50 cycles alternating current (AC); the United States runs on 110-volt, 60-cycle AC current. Unlike wall outlets in the United States, which accept plugs with two flat prongs, outlets in Portugal take Continental-type plugs, with two round prongs.

*Adapters, Converters, Transformers* To use U.S.-made electric appliances abroad, you'll need an adapter plug. Unless the appliance is dual-voltage and made for travel, you'll also need a converter. Hotels sometimes have 110-volt outlets for low-wattage appliances marked "For Shavers Only" near the sink; don't use them for a high-wattage appliance like a blow-dryer. If you're traveling with an older laptop computer, carry a transformer. New laptop computers are auto-sensing, operating equally well on 110 and 220 volts, so you need only the appropriate adapter plug. For a copy of the free brochure "Foreign Electricity is No Deep Dark Secret," send a stamped, self-addressed envelope to adapter-converter manufacturer Franzus Company (Customer Service, Dept. B50, Murtha Industrial Park, Box 142, Beacon Falls, CT 06403, tel. 203/723–6664).

**Luggage** *Regulations* Free airline baggage allowances depend on the airline, the route, and the class of your ticket; ask in advance. In general, on domestic flights and on international flights between the United States and foreign destinations, you are entitled to check two bags—neither exceeding 62 inches (158 centimeters) in length + width + height, or weighing more than 70 pounds (32 kilograms). A third piece may be brought aboard; its total dimensions are generally limited to less than 45 inches (114 centimeters), so it will fit easily under the seat in front of you or in the overhead compartment. In the U.S. the Federal Aviation Administration (FAA) gives airlines broad latitude to limit carry-on allowances and tailor them to different aircraft conditions. Charges for excess, oversize, or overweight pieces vary.

If you are flying between two foreign destinations, note that baggage allowances may be determined not by piece but by weight—generally 88 pounds (40 kilograms) of luggage in first class, 66 pounds (30 kilograms) in business class, and 44 pounds (20 kilograms) in economy. If your flight between two cities abroad *connects* with your transatlantic or transpacific flight, the piece method still applies.

*Safeguards* Before leaving home, itemize your bags' contents and their worth, and tag them inside and out with your name, address, and phone number. (If you use your home address, cover it so that potential thieves can't see it.) Put a copy of your itinerary inside each bag, so that you can easily be tracked. At check-in, make sure that the tag attached by baggage handlers bears the correct three-letter code for your destination. If your bags do not arrive with you, or if you detect damage, file a written report with the airline before you leave the airport.

## Taking Money Abroad

**Traveler's Checks** Traveler's checks are preferred in metropolitan centers, although you'll need cash in rural areas and small towns. The most widely recognized are **American Express, Citicorp, Diners Club, Thomas Cook,** and **Visa,** which are sold by major commercial banks. Both American

Express and Thomas Cook issue checks that can be countersigned and used by you or your traveling companion. Typically the issuing company or the bank at which you make your purchase charges 1% to 3% of the checks' face value as a fee. Some foreign banks charge as much as 20% of the face value as the fee for cashing travelers' checks in a foreign currency. Buy a few checks in small denominations to cash toward the end of your trip, so you won't be left with excess foreign currency. Record the numbers of the checks, cross them off as you spend them, and keep this list separate from the checks. Hold on to your receipts after exchanging traveler's checks in Portugal—it's easier to convert escudos back into dollars if you have them.

**Currency Exchange** Banks offer the most favorable exchange rates. If you use currency exchange booths at airports, rail and bus stations, hotels, stores, and privately run exchange firms, you'll typically get lower rates, but you may find the hours more convenient.

You can get good rates and avoid long lines at airport exchange booths by getting a small amount of currency at **Thomas Cook Currency Services** (630 5th Ave., New York, NY 10111, tel. 212/757–6915 or 800/223–7373 for locations in major metropolitan areas throughout the U.S.) or **Ruesch International** (tel. 800/424–2923 for locations) before you depart. Check with your travel agent to be sure that the currency of the country you will be visiting can be imported.

## Getting Money from Home

**Cash Machines** Many automated-teller machines (ATMs) are tied to international networks such as **Cirrus** and **Plus**. You can use your bank card at ATMs to withdraw money from an account and get cash advances on a credit-card account if your card has been programmed with a personal identification number, or PIN. Check in advance on limits on withdrawals and cash advances within specified periods. Ask whether your bank-card or credit-card PIN will need to be reprogrammed for use in the area you'll be visiting. Four digits are commonly used overseas. (Note that Discover is accepted only in the U.S.) On cash advances you are charged interest from the day you receive the money from ATMs as well as from tellers. Although transaction fees for ATM withdrawals abroad may be higher than fees for withdrawals at home, Cirrus and Plus exchange rates are excellent, because they are based on wholesale rates only offered by major banks. They also may be referred to abroad as "a withdrawal from a credit account."

Plan ahead: Obtain ATM locations and the names of affiliated cash-machine networks before departure. For specific foreign Cirrus locations, call 800/424–7787; for foreign Plus locations, consult the Plus directory at your local bank.

Many cash machines will convert foreign currency (bills) into escudos. Machines are located outside several of the bigger banks throughout the country (in Lisbon, in the Praça dos Restauradores, on the Rua de Ouro and Rua Augusta, and in the Praça do Comércio), and instructions are provided in English.

**Wiring Money** You don't have to be a cardholder to send or receive a **MoneyGram** from **American Express** for up to $10,000. Go to a MoneyGram agent in retail and convenience stores and American Express travel offices; pay up to $1,000 with a credit card and anything over that in cash. You are allowed a free long-distance call to give the transaction code to your intended recipient, who need only present identification and the transaction reference number to the nearest MoneyGram agent to pick up the cash. MoneyGram agents are in more than 70 countries (call 800/926–9400 for locations). Fees range from 3% to 10%, depending on the amount and how you pay.

You can also use Western Union. To wire money, take either cash or a cashier's check to the nearest agent or call and use MasterCard or Visa. Money sent from the United States or Canada will be available for pickup at agent locations in 100 countries within minutes. Once the money is in the system it can be picked up at any one of 25,000 locations (call 800/325–6000 for the one nearest you; 800/321–2923 in Canada). Fees range from 4% to 10%.

## Currency

Portugal's currency unit is the escudo, which is divided up into 100 centavos. The number of escudos is written to the left of the $ sign and the centavos to the right; thus, 2 escudos and 50 centavos is written 2$50. Coins are issued for 200$00, 100$00, 50$00, 20$00, 10$00, 5$00, 2$50, and 1$00. Bills in circulation are for 10,000$00, 5,000$00, 2,000$00, 1,000$00, and 500$00. Units of 1,000$00 are often referred to as "contos." At press time (summer 1994), the exchange rate was about 145$00 to the U.S. dollar, 108$00 per Canadian dollar, and 256$00 to the pound sterling.

## What It Will Cost

As Portugal moves to catch up with the rest of Europe, prices keep climbing; annual inflation runs around 8%. The weakening U.S. dollar has lost about 15% of its value against the escudo in recent years. Lisbon is still not as expensive as other international capitals, but it is not the extraordinary bargain it used to be. The coastal resort areas from Cascais and Estoril down to the Algarve can also be expensive, but lower-price hotels and restaurants catering mainly to the package-tour trade are certainly popular. The traveler who heads off the beaten track will find substantially cheaper food and lodging.

Transportation is still cheap in Portugal when compared with the rest of Europe. Gas prices are controlled by the government, and train and bus travel are inexpensive. Highway tolls are steep but may be worth the cost if you want to bypass the small towns and villages. Flights within the country on the state-owned TAP airlines are costly.

**Taxes** Value-added tax (or sales tax) is called IVA in Portugal. It is charged on services such as hotels and restaurants and on many categories of consumer products. Restaurant menus generally state at the bottom whether tax is included (*IVA incluido*) or not (*mas 8% IVA*). Higher-end restaurants are required to charge 8% IVA. When in doubt about whether tax is included in a price, ask: *Está incluido o IVA* (ee-vah)?

**Sample Prices** Coffee in a bar: 60$00 (standing), 120$00 (seated). Draft beer in a bar: 80$00 (standing), 125$00 (seated); bottle of beer, 125$00. Small glass of wine in a bar: 80$00; glass of Port: 175$00–2,000$00, depending on brand and vintage. Bottle of ordinary table wine (*vinho da casa*): 350$00; half bottle, 200$00. Coca-Cola: 70$00. Ham-and-cheese sandwich: 125$00. One-mile taxi ride: 200$00 (but the meter keeps ticking in traffic jams). Local bus ride: 140$00 if purchased from driver. Subway ride: 65$00. Ferry ride in Lisbon: 100$00–500$00 round-trip. Opera or theater seat: about 3,500$00–6,000$00, depending on location. Nightclub cover-charge 3,000$00–5,000$00. Fado performance: 2,000$00 cover-charge or 5,000$00–6,000$000 for dinner. Movie ticket: 400$00–500$00. Foreign newspaper: 240$00.

## Long-Distance Calling

The country code for Portugal is 351. AT&T, MCI, and Sprint have international services that make calling home relatively affordable and convenient and let you avoid hotel surcharges. Before you go, call the company of your choice to learn the number you must dial in Portugal to reach its network: **AT&T** USA Direct (tel. 800/874–4000), **MCI** Call USA (tel. 800/444–4444), or **Sprint** Express (tel. 800/793–1153). All three companies offer message delivery services to international travelers and have added debit cards so that you don't have to fiddle with change. (*See* Telephones in Staying in Portugal, *below*.)

## Passports and Visas

If your passport is lost or stolen abroad, report the loss immediately to the nearest embassy or consulate and to the local police. If you can provide the consular officer with the information contained in the passport, he or she will usually be able to issue you a new passport promptly. For this reason, keep a photocopy of the data page of your passport separate from your money and traveler's checks. Also leave a photocopy with a relative or friend at home.

**U.S. Citizens** All U.S. citizens, even infants, need a valid passport to enter Portugal for stays of up to 60 days. You can pick up new and renewal application forms at any of the 13 U.S. Passport Agency offices and at some post offices and courthouses. Although passports are usually mailed within four weeks of your application's receipt, allow five weeks or more from April through summer. Call the Department of State Office of Passport Services' information line (tel. 202/647–0518) for fees, documentation requirements, and other details.

**Canadian Citizens** Canadian citizens need a valid passport to enter Portugal for stays of up to 60 days. Application forms are available at 23 regional passport offices as well as post offices and travel agencies. Whether for a first or a subsequent passport, you must apply in person. Children under 16 may be included on a parent's passport but must have their own to travel alone. Passports are valid for five years and are usually mailed within two weeks of an application's receipt. For fees, documentation requirements, and other information in English or French, call the passport office (tel. 514/283–2152 or 800/567–6868).

**U.K. Citizens** Citizens of the United Kingdom need a valid passport to enter Portugal for stays of up to 60 days. Applications for new and renewal passports are available from main post offices as well as at the six passport offices, located in Belfast, Glasgow, Liverpool, London, Newport, and Peterborough. You may apply in person at all passport offices, or by mail to all except the London office. Children under 16 may travel on an accompanying parent's passport. All passports are valid for 10 years. Allow a month for processing.

A British Visitor's Passport is valid for holidays and some business trips of up to three months to Portugal. It can include both partners of a married couple. Valid for one year, it will be issued on the same day that you apply. You must apply in person at a main post office.

## Customs and Duties

**On Arrival**  Visitors age 15 and over are permitted to bring in 200 cigarettes, or 100 cigarillos, or 50 cigars, or 250 grams of loose tobacco. Those 17 years of age and older may bring in one liter of liquor over 22 proof and two liters of wine. Perfume is limited to 50 grams, eau de cologne to .25 liter. Dogs and cats are admitted, providing they have up-to-date vaccination records from the home country.

It is a good idea to carry along sales receipts for expensive personal belongings to avoid paying export duties when you leave.

All visitors to Madeira over 1 year old who are traveling from an infected area need a certificate of vaccination against yellow fever.

**Returning Home**  If you take any foreign-made equipment from home, such as cameras, it's wise to carry the original receipt with you or register it with U.S. Customs before you leave (Form 4457). Otherwise, you may end up paying duties on your return.

*U.S. Customs*  If you've been out of the country for at least 48 hours and haven't already used the exemption, or any part of it, in the past 30 days, you may bring home $400 worth of foreign goods duty-free. So can each member of your family, regardless of age; and your exemptions may be pooled, so one of you can bring in more if another brings in less. A flat 10% duty applies to the next $1,000 worth of goods; above $1,400, the rate varies with the merchandise. (If the 48-hour or 30-day limits apply, your duty-free allowance drops to $25, which may not be pooled.) Please note that these are the *general* rules, applicable to most countries, including Portugal.

Travelers 21 or older may bring back 1 liter of alcohol duty-free, provided the beverage laws of the state through which they reenter the United States allow it. In addition, 100 non-Cuban cigars and 200 cigarettes are allowed, regardless of your age. Antiques and works of art more than 100 years old are duty-free.

Gifts valued at less than $50 may be mailed to the U.S. duty-free, with a limit of one package per day per addressee, and do not count as part of your exemption (do not send alcohol or tobacco products or perfume valued at more than $5); mark the package "Unsolicited Gift" and write the nature of the gift and its retail value on the outside. Most reputable stores will handle the mailing for you.

For a copy of "Know Before You Go," a free brochure detailing what you may and may not bring back to the United States, rates of duty, and other pointers, contact the **U.S. Customs Service** (Box 7407, Washington, DC 20044, tel. 202/927–6724).

*Canadian Customs*  Once per calendar year, when you've been out of Canada for at least seven days, you may bring in C$300 worth of goods duty-free. If you've been away less than seven days but more than 48 hours, the duty-free exemption drops to C$100 but can be claimed any number of times (as can a C$20 duty-free exemption for absences of 24 hours or more). You cannot combine the yearly and 48-hour exemptions, use the $300 exemption only partially (to save the balance for a later trip), or pool exemptions with family members. Goods claimed under the C$300 exemption may follow you by mail; those claimed under the lesser exemptions must accompany you.

Alcohol and tobacco products may be included in the yearly and 48-hour exemptions but not in the 24-hour exemption. If you meet the age requirements of the province through which you reenter Canada, you may bring in, duty-free, 1.14 liters (40 imperial ounces) of wine or liquor *or* two dozen 12-ounce cans or bottles of beer or ale. If you are 16 or older, you may bring in, duty-free, 200 cigarettes, 50 cigars or cigarillos, and 400 tobacco sticks or 400 grams of manufactured tobacco. Alcohol and tobacco must accompany you on your return.

An unlimited number of gifts valued up to C$60 each may be mailed to Canada duty-free. These do not count as part of your exemption. Label the package "Unsolicited Gift—Value under $60." Alcohol and tobacco are excluded.

For more information, including details of duties on items that exceed your duty-free limit, ask the Revenue Canada Customs and Excise and Taxation Department (2265 St. Laurent Blvd. South, Ottawa, Ont., K1G 4K3, tel. 613/957–0275) for a copy of the free brochure "I Declare/Je Déclare."

*U.K. Customs*   If your journey was wholly within EU countries, you no longer need to pass through customs when you return to the United Kingdom. According to EU guidelines, you may bring in 800 cigarettes, 400 cigarillos, 200 cigars, and 1 kilogram of smoking tobacco, plus 10 liters of spirits, 20 liters of fortified wine, 90 liters of wine, and 110 liters of beer. If you exceed these limits, you may be required to prove that the goods are for your personal use or are gifts.

For further information or a copy of "A Guide for Travellers," which details standard customs procedures as well as what you may bring into the United Kingdom from abroad, contact HM Customs and Excise (Dorset House, Stamford St., London SE1 9PY, tel. 0171/928–3344).

## Traveling with Cameras, Camcorders, and Laptops

**Film and Cameras**   If your camera is new or if you haven't used it for a while, shoot and develop a few test rolls of film before you leave. Store film in a cool, dry place—never in the car's glove compartment or on the shelf under the rear window.

Airport security X-rays generally aren't harmful to film with ISO below 400. To protect your film, carry it with you in a clear plastic bag and ask for a hand inspection. Such requests are honored at U.S. airports and are up to the inspector abroad. Don't depend on a lead-lined bag to protect film in checked luggage—the airline may increase the radiation to see what's inside. Call the Kodak Information Center (tel. 800/242–2424) for details.

**Camcorders and Videotape**   Before your trip, put camcorders through their paces, invest in a skylight filter to protect the lens, and check all the batteries. Most newer camcorders are equipped with batteries that can be recharged with a universal or worldwide AC adapter charger (or multivoltage converter) usable whether the voltage is 110 or 220. All that's needed is the appropriate plug.

Videotape is not damaged by X-rays, but it may be harmed by the magnetic field of a walk-through metal detector, so ask for a hand-check. Airport security personnel may ask you to turn on the camcorder to prove that it's what it appears to be, so make sure the battery is charged. Note that rather than the National Television System Committee video standard (NTSC) used in the U.S. and Canada, Portugal uses PAL/SECAM technology. You will not be able to view your tapes through the local TV set or view movies bought there in your home VCR. Blank tapes bought in Portugal can be used for NTSC camcorder taping, but they are pricey.

**Laptops**  Security X-rays do not harm hard-disk or floppy-disk storage, but you may request a hand-check, at which point you may be asked to turn on the computer to prove that it's what it appears to be. (Check your battery before departure.) Most airlines allow you to use your laptop aloft except during takeoff and landing (so as not to interfere with navigation equipment). For international travel, register your foreign-made laptop with U.S. Customs as you leave the country. If your laptop is U.S.-made, call the consulate of the country you'll be visiting to find out whether it should be registered with customs upon arrival. Before departure, find out about repair facilities at your destination, and don't forget any transformer or adapter plug you may need (*see* Electricity, *above*).

## Language

Despite its Slavic-sounding inflections and nasal intonations, Portuguese is essentially a romance language of Latin origin, and is now the seventh most widely spoken language in the world. Roughly half the people a tourist comes in contact with (at least in the larger cities) will speak some English. Any attempt by visitors to speak Portuguese will be warmly appreciated. Written Portuguese resembles Spanish, although pronunciation can be markedly different (*see* the Glossary at the end of this guide).

## Staying Healthy

Sunburn and sunstroke are common problems in summer in mainland Portugal and virtually year-round in Madeira. On a hot, sunny day, even people not normally bothered by a strong sun should cover up with a long-sleeve shirt, a hat, and slacks or a beach wrap. Carry sunscreen for nose, ears, and other sensitive areas; be sure to drink enough liquids, and above all, limit your sun exposure for the first few days until you become accustomed to the heat.

No special shots are required before visiting Portugal (except for yellow-fever shots if you want to visit Madeira and have come from an infected area). If you need to purchase prescription drugs in Portugal, have your doctor write a prescription using the drug's generic name; brand names can vary widely.

**Finding a Doctor**  The **International Association for Medical Assistance to Travelers** (IAMAT, 417 Center St., Lewiston, NY 14902, tel. 716/754–4883; 40 Regal Rd., Guelph, Ont., N1K 1B5, tel. 519/836–0102; 57 Voirets, 1212 Grand-Lancy, Geneva, Switzerland) publishes a worldwide directory of English-speaking physicians whose qualifications meet IAMAT standards and who have agreed to treat members for a set fee. Membership is free.

**Medical Treatment**  In Portugal there is no free medical treatment for visitors unless their countries of origin have reciprocal health agreements, as with the United Kingdom. There is a **British Hospital** (Rua Saraiva de Carvalho 49, Lisbon, tel. 01/395–5067) for both in- and outpatients, with English-speaking doctors and nurses. There are local hospitals with emergency services in all the larger towns. Pharmacies are open weekdays from 9 to 1 and 3 to 7, Saturdays from 9 to 1; the addresses and phone numbers of those open after hours are posted on pharmacy doors and listed in newspapers.

**Assistance Companies**  Pretrip medical referrals, emergency evacuation or repatriation, 24-hour telephone hot lines for medical consultation, dispatch of medical personnel, relay of medical records, cash for emergencies, and other personal and legal assistance are among the services provided by several organizations specializing in medical assistance to travelers. Among them are **International SOS Assistance** (Box 11568, Philadelphia, PA 19116, tel. 215/244–1500 or 800/523–8930; Box 466, Pl. Bonaventure, Montréal, Qué., H5A 1C1, tel. 514/874–7674 or 800/363–0263), **Medex Assistance Corporation** (Box 10623, Baltimore, MD 21285, tel. 410/296–2530 or 800/874–9125), **Near Services** (450 Prairie Ave., Suite 101, Calumet City, IL 60409, tel. 708/868–6700 or 800/654–6700), and **Travel Assistance International** (1133 15th St. NW, Suite 400, Washington, DC 20005, tel. 202/331–1609 or 800/821–2828). Because these companies will also sell you death-and-dismemberment, trip-cancellation, and other insurance coverage, there is some overlap with the travel-insurance policies discussed under Insurance, *below.*

**Publications** *The Safe Travel Book* by Peter Savage ($12.95, Lexington Books, 866 Third Ave., New York, NY 10022, tel. 212/702–4771 or 800/257–5755, fax 800/562–1272) is packed with handy lists and phone numbers to make your trip smooth. *Traveler's Medical Resource* by William W. Forgey ($19.95, ICS Books, Inc., 1 Tower Plaza, 107 E. 89th Ave., Merrillville, IN 45410, tel. 800/541–7323) is also a good, authoritative guide to care overseas.

---

## Insurance

**For U.S. Residents** Most tour operators, travel agents, and insurance agents sell specialized health-and-accident, flight, trip-cancellation, and luggage insurance as well as comprehensive policies with some or all of these features. Before you make any purchase, review your existing health and homeowner policies to find out whether they cover expenses incurred while traveling.

*Health and Accident* Specific policy provisions of supplemental health-and-accident insurance for travelers include reimbursement for from $1,000 to $150,000 worth of medical and/or dental expenses caused by an accident or illness during a trip. The personal-accident or death-and-dismemberment provision pays a lump sum to your beneficiaries if you die or to you if you lose one or both limbs or your eyesight; the lump sum awarded can range from $15,000 to $500,000. The medical-assistance provision may reimburse you for the cost of referrals, evacuation, or repatriation and other services, or it may automatically enroll you as a member of a particular medical-assistance company (*see* Assistance Companies, *above*).

*Flight Insurance* Often bought as a last-minute impulse at the airport, flight insurance pays a lump sum when a plane crashes either to a beneficiary if the insured dies or sometimes to a surviving passenger who loses eyesight or a limb. Like most impulse buys, flight insurance is expensive and basically unnecessary. It supplements the airlines' coverage described in the limits-of-liability paragraphs on your ticket. Charging an airline ticket to a major credit card often automatically entitles you to coverage and may also include travel by bus, train, and ship.

*Baggage Insurance* In the event of loss, damage, or theft on international flights, airlines' liability is $20 per kilogram for checked baggage (roughly about $640 per 70-pound bag) and $400 per passenger for unchecked baggage. On domestic flights, the ceiling is $1,250 per passenger. Excess-valuation insurance can be bought directly from the airline at check-in for about $10 per $1,000 worth of coverage. However, you cannot buy it at any price for the rather extensive list of excluded items shown on your airline ticket.

*Trip Insurance* **Trip-cancellation-and-interruption insurance** protects you in the event you are unable to undertake or finish your trip, especially if your airline ticket, cruise, or package tour does not allow changes or cancellations. The amount of coverage you purchase should equal the cost of your trip should you, a traveling companion, or a family member fall ill, forcing you to stay home, plus the nondiscounted one-way airline ticket you would need to buy if you had to return home early. Read the fine print carefully, especially sections defining "family member" and "preexisting medical conditions." **Default or bankruptcy insurance** protects you against a supplier's failure to deliver. Such policies often do not cover default by a travel agency, tour operator, airline, or cruise line if you bought your tour and the coverage directly from the firm in question. Tours packaged by one of the 33 members of the United States Tour Operators Association (USTOA, 211 E. 51 St., Suite 12B, New York, NY 10022; tel. 212/750-7371), which requires members to maintain $1 million each in an account to reimburse clients in case of default, are likely to present the fewest difficulties.

*Comprehensive* Companies supplying comprehensive policies with some or all of the
*Policies* above features include **Access America, Inc.** (Box 90315, Richmond, VA 23230, tel. 800/284–8300); **Carefree Travel Insurance** (Box 310, 120 Mineola Blvd., Mineola, NY 11501, tel. 516/294–0220 or 800/323–3149); **Tele-Trip** (Mutual of Omaha Plaza, Box 31762, Omaha, NE 68131, tel. 800/228–9792); **The Travelers Companies** (1 Tower Sq., Hartford, CT 06183, tel. 203/277–0111 or 800/243–3174); **Travel Guard International** (1145 Clark St., Stevens Point, WI 54481, tel. 715/345–0505 or 800/826–1300); and **Wallach and Company, Inc.** (107 W. Federal St., Box 480, Middleburg, VA 22117, tel. 703/687–3166 or 800/237–6615).

**U.K.** Most tour operators, travel agents, and insurance agents sell poli-
**Residents** cies covering accident, medical expenses, personal liability, trip cancellation, and loss or theft of personal property.

For advice by phone or a free booklet, "Holiday Insurance," that sets out what to expect from a holiday-insurance policy and gives price guidelines, contact the Association of British Insurers (51 Gresham St., London EC2V 7HQ, tel. 0171/600–3333; 30 Gordon St., Glasgow G1 3PU, tel. 0141/226–3905; Scottish Providence Bldg., Donegall Sq. W, Belfast BT1 6JE, tel. 01232/249176; call for other locations).

## Car Rentals

Be sure to make your arrangements for car rentals before you leave home; cars rented on arrival in Portugal can cost up to twice as much.

If you are planning to begin your visit with a city stay, save money by arranging to pick up your car the day you are ready to start traveling. If you are already in Portugal and decide to rent a car, it may be cheaper to call home and have a friend or relative make the reservation for you, although cars must be reserved seven days in advance. Most major car-rental companies are represented in Portugal, including **Alamo** (tel. 800/327–9633); **Avis** (tel. 800/331–1084, 800/879–2847 in Canada); **Budget** (tel. 800/527–0700); **Hertz** (tel. 800/654–3001, 800/263–0600 in Canada); and **National** (tel. 800/227–3876), known internationally as InterRent and Europcar. In cities, unlimited-mileage rates range from $59 per day for an economy car to $99 for a large car; weekly unlimited-mileage rates range from $342 to $659. This includes the value-added tax (VAT), which in Portugal is 16% on car rentals.

**Requirements** Your own driver's license is acceptable. An International Driver's Permit, available from the American or Canadian Automobile Association, is a good idea.

**Extra Charges** Picking up the car in one city and leaving it in another may entail substantial drop-off charges or one-way service fees. The cost of a collision or loss-damage waiver (*see below*) can be high, also. Some rental agencies will charge you extra if you return the car *before* the time specified on your contract. Ask before making unscheduled drop-offs. Be sure the rental agent agrees *in writing* to any changes in drop-off location or other items of your rental contract. Fill the tank when you turn in the vehicle to avoid being charged for refueling at what you'll swear is the most expensive pump in town. In Europe manual transmissions are standard and air conditioning is a rarity and often unnecessary. Asking for an automatic transmission or air-conditioning can significantly increase the cost of your rental. Find out what the standard rentals are in the country you'll be visiting and weigh that factor when making your reservation.

**Cutting Costs** Major international companies have programs that discount their standard rates by 15% to 30% if you make the reservation before departure (anywhere from 24 hours to 14 days), rent for a minimum number of days (typically three or four), and prepay the rental. Several companies operate as wholesalers; they don't own their own fleets but rent in bulk from those that do and offer advantageous rates to their customers. Rentals through such companies must be arranged and paid for before you leave the United States. Among them are **Auto Europe** (Box 7006, Portland, ME 04112, tel. 207/828–2525 or 800/223–5555, 800/458–9503 in Canada); **Europe by Car** (mailing address, 1 Rockefeller Plaza, New York, NY 10020; walk-in address, 14 W. 49th St, New York, NY 10020, tel. 212/581–3040, 212/245–1713, or 800/223–1516; 9000 Sunset Blvd., Los Angeles, CA 90069, tel. 800/252–9401 or 213/272–0424 in CA); **Foremost Euro-Car** (5658 Sepulveda Blvd., Suite 201, Van Nuys, CA 91411, tel. 818/786–1960 or 800/272–3299); and **The Kemwel Group** (106 Calvert St., Harrison, NY 10528, tel. 914/835–5555 or 800/678–0678). You won't see these wholesalers' deals advertised; they're even better in summer, when business travel is down. Always ask whether the prices are guaranteed in U.S. dollars or foreign currency and if unlimited mileage is available. Find out about any required deposits, cancellation penalties, and drop-off charges, and confirm the cost of any required insurance coverage.

**Insurance and Collision Damage Waiver** Until recently, standard rental contracts included liability coverage (for damage to public property, injury to pedestrians, and so on) and coverage for the car against fire, theft, and collision damage with a deductible. Due to law changes in some states and rising liability costs, several car rental agencies have reduced the type of coverage they offer. Before you rent a car, find out exactly what coverage, if any, is provided by your personal auto insurer. Don't assume that you are covered. If you do want insurance from the rental company, secondary coverage may be the only type offered. You may already have secondary coverage if you charge the rental to a credit card. Only Diner's Club (tel. 800/234–6377) provides primary coverage in the U.S. and worldwide.

In general, if you have an accident you are responsible for the automobile. Car rental companies may offer a collision damage waiver (CDW), which ranges in cost from $4 to $14 a day. You should decline the CDW only if you are certain you are covered through your personal insurer or credit card company.

## Rail Passes

The **EurailPass**, valid for unlimited first-class train travel through 17 countries including Portugal, is an excellent value for travel around the Continent. Standard passes are available for 15 days ($498), 21 days ($648), one month ($728), two months ($1,098), and three months ($1,398). **Eurail Saverpasses** valid for 15 days cost $430 per person, for 21 days $550, for one month $678 per person; you must do all your traveling with at least one companion (two companions from April through September). **Eurail Youthpasses**, which cover second-class travel, cost $578 for one month, $768 for two; you must be under 26 on the first day you travel. **Eurail Flexipasses** allow you to travel first class for 5 ($348), 10 ($560), or 15 ($740) days within any two-month period. **Eurail Youth Flexipasses,** available to those under 26 on their first travel day, allow you to travel second class for 5 ($255), 10 ($398), or 15 ($540) days within any two-month period. Another option is the **Europass**, featuring a minimum of 5 and a maximum of 15 days (within a two-month period) of unlimited rail travel in your choice of three to all five of the participating countries (France, Germany, Italy, Spain, and Switzerland); cost for five days is $280 first class, $198 second class (3 countries); for 8 days, $394 first class, $284 second class (4 countries), and for 11 days, $508 first class, $366 second class (all five countries). **Portugal** may be added as an *Associate Country* for an additional $22 in first class or $16 in second class. Each extra rail day costs $38 for first class and $28 for second class. Apply through your travel agent or **Rail Europe** (226–230 Westchester Ave., White Plains, NY 10604, tel. 914/682–5172 or 800/848–7245; or 2087 Dundas East, Suite 105, Mississauga, Ont., L4X 1M2, tel. 416/602–4195), **DER Tours** (Box 1606, Des Plaines, IL 60017, tel. 800/782–2424, fax 800/282–7474), or **CIT Tours Corp.** (342 Madison Ave., Suite 207, New York, NY 10173, tel. 212/697–2100 or 800/248–8687; 310/670–4269 or 800/248–7245 in western U.S.).

## Student and Youth Travel

**Travel Agencies**  **Council Travel Services (CTS),** a subsidiary of the nonprofit Council on International Educational Exchange, specializes in low-cost travel arrangements abroad for students and is the exclusive U.S. agent for several discount cards. Also newly available from CTS are domestic air passes for bargain travel within the United States. CIEE's twice-yearly *Student Travels* magazine is available at the CTS office at CIEE headquarters (205 E. 42nd St., 16th Floor, New York, NY 10017, tel. 212/661–1450) and in Boston (tel. 617/266–1926), Miami (tel. 305/670–9261), Los Angeles (tel. 310/208–3551) and at 43 branches in college towns nationwide (free in person, $1 by mail). **Campus Connections** (1100 East Marlton Pike, Cherry Hill, NJ 08034, tel. 800/428–3235) specializes in discounted accommodations and airline fares for students. The **Educational Travel Centre** (438 N. Frances St., Madison, WI 53703, tel. 608/256–5551) offers low-cost domestic and international airline tickets, mostly for flights departing from Chicago, and rail passes. Other travel agencies catering to students include **TMI Student Travel** (1146 Pleasant St., Watertown, MA 02172, tel. 617/661–8187 or 800/245–3672), and **Travel Cuts** (187 College St., Toronto, Ont., M5T 1P7, tel. 416/979–2406).

**Discount**  For discounts on transportation and on museum and attractions ad-
**Cards**  missions, buy the **International Student Identity Card** (ISIC) if
you're a bona fide student or the **International Youth Card** (IYC) if
you're under 26. In the United States the ISIC and IYC cards cost
$16 each and include basic travel accident and illness coverage and a
toll-free travel assistance hot line. Apply to **CIEE** (*see* address
*above*, tel. 212/661–1414; the application is in *Student Travels*). In
Canada the cards are available for $15 each from **Travel Cuts** (*see
above*). In the United Kingdom they cost £5 and £4 respectively at
student unions and student travel companies, including Council
Travel's London office (28A Poland St., London W1V 3DB, tel. 0171/
437–7767).

**Hostelling**  A **Hostelling International** (HI) membership card is the key to more
than 5,000 hostels in 70 countries; the sex-segregated, dormitory-
style sleeping quarters, including some for families, go for $7 to $20
a night per person. Membership is available in the United States
through **Hostelling International-American Youth Hostels** (HI-AYH,
733 15th St. NW, Suite 840, Washington, DC 20005, tel. 202/783–
6161), the U.S. link in the worldwide chain, and costs $25 for adults
18 to 54, $10 for those under 18, $15 for those 55 and over, and $35 for
families. Volume 1 of the *AYH Guide to Budget Accommodation* lists
hostels in Europe and the Mediterranean ($13.95, including post-
age). HI membership is available in Canada through **Hostelling In-
ternational-Canada** (205 Catherine St. Suite 400, Ottawa, Ont., K2P
1C3, tel. 613/748–5638) for $26.75, and in the United Kingdom
through the **Youth Hostel Association of England and Wales** (Trevel-
yan House, 8 St. Stephen's Hill, St. Albans, Herts. AL1 2DY, tel.
01727/855215) for £9.

## Traveling with Children

The Portuguese are very family-oriented and love children, so take
them along on your trip. You'll see children of all ages accompanying
their parents everywhere, including bars and restaurants. Shop-
keepers will smile and offer your child a *bombom,* and even the cold-
est waiters tend to be friendlier when you have a child with you.
Kitchens are usually willing to fix something special for children,
but you won't find children's menus anywhere. On the road, even the
smallest *tasca* (town restaurant/bar) will be able to make a *sandes de
queijo* (cheese sandwich), and roast chicken (*frango assado*) is on
most menus. Museum admissions, buses, and metro rides are generally free for children under five, and half-price for children under 12.

**Publications**  *Family Travel Times,* published 10 times a year by **Travel With Your**
*Newsletter*  **Children** (TWYCH, 45 W. 18th St., New York, NY 10011, tel. 212/
206–0688; annual subscription $55), covers destinations, types of va-
cations, and modes of travel. TWYCH also publishes *Cruising with
Children* ($22) and *Skiing with Children* ($29).

*Books*  *Traveling with Children—And Enjoying It,* by Arlene K. Butler
($11.95 plus $3 shipping per book; Globe Pequot Press, Box 833, 6
Business Park Rd., Old Saybrook, CT 06475, tel. 800/243–0495, or
800/962–0973 in CT) helps plan your trip with children, from tod-
dlers to teens. *Innocents Abroad: Traveling with Kids in Europe*,
by Valerie Wolf Deutsch and Laura Sutherland ($15.95 or $4.95
paperback, Penguin USA, *see above*), covers child- and teen-friend-
ly activities, food, and transportation.

**Getting There**  On international flights, the fare for infants under age 2 not occupy-
*Airfares*  ing a seat is generally either free or 10% of the accompanying adult's
fare; children ages 2 to 11 usually pay half to two-thirds of the adult

fare. On domestic flights, children under 2 not occupying a seat travel free, and older children currently travel on the "lowest applicable" adult fare.

**Baggage** In general, infants paying 10% of the adult fare are allowed one carry-on bag, not to exceed 70 pounds or 45 inches (length + width + height) and a collapsible stroller; check with the airline before departure, because you may be allowed less if the flight is full. The adult baggage allowance applies for children paying half or more of the adult fare.

**Safety Seats** The FAA recommends the use of safety seats aloft and details approved models in the free leaflet **"Child/Infant Safety Seats Recommended for Use in Aircraft"** (available from the FAA, APA–200, 800 Independence Ave. SW, Washington, DC 20591, tel. 202/267–3479; Information Hot Line, tel. 800/322–7873). Airline policy varies. U.S. carriers allow FAA-approved models bearing a sticker declaring their FAA approval. Because these seats are strapped into regular passenger seats, airlines may require that a ticket be bought for an infant who would otherwise ride free. Foreign carriers may not allow infant seats, may charge the child's rather than the infant's fare for their use, or may require you to hold your baby during take-off and landing, thus defeating the seat's purpose.

**Facilities Aloft** Some airlines provide other services for children, such as children's meals and freestanding bassinets (only to those with seats at the bulkhead, where there's enough legroom). Make your request when reserving. Biennially, the February issue of *Family Travel Times* details children's services on three dozen airlines ($12; *see above*). "Kids and Teens in Flight" (free from the U.S. Department of Transportation's Office of Consumer Affairs (R-25, Washington, D.C. 20590, tel. 202/366–2220) offers tips for children flying alone.

**Lodging** Generally, children under six years stay free in the same room with parents, and children under 12 sharing the parents' room get a 50% discount. A travel agent should be able to confirm this for you.

**Baby-Sitting Services** The front-desk personnel in most Portuguese hotels will be able to find a reliable baby-sitter.

## Hints for Travelers with Disabilities

**Organizations** Several organizations provide travel information for people with disabilities, usually for a membership fee, and some publish newsletters and bulletins. Among them are the **Information Center for Individuals with Disabilities** (Fort Point Pl., 27–43 Wormwood St., Boston, MA 02210, tel. 617/727–5540 or 800/462–5015 in MA between 11 AM and 4 PM, or leave message; TTY 617/345–9743); **Mobility International USA** (Box 10767, Eugene, OR 97440, tel. and TTY 503/343–1284:; fax 503/343–6812), the U.S. branch of an international organization based in Britain (*see below*) that has affiliates in 30 countries; **Moss Rehab Hospital Travel Information Service** (tel. 215/456–9603, TTY 215/456–9602); the **Travel Industry and Disabled Exchange** (TIDE, 5435 DonnaAve., Tarzana, CA 91356, tel. 818/344–3640, fax 818/344–0078); and **Travelin' Talk** (Box 3534, Clarksville, TN 37043, tel. 615/552–6670, fax 615/552–1182).

**In the United Kingdom** Important information sources include the **Royal Association for Disability and Rehabilitation** (RADAR, 12 City Forum, 250 City Rd., London EC1V 8AF, tel. 0171/250–3222), which publishes travel information for people with disabilities in Britain, and **Mobility International** (228 Borough High St., London SE1 1JX, tel. 0171/

403–5688), an international clearinghouse of travel information for people with disabilities.

**Travel Agencies and Tour Operators** **Flying Wheels Travel** (143 W. Bridge St., Box 382, Owatonna, MN 55060, tel. 507/451–5005 or 800/535–6790) is a travel agency specializing in domestic and worldwide cruises, tours, and independent travel itineraries for people with mobility problems.

**Publications** Several free publications are available from the U.S. Consumer Information Center (Pueblo, CO 81009): "New Horizons for the Air Traveler with a Disability" (include Dept. 608Y in the address), a U.S. Department of Transportation booklet describing changes resulting from the 1986 Air Carrier Access Act and from the 1990 Americans with Disabilities Act; and the Airport Operators Council's *Access Travel: Airports* (Dept. 5804), which describes facilities and services for people with disabilities at more than 500 airports worldwide.

*Travelin' Talk Directory* (*see* Organizations, *above*) was published in 1993. This 500-page resource book ($35 check or money order with a money-back guarantee) is packed with information for travelers with disabilities. Twin Peaks Press (Box 129, Vancouver, WA 98666, tel. 206/694–2462 or 800/637–2256) publishes the *Directory of Travel Agencies for the Disabled* ($19.95), listing more than 370 agencies worldwide. Add $2 for shipping.

## Hints for Older Travelers

**Organizations** The **American Association of Retired Persons** (AARP, 601 E St. NW, Washington, DC 20049, tel. 202/434–2277) provides independent travelers who are members of the AARP (open to those age 50 or older; $8 per person or couple annually) with the Purchase Privilege Program, which offers discounts on lodging, car rentals, and sightseeing, and arranges group tours, cruises, and apartment living through AARP Travel Experience from American Express (400 Pinnacle Way, Suite 450, Norcross, GA 30071, tel. 800/927–0111 or 800/745–4567).

Two other organizations offer discounts on lodgings, car rentals, and other travel products, along with such nontravel perks as magazines and newsletters: the **National Council of Senior Citizens** (1221 F St. NW, Washington, DC 20004, tel. 202/347–8800 (membership $12 annually) and **Mature Outlook** (6001 N. Clark St., Chicago, IL 60660, tel. 800/336–6330; $9.95 annually).

For reduced rates, mention your senior-citizen identification card when booking hotel reservations, not when checking out. At restaurants, show your card before you're seated; discounts may be limited to certain menus, days, or hours. If you are renting a car, ask about promotional rates that might improve on your senior discount.

**Educational Travel** The nonprofit **Elderhostel** (75 Federal St., 3rd Floor, Boston, MA 02110, tel. 617/426–7788) has offered inexpensive study programs for people 60 and older since 1975. Held at more than 1,800 educational institutions, courses cover everything from marine science to Greek myths and cowboy poetry. Participants usually attend lectures in the morning and spend the afternoon sightseeing or on field trips; they live in dorms on the host campuses. Fees for two- to three-week international trips—including room, board, and transportation from the United States—range from $1,800 to $4,500.

**Interhostel** (University of New Hampshire, 6 Garrison Ave., Durham, NH 03824, tel. 800/733–9753 or 603/862–1147) caters to a slightly younger clientele—50 and over—and runs programs in some 25 countries. The idea is similar: Lectures and field trips mix with sightseeing, and participants stay in dormitories at cooperating educational institutions or in modest hotels. Programs usually last two weeks and cost $1,500–$2,100, excluding airfare.

**Publications**  *The 50+ Traveler's Guidebook: Where to Go, Where to Stay, What to Do* by Anita Williams and Merrimac Dillon ($12.95, St. Martin's Press, 175 5th Ave., New York, NY 10010) is available in bookstores and offers many useful tips. "The Mature Traveler" (Box 50820, Reno, NV 89513; $29.95), a monthly newsletter, contains many travel deals.

## Hints for Gay and Lesbian Travelers

Although the general age of consent in Portugal is 16, and homosexuality is not mentioned in the Code of Law, various articles of the penal code are enforced against gays. Portuguese police can be hostile, have been known to be physically abusive to gays, and are allowed to jail suspected criminals indefinitely pending investigation. Bearing in mind the above warning, decorum and discretion are of paramount importance. Lisbon is the most important city in the Portuguese gay scene, followed by Oporto, Albufeira, and Portimão. The action in Lisbon is concentrated around *Rua da Imprensa Nacional* near the Botanical Garden, but although this park seems idyllic by day, it is dangerous after dark. For more information, contact **Gay International Rights** (C.P. 110, 4702 Braga Codex, Portugal, tel. 053/79296).

**Organizations**  The **International Gay Travel Association** (Box 4974, Key West, FL 33041, tel. 305/292–0217 or 800/999–7925 or 800/448–8550), which has 800 member organizations, will provide you with names of travel agents and tour operators who specialize in gay travel.

**Tour**  The dominant travel agency in the market is **Above and Beyond** (3568
**Operators and**  Sacramento St., San Francisco, CA 94118, tel. 415/922–2683 or 800/
**Travel**  397–2681). Tour operator **Olympus Vacations** (8424 Santa Monica
**Agencies**  Blvd. No.721, West Hollywood, CA 90069; tel. 310/657–2220) offers all-gay-and-lesbian resort holidays. **Skylink Women's Travel** (746 Ashland Ave., Santa Monica, CA 90405, tel. 310/452–0506 or 800/225–5759) handles individual travel for lesbians all over the world and conducts two international and five domestic group trips annually.

**Publications**  The premiere international travel magazine for gays and lesbians is **Our World** (1104 North Nova Rd., Suite 251, Daytona Beach, FL 32117, tel. 904/441–5367; $35 for 10 issues). **Out & About** (tel. 203/789-8518 or 800/929–2268; $49 for 10 issues, full refund if you aren't satisfied) is a 16-page monthly newsletter with extensive information on resorts, hotels, and airlines that are gay-friendly.

## Further Reading

A good place to begin is your local library. Check the library index, perhaps for the travel section first, and then the history books.

*Portugal* (Scala Books, 1983), by Helmut and Alice Wohl, *Country Manors of Portugal* (Scala Books, 1987), by Marcus Binney, *Portugal, Garden of Europe* (Passport Books, 1991), by Julia Wilkinson, *The Last Old Place: A Search through Portugal* (S&S Trade, 1993), by Datus C. Proper, and *Fado* (Aster, 1980), by Mascarenhas Barreto) are a good visual introduction to the countryside, houses, and music of Portugal. *The Discoverers—An Encyclopedia of Explorers and Exploration,* edited by Helen Delpar (McGraw Hill, 1980) and *The Conquest of Paradise—Christopher Columbus and the Columbian Legacy,* by Kirkpatrick Sale (Knopf, 1990) will inform you about the Portuguese explorers and what they discovered. Look at your library for *They Went to Portugal* by Rose Macaulay (Penguin/Clarke, Irwin); it's good for dipping into or a serious read.

*Portugal—Social Life and Customs,* edited by Richard Herr and John Polt, and *Iberian Identity: Essays on the Nature of Identity in Portugal and Spain* (University of California International Studies, 1989) gives insight about the people of the Iberian peninsula.

*Time Off in Spain and Portugal* by Teresa Tinsley (Horizon Books Ltd./Harper & Row, 1989) is for travelers contemplating more than just a few days or weeks in the country—it includes historical facts as well as local contacts and advice on how to experience the everyday life of the Portuguese and be more than just a tourist.

Other books include:

**History** *A New History of Portugal* (Cambridge University Press, 1976); *A History of Portugal* (2 volumes; Columbia University Press, 1972) by A. H. Marques de Oliveira; *Portugal: Ancient Country, Young Democracy* (Wilson Center Publishers, 1990), edited by Kenneth Maxwell and Michael H. Haltzel; *The Discoverers* (Random House, Inc., 1983), by Daniel Boorstin; *The Portuguese Land and Its People* (Penguin Viking, 1991), by Marion Kaplan; *Portugal of the Portuguese* (The Gordon Press, 1976), by A. F. Bell.

**Literature** *The Lusiads* (Viking Penguin, 1975), by Luis de Camões, translated by W. C. Atkinson, was written by a contemporary of Cervantes and Shakespeare who wrote the definitive classic of his people during the time of the Discoveries. *Portugal, A Book of Folkways* (Cambridge University Press, 1936) is a collection of Portuguese folklore.

**Gastronomy** *Flavors of Portugal* (Diversity, Inc., 1989), by Elvira Ferreira, *The Food of Portugal* (William Morrow & Co., 1986), by Jean Anderson; *Portugal on Your Own, Making the Most of Local Food & Drink* (Hippocrene Books, Inc., 1986), by Carol Wright, *Wines of Spain and Portugal* (Price Stern, 1990), by Charles Metcalfe and Kathryn McWhirter.

# Arriving and Departing

## From North America by Plane

All transatlantic flights from the United States and Canada to Portugal pass through Lisbon, where you change for connecting flights to other destinations in the country or to Madeira or the Azores. Schedule and fare changes occur with breathtaking frequency, so consult with your travel agent on which bargains are currently available, and read the newspaper for special promotions.

Flights are either nonstop, direct, or connecting. A **nonstop** flight requires no change of plane and makes no stops. A **direct** flight stops at least once and can involve a change of plane, although the flight number remains the same; if the first leg is late, the second waits. This is not the case with a **connecting** flight, which involves a different plane and a different flight number.

**Airports and** Three airlines fly from the United States to Portugal: **TAP Air Portugal** (tel. 800/221–7370); **TWA** (tel. 800/892–4141); and **Delta** (tel.

800/241–4141). TAP flies to Lisbon's **Portela Airport** (tel. 01/802060) six times a week in winter; daily from New York and Newark from April till September; and twice weekly from Boston and Los Angeles. TAP also flies to Madeira and the Azores through Boston three times a week. TWA flies daily from New York in the summer, four times a week during the rest of the year. Delta flies from New York three times a week.

**Air Canada** (tel. 800/776–3000) has three flights a week from Toronto and Montréal; **TAP Air Portugal** has frequent service from both Montréal and Toronto, including flights to Madeira (through Lisbon) and the Azores (through Boston).

Although price will probably be your prime consideration in selecting an airline, try to avoid the delays involved in changing planes at New York's Kennedy Airport.

**Flying Time**  From New York to Lisbon: 6½ hours. From Atlanta to Lisbon (including one stop): 12 hours. From Los Angeles to Lisbon (including one stop): 15 hours. From Toronto or Montréal to Lisbon: eight hours.

**Cutting Costs**  The Sunday travel section of most newspapers is a good source of deals. When booking, particularly through an unfamiliar company, call the Better Business Bureau and your local or state Consumer Protection Bureau to find out whether any complaints have been registered against the company, pay with a credit card if you can, and consider trip-cancellation and default insurance (*see* Insurance, *above*).

*Promotional Airfares*  Less expensive fares, called promotional or discount fares, are round-trip and involve restrictions, which vary according to the route and season. You must usually buy the ticket—commonly called an APEX (advance purchase excursion) when it's for international travel—in advance (seven, 14, or 21 days are usual), although some of the major airlines have added no-frills, cheap flights to compete with new bargain airlines on certain routes.

For comparison, at press time round-trip New York–Lisbon fares were: Navigator Class, $2,684, economy, $778–$1,100. Note that TAP Air Portugal does not offer first-class service.

Read the newspapers, too; sometimes airlines advertise amazingly low fares. For example, at press time it was possible to book a round-trip New York–Lisbon flight on at least two major airlines for under $500 (with airport tax, the total cost was $528).

With the major airlines the cheaper fares generally require minimum and maximum stays (for instance, over a Saturday night or at least seven and no more than 30 days). Airlines generally allow some return date changes for a $25 to $50 fee, but most low-fare tickets are nonrefundable. Only a death in the family would prompt the airline to return any of your money if you cancel a nonrefundable ticket. However, you can apply an unused nonrefundable ticket toward a new ticket, again with a small fee. The lowest fare is subject to availability, and only a small percentage of the plane's total seats will be sold at that price. Contact the U.S. Department of Transportation's Office of Consumer Affairs (I–25, Washington, DC 20590, tel. 202/366–2220) for a copy of "Fly-Rights: A Guide to Air Travel in the U.S."

*Consolidators*  Consolidators or bulk-fare operators—"bucket shops"—buy blocks of seats on scheduled flights that airlines anticipate they won't be able to sell. They pay wholesale prices, add a markup, and resell the seats to travel agents or directly to the public at prices that still undercut the airline's promotional or discount fares (higher than a charter ticket but lower than an APEX ticket, and usually without the advance-purchase restriction). Moreover, some consolidators sometimes give you your money back. Carefully read the fine print detailing penalties for changes and cancellations. If you doubt the reliability of a company, call the airline once you've made your booking and confirm that you do, indeed, have a reservation on the flight.

The biggest U.S. consolidator, C. L. Thomson Express, sells only to travel agents. Well-established consolidators selling to the public include: **UniTravel** (Box 12485, St. Louis, MO 63132, tel. 314/569–0900 or 800/325–2222) and **Travac** (989 6th Ave., New York, NY 10018, tel. 212/563–3303 or 800/872–8800).

*Charter Flights* Charters usually have the lowest fares and the most restrictions. Departures are limited and seldom on time, and you can lose all or most of your money if you cancel. (The closer to departure you cancel, the more you lose, although sometimes you will be charged only a small fee if you supply a substitute passenger.) The charterer may legally cancel the flight for any reason up to 10 days before departure; within 10 days of departure, the flight may be canceled only if it is physically impossible to operate it. The charterer may also revise the itinerary or increase the price after you have bought the ticket, but if the new arrangement constitutes a "major change," you have the right to a refund. Before buying a charter ticket, read the fine print for the company's refund policy and details on major changes. Money for charter flights is usually paid into a bank escrow account, the name of which should be on the contract. If you don't pay by credit card, make your check payable to the escrow account (unless you're dealing with a travel agent, in which case his or her check should be payable to the escrow account). The U.S. Department of Transportation's Office of Consumer Affairs (I–25, Washington, DC 20590, tel. 202/366–2220) can answer questions on charters and send you its "Plane Talk: Public Charter Flights" information sheet.

*Discount Travel Clubs* Travel clubs offer members unsold space on airplanes, cruise ships, and package tours at as much as 50% below regular prices. Membership may include a regular bulletin or access to a toll-free hot line giving details of available trips departing from three or four days to several months in the future. Most also offer 50% discounts off hotel rack rates, but double-check with the hotel to make sure it isn't offering a better promotional rate independent of the club. Clubs include **Discount Travel International** (114 Forrest Ave., Suite 203, Narberth, PA 19072, tel. 215/668–7184; $45 annually, single or family), **Entertainment Travel Editions** (Box 1014, Trumbull, CT 06611, tel. 800/445–4137; price ranges $28-$48), **Great American Traveler** (Box 27965, Salt Lake City, UT 84127, tel. 800/548–2812; $29.95 annually), **Moment's Notice Discount Travel Club** (425 Madison Ave., New York, NY 10017, tel. 212/486–0503; $45 annually, single or family), **Privilege Card** (3391 Peachtree Rd. NE, Suite 110, Atlanta, GA 30326, tel. 404/262–0222 or 800/236–9732; domestic annual membership $49.95, international, $74.95), **Travelers Advantage** (CUC Travel Service, 49 Music Sq. W, Nashville, TN 37203, tel.800/548–1116; $49 annually, single or family), and **Worldwide Discount Travel Club** (1674 Meridian Ave., Miami Beach, FL 33139, tel. 305/534–2082; $50 annually for family, $40 single).

*Publications* Both Consumers Union's "Consumer Reports Travel Letter" (Box 53629, Boulder CO 80322, tel. 800/234–1970; $39 a year) and the newsletter "Travel Smart" (40 Beechdale Rd., Dobbs Ferry, NY

10522, tel. 800/327–3633; $37 a year) have a wealth of travel deals and tips in each monthly issue. *The Official Frequent Flyer Guidebook* by Randy Petersen (4715-C Town Center Dr., Colorado Springs, CO 80916, tel. 719/597–8899 or 800/487–8893; $14.99, plus $3 shipping and handling) yields valuable hints on getting the most for your air travel dollars, as does *Airfare Secrets Exposed*, by Sharon Tyler and Matthew Wonder (Universal Information Publishing, $16.95 in bookstores). Also helpful is *202 Tips Even the Best Business Travelers May Not Know* by Christopher McGinnis (Box 52927, Atlanta, GA 30355, tel. 404/659–2855; $10 in bookstores.)

**Enjoying the Flight** Fly at night if you're able to sleep on a plane. Because the air aloft is dry, drink plenty of fluids while on board. Drinking alcohol contributes to jet lag, as do heavy meals. Bulkhead seats, in the front row of each cabin—usually reserved for people who have disabilities, are elderly, or are traveling with babies—offer more legroom, but trays attach awkwardly to seat armrests, and all possessions must be stowed overhead.

**Smoking** Since February 1990, smoking has been banned on all domestic flights of less than six hours' duration; the ban also applies to domestic segments of international flights aboard U.S. and foreign carriers. On U.S. carriers flying to Portugal and other destinations abroad, a seat in a no-smoking section must be provided for every passenger who requests one, and the section must be enlarged to accommodate such passengers if necessary as long as they have complied with the airline's deadline for check-in and seat assignment. If smoking bothers you, request a seat far from the smoking section.

Foreign airlines are exempt from these rules but do provide no-smoking sections, and some nations, including Canada as of July 1, 1993, have gone as far as to ban smoking on all domestic flights; other countries may ban smoking on flights of less than a specified duration. The International Civil Aviation Organization has set July 1, 1996, as the date to ban smoking aboard airlines worldwide, but the body has no power to enforce its decisions.

## From the United States by Ship

**Cunard Line** (555 5th Ave., New York, NY 10017, tel. 212/880–7500 or 800/528–6273) operates the *Queen Elizabeth II (QE2)* on the only regular transatlantic crossings, sailing between New York City and Southampton, England, from April through December. On two crossings a year (May and August) the *QE2* stops in Madeira, via Southampton and the Canary Islands.

Other cruise lines whose ships are in Europe for the summer and the Caribbean for the winter make repositioning crossings: eastbound in spring and westbound in fall. Among them is **Royal Viking** (95 Merrick Way, Coral Gables, FL 33134, tel. 800/422–8000) whose crossings from Ft. Lauderdale, Florida, occasionally stop in Madeira on the way to Rome. Check the travel pages of your Sunday newspaper, or contact a travel agent for lines and sailing dates.

For details regarding freighter travel to or from Portugal, consult **Pearl's Freighter Tips** (Box 188, 16307 Depot Rd., Flushing, NY 11358), **Travel World/Freighter Tips** (180-10 Union Turnpike, Flushing, NY 11358, tel. 718/969–8400), and **Freighter World Cruises** (180 South Lake, Suite 335, Pasadena, CA 91101, tel. 818/449–3106 or 800/531–7774).

**From the United Kingdom**

**By Plane** It's important to distinguish between scheduled services to Portugal, operated chiefly by **TAP Air Portugal** and **British Airways,** and inexpensive charter flights operated by a whole range of companies that serve Lisbon, Oporto, Faro, Madeira, and the Azores (more frequently in summer months). If you're looking for bargains, don't mind traveling at inconvenient times, and are prepared for delays (up to 48 hours at peak periods), then consider a charter flight. But if you value reliability—and don't mind paying for it—you're better off with a scheduled flight.

In summer there are three flights daily from London Heathrow to Lisbon by British Airways and one daily from Heathrow to Lisbon by TAP Air Portugal (two flights daily on Thursday, Saturday, and Sunday). Flying time is between two and 2½ hours. Oporto receives daily direct flights by British Airways and TAP Air Portugal from London Heathrow. TAP has three flights a week from Heathrow to Madeira. All flights to the Azores connect through Lisbon.

Faro is served by two British Airways scheduled flights every day from London Gatwick, and by TAP on three days (Thursday, Saturday, and Sunday) from London Heathrow. The fantastic boom in the popularity of the Algarve as a vacation destination has also fostered a larger number of regular charter flights to Faro, and to a lesser extent Lisbon. This gives a wider choice, especially from regional airports in the United Kingdom. Charter seats are often sold off at a big discount at the last minute.

Charter flights offer substantial savings, though booking conditions can be strict. You'll need to buy your ticket some time in advance (between two and four weeks), and most charter flights are for periods of one to three weeks. On the other hand, there are charter flights to almost every Portuguese airport from practically every British regional airport. Most flights, naturally, are in summer. Prices vary so much that it's hard to give guidelines, but you can usually expect to pay between 10% and 15% less than on the cheapest scheduled flight. Check with a good travel agent, take your time, and shop around. Further bargains are available if you buy at the last minute off-season or only want a one-way ticket. Check the advertisements in *Time Out* and the Sunday paper.

For reservations and information: **British Airways** (tel. 0171/897–4000) and **TAP Air Portugal** (tel. 0171/828–0262).

**By Car** The least expensive route to Portugal by car, though not necessarily the fastest, is by cross-channel ferry to France. The drawbacks are that the shortest and cheapest ferry crossing (Dover–Calais) leaves you with the greatest amount of driving; this can be tiring and also expensive if you take toll roads through France and spend many nights en route. It is some 2,121 kilometers (1,318 miles) from Calais to Lisbon. For a distance such as this, unless time is short, consider going as far as possible by ferry or using Motorail for part of the journey to reduce the tiring drive to a minimum. **Brittany Ferries** (Millbay Docks, Plymouth, PL1 3EW, tel. 01752/221–321) offers a range of vacation tours for motorists to Portugal, with lodgings in hotels, private houses, or pousadas, and taking the Plymouth–Santander (northern Spain) ferry route.

**By Tunnel** The Channel Tunnel opened officially in May 1994, providing the fastest route across the Channel—35 minutes from Folkestone to Calais, or 60 minutes from motorway to motorway. It consists of two large 50-kilometer (31-mile)-long tunnels for trains, one in each direction, linked by a smaller service tunnel running between them. **Le Shuttle** (tel. 0345/353535 in the U.K., 800/388–3876 in the U.S.), a special car, bus, and truck train, which was scheduled to begin service in June 1994, operates a continuous loop, with trains departing every 15 minutes at peak times and at least once an hour through the night. No reservations are necessary, although tickets may be purchased in advance from travel agents. Most passengers stay in their own car throughout the "crossing"; progress updates are provided on display screens and radio. Motorcyclists park their bikes in a separate section with its own passenger compartment, while foot passengers book passage by coach (*see* By Train, *below*).

The Tunnel is reached from exit 11a of the M20/A20. Drivers purchase tickets from toll booths, then pass through frontier control before loading onto the next available service. Unloading at Calais takes 8 minutes. Ticket prices start at £130 for a low-season 5-day round trip in a small car and are based on season, time of day, length of stay, and car size regardless of the number of passengers. Peak season fares are not always competitive with ferry prices.

**By Train**    Train services to Portugal are not as frequent, fast, or inexpensive as plane travel. Getting to Lisbon by rail takes between two and 2½ days; the fastest connection to Paris is the *Hoverspeed City Link* rail-hovercraft-rail service from London's Victoria Station, with up to four departures daily to choose from. From Paris the luxurious overnight Paris–Madrid **TALGO** or the **Puerta del Sol** leave the Gare d'Austerlitz, transfer in Madrid to the Lisboa Express, and reach Lisbon in about nine hours. Advance reservations are obligatory in both trains; book well in advance to guarantee a place.

**Eurostar** (for information, tel. 071/922–4486 in the U.K., 800/942–4866 in the U.S.) high-speed train service was scheduled to begin in July 1994, with passenger-only trains whisking riders via the Chunnel between London (Waterloo) and the Continent—to Paris (Gare du Nord) in 3 hours and to Brussels (Midi) in 3¼ hours. The service of one train daily each way was scheduled to increase in January 1995 to 15 trains daily in each direction. At press time, ticket prices had not been set. Tickets are available in the United Kingdom through **Intercity Europe,** the international wing of BritRail (London/Victoria Station, tel. 071/834–2345 or 071/828–8092 for credit-card bookings), and in the United States through **Rail Europe** (tel. 800/942–4866) and **BritRail Travel** (1500 Broadway, New York, NY 10036, tel. 800/677–8585).

**Campus Travel** (52 Grosvenor Gardens, London SW1W OAG, tel. 0171/730–3402) and **Transalpino** (71–75 Buckingham Palace Rd., London SW1W 0RE, tel. 0171/834–9656) both offer excellent deals for those under 26. Otherwise book through **British Rail International** (tel. 0171/834–2345) or **French Railways SNCF** (179 Piccadilly, London W1V 0BA, tel. 0171/409–3518).

**By Bus**    The **Eurolines/National Express** consortium runs regular bus service to Lisbon (twice weekly); Faro and Lagos in the Algarve on the southern coast (twice weekly); and once weekly to Coimbra. Buses leave London Victoria Coach Station and reach Coimbra, Lisbon, and Faro on the third day. For more information and reservations: **National Express/Eurolines** (Coach Travel Center, 13 Regent St., London SW1Y 4LR, tel. 0171/730–0202), **Campus Travel** (52 Grosvenor Gardens, London SW1W 0AU, tel. 0171/730–8235), or any **National Express** appointed agent.

**Fly/Drive**    This has proved one of the more popular touring vacations in Portugal, as it combines swiftness in getting to the country (in practice you can be driving along the roads of Portugal within hours of leaving the United Kingdom) with total freedom of movement—plus the advantages of the "package" with none of its attendant restrictions. Prices are calculated per person as a rule, with two sharing both the car and accommodations (if pre-booked); if four go together, the costs are lower. Fly/drive can start at any of Portugal's three mainland airports—Lisbon, Oporto, and Faro, with Lisbon and Faro being the most popular. Fly/drive is also available in Madeira, but packages are based on staying in one hotel and exploring from there (and be advised that driving in Madeira is not for the fainthearted).

Prices include flight, fully insured car rental with unlimited mileage, and a variety of itineraries, with first and last nights' accommodations (or a fully worked out itinerary, if you prefer).

**British Airways** teams up with **Avis** for this, but there are a number of other car rental companies in the market. In some cases (the Algarve in particular) a car is offered as part of the package deal when you rent a villa or apartment. Full details are available from travel agents, car rental companies, and the airlines.

# Staying in Portugal

## Getting Around

By Plane **TAP Air Portugal** (Lisbon tel. 01/386–1020 ) and its sister carrier, **LAR,** (tel. 01/848–8509) are the main domestic airlines in Portugal, with flights from Lisbon to all major cities and many interregional flights, including to Madeira and the Azores. **Portugalia** (01/808–999) flies between Lisbon and Oporto and offers charter service to Funchal in Madeira. Travel in Portugal can be time-consuming; trains are slow and roads can be bad, so flying is sometimes the best option.

Portugalia operates a *Ponte Areo* (Air Bridge) commuter service between Lisbon and Oporto/Faro. Flights leave every hour or so, depending on the time of day, and no advance booking is needed; just show up at the airport, buy a ticket, and take the next flight out. At press time (summer 1994) the cost of a one-way ticket was 16,000$00 (approximately $84).

By Train The Portuguese railway system, **Caminhos de Ferro Portugueses** (CP; tel. 01/876–025 or 01/877–092 for route information) is surprisingly extensive. Trains are clean and leave on time, but many of those away from the Lisbon–Oporto main line are old-fashioned and infrequent. Many of the branch lines serving the agrarian interior, especially in the north, are meter-gauge.

Some express trains between Lisbon and Oporto run virtually nonstop and have either restaurant or buffet facilities. They are first-class and require advance reservations and supplementary fares. The fastest trains travel the 350 kilometers (215 miles) in less than three hours. Fares from Lisbon to Oporto are about $17–$30 first class and $9.25–$18 second class, depending on time of travel and number of stops made. Several of the Oporto–Lisbon trains take cars, as do some of the Algarve trains (summer only) and one train a day between Lisbon, Castelo Branco, Regua, and Guarda. Prices are reasonable, but cars must be at the station an hour beforehand and tickets are best purchased in advance.

One of the newest tourist attractions in the Alto Minho region of the north is the historic steam engines and 19th-century rail cars, with crews in period costume, that ply between Viana do Castelo and Caminha along a route similar to that inaugurated in 1878. Be sure to buy tickets at the station as there is a huge surcharge on the train.

*Fares* A *cartão jovem* (Inter-rail youth pass) for those 26 and under costs about $200 and offers a discount on second-class train tickets during a month-long period, except on peak travel days. Family tickets (for at least three people), and group tickets (for 10 or more people traveling a minimum of 75 kilometers/47 miles one way) are sold at discounts of between 20% and 30%. Tourist tickets can be purchased for periods of seven, 14, and 21 days.

If you are under 26, inquire about a *Billet International Jeune* (BIJ) discount travel plan. The special one-trip tariff is offered by **EuroTrain International,** with offices in London, Dublin, Paris, Madrid, Rome, Zurich, Athens, Brussels, Budapest, Hannover, Leiden, Vienna, and Tangier. You can purchase a EuroTrain ticket at one of these offices or through travel agents, youth travel specialists, and at mainline rail stations. **Tagus Turismo Juvenil** (20 Rua Camilo Castelo Branco, 1100 Lisbon, tel. 01/352–5509; 9 Praça de Londres, 1000 Lisbon, tel. 01/848–4957, fax 01/532715), a well-known student-travel agency, is another source for information and reservations.

Portuguese railways are covered by the Eurailpass. Details and up-to-date prices can be obtained in the United States at **Rail Europe** (610 5th Ave., New York, NY 10020, tel. 800/345–1990). **Wasteels Expresso** (Av. António Augusto de Aguiar 88, 1000 Lisbon, tel. 01/579180 and 01/579655) is reliable for all local and international train tickets and reservations.

Contact your nearest **Portuguese National Tourist Office** for their *Railroads of Portugal* booklet, which contains information on schedules, fares, and discounts.

*Smoking* CP provides no-smoking cars on all long-distance trips and most short runs; be sure to specify if you want a no-smoking seat or bunk, because many Portuguese will contentedly smoke all night long.

**By Bus** You can be sure a bus will go to almost any town not served by train—and the fare will be lower. **Rodoviaria Nacional** (Av. Columbano Bordalo Pinheiro 86, 1000 Lisbon, tel. 01/726–7123; Av. Casal Ribeiro 18, tel. 01/545439), the national bus company, runs regular services throughout Portugal.

Bus tours can give you a quick overview of large cities and the surrounding sights before you set off on foot to explore. Most of the following private companies in Lisbon offer tours in English: **Mundial Turismo** (Av. António Augusto de Aguiar 90–A, tel. 01/356–3521 or 01/575740), **Novo Mundo** (Rua Augusto dos Santos 9, tel. 01/352–7711), **Sol Expresso** (Rua Entrecampos 1, tel. 01/797–3748, for Algarve and Alantejo), **Star Travel Service** (Praça dos Restauradores 14, tel. 01/346–2501), **RN Tours/Gray Line** (Av. Fontes Pereira de Melo 33, tel. 01/538846 and 577523), **Abreu Tours** (Av. da Liberdade 160, tel. 01/347–6441), **Citirama** (Av. Praia da Vitoria 12, tel. 01/352–2594), **Viagens Rawes** (Travessa do Corpo Santo 15, tel. 01/347–0231); and **Melia** (Rua Rosa Araujo 2, tel. 01/315–7247). You can make bookings at hotels or travel agencies.

**By Car** Major work is being done on Portugal's highway system; a new superhighway runs between Lisbon and Oporto, and *autoestradas* (four-lane toll roads) circumvent many of the more congested areas of these cities. Most highway driving is still on two-lane roads with the risk of backups behind heavy trucks, but it is, even so, the best way to see the rural areas and get off the beaten track.

In the north, the IP5 has improved the drive from Aveiro to the Spanish border at Guarda, so you're unlikely to get stuck in a line behind a truck. The IP4 crosses east from Porto through Vila Real, opening up the way to Bragança. Heading southeast from Lisbon through the southern part of the Alentejo, the new E52 highway connects Beija to Vilaverde de Ficalho, near the Spanish frontier town of Rosal de la Frontera. In the south, a new Algarve highway from Albufeira to Vila Real de Santo António runs inland of the coastal routes, defusing many frustrating delays.

Tolls seem steep in Portugal, but time saved by traveling the autoestradas usually makes them worthwhile.

*Rules of the Road* Residents of EU countries can use their national driver's license in Portugal. Others should have an International Driver's Permit (*see* Car Rentals in Before You Go, *above*), although your national license and passport usually suffice. Driving is on the right, and a red warning-triangle must be carried to place on the road behind your car in case of a breakdown. Seat belts are obligatory, and children under 12 must ride in the back seat. Horns are banned in built-up areas (but that doesn't seem to stop the Portuguese). The city speed limit is 60 kilometers (37 miles) per hour; on the autoestrada the limit is 120 kph (74 mph); on the Nacional (national two-lane highway) the limit is 100 kph (62 mph), and on other roads it is 90 kph (56 mph) unless otherwise signposted.

Billboards warning you not to drink and drive dot the countryside, and punishable alcohol levels are low. Portuguese drivers are notoriously rash, and the country has one of the highest traffic fatality rates in Europe, so driving defensively is strongly recommended.

*Gas* Gas stations are plentiful throughout Portugal. Prices are controlled by the government and are the same everywhere. At press time gasoline cost 145$00 a liter (approximately ¼ gallon) for normal (92 octane) and 150$00 a liter for super (97 octane). Unleaded gas is now available for 155$00.

Credit cards are frequently accepted, especially along main roads.

*Breakdowns* The large car-rental companies, Hertz and Avis, have 24-hour breakdown service. If you are a member of an automobile club (AAA, CAA, or AA), you can get assistance from the Portuguese Automobile Club (ACP/Automovel Clube de Portugal, Rua Rosa Araujo 24, 1200 Lisbon, tel. 01/387–1880; Rua Gonçalo Cristovão 2–6, 4000 Oporto, tel. 02/316732).

**By Bicycle** Portugal is one of Europe's more mountainous countries. Although country roads can sometimes be crowded with speeding trucks, bicycle trips can take you along some unforgettably scenic routes. Ask the tourist office for a brochure, or contact the **Direção-Geral de Desportos** (Av. Infante Santo 74–4, 1300 Lisbon, tel. 01/607–095 or 01/674–181).

## Telephones

**Local Calls** Public phones can be frustrating, and phone numbers in Portugal are being changed to a seven-digit system (often without notice), so you might have trouble getting through. Ask either at your hotel or at a local phone office for help. The easiest way to make a local call is to go into a café or bar and ask the bartender if you may use the phone. Bar phones are metered, and the bartender will charge you after you've finished.

At a pay phone, insert coins and wait for a dial tone. The minimum cost for a local call is 10$00, and 50$00 to call another province, for which you must dial the area code. On the old pay phones, you line up the coins in a groove on top of the dial, and they drop down as needed. The new CrediFone or T-Sete phone booths take phone debit cards, which can be purchased at post offices for either 750$00 or 1,750$00. These phones have digital readouts, so you can see your time ticking away, and they are uncomplicated to use—the booths have instructions in several languages, including English. The phones accept Visa and MasterCard, and a countrywide "free-phone" information line can be reached at 145311, 145883, or 14562.

To make calls to other areas within Portugal, precede the provincial code with 0 (most phone booths have a chart inside listing the various province codes). The 0 is unnecessary when dialing from outside Portugal.

**International Calls** Calling abroad is awkward from public pay phones and can be expensive from hotels, which often add a considerable surcharge. The best way to make an international call is to go to the local telephone office and have someone place it for you. Every town has an office, and big cities have several. When the call is connected, you will be sent to a quiet cubicle and charged according to the meter. If the price is 500$00 or more, you may pay with Visa or MasterCard, or use the CrediFone card (*see* Local Calls, *above*). In Lisbon the main telephone office is located in the Praça dos Restauradores, right off the Rossio.

To make an international call yourself, dial 00 and wait for a tone. Then dial the country code (1 for the United States; 44 for the United Kingdom), followed by the area code and number. You can call the United States easily with your long-distance phone company's card, for a reasonable surcharge. Dial 05017-1-288, and you'll be connected with an **AT&T** operator in the States. For an **MCI** operator dial 05017-1-234, and to access **Sprint**, dial 05017-1-877. You can then make a collect or calling card call.

**Operators and Information** The national number for emergencies is 115; for general information dial 118; the international information and assistance operator is at 098. These are good numbers to keep handy, since Portugal is in the process of changing numbers and adding digits.

## Mail

**Postal Rates** Airmail letters to the United States and Canada cost 130$00 up to 15 grams, postcards 130$00. Letters to the United Kingdom and other countries in the European Union cost 70$00 up to 20 grams. Letters within Portugal are 50$00. Postcards are charged the same rate as letters. Stamps (*selos*) can be bought at post offices and government-run tobacco shops.

**Receiving Mail** Because mail delivery can often be slow and unreliable, it is best to have your mail sent to **American Express** (tel. 800/543-4080); call for lists of offices in Portugal. An alternative is to have mail held at a Portuguese post office; have it addressed to **Lista de Correios** (general delivery) in a town you will be visiting. Postal addresses should include the name of the province and district, for example, Figueira da Foz (Coimbra).

## Tipping

Service is included in café, restaurant, and hotel bills, but waiters and other service people are poorly paid, and you can be sure your contribution will be appreciated. However, if you received bad service, never feel obligated (or intimidated) to leave a tip. An acceptable tip is 10%–15% of the total bill, and if you have a sandwich or *petiscos* (appetizers) at a bar, leave less, just enough to round out the bill to the nearest 100. Cocktail waiters get 25$00–50$00 a drink, depending on the bar.

Taxi drivers get about 10% of the meter, but more for long rides or extra help with luggage, and there is an official surcharge for airport runs and baggage.

Hotel porters are tipped 100$00 a bag; 100$00 also goes for room service or a doorman who calls you a taxi. If you stay in a hotel for more than two nights, tip the maid about 100$00 per night. The concierge should be tipped for any additional help he or she gives you.

Tour guides should be tipped about 200$00, ushers in theaters or bullfights 100$00, barbers at least 100$00, hairdressers at least 200$00 for a wash and set. Washroom attendants are tipped 100$00.

## Opening and Closing Times

Banks  Banks are generally open weekdays 8:30–3. Money exchanges at airports and train stations are usually open all day (24 hours at Portela airport in Lisbon), and some hotels will be able to accommodate you, although at a slightly lower rate than at a bank.

Museums  Most museums open at 10, close for lunch between 12:30 and 2 and close at 5 (a few big ones stay open at midday—check beforehand). They are closed on Monday and holidays; palaces close on Tuesday and holidays.

Shops  One of the most inconvenient things about shopping in Portugal is that most shops close at midday for approximately two hours. Store hours are Monday–Friday 9–1 and 3–7, Saturday 9–1. In December Saturday hours are the same as weekdays. Shops are closed on Sunday, although some *hipermercados* (supermarkets) and shopping centers are open seven days a week, 10 AM–midnight.

## Shopping

Superbly woven baskets found in markets and gift shops make lightweight and practical gifts. Beautifully hand-embroidered table linens don't weigh much, nor do the embroidered organdy blouses or initialled handkerchiefs that are the specialty of Madeira. Traditional embroidered silk bedspreads are still made in Castelo Branco, and exquisite hand-made lace can be found in Vila do Conde near Oporto.

The country's lovely glazed tiles—*azulejos*—can be found in either single patterns or pictorial panels that can be shipped home by freight. Porcelain and pottery are also very attractive and sometimes irresistible; *Vista Alegre* is the oldest and most famous porcelain, with works near Aveiro.

Pottery differs from place to place. The brightly colored roosters (symbol of Portugal) are made in Barcelos, black pottery in Vila Real, polychrome in Aveiro, blue and white in Coimbra and Alcobaça. Caldas da Rainha is famous for green glazed plates and dishes made in the form of leaves, vegetables, fruit, and animals. In the Alentejo, particularly in Estremoz, you will find early Etruscan and Roman shapes reproduced in unglazed red clay pots and jars. There is also a large range of glazed cooking pots in all shapes and sizes, and colored figurines.

Marinha Grande is the center for glassware of every kind, and Atlantis crystal is particularly worth seeking out; its local factory is renowned.

The Alantejo is the home of natural cork; here you'll find picture frames, lidded buckets (*tarros*) in which food can be kept hot or cold, and other lightweight gifts. Carved wooden spoons and boxes and lambskin and goatskin slippers are also from this part of the country. Attractive lanterns, fire screens, and outdoor furniture are made from tin, brass, copper, and other metals in the Algarve and Trás-os-Montes. Primitive as well as sophisticated musical instruments (such as guitars, horns, flutes, and bells) are made in the Minho, Trás-os-Montes, and the Beiras. Coimbra is famous for guitars, and clay whistles are made in Estremoz.

Fine leather shoes, handbags, and belts can be bought all over the country, as can textiles such as cotton and wool blankets in cheerfully colored stripes. Needlepoint and embroidered carpets and rugs are the specialty of Arraiolas in the Alentejo, and Portalegre has the finest tapestry shops in Portugal.

Portuguese jewelry is also lovely: The gold is 19.25 carats here, and you can find modern brooches and earrings, as well as many exquisite pieces based on ancient designs. Fine-leather bookbinding is another specialty, along with other leather products, such as clothing, wallets, luggage, belts, and gloves. For children's gifts stop in at any stationery shop, where you'll find a wide selection of unusual pen-and-pencil boxes, notebooks, erasers, and other items not seen in the United States.

**Tax Refunds** A number of shops, particularly large stores and shops in holiday resorts, offer a refund of the 12% IVA sales tax on large purchases (the purchase must be a single item worth more than $500). Be sure to ask for your tax-free check; you show your passport, fill out a form, and the store mails you the refund at home. Or, simply present the signed form and the merchandise at the tax-free counter at the airport for a cash refund before you leave the country.

## Sports and the Outdoors

Tennis is becoming ever more popular. If your hotel doesn't have courts, most of the resort areas have a **Clube de Tenis** where you can swing a racket (usually for a small fee). Most courts are clay. Tennis pros offer classes almost all year long in the resorts; contact the tourism office for a list of courts in the resort areas. For further information, contact the **Federação Portuguesa de Tenis** (Portuguese Tennis Federation, Estadio Nacional, Caxias, 2480 Oeiras, tel. 01/419–5244 or 01/419–8472).

**Sailing, boating, windsurfing,** and other water sports are popular all along the Atlantic and Mediterranean coasts and around Madeira and the Azores. Yachting and sailing facilities can be found at the Cascais Yacht Club, the marinas of Lisbon, and the expanding Vilamoura Marina in the Algarve, which currently offers 1,000 berths. The tourism office publishes listings of facilities available all over the country. For further information contact the **Federação Portuguesa de Vela** (Portuguese Sailing Federation, Doca de Belem, 1300 Lisbon, tel. 01/641–2152 or 01/647–324), the **Associação Naval**

**de Lisboa** (Doca deBelem, tel. 01/363–5861), or **Federação Portuguesa de Atividades Subaquáticas** (Portuguese Underwater Sports Federation, Rua Almeida Brandão 39, 1200 Lisbon, tel. 01/ 396–4322); **Federação Portuguesa de Canoagem** (Portuguese Canoeing Federation, Rua António Pinto Machado 60, 4100 Porto, tel.02/ 697350). For surfing, head to Cascais (rent a board there at **Windsurf Portugal** (tel. 01/486–1883), and continue on to the awesome beach at Guincho, where shooting a curl is popular even in the mild winters.

Portugal's rivers, streams, and almost 1,300 kilometers (800 miles) of coastline make the country a paradise for **fishing,** with a great variety of catches. The best freshwater fishing is in the Rio Minho and Ria Lima (lamprey, trout, salmon) and in the Ria Vouga and the Serra da Estrela lakes and streams (trout). Off Madeira and the Azores, the Gulf Stream ensures some of the best deep-sea fishing in the world. The **Clube dos Amadores de Pesca da Costa do Sol** (Rua dos Fontainhos 16, 2750 Cascais, tel. 01/284–1691) is for fishermen in the Lisbon area; or, contact the tourist office for a booklet on fishing throughout the country.

Portugal also has year-round **golf.** Courses in Lisbon, Estoril, and the Algarve are reputed to be the best on the Continent, and challenging courses in the north of the country and on Madeira and the Azores are set amidst breathtaking scenery. Contact the tourism office for detailed descriptions of the courses and a list of greens fees or the **Federação Portuguesa de Golf** (Portuguese Golf Federation, 9 Rua Almeida Brandão 39, 1200 Lisbon, tel. 01/674–658), or the **Clube de Campo de Portugal** (Herdade de Aroeira, Fonte da Telha, 2825 Monte de Caparica, Aoeira, tel. 065/226–1802, fax 065/297–1358).

**Hiking** is a wonderful way to get in touch with nature in Portugal. The Iberian Peninsula is on a main route of migrating birds, where there is an astounding variety of species. The oldest nature reserve in the country is at Peneda-Gêres in the far north, where wild boar, civet cats, wolves, and wild horses roam the mountains.

For the equestrian, Portugal offers **horseback riding** along sandy beaches, mountain trails, and in small villages throughout the country. Most Algarve resorts have stables, as does the Campo Dom Carlos in Cascais. Contact the **Federação Equestre Portuguesa** (Portuguese Equestrian Federation, Av. Duque d'Avila 9–4, 1000 Lisbon, tel. 01/674–658 or 01/526–286).

## Beaches

Despite the tourist boom that has almost completely developed large stretches of the Algarve and the Costa de Prata, you can commune with the sea and the sky in relative solitude along the Costa Azul and the beaches of the Minho and Costa Verde. Decide whether you want the excitement and glamour of a world-class resort complete with casino and 24-hour nightlife; or whether your spirit would be more refreshed by amber cliffs and yellow sand leading into an indigo sea down south in the Algarve, or lush green mountains and oyster sand meeting the blue-gray ocean, as in the north.

## Dining

Although it is a small country, Portugal has a large, rich, and varied gastronomy. The Portuguese introduced coriander, pepper, ginger, curry, saffron, and paprika to Europe as a result of their explorations and establishment of trade routes with the East. They brought back tea from the Orient, coffee and peanuts from Africa, and pineapples, tomatoes, and potatoes from the New World.

Portugal's rivers and its proximity to the sea give it a fish- and seafood-oriented gastronomy: Be sure to try the *caldeirada* (national seafood stew) and fresh *sardinhas assadas* (grilled sardines). *Lulas recheadas*, squid stuffed with sausage and rice, is a unique combination of texture and flavor. Chicken and pork are good everywhere, and the mention of golden and crunchy *leitão da Bairrada* (roast suckling pig) in the north is enough to give anyone an appetite. Sautéed or grilled *bife à português* (steak), often cooked in a port wine sauce, is served throughout the country. *Bacalhau* (codfish) can be served 365 different ways (or so legend has it). Soups of all kinds are popular, and most restaurants serve *caldo verde*, a filling blend of shredded cabbage and potatoes. The famous pork and clam dish, called *porco à Alentejana*, is made with diced marinated pork and clams and served with potatoes or rice. Desserts tend to be sweet and egg-based, with *pudim flan*, a caramel custard, almost a national passion.

The country has a wealth of good wines. Apart from the unique port and Madeira, there are more than 100 different varieties, ranging from table wines to extra-special ones, all reflecting the individual character of their regions' soils.

Mealtimes are similar to those in the United Kingdom. Breakfast is lightest; and lunch, the main meal of the day, is served between 12 and 2:30, although nowadays, office workers in cities often grab a quick sandwich in a bar instead of stopping for a big lunch. About 5 there's an afternoon break for coffee or tea and a pastry, and dinner is eaten around 7.

As in many European countries, Portuguese restaurants use an *ementa (or prato) do dia*, or set menu. This can be a real bargain—usually 80% of the cost of three courses ordered separately.

**Ratings** The government rates restaurants from five forks (deluxe) down to one fork (basic). We use four categories (Very Expensive, $$$$; Expensive, $$$; Moderate, $$; and Inexpensive, $) to indicate average prices in escudos for a three-course meal excluding wine.

## Lodging

Portugal offers accommodations to suit every taste and budget, from palaces to pensions, from mansions to ultra-modern hotels. Many visitors design their itineraries around pousadas, (*see below*). Luxurious resorts provide self-contained surroundings that can tempt guests not to leave.

There are new high-rise hotels in cities, *residências* (in what were once private homes—the term *"residencial"* is also often used), and aparto-hotel-style pensions (with suites or one-bedroom units and kitchenettes) in the smallest of towns. Contact the Portuguese National Tourist Office (590 5th Ave., New York, NY 10036, tel. 212/354–4403 or 212/354–4404, fax 212/764–6137) for the list of **Hotels de Charme,** a newly associated group of 16 small hotels and pousadas throughout the country. By law prices must be posted at the reception desk and should indicate whether tax is included (IVA is 8% for hotels).

**Hotels** High season means not only the summer months, but also Easter week and anytime a town is holding a fiesta. However, in the off-season (November through March) many hotels' rates are as much as 20% lower. In Portugal, a Continental breakfast is usually included in the price of the room.

**Pousadas** The term **pousada** is derived from the Portuguese verb *pousar,* meaning "to rest." Portugal has an easily accessible network of more than 37 of these state-run hotels, which are located in wonderfully restored castles, palaces, monasteries, convents, and other charming historic buildings. Each pousada is set in a particularly scenic and tranquil part of the country and is tastefully furnished with traditional regional crafts and antiques and artwork. All have restaurants that present regional specialties; you may stop for a meal or a drink at a pousada without spending the night. Rates are reasonable, considering that most pousadas are four- and five-star hotels and a stay in a pousada can be the highlight of your visit. However, they are extremely popular with foreigners and Portuguese alike, so make reservations in advance, especially during summer months, since some have 10 or fewer rooms. For more information, contact the tourist office or **ENATUR** (Av. Sta. Joana a Princesa 10–A, 1700 Lisbon, tel. 01/848–1221); in the United States, **Marketing Ahead** (433 5th Ave., New York, NY 10016, tel. 212/686–9213 or 800/223–1356, fax 212/686–0271); in the United Kingdom, **Keytel International** (402 Edgeware Rd., London W2 1ED, tel. 0171/402–8182).

**Country Houses** Manors, farm estates, and country houses have been modified to receive small numbers of guests in a fairly new venture called *Turismo de Habitação* (Country House Tourism), mostly operating in the north of the country. These guest houses, which offer an alternative kind of comfort, are in bucolic settings removed from the cities, near parks or monuments and in historic villages. Breakfast is always included in the price. For more details contact your tourism office or **Promoçõese Idéias Turísticas** (PIT: Alto da Pampilheira, Torre D-2-8A, 2750 Cascais, tel. 01/486–7958 or 01/484–4464) for homes in the center and south; **Direção-Geral do Turismo, Divisão do Turismo no Espaço Rural** (Av. António Augusto de Aguiar 86, 1099 Lisbon, tel. 01/286–7958), or **TURIHAB** (Praça da República, 4990 Ponte de Lima, tel. 058/942–729 or 058/741–672), for accommodations in more rural areas of the country.

**Camping** More than 100 good campgrounds are available in Portugal, where camping has been on the upswing over the past few years. One of the largest is the *Monsanto Parque Florestal*, along the Estoril autostrada not far from the city center, with tennis, a swimming pool, a bank, a restaurant, cafés, a chapel, a library, a game room, and a mini-market. Another very pleasant site is five minutes from Guincho Beach, Cascais; it's operated by **Orbitur** (Avenida Almirante Gago Coutinho 25, Lisbon 1000, tel. 01/892–938), which also has several other well-equipped camps, some with four-person chalets to rent.

For a relatively complete list of campgrounds, contact the **Turismo** offices or the **Federação Portuguesa de Campismo e Caravanismo** (Portuguese Camping and Caravanning Federation, Av. 5 de Outubro 15–3, 1000 Lisbon, tel. 01/522–715 or 01/522–3308).

**Hostels** There are about 17 **Pousadas de Juventude** (Youth Hostels) around the country, providing clean, somewhat spartan, and reasonably priced lodgings. Young travelers with membership cards validated by any Youth Hostel Association belonging to the International Federation of Youth Hostels are welcome. Although it's best to purchase an AYHA membership card at home, you will be able to get one in an overseas hostel. Not all hostels require the ID, but some do, so it may be worth the investment. Hostels provide linens, breakfast, and sometimes dinner. The official limit is three consecutive days, but you may stay longer if space is available. To join the International Federation of Youth Hostels, apply in the United States to **American Youth Hostels, Inc.** (Box 37613, Washington, DC 20013, tel. 202/783–6161), in Canada to **Canadian Hosteling Association** (18 Dyward Market, Ottawa, Ont., K1N 7A1, tel. 613/748–5638), and in the United Kingdom to **Youth Hostels Association** (14 Southampton St., London WC2E 7HY, tel. 0171/836–8541). IFYH recently introduced the name **Hostelling International** as a new, more global logo—look for it on signs and in their advertising.

Spas Portugal has been favored with a profusion of thermal springs, whose waters reputedly can cure whatever ails you. In the smaller spas, hotels are rather simple; in the more famous ones, they are first-class. Most are open from May through October. For complete listings and reservations information, contact the Portuguese tourism office nearest you, **Marketing Ahead** (*see above*), or the **Associação Nacional dos Industriais de Aguas Minero-Medicinais de Mesa** (Rua de S. Jose 93–1, 1100 Lisbon, tel. 01/324523).

Home You can find a house, apartment, or other vacation property to ex-
Exchange change for your own by becoming a member of a home-exchange organization, which then sends you its annual directories listing available exchanges and includes your own listing in at least one of them. Arrangements for the actual exchange are made by the two parties, not by the organization. For more information contact the **International Home Exchange Association** (IHEA, 41 Sutter St., Suite 1090, San Francisco, CA 94104, tel. 415/673–0347 or 800/788–2489). Principal clearinghouses include: **Homelink International** (Box 650, Key West, FL 33041, tel. 800/638–3841), with thousands of foreign and domestic listings, publishes four annual directories plus updates; the $50 membership includes your listing in one book. **Intervac International** (Box 590504, San Francisco, CA 94159, tel. 415/435–3497) has three annual directories; membership is $62, or $72 if you want to receive the directories but remain unlisted. **Loan-a-Home** (2 Park La., Apt. 6E, Mount Vernon, NY 10552, tel. 914/664–7640) specializes in long-term exchanges; there is no charge to list your home, but the directories cost $35 or $45 depending on the number you receive. **Villa Leisure** (Box 30188, Palm Beach, FL 33420, tel. 407/624–9000 or 800/526–4244) facilitates swaps.

Apartment If you want a home base that's roomy enough for a family and comes
and Villa with cooking facilities, a furnished rental may be the solution. It's
Rentals generally cost-wise, too, although not always—some rentals are luxury properties (economical only when your party is large). Home-exchange directories do list rentals—often second homes owned by prospective house swappers—and some services search for a house or apartment for you (even a castle if that's your fancy) and handle the paperwork. Some send an illustrated catalogue and others send photographs of specific properties, sometimes at a charge; up-front registration fees may apply.

Among the companies are **At Home Abroad** (405 E. 56th St., Suite 6H, New York, NY 10022, tel. 212/421–9165); **Europa-Let** (92 North Main St., Ashland, Oregon 97520, tel. 503/482–5806 or 800/462–4486); **Interhome Inc.** (124 Little Falls Rd., Fairfield, NJ 07004, tel. 201/882–6864); **Property Rentals International** (1 Park West Cir., Suite 108, Midlothian, VA 23113, tel. 804/378–6054 or 800/220–3332); **The Invented City** (*see* IHEA, *above*); and **Vacation Home Rentals Worldwide** (235 Kensington Ave., Norwood, NJ 07648, tel. 201/767–9393 or 800/633–3284). **Hideaways International** (767 Islington St., Box 4433, Portsmouth, NH 03802, tel. 603/430–4433 or 800/843–4433) functions as a travel club. Membership ($99 yearly per person or family at the same address) includes two annual guides plus quarterly newsletters; rentals are arranged directly between members, not by the club staff.

In Britain try **Jean Harper Holidays** (20 Walton Rd., Stockton Heath, Warrington WA4 6NL, tel. 01925/64234) or **Bartle Holidays** (Wingfield, High Dr. Woldingham, Caterham, Surrey CR3 7ED, tel. 01883/652257).

## Credit Cards

The following credit card abbreviations are used throughout this guide: AE, American Express; D, Discover; DC, Diners Club; MC, MasterCard; and V, Visa.

# 2 Portraits of Portugal

# Family Affairs

By Marion
Kaplan

In modern Portugal, there are still a few dukes, marquises, and counts. Nobility has not been recognized since the fall of the monarchy in 1910, but the old families are still there— and social snobbery. I can gawp at the partying, if I want to, in the weekly Semanário's magazine, *Olá*, which concentrates on the rich at play, their plush homes and glossy lifestyles. Old families do not welcome the new rich to their clubs; there are no grandees among the northern industrialists. Wealth and power have shifted drastically. Yet despite the shock of revolution, the sudden development of a new class of money-market technocrats and impresarios, divisions are not just between old and new, rich and poor, success and failure. The aristocracy and landowning classes, feudal by history and rich by inheritance, have adapted, too.

Sons and daughters of the old families take little for granted. They go to university, marry correctly, enter the professions, participate actively in the modernizing of Portugal—outside the cut and thrust of party politics. These families have experienced and survived the shattering effects of revolution; the challenges of 1992 could never be as fearful as the shocks of 1974.

Family names ring across history and continents, yet it is no longer simple in the gusts and eruptions of new times—despite an astonishingly large and informative press—even for knowledgeable and socially aware Portuguese to be sure who is who.

For one thing, many Portuguese come from truly gigantic families. At a family reunion held in Lisbon's Estufa Fria greenhouse-park, 1,200 d'Oreys showed up.

In the house which had been her family's for three generations Maria Eugenia Sa da Bandeira—another historic and distinguished name—spoke of her large family to *Olá* magazine. "Imagine what it's like," she said, "buying shoes for fifteen, or toothbrushes." Another matriarch, Maria Simoes de Almeida, has seventeen children, a family that, with husbands and wives and their children, adds up to close to a hundred. In north Portugal's *vinho verde* country I have met many people for whom, for reasons that are as much custom as religion, anything but a large family would be unusual.

In Geraz do Lima the Casa dos Cunhas has belonged for centuries to the Sottomayor Correia de Oliveira family. One of the family is a lawyer, Antonio Correia de Oliveira, one of six children and, in his thirties, a father of six. "Not a lot," he said; "my grandparents had fifteen." I met dashing young Miguel Reymao, an agronomist who works for a bank. He is one of ten brothers and sisters whose family owns the Quinta de Luou, a member of the Association of Bottlers and Producers of Vinho Verde which aspires to a high quality and more individual wine.

No Reymao lives on the estate, a flourishing 21-hectare farm near Ponte de Lima which is run in the manner of many such properties by a *caseiro* (manager). The future of the family's pleasant country house? Tourism, perhaps.

Transforming old family concerns into EC-conscious companies capable of strong competition became a business priority as the 1980s ended. Jerónimo Martins, a family grocery founded in 1792 and in the same family until about 1920, created a new group in 1989, built on a supermarket empire and a Unilever association, and a new image which left family considerations behind. But no proud Portuguese company would ignore its history. Bold publicity reminded everyone that Jerónimo Martins had outlasted five political regimes, the French invasions, two world wars, four revolutions and the Chiado fire that, in August 1988, burned its most distinguished shop to cinders.

Of the Costa Salema family, Helena Roseta—one of eight brothers and sisters—is the most forthright and conspicuous. Born in 1947, she is a qualified architect, has been *Presidente da Câmara* (mayor) of Cascais, a Member of Parliament within the PSD party and an independent deputy on the Socialists' bench outside it. She is not the only achiever. Her husband, Pedro Roseta, a PSD deputy, has been ambassador to the Organization for Economic Cooperation and Development (OECD). Each of her brothers and sisters is a professional success, their husbands and wives often public figures—one sister is married to Antonio Capucho, a PSD minister, one of the d'Orey clan and elected to the European Parliament in 1989. Another sister, Margarida Salema, a lawyer, was selected by Cavaco Silva for the PSD list and also won a seat at Strasbourg. In a profile on the family the newspaper *O Independente* found not a dud among them—even the upcoming generation showed every sign of intellectual brilliance in fields as diverse as architecture and maritime biology. The family's modest explanation for its strong public presence: 'The family is big, the country small.'

With its deep roots and long blood lines, traditions and kinsfolk and, increasingly, professional success and the money that goes with it, the classic Portuguese family is a rock of ages. The family might appear to have sundered where sons and daughters have left villages and farms to study, to work, or to emigrate. But the glue holds. Wealth, class, and lifestyle affect only the degree of sophistication of joyous, loud reunions.

Children, whether from aristocratic families, the bourgeoisie, or smallholdings and farms, love and respect their parents, visit them frequently when they are away from home, very often marry into their own community—and occasionally never break away at all. In the rural setting in which I live, a young man quite often stays at home until he is married. He is doted on and spoiled. If he is talented he may start a small business, like many a local plumber or electrician—Edelberto Estrelo in Areeiro turned a teenage knack with wiring into a successful enterprise. His living room, packed with refrigerators, television sets, washing machines, and other *electrodomésticos*, grew to a spacious showroom—an extension of the family home. He does installations and repairs; his mother runs the shop. When he marries, his wife—if she has no profession or job of her own—will help out.

Young couples frequently live with one or other set of parents—separate housing is too often prohibitively costly. When babies arrive, grandmothers are instant babysitters. And when there is no handy mother-in-law, grandmother, older sister, cousin, or other relative, then babies fit in with daily activity—tucked into the corner of a minimercado (a modernized village store), or among the laundry in a *lavandaria*. Family life can sometimes be too close: mother-in-law may be a useful baby minder but she may be as interfering and troublesome as the mother-in-law jokes suggest. Mental breakdowns are not uncommon; family pressures are the prime cause.

From birth to death, in a traditional rural family, links bind tightly even across oceans where sons, daughters, cousins have settled and extended the family further. In marriages abroad Portuguese will most likely marry Portuguese. Beldora, the lissom and beautiful American-born granddaughter of my hard-working neighbours, married a young American whose Portuguese parents come from the same *freguesia* (parish). Love bloomed from a casual encounter and a comfortable convention made for a good marriage—and, a year later, a bonny baby daughter.

However, the Portuguese family is undergoing new challenges and trials every day. There is no enemy to fight, no cause to defend, no dastardly regime to overcome or escape; their concerns are closer to home, in the hopes, successes, and failures of children, in relationships between wife and husband. The post-revolution generation faces the acute problems of a developing country—in education, in housing, in jobs, in acquiring a suitably supercharged EC mentality. Suddenly, small Portugal is like an erupting volcano. Are families suffering? Many, yes. But there have been worse upheavals—emigration, Salazar's policies and repressions, the revolution itself. The family, close and united, the frame on which this new society is taking shape, on the whole stays strong.

# Portuguese Wine

**W**ith the exception of those classic Kings of Wines, Port and Madeira, the wines that Portugal produces are mainly honest and straightforward, unaccompanied by the snobbish mystique that shrouds French vintages. This is a country where the ordinary visitor who likes wine can enjoy an endless procession of delicious experiments for little more than the cost of a good beer. It is also possible to find wines of some age that in other countries would be very expensive, but can be enjoyed here at a very moderate cost.

Not that the history of wine in Portugal is shorter or less distinguished than the history of wine in other Continental countries. It stretches back beyond the Romans to the Phoenicians, flourished still under the teetotal Moslems, and went through a checkered time after the Moors were expelled. One of the mainstays of the wine trade's prosperity in Portugal—especially where Port was concerned—was the firm link with Britain. The trade between the two countries predates the 1386 Treaty of Windsor possibly by two centuries. After a long period of generally spasmodic development, with some regions flourishing while others, such as the Algarve, almost ceased production, the situation was taken in hand by Pombal—one of the many facets of Portuguese life that he tried to improve by diktat. In 1756 he put into operation a national plan for "demarcated" regions, geographically delineating growing areas and controlling their output and marketing, with the Port region the first to be demarcated.

Demarcation, and the attendant control of quality, really took off in the first years of this century, and there are now ten regions officially demarcated—the Algarve, Moscatel de Setúbal, Bucelas, Carcavelos, Colares, Bairrada, Dão, Douro, Vinho Verde, and the island of Madeira.

The official body that looks after wine production is the Junta Nacional do Vinho (J.N.V.), based in Lisbon. It controls all the facets of viniculture and of marketing, runs competitions, promotes cooperatives (important in the new political climate of the country), and empowers growers to use a seal of approval *(selo de origem)*, rather like the French *appelation d'origine*, which acts as a protection for the public. There are several areas which are undemarcated still, such as those around Évora, but which nonetheless produce excellent wines.

It is still too early to judge how the convoluted regulations on wine that the EU try to operate will affect Spain and Portugal, who are very recent recruits to the organization, but, as both countries represent a threat to the entrenched interests of the older members, especially France, it is certain that they will have a considerable impact in the long run.

## The Algarve and the Alentejo

Starting in the south, and working our way up-country, we will begin with a quick look at the wines produced in the southern-most demarcated region, the Algarve. The vast proportion of tourism to Portugal is down here, among the almond blossoms, concrete hotels, and wide sandy beaches. Most of the Algarve's wine is produced in a comparatively narrow strip of land stretching between the mountains and the sea. Algarve wine is largely red, with a tiny proportion of white, and is often not unlike a good table wine, a carafe type. Among the better makes are *Lagoa* and *Tavira*.

Higher up-country lies the Alentejo, usually known to visitors—at least in its southern reaches—simply as a wide tract of land to get across as quickly as possible when heading for the Algarve beaches. But this view isn't really fair to the province, which can be quite lovely at certain times of year, especially in spring. The Alentejo vineyards, not yet demarcated, are almost all in the top part of the province, around Évora and over towards the Spanish border. The wines they produce even have a Spanish look and taste to them—*Redondo*, *Borba* (with its lovely dark color and slightly metallic flavor), *Reguengos de Monsaraz*, and *Vidigueira*. They are all worth seeking out—the reds rich in color, the whites tending to be pale with a distinct tang. All are very high in alcohol content, so drink carefully.

## The Regions Around Lisbon

There are four demarcated regions within easy reach of Lisbon—Moscatel de Setúbal, Bucelas, Carcavelos, and Colares.

The Setúbal Peninsula lies below Lisbon, across the Tagus, and is now easily reached by a through highway. It is worth exploring for many reasons, not least to discover the peace of the wooded and rocky Serra d'Arrábida. The wines produced here are well known abroad, mainly through the 150-year efforts of the House of Fonseca, based on Azeitão in the heart of the peninsula. The Moscatel which Fonseca produces, together with the small vinegrowers who make up the local cooperative in Palmela—a few miles east of Azeitão and boasting a superb pousada—is best known as a fortified dessert wine, aged and with a mouthwatering taste of honey. If you manage to find some that is, say, 25 years old, then you will find it has a licorice color, and enjoy its sweet scent and taste. Fonseca and the cooperative produce many other wines as well as the Moscatel—fine reds (notably one called *Periquita*, or "little parrot"); rosés, of which *Lancers* and *Faisca* are much exported; and some ordinary whites, as distinct from the dessert ones, though nothing like as many as are produced elsewhere in the country.

Although Fonseca has a very old winery in Azeitão itself, there is a fascinating modern installation on the eastern edge of the little town. It is a series of great white tanks, looking for all the world like a collection of half-buried flying saucers.

The Bucelas region is situated around 30 km (19 mi) north of the capital, in the valley of the River Trancão. Though wine from here has a considerable history, and was very popular with the British soldiers under Wellington in the Peninsular War, this is quite a small demarcated region, and all the wine it produces appears under the *Caves Velhas* label. The Bucelas wine is usually straw colored, with a distinctively full nose and a fruity taste, which can sometimes verge on the citrus. It makes an extremely good companion for the lighter kind of white meats, veal and poultry, and is especially appropriate with fish.

Carcavelos consists of just one smallish vineyard, the Quinta do Barão, sandwiched between Lisbon and Estoril along a stretch of overdeveloped and popular coastline. This is not an easy wine to find, the yearly output being quite small, but if you are interested in wines with a history, it would be worth searching out for your collection. Carcavelos is another fortified dessert wine, topaz colored, with a nutty aroma and a slightly almond taste, mostly drunk as an aperitif.

The last of the four demarcated regions around Lisbon is Colares, on the westernmost tip of Portugal, beyond Sintra. It is a fairly hostile place for vine growing, with sandy soil and exposed to the Atlantic winds. Like Carcavelos, the spread of Lisbon's commuter belt has squeezed this region, which is a pity, as it has a long and distinguished history of wine production and still yields some very individual vintages, especially red. This is a wine that definitely improves with age, of a full ruby color, an aromatic nose, and an aftertaste which is likened to blackcurrants. It can be a little astringent when young, so it is always wise to try to find one of the older years. One label to seek out might be *Colares Chita*. The Colares whites are straw colored, slightly nutty in taste, and—like the reds—improve with age. They should be drunk well chilled.

## Bairrada and Dão

Higher up the Atlantic coast, and not far south of Oporto, is the region of Bairrada. It is not that long ago—1979—that Bairrada was demarcated, though, on the quality of its output, it probably should have been long before. This is a region made up mainly of smallholdings, gathered into six cooperatives. Taken all together, they turn out a fairly large quantity of wine. As there are several places of interest to the visitor—Coimbra, Conimbriga, Aveiro, and the Forest of Buçaco with its fantasy hotel—it may well be that you will easily come across the Bairrada wines. The reds are of an intense color, with a delicious nose and a fruity, rich and lasting taste. They mellow with age, and go very well with stronger dishes, such as game, roasts, and the more pungent cheeses. There are not too many whites in this region, and most of them are slightly sparkling *(espumantes)*, made often by the champagne method, though of course they cannot be called that, as the French champagne area has fought several legal battles to protect the name. Their characteristics mirror the reds in having a slightly darkish straw color, with a heavy, rather spicy nose. They go well with fish, pasta, and pâtés. One of the biggest names in the region, and one which has been largely exported, is *Aliança*, though several others such as *São Domingos*, and *Frei João* are worth tracking down. The hotel at Buçaco has its own wines in an extensive cellar, and they add a delicious dimension to a visit to that exceptional place.

The Dão demarcated region—pronounced something like "down" with an adenoidal twang—is also a name quite well known outside Portugal. This region is just south of the Douro in the mountainous heart of northern Portugal, crossed by the valleys of the Rivers Dão, Mondego, and Alva. Because of its terrain, the climate is very capricious here—cold, wet winters, scorchingly hot summers. Unlike the sandy or clay soils to the south, the terrain is made up of granite and schist, a rock which shatters easily, with the resultant changes in the kind of grapes that are cultivated. A very high proportion of wine here is red, matured—they are known as *vinhos maduros*—in oak casks for at least 18 months before being bottled. When they are fully mature, they have an attractively dark reddish-brown color, almost the hue of garnets, a "complex" nose, and a lasting velvety taste. They are best drunk at room temperature after being allowed to breathe well, and go excellently with the favorite roasts of Portugal, lamb and pork. Some of the best names to look for are *São Domingos*, *Terras Altas*, and *Porta dos Cavaleiros*, or any of the labels where the word Dão precedes the name of the supplier—*Dão Aliança*, *Dão Caves Velhas*, *Dão Serra*, or *Dão Fundação*. The Dão whites are less common. They spend shorter times maturing in casks, though still ten months or more, have the color of light straw, a full nose, and a dry, earthy flavor. The white *Grão Vasco* is certainly one to try, or *Meia Encosta*.

### Douro and Port

The secret of Port is found first of all in the nature of the arid, volcanic soil and the hothouse temperature of the Douro valley. Some 800 years ago, when the father of Afonso Henriques took possession of his new domain between Douro and Minho, he planted a stock brought from Burgundy. The vine, like Count Henri, adjusted itself to the alien soil. "Eating lava and drinking sunshine," the Burgundy vines stretched, little by little, to the river's edge. They fought a bitter fight, strangling in ravines, wandering in fits and starts, to force their roots through schistous soil. Nothing but the vine could survive in this torrid pass. With tireless obstinacy, the men of the Douro broke up slate, built terraces with stone-retaining walls, struggled against drought and phylloxera, and made the lost valley the most prosperous in Portugal.

It comes alive during the grape gathering, which lasts for several weeks, since the grapes ripen according to exposure and altitude. In the vineyards sited at lower levels, the gathering is often finished long before the higher plantations are ripe, for cold winds blow down from the Serra do Marão. The region, usually drowsy—the population is scattered because of water shortage—suddenly springs into activity at the time of picking. Workers hurry in from neighboring provinces. From dawn until dusk women are busy filling baskets, which the men carry on their backs, supporting as much as 150 pounds with the acid of a leather band looped over their foreheads. They descend in long files towards the *lagares* at the foot of the slopes, pile the fruit in these enormous vessels, ready for treading. Over 40 varieties of grape go into the making of Port, creating the wide diversity of taste that the finished wines can have. The harvesters gather about the vats before the *must* has begun to ferment; the atmosphere is steamy, the feverish excitement of new wine induces singing and dancing. In the spring the young wine goes down by road to the lodges in Vila Nova de Gaia. Since the building of a dam across the river the age-old transportation of the wine by *rabelos*, those strange boats of Douro that look somewhat like ancient Phoenician craft, has ceased.

Port, born as it is of a soil rich in lava, is divided into two great families—vintage and blended. When a year is outstanding—as in 1945, '47, '48, '55, '58, '63, '70, '75, '77, '80, '83, and '85—the wine is unblended and, after reinforcement and bottling, left to mature. These are the vintage wines, which will take upwards of 20 years to mature; the old bottles, dusty with cobwebs, are brought up from the cellar for weddings and christenings, and must be decanted before drinking.

By far the greater quantity of Port, though, even of good quality, is made of a carefully studied blend of new wine with old vintages, thereby obtaining a wide range of taste. For a long time, when England was the biggest market for Port, the first choice was given to full-bodied tawnies; these were served at the end of dinner, with cheese, or an apple and walnuts. However, there is a lot to be said for the white Ports, either sweet as an after-dinner drink, or dry, as an aperitif with ice and a twist of lemon.

The visitor to Oporto should definitely visit one of the Lodges to learn more about Port, taste it and, maybe, buy a bottle of one of the vintages that takes your fancy. It is quite an experience for anyone interested in wine to see these huge old cellars and find out some of the long, fascinating history that Port has gathered, like the cobwebs, over the centuries. Language will be no problem, as there has been an alliance for more than 200 years between the English and Portuguese in the Port trade, and many of the families are totally bilingual.

Of course, not all the wine produced in the Douro demarcated region is Port. The reds here are of a deep ruby color, extremely fruity, and with a rounded taste. They go well with richer foods, a variety of meats, casseroles, and stews—anything that tends to be well flavored with herbs. The whites are dry, by and large, a pleasant pale yellow color, with a "full" nose. They go well with salads, hors d'oeuvres, and chicken dishes. Look for *Mesão Frio, San Marco, Quinta da Cotto*, and *Santa Marta*.

**Vinho Verde**

This is the largest demarcated region in the country, divided into six subregions: Monção, Lima, Amarante, Basto, Braga, and Penafiel. The area lies inland from the Atlantic coast, threaded by a sequence of westward-flowing rivers, and enjoys a fairly mild climate with Portugal's highest rainfall.

Like *retsina* in Greece, vinho verde has come to mean Portuguese wine to many people. The name simply means "green wine," which refers to its delightful youth (as in Cleopatra's "salad days") and not to its color. For anyone who enjoys wine purely as a refreshing, mildly intoxicating beverage, a kind of celestial 7-Up, vinho verde is unquestionably *the* drink—gently sparkling (what the experts call *pétillant*), with a delicate fruity flavor, it embodies the coolness and fragrance of summer gardens. Vinho verde goes especially well with fish or any kind of seafood. The reds are important to the region, but will mostly be found on their home ground; they don't travel much. They also are refreshingly thirst-quenching, sharp rather than heavy, with a vermilion-to-purple color. Naturally, they go ideally with almost any meat dish. Try for *Alvarinho* and *Quinta de São Claudio*.

The vineyards are particularly noticeable in the Vinho Verde district, as this is an area where they are frequently terraced, climbing up the hill-sides away from the rivers like agricultural fortifications. Also, in places they actually arch over the roads, and often march alongside as you drive, the vines held high on colonnaded rows of pillars, reaching up to the sun. The grapes hang so high that they ripen in direct sunlight, without any rising heat from the ground.

## Madeira

Like Port, Madeira—our last demarcated region—deserves a chapter all to itself. This is a volcanic island, rising up to the misty retreat of Curral das Freiras, huddled in an old crater. The soil is clearly volcanic, and the beaches, such as they are, black. The temperate climate here, which can be humid in summer, provides exactly the conditions in which vines can thrive—although they seldom grow below 300 feet above sea level, that warmer zone being taken up by bananas and sugarcane production.

The history of viniculture on Madeira is almost as long as the history of humans on the island, and that started in 1419. Like Port, Madeira—the wine and its preparation—is a way of life, and a way of life in which Portuguese and British families are bound together. When Charles II married Catherine of Bragança in 1662 he, perhaps foolishly, declined to accept the island as part of her dowry.

Again like Port, the modern wine has changed a great deal from the traditional drink that was much favored by George Washington, among many other famous people. The modern, light, dry versions have become popular as the public's tastes have altered. Madeira is a fortified wine, and most often blended, too. The main styles are: *Boal* and *Malmsey* or *Malvasia*, the sweeter, heavier ones, which make excellent dessert wines; *Verdelho*, not so sweet, and useful as a light between-times drink, say as an alternative to sherry; and *Sercial*, dry and light, which makes an excellent aperitif. None of these, of course, is the kind of wine you are likely to drink as accompaniment to the main course of a meal, but they are all attractive occasional wines and when they are really aged, as they often are, can provide the dedicated drinker with a rare experience.

The labels to look for—and they date back in some cases for a couple of centuries—include *Blandy, Cossart Gordon, Rutherford and Miles, Leacock,* and *Miles and Luis Gomes* (you see what we mean about British and Portuguese families). A visit to a wine lodge in Funchal is an educational and delectable way of passing a couple of hours during your vacation.

## Portuguese Wine Words

| | |
|---|---|
| Adamado | Medium Sweet |
| Adega | Wine vaults |
| Adega Cooperativa | Wine Cooperative |
| Aguardente | Brandy |
| Branco | White |
| Bruto | Extra dry (for sparkling wines) |
| Caves | Wine cellars |
| Colheita | Grape harvest (thus a vintage, e.g., Colh. 1980) |
| Doce | Sweet |
| Espumante | Sparkling wine |
| Garrafeira (or Reserva) | Fine and mature wine. Special vintage |
| Generoso | A sweet dessert wine, highly alcoholic |
| Meio Seco | Medium dry |
| Região Demarcada | Demarcated Region (see text for explanation) |
| Rosado | Rosé |
| Seco | Dry |
| Tinto | Red |
| Velho | Old |
| Vinho da Mesa | Table wine |
| Vinho da Casa | House wine |

# 3 Lisbon

By Jules
Brown

With a total population of about 1 million, Lisbon is one of Europe's smallest capital cities, and, to many visitors, it immediately becomes one of the most likeable. Lying north of the Rio Tejo (River Tagus) estuary and spread over a string of seven hills, Lisbon offers a variety of faces to anyone with the energy to negotiate its switchback streets. In the oldest parts of the city, tiny, stepped alleys are lined with pastel-color houses, across which drying laundry is strung; here and there you come across a *miradouro*, a natural vantage point with spectacular views of the city and river. In the grand 18th-century center, wide boulevards are bordered by black-and-white mosaic cobblestone sidewalks. There's a legacy of fine Art Nouveau buildings, too, and everywhere—on church walls, around fountains, and in restaurants and bars—you'll see the striking blue-and-white *azulejos* (painted and glazed ceramic tiles) for which the country is famous.

Lisbon's earliest history is a little unclear, but historians believe the city was probably founded by the Phoenicians. It was not until 205 BC, however, when the Romans linked it by road to the great Spanish cities of the Iberian peninsula, that Lisbon prospered. The Visigoths followed in the 5th century and built the earliest fortifications on the site of the Castelo de São Jorge, but it was with the arrival of the Moors in the 8th century that Lisbon came into its own. The city became a flourishing trading center during the 300 years of Moorish rule, and the Alfama—the oldest district of Lisbon—retains its intricate Arab-influenced layout, although no original buildings exist. In 1147 the Moorish period ended when the Christian army, led by Dom Afonso Henriques, took the city after a siege that lasted 17 weeks. To give thanks for the end of Moorish rule, Henriques planned a great cathedral, and the building was dedicated three years later.

The next great period in the city's history—"the Discoveries"—came in the 16th century, after the voyages of discovery led by the great Portuguese navigators, to India, Africa, and Brazil. The wealth realized by these expeditions was phenomenal: Gold, jewels, ivory, porcelain, and spices helped finance grand new buildings and impressive commercial activity. Late–Portuguese Gothic architecture—called Manueline (after the king Dom Manuel I)—assumed a rich, individualistic style, characterized by elaborate sculptural details, often with a maritime motif. Torre de Belém and the Mosteiro dos Jerónimos (Belém's tower and monastery) are supreme examples of this period.

With independence from Spain in 1640 and assumption of the throne by successive dukes of the House of Bragança, Lisbon became ever more prosperous, only to suffer calamity on November 1, 1755, when the city was hit by the last of a series of earthquakes. Two thirds of Lisbon was destroyed, and tremors were felt as far north as Scotland; 40,000 people in Lisbon died, and entire sections of the city were swept away by a tidal wave.

Under the direction of the prime minister, the Marquês de Pombal, Lisbon was rebuilt quickly and ruthlessly. The old medieval quarters were leveled and replaced with broad boulevards; the city's commercial center, the Baixa, was laid out in a grid; and the great Praça do Comércio, the riverfront square, was planned. Essentially this is how downtown Lisbon appears to visitors today. Its 18th-century character largely consists of an elegant layout that remains as pleasing and efficient in modern times as it was intended to be 250 years ago. And aside from the attraction of the architecture, the

Gulbenkian Museum and a host of others are here—Lisbon has a lot to recommend it for a leisurely stay.

Of course, there are parts of Lisbon that lack charm, particularly the modern city that extends beyond the center in a series of often dreary suburbs. Even some of the elegant downtown sections are losing their appeal, as restorations and renovations replace turn-of-the-century buildings with shiny new office blocks. But the beauty of much of the city should compensate. In parts of Lisbon—especially in the Alfama and the Bairro Alto—the centuries seem to collide: Out of 17th-century buildings trip designer-clad youths; the fish market at Cais do Sodré resonates with traditional sights and smells; and just a few minutes' walk from Lisbon's 18th-century aqueduct sits Portugal's modernistic Amoreiras shopping center.

Visitors are often surprised to find that because of the hills, places appearing close to one another on a map are on different levels and actually quite far apart. But the novel transportation system, an entertainment in itself, will complement your walking tours. It consists of trams and buses and a subway system, with funicular railways and elevators to take you up the steep hills. And whatever your vantage point, the river is never far away: Chances are either you'll be looking over it or walking alongside it, close to the fishing boats, container ships, and passenger ferries that make up its traffic.

It's best not to visit at the height of summer, when the city positively steams and lodgings are at their most expensive—and most crowded. Winters are generally mild and usually accompanied by bright blue skies, but for optimum Lisbon weather, visit on either side of summer, in May or late September through October.

# Essential Information

## Important Addresses and Numbers

**Tourist Information**  Lisbon's main tourist office is in the **Palácio Foz** (Praça dos Restauradores, tel. 01/346–3314), at the Baixa end of Avenida da Liberdade, open daily 9–8. The staff speaks English, and there are plenty of free brochures and maps. You can also reserve a hotel room from here. There is also a useful tourist office at the **airport** (tel. 01/849–4323 or 849–3689); open daily 6 AM–2 AM. Both offices closed Christmas and New Year's.

**Embassies**  **United States** (Av. das Forças Armadas, tel. 01/726–6600), **Canada** (Av. da Liberdade 144–3, tel. 01/347–4892), **United Kingdom** (Rua S. Domingos a Lapa 37, tel. 01/396–1191).

**Emergencies**  **Police** (tel. 01/346–6141), **ambulance** (tel. 01/301–7777), **fire** (tel. 01/606060), **SOS Emergencies** (tel. 115). For general problems, or in case of theft, the **Tourism Police** (Rua Capelo 13, tel. 01/346–6141) has an office open 24 hours. If you need to make a claim against your travel insurance, you must file a report here.

*Doctors*  Ask the staff at your hotel or at the embassy to recommend a reliable local doctor: Many doctors who have trained abroad speak English. Also, you can contact the British Hospital (*see below*), whose switchboard staff speaks English.

*Hospitals*  **British Hospital** (Rua Saraiva de Carvalho 49, tel. 01/395–5067 or 397–6329) has English-speaking doctors and nurses. Other hospitals include the **Hospital São José** Rua José A. Serrano, tel. 01/886–

0131); **Hospital de São Francisco Xavier** (Est. Forte A. Duque, tel. 01/301–7351); and **Hospital Santa Maria** (Av. Prof. Egas Moniz, tel. 01/797–5171; emergency 01/793–2762).

**Late-Night Pharmacies** Hours of operation and listings of druggists that stay open late are posted on most pharmacy doors. For information on the nearest drugstore open weekends or after hours, call 118. Local newspapers also carry a current list of pharmacies that have extended hours.

**Where to Change Money** Most major banks have offices in the **Baixa,** and there are currency-exchange facilities at the **airport** and at **Santa Apolónia train station.** Throughout the city you will find automatic currency-exchange machines (equivalent to ATMs in the United States), but they only take European money cards; Cirrus and Plus networks cannot be accessed in Lisbon or anywhere in Portugal.

**Mail and Telephones** The **main post office** (Praça do Comércio) receives Poste Restante mail (General Delivery) and is open weekdays 9–7. You'll need your passport to collect your mail.

The **post office** on the eastern side of Praça dos Restauradores, at No. 58, is open Monday–Saturday 8 AM–10 PM, Sunday 10 AM–6 PM. The **telephone office** here is the best place to make long-distance calls, but expect to take a numbered ticket and wait your turn in line. There's a second **telephone office** on the northwestern corner of the Rossío, at No. 65, that's open daily 8 AM–10 PM. At both of these locations you can use your Visa card. You can also make direct-dialed, long-distance calls from most city phone cabins on the street, though it's easiest if you use a phone card (750$00 or 1,725$00), available from post offices.

If you have an AT&T, MCI, or Sprint calling card, you can dial the appropriate access number from your hotel phone (and some public phones) to be connected with an English-speaking operator to make an international call. For AT&T dial 05017–1–288; for Sprint dial 05017–1–877; for MCI dial 05017–1234. Be aware that you cannot get this service from all phones in the city.

**English-Language Bookstores** Many bookstores downtown carry at least a few English-language novels and guidebooks. **Livraria Bertrand** (Rua Garrett 75), **Livraria Britanica** (Rua de São Marcal 168), and **Livraria Bucholz** (Rua Duque de Palmela 4) have a broader selection than most. For American and European newspapers, go to one of the several small newsstands at the bottom of Praça dos Restauradores and on the Rossío, but expect periodicals to be a day or two out of date.

**Travel Agencies** You can save yourself a lot of time by purchasing train or bus tickets from one of Lisbon's many travel agencies. Major agencies include: **American Express** (c/o Top Tours, Av. Duque de Loulé 108, tel. 01/315–5877), **Wagon-Lits** (Av. da Liberdade 103, tel. 01/342–6434), **Marcus & Harting** (Rossío 45–50, tel. 01/346–9271), and **Viagens Rawes** (Travessa do Corpo Santo 15, tel. 01/347–4089). All main branches generally have an employee who speaks English.

## Arriving and Departing by Plane

**Airport and Airlines** International and domestic flights land at Lisbon's small but recently modernized **Portela Airport** (tel. 01/802060; call 01/802262 for arrival/departure information), north of the city. There is a tourist office here and an exchange bureau for changing money on your arrival. The airport is only about 20 minutes from the city center by car or taxi.

**TAP,** the Portuguese national airline, flies from New York, Newark, Boston, Los Angeles, Montréal, and Toronto, with some direct flights to Lisbon. Also, **TAP, British Airways, TWA, Delta,** and **Air Canada** link the city with London and other European capitals (*see* Arriving and Departing in Chapter 1, Essential Information).

**Between the Airport and Downtown**
There are no trains or subways between the airport and the city, but getting downtown by bus or taxi is a simple matter and is relatively inexpensive.

*By Bus*
There is a special express-bus service into the city center called the **Linha Verde** (Green Line, No. 90), which departs every 15–30 minutes 7:30 AM–10:30 PM and takes 30 minutes. The bus leaves from immediately outside the terminal building, costs 250$00, and stops at several useful points, including Praça Marquês de Pombal, the Avenida da Liberdade, the Rossío, and Santa Apolónia train station.

City Buses 44 and 45 costing about 140$00 one-way are cheaper than Linha Verde. They depart every 15–30 minutes 6 AM–1 AM from the main road in front of the terminal building and pass through Praça dos Restauradores on the way to the Cais do Sodré train station. (From there you can continue by rail to Estoril and Cascais.)

*By Taxi*
Taxis in Lisbon are so cheap and the airport is so close to the city center that many visitors make a beeline straight for a cab (lines form at the terminal). Expect to pay 1,500$00–2,000$00 to most destinations in the city center and around 6,000$00 if you're headed for Estoril or Sintra. Note that you will probably have to pay about 300$00 extra for each piece of luggage.

*By Car*
Car-rental firms and the tourist-information office at the airport provide free maps of Lisbon and the Lisbon Environs. The drive to the city center takes 20–30 minutes, depending on traffic conditions. It's best to follow the Linha Verde bus route (*see* By Bus, *above*). However, signs to the city center are posted along Avenida Marechal Craveiro Lopes, through Campo Grande, down Avenida da República, and to Praça Marquês de Pombal, and the main Avenida da Liberdade.

## Arriving and Departing by Car, Train, and Bus

**By Car**
Lisbon sees some of the most reckless driving in all of Portugal. Add to this the notoriously difficult parking situation in the city center and the cramped old-town quarters, and there's much to be said for not using a car in the capital. Nevertheless, most of the country's highways originate in Lisbon, including the fast roads west to Estoril, south to Setúbal, and north to Oporto.

*Car Rentals*
Major car-rental companies have offices at the airport and at Santa Apolónia station (*see below*). In central Lisbon you'll also find: **Avis** Rua da Glória 14, tel. 01/346–2676), **Budget** (Av. Fontes Pereira de Melo 62, tel. 01/353–7717), **Europcar** (Av. António Agusto de Aguiar 24, tel. 01/353–6757), and **Hertz** (Av. 5 de Outubro 10, tel. 01/353–2894). Smaller local companies are also represented in Lisbon; the tourist office has full details.

**By Train**
International trains from France and Spain and long-distance domestic services from Oporto and the north arrive at and depart from the **Santa Apolónia station** (Av. Infante D. Henrique, tel. 01/888–4142), on the riverfront, to the east of Lisbon's center. One daily train runs to and from Paris; two daily trains to and from Madrid; and frequent daily trains to and from Oporto from 7 AM to midnight. To reach the Rossío or Avenida da Liberdade from the station, take a

taxi or Bus 9 or 46 from outside the station. The Linha Verde bus also runs from here into the center.

Local trains to Sintra and all destinations in Estremadura use the central **Rossío station** (tel. 01/346–5022), an unmistakable neo-Manueline building that stands between Praça dos Restauradores and the Rossío itself. It's under long-term renovation, but it's still in operation. Trains to Sintra run daily every 15 minutes from 6 AM to 2:40 AM; three trains daily run to towns in Estremadura. The train-information office is on street level, but for tickets and platforms take the escalators (through the shopping center in the station building) to the top floor.

Trains traveling along the coast to Estoril and Cascais arrive at and depart from the waterfront **Cais do Sodre station** (tel. 01/347–0181), a 10-minute walk west of the Praça do Comércio. Departures both ways are very regular—every 15–30 minutes, 5:30 AM–2:30 AM.

Traveling by train to the Algarve and the south of the country is somewhat more complicated than train travel to other destinations. The **Barreiro station** (tel. 01/207–3028) is on the opposite side of the Rio Tejo but is linked to Lisbon by a ferry that docks at the **Terminal Fluvial** (also known as Sul e Sueste) adjacent to Praça do Comércio. The fare is included in the train-ticket price. There are seven daily trains to the Algarve, the first of which leaves at 6:40 AM, and the last one—an overnight service—at about midnight. For information about train service from any station in Lisbon (or the rest of the country) call 01/888–4025 daily 8 AM–11 PM.

**By Bus**   Most international buses and domestic express buses, including those to and from the Algarve, operate from within the **main bus terminal** (Av. Casal Ribeiro 18, tel. 01/545439), which is very near Praça Duque de Saldanha. The Saldanha and Picoas metro stations are just a few minutes' walk away. Terminals at **Praça de Espanha** (Pavalha metro) and **Campo Pequeno** (Campo Pequeno metro) serve Setúbal and the northwest coast of Portugal respectively; buses to and from Mafra operate from Largo Martim Moniz, northeast of Praca da Figueira.

For bus transportation schedules it's best to inquire in advance at the main tourist-information office, since routes and companies change frequently (particularly on the popular summer express runs to the Algarve). Most travel agents can sell you a bus ticket in advance; if you buy from the company ticket office at the main terminal, give yourself plenty of time to purchase before you depart. In summer it's wise to reserve a ticket at least a day in advance for destinations in the Algarve. There are four daily departures from Lisbon for the Algarve and Oporto; towns closer to the capital receive more frequent service.

## Getting Around

The best way to see central Lisbon is on foot (in combination with various forms of public transport). It's a small city by any standard, and most of the points of interest are contained within the well-defined older quarters. A stroll through the Baixa—the gridded 18th-century downtown shopping area—can take less than a half hour; from there you can walk to the Bairro Alto to the west or the Alfama to the east. The latter two areas are the most interesting of the old-town quarters. A 30-minute walk north up the central Avenida da Liberdade takes you to the large Parque Eduardo VII; the Gulbenkian Foundation is about 15 minutes farther.

If you plan to walk the city, it's important to remember that Lisbon is hilly and has cobblestone sidewalks that can make walking tiring (especially in the hot summer) even when you wear comfortable shoes. At some point you'll probably want to use the public-transportation system, if only to sample the old trams and funicular railways and elevators that link sections of the city.

There are ways to reduce public-transportation costs, especially if you're staying in Lisbon for more than a few days. Various transport passes are available for use either on the metro or on the city's buses; details are given below under the relevant headings. Another option is a *Passe Turístico* (tourist pass) that gives unlimited rides on all city transportation. It costs 1,350$00 for four days or 1,900$00 for a week and is available at Cais do Sodré station at the booth by the Elevador de Santa Justa and other terminals; take your passport along to qualify for the pass.

A note of warning: Avoid traveling on public transportation during rush hours, especially on the metro, which gets jammed. Also, be aware that pickpockets ply their trade on crowded trains, buses, and trams. Keep an eye on your possessions, and carry bags and purses with the zipper side facing your body.

**By Tram** Taking an *elétrico* (tram) is one of the most amusing and enjoyable ways to get around Lisbon. The system, built by British engineers at the end of the last century, is one of the best in Europe and is easy to use. Stops are indicated by *paragem* (stop signs) on the sidewalks, and every stop has a route map for each tram that passes that way. The system operates 6:30 AM to midnight, and tickets cost 140$00 per journey; insert your ticket in the ticket-punch machine by the driver. Useful routes and an inexpensive tour of the city include Trams 13, 24, 28, 29, and 30; Trams 15, 16, and 17 will take you to Belém; Tram 12 goes to the Alfama.

**By Bus** *Carris* (buses) are generally quicker than trams. There's a flat fare of 140$00 for most city journeys, though you can also buy a one-day bus pass (350$00) or a three-day pass (820$00) from kiosks near principal bus stops on main routes. Again, each stop is posted with full details of routes, so it's simple to determine the correct bus to take. City buses operate 6 AM to midnight, and useful buses include 90, which links the airport with the main downtown areas, and 52 and 53, which make the spectacular journey across the Ponte 25 de Abril over the Rio Tejo. When you board, insert your ticket in the ticket-punch machine located behind the driver and wait for the pinging noise. For information on bus routes, call 01/363–2044.

**By Metro** The Metropolitano is modern and efficient but covers a limited route and is used mostly by local commuter traffic. However, you may find it convenient for transport to and from the Gulbenkian Foundation, and to Praça de Espanha for the bus across the Ponte 25 de Abril to Setúbal; there are stops en route along Avenida da Liberdade and at the Parque Eduardo VII. The metro operates 6:30 AM to 1 AM, and tickets cost 65$00 per journey if you buy them at the ticket office inside the station, 55$00 if you use the automatic ticket machine (instructions are in English); a block of ten tickets costs 450$00 from the ticket machines or 475$00 from the ticket office. There's also a one-day (200$00) or seven-day (600$00) Passe Metropolitano (Metro Pass), available at stations, for use just on the metro system. For metro information, call 01/355–8547. Insert your ticket in the ticket-punch machine at the barrier.

**By Funicular and Elevator** Small funicular-railway systems and an ingenious vertical lift (both are called the *elevador*) link some of the high and low parts of Lisbon. The lift, the Elevador de Santa Justa, whisks passengers from Rua de Santa Justa in the Baixa grid up to Largo do Carmo in the Bairro Alto. Of the funicular railways, the most useful are the Elevador da Glória, which runs from Calçada da Glória, just behind Praça dos Restauradores, to Rua de São Pedro de Alcântara in the Bairro Alto, and the Elevador da Bica, which runs from Rua do Loreto down to Rua Boavista, northwest of Cais do Sodré. Hours of operation for all three coincide with those of the other public-transportation systems; tickets cost 140$00 per journey, and departures are every few minutes from 7 AM to 11 PM.

**By Taxi** Taxis are plentiful and cheap, and if two to four people are traveling together a cab is often the cheapest option. Drivers are generally reliable and use meters; small tips are appreciated. Rates start at 250$00, and most city journeys will run 500$00–600$00; supplementary charges are added at night, for luggage, and for journeys outside the city limits. You may hail cruising vehicles, but it's sometimes difficult to get drivers' attention, especially late at night; there are taxi stands at most main squares. When you hail a cab, remember that when the green light is on it means the cab is already occupied. To phone a cab, try **Radio Taxis** (tel. 01/815–5061) or **Rossío Taxis** (tel. 01/827536).

**By Ferry** Ferries crossing the Rio Tejo leave from jetties at Praça do Comércio (Fluvial terminal), Cais do Sodré, and Belém, and cost 95$00–275$00 one-way. The journey is worth making at least once for the spectacular view it affords of Lisbon from the water. For details of Lisbon-area destinations accessible by ferry, *see* Essential Information in Chapter 4, Lisbon's Environs.

## Guided Tours

**Orientation** Many companies organize half-day tours of Lisbon and its environs and full-day trips to more distant places of interest. Listed below are a handful of reliable sources, and reservations can be made through any travel agency or hotel; some tours will pick you up at your door. A half-day tour of Lisbon costs about 4,500$00; a full-day trip out of the city to places such as Obidos, Nazaré, and Fátima costs about 12,000$00.

Try **Capristanos** (Av. Duque de Loule 47, tel. 01/543580), **Citirama** (Av. Praia da Vitória 12, tel. 01/352–2594, **Marcus & Harting** (Rossío 45–50, tel. 01/346–9271), and **Portugal Tours** (Rua D. Estefania 124–2, tel. 01/352–2902), and **RN Gray Line Tours** (Av. Fontes Pereira de Melo 14, tel. 01/577523).

**Personal** For names of personal guides, contact Lisbon's main tourist office
**Guides** (*see* Important Addresses and Numbers, *above*). Beware of unauthorized guides who approach you outside popular monuments and attractions: They are usually more concerned with "guiding" you to a particular shop or restaurant. But this is not to suggest that persons offering you a tour of the interior of a church or museum should be ignored. Often knowledgeable people associated with the particular institution volunteer their services for a tip of 200$00 or so.

# Exploring Lisbon

## Orientation

The center of Lisbon stretches north from the spacious Praça do Comércio—one of the largest riverside squares in Europe—to the

Rossío, a smaller square lined with shops and sidewalk cafés. The district in between is known as the Baixa (Lower Town), an attractive grid of parallel streets that was built after the 1755 earthquake and tidal wave destroyed much of the city.

The Alfama, the old Moorish quarter that survived the earthquake, lies east of the Baixa. Located in this part of town are the Sé (the city's cathedral) and, on the hill above, the Castelo de São Jorge (St. George's Castle). West of the Baixa, sprawled across another of Lisbon's hills, is the Bairro Alto (Upper Town), a fascinating area of intricate 17th-century streets, peeling houses, and churches. Five kilometers (3 miles) farther west is Belém, site of the famous Jerónimos Monastery, as well as several royal palaces and museums.

The modern city begins at Praça dos Restauradores, adjacent to the Rossío. From here the main Avenida da Liberdade stretches northwest to the landmark Praça de Marquês de Pombal, headed by the green expanse of the Parque Eduardo VII beyond.

The account of Lisbon below is divided into a series of walking tours that take you through the old- and new-town areas. Each quarter is pleasingly self-contained and can easily occupy half a day or more. By using taxis and public transportation you can combine two or three tours in a single day, but beware of trying to see too much too quickly. Walking in the summer heat is tiring, and, besides, some of Lisbon's greatest attractions and pleasures are to be found in the "hidden" squares and streets and in some of the agreeable café-bars for which the city is known. In Lisbon, slower is always better.

## Highlights for First-Time Visitors

Amoreiras Shopping Center (*see* Tour 4)
Castelo de São Jorge (*see* Tour 1)
Elevador de Santa Justa (*see* Tour 2)
Fundação Calouste Gulbenkian (*see* Tour 4)
Igreja de São Roque (*see* Tour 3)
Instituto do Vinho do Porto (*see* Tour 3)
Mosteiro dos Jerónimos (*see* Tour 5)
Museu de Arte Antiga (*see* Tour 5)
Rossío Square (*see* Tour 2)
Torre de Belém (*see* Tour 5)

## Tour 1: The Alfama District

*Numbers in the margin correspond to points of interest on the Lisbon map.*

The Moors, who imposed their rule on most of the southern Iberian peninsula during the 8th century, left their mark on much of Lisbon but nowhere so evidently as in the Alfama district. Here narrow, twisting streets wind up to an imposing castle set on one of the city's highest hills. This is a grand place to get your bearings and take in supreme views over the whole of Lisbon. The Alfama's streets and alleys are very steep, and its levels are connected by flights of stone steps, which means it is easier to tour the area from the top down. Take a taxi up to the castle or approach it by tram (Tram 28 from Rua Conceição in the Baixa or Tram 12 from Largo Martim Moniz, just northeast of the Rossío) and stroll down toward the center of town.

❶ Although the **Castelo de São Jorge** (St. George's Castle) was constructed by the Moors, the site on which it stands dates to the 5th century, when the Visigoths first raised a fortification here. At the castle's entrance is a statue of Dom Afonso Henriques, who in 1147 besieged the castle and ultimately drove the Moors out of Lisbon. Within the preserved Moorish walls and the castle's ramparts and towers (restored to their former glory in 1938) are remnants of a palace that was the residence of the kings of Portugal until the 16th century. The well-kept grounds are home to swans, turkeys, ducks, ravens, and other birds, and the outer walls encompass the small medieval village of Santa Cruz and its surviving church, a few simple houses, and rather more restaurants and shops. *Open Apr.–Sept., daily 9–9; Oct.–Mar., daily 9–7.*

After leaving the castle, give yourself time to wander the warren of streets that make up the **Alfama,** the most ancient part of Lisbon. Because its foundation is dense bedrock, the district—a jumble of whitewashed houses with flower-laden balconies and red-tile roofs—has managed to survive the wear and tear of the ages, including the great earthquake of 1755. Nevertheless, time has taken its toll, and what in the Moorish period was the most exclusive part of the city is now a somewhat run-down working-class neighborhood but is full of interest nonetheless. June is a particularly joyous time to visit, during the festivals of the *Santos Populares* (Popular Saints), when the entire quarter turns out to eat, drink, and be merry.

Although the Alfama has a notoriously confusing layout, it is relatively compact, and you'll keep circling back to the same main squares and streets. Follow the castle walls around, and you'll
**2** emerge close to the **Museu da Marioneta** (Puppet Museum), with its unique collection of Portuguese and foreign puppets. The intricate workmanship that went into the creation of these dolls is remarkable. Occasionally the museum staff performs a traditional puppet show, but schedules are not regular so you should inquire at the museum about upcoming events. *Largo Rodrigues de Freitas 19, tel. 01/ 878396. Admission: 300$00 adults, children under 10 free. Open Tues.–Sun. 10–1 and 2–6.*

From the puppet museum it's a 10-minute walk down Rua de Santa
**3** Marinha and Rua São Vicente to the twin-tower **Mosteiro de São Vicente** (St. Vincent's Monastery). The bright, Italianate facade heralds an airy church with a barrel-vault ceiling. Although there's nothing left of the original 12th-century monastery, the present church (completed in 1704) features a tiled cloister, and the former monastery refectory is the pantheon of the Bragança dynasty. In the pantheon, among the great, solid tombs and weighty inscriptions, lies Catherine of Bragança, who married Charles II of England in 1661. *Largo de São Vicente. Admission to church free; cloister 200$00 plus tip for guide. Open daily 10–1 and 2:30–5.*

**Time Out** Behind São Vicente is the **Feira da Ladra,** Lisbon's flea market, which is open every Tuesday morning 8 AM–1 PM and all day Saturday. There is the occasional antique here waiting to be discovered, but the browser will find mainly junk, army clothing, and bric-a-brac. Still, this can be an amusing way to spend an hour or so.

From outside the São Vicente church, tired legs can catch Tram 28 (or walk 10 minutes) to the Alfama's prettiest square, **Largo das Porta's do Sol.** The terrace offers glorious views of the streets below, dotted with drying laundry draped across the stepped alleys.

**4** Just off the square you'll find the **Museu Escola de Artes Decorativas** (Museum and School of Decorative Arts), a beautifully restored 17th-century palace in which tour guides exhaustively point out

# Lisbon

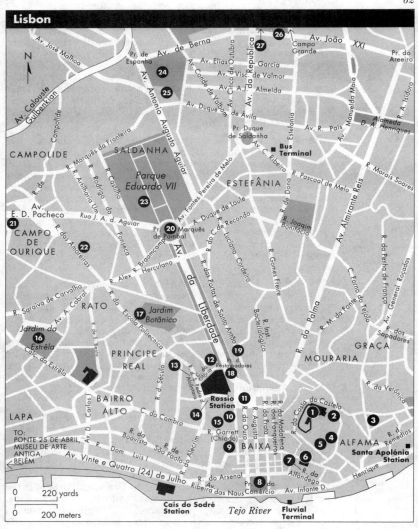

Amoreiras, **21**
Aqueducto das Aguas Livres, **22**
Campo Pequeno, **26**
Casa dos Bicos, **7**
Castelo de São Jorge, **1**
Centro de Arte Moderna, **25**
Chiado, **9**

Convento do Carmo, **15**
Elevador da Glória, **12**
Elavador de Santa Justa, **10**
Igreja de São Roque, **14**
Igreja de Santa Luzia, **5**
Instituto do Vinho do Porto, **13**

Jardim Botânico, **17**
Jardim da Estrêla, **16**
Mosteiro de São Vicente, **3**
Museu Escola de Artes Decorativas, **4**
Museu Calouste Gulbenkian, **24**
Museu da Cidade, **27**
Museu Etnografico, **19**

Museu da Marioneta, **2**
Parque Eduardo VII, **23**
Praça do Comércio, **8**
Praça Marquês de Pombal, **20**
Praça dos Restauradores, **18**
Rossío , **11**
Sé, **6**

every furnishing, including the lovely *arraiolos* (traditional, hand-embroidered Portuguese carpets that are brightly colored and based on imported Arabic designs). The more than 20 workstations next to the museum teach rare handicrafts, such as bookbinding, carving, and cabinetmaking. The museum has been closed for restoration, but is due to reopen in the near future; call for new hours and admission cost. *Rua de São Tomé 90, tel. 01/886–2183.*

**⑤** Continue down the hill about 110 yards to the **Igreja de Santa Luzia** (Church of Santa Luzia), with its fine exterior azulejos upon which the story of the siege of the castle and the conquest of Lisbon from the Moors is told. The adjacent terrace, the **Miradouro Santa Luzia,** offers another sweeping view of the Alfama and the river.

**Time Out**     At both Largo das Portas do Sol and the Miradouro Santa Luzia, you'll find a number of small café-bars with outside seats from which you can watch the ships' activities on the Rio Tejo. **Cerca Moura** (Largo das Portas do Sol 4)—named after the Moorish walls that surround the district—is one of the best, with a full menu of drinks and snacks from which to choose.

Head southwest from the miradouro along Rua do Limoeiro, which eventually becomes Rua Augusto Rosa. This route takes you past **⑥** the **Sé**—Lisbon's cathedral—which was founded in 1150 to commemorate the defeat of the Moors; to rub salt in the wound, the conquerors built the sanctuary upon the site where Moorish Lisbon's main mosque once stood. Aside from the austere Romanesque interior and a fine rose window, there's little to detain you, save a splendid 13th-century cloister. The ticket for the cloister also allows you entry to the sacristy, which contains the relics of the martyr St. Vincent. According to legend, the relics were carried from the Algarve to Lisbon in a ship piloted by ravens. *Largo da Sé. Admission to cathedral free; cloister 300$00. Cathedral open daily 9–noon and 2–6, sacristy open daily 10–1 and 2–6.*

Opposite the cathedral is the small church of Santo António da Sé, which retains a room (now a chapel) in which Saint Anthony was born, in 1195. The **Museu Antoniano,** in the chapel, features a curious collection of icons, books, and relics relating to the life of the saint. *Largo de Santo António da Sé, tel. 01/860–0447. Admission: 140$00; free Sun. Open Tues.–Sun. 10–1 and 2–6.*

**⑦** To complete your tour of this district, walk around and below the cathedral to the **Casa dos Bicos,** a mansion that survived the 1755 earthquake. Its main attraction is its striking facade of pointed white-stone diamonds. The building is at the end of Rua dos Bacalhoeiros, a street close to the dockside and lined with modest fish-and-seafood restaurants. From here it's an easy walk to the adjacent Baixa district, or retrace your steps to the cathedral, outside which Tram 28 stops before heading to the Baixa.

## Tour 2: The Baixa District and the Chiado

The earthquake of 1755, a massive tidal wave, and subsequent fires killed thousands of people and reduced proud 18th-century Lisbon to rubble. But within 10 years, frantic rebuilding under the direction of the king's minister, the Marquês de Pombal, had given the city a new look: a neoclassical, grid design.

This can be seen perfectly today in the impressive **Baixa** district (Lower Town), which stretches from the riverfront to the square known as the Rossío. Pombal intended the various streets to house certain trades and crafts and the street names to tell the story, as do Rua dos Sapateiros (Cobblers' Street), Rua da Prata (Silversmiths' Street), and Rua do Ouro (now the Rua Aurea: Goldsmiths' Street).

**❽** Begin your tour in the enormous **Praça do Comércio,** the riverfront square that completed Pombal's design. Known also as the Terreiro do Paço, after the royal palace (Paço) that once stood here, it is indeed a regal space, lined with serene 18th-century buildings. The equestrian statue is of Dom José, who was king at the time of the earthquake and during subsequent rebuilding. Steps—once used by occupants of the royal barges that docked here—lead up from the water onto the square. The square itself is a hub for public transportation (trams to Belém leave from here), and at times it may look like nothing more than a parking lot. Indeed, the best views are from any of the ferries that regularly cross the Tejo at this point.

**Time Out** One of the original buildings on the square houses the elegant **Café Martinho da Arcada** (Praça do Comércio 3; *see* Dining, *below*), situated, as its name suggests, in the 18th-century arcade. A literary haunt since 1782, the main rooms now contain an expensive restaurant full of old-style atmosphere; there's also a more modest adjacent café-bar.

From the square a riverside path runs to the train station at **Cais do Sodré** and offers pleasant views of the Tejo. If you want a rest, settle on a park bench and watch the fishermen throwing out their lines. It's a 10-minute walk to Cais do Sodré from the Praça do Comércio, where there's an open-air produce market on the waterfront (and a handy taxi stand and bus stop in case you don't want to continue on foot).

Back at the Praça do Comércio, the most practical tour to make is through the grid of streets that makes up Lisbon's main shopping and banking district. The central street—**Rua Augusta**—and some of the cross streets have been closed to cars, making window shopping easy. Most days there's a small crafts market close to the Praça do Comércio, and scattered throughout the shopping district you'll find some of the best shoe shops in Europe; glittering jewelry stores; and a host of cafés and delicatessens selling wines, cheeses, and pastries.

**❾** The western side of the grid, the streets leading uphill to the Bairro Alto, is known as the **Chiado,** Lisbon's most chic shopping district. In 1988 this area suffered great damage from a calamitous fire that destroyed many of the older shops in the vicinity of Rua Garrett. Today, though, an ambitious rebuilding program is under way. Despite the damage—some of which you can see from Rua do Carmo—the Chiado remains a fashionable place to shop.

**Time Out** Rua Garrett, the Chiado's principal street, is lined with old department stores and a series of comfortable, turn-of-the-century, wood-paneled coffee shops that attract locals and tourists. The most famous of these is the **A Brasileira** (Rua Garrett 120), which features a life-size statue of Portugal's national poet, Fernando Pessoa, seated at a table. This is a fine place for coffee or a beer anytime but Sunday, when the café is closed.

At Rua Garrett you aren't far from the Bairro Alto (*see* Tour 3, *below*), but the steep walk can be arduous. It may be better to drop back down to the Baixa, where—at the junction of Rua Aurea and
**❿** Rua de Santa Justa—you'll find the extraordinary **Elevador de Santa**

**Justa,** a lift engineered in 1902 inside its own Gothic-style tower. In less than a minute the lift whisks passengers up to Largo do Carmo in the Bairro Alto. *Cost: 140$00. Open daily 7 AM–11 PM.*

**⑪** If you walk north beyond the elevador, you'll enter the **Rossío,** Lisbon's main square since the Middle Ages. On the northern side of the praça—known officially as Praça Dom Pedro IV (whom the central statue commemorates)—is the mid-19th-century **Teatro Nacional** (National Theater), built on the site of the earlier Palace of the Inquisition. Unless you come to the theater for a performance (productions are in Portuguese), you'll probably do what the locals do when they come to the Rossío: sit at one of the sidewalk cafés lining the east and west sides of the square. The **Café Nicola** (*see* Dining, *below*), on the west side, is one of the more traditional spots.

The Rossío, filled with hawkers, newspaper stands, and shoppers taking a break, is a lively place to end your tour. It's also a good place to have your shoes shined by one of the roaming shoe-shiners who solicit their trade in the cafés. Before you agree to take their services, though, make sure you establish the price.

## Tour 3: The Bairro Alto

Lisbon's **Bairro Alto** (Upper Town) extends west of the Baixa and, like the latter, is laid out in a grid. Unlike the Baixa, however, the streets of the Bairro Alto are narrow and cobbled and follow the contours of the hills, which makes getting around the district both pleasurable and confusing. Although the district dates to the 17th century, most of the buildings are from the 18th and 19th centuries and house restaurants, nightclubs, bars, churches, and antiques shops. Historically the area has been slightly bohemian, but, with the opening of smart boutiques and trendy eateries, some gentrification has come. Yet the back streets are still lively with the sounds of daily life: Children scuffle amid the drying laundry, women carry huge bundles from shop to shop, and old men clog the doorways of neighborhood barrooms.

**⑫** You can approach the Bairro Alto using the Elevador de Santa Justa (*see* Tour 2, *above*), but this tour starts at the **Elevador da Glória,** a funicular railway located on the western side of Avenida da Liberdade, by Praça dos Restauradores. The elevator runs up the steep Calçada da Glória and takes only about a minute to reach the São Pedro de Alcântara miradouro, a viewing point that looks out over the castle and the Alfama (*see* Tour 1, *above*). *Cost: 140$00. Open 7 AM–midnight.*

**⑬** Immediately across the street from the miradouro is the wonderful **Instituto do Vinho do Porto** (Port Wine Institute), where, in the cozy, clublike lounge, visitors can sample more than 300 types and vintages of port, from extra-dry white varieties to red vintages. Service can be a bit slow, but eventually someone will bring you a wine list, and you may order by the glass or bottle. *Rua de São Pedro de Alcântara 45, tel. 01/342-3307. Prices of tastings start at 150$00 a glass. Open Mon.–Sat. 10–10.*

**Time Out** While in the Bairro Alto you may want to sample an *ementa turística* (tourist menu) that's offered in many of the small restaurants and bars. Typically, menus in this district include a set lunch of three courses, wine, and coffee and cost less than 2,000$00. **O Tacão Pequeno** (Travessa da Cara 3A), on a side street opposite the upper station of the funicular railway, is a cheerful dining room that's often packed with people enjoying the hearty local food.

From the institute, turn right and walk down Rua São Pedro de
⑭ Alcântara. At Largo Trindade Coelho, on your left, is the **Igreja de São Roque** (Church of St. Roque), a Renaissance church built by Felipe Terzi, the architect who designed São Vicente (*see* Tour 1, *above*) in the Alfama. Curb your impatience with its plain facade and venture inside. Its side chapels are superbly decorated. The last chapel on the left before the altar, the 18th-century **Capela de São João Baptista** (Chapel of St. John the Baptist) is extraordinary: Designed and built in Rome, with rare stones and mosaics that resemble oil paintings, the chapel was taken apart, shipped to Lisbon, and installed in 1747. You may find a guide who will escort you around the church and switch on the appropriate lights so the beauty of the chapels is revealed. Adjoining the church, the **Museu de Arte Sacra** (Museum of Sacred Art) displays a collection of 16th- to 18th-century paintings and a series of Italian clerical vestments and liturgical objects. *Largo Trindade Coelho, tel. 01/346-0361. Church open daily 8:30-6. Museum open Tues.-Sun. 10-5. Admission to museum: 150$00; free Sun.*

Continue to follow Rua Nova da Trindade south down the hill and turn left at Rua Trindade toward the pretty Largo do Carmo, on
⑮ which stands the partially ruined **Convento do Carmo** (Carmo Convent). The convent—once Lisbon's largest—was severely damaged in the 1755 earthquake, but open-air summer orchestral concerts are held beneath its majestic archways. Its sacristy houses the **Museu Arqueológico do Carmo** (Archaeological Museum), a small but worthy collection of ceramic tiles, medieval tombs, ancient coins, and other city finds. *Museu Arqueológico, Largo do Carmo, tel. 01/346-0473. Admission: 300$00. Open April-Sept., Tues.-Sat. 10-6; Oct.-March, Tues.-Sat. 10-1 and 2-5.*

Down a narrow alley behind the Carmo Convent is the upper station of the Elevador de Santa Justa; if you wish, you can return directly to the Baixa from there.

To complete your tour of the Bairro Alto, take the tram across the
⑯ quarter to the **Jardim da Estrêla** (Estrêla Gardens) on the western edge of the district; Tram 28 runs from Rua do Loreto, near Praça Luis de Camões, which is just west of Largo do Carmo. Inside the attractively laid out gardens, old men sit at tables playing card games, while towering over the southwestern side is the 18th-century **Basilica da Estrêla** (Estrêla Basilica. Open 7:30-1 and 3-8). This spacious Baroque church has an unusually restrained interior and offers views of the city from its *zimborio* (dome). Across the gardens, on Rua de São Jorge, is the **English Cemetery,** established in the early 18th century to allow Protestants to be buried with due reverence in a Catholic city. The most famous resident buried here is British author Henry Fielding, who died in Lisbon in 1754 and is known for his classic novel *Tom Jones.* You must ring for entrance at the cemetery gates.

⑰ Lisbon's botanical gardens, the **Jardim Botânico,** are about 1 kilometer east of the Estrêla Gardens, in the **Rato** district just north of the Bairro Alto. An alternative approach (but of the same distance) is to head north from the Port Wine Institute (*see above*), instead of south. Whichever way you get there, the botanical gardens, set on a hillside and inhabited by varieties of birds, make a pleasant stop. The four hectares of garden—laid out in 1874—contain nearly 15,000 species of subtropical plants and also house a 19th-century meteorological observatory. *Rua da Escola Politécnica 58, tel. 01/ 396–1521. Open May–Oct., daily 9–7; Nov.–Apr., weekdays 9–6; guided tours year-round Sat. at 11. Reservations required for tours.*

## Tour 4: The Modern City

**⑱** **Praça dos Restauradores,** the square adjacent to the Rossío Station, marks the beginning of the modern city. Here the broad, tree-lined Avenida da Liberdade starts its northwesterly ascent. There's little of interest in the square, save the 18th-century **Palácio Foz** on the west side, which houses the main tourist office. On the eastern side, a block east from the square and running parallel to it, is **Rua das Portas de Santo Antão,** famous for its row of seafood restaurants, most of which display in their windows great tanks of lobsters and fish on ice slabs.

**⑲** Also on this road is the **Museu Etnografico,** sponsored by the Lisbon Geographical Society. The building is currently being beautifully restored. When it finally reopens, you'll again be able to see its bizarre collections—shrunken heads, shells, and African musical instruments retrieved from Portugal's former colonies are displayed here. *Rua das Portas de Santo Antão 100.*

The city's main avenue—**Avenida da Liberdade**—is 1½ kilometers (1 mile) long and about 325 feet wide in places. Sadly, the thoroughfare that was laid out in 1879 isn't as grand as it once was: Many of the turn-of-the-century mansions and Art Deco buildings that graced the route have been demolished; others are covered in scaffolding as "renovation" work—the practice of turning historic buildings into soulless office blocks—continues. Nevertheless, you should take a leisurely stroll up the avenue from Praça dos Restauradores. Among the many cafés serving coffee and cool drinks is the open-air *esplanada* (garden-café), in its central, tree-shaded location at the south end.

**⑳** It takes about 30 minutes on foot (or two stops on the metro) to reach the top of the avenue and the **Praça Marquês de Pombal,** a large roundabout also known as the Rotunda. Dominating the site is a central statue of the Marquês, designer of the new Lisbon that emerged from the ruins of the 1755 earthquake. From here you can take the metro north to the Gulbenkian Foundation (*see below*) or back to the Rossío (*see* Tour 2, *above*).

**㉑** Alternately, go uphill to the west along Rua Joaquim António Aguiar to Lisbon's most ambitious post-modern building, the gigantic, pink-and-blue, commercial-and-residential complex called **Amoreiras.** Take the 1-kilometer (⅔-mile) walk, or jump in a cab. Designed by Tomás Taveira and visible from just about everywhere in the city, Amoreiras is adored as well as disdained. Inside there's a huge shopping center, a 10-screen movie theater, a "food street" of restaurants and bars, and information boards at every turn to help you cope with the complex's enormity. On weekends it seems all of Lisbon turns out to parade the corridors. *Av. Eng. Duarte Pacheco, tel. 01/692558. Shops and restaurants open daily 9 AM–11 PM.*

**㉒** Rua das Amoreiras runs south from the shopping center to the Largo do Rato. As you approach the quiet Largo das Amoreiras, look up at the **Aqueduto das Aguas Livres,** an 18th-century aqueduct supported by 14 arches, which formerly provided clean drinking water for the city. Nineteenth-century lore tells of one character who had a penchant for hurling his victims the 200 feet to the ground below.

For organized visits to the aqueduct, call 01/813–5522 or ask at the tourist information office.

Back at the Rotunda is the entrance to Lisbon's main park, the
㉓ **Parque Eduardo VII,** which was established at the beginning of this
century and named in honor of King Edward VII of England, who
visited Lisbon in 1903. Bordering the common, particularly on the
western side, are several of Lisbon's luxury hotels, including the
Ritz and the Lisboa Meridien. (Many of the hotels have private terraces that guarantee you a room with a view.) The park is best
known for its two *estufas,* the *estufa fria* (cold greenhouse) and
*estufa quente* (hot greenhouse), which contain rare flowers, trees,
and shrubs from tropical and subtropical climes. The estufa fria is
also one of the city's most bizarre concert venues, used on occasion
by orchestras and soloists. *Tel. 01/682278. Admission to estufas:
75$00. Open Apr.–Sept., daily 9–6; Oct.–Mar., daily 9–5.*

Leave the park on the east side, and head north along Avenida António Augusto Aguiar. A 15-minute walk will bring you to the Praça de
Espanha, to the right of which, in the Parque de Palhava, is the celebrated **Fundação Calouste Gulbenkian,** set on its own lush grounds.
The museum of this cultural-trust foundation houses treasures collected by Armenian oil magnate Calouste Gulbenkian (1869–1955)
and donated to the people of Portugal in return for tax concessions.
㉔ The **Museu Calouste Gulbenkian** is the main part of the foundation's
buildings and is easily Portugal's finest museum. The collection it
houses is split in two: One part is devoted to Egyptian, Greek, Roman, Islamic, and Oriental art and the other to European acquisi-
tions. Both holdings are relatively small, but the quality of the
pieces on display is magnificent, and you should aim to spend at least
two hours here, or even the better part of a day. English-language
notes are available throughout the museum.

You might first visit the astounding Egyptian room, highlighted by
a haunting gold mummy mask. Greek and Roman coins and statuary,
Chinese porcelain, Japanese prints, and a set of rich 16th- and 17th-
century Persian tapestries follow. No less comprehensive is the European art section, with pieces representing all major schools from
the 15th through the 20th centuries. A room of vivid 18th-century
Venetian scenes by Francesco Guardi and paintings by Rembrandt,
Rubens, Monet, and Renoir stimulate the senses, as do the Italian
and Spanish ceramics, gleaming French furniture, textiles, and Art
Nouveau jewelry. In short, this collection rates as one of the most
satisfying and complete holdings of artistic brilliance in the world.

If it's all too much to take in at one time, break up your visit with a
stop in the pleasant café-restaurant in the basement. There's an exhibition room here, too, that features temporary displays of art.
Later, on your way out of the museum, at the main desk, you can buy
superb (and inexpensive) posters and postcards. The foundation also
houses two concert halls, where music and ballet festivals are held in
winter and spring. Thanks to the Gulbenkian Foundation, modestly
priced tickets are available at the box office. *Av. de Berna 45, tel.
01/795–0236. Admission: 200$00, free Sun. Open June–Sept.,
Tues., Thurs., Fri., and Sun. 10–5; Wed. and Sat. 2–7:30. Oct.–
May, Tues.–Sun. 10–5.*

In the gardens outside the museum, sculptures hide in every recess.
You may want to spend a little time here before following signs
㉕ through the garden to the foundation's **Centro de Arte Moderna,**
where modern and contemporary Portuguese and foreign art are
displayed on two floors. There's also a special section set aside for

drawings and prints. Although the range of exhibits here is more limited than that of the Gulbenkian, modern-art fans will appreciate this venue for the finest collection of its sort in Portugal. Naturally, Portuguese artists are best represented: Look for pieces by Amadeo de Sousa Cardoso, whose painting style varied greatly in his short life; abstract works by Viera da Silva; and the childhood themes explored in the paintings of Paula Rego. *Rua Dr. N. Bettencourt, tel. 01/795–0241. Admission: 200$00, free Sun. Open June–Sept., Tues., Thurs., Fri., and Sun. 10–5; Wed. and Sat. 2–7:30. Oct.– May, Tues.–Sun. 10–5.*

From the Modern Art Museum, walk back through the grounds of the Gulbenkian Foundation and exit east on to Avenida de Berna. Where the street crosses Avenida da República you'll find the area ❷❻ (and metro stop) known as **Campo Pequeno.** This site—impossible to overlook—is the city's circular, red-brick, Moorish-style bullring, which sports small cupolas atop its four main towers. The bullring holds about 9,000 people who crowd in to watch the twice-weekly bullfights (*see* Sports, *below*).

North of the downtown area, the modern city stretches into sub-❷❼ urbs, with little to tempt the tourist except perhaps the **Museu da Cidade** (City Museum), in Campo Grande. From the bullring take the metro to Campo Grande (the museum is just a few minutes' walk away), or Bus, which stops close to the 18th-century Palácio Pimenta. The museum houses a collection of prints and paintings of Lisbon before the earthquake and a famous portrait of poet Fernando Pessoa, painted by the modernist Almada Negreiro, whose works are also displayed in the Gulbenkian's Centro de Arte Moderna. *Campo Grande 245, tel. 01/759–1617. Admission: 290$00. Open Tues.–Sun. 10–1 and 2–6.*

### Tour 5: Belém and the Museu de Arte Antiga

To see the best examples of the uniquely Portuguese, late-Gothic architecture known as Manueline, you should head for **Belém,** at the far southwestern edge of Lisbon. If you are traveling in a group of three or four, taxis are the cheapest means of transportation. Otherwise, for a more scenic—if bumpier—20–30-minute journey, take Tram 15, 16, or 17 from Praça do Comércio, which stop close to your destination.

*Numbers in the margin correspond to points of interest on the Belém map.*

❷❽ The enormous bulk of Belém's famous **Mosteiro dos Jerónimos** (Jerónimos Monastery), the construction of which began in 1502, makes it Lisbon's most impressive building. Conceived and commissioned by Dom Manuel I to honor the discoveries of Vasco de Gama, the edifice was financed largely by treasures brought back from the so-called *descobrimentos*—the "discoveries" of Africa, Asia, and South America made by the Portuguese. The Manueline design of the monastery was created by Diogo de Boitac and his successor João de Castilho, a Spaniard. The latter architect was responsible for the superb southern portal that forms the main entrance to the church: The figure on the central pillar is Henry the Navigator, and the canopy shows a hierarchy of statues contained within niches. The spacious Gothic interior contrasts with the riot of decorative Renaissance detail on the six nave columns, which disappear into a complex latticework ceiling.

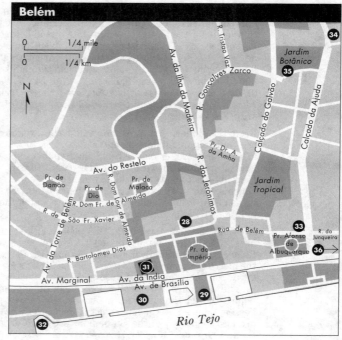

Don't leave the monastery without visiting the Gothic- and Renaissance-style **double cloister,** the lower level of which was also designed to stunning effect by Castilho. The arches and pillars are
heavily sculpted with marine motifs typical of the Manueline style.
*Praça do Império, tel. 01/362–0034. Admission to church free; clois-
ter 400$00 June–Sept., 250$00 Oct.–May, free Sun. Church open
June–Sept., Tues.–Sun. 10–6:30; Oct.–May, Tues.–Sun. 10–1 and
2:30–5. Cloister open June–Sept., daily 10–6:30.; Oct.–May, daily
10–5.*

There are two museums in the complex of buildings adjoining the
monastery. For enthusiasts only, the recently restored **Museu
Nacional de Arqueologia** (National Museum of Archaeology. Admission: 250$00, free Sun.; open Tues.–Sun. 10–5:30) presents Portu-
guese archaeological relics from Paleolithic to medieval times. Far
more inviting to the layperson is the **Museu da Marinha** (Maritime
Museum. Admission: 250$00, children 10–18 150$00; open Tues.–
Sun. 10–5), at the western edge of the building. The Maritime Museum is large, and there's something here for everyone, including early maps, navigational equipment, real and model ships, uniforms,
and other items that reflect Portugal's seafaring tradition.

**Time Out**   For a real taste of Lisbon, stop at the impressive **Fabrica dos Pasteis
de Belém** (Rua de Belém 86–88), a pastry shop and café that serves
delicious hot-custard pastries sprinkled with cinnamon and pow-
dered sugar. Although you can buy these treats throughout Lisbon,
they're made best here.

**㉙** Across from the monastery, at the water's edge (walk through the park and take the pedestrian underpass), stands the **Monumento dos Descobrimentos** (Monument of the Discoveries). Built in 1960, this tall, white, angular slab was designed as a modern tribute to the country's seafaring explorers, and it was built on what was the departure point for many voyages. Facing the water, at the prow, is Henry the Navigator; lined up behind him are the Portuguese explorers of Brazil and Asia, as well as other national heroes, including Camões the poet, who can be recognized by the book in his hand. Walk inside and take the elevator to the top for river views. *Admission: 275$00. Open Tues.–Sun. 9:30–7.*

**㉚** If you walk west for a couple of minutes along the waterfront you'll come to a squat modern building that houses the **Museu de Arte Popular.** Housed here are examples of the country's folk art, as well as a collection of ceramics, costumes, furniture, domestic and farm implements, and other ethnographic pieces. Displays are organized according to the province from which the objects came. *Av. Brasília,tel. 01/301–1282. Admission: 300$00, free Sun. Open Tues.–Sun. 10–12:30 and 2–5.*

**㉛** The museum is looking a little shabby these days, especially since the opening of the **Centro Cultural de Belém** across the road. Built of pink granite and marble, the Centro's design partly echoes that of the landmark Torre de Belém, a few blocks west (*see below*). It contains exhibition space, a restaurant, and a concert hall, and it has fine views of the monastery and the river from its attractive roof gardens and terrace bar. Stop by reception to pick up an events brochure (*see also* The Arts and Nightlife, *below*). *Av. da India, tel. 01/ 301–9606. Exhibition hall and café open daily 11–8; terrace bar open weekdays 3–9PM.*

**㉜** Another kilometer (⅔ miles), or about a 15-minute walk, farther west along the waterfront will bring you to the fanciful **Torre de Belém** (Belém Tower). Its openwork balconies and domed turrets make this perhaps the purest Manueline structure in the country. Although it was built in the early 16th century on an island in the middle of the Rio Tejo, today the chalk-white tower stands near what has become the north bank—evidence of the changing course of the river. Built to defend the entrance to the port, the tower served as a prison from the late 16th through the 19th century; its inmates were incarcerated in the dungeons. Cross the wood gangway and walk inside, not necessarily to see the rather plain interior but to clamber up the steep stone steps to the very top. From this vantage point you'll have a bird's-eye view of the Tejo and central Lisbon. *Av. da India, tel. 01/301–6892. Admission: 400$00 June–Sept., 250$00 Oct.–May. Open June–Sept., Tues.–Sun. 10–6:30; Oct.–May, Tues.–Sun. 10–1 and 2:30–5.*

**㉝** Make your way back to the center of Belém via Avenida da India. On the north side of Praça Afonso de Albuquerque is the **Museu Nacional de Coches,** which houses one of the largest collections of coaches in the world in buildings that once accommodated a riding school. The oldest vehicle on display was made for Phillip II of Spain in the late 16th century, and among the most stunning exhibits are three gold coaches created in Rome for King John V in 1716. This collection of gloriously painted, gilded Baroque coaches is dazzling, and it's one of the most popular collections in Lisbon. *Praça Afonso de Albuquerque, tel. 01/363–8022. Admission: 400$00 June–Sept., 250$00 Oct.–May, free Sun. Open June–Sept., Tues.–Sun. 10–1 and 2:30–6:30; Oct.–May, Tues.–Sun. 10–1 and 2:30–5:30.*

Calçada da Ajuda, on the east side of the coach museum, leads north
**34** up the hill to the overblown, fussily designed **Palácio da Ajuda**
(Ajuda Palace). It's a 20-minute walk, but Bus 14 stops here. In 1802
construction began on the palace, which was intended as a royal residence; its last royal occupant died here in 1911. Today the building
is home to a museum of 18th- and 19th-century paintings, furniture,
and tapestries, but unless you're especially interested in such
works, this attraction is not an essential sight. *Largo da Ajuda, tel.
01/363–7095. Admission: 250$00, free Sun. 10–2. Open Thurs.–
Tues. 10–5.*

**35** Just southwest of the palace is the **Jardim Botânico da Ajuda** (Ajuda
Botanical Gardens), the oldest botanical garden in Portugal (laid out
in 1768) and an enjoyable place to spend a half-hour or so. The many
species of flora, labeled in Latin, are contained in several green-
houses covering 10 acres. *Calçada da Ajuda. Admission: 50$00.
Open June–Sept., Tues.–Sun. 10–7; Oct.–May, Tues.–Sun. 10–6.*

Having completed your tour of Belém, take a taxi or public transportation (*see above*) toward downtown Lisbon. About halfway you'll
pass under the magnificent **Ponte 25 de Abril,** spanning the Rio Tejo.
Standing 230 feet above the water and stretching almost 2.5 kilometers (1.6 miles), this is the longest suspension bridge in Europe. The
bridge was completed in 1966 but later retitled; its name commemorates the 1974 revolution, in which the Portuguese army overthrew
Prime Minister Marcelo Caetano, successor to the long-serving au-
tocrat Dr. Salazar. Drive across the bridge on a clear day, if you can:
The view extends for miles and the experience is unforgettable.
Traveling to Setúbal (*see* Chapter 4, Lisbon's Environs), for example, will afford you the chance to enjoy the panoramic view.

Shortly after passing under the bridge, you approach the wealthy
district of **Lapa,** with its many foreign embassies, as well as the
**36** **Museu de Arte Antiga** (Ancient Art Museum), the only museum in
Lisbon to approach the status of the Gulbenkian (*see* Tour 4, *above*).
Buses 27 and 49 run from Rua de Belém across from the monastery
and stop near the museum on their way back to downtown Lisbon
(Tram 19 from Rua do Arsenal, near Praça do Comércio, stops outside the museum, if you are making a separate trip). Housed in a
17th-century palace, the museum features a beautifully displayed
collection of Portuguese art dating mainly from the 15th through
19th centuries that superbly complements the Gulbenkian's general
collection. Indeed, Gulbenkian himself donated several pieces to
this museum, which opened in 1883.

Of all the holdings, the religious works of the Portuguese School of
artists (characterized by fine portraiture with a distinct Flemish influence) stand out, especially the acknowledged masterpiece of
Nuno Gonçalves, the *Saint Vincent Altarpiece*. Painted between
1467 and 1470 for the Saint Vincent chapel in Lisbon's cathedral, the
altarpiece has six panels showing the patron saint of Lisbon receiving the homage of king, court, and citizens. Sixty different figures
can be identified, including Henry the Navigator, the archbishop of
Lisbon, and sundry dukes, monks, fishermen, knights, and religious
figures. In the top left corner of the two central panels is a figure
purported to be that of Gonçalves himself.

Besides the Portuguese works, there are pieces by Flemish painters
who influenced the Portuguese. There are also extensive collections
of French silver, Portuguese furniture and tapestries, Oriental ceramics, and other works from former Portuguese colonies. *Rua das*

*Janelas Verdes, tel. 01/397–6001. Admission: 250$00, free Sun.
10–1 Open Tues.–Sun. 10–1 and 2–5.*

## Lisbon for Free

There's a lot to do in Lisbon that's free or close to it. Indeed, on some
walking tours around the city, it may be difficult to spend your money. The city's churches, for instance—including the Sé (Cathedral;
*see* Tour 1)—charge no admission fee, although there often is a small
charge to enter the cloisters.

Walking around the alleys, streets, and squares in the historic districts of the Alfama (*see* Tour 1), the Baixa (*see* Tour 2), and the
Bairro Alto (*see* Tour 3) carries no charge, of course, and for the
price of a cup of coffee you can pull up a chair at a sidewalk café anywhere in downtown Lisbon and watch the fascinating world go by.
For an equally marginal cost you can ride an elevador from the Baixa
to the Bairro Alto (*see* Tours 2 and 3) or see the city from the windows of a rattling tram (*see* Getting Around in Essential Information, *above*).

**Historic Sites** Some of Lisbon's most compelling historic sites are free, including
the dramatic heights of the **Castelo de São Jorge** (*see* Tour 1), the
**Capela de São João Baptista** (*see* Tour 3), and the Manueline **Mosteiro
dos Jerónimos** (although not the cloisters; *see* Tour 5).

**Museums** Several museums have free admission on Sunday, including the famous **Museu Calouste Gulbenkian**, the adjacent **Centro de Arte
Moderna** (*see* Tour 4), and the **Museu de Arte Antiga** (*see* Tour 5). At
some of these museums free admission is limited to certain hours, so
check with the tourist office or with the museum itself before you
go.

**Parks and** Enjoy Lisbon for free at the twice-weekly **Feira da Ladra** (flea mar-
**Public Places** ket; *see* Tour 1), on the edge of the Alfama, or by dawdling in the
main square, the **Rossío** (*see* Tour 2). The gardens and church at
**Estrêla** (*see* Tour 3) are a pleasant spot, and a stroll up the main
Avenida da Liberdade ends with a rest in the city's main park,
**Parque Eduardo VII** (*see* Tour 4). Not far from here is an opportunity
to window-shop until you drop at the **Amoreiras** shopping center (*see*
Tour 4), open for business daily 9 AM–11 PM.

## What to See and Do with Children

Keeping children amused in Lisbon should be no problem; kids love
the rickety trams, funicular railways, ferries, and parks, and most
bars and restaurants accommodate families with children. One attraction you can bet youngsters will enjoy is the summertime **Feira
Popular**, a fair with rides, games, and a lot of food. *Entrecampos,
opposite Entrecampos metro station. Admission: 100$00. Open
May–Sept., weekdays 7 PM–1 AM, weekends and holidays 1–1.*

**Museums** Not all of Lisbon's museums and galleries are appropriate for children, but plenty of them host special exhibits geared toward young
visitors; also, most charge lower admission fees (or no fee at all) for
kids under 10. The following museums may be of particular interest
to families.

**Museu da Marinha** (*see* Tour 5)

**Museu da Marioneta** (*see* Tour 1)

**Museu de Arte Popular** (*see* Tour 5)

**Museu Etnografico** (*see* Tour 4)

**Museu Miltar** (Military Museum). The extensive collection of weapons, uniforms, and armor from the 15th century should intrigue any adventure-seeking child. Adults can study the historical text that accompanies the displays. *Largo do Museu da Artilharia (opposite Santa Apolónia station), tel. 01/888–2131. Admission: 150$00 adults, 75$00 10–16. Open Tues.–Sat. 10–4, Sun. 11–5.*

**Museu Nacional de História Natural** (Natural History Museum). Divided into three sections, this museum presents mineral and geological displays, zoological and anthropological exhibits, and a botanical garden (*see* Tour 3, *above*). *Rua da Escola Politécnica 58, tel. 01/396–1521. Admission free. Mineral/geological and zoological/anthropological sections open Mon.–Fri. 9–noon and 1:30–5:30. Botanical gardens open May–Oct., daily 9–7; Nov.–Apr., Mon.–Fri. 9–5.*

**Planetário Calouste Gulbenkian** (Planetarium). In Belém, behind the Maritime Museum, the planetarium presents interesting astronomical shows and displays several times a week. A bulletin posted in the window announces the current program, or you can get updates from the Palácio da Foz tourist office. *Praça do Imperio, tel. 01/362–0002. Admission: 250$00 adults, 150$00 children. Schedules vary, so check in advance.*

Parks  **Jardim da Estrêla** (*see* Tour 3, *above*)

**Jardim do Campo Grande** (metro: Entrecampos), in the north of the city, has a playground, tennis courts, a boating lake (rentals available), and two cafés.

**Jardim Zoológico.** With a menagerie of 2,000 animals, the city zoo is always a popular spot. In addition to the usual exhibits there is a children's zoo, with miniature houses and small animals, a dolphin show at 11 and 3, and a cemetery for dogs. There are snack bars and restaurants on site, or you can pack a lunch for a picnic. *Estrada de Benfica 158 (metro: Sete Ríos), tel. 01/726–8041. Admission to zoo: 390$800 adults, 250$00 children. Admission to dolphin show: 800$00 adults, 600$00 children. Open daily 9–8.*

**Parque Eduardo VII** (*see* Tour 4, *above*)

## Off the Beaten Track

To fully understand the craftsmanship that goes into making the ubiquitous azulejos, visit the engaging **Museu do Azulejo** (Azulejo Museum), in the 16th-century Madre de Deus convent and cloister. Some of the ceramics on display date to the 1700s, with representative examples from each century to the present. A highlight of the display is the 118-foot, 18th-century *Panorama of Lisbon*, a beautifully detailed study of the city and waterfront and reputedly the country's longest azulejo work. While you're here you may want to take a look at the richly furnished convent-church, too, since it contains some noteworthy gilt Baroque decoration. To reach the museum, take Tram 3 or 16 from Praça do Comércio to the eastern suburb of Xabegras (20 minutes away). *Rua Madre de Deus 4, tel. 01/814–7747. Admission: adults 200$00, senior citizens and children under 14 free. Open Tues.–Sun. 10–12:30 and 2–5.*

Northwest of the city, in the suburb of São Domingo de Benfica (near the zoo), stands the **Palácio dos Marqueses da Fronteira,** one of the most beautiful private houses in the capital. Built in the late 17th century, the building contains splendid reception rooms with 17th-

and 18th-century decorative tiles, contemporary furniture, and paintings. The grounds, which contain a terraced walk, a topiary garden, and statuary and fountains, are stunning. *Largo de São Domingo de Benfica 1 (metro: Sete Ríos), tel. 01/778–2023. Admission to gardens, 300$00; to palace and gardens, 1,000$00. Open Mon.–Fri. for 1-hour guided tour; arrive between 10:45 and 11AM. On Sat., full guided tour costs 1,000$00 (gardens) or 1,500$00 (palace and gardens); arrive at 10:45AM. Call ahead for details and restrictions.*

# Shopping

Shopping in Lisbon can be a pleasant, even refreshing experience, not least because there are still many independent boutiques and few large stores. Handmade goods such as leather handbags, shoes, gloves, embroidery, ceramics, and basketwork are sold throughout the city at relatively reasonable prices. Most shops are open weekdays 9–1 and 3–7 and Saturday 9–1; shopping malls and supermarkets often remain open until at least 10, and some are open on Sunday, also.

## Shopping Districts

In 1988 a fire destroyed much of the Baixa's **Chiado** district (*see* Tour 2, *above*), Lisbon's smartest shopping area, but there are still plenty of choice stores on and around the Chiado's Rua Garrett. The rest of the district, made up of the grid of streets from the Rossío to the Rio Tejo, remains a fine place to shop, with small stores given over mainly to fashion, jewelry, shoes, and delicatessen foods. Excellent shops continue to open in the new residential districts near the airport, at **Praça de Londres** and **Avenida de Roma**.

Of the shopping centers, easily the best is the **Amoreiras** (Av. Eng. Duarte Pacheco), west of Praça Marquês de Pombal, which contains a multitude of shops selling clothes, shoes, food, crystal, ceramics, and jewelry. It also has a hairdresser, restaurants, and 10 movie screens. For more information *see* Tour 4, *above*.

## Markets

Lisbon has several markets and, although you are unlikely to find authentic antiques, you may find something traditional to take home. The best-known market is the **Feira da Ladra** (No metro; Campo de Santa Clara in the Alfama), a flea market held on Tuesday morning (8 AM–1 PM) and all day Saturday. Others worth considering are the clothes market at **Praça de Espanha** (metro: Palhavã; open Mon.–Sat. 9–5.); the covered produce market at **Praça do Chile** (metro: Arroios; open Mon.–Sat. 9–5); the fish-and-flower market opposite **Cais do Sodré** (no metro; open daily dawn–dusk); and the food market opposite the Sheraton Hotel on **Avenida Fontes Pereira de Melo** (metro: Picoas; open Mon.–Sat. 9–5).

## Specialty Stores

**Antiques**  Most of Lisbon's antiques shops are concentrated in the district of Rato and in the Bairro Alto along one long street, which changes its name four times as it runs southward from Largo do Rato: Rua Escola Politécnica, Rua Dom Pedro V, Rua da Misericórdia, and Rua do Alecrim. Also look on the nearby Rua de São Bento for more stores. Two of the best-known shops are **Solar** (Rua Dom Pedro V

68–70), and **Abside** (Travessa dos Fieis de Deus 14–16), the latter in the Bairro Alto.

**Ceramics** **Viuva Lamego** (Largo do Intendente 25) offers the largest selection of tiles and pottery in Lisbon, at competitive prices. **Vista Alegre** (Largo do Chiado 18) founded its porcelain factory in 1824, and you can buy perfect reproductions of their original table services and ornaments. The **Fábrica Sant'Ana** (Rua do Alecrim 95), founded in the 1700s, sells wonderful hand-painted ceramics and tiles based on antique patterns; the pieces sold here may be the finest you'll find in the city. Also try **Aresta Viva** (Rua Antero de Quental 22), producers of handmade and hand-painted tiles, some based on 16th-century designs seen at the Museu do Azulejo (*see* Off the Beaten Track, *above*). For handcrafted modern pottery, **Casa Ribeiro da Silva** (Trav. Fieus de Deus 69) is worth a visit.

**Clothing** Although Lisbon isn't on the cutting edge of fashion and design, there are young Portuguese clothing designers whose products are featured alongside the more established fashion names in a variety of stores. **Praça de Londres** and **Avenida de Roma**—both in the modern city—comprise the newest fashionable shopping district. For big international names under one roof, **Amoreiras** shopping center (*see* Shopping Districts, *above*) can't be beat. Designer clothes stores are starting to creep into the Bairro Alto: **Manuel Alves** and **José Manuel Goncalves** have stores at Rua da Rosa 39 and 85 respectively; while **Eldorado** (Rua do Norte 25) sells antique clothing.

**Food and Wine** There are some excellent delicatessens in the Baixa that sell fine foods, including delicious regional cheeses, and a wide selection of wines, especially varieties of port—one of Portugal's major exports. **Manuel Tavares** (Rua da Betesga 1a), just off the Rossío in the Baixa, has a particularly good selection of vintage ports and wines; while the **Instituto do Vinho do Porto** (*see* Tour 3, *above*) offers more than 100 varieties to sample and bottles for sale. Other places that sell local wines are delicatessens, supermarkets, and—oddly—any shop that sells *bacalhau* (dried cod), which you'll see stacked outside on the sidewalk or hanging in the window. Rua do Arsenal has several such stores.

Other popular gourmet items are fresh chocolates, marzipan, dried and crystallized fruits, and pastries, on sale in most of the city's *pastelarias* (cafés specializing in cakes and pastries). Try the pastelaria **Suiça** (Rossío 96, eastern side), which has a particularly large selection of sweets.

**Handicrafts** **Rua da Conceição,** one of the crossroads in the Baixa, is known for buttons, wools, cottons, and all sewing materials. For embroidered goods and baskets from the Azores, try **Casa Regional da Ilha Verde** (Rua Paiva de Andrade 4). **Tito Cunha** (Rua Aurea 286) has a similar range of goods from Madeira, and near the Castelo de São Jorge, you'll find **A Bilha** (Rua do Milagre de Santo António 10), which sells embroidery, lace, copper, gold, and silver. **Casa Quintão** (Rua Ivens 30) has a large selection of arraiolos (here you can also buy a kit for making your own rug), and another showroom for traditional carpets is **Almoravida** (Rua da Senhora da Glória 130).

**Jewelry** The Baixa is a good place to look for jewelry: Rua Aurea (formerly Rua do Ouro) was named for the goldsmiths'shops installed here under Pombal's 18th-century city plan—the trade has flourished here ever since. **Sarmento** (Rua Aurea 251) has a large display of characteristic Portuguese gold- and silver-filigree work. For antique silver and jewelry visit **António da Silva** (Praça Luis de Camões 40) or **Barreto & Gonçalves** (Rua das Portas de Santo Antão 17).

**Leather Goods** Shoe shops can be found all over the city, but they may have limited selections of large sizes because the Portuguese tend to have small feet. However, all the better shops can make shoes to order.

Fine leather handbags and luggage are sold at **Galeão** (Rua Augusta 190) and **Casa Canada** (Rua Augusta 232) also has a large selection, although most of the products are not manufactured in Portugal. Gloves are sold or made to order in specialty shops in the Rua do Carmo and Rua Aurea. **Coelho** (Rua da Conceição 85) is excellent for leather belts and can also make leather-back fabric belts from your own material.

# Sports

## Participant Sports

There are few sports facilities in Lisbon itself; for most outdoor activities—scuba diving, fishing, horseback riding, water sports— you'll have to go outside the city (*see* Sports and Fitness in Chapter 4, Lisbon's Environs).

**Golf** There are a half-dozen golf courses in Lisbon's environs, most of which are concentrated along the Estoril Coast. Indeed, if you're planning to play golf, it's best to arrange to stay at one of the hotels outside Lisbon that offers special golf packages (*see* Dining and Lodging in Chapter 4, Lisbon's Environs). The nearest golf course is at **Lisboa Sport Club** (Casal da Carregueira, near Belas, tel. 01/431– 0077), about 20 minutes by car from the city.

**Swimming** If your hotel doesn't have a pool you can visit one of the city's municipal pools: **Piscina do Areeiro** (Av. de Roma, tel. 01/848–6794), **Piscina do Campo Grande** (Campo Grande, tel. 01/796–6305), or **Piscina dos Olivais** (Av. Dr. Francisco Luís Gomes, 5 kilometers/3.1 miles northeast of town, tel. 01/851–4630). The **Lisboa Sport Club** (*see above*) also has a swimming pool.

Another option is the new **Aquaparque de Lisboa** (Av. das Descobertas, tel. 01/301–5017, open daily 9:30–8), a complex of pools, slides, waterfalls, cafés, and restaurants in Restelo Park, near Belém.

**Tennis** There are public tennis courts at **Campo Grande** (Estádio 1 de Maio at Alvalade). To play, inquire at the main tourist office in Praça dos Restauradores (*see* Important Addresses and Numbers in Essential Information, *above*).

## Spectator Sports

**Bullfighting** For those not disturbed by bullfights, the events are held Sunday and Thursday between Easter and September in the ornate Praça de Touros (bullring) at **Campo Pequeno.** Some people defend the Portuguese bullfight as entertainment because the bull is not killed in the ring but is wrestled to the ground by a group of *forçados* (a team of eight men who fight the bull) dressed in traditional red-and-green costumes. Nonetheless, any bull injured during the contest is later killed. The first-class riding skills displayed by the *cavaleiro* (horseback fighter) during the fight are undeniable. After the cavaleiro performs, the forçados goad the bull into charging them, and one man throws himself across the horns (which have been padded) while the other men pull the bull down by grabbing hold of whatever bits they can, including the tail. *Av. da República (metro: Campo*

*Pequeno), tel. 01/793–6601. Admission: 2,000$00–8,000$00, depending on seats. Exhibitions Easter–Sept., Thurs. and Sun.*

**Soccer** Soccer is Portugal's most popular sport, and Lisbon has three teams, which play at least weekly during the September–May season. The most famous team is **Benfica,** for whom the great Eusebio played in the 1960s, when he took his team to five European championship finals. Matches are held in the northwest part of the city, at the huge Estádio da Luz (Av. Gen. Norton Matos, tel. 01/726–6129), one of Europe's biggest stadiums. A great rival of Benfica, the **Sporting Clube de Portugal,** plays at the Estádio José Alvalade (tel. 01/758–9021) near Campo Grande in the north of the city. Third best of the teams is Belém's **Belenenses,** which plays at Estadio do Rastelo (tel. 01/301–0461). You can buy tickets on the day of a game at the stadiums, but for most big matches (certainly when Benfica and Sporting play each other, or when either play Oporto's main team, FC Porto), you should purchase tickets in advance from the booth in Praça dos Restauradores. Plan to arrive at the stadium early, because there's usually a full program of entertainment first, including children's soccer, marching bands, and fireworks. (Note: Always be wary of pickpockets in the crowd.)

# Dining

Although only a few of Lisbon's restaurants can compare with the best establishments in other European capitals, there's no doubt that dining here is taken seriously. Fresh ingredients—especially fish and shellfish—are used everywhere, and you can find excellent meals all over the city, often in seemingly modest places. Sometimes the dining experience is boosted by the setting: Many restaurants are housed in ancient, converted buildings; some have city and river views; and others offer outdoor dining in summer.

With the exception of some very expensive restaurants, many of which feature French-influenced fare, a large number of places serve Portuguese cuisine, characterized by grilled sardines, simple steaks and cutlets, fresh seafood (always ask the price before ordering), and salads. Local specialties include *açorda* (a thick bread and shellfish stew) and different varieties of bacalhau. In addition, the capital manages to attract the best of the country's regional foods and specialties, too—you'll be able to enjoy game, lampreys from the Minho, and other seasonal delights (though often at a higher price than in their respective Portuguese regions). If you want more variety, however, try restaurants that specialize in colonial Portuguese food—principally Brazilian, but also Mozambican and Goan (Indian) cuisine. Wine is excellent and reasonably priced everywhere, especially the *vinho da casa* (house wine), which—in cheaper and more expensive restaurants alike—is carefully selected for its quality. Don't forget to finish your meal with a glass of port—having established at the Instituto do Vinho do Porto (*see* Tour 3, *above*) which one you prefer.

Almost all restaurants offer an *ementa turistica*, usually at lunchtime. Meals vary in quality but generally include three courses, a drink, and coffee, all for about 2,000$00–2,500$00. The selections are nearly always of good value but can be limited in scope. At all restaurants, be wary of eating anything brought as an appetizer that you haven't specifically ordered. You'll be charged extra, even if you eat just one olive, and it's surprising how much this can add to the cost of a meal. Lisbon's restaurants usually serve lunch from noon until 3 and dinner from 7:30 until 11; many establishments are closed Sunday.

Unless otherwise noted below, restaurants don't accept reservations; this is especially true of inexpensive places. In the traditional *cervejarias* (beer hall/restaurants), which frequently have huge dining rooms, you'll probably have to wait for a table, but usually not for more than 15 or 20 minutes. In the Bairro Alto, many of the reasonably priced *tascas* (taverns) are on the small side: If you can't reserve a table, either wait in line or move on to the next place. Throughout Lisbon, dress for meals is usually casual, but exceptions are noted below.

Highly recommended restaurants are indicated by a star ★.

| Category | Cost* |
|----------|-------|
| $$$$ | over 6,000$00 |
| $$$ | 3,500$00–6,000$00 |
| $$ | 2,000$00–3,500$00 |
| $ | under 2,000$00 |

*per person, excluding drinks and service.*

$$$$ **António Clara.** This classic French restaurant, named for its owner, is housed in an attractive Art Nouveau building in the north of Lisbon, in the modern part of the city. In addition to French fare, international dishes with a flourish are served in an elegant room that has a decorated ceiling, oil paintings, heavy draperies, and a huge chandelier. The menu is seasonal (fish is always well presented), the service extremely attentive, and there's a fine wine list. A private dining club for business people and the piano bar attract an upmarket clientele. *Av. da República 38, tel. 01/796–6380. Reservations required. Jacket and tie required. AE, DC, MC, V. Closed Sun.*

$$$$ **Aviz.** One of the best and classiest restaurants in Lisbon, Aviz has a
★ rich but subtle Belle Epoque decor, which includes turn-of-the-century furnishings, fine wood paneling, leather chairs, and crisp linen tablecloths. This exclusive restaurant is hidden on a side street off the Baixa's Rua Garrett. The mainly French and international menu is enhanced by Portuguese elements such as bacalhau. *Rua Serpa Pinto 12–13, tel. 01/342–8391. Reservations required. Jacket and tie required. AE, DC, MC, V. Closed Sat. lunch and Sun.*

$$$$ **Casa da Comida.** Imaginative French and Portuguese food is served in what was once a private residence. This grand house, with its flower-filled patio, offers a variety of options, from seafood to grilled steak with anchovy butter. You may have to look closely to find the entrance, situated just off the pretty Praça das Amoreiras. *Travessa das Amoreiras 1, tel. 01/685376. Reservations advised. AE, DC, MC, V. Closed Sat. lunch andSun.*

$$$$ **Gambrinus.** One of Lisbon's older and smarter restaurants, Gambrinus is renowned for its fish and shellfish. Situated on a busy street that bulges with fish restaurants, this establishment is understated—a quality that only adds to its appeal: Once inside the front door you'll find many small dining rooms; your waiter will regale you with a list of the day's seafood specials, which vary enormously in price—prawns, lobster, and crab are always available and always excellent. (There are meat dishes, too.) For a less formal but satisfying meal, you can eat at the wood-paneled bar during lunchtime. *Rua Portas*

# Lisbon Dining

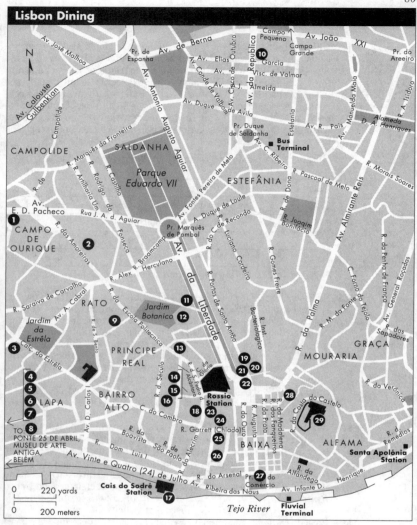

Alcântara, **4**
O Alexandre, **7**
Andorra, **19**
António Clara, **10**
Aviz, **25**
Bonjardim, **21**
Brasuca, **16**
Café Martinho da Arcada, **27**
Cais da Ribeira, **17**

O Cantinho do Aziz, **28**
Casa da Comida, **2**
Casa Faz Frio, **13**
Cervejaria Trindade, **23**
Comida de Santo, **9**
Farah's Tandoori, **3**
Gambrinus, **22**
Já Sei, **5**
O Madeirense, **1**

O Manel, **12**
Michel, **29**
A Quinta, **24**
Ribadouro, **11**
São Jerónimo, **6**
Sinal Vermelho, **14**
Solmar, **20**
Sua Excêlencia, **8**
Tagide, **26**
Tavares Rico, **18**
Vá e Volte, **15**

*de S. Antão 23–25, tel. 01/346–8974. Reservations advised. AE, DC, MC, V.*

**$$$$ Tagide.** Delicious Portuguese food and wine are served in this fine old tiled house that looks out over the Baixa and Rio Tejo. Renovations have created an elegant dining room—a lovely backdrop for sampling the impressive list of Portuguese regional dishes, including the famous *presunto* (smoked ham) from Chaves. Also offered is a smaller but no less succulent selection of French-influenced international dishes. Try to sit at a table by the window. *Largo Academia das Belas Artes 18–20, tel. 01/346–0570 or 01/342–0720. Reservations advised. AE, DC, MC, V. Closed weekends.*

**$$$$ Tavares Rico.** ★ Superb food, an excellent wine list, and a handsome Edwardian dining room have made this one of Lisbon's most famous and formal restaurants. Tavares Rico—founded as a café in the 18th century—has been pleasing customers with the splendor of its furnishings, the quality of its service, and its French-inspired menu, which features seasonal ingredients. A wise choice for an entrée is the sole cooked in champagne sauce. *Rua Misericórdia 35–37, tel. 01/342–1112. Reservations required. Jacket and tie advised. AE, DC, MC, V. Closed Sat. dinner and Sun.*

**$$$ Alcântara.** This large bar-restaurant has a glorious modern design that impressively and effectively combines wood, velvet, and steel. Old Portuguese specialties highlight the menu, and fish is always a good choice. There's a large wine list, too, and a splendid bar if you want to sip an aperitif before dinner. The restaurant is outside the city center, near Ponte 25 de Abril, and the kitchen stays open until 2 AM. *Rua Maria Luísa Holstein 15, near Rua Coz. Económica, tel. 01/363–7176. Reservations advised. AE, DC, MC, V. No lunch. Closed Tues.*

**$$$ Café Martinho da Arcada.** This famous café-restaurant, founded in 1782 beneath the arcades of Praça do Comércio in Baixa, was once frequented by the Portuguese poet Fernando Pessoa and other literary stars. In the wood-paneled dining room you can choose from a Portuguese menu that offers dishes from various regions and some that reveal a French influence as well. Try a *cataplana* (clam stew) from the Algarve, especially if you won't be heading south on this trip. *Praça do Comércio 3, tel. 01/879259. Reservations advised. MC, V. Closed Sun.*

**$$$ Cais da Ribeira.** Converted from an old fisherman's warehouse, this small restaurant perched on the waterfront behind Cais do Sodré station specializes in fish grilled over charcoal and a filling *caldeirada* (fish stew). The pretty, split-level wooden interior makes good use of the old warehouse shell. Whatever you order, the views over the river will complement your meal nicely. Remember that this is not the most desirable area for walking late at night: You can get a taxi just around the corner, in front of the train station. *Cais do Sodré, tel. 01/342–3611 or 01/347–6653. Reservations advised. AE, DC, MC, V. Closed Sat. dinner and Sun.*

**$$$ Já Sei.** Because of its prime location above the river at Belém, this is a fine lunchtime stop, especially in summer if you sit on the attractive outdoor terrace. Smooth service and impressive meals—*arroz de marisco* (seafood rice) for two, for example—make this a memorable choice. *Av. Brasília 202, Belém, tel. 01/301–5969. Reservations advised. AE, DC, MC, V. Closed Sun. dinner and Mon.*

**$$$ Michel.** ★ Innovative French cooking with Portuguese flourishes is served in this intimate and attractive green-painted restaurant just outside the walls of St. George's Castle. Curtains—which add to the dignified ambience—shut out the sun beaming in from the dusty square outside. Choose from such dishes as bass fillet with champagne sauce, and *porco a alentejana* (pork with clams), a Portuguese classic. *Largo S. Cruz do Castelo 5, tel. 01/886–4338. Reservations advised. AE, DC, MC, V. Closed Sun.*

$$$ **O Madeirense.** Even though it's set inside the Amoreiras shopping center, Lisbon's only Madeiran restaurant goes overboard making patrons feel they're on the island itself: Rural scenes adorn the walls, the wait staff are in traditional costume, and the place is filled with wood, rattan, and rubber plants. But this is no mere theme restaurant: The cooking is assured, and the consistent quality of the food and service appeals to the mainly business clientele. Start with a glass of Madeira wine while you ponder the menu: the *espedata* is traditional—a skewer of filet steak, rubbed with salt and spices, is hung above the table from a stand so you can serve yourself at will. Tuna and swordfish make an appearance on the menu, too, and you might try the fried corn cubes, presented as an appetizer. *Loja 3027, Amoreiras Shopping Center, Av. Eng. Duarte Pacheco, tel. 01/ 690827. Reservations advised for Sun. lunch. AE, DC, MC, V.*

$$$ **O Manel.** Tucked away in a strange little enclave of theaters and restaurants behind the Lisboa Plaza hotel, O Manel is a fish and shellfish house that attracts the capital's politicians and media types. You have to know it's here to find it, but once you've made your way, you're greeted by a roaring fire, two small dining rooms, and great food—the açorda with prawns is immensely filling; other fish (and meat) is grilled to perfection. There's a wine list, but the house wine is very drinkable; the staff are short on English but happy to help. To get here, walk through the gates on Travessa do Salitre into the theater complex—it looks like an amusement park, and you may have to pay a nominal entrance fee, but it's the right place—bear left into the car park and then turn right. Anyone can direct you if you get stuck. *Parque Mayer, Av. de Liberdade, tel. 01/346–3167. Reservations advised on weekends. DC, MC, V.*

$$$ **São Jerónimo.** Contemporary decor and classy presentation of Portuguese food attract Lisbon's elite to São Jerónimo. Favorites include grilled shrimp and other fresh seafood dishes, and there are daily changing regional specials, too. This quiet restaurant beside the monastery in Belém offers discreet, stylish dining. *Rua dos Jerónimos 12, Belém, tel. 01/364–8797. Reservations advised. Jacket and tie advised. AE, DC, MC, V. Closed Sun.*

$$$ **Solmar.** Best known for its fish and shellfish (and the excellent seafood soup), Solmar's menu may surprise some with its occasional offering of boar or venison (when in season). Competent waiters move briskly about the two-floor dining area: A central fountain is the focus, and a huge mosaic of an underwater scene carries out Solmar's oceanic theme. Some have complained that Solmar is resting on its laurels, but the cooking is more hit than miss, and it's an ideal lunch stop for sightseers. *Rua Portas de S. Antąo 108, tel. 01/342–3371. AE, DC, MC, V.*

$$$ **Sua Excêlencia.** In this cozy little pink town-house restaurant, the English-speaking owner will personally talk you through the outstanding Portuguese dishes on the menu. Specialties include smoked swordfish (an Algarve favorite), baked bacalhau, and Angolan-style chicken. And a good-value tourist menu costs less than 4,000$00. This is a handy place for those staying at York House or As Janelas Verdes (*see* Lodging, *below*), and it provides an intimate dining experience after a hectic day's sightseeing. *Rua do Conde 42, tel. 01/603614. Reservations advised. MC, V. Closed Wed., lunch Sat. and Sun., and Sept.*

$$ **Brasuca.** Eating in this comfortable Brazilian restaurant set in an old mansion on the edge of the Bairro Alto is almost like being invited into someone's home. The dining room still has domestic features that make it an intimate retreat, and the staff is genuinely

welcoming. Before indulging in the Brazilian specialties and main-stream Portuguese fare—spicy meat or fish stews and grilled meats are a good choice—try a traditional (but strong!) *caipirinha* (Brazil-ian-rum cocktail). The restaurant is off Rua Seculo, not the easiest place to find, but worth searching for. *Rua João Pereira da Rosa 7, tel. 01/342-8542. Reservations advised. AE, DC, MC, V. Closed Mon.*

**$$ Cervejaria Trindade.** Relatively inexpensive and hearty Portuguese
★ cuisine, including açorda and grilled seafood, makes the relatively short wait for a table here worthwhile. The walls inside this 19th-century Bairro Alto beer hall/restaurant are adorned with colorful tiles, and high vaulted ceilings and frenetic service add to the res-taurant's feeling of enormousness. The garden is an enjoyable spot for dining in summer. *Rua Nova da Trindade 20, tel. 01/342-3506. AE, DC, MC, V.*

**$$ Comida de Santo.** Excellent Brazilian food served in an attractive, brightly painted dining room, and lively Brazilian music ensure a steady clientele and keep this place packed until closing time, at 1 AM. Come early and enjoy classic dishes, such as *fejoada* (meat-and-bean stew) or *vatapa* (a spicy shrimp dish). *Calçada Engenheiro Miguel Pais 39, tel. 01/396-3339. AE, DC, MC, V.*

**$$ Farah's Tandoori.** A small, simple place, Farah's is known as one of the best and friendliest Indian restaurants in Lisbon. All the cur-ries, served with Indian bread if you choose, are sure bets for a good meal. Specialties include coconut prawns, *birianis* (mixed rice dishes) and a good tandoori chicken. Two dining floors make finding a table a manageable task. Take a taxi—it's in an anonymous side street off Rua Buenos Aires and is a bit tricky to find at night. *Rua de Sant'Ana à Lapa 73, tel. 01/609219. MC, V. Closed Tues.*

**$$ O Alexandre.** There are only a half dozen tables in this tiny restau-rant, and you'll do better sitting outside on the attractive sidewalk terrace, from which there are superb views of the Jerónimos Monas-tery. The Alexandre does a brisk lunchtime business, serving fish and seafood platters to a largely local clientele. Try the grilled *peixe espada* (swordfish) or one of the more unusual squid or octopus dishes. Note that the restaurant closes at 10PM. *Rua Vieira Portuense 84, Belém, tel. 01/363-4454. No reservations. MC, V. Closed Sat.*

**$$ Ribadouro.** Go to this bustling basement restaurant on the main ave-nue for the finely prepared seafood, including crab and crayfish. The surroundings are functional, not fancy, but the layout allows you to watch the delectable crustaceans being prepared at the counter. Try to arrive before 8, although even on the busiest nights you shouldn't have to wait too long to be seated. If you eat at the bar, prices are even more reasonable. *Av. da Liberdade 155, tel. 01/549411. AE, DC, MC, V.*

**$$ Sinal Vermelho.** This restaurant in the heart of the Bairro Alto up-
★ dates the traditional Lisbon *adega* (tavern). The split-level dining room is traditionally tiled, and the food is thoroughly Portuguese, but the prints on the wall are modern, the clientele firmly profes-sional (and in-the-know tourist), and the wine list wide-ranging (if completely Portuguese). Go for the fresh fish and seafood, which is rarely disappointing; the meat dishes are less inspiring, though if you're feeling adventurous you might try the tripe or the kidneys. *Rua das Gáveas 89, tel. 01/346-1252. Reservations advised on week-ends. MC, V. Closed Sun.*

**$ Andorra.** On the renowned Baixa street of fish restaurants sits the Andorra. It's a perfect place for a simple lunch, with an outdoor terrace where you can watch the lively street scenes and smell the charcoal-grilled sardines. The friendly staff serves up plates of well-cooked Portuguese favorites, and you can choose from a short wine list that caters for most tastes. If it's a dull day you can sit at tables in the functional but pleasant dining room. *Rua Portas de S. Antão 82, tel. 01/342–6047. MC, V. Closed Sun.*

**$ A Quinta.** This homey, country-style restaurant at the top of the Elevador de Santa Justa commands fine views of the Baixa. The eclectic menu features Portuguese specialties, such as stuffed squid or sardines, and quirky international fare—from steak-and-kidney pie and goulash to spaghetti and Wiener schnitzel. *Passarela do Elevador de Santa Justa, next to Largo do Carmo, tel. 01/346–5588. AE, DC, MC, V. Closed Sat. dinner and Sun.*

**$ Bonjardim.** Set in an alley between Praça dos Restauradores and
★ Rua Portas de Santo Antão and known locally as Rei dos Frangos (the King of Chickens), Bonjardim specializes in superbly cooked spit-roasted chicken, best eaten with fries and a salad. The restaurant is crowded at peak times (8–10 PM), but you shouldn't have to wait long, and watching the frenzied waiters is entertainment in itself. *Travessa de S. Antão 11, tel. 01/342–4389. AE, DC, MC, V.*

**$ Casa Faz Frio.** Here is an *adega típica* (traditional wine cellar) located on the edge of the Bairro Alto, complete with wood beams, blue tiling, and bunches of garlic suspended from the ceiling. The list of Portuguese dishes changes daily, and although there's not a large choice there's usually bacalhau, rissoles, grilled pork, and quail. Surroundings are simple but convivial, and you'd be hard pushed to spend more than 2,000$00 including drinks and coffee. *Rua de Dom Pedro V 96–98, tel. 01/346–1860 No credit cards.*

**$ O Cantinho do Aziz.** Hidden in the ring of tiny streets below the castle, this small, family-run Mozambican restaurant offers "Comida Indio-Africana"—plenty of rich curried meat and fish dishes accompanied by coconut-flavored rice. The surroundings are rudimentary and the TV occasionally deafening, but the tasty food comes with a smile. Climb the flight of steps from Poco do Borratem, near Praça da Figueira, and turn left when you reach the white wall at the top. *Rua de S. Lourenço 3–5, tel. 01/876472. No credit cards. Closed Sun.*

**$ Vá e Volte.** For one-plate budget Bairro Alto fare, look no further. In a restaurant that's little more than a bar with a couple of small dining rooms, the owner, his wife, the cook, and the small staff keep the meals coming with speed and good humor. Fried or grilled fish or meat dishes are served with enough salad, potatoes, and vegetables to keep the wolf from the door, and the *arroz doce* (rice pudding) is homemade. The house wine is fine, but even if you choose a regional specialty from the wine list, the price won't break the bank. *Rua do Diario de Noticias 100, tel. 01/342–7888. MC, V.*

## Café-Bars and Pastelarias

Lisbon has some glorious old cafés, and you should make every effort to visit at least a few. Most are wonderfully decorated and have rich interiors of burnished and carved wood, mirrors, and traditional tiling. Also, many cafés have outdoor seating, so you can order a coffee, beer, or snack, and watch the city pass by. Pastelarias are perhaps the city's greatest contribution to the gastronomic arts: Be sure to sample some pastries and cakes at one of the places listed below, all of which serve drinks, too.

**Café a Brasileira.** Rather less exclusive than it once was, this coffeehouse in the heart of the shopping district is still the most famous of Lisbon's old haunts. For a feel of bygone days it's best to come before dark, because at night every table (and the long bar) is taken over by beer-drinking young people. *Rua Garrett 120.*

**Café Nicola.** With its grand interior and suitably aloof waiters, this "in" café is one of the prime and priciest spots for sitting down and taking in downtown Lisbon. *Rossío, west side.*

**Café Martinho da Arcada.** A stand-up café under the arches, next to the famous restaurant of the same name (*see above*), this is a welcome stop for a coffee and specialty *pastéis de nata* (cream cake) before catching your tram to Belém. Tradition oozes from the tiled walls and the waiters rush to and fro, while the hard-working cooks fry scrumptious rissoles and pastries behind the bar. *Praça do Comércio 3. Closed Sun.*

**Casa Chineza.** Join the locals for a midmorning stand-up snack and coffee at this traditional Baixa pastelaria. Enjoy the pastry, admire the fine decor, and then on with the shopping! *Rua Aurea 274–278.*

**Leiteria a Camponeza.** This is an old-fashioned Baixa *leiteria* (specializing in milk products and pastries), whose blue-tiled walls display bucolic scenes. The coffee, cakes, and sandwiches are all good. *Rua dos Sapateiros 155–157. Closed Sun.*

**Pastelaria Suiça.** This huge café-pastelaria stretches all the way back to the adjacent Praça da Figueira. The renowned cakes draw such crowds that it may be easier to order pastries to go from the inside counter. Outdoor tables are at a premium, especially on nice days. *Rossío 96, east side.*

**Versailles.** Located in the modern part of the city, the Versailles (founded in 1929) has retained its grand furnishings. Homemade cakes and hot chocolate are house specialties. *Av. de República 15.*

# Lodging

A spate of new hotels has gone up in Lisbon in recent years, and old favorites have been modernized, so guests of the city can now choose from a range of accommodations. However, hotels in Lisbon are not the bargain that, by and large, restaurants are, and staying in the top-rated hotels may cost as much here as in any European capital.

Nevertheless, it's still possible to find reasonably priced rooms among the city's dozens of modest *pensões* (guest houses), many of which cost less than 8,000$00 a night. If you plan to stay in a pensão, be aware that the toilet may be down the hall, and you may have to share a shower room with other guests. The quality varies greatly from one guest house to another, but the best are spotless and friendly, and many are concentrated downtown around the Rossío, Praça dos Restauradores, and in the Bairro Alto. In summer it's often difficult to find a pensão with vacancies, so you may have to go door to door looking for a suitable place. The tourist office can make reservations for you, but they usually don't recommend the very cheap places, and you won't be able to see your room first.

There is no real tourist season in Lisbon because the capital is host to trade fairs and conventions year-round, so it's best to secure a room in advance of your trip. Particularly busy periods are Easter–June and September–November; at the budget end of the scale, pensões are very busy over the high summer months. If you've arrived without accommodations, stop by the hotel-reservations desk at the airport or at the main downtown tourist-information office (Palácio Foz, Praça dos Restauradores, tel. 01/346–3314; open Mon.–Sat. 9–8, Sun. 10–6). The staff at both locations speaks English, and there's no fee for their services.

Despite the high year-round occupancy, substantial discounts abound from November through February, sometimes as much as 30%–40%. Even pensões drop their prices by a couple of thousand escudos at this time. So it's always worth asking.

All lodgings listed below include private baths in rooms unless otherwise noted. Breakfast is usually included, but not always at hotels in the $$ and $ categories; particularly good deals are noted below.

Highly recommended hotels are indicated by a star ★.

| Category | Cost* |
|---|---|
| $$$$ | over 40,000$00 |
| $$$ | 20,000$00–40,000$00 |
| $$ | 14,000$00–20,000$00 |
| $ | under 14,000$00 |

*All prices include tax and service and are for two people sharing a standard double room.*

$$$$  **Lisboa Sheraton and Towers.** Typical of Sheraton properties, this 30-floor hotel has a huge reception area with a comfortable bar, but less-impressive—although still eminently likable—guest quarters. A separate desk in the lobby and a private lounge accommodate visitors staying in the more deluxe Towers section; guest rooms in the Towers are about the same size as the others, but their appointments are luxurious and the views better. The range of facilities available to all guests is extensive. The only drawback is location—you're not far from Parque Eduardo VII, but for other sights, your days will start and end with a taxi ride. *Rua Latino Coelho 1, 1000, tel. 01/575757, fax 01/547164. 384 rooms. Facilities: restaurant, bar, pool, gym, sauna, shops, garage. AE, DC, MC, V.*

$$$$  **Meridien Lisboa.** The stepped facade and decorative metal canopy above the entrance are just two of the details that make this mid-'80s accommodation one of the most distinctive modern luxury hotels in Lisbon. Most rooms are small, but they're bright, soundproof, and attractively decorated; ask for one in front with a view of the Parque Eduardo VII. *Rua Castilho 149, 1000, tel. 01/690400, fax 01/693231. 331 rooms. Facilities: restaurant, bar, health club with sauna, shops, garage. AE, DC, MC, V.*

$$$$  **Ritz Lisboa.** One of the finest hotels in Europe, this hotel, part of the
★  Intercontinental Hotel chain, is renowned for its excellent service and comfortable surroundings. You know you're in good hands from the minute you step into the spacious marble reception area and find, as well, a glittering array of jewelry stores and a bar with a summer terrace overlooking the park. There's more space in the Ritz's corridors and lobby areas than in most hotels' rooms, and the guest rooms and suites live up to the public areas. Large, light, and airy, they have luxurious bathrooms, private terraces, and elegant furniture. In a similar vein, the public rooms feature tapestries, antique reproductions, and fine paintings. Rooms in the back looking over the park are the best choice; on a clear day you can see the castle and the river from the upper floors. There's a lunchtime buffet at the Veranda restaurant, which, like the bar and lounge, has a wonderful summer terrace. The famous Ritz Grill is currently closed for renovations. *Rua Rodrigo da Fonseca 88, 1000, tel. 01/692020, fax 01/691783. 304 rooms. Facilities: restaurant, bar, shops, garage. AE, DC, MC, V.*

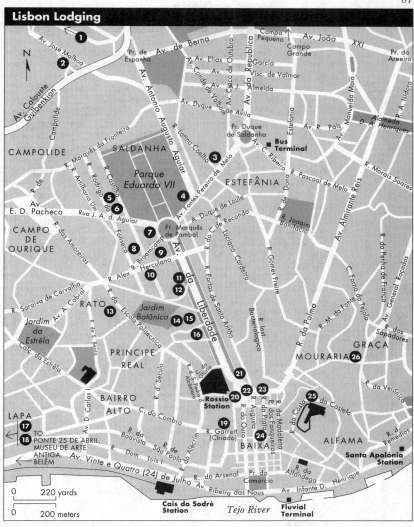

## Lisbon Lodging

Albergaria Senhora do Monte, **26**
Altis, **10**
Arco Bandeira, **22**
As Janelas Verdes, **18**
Avenida Palace, **20**
Beira-Minho, **23**
Casa de São Mamede, **13**

Duas Nações, **24**
Eduardo VII, **4**
Fénix, **7**
Flamingo, **8**
Flórida, **9**
Hotel Borges, **19**
Lisboa Penta, **1**
Lisboa Plaza, **15**

Lisboa Sheraton and Towers, **3**
Meridien Lisboa, **5**
Ninho das Aguias, **25**
Novotel Lisboa, **2**
Principe Real, **14**
Residencial Florescente, **21**

Ritz Lisboa, **6**
Sofitel Lisboa, **16**
Tivoli Jardim, **12**
Tivoli Lisboa, **11**
York House, **17**

**$$$$ Tivoli Lisboa.** Located on Lisbon's main avenue, this well-run prop-
★ erty has a large public area and bar furnished with inviting arm-
chairs and sofas. A pianist plays here nightly. The hotel has been
completely redecorated since 1992, and its reasonable room rates,
and pleasant, well-equipped—although modestly sized—guest
quarters make the Tivoli a popular choice. Rooms in the rear are
most quiet. In warmer months the outdoor pool and garden offer
respite from the bustling city; the grill on the top floor presents
wonderful views of the city and the Tejo. There's also a good restaurant off the lobby, where a filling morning buffet is presented. *Av.
da Liberdade 185, 1200, tel. 01/353–0182, fax 01/579461. 344 rooms.
Facilities: restaurant, grill, bar, pool, garden, tennis court, shops,
garage. AE, DC, MC, V.*

**$$$ Altis.** A member of the Best Western group of hotels, this large mod-
ern lodging has a broad range of facilities, including an indoor pool
and an art gallery. The mezzanine bar and lounge, above the lobby,
is a relaxing spot. Rooms are welcoming, if unexceptional; those on
higher floors have some fine views of Parque Eduardo VII, as does
the grill restaurant, the Don Fernando Grill, on the top floor. *Rua
Castilho 11, 1200, tel. 01/522496, fax 01/548696. 307 rooms. Facili-
ties: 2 restaurants, 4 bars, pool, gym, sauna, art gallery, shops, ga-
rage. AE, DC, MC, V.*

**$$$ As Janelas Verdes.** Owned and managed by the capable family firms
that founded the Tivoli Lisboa and the Lisboa Plaza, As Janelas
Verdes joins the capital's select band of historic buildings now converted into fine hotels. The late-18th-century mansion is on the
same street as York House (indeed, it used to be the annex of that
hotel; *see below*) and the Museum of Ancient Art; and it was once the
home of famous Portuguese novelist Eça de Queirós. Its 17 guest
rooms have been marvelously restored, and are individually furnished to a high standard. Fittings and furnishings throughout are
in keeping with the building's historic character; and in the lovely
ivy-covered patio garden you can eat breakfast and imagine yourself
in a different age. The hotel isn't particularly central, though you
are halfway to Belém (the tram stops nearby), and close to the Sua
Excêlencia restaurant. *Rua das Janelas Verdes 47, 1200, tel. 01/
396–8143, fax 01/396–8144. 17 rooms. Facilities: patio garden,
lounge. AE, DC, MC, V.*

**$$$ Avenida Palace.** Situated between the Rossío and Praça dos
Restauradores, right next to the Rossío Station building, this is
Lisbon's most central big hotel. Furnishings and decor throughout
are turn-of-the-century, and the grand public areas—lobby, central
staircase, and corridors—are all suitably overwhelming in scale.
Rooms are not of the same dimensions (and single travelers may oc-
casionally find themselves rather poorly served), but all have high
ceilings, individual furnishings, and smart if small bathrooms lined
with marble. Street noise can be a problem, but the hotel's proximi-
ty to the best downtown restaurants and bars may be compensation
enough. *Rua 1 de Dezembro 123, 1200, tel. 01/342–2884, fax 01/
322884. 92 rooms. Facilities: bar, parking. AE, DC, MC, V.*

**$$$ Eduardo VII.** This reasonably priced Best Western hotel is well situ-
ated in the center of the city, near the park of the same name. Its
anonymous 1930's exterior opens up to reveal 10 floors of shipshape
rooms that are short on space, but smart and comfortable. The hotel
is at the bottom of this price category, unless you reserve one of the
few suites—the only quarters with a real sense of space. The hotel's
singular attraction is its top-floor Varanda restaurant and Lanterna
bar, which both have superb views of the Lisbon skyline—a fine
treat. *Av. Fontes Pereira de Melo 5, 1000, tel. 01/353–0141, fax 01/*

*353–3879. 140 rooms. Facilities: restaurant, bar, shops. AE, DC, MC, V.*

$$$ **Lisboa Penta.** The city's largest hotel is about midway between the airport and city center, next to the U.S. Embassy and near the Gulbenkian Foundation. The Penta provides shuttle-bus service downtown between 8AM and 7:30PM, but this is probably not the best choice for a tourist planning to do a lot of sightseeing in the center. Business travelers seem content here. The rooms are rather small, but each has a terrace that overlooks either the pool or garden. *Av. dos Combatentes, 1600, tel. 01/726–5050 or 01/726–4054, fax 01/726–4281. 588 rooms. Facilities: restaurant, bar, outdoor pool, health club with sauna, squash courts, shops, garage. AE, DC, MC, V.*

$$$ **Lisboa Plaza.** This family-owned hotel behind Avenida da Liberdade
★ is a most comfortable and welcoming lodging. It's been in business for more than 40 years, and the experience shines through every aspect of its operation. Service is friendly and helpful, and an ongoing renovation program has smartened up the air-conditioned guest rooms and public areas without detracting from their character. Pastel colors, prints on the walls, attractive ornaments, dried flower arrangements, and smart, well-stocked bathrooms all add to the charm. The best rooms are at the back, looking up to the botanical gardens; those at the front are closer to the main road and don't have the views, but double-glazing keeps everything nice and quiet. The bar is a particularly pleasant place to unwind after sightseeing, and an excellent buffet breakfast is included in the room rate. *Travessa do Salitre 7, 1200, tel. 01/346–3922, fax 01/347–1630. 106 rooms. Facilities: restaurant, bar, business services, parking. AE, DC, MC, V.*

$$$ **Principe Real.** This small hotel close to the botanical gardens has a large repeat clientele who enjoy the friendly atmosphere and excellent central location. Each of the comfortable rooms is decorated in a different style with harmonious color schemes. The lack of facilities is more than made up for by fine personal service. *Rua da Alegria 53, 1200, tel. 01/346–0116, fax 01/342–2104. 24 rooms. Facilities: bar. AE, DC, MC, V.*

$$$ **Sofitel Lisboa.** One of the latest additions to the Avenida da Liberdade, the Sofitel is a handsome modern hotel with a high-tech edge to its design. Business travelers especially seem happy to have discovered such up-to-the-minute lodgings in so central a location. Rooms are pleasingly contemporary in style, decorated in attractive colors, and comfortably appointed. The intimate piano bar makes a good stop after a day's downtown touring, while the Cais da Avenida restaurant, with an entrance on the avenue, can seat diners right by the window for sidewalk views of the attractive central artery. *Av. da Liberdade 123–125, tel. 01/342–9202, fax 01/342–9222. 170 rooms. Facilities: restaurant, bar, business services, garages. AE, DC, MC, V.*

$$$ **Tivoli Jardim.** A less-expensive annex to the Tivoli Lisboa, the Jardim sits behind its counterpart, and guests are welcome to use the Tivoli Lisboa's swimming pool and tennis courts. Guest rooms aren't as extravagantly decorated here, but still they are bright; public areas—clad in marble and Portuguese tiles—are dramatically designed. As at the pricier lodging, you get comfort and value for your money. *Rua Júlio Cesar Machado 7–9, 1200, tel. 01/539971, fax 01/355–6566. 119 rooms. Facilities: restaurant, snack bar, parking, access to pool and tennis court. AE, DC, MC, V.*

$$$ **York House.** A former 17th-century convent, this attractive
★ *residência* or *residencial* (inn that is housed in what was once a private home) is near the Museum of Ancient Art and has its own shady courtyard garden, where drinks are served. Despite its somewhat

inconvenient location, west of the center, the York House has a loyal following (especially among English visitors), and you'll need to book well in advance. The reason is obvious—from the vinecovered staircase that climbs to the garden from the street, to the wonderfully individual rooms with original features and good reproduction furniture, the whole inn is a delight. Rooms have four-poster beds and lovely rugs, and corridors, too, are tiled and spread with rugs—surely an improvement on the austerity of convent days here. From November to March, room rates drop to $$, making it even more attractive. *Rua das Janelas Verdes 32–1, 1200, tel. 01/396–2435, fax 01/397–2793. 36 rooms. Facilities: restaurant, bar, garden. AE, DC, MC, V.*

$$ **Albergaria Senhora do Monte.** This small, unpretentious hotel in the
★ oldest part of town near St. George's Castle offers some of the best views of Lisbon, especially at night, when the castle is softly illuminated. When you book a room, specify that you want one with a terrace so you can take advantage of the scenery. The top-floor grill has a picture window, the neighborhood is quiet, and parking is available. Without a car, you'll face a steep walk every time you return to the Albergaria; Tram 28 runs nearby. *Calçada do Monte 39, 1100, tel. 01/887–7783, fax 01/877783. 27 rooms. Facilities: bar, grill. AE, DC, MC, V.*

$$ **Fénix.** Located at the top of Avenida da Liberdade, on Praça Marquês de Pombal, this recently renovated—and much improved—hotel has marble trappings in its bright, air-conditioned public rooms, large guest rooms, and a pleasant first-floor bar. Rooms at the front have good views over the Rotunda and its swirling traffic (double-glazing keeps out the noise); all rooms have plenty of closet space, comfortable armchairs, gleaming bathrooms, TV, and phones. The basement restaurant, O Bodegon, serves good Spanish and Portuguese food in rustic surroundings. *Praça Marquês de Pombal 8, 1200, tel. 01/386–2121, fax 01/386–0131. 119 rooms. Facilities: restaurant, bar. AE, DC, MC, V.*

$$ **Flamingo.** Best Western seems to specialize in snapping up comfortable old city center hotels that have perhaps seen better days but still offer good-value lodgings that are popular with tourists. This small hotel near the top of the Avenida da Liberdade has a friendly staff and cheerful guest rooms, which are a bit on the small side, but pleasant nonetheless. Those in front tend to be noisy. Amenities include a Portuguese-Continental restaurant; a comfortable, relaxing bar; and a pay parking lot next door, a bonus in this busy area. *Rua Castilho 41, 1200, tel. 01/382–2191, fax 01/352–1216. 39 rooms. Facilities: restaurant, bar. AE, DC, MC, V.*

$$ **Flórida.** This hotel has a pleasant atmosphere and a fair location, near the Parque Eduardo VII. Public areas are smart, if rather stuck with 1970's style; the guest rooms are comfortable—although not big—and have decent marble bathrooms. Breakfast is the only meal available, but there is a bar that stays open late. *Rua Duque de Palmela 32, 1200, tel. 01/576145, fax 01/543584. 112 rooms. AE, DC, MC, V.*

$$ **Novotel Lisboa.** The attentive staff and quiet, welcoming atmosphere contribute to the comfortable feel of this modern hotel near the U.S. Embassy. Although not centrally situated, the recently renovated hotel benefits from the nearby Palhavã metro station and its range of facilities. Public rooms are spacious, and guest rooms are attractively furnished. *Av. Jóse Malhoa, Lote 1642, 1000, tel. 01/726–6022, fax 01/726–6496. 246 rooms. Facilities: restaurant, bar, terrace, pool, garage. AE, DC, MC, V.*

$ **Arco Bandeira.** The plain rooms in this friendly fourth-floor pensão are reasonably quiet, given its location, at the bottom of the Rossío (under the arch at the top of Rua dos Sapateiros). Common areas, including the shared bathrooms, are spotless; some rooms have excellent views of Praça da Figueira, and the staff is very friendly and used to tourists. You'll pay under 6,000$00 per room most of the year, making this pensão a bargain budget choice. *Rua dos Sapateiros 226, 1100, tel. 01/342–3478. 8 rooms. No credit cards.*

$ **Beira-Minho.** The best rooms in this second-floor pensão have sweeping views of one of Lisbon's busiest squares, and prices begin at about 5,000$00. The Beira-Minho's location makes this a good base for city-center sightseeing, and it's just across from the Pastelaria Suiça, an excellent place for breakfast. *Praça da Figueira 6, 1100, tel. 01/346–1846. 19 rooms, 12 with bath. No credit cards.*

$ **Casa de São Mamede.** Located behind the botanical gardens and halfway between the main avenue, Avenida da Liberdade, and the Amoreiras shopping center, this attractive, friendly, old-fashioned residência (originally built as a private home) is a fine value. There's a real charm to the public areas—which still reflect the history of the building—and if some of the guest rooms appear frayed at the edges, then so be it: this is historic Europe at budget prices. *Rua da Escola Politécnica 159, 1200, tel. 01/396–3166, fax 01/395–1896. 30 rooms. MC, V.*

$ **Duas Nações.** What you're really paying for in this fairly basic, sometimes noisy pensão is its superb location, in the heart of the Baixa grid. Here, you're within walking distance of all the downtown sights, shops, and restaurants. Duas Nações is comfortable enough but has few amenities, although the dining room, retaining its original large dimensions and decor, raises eyebrows in surprise. Guest rooms are functional, plain, and without individual spark—but that's hardly a unique complaint in Portugal. Quieter rooms face the back. *Rua da Vitória 41, 1100, tel. 01/346–0710. 66 rooms, 42 with bath. Facilities: bar. No credit cards.*

$ **Hotel Borges.** Set in the heart of the Chiado district, this dependable
★ hotel, much favored by European tour groups, and characterized by old-fashioned charm and good, modern service, is convenient for guests who plan to shop till they drop. The Borges offers decent-size rooms and an option for breakfast, but taking a coffee and pastry at the famous Café Brasileira (just steps away) is a better bet. *Rua Garrett 108–110, 1200, tel. 01/346–1951, fax 01/342–6617. 99 rooms. Facilities: restaurant, bar. MC, V.*

$ **Ninho das Aguias.** Perched below the castle, within walking distance of the Alfama, this budget-price pensão is a good find, although it's a bit far from the center of Lisbon. Rooms are simply furnished, and the main attraction is the garden terrace, which has a superb view of the city center. *Costa do Castelo 74, 1100, tel. 01/886–7008, 16 rooms, 6 with bath. No credit cards.*

$ **Residencial Florescente.** One block from Praça dos Restauradores, on a street well-known to seafood-lovers because of its many restaurants, this residencial is in a prime position. Rooms are spread across four floors—there's no elevator—and the best are airy and freshly painted, with their own small bathrooms and TV. There is a great variety of rooms, however, and you may not be too impressed with the cheaper choices on the upper floors, where you share bathrooms, so ask to see a selection if necessary. You'll not do better for inexpensive, central lodgings, and though not even breakfast is served, you couldn't be better placed for downtown cafés and restaurants. *Rua Portas de Santo Antão 99, 1100, tel. 01/342–6609, fax 01/342–7733. 100 rooms, 50 with bath or shower. No facilities. MC, V.*

# The Arts and Nightlife

Lisbon has an extensive arts-and-nightlife scene, and you'll find full details of films and events in the weekly *Sete* magazine, available at most newsstands. Although written in Portuguese, listings are fairly easy to decipher, or you can ask the tourist-information office or someone at your hotel reception desk to interpret.

Tickets to musical and theatrical performances are best purchased at the box offices, but you can also get them at booths around the city: There's one in Praça dos Restauradores, near the post office.

## The Arts

The prime mover behind Lisbon's artistic and cultural scene is the **Fundação Calouste Gulbenkian** (*see* Tour 4, *above*), which not only presents exhibitions and concerts in its buildings but also sponsors events throughout the city. The foundation publishes a frequently updated schedule of activities, which you can pick up at the reception desk. The tourist-information office can also assist with queries about upcoming events. The new **Centro Cultural de Belém** (*see* Tour 5, *above*) also puts on a full range of reasonably priced concerts and exhibitions, featuring national and international artists and musicians. Its monthly program of events is available at the reception desk inside the center.

Art Galleries   Lisbon's major art museums often put on temporary exhibitions alongside their permanent collections, and you'll find details in *Sete* and in the local press. Other galleries of interest include: **Galeria de Arte Cervejaria Trindade** (Rua Nova da Trindade 20, tel. 01/342–3506), **Galeria de Arte Hotel Altis** (Rua Castilho 11, tel. 01/527496), **Galeria de São Bento** (Rua do Machadinho 1, tel. 01/397–4325), and **Galeria Valentim de Carvalho** (Palácio Alcáçovas, Rua Cruz dos Poiais 111, tel. 01/608619).

Concerts   Classical-music concerts are staged from about October through June by the **Fundação Calouste Gulbenkian** (*see* Tour 4, *above*), which has three concert halls. Of particular interest is the annual **Early Music and Baroque Festival,** held in churches and museums around Lisbon every spring. You may also be in town during a performance of the **Nova Filarmonica,** one of Portugal's national orchestras, which gives concerts around the country throughout the year. Consult *Sete* and local newspapers for details.

Other venues where regular concerts take place include the **Centro Cultural de Belém** (*see* Tour 5, *above*), the **Teatro Nacional de São Carlos** (*see* Theater, *below*), the **Sé** (see Tour 1, *above*), the **Igreja do Carmo** (Largo do Carmo, for summer outdoor concerts), and the **Basilica da Estrêla** (*see* Tour 3, *above*).

Film   Surprisingly, all films shown in Lisbon appear in their original language accompanied by Portuguese subtitles, and you can usually find the latest Hollywood releases playing around town. Ticket prices are low and even cheaper on Monday; it's best to get to the movie theater early on any day to be assured a seat. Some of the theaters are in preserved Art Deco buildings and are attractions in their own right. There are dozens of movie houses throughout the city, including a large selection on and around Praça dos Restauradores and Avenida da Liberdade. A more modern facility, in the **Amoreiras shopping center** (Av. Eng. Duarte Pacheco, tel. 01/691275), has 10 screens.

Theater  Plays are performed in Portuguese at the **Teatro Nacional de Dona Maria II** (Praça Dom Pedro V, tel. 01/342–2210), Lisbon's principal theater. Performances are given August–June, and there's the occasional foreign-language production, too. The **Teatro Nacional de São Carlos** (Rua Serpa Pinto 9, tel. 01/346–5914) hosts an opera season September–June.

If you're traveling with children it's worth inquiring about productions at the **Teatro Infantil de Lisboa** (Rua Leão de Oliveira 1, tel. 01/363–9974), a children's theater that stages productions in Portuguese but uses mime and other media that can be understood by children of all nationalities.

## Nightlife

Lisbon has an extremely active nightlife, revolving mostly around the bars and discos of the Bairro Alto, and those along Avenida 24 de Julho, northwest of Cais do Sodré, where a 20- to 30-year-old crowd hangs out. In both districts, you'll find dozens of places to eat, drink, and dance the night away. On weekends the mobs are shoulder to shoulder in the street, as each passing hour heralds a move to the next trendy spot. For a less boisterous evening out, visit one of the adegas tipicas in the Bairro Alto to hear *fado*. Still other venues host a variety of live events, from rock-and-roll to African-music performances.

Bars  For late-night partying, there are two main areas. The **Bairro Alto**, long the principal center of Lisbon's nightlife, is still best if you don't want to walk too far between drinks. Most bars here stay open until 3 or so. Recently, though, many new designer bars have opened along and around **Avenida 24 de Julho**: because this isn't a residential area (as the Bairro Alto still is), bars here can stay open until 5AM or 6AM. Whichever district you choose, note that not all bars have signs outside, so to discover the latest hot spots it may be necessary to follow the crowds or try a half-open door. Don't expect to have a quiet drink: The company is generally young and excitable.

Without question the best place to start off your evening is the Bairro Alto's refined **Instituto do Vinho do Porto** (Rua de São Pedro de Alcântara 45, tel. 01/347–5707, open Mon.–Sat. 10–10), a formidable old building in which you can sink into an armchair and sample a selection of port. Farther up the street is **Harry's Bar** (Rua de São Pedro de Alcântara 57, tel. 01/346–0760), which attracts a mixed tourist and local clientele. Also in this area is the **Pavilhão Chinês** (Rua Dom Pedro V 89, tel. 01/342–4729), a comfortable bar that is decorated with extraordinary bric-a-brac from around the world—statues, tankards, ceramics, baubles, and toys.

Back in the heart of the Bairro Alto, the well-heeled young crowd the loud and fashionable **Cena de Copos** (Rua da Barroca 103–105, tel. 01/347–3372); **Apollo XIII** (Trav. da Cara 8, tel. 01/342–4952) is mainly for students; **Pintaí** (Largo Trindade Coelho 22, tel. 01/342–4802) serves up mighty Brazilian cocktails; while **A Tasca** (Trav. de Quiemada 13–15, no phone) is a bright bar with tequila as its specialty drink. Down on Avenida 24 de Julho, current favorites include **Caré 24 de Julho** (no. 114, no phone) and **Café Central** (no. 110, no phone). **Cerca Moura** (Largo da Portas do Sol 4, tel. 01/874859), in the Alfama, is a pleasant, quieter bar, with outdoor seating and views of the river.

Discos and  Again, the split of discos and clubs is between the Bairro Alto and
Clubs  the Avenida 24 de Julho district, with a smattering of cool, up-mar-

ket places in the suburbs of Santos and Alcântara (note that new discos open and close frequently in Lisbon). Most charge about 1,500$00–2,000$00 (more on weekends), which usually includes one drink. Some clubs have strict door policies, and bouncers may scrutinize you and your clothes—it's best to ask around first about the age of the patrons. Clubs are open from about 11 until 4 or 5, although few get going until well after midnight. "In" spots in Bairro Alto are **Fragil** (Rua da Atalaia 126, tel. 01/346–9578), which attracts a partly gay crowd; and **Sudoeste** (Rua Barroca 135, tel. 01/342–1672), a small place that plays grunge, rap, and dance music. In the Avenida 24 de Julho area, **Kremlin** (Escadinhas da Praia 5, tel. 01/608768) continues to attract the trendiest Lisboetas; **Plateau** (Escadinhas da Praia 3, no phone) is similar, and stays open until 6 AM. Or try **Kapital** (Av. 24 de Julho, opposite Santos train station, no phone) which is typical of the new high-fashion, high-price venues down here.

The two top places in Alcântara are still the exclusive **Banana Power** (Rua Cascais 51, tel. 01/631815), which also has a restaurant, and the ritzy **Alcântara Mar** (Rua da Cozinha Económica 11, tel. 01/649440), which is closed Monday and Tuesday.

**Fado** One of Lisbon's most famous nighttime diversions is going to an adega tipica to hear fado, a haunting, blues-style music rooted in African slave songs. During colonial times fado was exported to Portugal; later, Lisbon's Alfama was recognized as the birthplace of the style; and today most performances occur in the Bairro Alto. In the adegas tipicas food and wine are served, and fado plays late into the night: The singing starts at 10 or 11, and the adegas often stay open until 3. Unfortunately, it's becoming increasingly difficult to find an authentic adega tipica, since tourism has encouraged proprietors to charge admission fees and dilute real fado with other, more "accessible" forms of music. It's best to ask around for a personal recommendation of an adega tipica, but here are some suggestions: **Senhor Vinho** (Rua do Meio á Lapa 18, tel. 01/397–2681, closed Sun.); **Lisboa a Noite** (Rua das Gaveas 69, tel. 01/346–8557, closed Sun.), which is more expensive than most; the **Adega do Machado** (Rua do Norte 91, tel. 01/346–0095, closed Mon.), a typical, bustling tourist place; **Adega do Ribatejo** (Rua Diario de Noticias 23, tel. 01/346–8343), a popular local haunt; and **Timpanas** (Rua Gilberto Rola 24, tel. 01/397–2431, closed Mon.), which is farther out of the center but is one of the most authentic.

**Gay and Lesbian** Lisbon has a well-established gay and lesbian scene, mostly concentrated in and around the Bairro Alto. **Trumps** (Rua Imprensa Nacional 104b, tel. 01/397–1059) is the city's biggest gay disco; **Memorial** (Rua Gustavo Sequeira 42, tel. 01/396–8891) is popular with both gay and lesbian visitors; while **Tatoo** (Rua de Sao Marcal 15, tel. 01/393–2726) is a boisterous club and bar. **Fragil** (*see* Discos and Clubs, *above*) while not exclusively gay, does attract a good, mixed crowd of people.

**Live Music** For a change from fado, there are plenty of places offering live rock, pop, and jazz. Big-name American and British bands, as well as the superstar Brazilian singers so beloved in Portugal, often play in Lisbon's large concert halls and stadiums. *Sete* has details of upcoming performances, and keep an eye out for advertising posters around the city. Advance tickets may be bought at the venue or at the ticket booth in Praça dos Restauradores.

African music is immensely popular in Lisbon, with touring groups from Cabo Verde and Angola playing regularly alongside home-grown talent. The **Ritz** (Rua da Glória 55, tel. 01/342–5140) is Lisbon's biggest African club. It's on the edge of the Bairro Alto in a rather seedy area but is renowned as a friendly place where you can dance to live music. In the Alfama **Pê Sujo** (Largo de São Martinho 6, tel. 01/886–5269, closed Mon.) is a similar club specializing in live Brazilian music aided and abetted by superb caipirinhas.

# 4 Lisbon's Environs

By Jules
Brown

The region that is considered Lisbon's environs stretches about 50 kilometers (31 miles) north and south of the Rio Tejo (River Tagus) from the capital, and encompasses a succession of coastal resorts and historic towns, each with unique traditions and characteristics. The region is, properly speaking, the most southerly part of the province of Estremadura, which reaches as far north as Alcobaça (*see* Chapter 5) and borders on the province of Ribetejo to the east, and it is best seen by using the capital as a base.

This was the first land taken back from the Moors in the 12th century under the Christian Reconquest, which had originated farther to the north in the region of the River Douro: Estremadura means "farthest from the River Douro," an indication of the early extent of the Christian advance against the Moors. The scenery is highly varied and includes glistening coastline, broad river estuaries, wooded valleys, and green mountains. Because of its proximity to Lisbon, the area tends to be heavily populated and geared toward the capital's needs: Beaches, restaurants, and hotels are filled with people escaping from the city, and coastal roads are often congested with slow-moving traffic. All of the main towns and most of the sights in the area are accessible by public transportation from the capital, and it's possible to visit them on day trips.

Lisbon and Lisbon's environs are complementary: It's necessary to visit both the city and its surrounding towns to get a real sense of how they have served each other through history. Even the country's earliest rulers appreciated the importance of one to the other. It was the Moors who first built a castle northwest of the capital at Sintra, as a defense against Christian forces under Dom Afonso Henriques, which had moved steadily southward since the victory at Ourique in 1139. The castle at Sintra fell to the Christians in 1147, a few days after they defeated the Moors in Lisbon.

Once the Christian Reconquest had been consolidated in Estremadura, there was a less pressing need for defensive measures. The early Christian kings instead adopted the lush hills and valleys of Sintra as a summer retreat, and designed estates and glorious palaces that survive today. Similarly, Lisbon's 18th- and 19th-century nobility desired a more leisurely life outside the city and so developed small resorts along the Estoril coast; the amenities and ocean views are still greatly sought after. In this century, too, Lisboans search for local retreats: Across the Rio Tejo are the tourist beaches of the Costa da Caparica and the southern Setúbal Peninsula.

In whichever direction you travel and whatever your interests, you should be delighted with all the environs has to offer. The palaces, gardens, and luxury *quintas* (country manor houses) of Sintra are justly celebrated. At Cascais and Estoril life revolves around the sea, and visitors can take part in time-honored pastimes: a stroll along the shore, a seafood meal, a game of tennis, a flutter at the casino. To the north, around Guincho's rocky promontory and the Praia das Maças coast, the Atlantic Ocean is often windswept and rough, but there's good sailboarding and surfing, as well as excellent views for coastal drives.

The best of the sand beaches lie to the south of the Rio Tejo, on the Setúbal Peninsula, a scenic area known for its rural traditions, festivals, and agriculture. Visitors can sample some of the county's best wines, explore the attractive dramatic mountain scenery of the Serra da Arrábida (Arrábida Mountains), and indulge themselves by lodging in one of two ancient castles, now converted into *pousadas* (luxury state-run hotels). At the large port of Setúbal, architectural

history was made in the late-15th century with the building of the
first church in the Manueline style—a design that was later to come
into full bloom with the building of Lisbon's Jerónimos Monastery
(*see* Tour 5 in Chapter 3) in the early 16th century.

Another reason for the region's ever-increasing popularity is its
comprehensive sports facilities. Swimming and water sports are
omnipresent, with the local climate encouraging a dip almost year-
round. The superb golf courses lying between Lisbon and Estoril attract international players, and nearly everywhere you'll find good
fishing, horseback riding, country walking, and tennis. Even grand
prix racing is highly profiled at Estoril. The Lisbon environs can
also be good for shopping and souvenir-hunting: The area is the site
of several traditional annual country fairs, where you'll be able to
find a variety of local handicrafts and foods.

# Essential Information

## Important Addresses and Numbers

**Tourist** Lisbon's main tourist office in the Palácio Foz (Praça dos
**Information** Restauradores, tel. 01/346–3314) can help with general inquiries
concerning travel to the city's environs.

The local offices listed below are usually open June–September, daily 9–1 and 2–6, sometimes later in the tourist-resort areas. Hours
are greatly reduced after peak season, and most offices are closed
Sunday.

There are also tourist offices in **Cabo da Roca** (tel. 01/928–0081),
**Cascais** (Av. Marginal, tel. 01/486–8204), **Colares** (Alameda Coronel
Linhares de Lima, tel. 01/929–2638), **Estoril** (Arcadas do Parque,
tel. 01/468–0113), **Sesimbra** (Av. dos Naufragios, tel. 01/223–1926),
**Setúbal** (Largo do Corpo Santo, tel. 065/524284), **Sintra** (Praça da
Republica 23, tel. 01/923–1157), and **Queluz** (tel. 01/436–3415).

**Emergencies** For all general emergencies dial **115**. For the **police**, call Sintra (tel.
01/923–0761); Cascais (tel. 01/483–0061); or Estoril (tel. 01/468–
1396). For local **medical** matters, contact the Sintra Health Center
(Rua Visconde de Monserrate 2, tel. 01/923–3400), or Cascais Hospital (tel. 01/486–5891). In all the towns in Lisbon's environs, a notice
on the door of every **farmácia** indicates the name and address of the
nearest all-night pharmacy.

If you can afford to wait for attention, it's often easier to contact
emergency and medical services in Lisbon (*see* Important Addresses and Numbers in Chapter 3).

**Mail** There are main post offices in **Cascais** (Rua Manuel J. Avelar, tel.
01/483–3175) and **Sintra** (Praça da República 26, tel. 01/924–1590).

## Arriving and Departing by Plane

Lisbon is the initial point of arrival for almost all the destinations
covered here *(see* Essential Information in Chapter 3); from the city
you may drive or take public transportation to the surrounding
towns. If you are traveling north from the Algarve, tour the Setúbal
peninsula (*see* Tour 4, *below*) before moving north.

## Getting There and Getting Around

**By Train**  Electric commuter trains travel the entire Estoril coast, with departures every 15–30 minutes from the waterfront Cais do Sodré station (tel. 01/347–0181), in Lisbon, just 10 minutes west (by foot) of the Praça do Comércio. The scenic trip to Estoril, with splendid sea views, takes about 30 minutes, and four more stops along the seashore bring you to Cascais, at the end the line. A one-way ticket to either costs 155$00; service operates daily 5:30 AM–2:30 AM. Trains from Lisbon's Rossío station (tel. 01/346–5022), situated between Praça dos Restauradores and the Rossío, run every 15 minutes to Queluz (a 20-minute trip) and on to Sintra (40 minutes total). The service operates 6 AM–2:40 AM, and one-way tickets cost about 155$00.

For current information about all train services in Lisbon's environs, call 01/888–4025.

Although you can reach Setúbal by train and ferry, it's much easier to take the bus (*see below*). In summer an inexpensive narrow-gauge railway runs for 8 kilometers (5 miles) along the Costa da Caparica from the town of Caparica, on the Setúbal Peninsula. It makes 20 stops at beaches along the way.

**By Bus**  Although the best way to reach Sintra and most of the towns on the Estoril coast is by car or by train from Lisbon, there are some useful bus connections between towns. At Cascais the bus terminal outside the train station operates regular summer services to Guincho (15 minutes) and Sintra (one hour). From outside the train station at Sintra, there are half-hourly bus departures in summer to the nearby coastal resorts of Praia das Maças and Azenhas do Mar (30 minutes) in the west, and north to Mafra in the Estremadura (one hour). There's also regular year-round service from Sintra to Cascais and Estoril (one hour).

Buses 52 and 53 to Caparica (45 minutes from Lisbon) depart from Praça de Espanha (metro: Palhavã) in Lisbon and travel over the Ponte 25 de Abril bridge, which provides superb panoramic views. Regular buses to Caparica also leave from the quayside at Cacilhas, the suburb immediately across the Tejo from Lisbon, which you can reach by ferry from the Terminal Fluvial, adjacent to Praça do Comércio. Both services can be very crowded in the summer months.

Buses to Setúbal (one hour; cost 500$00) leave regularly from Lisbon's Praça de Espanha (metro: Palhavã). At Setúbal you can connect with local services north to Palmela (20 minutes), and southwest to Sesimbra (30 minutes). Six buses daily run a 30-minute trip from Sesimbra to the southwestern cape of Cabo Espichel.

**By Car**  Driving is certainly the most flexible way to see Lisbon's environs; fast highways connect Lisbon with Estoril and Setúbal, and the quality of other roads in the region is generally good. Take special care on hilly and coastal roads, though, and if possible, avoid driving (or at least driving to Lisbon) at the end of a weekend or during public holidays. Bear in mind, too, that parking can be problematic, especially in the summer along the Estoril coast. When you do park, *never* leave anything visible in the car, and it's wise to clear the trunk as well.

*Car Rentals*  There are more choices for car rentals in Lisbon (*see* Arriving and Departing by Car, Train, and Bus in Chapter 3), though the tourist offices in Cascais, Estoril, Sintra, and Setúbal can advise you of the local possibilities. Two choices are **Avis** (Tamariz, Estoril, tel. 01/

468–5728) and **Europcar** (Av. Marginal, Centro Comércial Cisne, Bloco B, Logas 4 and 5, Cascais, tel. 01/486–4438).

**By Boat**  Ferries cross the Rio Tejo from Lisbon to the suburb of Cacilhas, every 10–15 minutes (7 AM–9 PM) from Fluvial terminal, adjacent to Praça do Comércio, or Cais do Sodré (24-hour service). One-way tickets cost 95$00, and the journey takes about 15 minutes. From Setúbal there's 24-hour ferry service, at least hourly, for cars and foot passengers across to the Tróia Peninsula; the journey takes about 20 minutes.

**By Taxi**  If you don't have your own car, it may pay in convenience to take a taxi to some attractions in the area. Cabs can be reasonably inexpensive, and you can usually agree on a fixed price that will include the round-trip to a specific attraction (the driver will wait for you to complete your tour). Tourist offices can give you an idea of what fares are reasonable for various local trips.

**On Foot**  The Estoril coast and much of Sintra are ideal for walking. Most of the tours in this chapter are designed as walks, and the tourist offices will provide maps and brochures that detail local footpaths. If you visit Costa da Caparica in the summer, be prepared to walk a good distance before you find a relatively uncrowded beach.

## Guided Tours

**Catur** (Largo da Academia Nacional de Belas Artes 12, Lisbon, tel. 01/346–7974) offers a seven-hour excursion (9,000$00, includes lunch) to principal sites in Lisbon's environs. **Citirama** (Av. Praia da Vitória 12–B, Lisbon, tel. 01/352–2594) has half-day trips to Queluz, to Sintra, and to Estoril, and a tour of the area's royal palaces (each 7,000$00); nine-hour tours of Mafra, Sintra, and Cascais (12,000$00, including lunch); and even an evening visit to Estoril's famous casino (13,000$00, including dinner). **Gray Line/RN Tours** (Av. Sidonio Pais 2, Lisbon, tel. 01/538846) offers half-day trips into the Arrábida Mountains and to local craft centers for around 7,000$00.

For guided tours of the Sintra area, it's best to ask first at the tourist information center (*see* Important Addresses and Numbers, *above*). In previous years, inclusive half-day tours have encompassed visits to all the principal sights and a wine-tasting in Colares. The office has current schedules and prices, and can sell tickets. **Sintratur** (Rua João de Deus 82, Sintra, tel. 01/923–3780) runs old-fashioned horse and carriage rides in the Sintra area. A short tour of Sintra costs 2,500$00; longer trips cost between 7,000$00 and 14,000$00 and take in attractions as diverse as the Moorish castle and the nearby coastal resorts.

*See also* Guided Tours in Chapter 3.

# Exploring Lisbon's Environs

## Orientation

Several of the destinations in this chapter make ideal day trips from Lisbon, particularly the seaside resorts of the Estoril coast, the palace at Queluz, and the beaches of the Costa da Caparica. Plan ahead to see some of the sights on day trips from Lisbon and others in a regional tour that might last several days. West of Lisbon consider Sintra and the Serra de Sintra for possible overnight stops; the beautiful surroundings can occupy two or three days' leisurely exploring. Estoril and Cascais—both easy day trips—have lively resorts and beaches that may tempt you to stay longer than planned. Setúbal has a splendid pousada that makes a popular overnight stop for those driving on toward the Algarve.

With a car it's possible to cover the areas north and south of the Rio Tejo in two days, although a week would not be too long to spend. Traveling by public transportation also allows you to get around with relative ease between the major destinations.

## Highlights for First-Time Visitors

Cabo da Roca (*see* Tour 2)
Cascais (*see* Tour 1)
Costa da Caparica (*see* Tour 4)
Estoril Casino (*see* Tour 1)
Igreja de Jesus, Setúbal (*see* Tour 4)
Monserrate Gardens (*see* Tour 2)
Palácio Nacional de Pena (*see* Tour 2)
Palácio Nacional de Queluz (*see* Tour 3)
Palácio Nacional de Sintra (*see* Tour 2)
Sesimbra (*see* Tour 4)

## Tour 1: The Estoril Coast

*Numbers in the margin correspond to points of interest on the Estoril Coast, Sintra, and Queluz map.*

The **Estoril coast** extends for 32 kilometers (20 miles) west of Lisbon, taking in the major towns of Estoril and Cascais, as well as some smaller settlements that are part city suburb, part beach town. A favored residential area (thanks to its special microclimate), the coast has milder winters than nearby Lisbon. Partly for that reason, this entire stretch is also known as the Portuguese Riviera.

Over the years the casino at Estoril and the beaches there and in Cascais have been playgrounds for the wealthy, as well as homes for expatriates and exiled royalty of Europe. Today parts of the coastline and several of the hotels are still exclusive, but many of the easternmost towns (particularly those nearest Lisbon) are now firmly part of the city's commuter belt. Even in Estoril and Cascais—whose rich villas still imply wealth—you can count on sharing a visit in summer with great throngs of tourists.

Besides the crowds, the Estoril coast has had to face the problem of pollution due to an inadequate sewage system. Many of the beaches have been profoundly affected, but the quality and cleanliness of the water and sands differ greatly from beach to beach. The problem is a long-standing one, brought about by development, and although plans are underway to rectify the situation, you are strongly advised to avoid swimming in an area unless the water has been declared safe. The best way to determine this is to look for a blue Council of Europe flag, which signals a high standard of unpolluted water and beach. Consult local tourist offices if you are unsure.

None of this is to suggest that the Estoril coast should be avoided. Many of the beaches are still fine, the waterfront towns—especially Cascais—are attractive, and the train ride along the shore offers some of the most appealing views in the region. Unless you intend to tour the wider region over several days, taking the train can be better than joining the crowded roads. If you do choose to drive, leave Lisbon by car via the Estrada Marginal road (follow signs for Cascais/Estoril) and take the curving coastal route to Estoril (the

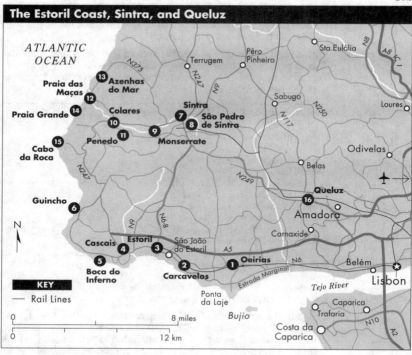

N6), or the parallel, faster Auto-Estrada da Oeste highway (A5), which runs from the Praça Marquês de Pombal in Lisbon to Estoril.

**❶** The first point of interest along the coastal route is at **Oeiras,** 17 kilometers (10½ miles) west of Lisbon. The suburb features the 18th-century Palácio do Marquês de Pombal, originally the country mansion of the man who redesigned Lisbon after the great earthquake of 1755. Unfortunately, only the grounds (including an interesting fishing pavilion and a water tank with the familiar blue-and-white tiling) are open to the public—sometimes.

**❷** The town of **Carcavelos,** a couple of kilometers (just over a mile) farther west, has a small beach lined with café-bars and a busy Thursday market. After another 5 kilometers (3 miles) along the coastal road you'll enter the increasingly built-up environs of Estoril, at **São Pedro** and **São João do Estoril.** Both suburbs have their own beaches and train stations. From São João do Estoril, you can pick up the seafront promenade path that runs through Estoril to Cascais. This is a fine walk (about 5 kilometers/3 miles) with excellent seaside views and no shortage of places to stop for a cold drink or coffee.

**❸** The town of **Estoril,** 26 kilometers (16 miles) west of Lisbon, is filled with grand homes and gardens but otherwise has few specific attractions to interest visitors. Many of the mansions date from the last century, when the resort was preferred by the European aristocracy, and Estoril has managed to maintain a ritzy, jet-set veneer: The town still boasts numerous plush accommodations, restaurants, and sports facilities.

Perhaps the most distinctive attraction in Estoril is its **casino,** which opened in the center of town in 1968 and includes a restaurant, bar, concert venue, movie theater, and art gallery. If you fancy gaming, you won't want to miss a throw of the dice in the gambling salons, which have all the usual games, including banks of American and European slot machines. (To enter the casino, all foreign visitors must show their passports to prove they are 21.) If you're making a night of it, there's dinner and an international floor show, too. Every summer musical concerts and ballets are staged here, and a schedule is available at the tourist office. *Parque do Estoril, tel. 01/268–4521. Admission: 400$00. Casino and restaurant open 3 PM–3 AM, floor show nightly at 11. Reservations required for restaurant and show. Jacket and tie required at all times. AE, DC, MC, V.*

The casino is set at the top of the formal gardens of the **Parque do Estoril,** a park that overlooks the sea and is lined on both sides by several pleasant cafés. People-watching is a famous pastime in this exclusive resort, and a prime spot is from one of the al fresco restaurants along the beachfront **Tamariz esplanade.** The best and longest local beach is at the adjacent **Monte Estoril,** which adjoins Estoril's beach: Here you'll find rest rooms and beach chairs for rent, as well as plenty of shops and snack bars.

**Time Out**   Facing the park is Estoril's luxurious **Hotel Palácio** (*see* Dining and Lodging, *below*), worth visiting, if for no reason other than to take tea in one of its ample salons. During World War II the palace was an espionage center where—in neutral Portugal—the Germans and Allies kept watch on each other, and where exiled European courts awaited the end of the war.

**❹**   Walk along the seafront promenade and around the bay to **Cascais,** just 3 kilometers (2 miles) to the west. Once a mere fishing village, this pretty town—with three small, sandy bays—is now a heavily developed tourist resort packed with shops, restaurants, and hotels. Regardless of the masses of people, Cascais (unlike Estoril) has retained some of its erstwhile small-town character and boasts a selection of sights both in and around the town. (However, what Cascais does have in common with Estoril is polluted water: The beaches are very attractive, but stay out of the sea.) Aside from the harbor, with its fishing boats and yachts, the nicest part of town is the area of old streets and squares off Largo 5 Outubro, behind the Hotel Baia, where you'll find lace shops, cafés, and restaurants galore. In summer, parking in Cascais is a real headache.

Walk south from the Hotel Baia, along Rua Marquês Porçada, to the Baroque **Igreja de Nossa Senhora da Assunção** (Church of Our Lady of the Assumption) with its plain white facade. Inside are fine paintings by Portuguese artist Josefa de Óbidos and an elegant golden altar. *Largo da Assunção. Admission free. Open daily 9–1 and 5–8.*

Opposite the church is one of the entrances to the municipal **Parque do Marechal Carmona** (open daily 9–6), in which there is a shallow lake, a café, a small zoo, and tables and chairs set out under the trees for picnickers. Walk through the park to its southern edge, and you'll find the **Museu Conde de Castro Guimarães,** a stately 19th-century home set on spacious grounds. The small, charming museum houses 18th- and 19th-century paintings, ceramics, furniture, and some archaeological artifacts that were excavated nearby. *Estrada da Boca do Inferno. Admission: 150$00, free Sun. Open Tues.–Sun. 11–12:30 and 2–5.*

Back on the north side of the park, opposite the Pavilhão de Cascais (Cascais Pavilion), stands a modern, single-story building that houses the **Museu do Mar** (Museum of the Sea). Here, you'll find model boats and fishing equipment, traditional costumes worn by 19th-century locals, an analysis of the fish caught in the waters off Cascais, and some splendid old photographs and paintings of the area. *Av. da República (no phone). Admission: 120$00, free Sun. Open Tues.–Sun. 10–4:45.*

**Time Out**   A short walk west from the park along the coastal road will bring you to the café-terrace **Esplanada Santa Marta**, which overlooks the tiny Santa Marta beach and the adjacent lighthouse. This is a perfect spot for a cool drink on the way to or from the Boca do Inferno, a 20-minute walk beyond.

**⑤** Continue on the coastal road for a little less than 2 kilometers (1¼ miles) to Cascais's most famous attraction, the **Boca do Inferno** (Mouth of Hell). Year-round the sea pounds this impressive natural grotto, one of several in the rugged local coastline. Walk along the fenced paths to the viewing platforms above the grotto, and peer down into the abyss: It's a lively spot anytime, though it's best when the incoming tide thrusts waves high onto the surrounding cliffs. A path leads down to secluded spots on the rocks below, where fishermen cast their lines. Afterward, visit the daily roadside market of handicrafts, lace, and leather goods or one of the nearby cafés.

**⑥** From the Boca do Inferno it's a scenic 9-kilometer (5½-mile) drive along the coastal road to the superb surfing beach at **Guincho.** Here rollers from the Atlantic pound onto the sand even on the calmest of days, providing perfect conditions for windsurfing (the annual world championships are often held here during the summer). But beware: The undertow at Guincho beach is notoriously dangerous, and even the best swimmers should take heed.

From Guincho you can return along the coastal road to Cascais and Estoril, or cut inland and drive north on the N247 to Cabo da Roca and east to Sintra *(see* Tour 2, *below).*

## Tour 2: Sintra and Environs

**⑦** Long considered one of the most beautiful places in Portugal, **Sintra,** 30 kilometers (18 miles) northwest of Lisbon, should not be missed. The district's lush woods and valleys on the northern slopes of the **Serra de Sintra** (Sintra Mountains) have been inhabited since prehistoric times, though the Moors were the first to build a castle on their peaks. Later Sintra became the summer residence of Portuguese kings and aristocrats, and its late medieval National Palace *(see below)* was the greatest expression of the royal wealth and power of the time. In the 18th and 19th centuries the area's charms were becoming widely known, as a succession of English travelers, poets, and writers—including an enthusiastic Lord Byron—were drawn by the region's beauty. The poet Robert Southey described Sintra as "the most blessed spot on the whole inhabitable globe." Today the town's palaces, gardens, wooded paths, and viewpoints are still scintillating, and horse-drawn carriages and elegant old hotels in the vicinity add to Sintra's 19th-century air.

The main drawback, especially in the summer, is the number of tour buses that sometimes clog the main square of the **Vila Velha** (Old Town). In front of the National Palace, cars and buses jostle for space, while hawkers wander the central area trying to interest tourists in toys and souvenirs. However, even in the height of summer, Sintra exudes charm, and with a little effort you can escape the crowds by taking one of several lovely rural walks through the surrounding countryside. Ask the Sintra tourist office for their guide-book to local walks.

In the center of Sintra's old town stands the **Palácio Nacional de Sintra** (National Palace of Sintra), also called the Paço Real, whose conical twin chimneys are one of the region's most recognizable landmarks. There has probably been a palace here since Moorish times, although the present-day structure dates from the 14th century. The property was the summer residence of the House of Avis, Portugal's royal line, and it displays a combination of Moorish, Gothic, and Manueline architectural styles. To see the interior you must join one of the guided tours, which is a pity, since several of the rooms are exceptional and may demand more time than you're given. The kitchen, with its famous chimneys, is visited first, followed by a succession of rooms and a chapel decorated with some spectacular examples of mozarabic (Moorish influenced) azulejos from the 15th and 16th centuries. The Sala das Armas's ceiling is painted with the coats-of-arms of 72 noble families; another grand room has a ceiling of painted swans. One of the oldest rooms figures in a well-known tale about an encounter between Dom João I (1385–1433), for whom the palace was largely rebuilt, and a lady-in-waiting whom he kissed. The king had the room painted with as many magpies as there were chattering court ladies, in order to stop their gossiping by satirizing them as loose-tongued birds. *Largo Rainha D. Amelia, tel. 01/923–0085. Admission: 400$00 June–Sept., 200$00 Oct.–May, free Sun. 10–12:30. Open Thurs.-Tues. 10–1 and 2–5.*

**Time Out**  Well placed in Sintra's central square for fine views of the National Palace, the **Café Paris** makes a pleasant stop for a drink, or even a meal. Outside seating can be difficult to score; the lucky ones can soak up the bustling street scenes. *Largo Rainha D. Amelia, tel. 01/923–2375.*

If you stand on the steps of the palace and look at the peaks above, you can spot the battlemented ruins of the 8th-century **Castelo dos Mouros** (Moorish Castle), which defied hundreds of assaults until it was finally conquered by Dom Afonso Henriques in 1147. For a closer look follow the steep, partially cobbled road that leads up to the ruins; or you may rent one of the horse-drawn carriages outside the palace for a more romantic trip (7,000$00). Vast, panoramic views from the castle's serrated walls help explain why Moorish architects chose the site. *Estrada da Pena. Admission free. Open daily June–Sept. 10–6, Oct.–May 10–5.*

Several kilometers farther up the same road is the drawbridged **Palácio Nacional da Pena** (Pena Palace), the most enjoyable of Sintra's palaces, with its turrets, ramparts, and domes. It's a long but very pleasant walk here from the center of Sintra (about 1½ hours), although you can see the palace on one of the local tours or even come by horse and carriage, which costs 8,500$00 (*see* Guided Tours, *above*). Commissioned by the King Consort Ferdinand of Saxe–Coburg in 1840, to be built where a 16th-century convent once stood, the palace is a collection of clashing styles, from Arabian to Victorian. A splendid park surrounds the palace, filled with a lush variety of trees and flowers from every corner of the Portuguese empire, and perched atop a nearby crag, overlooking the grounds, is an enormous statue of Baron Eschwege (the building's German architect) cast as a medieval knight. The final kings of Portugal lived here, the last of whom—Dom Manuel—went into exile in England in 1910 after a republican revolt. The pseudo-medieval structure, with its ramparts, towers, and great halls, is decorated in late Victorian and Edwardian furnishings—a rich, sometimes vulgar, and often bizarre collection of furniture, ornaments, and paintings that makes the guided tour surprisingly interesting. *Estrada da Pena, tel. 01/ 923–0227. Admission to palace: 400$00 June–Sept., 200$00 Oct.– May, free Sun. 10–2. Open Tues.–Sun. 10–1 and 2–5. Admission to park: 200$00, plus an extra charge for cars and carriages. Open same hours as palace.*

Above the palace beyond the statue, a path leads to **Cruz Alta,** a 16th-century stone cross that rests 540 meters (1782 feet) above sea level, at the highest point of the Sintra Mountains. Naturally, the views from this altitude are stupendous, although you may find the climb arduous, especially in the summer sun. However, the walk from the Pena Palace back down to Sintra is delightful: You travel through shaded woods and have several opportunities to rest at viewpoints and take in the panoramic scenes.

If you want to speed up this tour take the high road (N247–3) west from Pena Palace for 4 kilometers (2½ miles) to the Convento de Santa Cruz dos Capuchos (*see below*). Otherwise, once you've returned to downtown Sintra, you might check out the souvenir and antique shops in the central streets (*see* Shopping, *below*) or visit a museum. The **Museu Regional** (Regional Museum), housed in the same building as the tourist information office, close to the Paço Real, not only displays a permanent collection of local archaeological, ethnological, and historical objects, but also hosts a variety of interesting temporary exhibitions. It also has a picture gallery that specializes in works associated with Sintra. *Praça da República 23. Admission free. Picture gallery open weekdays 9:30–noon and 2–6, weekends 2–6; museum open Tues.–Fri. 9:30–noon and 2–6, weekends 2–6.*

Just down the road, in the **Museu do Brinquedo** (Toy Museum), you'll find an appealing collection of locally made dolls and traditional Portuguese toys. *Largo Latino Coelho 9, tel. 01/924–2171. Admission: 200$00. Open Tues.–Sun. 10–12:30 and 2:30–5.*

**❽** The other local excursion is to the nearby village of **São Pedro de Sintra** (located just over a kilometer—under a mile—southeast). The walk there along the main road is not much fun: local buses leave from outside Sintra train station (weekdays every 30–40 minutes, reduced service on weekends); you can catch one as it passes the tourist office; or catch a taxi; or cut out much of the distance by climbing up through the lush gardens of the **Parque Liberdade** (June–Sept., daily 9–8; Oct.–May, daily 9–6), which starts just east of Sintra. São Pedro is most famous for its **Feira da Sintra** (Sintra Fair), held every second and fourth Sunday of the month. Dating back to the time of the Christian Reconquest, the fair is one of the best in the country, with livestock and agricultural displays, and local crafts, antiques, bric-a-brac, and food for sale. Even on non-fair days, it's worth coming to São Pedro to see the delightful village church in its own enclosed little square, and the vast Praça Dom Fernando II (also called the Largo da Feira), where the fair is held under the plane trees. There are several good restaurants in São Pedro, too (*see* Dining and Lodging, *below*), which makes it an attractive lunch stop.

Most of the other local points of interest lie to the west of Sintra and can be reached via the road to Colares (*see below*).

**Time Out** On your way west follow signs to Seteais (a 20-minute walk from Sintra), where you can stop for a meal or afternoon tea at the 18th-century **Palácio de Seteais** (*see* Dining and Lodging, *below*). Built by the Dutch Consul in Portugal, the imposing building—once a palace—is now a luxury hotel, with an excellent (and very expensive) restaurant and beautiful formal gardens. The lunch menu offers a variety of specialties. *Rua Barbosa do Bocage 8, tel. 01/923–3200. Reservations advised. Jacket advised.*

Beyond the palace the road continues through a leafy neighborhood of private manor houses; some of the homes are part of the *Turismo de Habitação* system, an organization that lists lodgings for rent. About 3 kilometers (1.8 miles) from Seteais are the world-renowned gardens of **Monserrate,** laid out by Scottish gardeners in the mid-1800s at the behest of a wealthy Englishman, Sir Francis Cook. The architecturally extravagant, Moorish-style domed pavilion—the ground's centerpiece—is closed to visitors, but the gardens, with their streams, waterfalls, and imported Etruscan tombs, demand a stop. In addition to the dazzling array of tree and plant species, you'll see one of the largest collections of ferns in the world. *Estrada da Monserrate, tel. 01/923–0137. Admission: 200$00. Open daily June–Sept. 10–6, Oct.–May 10–5.*

Past Monserrate the road leads west for 3 kilometers (2 miles) to the small village of **Colares,** associated with the locally produced red wine. The town is also known for its parish church, which is adorned with ceramic tiles, and its main square, which is bordered by some 18th-century houses. The village's winding streets are alive with colorful flowers and trees. For terrific views of the sea and surrounding mountains, take the winding road that climbs up to the nearby village of **Penedo,** less than 2 kilometers (1½ miles) away.

Just out of Colares, the road from Sintra meets the N375, which runs east for 4 kilometers (2½ miles) to the tiny **Convento de Santa Cruz dos Capuchos** (Capuchos Convent), a friary built in 1560 by Franciscan monks. The 12 diminutive cells, the chapel, and the refectory—all hacked out of solid rock—are insulated with cork, hence the nickname the "Cork Convent." *Tel. 01/923–0137. Admission 200$00. Open daily, June–Sept. 10–6; Oct.–May 10–5.*

From the convent, follow the N375 back to where you turned beyond Colares; continue northwest and follow the hilly route to the Atlantic-facing resort village of **Praia das Maças** and to the similar resorts of **Azenhas do Mar** to the north and **Praia Grande** to the south. All three have good beaches (Praia Grande's is the longest) and a selection of small restaurants. If you're visiting Praia das Maças between July and September, a 19th-century tram (the Elétrico de Sintra; tel. 01/923–0662 for information) leaves hourly (8 times daily; closed Mon.) from **Banzão** (just outside Colares) and offers particularly engaging views as it approaches the beach.

**Time Out** At Praia Grande the **Angra** (tel. 01/929–0069) restaurant, with its beachfront views and rooftop terrace, is an ideal, moderately priced stop for lunch or dinner.

Retrace your steps to Colares and drive southwest on the N247; turn right after 3 kilometers (2 miles) for the minor road (N247–4), which leads, after another kilometer or so, to the windswept **Cabo da Roca** and its lighthouse, continental Europe's westernmost point. Here, where the immense wild ocean stretches away from the rugged, barren land, you can purchase a certificate from the gift shop that verifies your visit. Also on site is a tourist desk. Many people visit just to say they've been to the western edge of the continent, but even without the certificate the memory of this desolate granite cape will linger.

Cabo da Roca marks the end of Tour 2, and from here you can drive back through Colares to Sintra for Tour 3. Alternatively, at the junction where the cape road (N247–4) and the main road (N247) meet, take a minor road (signposted to Peninha) that cuts inland and across the Serra de Sintra. This is the scenic route that runs 15 kilometers (9 miles) back to Sintra, passing the peak of Peninha, with a good overlook, and a turn-off for the Capuchos Convent, before climbing to the Pena Palace and finally down to Sintra.

### Tour 3: Queluz and the Palácio Nacional

Located halfway between Lisbon and Sintra (just off the N249) is **⑯** the town of **Queluz,** with its magnificent **Palácio Nacional de Queluz** (Queluz Palace). The 15-kilometer (9-mile) drive from Portugal's capital takes about 20 minutes, making this a good half-day option or a fine stop on the way to or from Sintra. If you take the train, get off at the Queluz-Belas station and walk about a kilometer (just over ½ mile) to the palace.

One of the most attractive of the royal residences near Lisbon, the Queluz Palace—a salmon-pink rococo edifice that was ordered by Dom Pedro III in 1747 and took 40 years to complete!—was inspired, in part, by the palace at Versailles. Intended as a royal summer residence, the building is surrounded by formal landscaping and waterways designed by a Frenchman, Jean-Baptiste Robillon. The ponds, canal, statues, fountains, hedges—and the palace—all fit a carefully executed baroque plan that implies harmony and wholeness. In 1934 a disastrous fire caused much damage, but the palace has been restored and is used today for formal banquets, music festivals, and as accommodations for visiting heads of state. On the guest list have been dignitaries such as Queen Elizabeth II and President Eisenhower. In summer a month-long festival—the Noites de Queluz (Queluz Nights)—complete with costumed cast and orchestra, is staged in the gardens. This event mimics the concerts, fireworks displays, and other activities held in the gardens to amuse Queen Maria I (wife of Dom Pedro III), who lived in the palace throughout her long reign (1777–1816) and whose eccentric behavior earned her the name "Mad" Queen Maria.

Visitors may tour the richly furnished interior and walk through the elegant state rooms: the frescoed Music Salon, the Hall of Ambassadors, the mirrored Throne Room with its crystal chandeliers and gilt trimmings, and so on. The room appointments, gathered from all corners of the globe, including fine woods and precious metals from the old Portuguese colonies, are as ornate and spectacular as you might expect. *Tel. 01/435–0039. Admission: 400$00 June–Sept., 200$00 Oct.–May. Open Mon. and Wed.–Sun. 10–1 and 2–5.*

**Time Out**   Reserve a table in advance to enjoy lunch in the old palace kitchens, now the **Restaurante de Cozinha Velha** (tel. 01/435–0232). In addition to the excellent food, the fixtures and fittings that date to the 18th century make this an experience to savor. If you miss lunch, try to visit during afternoon tea. *See* Dining and Lodging, *below.*

## Tour 4: The Setúbal Peninsula

*Numbers in the margin correspond to points of interest on the Setú-bal Peninsula map.*

The extensive **Setúbal Peninsula**, south of the Rio Tejo, is visited mostly for its beaches on the Costa da Caparica, which provide the cleanest ocean swimming closest to Lisbon. Other area attractions include the major port of Setúbal and the scenic mountain range that separates the port from the peninsula's southernmost beaches and fishing villages.

If you're intent on spending the day at the beach or simply touring the town of Setúbal, traveling by public transportation may be your easiest course of action. However, if you want to see most or all of the sites covered in this tour, renting a car will be your best move. If you travel by bus or car, you'll approach the Setúbal Peninsula (and the sites covered below) by crossing the Ponte 25 de Abril suspension bridge from Lisbon. From this route you're guaranteed stupendous views of the capital.

Having crossed the bridge, you're now on the main highway to Setú-bal, but since we're headed first for the north part of the peninsula, as you leave the bridge, follow the signs off the highway to the **Cristo Rei.** The huge statue of Christ, built in 1959, was designed after the famous statue of Christ the Redeemer in Rio de Janeiro. The figure, with outstretched arms that seem to embrace the city, is a water-front landmark that can be seen easily from almost anywhere in Lisbon. Take the elevator to the top for remarkable panoramic views. Buses to Setúbal make a stop on the highway close to the turn-off for the Cristo Rei, so you can cross the highway by bridge and climb up to the statue. *Admission: 150$00. Open daily 9–7.*

**17** The suburb above which the statue stands, **Cacilhas,** is noted for the numerous seafood restaurants lining its main street, Rua do Ginjal. Waiters armed with menus linger outside their doors, ready to pounce on passersby who can't decide where to eat. At night, and especially on weekends, this is a popular destination for city folks who take the ferry across the river. Ferries depart regularly from Lisbon's Cais do Sodré station and the quay at Praça do Comércio; *see* Arriving and Departing by Train, Bus, Car, and Boat, *above.* Incidentally, buses from the ferry station on the Cacilhas dockside can take you to the Cristo Rei statue.

**18** Buses also connect Cacilhas with the **Costa da Caparica** by way of **Caparica,** 14 kilometers (8½ miles) southwest of Lisbon. If you're driving, either return to the highway and follow the signs or take the minor N377 from Cacilhas—a slower, more scenic route—to reach the 20-kilometer (12-mile) stretch of beach on the northwestern coast of the Setúbal Peninsula. Formerly a fishing village, Caparica is now a lively resort, packed with Portuguese tourists who come to enjoy the relatively unpolluted waters.

Several new resorts near Caparica are on the verge of a tourism boom, but you may be able to avoid the crowds if you keep heading south toward the less accessible, lonely dunes and coves at the end of the peninsula. During the summer a small narrow-gauge train departs from Caparica and travels along an 8-kilometer (5-mile) stretch of coast, making stops en route. Each beach is unique: The areas nearest Caparica are family oriented, while the more southerly resorts tend to attract a younger crowd (among these beaches are some nudist spots as well).

## The Setúbal Peninsula

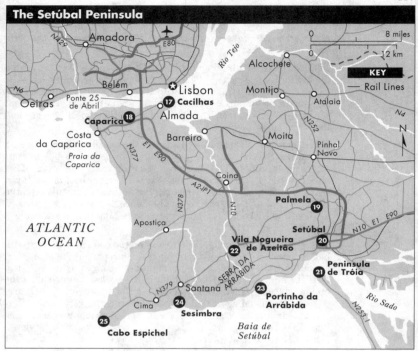

Map labels: N429, Amadora, E80, Rio Tejo, Alcochete, Belém, Montijo, Atalaia, N6, Oeiras, Ponte 25 de Abril, Lisbon, Cacilhas (17), Almada, Caparica (18), Barreiro, Moita, Pinhal Novo, N252, N4, Costa da Caparica, Praia da Caparica, N377, E1 E90, Coina, A2-IP1, N10, Palmela (19), N378, ATLANTIC OCEAN, Apostiça, Setúbal (20), N10 E1 E90, Vila Nogueira de Azeitão (22), Peninsula de Tróia (21), SERRA DA ARRÁBIDA, N379, Santana, Portinho da Arrábida (23), Rio Sado, Cima, Sesimbra (24), N253-1, Cabo Espichel (25), Baía de Setúbal, KEY — Rail Lines, N, 0–8 miles, 0–12 km.

From the Costa da Caparica, head back to the highway (E1) and drive southeast to **Palmela,** a small town 25 kilometers (15 miles) from Lisbon, in the center of a prosperous wine-growing area. Every September the community holds a harvest festival. Palmela's cobbled streets are prettily laced with engaging, low, whitewashed houses, and dominating the village are the remains of a 12th-century castle that was captured from the Moors and enlarged by successive kings. In the 15th century the monastery and church of Sant'Iago were built within the castle walls. The buildings were damaged in the 1755 earthquake and lay abandoned for many years until, after extensive restoration, a pousada was opened in the monastic buildings. The views from this height are extensive.

The main highway continues south to **Setúbal,** 40 kilometers (24½ miles) from Lisbon, at the mouth of the Rio Sado. This is the country's third-largest port, and, although it's one of Portugal's oldest cities, its character has become largely industrial. Nevertheless, if you do stop here overnight before driving on to the Algarve, consider lodging in the 16th-century Castelo de São Filipe (*see* Dining and Lodging, *below*), now one of Portugal's finest pousadas. Even if you decide to go on, you may want to dine here or just pause to take in the views from the castle's privileged position over the city.

Despite the industrial surroundings, the cobbled pedestrian streets in the center around the cathedral are attractive, opening into pretty squares with cafés. The downtown tourist office on Largo do Corpo Santo is built over the remains of a Roman warehouse whose walls can be seen through the glass floors in the office. Stroll down to the port, too, an agreeable clutter of fishing boats and warehouses fronted by gardens. And just back from here, to the west, is the colorful market and its neighborhood restaurants.

Aside from the castle, the major historic relic in Setúbal is the 15th-century **Igreja de Jesus** (Church of Jesus), one of Portugal's earliest examples of Manueline architecture, built with local marble. Setúbal's sanctuary, which predates the Jerónimos Monastery at Belém, displays twisted, ropelike pillars that support the vault—the details of which would soon become the hallmark of Manueline style. The church's original monastic buildings and Gothic cloister now house a **municipal museum,** which contains a fascinating collection of 15th- and 16th-century Portuguese paintings, several by the so-called Master of Setúbal. Other museum attractions include some lovely azulejos, local archaeological finds, and a coin collection. Both church and museum are undergoing extensive renovation, but you can still admire the original, badly worn main doorway, and deplore the addition of a concrete expanse out front that makes the church square look like a roller-skating rink. *Praça Miguel Bombarda. Contact the tourist office for information on the reopening.*

**㉑** Across the estuary from Setúbal is the **Península de Tróia,** a long spit of land blessed with fine beaches and clean water. Ferries to the peninsula leave from Setúbal's port at least hourly day and night. To answer the demands of tourists, the point has been much developed in recent years, evidenced by the large sports complex—**Tróia Tourist Complex**—which includes a golf course, tennis courts, and other amenities. The area has managed to retain a little of its history, though: The peninsula is the site of the Roman town of Cetobriga, destroyed by a tidal wave in the 5th century, and you can visit the scant ruins (opposite the marina). As with Caparica, the farther south you go, the thinner the crowds.

From Setúbal, drive west along the N10 and almost immediately you'll enter the **Serra de Arrábida,** a 5,000-foot-high mountain range whose wild crags fall steeply to the sea. There is profuse plant life at these heights, particularly in the spring, when the rocks are carpeted with wildflowers. The entire region is now a national park.

Ten kilometers (6 miles) from Setúbal is the **Quinta da Bacalhoa,** a late-16th-century L-shaped mansion whose box-hedged gardens sport striking azulejo-lined paths. You can't tour the villa (which is a private house), but the gardens are open to the public. A pavilion with three pyramidal towers houses the oldest azulejo panel in the country: It depicts the story of Susannah and the Elders and dates from 1565. *Admission free; tips expected. Gardens open Mon.–Sat. 1–5.*

**Time Out**  Follow the road to the adjacent village of Vila Fresca de Azeitão, not far from the mansion, to find the 16th-century **Quinta das Torres** (tel. 065/208–0001), now an inn with a restaurant. The fine old building has been beautifully restored and features antique furniture and tapestries at every turn. The locally produced food served here is well prepared and moderately priced.

Two kilometers (1¼ miles) to the west of Vila Fresca de Azeitão is
**㉒** the town of **Vila Nogueira de Azeitão,** whose grandest building is the 16th-century **Tavora Palace,** once owned by the Duke of Aveiro. In the 18th century, the Marquês de Pombal accused the duke of collaborating in the assassination plot against the king, Dom José. Subsequently the duke was executed by the Marquês, and the Tavora coat of arms was erased from the Sala das Armas in Sintra's National Palace. Unfortunately, the palace is not open for visits.

On a more upbeat association, the village is known for its winemaking. Visitors may tour the wine vaults of the **José Maria da Fonseca Company,** one of the country's major wine exporters, and view all stages of the production process. There's the New Winery, very near the Tavora Palace, and the Old Winery, right in the center of the village. Both are signposted. Among the vintages for sale is the dessert wine called Moscatel de Setúbal. *Tel. 065/219–1500. Open weekdays 9–noon and 2–5. Admission free.*

**Time Out** On the first Sunday of every month, Vila Nogueira de Azeitão holds an interesting **country market,** where you can buy the locally made *queijo fresco* (sheep's milk cheese), which is popular in and around Lisbon. This cheese is a good choice for a picnic lunch, and you can buy excellent fresh bread from one of the market's bakery stalls.

**㉓** Continuing west from Azeitão on the N379, after about 2 kilometers (1¼ miles), veer left toward the small fishing village of **Portinho da Arrábida,** about 8 kilometers (5 miles) farther on, at the foot of the **Serra de Arrábida.** The village is a popular destination for Lisboans, who appreciate the good local beaches. In summer, when the number of visitors makes parking nearly impossible, leave your car above the port and take the steep walk down to the water, where you'll find several modest seafood restaurants that overlook the port.

You can return from Portinho da Arrábida by either of two parallel roads leading from the village toward Setúbal. The lower, coastal road hugs the shore nearly all the way; the upper road gives access to the ramshackle, white-walled **Convento de Arrábida,** an atmospheric 16th-century monastery built into the hills of the Serra de Arrábida. From here the views are glorious, but you'll have to contact the tourist office in Setúbal in advance to arrange a visit to the monastery.

**㉔** Alternatively, continue southwest on N379 to the junction at Santara, and turn left for the 3-kilometer (2-mile) drive south to **Sesimbra,** a lively fishing village surrounded by mountains and isolated bays and coves, to which many Lisboans retreat in the summer. It is only about 40 kilometers (24½ miles) south of the capital, a location that has contributed to the area's popularity. Despite highrise apartments that now mar the town, Sesimbra has some central narrow streets that are still thoroughly agreeable. Perched on a hilltop, northwest of town, an old castle with five towers overlooks the port, which is guarded by a 17th-century fortress and littered with nets, anchors, and coils of rope. Packed with colorful fishing boats—which unload their catches at an entertaining daily fish auction—the port is the liveliest spot in town.

**㉕** Twelve kilometers (7 miles) to the west, the N379 ends at **Cabo Espichel,** a salt-encrusted headland on which 18th-century arcaded pilgrimage houses border a huge open space; at one end is a forsaken pilgrimage church. This is the southwestern point of the Setúbal Peninsula, a rugged and lonely place to end your tour. To the north, unsullied beaches extend as far as Caparica, with only local roads and foot paths connecting them. Drivers heading north toward Lisbon should retrace their route to Santana and follow the N378, which joins the E1/A2 after 20 kilometers (12 miles).

**What to See and Do with Children**

Take the narrow-gauge railway along Costa da Caparica (*see* Tour 4)
Pena Palace (*see* Tour 2)
Ferry ride to Cacilhas (*see* Tour 4)
Climb up to the Cristo Rei statue on a clear day (*see* Tour 4)
Walk along the ocean promenade between Estoril and Cascais, stopping for lunch or drinks at a café on the way (*see* Tour 1)

# Shopping

Throughout Lisbon's environs there are shopping opportunities galore, from ceramics sold in smart Cascais boutiques to weavings and leather goods featured at roadside stalls and weekly village markets. Quality and prices vary greatly, so you'd do well to shop around before buying. Prices are fixed almost everywhere, although with a firm command of the Portuguese language you may be able to negotiate a small discount at some of the local markets and roadside stalls. Bargaining is not practiced in stores or boutiques.

### Cascais

Cascais, the best shopping area on the Estoril coast, has many pedestrian streets lined with shops that are all within easy walking distance of one another. For smart fashions, gifts, and handmade jewelry, browse around **Rua Frederico Arouca.**

**Markets** are held north of town at Rua Mercado (off Avenida 25 de Abril) on Wednesday and Saturday, selling fruit, vegetables, cheese, bread, and flowers. Also, on the first and third Sunday of each month, a larger market with the same kind of goods is held at the **Praça de Touros** (bullring) on Avenida Pedro Álvares.

For local crafts you may want to walk about 25 minutes from the center of town to the daily market at the entrance of **Boca do Inferno,** where specialty items such as lace and ceramics are sold.

### Estoril

Each July and August Estoril holds the **Feira do Artesanato,** an open-air handicrafts fair, near the casino. Every evening, from 5 to midnight, stalls sell local arts and crafts and traditional Portuguese foods.

### Setúbal Peninsula

The city of Setúbal has the usual range of shops and services, but it's not the most attractive place in which to browse. On the first Sunday of each month a **country produce market** is set up in the center of Azeitão.

### Sintra

Sintra is a center for **antiques** and **curios,** with several of its streets dedicated to shops crowded with rare items, art, and crafts. **Almorábida** (Rua Visconde Monserrate 12–14), in front of the National Palace, is an outlet for genuine Arraiolos carpets, as well as lace, copper, and other artifacts. At **A Esquina** (Praça da República 20), the shop is stacked from floor to ceiling with hand-painted ceramics, many of them reproductions of 15th- to 18th-century designs signed by the artists. For hand-embroidered linen tablecloths, bed-spreads, towels, and sheets, visit **Violeta** (Rua das Padarias 19), and let the helpful staff show you the wares. In nearby São Pedro de Sintra a **country fair** displaying produce, crafts, and antiques takes place on the second and fourth Sunday of every month.

On the N9 road between Sintra and Mafra, the small town of Pêro Pinheiro is known for its **marble,** evidenced on both sides of the road by shops selling stacks of cachepots, plaques, and other decorative garden objects.

# Sports and the Outdoors

### Participant Sports

**Fishing**  Sesimbra, a deep-sea fishing center, is renowned for the huge sword-fish that are landed in the area. You may ask around for local people who rent boats, or contact the **Clube Naval de Cascais** (Esp. Príncipe Luís Filipe, in front of Hotel Baia, tel. 01/483–0125), which orga-nizes deep-sea fishing outings.

**Golf**  The entire region boasts excellent golf courses, among them: **Clube de Golfe do Estoril** (Av. da República, Estoril, tel. 01/468–0176), which has an immaculate 18-hole championship course, with special rates and privileges for guests staying at the Hotel Palácio; **Quinta da Marinha** (4 kilometers/2½ miles west of Cascais, tel. 01/468–9881), with its new 18-hole course designed by Robert Trent Jones; and the **Penha Longa** (tel. 01/924–0014), 9 kilometers (5 miles) from Estoril, with superb views, an 18-hole course, golf clinics, and put-ting greens. On the Estoril-Sintra road the **Estoril Sol** (Lagoa Azul, Linhó, tel. 01/923–2048) has a scenic nine-hole course; and the **Lis-bon Sports Club** at Belas (tel. 01/431–2482), 27 kilometers (17 miles) northeast of Estoril, is a quiet spot amid green hills, with a fine 18-hole course.

**Horseback Riding**  There's a particularly good equestrian center at the **Quinta da Marinha** (Cascais, tel. 01/486–9282), with year-round riding. Les-sons are also offered at the **Centro Hipico da Costa do Estoril** (tel. 01/487–2064) and the **Clube de Campo Dom Carlos I** (Quinta da Marinha, tel. 01/487–1403). In Sintra, several local riding schools of-fer lessons; the local tourist office can provide addresses.

**Swimming**  Most good hotels along the Estoril coast have indoor and outdoor swimming pools, and it's recommended that you use them rather than the sea since the water on this stretch of the coast is polluted. The **Costa da Caparica** and the **southern side of the Setúbal Peninsula** have considerably cleaner waters and beaches. On the coast near Sintra there are public swimming pools (open June–Sept.) at Praia das Maças (tel. 01/929–2029), Praia Grande (tel. 01/929–2145), and Azenhas do Mar (tel. 01/929–2477).

**Tennis**  Many of the hotels in the region have tennis courts. Some other op-tions are: the **Clube de Tenis do Estoril** (Av. Amaral, Estoril, tel. 01/466–2720), **Oeiras Tennis Club** (Rua Miguel Bombarda, tel. 01/247–1010), the **Quinta da Marinha** (*see* Golf, *above*, tel. 01/486–9881), and the sports complex on the **Tróia Peninsula,** which has 12 tennis courts. In Sintra, you can play tennis at the court in Parque Liberdade (tel. 924–1139) or at the Lourel municipal courts (Campo Raso, no phone).

**Water Sports**  **Sailboarding** and **surfing** are popular sports along the Estoril coast. The beaches at Carcavelos and São Pedro do Estoril appeal to sailors and surfers, but the experts head for Guincho beach, one of the venues of the World Windsurfing Championships. Rental equipment is available from **Windsurfing Guincho** (Bairro da Assunção, Zona C, Lote 10, Loja P, 2750 Cascais, tel. 01/284–7180).

There are sailing clubs at Cascais, Sesimbra, and Setúbal, and local tourist offices can provide you with information on others. It's often possible to arrange a week-long sail with some of the clubs in the coastal towns. Check with your local sailing organization to see if it has reciprocity with any Portuguese marinas. The **Clube Naval de Cascais** (Esp. Príncipe Luís Filipe, tel. 01/483–0125) provides shelter for yachts in Cascais Bay.

### Spectator Sports

**Grand-Prix Racing and Rallying**  The **Autódromo do Estoril** (Estoril Autodrome), on the Estoril–Sintra road, 5 kilometers (3 miles) north of Estoril, hosts Formula 1 car racing and can accommodate 40,000 spectators. The racetrack is also the start and finish point of the annual **Port Wine Rally,** an international car competition. Details about both events can be obtained from the Estoril tourist office.

# Dining and Lodging

**Dining**  Interesting and sometimes unusual preparations of fresh fish and seafood are served in restaurants throughout the area around Lisbon. Even the inland villages are close enough to the sea that you can be assured of quality and freshness in their restaurants. City dwellers make a point of crossing the Tejo to the suburb of Cacilhas to eat platefuls of *arroz de marisco* (rice with seafood); *linguado* (sole) is especially popular, as are the mounds of shellfish displayed in restaurant windows.

In Sintra *queijadas* (sweet cheese tarts) are popular; in the Azeitão region of the Setúbal Peninsula, locals swear by the queijo fresco, a delicious white sheep's-milk cheese. Lisbon's environs also produce good wines, many of which are offered as the house vintages in local restaurants. From Colares comes a light, smooth red, a fine accompaniment to a hearty lunch; Palmela, the demarcated wine-growing district of Setúbal, produces distinctive amber-colored wines of recognized quality; in the Setúbal Peninsula, the famous Fonseca winery produces a dessert wine called Moscatel de Setúbal.

Dress in restaurants throughout the region is usually casual, especially in the coastal resorts, but any exceptions are noted below. Reservations are not necessary unless specified, although you should be prepared to wait in line at the more popular seafood restaurants.

Restaurant prices correspond to Lisbon's dining chart, in Chapter 3. Highly recommended restaurants are indicated by a star ★.

**Lodging**  Many visitors are content to use Lisbon as a base from which to explore the environs. However, spending at least one night away from the capital, staying either at one of the popular resorts on the Estoril coast or Setúbal Peninsula, or at the rural retreat of Sintra may give you some perspective on the country. Regardless of where you stay, it's essential that you book a room in advance in the summer. If you do opt to spend a night or two outside Lisbon, you'll have an opportunity to experience two types of accommodations not available in the capital itself: pousadas and members of the *Turismo de Habatição* scheme.

The state-run pousadas often are located in converted historic buildings, and they generally have superior facilities and restaurants. The two in this region are at Setúbal and Palmela: Both are well worth a stay. For more information contact **Enatur Pousadas de Portugal** (Av. Santa Joana Princesa 10, 1700 Lisbon, tel. 01/848–1221, fax 01/805846).

The second type of lodging in the region is the Turismo de Habitação system—old manor houses and country estates that offer rooms and sometimes meals. All lodgings listed with this association are located in rural areas and provide comfortable accommodations. Some members of Turismo de Habitação are reviewed below, but since they typically have few rooms, availability is limited. For a full listing and more information, contact the **Associação Portuguesa de Turismo de Habitação** (Rua de João Penha 10, 1200 Lisboa, tel. 01/690549, fax 01/388–8115). Tourist offices can also advise you about vacancies at local manor houses.

Hotel rates correspond to Lisbon's lodging chart, in Chapter 3. Highly recommended hotels are indicated by a star ★.

**Cascais**
*Dining*

**João Padeiro.** Not only does this basement restaurant serve excellently prepared sole, but it's also renowned for succulent lobsters accompanied by homemade mayonnaise. If you're a meat-eater, you'll find a few choices on the menu, too, with pork being the most reliable dish. It's an odd building, with its roof slates at head height; walk down the narrow steps into the distinctive wood-and-leather-paneled interior, which although rather dim, is enlivened by cheery decorations. Service is brisk and assured, and the location—along the main road next to the tourist office—couldn't be more convenient for visitors who are unfamiliar with the town. *Rua Visconde da Luz 12, tel. 01/483–0232. Reservations advised. AE, DC, MC, V. Closed Tues. $$$*

**Beira Mar.** One of several well-established and unpretentious restaurants situated behind the fish market, the Beira Mar has a comfortable interior decorated with blue-and-white azulejos. The menu includes a wide variety of fish and meat dishes, but the best seafood and shellfish are from the usually impressive central display of the day's catch. *Rua das Flores 6, tel. 01/483–0152. AE, DC, MC, V. Closed Tues. $$*

**Joshua's Shoarma Grill.** This popular local spot, in an old town house close to the tourist office, specializes in tasty Middle Eastern food, including kebabs, pita bread, falafel, hummus, and the like. Main courses are served with rice and salad, and are very filling—try the *combinado*, with two or three different kinds of barbecued meat. *Rua Visconde da Luz 19, tel. 01/284–3064. MC, V. $$*

**O Pescador.** Fish and shellfish, picked fresh from the market, are the reliable items served in this folksy restaurant, where a cluttered ceiling and maritime-related artifacts distract the eye. The sole is a house specialty, and this is also a good place to try *bacalhau* (cod). *Rua das Flores 10, tel. 01/483–2054. AE, DC, MC. $$*

*Dining and Lodging*
★

**Hotel Albatroz.** Situated on a rocky outcrop, this attractive old house—once the summer residence of the Dukes of Loulé—is the most luxurious of Cascais's hotels. Though the Albatroz has been expanded and modernized, its genteel character has been retained, particularly in the charming bedrooms and the pleasant terrace bar. Public areas are grand, while the traditionally decorated guest rooms combine elegance with comfort. An outdoor pool and terrace overlook the ocean. Given its quality, most of the time this hotel is fully booked, so advance reservations are recommended, especially in summer. The hotel restaurant (also called the Albatroz), where fish dishes are the specialty, boasts superior views of the sea and the coast toward Lisbon. *Rua Frederico Arouca 100, 2750, tel. 01/483–2821, fax 01/484–4827. 40 rooms with bath. Facilities: restaurant, bar, pool, garage. AE, DC, MC, V. $$$$*

**Dom Manolo.** In this bustling Spanish-owned grill-restaurant, the waiters charge back and forth delivering excellent spit-roasted chicken to a largely local clientele. Accompany it with fries or salad, or both, and if you're still hungry, have a slab of the homemade crème caramel. These are not sophisticated surroundings: there are paper tablecloths, holiday posters tacked to the walls, and billowing smoke as the cooks battle with the huge spit-roast machinery at the front of the restaurant. But for inexpensive, down-to-earth food and company, it's hard to beat. *Av. Marginal 13, tel. 01/483–1126. No credit cards. $*

*Lodging* **Casa da Pérgola.** This charming town house, which has been in the hands of the same family for over a century, provides an intimate lodging experience. The decor throughout is refined, the central location excellent, and the style thoroughly 19th-century. The house is part of the Turismo de Habitação scheme, and has a limited number of rooms: you'll need to book well in advance. *Av. de Valbom 13, 2750, tel. 01/484–0040. 6 rooms with bath. Facilities: lounge, dining room. Closed Nov.–Feb. $$*

**Hotel Baia.** This modern stone hotel fronted with white balconies overlooks fishing boats on the quayside and the glistening blue waters of Cascais Bay. Following renovations, the Baia presents an air of efficiency, and the comfortable rooms are well-appointed, turned out in crisp colors, and have simple, attractive furnishings. Ask for one of the 66 that have balconies and sea views. There's a private esplanade along the ground floor, with a lounge, restaurant, grill, café, and bar. *Av. Marginal, 2750, tel. 01/483–1033 or 01/483–1034, fax 01/483–1095. 114 rooms with bath. Facilities: restaurant, grill, café, bar, roof terrace and pool. AE, DC, MC, V. $$*

**Estoril** **A Choupana.** Just east of the town in adjacent São João do Estoril,
*Dining* this long-established restaurant with beach views offers high-quality fresh fish, seafood, and local dishes in comfortable, plant-filled surroundings. Live music accompanies dinner, and there's nightly dancing until 2. Parking is available, and you can get a taxi from the train station. *Estrada Marginal, São João do Estoril, tel. 01/468–3099. Reservations advised. AE, DC, MC, V. $$$*

**The English Bar.** Despite the name and the mock-Tudor embellishments, this friendly restaurant—not bar— serves first-class Portuguese and international cuisine. Fish is always available, and the sole is a reliable choice; shellfish soup makes a fine starter. It's near Monte Estoril's Aparthotel Estoril Eden, only a few minutes' walk from the central beach (via the pedestrian underpass that starts behind Monte Estoril train station), and there are good views of the ocean from its windows. *Av. Sabóia 9, off Av. Marginal, tel. 01/468–0413. Reservations advised. AE, DC, MC, V. Closed Sun. $$$*

**Furusato.** This excellent new Japanese restaurant sits within a lovingly restored 19th-century house overlooking the central Praia do Tamariz and its promenade. Japanese cuisine is a rarity in Portugal, and Furusato serves a full range, including sushi, tempura, and teppanyaki dishes. *Praia do Tamariz, tel. 01/468–4430. AE, DC, MC, V. $$$*

**Frolic.** A bright, welcoming café-restaurant, set beside the Hotel Palácio, Frolic has a covered outdoor terrace overlooking the palm trees in the park opposite. Come for just a snack—the cakes and pastries are all homemade—or stop for a meal. There are Portuguese specialties and even pizzas; and it's open for late-night drinks until 2 AM. *Av. Clotilde, tel. 01/468–1219. AE, DC, MC, V. $–$$*

**Dining and**
**Lodging**
★

**Hotel Palácio.** During World War II exiled European courts came to live in this luxurious 1930s hotel to await the end of the war. The hotel faces the town's central park and has pastel rooms decorated with Regency-style reproduction furniture and attractive and elegant public rooms. The bar and lounge are particularly comfortable, with views over the outdoor pool to the park beyond. The staff is deft and courteous, and reception can assist with anything from car rental to organizing tennis lessons. The Palácio also boasts one of Portugal's most famous restaurants—the Four Seasons Grill—which serves buffets around the garden pool in summer and adjusts its menus seasonally, using the freshest ingredients in its quest for perfection. The hotel is a two-minute walk from the beach, and golfers can tee-up on the championship golf course. *Rua do Parque, Parque do Estoril, 2765, tel. 01/468–0400, fax 01/468–4867. 162 rooms with bath. Facilities: restaurant, bar, outdoor pool, tennis courts, golf, shops, parking. AE, DC, MC, V. $$$–$$$$*

**Lodging**

**Aparthotel Estoril Eden.** The comfortable, tastefully decorated rooms in this modern apartment hotel are reasonably sized and come with kitchenettes, TVs, and VCRs, making the Eden a good bet for families. Superb views of the sweeping Estoril coast from the rooms' balconies, which are equipped with tables and chairs, are an added attraction to the convenient Monte Estoril beach location. It's just a few minutes' walk to the ocean via an underpass that starts behind Monte Estoril train station. *Av. Sabóia 209, 2765, tel. 01/467–0573, fax 01/467–0848. 162 units with bath and kitchenette. Facilities: restaurant, bar, indoor and outdoor pools, sauna, gym, garden, parking. AE, DC, MC, V. $$$*

★

**Estalagem Lennox Country Club.** Set on a hillside a few minutes' walk above the casino, this extremely attractive hotel is a real favorite with golfers, who can take advantage of special packages. The ten rooms in the main building are named after famous golf courses, and the Lennox even sponsors its own challenge cup every year. But non-golfers will feel equally at home here, sitting out on the balconies soaking up the sea views, or relaxing by the poolside bar. Complimentary afternoon tea and cakes are served to all guests, and if you take meals here, house wines are included in the price. The most spacious rooms, on the top floor of the main building, have huge balconies and separate, small lounges. The other rooms here, including the 22 in the garden annex, are all comfortable and pleasingly decorated. There's also an indoor bar and a very cozy little lounge. *Rua Eng. Álvaro Pedro de Sousa 5, 2765, tel. 01/468–0424, fax 01/467–0859. 32 rooms with bath. Facilities: terrace bar, pool, golf packages, restaurant, lunch buffet, parking. AE, DC, MC, V. $$$*

**Hotel Lido.** Set on a quiet street well away from the beach, overlooking the lush green hillside above Estoril, the Lido is justly popular for its good-value rooms and amenities, which include a pool, garden, and decent restaurant. All guest rooms have balconies, and there's a fifth-floor lounge bar. The hotel is signposted for drivers from the casino—it's less convenient for tourists without a car since you're a steep 15-minute walk from the center of Estoril. *Rua do Alentejo 12, 2765, tel. 01/468–4123, fax 01/468–3665. 62 rooms with bath. Facilities: restaurant, bar, pool, garage. AE, DC, MC, V. $$*

**Guincho**
**Dining and**
**Lodging**

**Estalagem do Forte Muchaxo.** The sound of the sea echoes through the dining room of this attractive, rustic restaurant nestled in the rocks over Guincho beach. Begun as a simple hut where fishermen could go for drinks and coffee, it's one of the area's oldest and best-known eating places. Today it features beautifully presented and consistently well-prepared fish specialties and Portuguese fare. The lovely location of this restaurant and inn may draw you here from Cascais (10 kilometers/6 miles away); there are rooms available for overnight guests, most with splendid ocean views, and there's also a pool and lounge room for relaxing. *Praia do Guincho, on the beach, 2750 Cascais, tel. 01/487–0221, fax 01/487–0444. 24 rooms with bath. Facilities: restaurant, pool. AE, DC, MC, V. $$*

**Palmela**
*Dining and Lodging*

**Pousada de Palmela.** On a hill at the end of the Arrábida range, this historic building was originally a fortress and later became a monastery. In 1979 it was converted into a pousada, and the designers made use of the flagstone corridors and old cloister (now a lounge); most of the pleasant rooms provide superb views of the valley and the sea. The monks' former refectory is now a dependable restaurant, serving traditional Portuguese fare. *2950, tel. 01/235–1226, fax 01/233–0440. 28 rooms with bath. Facilities: restaurant, bar, garden, parking. AE, DC, MC, V. $$$*

**Queluz**
*Dining*
★

**Restaurante de Cozinha Velha.** Formerly the great kitchen of the adjoining Queluz Palace, this magnificent restaurant takes full advantage of its heritage: an imposing open fireplace and vast oak table catch the eye, old cooking utensils hang from the walls, and tables and chairs are fine reproduction antiques. The cooking hits the mark, with the Portuguese specialties occasionally tempered by a French touch; a spicy *cataplana* (stew) of salmon, monkfish, clams, and shrimp is just one superb main course. Certain dishes have been inspired by 18th-century recipes, notably some of the desserts, which are always a Portuguese obsession. Service is excellent, and the English-speaking staff can guide you around the impressive wine list. *Palácio Nacional de Queluz, tel. 01/435–0232. Reservations advised. AE, DC, MC, V. $$$*

**Sesimbra**
*Lodging*

**Hotel do Mar.** The fishing village of Sesimbra—west of Setúbal—is rapidly becoming a popular resort area, typified by comfortable hotels such as this one. Its many public rooms and amenities provide the mostly Portuguese guests with a complete vacation within the confines of the hotel. A low, stepped building tucked into the seaside cliffs, this property features reasonably sized modern rooms with balconies that overlook either the sea or the private garden and pool area. *Rua General Humberto Delgado 10, 2970, tel. 01/223–3326, fax 01/223–3888. 120 rooms with bath. Facilities: restaurant, coffee shop, bar, garden, terrace, pool, tennis courts, children's playground, parking. AE, DC, MC, V. $$*

**Setúbal**
*Dining*

**O Baluarte do Sado.** There are several cafés and restaurants around the market, near the port, but this is the best, and the friendly owner speaks English. At the back of a parking lot, the simple dining room with a plain tiled floor and more elaborately tiled walls is the background for excellent grilled meals—the charcoal range out front is kept busy with orders for barbecued cuts of various fish, squid, and beef. Or you might order an arroz de marisco or *caldeirada* (fish stew) for two; accompaniments are mixed salads, new potatoes when in season, and fries. Sunday lunchtime is especially popular with local families. Everyone drinks the house wine— the white goes well with all fish meals. *Praça da República 1, tel. 065/38780. No credit cards. $$*

**Rio Azul.** Locals frequent this popular seafood restaurant—hidden on a side street off Rua L. Todi, on the way to the castle, west of the harbor. It's a little tricky to find but is signposted from the main road. As you'd expect at a *marisqueira*, the dishes to go for are the fresh fish grilled to perfection and the arroz de marisco, a house specialty. *Rua Placido Stichini 1, tel. 065/522828. AE, DC, MC, V. Closed Wed. $$*

*Dining and*   **Pousada de São Filipe.** Perched atop a hill where it overlooks the
*Lodging*      town and the Rio Sado, this 16th-century castle-turned-picture-
★              book pousada makes an exciting overnight stop and is given excellent
reviews by most visitors. The approach to the main entrance from
the car park is magnificent, up a tunneled flight of stairs and past a
lovely 18th-century chapel decorated with azulejos depicting the life
of São Filipe. Winter nights can be chilly, but the historic location,
splendid views from the rooms and ramparts, and the hotel's unique
features compensate considerably for any fleeting moments of dis-
comfort. The interior is also awash with azulejo tiling, especially in
the welcoming bar; a canopied terrace in front of reception affords
fine views of town, bay, and Troia. And the appealing restaurant,
traditionally decorated, has a menu strong on Portuguese cuisine
that is especially good with fish. *Castelo de São Filipe, 2900, tel.
065/523844, fax 065/524981. 14 rooms with bath. Facilities: restau-
rant, bar, parking. AE, DC, MC, V. $$$*

*Lodging*   **Quinta do Patricio.** This manor house—a member of Turismo de
Habitação—is close to the castle and provides a small-scale, pretty
alternative to the grandness of the pousada. Furnishings through-
out the property are homey, with bright-colored rugs and paint-
ings, and from the garden you'll get some nice views of the town.
Meals are available upon request; reservations made well in advance
are essential. *Estrada de São Filipe, 2900, tel. 065/364–0310 or 065/
37019. 6 rooms and 1 apartment with bath. Facilities: bar, garden.
No credit cards. $$*

*Sintra*   **Cantinho de São Pedro.** Imaginative Portuguese cuisine with a
*Dining*   French influence is presented at this busy restaurant in São Pedro
de Sintra, an old village about a kilometer (about ½ mile) away. Locals consider the food well worth the wait for a table. Try the trout
with almonds and cream, or look for the fresh shellfish on the list of
*pratos do dia* (dishes of the day). The restaurant is a rustic little
plant-filled building in a small courtyard of artisans' workshops, just
off the main square. *Praça Dom Fernando II 18, São Pedro de
Sintra, tel. 01/923–0267. AE, DC, MC, V. Closed Mon. $$$*
**Solar de São Pedro.** Right on the square, the distinctive Solar de São
Pedro has grandstand views of the bi-monthly Sunday market—
you'll have to book ahead for lunch if you want to eat then. There's a
small menu of Portuguese specialties, but the São Pedro is best-
known for the eclectic international food like its fresh fish and
grilled steaks. It's all a good value, although meals that include fish
tend to be expensive. *Praça Dom Fernando II 12, São Pedro de
Sintra, tel. 01/923–1860. Reservations advised. AE, DC, MC, V.
Closed Wed. $$–$$$*
**Toca do Javali.** A few hundred meters past the market square in São
Pedro, you climb down the steps into this highly attractive restau-
rant to be greeted by wild boar. That's what *javali* means, and in the
cool, whitewashed, beamed interior, wild boar is either underfoot (a
skin is spread under every table) or on your plate. A separate game
menu (caça) suggests roast boar, or boar ragout, as well as partridge
and pheasant when in season; there are also regular dishes. In sum-
mer you can eat in the delightful terraced garden; otherwise, go for
a window table in the simple, traditional interior. At lunchtime, an
enormously good-value set meal consists of soup, main course, fruit
and wine for under 1,200$00. *Rua 1 de Dezembro 18, São Pedro de
Sintra, tel. 01/923–3503. AE, MC, V. Closed Wed. $$–$$$*
**Alcobaça.** Up a tiny side street, the Alcobaça is one of the few restau-

rants in the center of town to offer consistent good value. The friendly owner takes your order and then bustles around the small dining room to make sure everyone is happy. You will be, once you've tried the excellent grilled chicken or sampled the large, bubbling serving of arroz de marisco. The fresh clams *bulhão pato* (in parsley and garlic sauce) are also very tasty. These simple surroundings attract Portuguese tourists in search of honest home cooking, so trust their judgment and go right in. *Rua das Padarias 7–11, tel. 01/923–1651. MC, V. $$*

*Dining and Lodging* ★ **Hotel Palácio de Seteais.** This luxurious 18th-century palace, on pristine grounds, is a kilometer or so (just over ½ mile) from the center of Sintra. The palace's name, Seteais—meaning "seven sighs"—supposedly tells of the relief felt by the Portuguese after the signing of the 1807 Treaty of Sintra with the French. Today the sighs are more likely to be of admiration for the conservation of such a beautiful building. You'll enter under a superb, classical arch that joins the palace's two wings: Its public rooms are gloriously decorated with period and reproduction furnishings, delicate frescoes, and Arraiolos carpets; the guest rooms are individually styled, some with hand-painted wallpapers. If you're not planning an overnight stay, at least have yourself pampered in the splendid restaurant, which serves a four-course set meal of impressively garnished Continental-style dishes. In summer, coffee or afternoon tea taken on the terrace is an added delight. *Rua Barbosa do Bocage 8, 2710, tel. 01/923–3200, fax 01/923–4277. 30 rooms with bath. Facilities: restaurant, bar, gardens, pool, tennis, horseback riding, parking. AE, DC, MC, V. $$$$*

**Quinta das Sequóias.** This lovely 19th-century manor house (formerly the Casa da Tapada) is just 1 kilometer (about ½ mile) beyond the Palácio de Seteais, set in 40 acres of wooded grounds; look for the sign on the left-hand side of the road. Superbly managed by owner Candida Gonzalez, it's a supreme example of the quality offered by the Turismo de Habitação scheme: the half-dozen rooms, renovated from top to bottom have charming furniture and modern bathrooms. Careful thought has gone into the architectural redesign—one of the bathrooms has been cleverly built around monolithic boulders, while a new tower contains a guest room as well as a flower-filled ground-floor sitting area. Antique touches proliferate: here an old parasol in a corner, there a period jewelry box or some rustic kitchen utensils. A fine buffet breakfast (and dinner if requested) is served in a large, galleried dining room that overlooks Sintra's Pena Palace; other rooms have distant views of the hills and coast. The outdoor pool, jacuzzi, and terrace form part of the landscaped gardens, and from the grounds you can walk to the gardens at Monserrate or the Capuchos convent. *Quinta das Sequóias, Apartado 4, 2710 Sintra, tel. and fax 01/923–0342. 6 rooms with bath. Facilities: bar, evening meals on request, pool, Jacuzzi, gardens, billiard table, videos, parking. AE, DC, MC, V. $$–$$$*

*Lodging* **Quinta da Capela.** A member of Turismo de Habitação, this 16th-century manor home built by the Dukes of Cadaval presents superb rooms adorned with rugs and period furniture; just one comes without a private bathroom. There is also a lovely garden, an old chapel on the grounds, and a pool. The manor house is located just 3 kilometers (2 miles) west of Sintra, off the road to Colares. *Estrada de Monserrate, 2710 Sintra, tel. 01/929–0170. 7 rooms, 6 with bath, 2 apartments. Facilities: kitchen, garden, pool, gym, sauna, parking. MC. Closed Nov.–Feb. $$$*

**Tivoli Sintra.** The ultramodern Tivoli (a member of the chain of hotels in Lisbon by the same name) is right in the middle of town, very close to the National Palace. Comfortable chairs in its lounge and many of the smart rooms have excellent views of the local valley, and there's a welcoming restaurant, the Monserrate. Given the hotel's marvelous location, room rates are reasonable, especially in the winter when they're reduced by at least 15%. Overall this is one of the region's best-value choices. *Praça da República, 2710, tel. 01/923–3505, fax 01/923–1572. 75 rooms with bath. Facilities: restaurant, bar, garage. AE, DC, MC, V. $$–$$$*

**Hotel Central.** Dating from the turn of the century and exuding a certain faded charm, the Central appeals despite its lack of facilities. This was once *the* hotel in Sintra, and the interior reflects those bygone days: a smell of polished wood prevails, and Portuguese tiles and solid old furniture are everywhere. Its location opposite the National Palace is prime (although rooms that face the square can be noisy). Amenities include a large terrace with tables facing the palace and a simple Portuguese restaurant, whose wooden floors gleam and whose leaded picture windows look out over the back of town. Rooms here are inexpensive in winter. *Praça da República 35, 2710, tel. 01/923–0963. 14 rooms, 9 with bath. Facilities: restaurant, bar. AE, DC, MC, V. $$*

# The Arts and Nightlife

## The Arts

**Cascais**  The **Cascais music festival,** held every July and August, lures well-known orchestras and soloists to the town. Cascais also holds an annual summer **jazz festival** in July.

There are **three cinemas** in Cascais that present first-release films in English: two in the Pão d'Açucar shopping center on Estrada Marginal near the train station and one on Rua 25 de Abril.

**Estoril**  **Estoril Casino** (Parque do Estoril, tel. 01/468–4521) has regularly changing art exhibitions, a movie theater showing the latest films, and year-round theatrical and ballet performances. Call for details about performances and tickets, or ask at Estoril's tourist office (*see* Important Numbers and Addresses, *above*).

**Queluz**  Every summer the **Noites de Queluz** (Queluz Nights) is held in the palace gardens. Characteristic of the 18th century, performances reflect the music and costumes popular when the palace was built. For more information, contact the Sintra Tourist Board (*see* Important Numbers and Addresses, *above*).

**Setúbal Peninsula**  The **Feira de Santiago** takes place in Setúbal at the end of July and includes various folkloric events, a fair with rides and food stalls, and other entertainment.

Setúbal has two cinemas: the **Centro Comércial Jumbo** (tel. 065/591590), and **Cinema Charlot** (Rua Dr. A. M. Gamito 9–11, tel. 065/36759). In September Palmela sees the **Festa das Vindimas** (Grape Harvest Festival), with a symbolic treading of the grapes and a blessing of the harvest. Dancing, fireworks, wine tastings, and other celebrations accompany the festival.

Sesimbra celebrates saints' days and other religious holidays throughout the year, with particularly large festivals in June, July, and September. Some of the dates change every year, so contact the local tourist office for more information.

**Sintra** The excellent **Sintra Festival** runs from June through September every year, and features piano recitals, operas, and ballet performances that take place in the town's palaces, churches, and parks. Performances in the gardens of the Palácio de Seteais are especially popular. The **Sintra Tourist Board Cultural Department** (Praça da República 23, tel. 01/923–5079) can provide more details and an events brochure.

Besides its twice-monthly country fairs, the village of São Pedro de Sintra, hosts the large, annual **Festa de São Pedro** on June 29 (St. Peter's Day), with all of the riotous hullabaloo that the Portuguese inject into their religious festivities.

## Nightlife

Not surprisingly, the resorts on the Estoril coast are responsible for most of the region's nightlife. Generally the towns have a plethora of bars, and most have at least one disco. (You may find, however, that the dance clubs are a bit tame compared to those in Lisbon.)

**Cascais** Cascais, a town that attracts a young crowd, is the best bet for a long night's entertainment, with plenty of bars and discos on and around the central, pedestrian Rua Frederico Arouca that attract young people. For drinks, try the English-style pub, the **John Bull** (Praça Costa Pinto 32, tel. 01/483–3319) and the trendy **Belbuerguer** (Trav. Visconde da Luz 20, tel. 01/483–2312). For discos go to **Van Gogo** (Travessa de Alfarrobeira 9, tel. 01/483–3378), a converted fisherman's house that's open daily 11 PM–4 AM; or **Coconuts** (Estrada de Guincho, tel. 01/484–4109), with its outdoor bar, located just out of town near the Estalagem do Farol.

To hear fado, try one of these clubs: **Arreda** (Rua Alexandre Herculano 3, tel. 01/483–3864), or **Pigalo** (Trav. Frederico Arouca, tel. 01/483–2802).

**Estoril** The **Casino** (Parque do Estoril, tel. 01/468–4521. Open 3 PM–3 AM) is the obvious place for nightlife. Quite apart from the gaming tables and slot machines, there's a nightclub with floor shows, and a restaurant. Don't forget to take your passport to prove your age if you intend to gamble. Tour companies organize evening excursions to the Casino, which include dinner and a show (*see* Guided Tours in Essential Information, *above*).

Nightlife elsewhere in Estoril is based around several well-known bars and clubs. Two to try are: **Frolic** (Parque do Estoril, tel. 01/468–1219), in front of the casino, next to the café-restaurant of the same name, which attracts an older, sophisticated clientele; and **Forte Velho** (Av. Marginal, in São João do Estoril, tel. 01/468–1337), an old fort on the edge of town that's been converted into a disco. Both are open 10 PM–3 AM.

# 5 Évora and Central Portugal

*By Dennis Jaffe*

*An American who has lived in Europe since 1975, Dennis Jaffe with his wife, Tina, has written* Biking Through Europe *and the* Camper's Companions to Northern and Southern Europe. *He has also written extensively about Portugal, Turkey, Germany, and Switzerland.*

The region we call central Portugal encompasses three provinces: the Alentejo, the Estremadura, and the Ribatejo, each with its own geography, traditions, and character.

The **Alentejo**, which means "the land beyond the Rio Tejo (River Tagus)," in Portuguese, is a vast, sparsely populated region of heath and rolling hills punctuated with stands of cork and olive trees. It is the country's largest province, stretching from the rugged west coast beaches all the way east to Spain and from the Tejo in the north to the low mountains on the border of the Algarve, Portugal's southernmost province. Over the centuries this pastoral countryside has been the scene of innumerable battles: between Romans and Visigoths, Moors and Christians, Portuguese and Spaniards, Portuguese and French, and finally (in the 1830s) between rival Portuguese factions in a civil war. Few hilltops in the region are without at least a trace of a castle or fortress.

One of the Alentejo's major industries is cork, of which Portugal is the world's largest producer. This is not, however, an industry for people in a hurry. It takes two decades before the trees can be harvested, and they may be carefully stripped only once every nine years. The numbers painted on the trees indicate the year of the last harvest. Exhibits at several regional museums chronicle this delicate process and display associated tools and handicrafts.

The undulating fields of wheat and barley surrounding Beja and Évora, the rice paddies of Alcácer do Sal, and the vineyards of Borba and Reguengos are representative of this rural province. Traditions here are strong. Herdsmen tending flocks of sheep and goats wear the *pelico* (a traditional sheepskin vest), and women in the fields wear broad-brim hats over kerchiefs and colorful, patterned dresses over trousers. Dwellings are dazzling white; more elegant houses have wrought-iron balconies and grillwork. The windows and doors of modest cottages and hilltop country *montes* (farmhouses) are trimmed with blue or yellow, and colorful flowers abound. The best time to visit the Alentejo is spring, when temperatures are pleasant and the fields are carpeted with wildflowers. Summer can be brutal, with the mercury frequently topping 100°F. The Portuguese say, "In the Alentejo there is no shade but what comes from the sky."

The **Estremadura** occupies a narrow stretch of land along the coast, extending north from Lisbon to include the onetime royal residence of Leiria, 119 kilometers (73 miles) from the capital city. Closely tied to the sea, which at no point in the province is more than a few miles away, the region is known for its fine beaches, coastal pine forests, and picturesque fishing villages. Some of these—such as Nazaré—have evolved, for better or worse, into popular international resorts. Fruits and vegetables grow in fertile coastal valleys and livestock contentedly graze in rich pastures, but the Estremadura hasn't always been so peaceful. During the Wars of Reconquest, which raged from the 8th to the 13th centuries, it was the scene of a series of bloody encounters between Christians and Moors. In the aftermath of the wars Portuguese sovereignty was secured with the rout of the Spanish at Aljubarrota, in 1385, and the turning back of Napoleon's forces in 1810, at Torres Vedras. The bloodshed left a positive legacy for today's traveler: Alcobaça and Batalha, masterpieces of religious architecture, were built to commemorate Portuguese victories.

The **Ribatejo** developed along both sides of the Tejo, and it is this waterway, born in the distant mountains of Spain, that has shaped and sustained the province that carries its name. In the north the inhabitants tend small groves of olive and fig trees, and the peaceful, sparsely populated landscape has changed little since the Romans settled.

Over the centuries Romans, Visigoths, Moors, and Christians built and rebuilt various castles and fortifications to protect the strategic Tejo. Some fine examples may be seen along the river at Belver, Abrantes, and Almourol. Tomar, spanning the banks of the Nabão (a tributary of the Tejo) is dominated by the hilltop Convent of Christ, an extraordinary example of medieval architecture built in the 12th century by the Knights Templar. In the brush-covered hills at the western edge of the province lies Fátima, one of Christendom's most important pilgrimage sites. As it flows south approaching Lisbon, the river expands, often overflowing its banks during the winter rains, and the landscape changes to one of rich meadows and pastures and broad, alluvial plains, where rice and other cereals grow in abundance.

The Ribatejans are said to be more reserved than their fellow Portuguese; that is, until they step into the arena to test their mettle against a ton or so of charging bull. The Ribatejo is bullfight country, the heartland of one of Portugal's richest and most colorful traditions. On the vast plains along the east bank of the Tejo, you'll encounter men on horseback carrying long wooden prods and often wearing the traditional waistcoats and stocking caps of their trade. These are *campinos*, the Portuguese "cowboys" who tend the herds of bulls and horses bred and trained for arenas throughout the country.

# Essential Information

## Important Addresses and Numbers

**Tourist Information** The regional tourist office for Évora is the **Região de Turismo de Évora** (Rua 24 de Julho, 1, tel. 066/742534.)

*Estremadura* In the Estremadura the principal tourist offices are in **Alcobaça** (Praça 25 de Abril, tel. 062/42377), **Batalha** (Largo Paulo VI, tel. 044/96180), **Caldas da Rainha** (Rua Eng. Duarte Pacheco, tel. 062/831003), **Ericeira** (Rua Eduardo Burnay 33, tel. 061/63122), **Leiria** (Jardim Lúis de Camões, tel. 044/823773), **Lourinhã** (Praia da Areia Branca, tel. 061/422167), **Mafra** (Av. 25 de Abril, tel. 061/812023), **Nazaré** (Av. Vieira Guimarães, tel. 062/561194), **Óbidos** (Rua Direta,tel.062/959231), **Peniche** (Rua Alex. Herculano, tel. 062/789571), **Pombal** (Largo da Cardal, tel. 036/23230), **Torres Vedras** (Rua 9 de Abril, tel. 061/314094), and **Vila Franca de Xira** (Rua Dr. Manuel de Arriagá 24, tel. 063/26043).

*Lower Alentejo* In the Lower Alentejo there are tourist offices in **Beja** (Praça da República 12, tel. 084/321369), **Moura** (Largo Santa Clara, tel. 085/22301), **Odemira** (Trav. do Botequim 6, tel. 083/ 22247), **Serpa** (Largo D. Jorge de Melo 2–3, tel. 084/90335), and **Sines** (Jardim das Descobertas, tel. 069/634472).

*Ribatejo* In the Ribatejo you will find tourist offices in **Abrantes** (Largo da Feira, tel. 041/22555), **Constância** (Câmera Municipal, tel. 049/99205), **Fátima** (Av. D. Correia da Silva, tel. 049/531139), **Santerém** (Rua Capelo e Ivens 63, tel. 043/23140), **Tomar** (Rua Serpa Pinto 1, tel. 049/323113), and **Torres Novas** (Largo do Paço, tel. 049/812910).

*Upper Alentejo* For the Upper Alentejo the regional office is the **Região de Turismo de São Mamede** (Estrada de Santana 25, 7300 Portalegre, tel. 045/

21815). There are local offices in **Alcácer do Sal** (Solar dos Salemas, tel. 065/622603), **Alter do Chão** (Câmera Municipal, tel. 045/62454), **Arronches** (Câmera Municipal, tel. 045/52210), **Campo Maior** (Rua Mayor Talaya, tel. 068/686104), **Castelo de Vide** (Rua Bartolomeu A. da Santa 81/3, tel. 045/91361), **Elvas** (Praça da República, tel. 068/622236), **Évora** (Praça do Giraldo 73, tel. 066/22671), **Marvão** (Rua Dr. Matos Magalhães, tel. 045/93226), **Monforte** (Praça da República, tel. 045/53448), and **Portalegre** (Rua de Elvas, tel. 045/21815).

**Emergencies** For emergencies in central Portugal, as well as throughout the country, dial **115.**

*Hospitals* The following cities have hospitals with emergency rooms, and their approaches are marked HOSPITAL; the emergency room is marked URGÊNCIAS. Beja (Hospital Distrital, Rua Dr. António F C Lima, tel. 084/322133), Caldas da Rainha (Hospital Distrital, Parque Rainha Dona Leonor, tel. 062/832133), Évora (Hospital Distrital, Largo Sr. Pobreza, tel. 066/22132), Leiria (Hospital Distrital, Largo D. Mel. Aguiar, tel. 044/812255), Tomar (Hospital Distrital, Av. Dr. Candido Madueira, tel. 049/321100).

*Late-Night Pharmacies* All sizable towns have at least one pharmacy open weekends, holidays, and after normal store hours. Local newspapers usually keep a schedule, and notices are posted on the door of every pharmacy.

**Travel Agencies** Many travel agencies in the region are small, with limited services, and no English spoken. The following agencies have English-speaking personnel and a full range of services. In Évora, **RN Tours** (Rua República 131, tel. 066/24254); in Leiria, **Viajes Melia** (Av. Cidade Maringá 25, tel. 044/32286).

## Arriving and Departing by Plane

The Estremadura and Ribatejo are best served by Lisbon's international airport. Évora and the Alentejo can be conveniently reached either from Lisbon or Faro. Évora is 160 kilometers (100 miles) from Lisbon and 245 kilometers (147 miles) from Faro.

**Airports and Airlines** For flight information concerning Lisbon, *see* Chapter 3; for information about Faro's airport, *see* Chapter 6.

## Arriving and Departing by Car, Train, and Bus

**By Car** The Estremadura and the Ribatejo can be reached easily from Lisbon, since both provinces begin as extensions of the city's northern suburbs. From Oporto there is easy access via the A1 tollway.

Three main roads connect the Alentejo with Spain: The N521 runs 105 kilometers (64 miles) from Caceres, Spain, to the Portuguese border near Portalegre; the N4 covers the 15 kilometers (9 miles) between Elvas and the Spanish city of Badajoz; and to the south the N433 runs from Seville, Spain, to Beja, 225 kilometers (136 miles) away. The Alentejo can also be easily reached from the Algarve, its southern neighbor. The smoothest of the main routes is the IP-1/N264, which extends north from Albufeira.

**By Train** The train station for Marvão is in the town of Beira 10 kilometers (6 miles) away and is served by the *Lusitania Express* and the *Lúis de Camões* which run daily between Lisbon (Santa Apolónia Station) and Madrid. The *Lúis de Camões* leaves Lisbon's Santa Apolonia Station at 11:55 AM and arrives at Madrid's Atocha Station at 8:06PM. The *Lusitania Express* departs Lisbon at 10:25 PM and arrives in

Madrid's Chamartin Station at 8:40 the following morning. First-class seats cost 8,975$00. Second-class seats cost 5,140$00. Youth (under 26) seats cost 5,140$00. The *Sud Express*, linking Paris with Lisbon (Santa Apolónia Station)—via the Spanish cities of Burgos and Salamanca—stops at Pombal and Fátima. It leaves Lisbon daily at 5:05PM and arrives at Paris's Austerlitz Station at 7 PM the following day. First-class costs 29,580$00; second-class costs 17,800$00. Those under 27 pay 16,410$00. Sleepers (couchettes) cost 2,075$00 extra. Although the schedule reads "Fátima," the actual station is some 25 kilometers (15 miles) away, but a bus—on a coordinated schedule—runs between the town and the station.

**By Bus** **Euroline** has regular bus service between Lisbon and Spain's Costa del Sol, Seville, Madrid, and Barcelona. Euroline coaches also stop in the Alentejo towns of Elvas and Estremoz. Euroline buses from France and northern Europe stop in Pombal, Leiria, Abrantes, and Santarém. For information and reservations in Lisbon contact a travel agent or: **Intercentro Eurolines** (Rua Eng. Viera da Silva, 8-E, tel. 01/547300).

## Getting Around

**By Car** A car is by far the most efficient way to tour this region, especially in the Alentejo, where distances are great and bus and train service infrequent. Driving will give you access to many out-of-the-way beaches and villages. The roads are generally good and traffic is light, except for weekend congestion along the coast. There are no confusing big cities in which to get lost, although parking can be a major problem in some of the towns. The best map for motorists, both in scale and ease of reading, is the Michelin map #440, Portugal–Madeira, available at bookshops throughout Portugal; in the United States go to any major book shop or contact **Michelin Travel Publications** (1 Parkway S, Greenville, SC 29615, tel. 803/458-6330).

*Car Rental* Major car-rental agencies are located in Évora, Beja, Leiria and Nazaré.

**By Train** Travel by train within central Portugal, and particularly in the vast Alentejo, is not for people in a great hurry. Service to many of the more remote destinations is infrequent—and in some cases nonexistent. Even major tourist attractions such as Fátima, Nazaré, and Mafra have no direct rail links.

The Alentejo towns of Alcácer do Sal, Évora, and Beja are connected with Lisbon (Terreiro do Paço) by several trains daily. There is frequent service on the Lisbon– (Santa Apolónia Station) Oporto line to Santarém. Torres Vedras, Caldas da Rainha, and Leiria, in the western part of the region, are served from Lisbon's Rossío Station.

**By Bus** There are few, if any, places in this region that are not served by at least one bus daily. Express coaches run by several regional bus lines travel regularly between Lisbon and the larger towns such as Évora, Santarém, Leiria, and Abrantes. If you have the time and patience, bus travel, which offers an opportunity to come in close contact with locals, can be a rewarding and inexpensive way to get around. The main bus terminal in Lisbon is on Avenida Casal Ribeira 18. For schedules call tel. 01/545439.

## Guided Tours

**General Interest** Walking tours of Évora and bus tours of the Alentejo are available from **Mendes and Murteira** (Rua Corredoura 8, 7000 Évora, tel. 066/23616).

Few regularly scheduled sightseeing tours originate within the region but Évora, Nazaré, Óbidos, Tomar, Mafra, and the other major attractions are covered by a wide selection of one-day tours from Lisbon. For information contact **RN Tours** (Av. Fontes Pereira de Melo 12–14, tel. 01/356–0015) or **Cityrama** (Av. Praia da Vitoria 12–B, tel. 01/355–8567).

**Special Interest** Boat trips on the São Cristovão, along the Rio Zêzere, depart daily in summer from the dam at Castelo de Bode and include lunch. The 4½-hour cruise costs 5,000$00. For reservations and information in Tomar, contact Hotel dos Templários (Largo Candido dos Reis 1, 2300 Tomar, tel. 049/312121) or the Estalagem Lago Azul (Estrada Nacional 378, Castanheira, 2240 Ferreira do Zêzere, tel. 049/361445).

**Frescuras** (Estrada da Luz 197, 1600 Lisbon, tel. 01/726–2183) offers four-wheel-drive tours of the back roads and remote villages of the Alentejo, the west-coast beaches and the marshlands, and the bull-breeding areas of the Ribatejo. Hot-air balloon flights and four-wheel drives through the Alentejo are offered by **Turibalão Lda.** (Rua Miguel Bombarda 44 r/c, 7000 Évora, tel. 066/26323). **Cavalgada** (Apartado 68, 7050 Montemar O Novo, tel. 066/82071) sponsors half-, full-, and two-day horseback trips. **Promoções e Idéias Turisticas** (PIT: Rua Fredrico Arouca, 72, 2750 Cascais, tel. 01/484–4207, fax 01/484–2901) will arrange custom tours with overnight accommodations in historic manor houses.

# Exploring Évora and Central Portugal

## Orientation

For convenience the following tours are designed so that each falls easily within the confines of one of the three provinces: the Alentejo, the Estremadura, or the Ribatejo. However, these itineraries are not carved in stone: At times you may be tempted to cross from one tour to another or to link up with tours in another chapter. By all means do so!

Our first tour explores the rich architectural treasures of Évora, the capital of the Alentejo and our second, the area around Évora. We then cover the upper Alentejo, heading northeast across the rolling hills and past the fortresses of Estremoz and Elvas to the Alentejo's mountain range, the Serra de São Mamede, along the Spanish border.

The lower Alentejo—which includes the rice paddies and salt marshes around Alcácer do Sal and the rugged west-coast beaches—is the subject of our fourth tour. The last two circuits, through the Estremadura and Ribatejo, suggest visits to some of Portugal's most outstanding monuments and architectural treasures, including Mafra, Alcobaça, Óbidos, Tomar, and Batalha. Featured in the latter tour are such diverse places as the bull-fighting centers of Vila

Franca de Xira and Santarém, the shrine at Fátima, and the fishing port of Nazaré.

## Highlights for First-Time Visitors

Castle of Almourol (*see* Tour 6)
Cathedral of Évora (*see* Tour 1)
Convent of Christ in Tomar (*see* Tour 6)
Convent of the Conception in Beja (*see* Tour 4)
Fortified town of Marvão (*see* Tour 3)
Fortified town of Monsaraz (*see* Tour 3)
Monastery at Alcobaça (*see* Tour 5)
Monastery at Batalha (*see* Tour 5)
Monastery at Mafra (*see* Tour 5)

## Tour 1: Évora

*Numbers in the margin correspond to points of interest on the Central Portugal and Évora maps.*

Shepherds and farmers in traditional garb, with wizened faces bearing markings of a lifetime in the baking Alentejo sun, stand about Giraldo square; a group of pretty young college girls dressed in jeans and T-shirts chat animatedly at a sidewalk café; a local businessman in coat and tie purposefully hurries by; and clusters of tourists, the ubiquitous cameras in hand, capture the historic monuments on film. This is all part of a typical summer's day in downtown
❶ **Évora,** the flourishing capital of the rich agricultural Alentejo province, a university center, and one of the world's great architectural treasures (so classified by UNESCO in 1986).

Atop a small hill in the heart of the cork-, olive-, and grain-producing region, Évora—with its astonishing variety of inspiring architecture—stands out from provincial farm towns the world over; the entire inner city is a monument.

Although the region was inhabited some 4,000 years ago—as attested to by the dolmens and phallic menhirs in the surrounding countryside—it was during the Roman epoch that the town called "Liberalitas Julia" in the province of Lusitania first achieved importance. A large part of present-day Évora is built upon Roman foundations, of which the "Temple of Diana," with its graceful Corinthian columns, is the most conspicuous reminder.

The Moors were another group that made a great historical impact on the area. They arrived in 715 and remained more than 450 years. They were driven out in 1166, thanks in part to a clever ruse perpetrated by Geraldo Sem Pavor (Gerald the Fearless), the Portuguese counterpart to El Cid. Geraldo was able to trick Évora's Moorish ruler into leaving unguarded a strategic watchtower that protected one of the entrances to the town. With a small force, Geraldo took control of the tower, which prompted the main body of Moorish troops to leave its post at the principal entrance to the city, in an attempt to regain control of the watchtower. With the main entrance now undefended, the bulk of Geraldo's forces was able to storm the city unopposed.

Toward the end of the 12th century, Évora's fortunes increased, as the town became the favored location for the courts of the Burgundy and Avis dynasties; situated less than 164 kilometers (100 miles) from Lisbon, it attracted many of the great minds and creative talents of Renaissance Portugal. Gil Vicente, the founder of Portuguese theater; the sculptor Nicolas Chanterene; and Gregorio Lopes, the painter known for his renderings of court life, were some of the more prominent residents of the time. This concentration of royal wealth and Renaissance creativity superimposed upon the existing Moorish town was instrumental in the development of the delicate Manueline-Mudejar architectural style. You can see fine examples of this in the graceful lines of the Palace of Dom Manuel and the turreted São Bras Hermitage.

Évora is, above all, a town for walking. Wherever you glance as you stroll the maze of narrow streets and alleys of the old town, amidst arches and whitewashed houses, you'll come face to face with reminders of the town's rich architectural and cultural heritage.

**2** Begin your walking tour in the **Praça do Giraldo,** the bustling, arcade-lined square in the center of the old town named after the city's liberator, Gerald the Fearless. During Caesar's time the square, marked by a large arch, was the Roman forum; in 1571 the arch was destroyed to make room for the fountain across from the entrance to the church. The graceful, flattened sphere made of white Estremoz marble was designed and executed by the Renaissance architect Afonso Alvares.

**3** Note the striking white Renaissance facade of the **Igreja de St. Antão,** which stands at the top of the square. A medieval hermitage of the Templar Knights was razed in 1553 to make way for the present church, which, with its massive round pillars and soaring vaulted ceilings, is the finest example of the German style *Hallenkirche* to be found in the Alentejo. The marble altar in bas-relief is a holdover from the primitive hermitage.

**Time Out** The **Café Arcadia,** opposite the fountain on the Praça do Giraldo, is an Évora institution. The large hall, divided into snack bar and restaurant sections, is decorated with photos of the big bands that played here in the 40s. Outside tables set on the square are just the place from which to watch Évora on parade.

From the square head up the narrow, cobblestoned Rua 5 de Outubro. This pedestrian thoroughfare lined with shops, hanging lanterns, and whitewashed houses with wrought-iron balconies is one of the town's most attractive streets. The massive twin towers **4** and the battlement-ringed walls give the Sé (cathedral) a fortress-like appearance, a type of construction also seen in the Lisbon and Coimbra cathedrals. The Se, one of Portugal's most striking architectural achievements, is a transitional Gothic-style building constructed in 1186 from huge granite blocks. It has been enhanced over the centuries with an octagonal, turreted dome above the transept, a blue tiled spire atop the north tower, a number of fine Manueline windows, and several Gothic rose windows. At the entrance the Gothic arches are supported by marble columns bearing delicately sculpted 14th-century statues of the Apostles. With the exception of a fine baroque chapel, the granite interior is somber. The cloister, a 14th-century Gothic addition with Mudejar vestiges, is one of the finest of its genre in the country. Statues of the Evangelists decorate the four corners. Housed in the towers and chapter room are the Treasury and Museum of Sacred Art. Of particular interest is a 13th-century ivory triptych, The Virgin of Paradise, whose body opens up to show exquisitely carved scenes of her life and whose head is a 16th-century wooden replacement, strangely out of proportion. *Admission to museum: 250$00. Open Tues.–Sun. 9–noon and 2–5. Closed Mon. and holidays.*

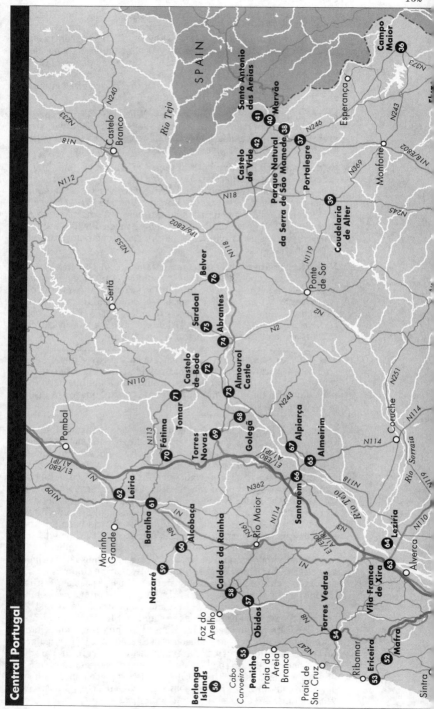

**Central Portugal**

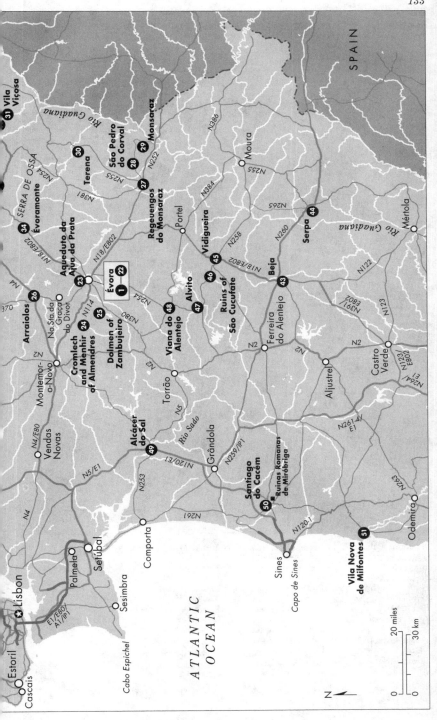

# Évora

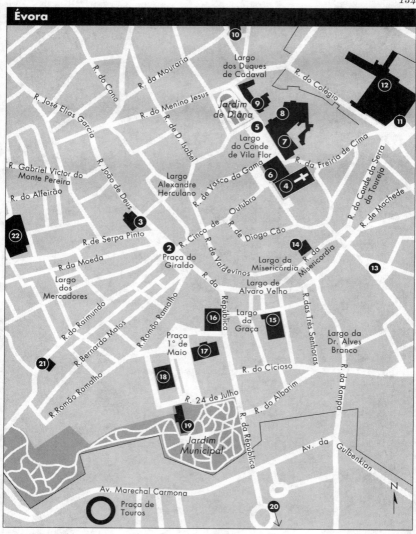

Biblioteca Pública, **7**
Ermida de São Bras, **20**
Igreja a Nossa Senhora da Graça, **15**
Igreja de Espirito Santo, **11**
Igreja de Misericordia, **14**
Igreja de Santa Clara, **22**
Igreja de Santo Antão, **3**

Ingreja de São Francisco, **17**
Igreja de São Mamede, **10**
Igreja e Convento dos Lóios, **8**
Largo da Porto de Moura, **13**
Municipal Market, **18**
Museu de Artes Decorativas, **21**

Museu do Artesanato, **16**
Museu Regional de Évora, **6**
Palácio de Dom Manuel, **19**
Palácio dos Duques de Cadaval, **9**
Praça do Giraldo, **2**
Sé, **4**
Templo Romano, **5**
Universidade de Évora, **12**

Leave the cathedral and turn right. After a few steps the view opens onto a large plaza dominated by the well-preserved ruins of the **❺ Templo Romano,** or Roman temple. The edifice, considered one of the finest of its kind on the Iberian peninsula, makes use of the Corinthian style, and was built during the second and third centuries. Although it has been referred to as the Temple of Diana, historians are uncertain as to which of the many Roman deities it was actually dedicated. The temple, largely destroyed during the invasions of the barbarian tribes in the early 5th century, has been used at various times as a fortification and, in the 14th century as a municipal slaughterhouse. It was uncovered and restored to its present state just over 100 years ago.

The stately late-17th-century baroque building across from the temple was once a palace that accommodated bishops but is now home to **❻** the **Museu Regional de Évora** (Museum of Évora). It contains a rich collection of sculpture and paintings as well as a number of interesting archaeological and architectural artifacts. The first-floor galleries arranged around a pleasant garden include several excellent carved pillars and a fine Manueline doorway. Among the early Portuguese paintings on display in the upstairs gallery are works attributed to the 16th- century Mestre de Sardoal. *Largo do Conde de Vila Flor, no phone. Admission: 300$00. Open Tues.–Sun. 10–12 and 2–5. Closed Mon. and holidays.*

Diagonally across the square from the museum, in the former town **❼** hall, is the **Biblioteca Pública** (Municipal Library), with an outstanding collection of rare books and manuscripts. *Open Mon.–Sat. 9–1 and 2–6.*

Around the corner from the library and adjacent to the Pousada dos **❽** Lóios (*see* Dining and Lodging, *below*) is the **Igreja e Convento dos Lóios** (Church and Convent of Lóios). To enter the church go down several steps and through a portal framed by a series of fan-shaped arches in the flamboyant Gothic style. The sanctuary, dedicated to St. John the Evangelist, was founded in the 15th century by the Venetian-based Lóios Order. Its interior walls are covered with 18th-century heroic *azulejo* panels created by Oliveira Bernardes, the foremost master of this unique Portuguese art form. The blue-and-white tiles depict scenes from the life of the church's founder, Rodrigo de Melo, who, along with members of his family, is buried here. The bas- relief marble tombstones at the foot of the high altar are the only ones of their kind in Portugal. Note the two metal hatches on either side of the main aisle: One covers an ancient cistern, which belonged to the Moorish castle that predated the church (an underground spring still supplies the cistern with potable water), and beneath the other hatch lie the neatly stacked bones of hundreds of monks, which have been collected over the centuries. This bizarre ossuary was uncovered in 1958 during restoration work. Enhanced by the 16th-century Renaissance gallery, the cloister is now an integral part of the Pousada dos Lóios. *Largo Conde de Vila Flor. Admission: 350$00. Open Tues.–Sun. 10–12:30 and 2–5. Closed Mon. and holidays.*

As you leave the church, just to your right will be two stone towers with pointed battlements. A part of a medieval castle that once pro **❾** tected the town, these towers were incorporated into the **Palacío dos Duques do Cadaval** (Palace of the Dukes of Cadaval), a former residence of Kings João I and João IV. A small ground-floor gallery contains historic documents, paintings, and the unusual Flemish-style bronze tomb of Rui de Sousa, a signatory of the Treaty of Tordesilhas. In 1494 the treaty divided the world into two spheres of influence: Spanish and Portuguese. Today the palace is being used by the city road department. *Admission, opening times, and ticket for the gallery are the same as those for the Lóios Church.*

Opposite the Roman temple a restful, tree-lined park looks out over an aqueduct and the plains. From this park—in one sweeping glance that takes in the temple, the spires of the Gothic cathedral, the Church of Lóios, and the 20th-century pousada housed in the convent—you can span nearly two thousand years of Portuguese history.

**Time Out** A snack bar at the corner of the park that overlooks the temple is a great spot to sit and reflect upon the architectural marvels spread out before you.

Once you're refreshed and suitably inspired, go down the hill past the palace, turn right at the bottom, and continue along the Rua Duques de Cadaval. The small church to your left is the **Igreja de São Mamede** (Church of St. Mamede), which contains a vaulted ceiling decorated with baroque frescoes. Note the fine azulejos that cover the wall of the nave. On the east wall is a marble bust of the Renaissance humanist Andre de Resendeby, created by João Cuteliero, a well-known contemporary Portuguese sculptor.

From the church follow the Rua de Colégio until it converges on the square called the Largo de Colégio. Along the way, to your right, you'll have a good view of the ancient town walls, and in some places, vestiges of the Roman foundations are visible. At the square is the 16th-century **Igreja de Espirito Santo** (Espirito Santo Church), a squat structure with five arches in front that was originally a part of the ancient Évora University. The interior contains some fine azulejos and paintings, including artist Gregorio Lopes's painting of *The Last Supper*.

Take a left turn after you leave the church to get to one of several campuses of **Universidad de Évora.** From 1555 until its closure by the Marquis of Pombal in 1759, this was a Jesuit college; in 1979, after a lapse of more than 200 years, Évora University resumed classes. Although the enrollment is small, the college's presence has given new life and vigor to this ancient city. The large courtyard is flanked on all sides by a series of graceful buildings with double-tier, white-limestone arched galleries in Italian Renaissance style. From the main entrance you'll see the imposing Baroque facade of the gallery, known as the **Sala dos Actos** (Hall of Acts), which is crowned with allegorical figures and coats of arms carved in white marble that was quarried in the region. Lining the gallery's interior are azulejos that represent historical, mythological, and biblical themes.

From the university return to the Largo do Colégio, then take a downhill stroll on Rua do Conde da Serra da Toureja. This is a lovely part of town with whitewashed houses and wrought-iron grillwork. At the **Largo da Porta de Moura**—perhaps Évora's most beautiful square—paired stone towers guard one of the principal entrances to the walled old town. Spires of the cathedral rise above the towers, and in the center of the square is an unusual Renaissance fountain. The large white marble sphere supported by a single column bears a Latin inscription dated 1556; overlooking the fountain is the **Cordovil Mansion** (closed to the public), on whose terrace are several particularly attractive arches decorated in the Manueline-Mudejar style.

Return to the post office near the square, via Rua da Misericórdia. The small church at the end of the road, along Largo da Porta de Moura, is the 16th-century **Igreja de Misericórdia** (Misericordia Church). Go inside to see the large azulejo panels depicting scenes from the life of Christ; the unsigned 18th-century tiles are thought to be the work of the renowned tile-maker António de Oliveira de Bernardes.

Follow the Rua da Misericórdia into the Largo de Alvaro Velho, an inviting square lined with metalsmith shops. Just past the Hotel Planice turn down the Travessa Manuelinho. The **Igreja a Nossa Senhora da Graça** (Church of Our Lady of Grace) is a splendid piece of classical Italian-style architecture. Note the impish figures perched above the portal: According to local legend, these four figures represent the first victims put to death in the Inquisition in Évora in 1543.

Cross the Largo da Graça, and continue to the Rua da República. On your left is the **Museu do Artesanato** (Crafts Museum), whose exhibits include a comprehensive collection of handicrafts from the Alentejo. At press time, the museum was closed for remodeling, but it is expected to reopen in the spring of 1995. *Rua da República, tel. 066/742534. Admission: 200$00. Open Tues.–Sun. 10–12:30 and 2–5. Closed Mon. and holidays.*

The imposing building across from the museum is the **Igreja de São Francisco** (Church of St. Francis). After the cathedral this is the grandest of Évora's churches. Its construction in the early 16th century, on the site of a former Gothic chapel, involved the greatest talents of the day; these included Nicolas Chanterene, Oliver of Ghent, and the Arruda brothers, Francisco and Diogo. The magnificent religious architecture notwithstanding, the bizarre **Casa dos Ossos** (House of the Bones) is the main attraction. The translation of the chilling inscription over the entrance reads: "We bones who are here are waiting for yours." The bones of some 5,000 skeletons dug up from cemeteries in the area line the ceilings and supporting columns. With a decorative flair worthy of Charles Addams. a 16th-century Franciscan monk placed skulls jaw-to- cranium, so they formed arches across the ceiling; and arm and leg bones are neatly stacked to shape the supporting columns. *Admission to the Bones Chapel: 50$00. Open Tues.–Sat. 9–12:30 and 2:30–5; Sun. 10–11:30 and 2:30–5.*

As you walk out of the church across the tiered portico and onto the Praça 1 de Maio, you'll see a large sprawling building, the **municipal market,** across the square. Wander around the stalls crammed with fresh fruits and vegetables and fish and meat to get a good idea of what the Alentejo produces and consumes. Mornings, except for Sunday, the pavement in front of the market overflows with displays of colorful pottery.

The extensive **Jardim Municipal** (Municipal Gardens), across from the market, offer a pleasant respite from the rigors of sightseeing. They are landscaped with a variety of exotic plants and trees from all over the world. At the entrance is the **Palácio de Dom Manuel** (Dom Manuel's Palace). Only a part of the former royal palace remains—restored after a fire in 1916.

The existing wing displays a row of paired, gracefully curved Manueline windows, and on the south side of the building there's a notable arcade of redbrick Mudejar sawtooth arches. Currently used as an art gallery, the palace has witnessed a number of historic events since its construction in the late 15th century. It was here, for instance, in 1497, that Vasco da Gama received his commission to command the fleet that discovered the sea route to India.

**Time Out**  In the Municipal Gardens is a snack bar where you can get sandwiches and drinks. From a park bench or the Victorian gazebo, you'll have a lovely view of the Church of St. Francis.

From the palace you may head south on the Avenida Dr. Barahona to the St. Blaise Chapel (a 15-minute walk), or go on to the Museum of ⑳ Decorative Arts. The **Ermida de São Bras** (St. Blaise Chapel), a curious structure built in the late 15th century, was the first important building in the Alentejo to join Gothic and Moorish elements to form the Gothic-Mudejar style. The fortified church is characterized by massive battlement-topped walls and a series of round towers crowned with steep spires.

To continue the tour, walk through the Municipal Gardens following the line of the ancient fortifications. At the Rua do Raimundo turn right, and continue for several minutes until you see a small church sandwiched between a garage and a car dealership. The church, the ㉑ **Igreja das Mercês**, is now the **Museu de Artes Decorativas** (Museum of Decorative Arts). Inside the late 17th-century building are several good examples of azulejos with scenes from the life of St. Augustine, the patron saint of the founding order of this church. There are also two unusual confessionals concealed behind tile panels. *Rua do Raimundo. tel. 066/22604. Admission: free. Open Tues.–Sun. 10–12:30 and 2–5. Closed Mon. and holidays.*

From the museum, cross the street, turn left, and then right onto the Travessa da Palmeira, a narrow alleyway bordering the old Quinta da Palmeira. Stay on this until it runs into the Rua de Serpa Pinto, then turn right on this busy thoroughfare and you'll come to ㉒ the baroque facade of the **Igreja de Santa Clara** (Santa Clara Church). The interior is adorned with paintings, including a fine rendition on wood of the Procession of Santa Clara by the 16th-century Évora painter Francisco João. Now return to the Praça do Giraldo, along the Rua de Serpa Pinto, or wander along one of the narrow passageways that leads through the old town.

---

**Tour 2: Around Évora**

---

㉓ The graceful arched **Aqueduto da Agua da Prata** (Aqueduct of the Silver Water), which once carried water 18 kilometers (11 miles) to Évora from the springs at Graça do Divor, is best seen along the road to Arraiolos. You can also see a section of it within Évora, along the Rua do Cano in the northwest corner of the city (walk east on Rua do Muro for about 200 yards from the entrance of N114–4, the Arraiolos road). Constructed in 1532 under the patronage of Dom João III, the aqueduct was designed by the famous architect Francisco de Arruda. Extensive parts of the system remain intact and can be seen.

A trip through the countryside surrounding Évora will take you to some of the earliest inhabited sites in Portugal, including the ㉔ **Cromlech** and the **Menhir of Almendres**. Follow N114 toward Montemar-O-Novo, and after 14 kilometers (8½ miles) turn off to Guadalupe, the site of a 17th-century chapel. In Guadalupe, near the grain-storage bins of the Agricultural Cooperative, is the Menhir of Almendres, a massive 8-foot-tall Neolithic stone obelisk. Several hundred yards in the same direction is the Cromlech, some 95 granite monoliths arranged in an oval configuration in the middle of a

large field. From the N380—the road to Alcaçovas—take the turn-
㉕ off to Valverde and the 20-foot-high **Dolmen of Zambujeiro,** the largest of its kind ever discovered on the Iberian peninsula. This
prehistoric monument is typical of those found throughout Neolithic
Europe: Several great stone slabs stand upright, supporting a flat
stone that serves as a roof. These structures were designed as burial
chambers.

㉖ **Arraiolos,** 22 kilometers (13 miles) northwest of Évora and dominated by the ruins of a once-mighty fortress, is a typical hilltop
Alentejo village of whitewashed houses and narrow streets. What
distinguishes Arraiolos is its worldwide reputation as a carpet-pro-
ducing center. In the 16th century, as Portuguese trade with the
East grew, an interest developed in the intricate designs of the carpets from India and Persia, and these patterns served as models for
the earliest hand-embroidered Arraiolos carpets. The colorful rugs
are not mass-produced in factories but are handmade by locals in
their homes and cottages. An authentic Arraiolos rug, made of locally produced wool, has some 44,000 ties per square meter. To discour-
age imitations, in 1992 the town council designed a special blue seal
of authenticity to be affixed to each carpet. There is a permanent exhibition of carpets in the **town hall.** *Admission free. Open weekdays
9–12:30 and 2–5; weekend hours vary, so call the tourist office
(Praça Lima Brito, tel. 066/42105) for information.*

## Tour 3: The Upper Alentejo

From Évora take N18 for 35 kilometers (21 miles) southeast to
㉗ **Reguengos de Monsaraz,** a sleepy little Alentejo town arranged
around a large square. Note the unusual pentagonal bell tower on
the 19th-century Victorian church. Reguengos, in the center of a
large wine-producing region, is also known for its handwoven rugs.

Five kilometers (3 miles) out of Reguengos on the road to Monsaraz
㉘ is the tiny hamlet of **São Pedro do Corval,** one of Portugal's major
centers for inexpensive hand-painted pottery.

Continue on the same route toward the fortified hilltop town of
㉙ **Monsaraz.** Just before the road begins to climb, you'll see an intriguing Moorish-style domed fountain across from the public laundry
area, dated 1723 in Roman numerals. The road now snakes up the
hill to a parking area outside the village walls; no cars except those
of residents are permitted inside. The entire village is a living museum of narrow, stone-surfaced streets lined with ancient white
houses. The town's 150 or so permanent residents (mostly older people) live mainly from tourism, and because they do so graciously and
unobtrusively, Monsaraz has managed to retain its essential character.

Old women clad in black still sit in the doorways of their tiny cottages and chat with neighbors, their ever-present knitting in hand
(as they have in villages all over the country for generations). At the
south end of the walls stand the well-preserved towers of a formidable castle. The view from atop the pentagonal tower sweeps across
the Alentejo plain to the west and to the east over the Rio Guadiana
to Spain. Within the castle perimeter is an unusual arena with
makeshift slate benches at either end of an oval field. Bullfights are
held here several times a year and always in the second week of September (during the festival of Senhora Jesus dos Passos, the village's patron saint).

The small **museum** next to the parish church displays religious artifacts and the original town charter signed by Dom Manuel in 1512. The former tribunal contains an interesting 15th-century fresco, which depicts Christ presiding over figures representing truth and deception. *Admission: 150$00. Open Wed.– Mon. 10–12 and 2–5; closed Tues.*

The area around Monsaraz is dotted with megalithic monuments. The **Menhir of Outeiro,** 3 kilometers (2 miles) north of town is one of the tallest ever discovered. Return to Reguengos, pick up N255, and head north 28 kilometers (17 miles) across the cork- and olive- tree-covered hills to **Terena.** This little jewel of a town, with a charter dating to 1262 and a castle on a hill, is a place where tourists are still a pleasant curiosity. Drive—or better yet, stroll—along the narrow Rua Direita past the white houses, some with Gothic doorways, others with baroque or Renaissance ones. The small, well-preserved castle was one of several built in this area to defend the border with Spain, which lies across the Rio Guadiana, 11 kilometers (7 miles) east.

**Vila Viçosa,** a quiet town with a moated castle, occupies a gentle elevation in the heart of the fertile Borba plain. It has been closely linked with Portuguese royalty since the 15th century, but this association was not always a happy one: In 1483 King João II, seeking to strengthen his grip on the throne, moved to eliminate the second Duke of Bragança, his brother-in- law and most formidable rival, who, from Vila Viçosa, controlled more than 50 cities, castles, and towns. After much intrigue and counter intrigue, the unfortunate Duke was beheaded in the main square of Évora.

Court life in Vila Viçosa flourished in the late 16th and early 17th centuries, when the huge palace constructed by the fourth Duke of Bragança (Jaime) was the scene of great royal feasts, theater performances, and bullfights. This all came to an abrupt end in 1640, when King João IV, the eighth Duke of Bragança and the first Portuguese to occupy the throne after 60 years of Spanish domination, elected to move his court to Lisbon. Thereafter, Vila Viçosa slipped into relative oblivion. In more recent times Portugal's last king, Carlos I, and the young Prince Luís Filipe spent their last night in the palace. The following day, February 1, 1908, in response to a royal decree that mandated exile for "political" crimes, they were assassinated by members of a secret political society while they were crossing Lisbon's Terreiro do Paço in an open carriage.

The **Paço Ducal** (Ducal Palace), still in the hands of the Braganças, draws a great many visitors. Built of locally quarried marble, the main wing extends for some 360 feet and overlooks the expansive Palace Square and the bronze equestrian statue of Dom João IV. The interior of the palace was extensively restored in the 1950s and contains all that you'd expect to find: Azulejos, Arraiolos rugs, frescoed ceilings, priceless collections of silver and gold objects, Chinese vases, Gobelin tapestries, a long dining hall adorned with antlers and other hunting trophies. The enormous kitchen is equipped with spits large enough to accommodate several oxen and enough gleaming copper to keep a small army of servants busy polishing. The apartments where the unfortunate Dom Carlos spent his last night have been maintained as they were. Carlos was quite an accomplished painter—some say a better painter than he was a king—and many of his works (along with private photos of Portugal's last royal family) line the walls of the apartments.

Following the tour of the palace you can visit the adjacent **Museu dos Coches** (Coach Museum), which features a collection of horse-drawn coaches and antique automobiles and is a pleasant postscript to your visit of the palace. However, if you've already seen the coach museum in Lisbon, you can skip this one. Vila Viçosa's is interesting but isn't in the same league. *Admission to palace: 750$00; to museum, 200$00. Open Oct.– May, Tues.–Sun. 9:30–1 and 2–5; June–Sept., Tues.–Sun. 9:30–1 and 2–6; closed Mon. and holidays.*

Located at the north end of the palace square is the **Knot Gate** with its massive stone ropes—an intriguing example of the Manueline style.

**32** Between Vila Viçosa and the town of **Borba** (4 kilometers [2½ miles] on N255) you'll see mountainous dirt-and-rock piles strewn about the countryside. These tailings, evidence of the many local quarries, are the residue of centuries of extracting the high-quality marble. Which explains the generous use of marble throughout the region, even in the most modest of buildings.

The village boasts a pleasant conglomeration of modest white-washed houses, noble mansions, and small churches—all beautifully decorated with marble. Borba's most notable monument is the 18th-century **Fonte das Bicas**, a neoclassical, white-marble fountain built to honor Queen Maria I, known as Maria the Pious, who reigned from 1777 to 1816. Borba is also one of the Alentejo's major wine producers, and the town's vintners have won many national prizes.

**33** **Estremoz**, which lies on the ancient road that connected Lisbon with Mérida, Spain, has been a site of strategic importance since Roman times, and the castle, which overlooks the town, was a crucial one of the Alentejo's many fortresses. Estremoz is most closely associated with the Queen Saint Isabel, though she spent only a short time here. Married to Dom Dinis—a Portuguese king—in 1282, she arrived in 1336 and after a brief stay became ill and died. The luxurious Pousada da Rainha Santa Isabel (*see* Dining and Lodging, *below*), which occupies the castle, was named for her. It was also in Estremoz, in 1367, that the Queen's grandson Pedro, the lover and secret husband of Inês de Castro, died. The Portuguese people loved Queen Saint Isabel, and over the ages have handed down many tales and legends of her humility and charity. A statue in the castle square commemorates her. From atop the castle tower you'll have a magnificent view over the Alentejo plains.

Across from the castle, housed in a 16th-century alms house, is the **Municipal Museum.** Its displays chronicle the development of the region and range from Roman artifacts to contemporary pottery. *Admission: 130$00. Open Tues.–Sun. 9–11:45 and 2–6; closed Mon. and holidays.*

The lower town, a maze of narrow streets and white houses radiates out from the Rossío, a huge, unpaved square. Stands lining it sell the colorful pottery for which Estremoz is so well known. In addition to the multicolored, hand-painted plates, pitchers, and dolls, note the earthenware jugs decorated with bits of local white marble.

**Time Out** There are several refreshment stands and snack bars along the Rossío, but for more substantial fare try the **Café Alentejo.** From this popular 50-year-old café and restaurant, you can watch the goings-on in the square.

The tiny **Rural Museum,** on the opposite side of the Rossío from the Café Alentejo, is chock-full of handmade miniatures depicting various aspects of Alentejo country life. The museum was once a *Casa do Povo* (a sort of Portuguese senior citizens' center), where all the exhibits were originally made. Note that the finely carved bulls' horns are crafted in a fashion similar that of the scrimshaw carvings of New England whalers. *Rossío. Admission: 100$00. Open Oct.–May, Tues.–Sun. 10–1 and 3–5; June–Sept., Tues–Sun. 10–1 and 2–6; closed Mon. and holidays.*

**34** **Évoramonte,** on N18, 17 kilometers (10 miles) southwest of Estremoz, is a medieval town that sits along the western flank of the **Serra da Ossa** at an altitude of 1,550 feet. Drive up to the castle for a spectacular panoramic view that extends as far as the **Serra da Estrela.** The Évoramonte castle, built in Italian-Renaissance style, is distinguished by a massive, round tower at each of its four corners. Also note the heavy Manueline ropes that run, like ribbons on a Christmas package, around the outside of the castle; they're joined together at the entrance with two tidy cement knots. (An interesting gastronomic aside: It was in Évoramonte that the famous *sopa Alentejana* is said to have originated. The convention held here in 1834 to end the civil war between the Liberals and Miguelists took so long to conclude that at the end only stale bread was left to eat—and thus was born the popular Alentejo soup, made with stale bread, garlic, olive oil, coriander, and water.)

**35** Return to Estremoz, and follow N4 38 kilometers (23 miles) to **Elvas,** another of the white, fortified Alentejo towns. Only about 6 kilometers (less than 4 miles) from the Spanish town of Badajoz, Elvas, since its founding, has been an important bastion in warding off attacks from the east. The extensive fortifications, 17th-century Portugal's most formidable, are characterized by a series of walls, moats, and reinforced towers. The enormousness of the complex can be best appreciated by driving around the periphery of the town. Another distinguishing landmark, the 8-kilometer (5-mile) **Amoreira Aqueduct**—which took more than a century to build —is still in use today. It was started in 1498 under the direction of one of the era's great architects, Francisco de Arruda—who also designed the Aqueduto da Agua da Prata (*see above*)—but not until 1622 did the first drops of water flow into the town fountain.

The former **Gothic Cathedral,** within the town walls, is worth a visit, if for no other reason than to see the 16th-century Manueline refurbishment designed by Francisco de Arruda. The blue and yellow azulejos lining the interior walls were added in the 17th century. From the Cathedral, which sits at the head of the Praça da República, walk up the hill past a pillory and two stone towers (spanned by a graceful Moorish loggia) to the castle. At the battlements you'll have a sweeping view of the town and its fortifications. *Praça da República. Admission: Open Fri.–Wed. 9:30–12:30 and 2:30–5:30; closed Thurs.*

**36** From Elvas head north 19 kilometers (11½ miles) on N373 to **Campo Maior,** and you'll traverse rows of gentle hills covered with the Alentejo's ubiquitous cork and olive trees. This is a quiet, sparsely populated corner of the country where little has changed over the years. You may notice the smell of roasting coffee lingering in the air: It isn't coming from a nearby café but from the several coffee-roasting plants in the area. Campo Maior is the center of Portugal's coffee industry.

Try to make it to this town during the first week of September, when nearly 100 streets and squares are covered with a rainbow-colored mantle of paper flowers and decorations. The decorations for each neighborhood are a closely held secret for months as the women nimbly assemble the paper flowers and the men construct the wooden framing. When the festival opens, all is revealed in a blaze of color and festivity. Check with the local or regional tourist office for exact dates.

At the top of the hill is a castle that was reconstructed after a disastrous explosion in 1732. As you walk around the fortifications, you'll notice some tiny whitewashed dwellings with laundry fluttering about like flags in the breeze. The little buildings are the old army barracks, the only part of the military complex that is still occupied. Before leaving Campo Maior, take time to stroll through the lower part of town, where the narrow streets are lined with many fine examples of wrought-iron grilles and balconies, giving the town a Spanish appearance.

**37** Take N371/N246 to **Portalegre,** the gateway to the Alentejo's most mountainous region, where the parched plains of the south give way to a greener, more inviting landscape. The town of Portalegre, which sits at the foot of the Serra de São Mamede, lacks the charm of the whitewashed hamlets in the south of the province but has long been noted for the quality of its tapestries. Near the town center, on the second floor of an unmarked, dilapidated Jesuit monastery (Rua Guilherme Gomes Fernandes 26) is a tapestry factory you can tour. Go up the stairs, turn left, and ring the bell. The workshop, Dickensian in appearance, is an ancient, wood-floored hall with two long rows of looms. World-famous tapestries—either copies of classical patterns or originals made to order—are handmade here. Note that this is not a place for bargain hunters: It takes approximately two years to complete a piece, and the current price is about $5,500 per square meter. *Rua Guilherme Gomes Fernandes 26, tel. 045/ 23283. Admission free. Open weekdays 9:30–11 and 2:30–4:30.*

**Time Out** Located in the municipal park in the town center, the **O Tarro** restaurant and snack bar has a pleasant terrace, which overlooks a pond and the sprawling park.

To explore Portalegre, start at the park in the center of the lower town and walk uphill past a maze of shops and old houses to the twin-towered **cathedral.** The 18th-century facade of this, the town's most prominent landmark, is highlighted with marble columns and wrought-iron balconies. *Open Mon.–Sat. 8:30–11:30 and 2–6; Sun. 8:30–11:30.*

The **Municipal Museum,** in a former seminary next to the cathedral, contains a wealth of religious art including a gilded, 16th-century Spanish pietà. *Admission: 100$00. Open Tues.–Sun. 9:30–12:30 and 2–6; closed Mon. and holidays.*

From the cathedral square, head east about 400 yards to the ruins of a once-formidable castle, whose tower walls afford a splendid view of the cathedral and its surroundings.

The **José Regio Museum,** just off the Avenida Poeta JoséRegio, roughly midway between the cathedral and the castle, was named for a local poet who died in 1969. He bequeathed his varied collection of religious and folk art to the museum, which is in his former home. *Praça Municipal, tel. 045/23625. Admission: 150$00. Open Tues.– Sun. 9:30–12:30 and 2–6; closed Mon. and holidays.*

Portalegre is also the gateway to a recently established national **38** park, the 80,000-acre **Parque Natural da Serra de São Mamede,** which extends north to the fortified town of Marvao and the spa of

Castelo de Vide and south to the little hamlet of Esperança, hugging the Spanish border. Rural in character, the sparsely inhabited park is made up of small family plots, and sheepherding is the major occupation. The region is rich in wildlife, including many rare species of birds, wild boar, deer, and wildcat. This is not a spectacularly scenic park like Yellowstone or Yosemite but a quiet place for hiking, riding, or simply communing with nature. For information about activities contact the **park office** (Praceta Herois da India 8, 7301 Portalegre, tel. 045/23631, fax 045/27501).

**39** If you're interested in horses, you must visit the **Coudelaria Real** (National Stud Farm), formerly the Royal Stud Farm, founded by Dom João V in 1748 to furnish royalty with high-quality mounts. The Coudelaria—the most important stud farm in Portugal—is on a dusty track 3 kilometers (2 miles) northwest of Alter do Chão. From Portalegre take N119 west for 21 kilometers (13 miles), then turn south toward Alter do Chão (which has an interesting castle opposite its main square). The road to the farm is marked COUDELARIA If, at the farm, you try to speak Portuguese or you seem interested in horses, the sympathetic employees may show you around. Otherwise, you can roam the farm yourself and look at the horses or maybe catch a training session. Of special interest is the annual horse auction held in late April. *Follow signs to Coudelaria. Open daily 9:30–12 and 2–4:30.*

For the most scenic approach to the Serra de São Mamede, backtrack to Portalegre on N119, then take N359 18 kilometers (11 miles) to Marvão. (Another route is to take N245 north to the intersection at N246 to Castelo de Vide and Marvão.) The narrow but well-surfaced serpentine N359 rises to an elevation of 2,800 feet, past stands of birch and chestnut trees and small vegetable gardens bordered by ancient stone walls. At **Portagem** take note of the well-preserved Roman bridge.

**40** The views of the mountains as you approach the fortress town of **Marvão** are spectacular, and the town's castle, perched atop a sheer rock cliff, commands a 360-degree panorama. Although it's possible to drive through the constricted streets of this medieval mountaintop village, Marvão is best appreciated on foot. First head for the castle, and climb to the tower. From there you can trace the course of the massive Vauban-style stone walls (characterized by concentric lines of trenches and walls, a hallmark of the 17th-century French military engineer Vauban), adorned at intervals with bartizans, to enjoy breathtaking vistas from different angles. Given its strategic position, it's no surprise that Marvão has been a fortified settlement since Roman times or earlier. The present castle was built under Dom Dinis in the late 13th century and modified some four centuries later, during the reign of Dom João IV.

At the foot of the path leading to the castle is the **Municipal Museum** housed in the recently renovated 13th-century Church of Saint Mary. The small gallery contains a diverse collection of religious artifacts, azulejos, costumes, ancient maps, and weapons. *Admission 200$00. Open daily 9–12:30 and 2–5:30.*

The village, with some 300 mostly older inhabitants, is laid out in several long rows of tidy, white stone dwellings terraced into the hill. The newly remodeled Pousada de Santa Maria (*see* Dining and Lodging, *below*) and the few guest houses and restaurants are well integrated into the village and do not detract from Marvão's pleasing traditional architecture. Head north on the small country road

**41** and follow signs to **Santo António das Areias,** where some two dozen prehistoric dolmens are scattered among the chestnut groves.

An intriguing backcountry lane connects Marvão with Castelo de Vide. About halfway down the hill from Marvão, turn to the right toward Escusa, and continue through the chestnut- and acacia-cov-
**42** ered hills to **Castelo de Vide.** This hilltop spa town is graced with flowers, which sprout from nearly every nook and cranny. When you encounter the local people it will be clear that the beauty of Castelo de Vide has reached the hearts of its residents, who have kind and gentle natures. Start out in the Praça Dom Pedro V, the large, ba-roque square bordered by the Church of Santa Maria and the town hall. From here wander down the alleyway to the right of the church; this route will take you to the village fountain, which taps one of the many springs in the area. (The waters are alleged to cure a wide variety of disorders ranging from diabetes to dermatitis.) The canopied, clam-shaped marble fountain is the town symbol.

Follow the cobblestone alley leading from the fountain up to the *Juderia* (Jewish Quarter). On the Rua da Juderia you'll come to a **medieval synagogue,** a modest, one-story building that was once the center of a thriving Jewish community. In medieval times, as the town prospered, many Jews and Marranos (Jews forced to convert to Christianity) settled here. As you walk along, notice the many houses with Gothic doorways and their various designs. (The tour-ist brochures proclaim that Castelo de Vide has the largest number of Gothic doorways of any town in Portugal.) From the Juderia it's a short climb to the ruins of the castle. Go up into the tower and inside the well-preserved keep to the large Gothic hall with a picture win-dow looking down on the town square and the church. *Admission free. Open Oct.–May, daily 10–5:30; June–Sept., daily 10–8.*

## Tour 4: The Lower Alentejo

Spread across a small knoll midway between Spain and the seais
**43** **Beja,** the Lower Alentejo's principal agricultural center. In the town's streets and squares, shepherds wearing broad-brimmed hats and the traditional sheepskin vests mingle with the townspeople. In the fields at the edge of town, gypsies often set up camp, with make-shift tents, horse carts, and open campfires. These scenes from a rapidly disappearing way of life contrast sharply with the modern improvements taking place in the region , and much of the old part of Beja still retains a significantly Arabic flavor, the legacy of more than 400 years of Moorish occupation. Students of the Portuguese language even claim that the local dialect has Arabic characteristics.

In the first century, Beja, founded by Julius Caesar and known as Pax Julia, was an important town in the Roman province of Lusita-nia. The name Pax Julia was chosen because it was here, after a long struggle, that peace was finally established between the Lusitanian chiefs and Julius Caesar. Roman artifacts can be seen at the Museu Regional on the second floor of the Convento da Conceição and at the excavations in nearby Pizões.

On a broad plaza in the center of the old town, the convent, once a Moorish *mesquita* (mosque), was founded in 1459 by the parents of King Manuel I. Favored by the royal family, the Franciscan convent thrived and became one of the richest of the period. The **Church of Santa Maria,** across the square, can be easily recognized by its mas-sive round pillars, Mudejar arches, and its bell tower similar in de-sign to that of the famed Giralda Tower in Seville. The church and cloisters display some fine azulejos from the 16th and 17th centuries, including panels depicting scenes from the life of St. John the Baptist, and a section of multicolored Moorish tiles. Upstairs, at the far end of the second-floor gallery, is the famous "Mariana Window," named after a young Beja nun, Mariana Alcoforado. As the story goes, Mariana fell in love with a French count named Chamilly, who was in the Alentejo fighting the Spaniards. When he went back to France, the nun waited longingly and in vain at the window for him to return. The publication in France in 1669 of five passionate love letters known as *The Portuguese Letters*, written by Mariana to the count and documenting the scandalous affair, brought a measure of lasting international literary fame to this provincial Alentejo town.

The recently established **Visigoth Museum** next door in the 6th-century Visigoth Church of Santo Amaro houses an impressive collection of artifacts, such as tombstones, weapons, and pottery, that help document the Visigoth presence in the region. *Largo da Conceiça⁻o. Admission to convent and museum: 100$00. Open Tues.–Sun. 9:45–1:30 and 2–5:15.*

---

**Time Out** | The **Café Pastelaria Santa Maria,** opposite the church, has outside tables looking out on the convent square and is a pleasant spot for cake and coffee or a light lunch.

---

**Beja Castle** is an extensive system of fortifications, whose crenellated walls and towers chronicle the history of the town from its Roman occupation through its 19th-century battles with the French. The castle keep houses a military museum where weapons going back to the 16th century are displayed. *Admission free. Open Oct.–May, daily 9–12 and 1–4; June–Sept., daily 10-1 and 2-6.*

**㊹ Serpa,** 29 kilometers (18 miles) east of Beja on N260, is a sleepy agricultural town that seems to have missed the train of progress and development that's changed much of Portugal. Here men pass the time of day by gathering together in the compact Praça da República, under the shadow of the ancient stone clock tower. Unemployment is high, and there is little else for many of them to do. In tiny cubbyholes along narrow, cobbled streets, carpenters, shoemakers, basket weavers, and other craftsmen work in much the same manner as their forefathers did generations earlier.

From the 13th-century castle walls, you can get a bird's-eye view of the town. Note how an aqueduct forms an integral part of the walls. As for the huge ruined sections of wall tottering precariously above the entrance, they're the result of explosions ordered by the Duke of Ossuna during the 18th-century War of the Spanish Succession. Within the castle walls there's a small municipal museum with a particularly unusual exhibit—a life- size bronze-colored papier-mâché replica of *The Last Supper. Admission: 100$00. Open Tues.–Sun. 9–12:30 and 2– 5:30; closed Mon. and holidays.*

Now head north on N265, a narrow road that parallels the Rio Guadiana as it runs through an isolated stretch of rolling hills and cork **㊺** trees. At the intersection with N258, follow signs to **Vidigueira,** a quiet farm town in the middle of the Alentejo plain, best known as the one-time home of Vasco da Gama, the Portuguese explorer whose voyage in 1497 opened the sea route to India. A statue of him stands in the main square. At the edge of town, in a setting of gardens and ponds, is the Carmelite chapel where the explorer's body lay from the time it was returned from India in 1539 until it was moved in 1898 to Lisbon's Jeronimos Monastery.

Five kilometers (3 miles) west of Vidigueira on N258, standing in an olive orchard, are the 2,000-year-old ruins of a Roman villa. The two-story building, the **Ruins of São Cucufate,** was part of an extensive Roman settlement. (Coins and other artifacts that have turned up indicate a first-century Roman presence here.) It's believed that the ground floor was used as a barn, with the living quarters above it. Remnants of the original heating and drainage systems are visible. The building was later adapted and used in the 13th century as a convent; the frescoes were done in the late 15th and early 16th centuries, and have not been restored. *N258. Admission free; donations accepted. Open Tues.–Fri. 10–12 and 2–5; closed Sat., Sun., and Mon.*

Continue on N258 to **Alvito,** a typical, sleepy Alentejo town that occupies a low hill above the Rio Odivelas. Noted for its fortress-like 13th-century parish church, the town also boasts a rectangular, early 16th-century castle, with round towers at three of its corners and a number of fine Mudejar windows, which has recently been converted into a pousada. In the village a surprising number of modest houses bear graceful Manueline doorways and windows.

The castle at **Viana do Alentejo,** 10 kilometers (6 miles) north of Alvito on N257, with its rough stone walls, brick battlements, and round turrets, is one of the most attractive in the Alentejo. It was constructed in 1313 to the very specific orders of Dom Dinis, who decreed that the pentagonal walls be tall enough that a horseman with a lance measuring nine covados (an ancient unit of measure that equals 66 centimeters, or 26 inches) wouldn't injure anyone on the battlements. The fortified parish church within the walls of the castle—designed by the famous Diogo de Arruda— has an eye-pleasing combination of battlements, spires, and ornate Manueline elements. Below the castle a delightful Renaissance fountain enhances the town square. Viana do Alentejo is also noted for a primitive-style pottery, sold in several of the small shops in town.

Take N383 southwest and west to Torrão, then follow N5 west, close to the Rio Sado through a sparsely populated region of pine and olive trees, to **Alcácer do Sal,** whose hilltop castle is its most prominent attraction and whose buildings form long, horizontal rows reaching down the hill to the riverbank. Because of its favored location and its salt, Alcácer was one of the first inhabited sites in Portugal; parts of the castle foundations are around 5,000 years old. The Greeks were here, and, of course, the Romans, who established the town of Salatia Urbs Imperatoria—a key intersection in their system of Lusitanian roads. During the Moorish occupation, under the name of Alcácer de Salaria, this became one of the most important Muslim strongholds in all of Iberia. In the 16th century Alcácer prospered as a major producer of salt, and a brisk trade was conducted with the northern European countries, which used it to preserve herring.

Drive west on N253 through the **Reserva Natural do Sado** (Sado River Nature Reserve). The riverbanks are lined with extensive salt pans and rice paddies, and the reserve gives shelter to wildlife such as dolphin, otter, white stork, and egret. From the beach town of Comporta, head south along the coast on N261 through a mostly deserted stretch of dunes and pine trees with some wonderful, undeveloped sandy beaches.

**Santiago do Cacém,** about 16 kilometers (10 miles) inland at the junction of N120 and N261, is a quiet regional market town. The castle, built by the Knights of the Order of Santiago (St. James) on the site of Moorish ruins, dominates the town and affords sweeping views to the sea, marred only by the oil refineries at Sines. Inside the parish church, which is surrounded by the fortifications, you can see a sculpture of Saint James battling the Moors. The old town, which occupies a maze of narrow streets just below the castle, has a number of well-preserved 17th- and 18th-century manor houses. The **regional museum,** housed in a former prison in the center of town, offers several well-organized exhibits portraying various aspects of Alentejo life, including one that shows the stages of and implements used in cork production. *Admission: 100$00. Open Sun.–Thurs. 10– 12:30 and 2–5:30; closed Fri., Sat., and holidays.*

At the edge of town, just off of the road to Lisbon, you can explore the excavations of the Roman city of **Miróbriga.** Originally this site was settled by the Celts in the 4th century BC; later, in the 1st century, it became a Roman town. The ruins, although not nearly as extensive or well-preserved as those at Conimbriga near Coimbra, contain the interesting sanctuaries of Venus and Esculapius (god of medicine). The excavations—some of which were done in the 1980s by a team from the University of Missouri—are not cur rently being worked. *Rd. to Lisbon. Admission: 100$00. Open Oct.–May, Tues.– Sun. 9–noon and 1–5:30; June–Sept., Tues.–Sun. 9–1 and 2:45– 6:45.*

From Santiago do Cacém head south either along the motorway past the refineries and power plant at Sines if you're in a hurry, or along the more scenic inland N120 to **Vila Nova de Milfontes.** Although the town itself is just another small beach resort without any special architectural merit, its location at the broad mouth of the Rio Mira is delightful, and it has soft sandy beaches on both sides of the river. Overlooking the sea is an ivy-covered fortress built on Moorish foundations in the late 16th century to protect Milfontes from the Algerian pirates who regularly terrorized the Portuguese coast. With the subsidence of the pirate threat, the fortress was abandoned and the ruins were sold at auction in 1906; in 1939 it was taken over by the present owner, who has converted it into a delightful inn called the Castelo de Milfontes (*see* Dining and Lodging, *below*).

## Tour 5: The Estremadura

In 1711, after nearly three years of a childless union with his Hapsburg queen, Mariana, a despairing João V vowed that should the queen bear him an heir, he would build a Franciscan monastery dedicated to St. Anthony. In December of that same year, a girl—later to become queen of Spain—was born; João's eventual heir, José I, was born three years later. True to his word, the King built the enormous **Palácio Nacional de Mafra** (Monastery and Royal Palace) that looms above the small farming community of **Mafra,** some 25 kilometers (15 miles) northwest of Lisbon. The original project—entrusted to the Italian-trained German architect Friedrich Ludwig—was to be a modest-size facility that could house 13 friars. What finally emerged after 18 years of construction was an immense, rectangular complex that contained a monastery large enough for 300 monks, an imposing basilica, and a grandiose royal palace, which has been compared to Spain's El Escorial outside Madrid. The numbers involved in the construction are mind- boggling: At times 50,000 workers were used; there are 4,500 doors and windows, 300 cells, 880 halls and rooms, and 154 stairways. Perimeter walls that total some 19 kilometers (12 miles) surround the park. The story of the monastery is the subject of a bizarre but fascinating novel titled *Baltasar and Blimunda* by the Portuguese author José Saramago.

There are many interesting details to note as you take the two-hour guided tour, but the highlight is the magnificent baroque library: The barrel-vaulted, two-tiered hall contains some 40,000 volumes of mostly 16th-, 17th-, and 18th-century works, and a number of ancient maps. The Basilica, constructed entirely of limestone and containing 11 chapels, was patterned after St. Peter's Basilica in the Vatican. The balcony of the connecting corridor overlooks the high altar and was a favorite meeting place for Dom João and Mariana. This midway point between the "his" and "hers" royal bedrooms was considered neutral territory. When you're in the gilded **throne room,** pay attention to the life-size renditions of the seven virtues, as well as the impressive figure of Hercules, by Domingos Sequeira. On display in the game room is an early version of a pinball machine. Note the hard- planked beds in the monastery infirmary; the monks used no mattresses.

You'll be fortunate if you arrive on a Sunday afternoon when, between 4 and 5 o'clock, the sonorous tones of the 92-bell carillon— played by Francisco Gato, a TAP Air Portugal pilot—ring out across the countryside. *Admission: 300$00. Open: Wed.–Mon. 10–1 and 2–5; closed Tues.*

**Time Out**    The **Pasteleria Dom João V,** directly across the street from the monastery, offers a welcome respite from the rigors of sightseeing. Homemade pastries and ice cream are specialties.

**㊳ Ericeira,** an old fishing village on the rocky coast 11 kilometers (7 miles) northwest of Mafra, is a popular seaside resort. The core of the village fans out from the sheer cliff, beneath which the fishing boats are hauled up onto a small, sheltered beach. Either end of the village has good sand for sunbathing, but the south end is preferred by surfers.

Take N247 for 20 kilometers (12 miles) north along the rugged coast
**㊴** to the turnoff for **Torres Vedras.** Today a bustling commercial center crowned with the ruins of a medieval castle, the town is best known for its extensive fortifications—a system of trenches and fortresses erected by Wellington in 1810 as part of a secret plan for the defense of Lisbon. It was here, at the Lines of Torres Vedras, that the surprised French Army under Napoleon's Marshal Masséna was routed. Remnants of the fortifications can be seen throughout the region.

As you continue north along N247 for 43 kilometers (25 miles) to Cape Carvoeiro, the rocky coast is interrupted by fine beaches at
**㊵** Santa Cruz, Ribamar, and Areia Branca. **Peniche,** in the lee of the rocky peninsula, is a major fishing and canning port with a bustling harbor watched over by a sprawling 16th-century fortress. The town, a popular summer resort, is also known for its lace. The most interesting of the area's several churches is the 13th-century Church of São Leonardo in nearby **Atouguia da Baleia.**

For a good view of the fortress and the harbor, drive out to **Cape Carvoeiro.** The narrow road winds around the peninsula, along the rugged shore, and past the lighthouse and bizarre rock formations. Within the fortress walls there's a small museum. *Admission free. Open Tues.–Sun. 10–12 and 2–5; closed Mon.*

The harbor at Peniche is the jumping-off point for excursions to the
**㊶** offshore **Berlenga Islands.** The six small islands are a nature reserve and a favorite place for fishermen and divers. Berlenga, the largest of the group, is the site of the **Forte de São João Baptista,** a 17th-

century fortress built to defend the area from pirates. There's also a hostel on the island. For more information about accommodations, contact the Peniche tourist office (Rua Alex Herculano, tel. 062/ 79571). *Boats leave Peniche for Berlenga between June and Sept. at 9AM and noon and return at 11:30 AM and 6 PM. Trip takes approximately 1 hour and costs 1,500$00.*

**57** **Óbidos,** once a strategic seaport but now left high and dry 10 kilometers (6 miles) inland by the silting of its harbor, is surrounded by fertile farmland. Cottages and cultivated fields abut the town walls where fishing boats and trading vessels once docked. As you approach Óbidos from the distance, you can see the bastions and crenellated walls standing as a hilltop sentinel guarding the now-peaceful valley of the Ria Arnoia. Enter the town through the massive, arched gates, and it may seem that you've been transported into medieval Portugal. The narrow Rua Direita, lined with boutiques and flower-bedecked white houses, runs the length of the town from the main gates to the foot of the castle: You may want to do a bit of shopping for ceramics and clothing on this street. The rest of the town is crisscrossed by a labyrinth of stone footpaths, tiny squares, and decaying stairways. Explore any route or all of them, for the town is small and you can't really get lost. Each nook and cranny will offer its own reward. Just be sure to include the castle in your explorations: Extensively restored after suffering severe damage in the 1755 earthquake, the multitowered complex—one of the finest medieval castles in Portugal—displays both Arabic and Manueline elements. Parts of the castle have been a pousada since 1952.

Óbidos has a long association with women prominent in Portuguese history. So enchanted was the young Queen Isabel with Óbidos—which she visited with her husband, Dom Dinis, shortly after their marriage in 1282— that the king gave it to her as a gift along with Abrantes and Porto de Móso; the town remained the property of the queens of Portugal until 1834. In the 14th century Inês de Castro sought refuge in this castle, and another queen associated with Óbidos was Leonor (the wife of João II), who came here in the 15th century to recuperate after the death of her young son; the town pillory bears Leonor's coat of arms. The 17th-century artist Josefa de Óbidos came to Óbidos as a small child and lived here until her death in 1684. Some of her work may be seen in the azulejos-lined **St. Mary's Church,** which dates back to the 8th century.

**58** Five kilometers (3 miles) north of Óbidos on N8 lies the spa of **Caldas da Rainha** (The Queen's Baths), the hub of a large farming area, but best known for its sulfur baths. In 1484 Queen Leonor, en route to Batalha, noticed some people bathing in a malodorous pool. Having heard of the healing properties of the sulfurous water, the queen interrupted her journey to soak in the pool and became convinced of their beneficial effects. She decided to build a hospital on the site, and reputedly was so enthusiastic that she sold her jewels to help finance the project. There is a large bronze statue of Leonor in front of the hospital. The expansive, wooded park surrounding the spa contains two interesting museums: The **Malhoa Museum,** primarily dedicated to the works of the local 19th- and 20th-century painter José Malhoa, and the **Rafael Bordalo Pinheiro Ceramics Museum,** in the house of that 19th-century ceramist. *Admission: 300$00. Open Tues.–Sun. 10–noon and 2–5.*

From Caldas head west along the lagoon to the beach town of **Foz do Arelho,** then take the coast road 26 kilometers (16 miles) north to
**59** **Nazaré.** Not so long ago tourists could mingle on the beach with the

black-stocking-capped fishermen and even help as the oxen hauled the fishing boats in from the crashing surf. But Nazaré, one of the first quaint Portuguese fishing villages to feel the impact of tourism, is no longer a village and has long ceased to be quaint. The boats now motor comfortably into a safe, modern harbor, and the oxen have been put to pasture. But tourists still flock here, and in summer the broad, sandy beach is covered with a multicolored quilt of tents and awnings, and the beachfront boulevard is lined with the usual assortment of restaurants, bars, and souvenir shops. To find what's left of the Nazaré once hailed by many as "the most picturesque fishing village in Portugal," come in the winter, and either climb the precipitous trail or take the funicular to the **Sitio,** the 361-foot cliff overlooking the beach. Clustered at the cliff's edge is a small community of fishermen who live in tiny cottages and seem unaffected by all that's happening below.

⑥ From Nazaré head southeast on N8-5 to **Alcobaça,** site of one of Portugal's most impressive religious monuments. Like the monastery at Mafra, the Monastery of Saint Mary of Alcobaça was built as the result of a kingly vow, this time in gratitude for a battle won. In 1147, faced with stiff Muslim resistance during the battle for Santarém, Portugal's first king, Afonso Henriques, promised to build a monastery dedicated to St. Bernard and the Cistercian Order. The Portuguese were victorious, Santarém was captured from the Moors, and shortly thereafter a site was selected. Construction on the monastery was begun in 1153 and concluded in 1178. The church, the largest in Portugal, is awe-inspiring: The unadorned, 350-foot- long structure of massive granite blocks and cross-ribbed vaulting is a masterpiece of understatement: There's good use of clean, flowing lines, with none of the clutter found in the later rococo and Manueline architecture. At opposite ends of the transept, placed foot-to-foot some 30 paces apart, are the delicately carved tombs of King Pedro I and Inês de Castro, their serene faces looking upward. The story of Pedro and Inês, one of the most bizarre love stories in Portuguese history, was immortalized by Camões in *Os Lusiads*, a renowned piece of Portuguese literature.

Pedro, son of King Afonso IV and heir to the throne, fell in love with the beautiful young Galician Inês de Castro, a lady-in- waiting to Pedro's Castilian wife, Constança. Fearful of any Spanish influence on his heir, the king banished Inês from the court. Upon the death of Constança, Pedro and Inês secretly married, and she lived in Coimbra, in a house later known as the *Quinta das Lagrimas* (The House of Tears); two sons were born of this union. King Afonso, ever wary of foreign influence on Pedro, had Inês murdered. Subsequently, Pedro took the throne and had Inês's murderers pursued: Two of the three were captured and executed, their hearts wrenched from their bodies. Pedro publicly proclaimed that he had been married to Inês and arranged an elaborate and macabre funeral for his wife. Before the procession, Inês's fleshless body, in royal garb, was enthroned beside him, and the courtiers were forced to kiss her lifeless hand. She was then placed in the tomb in Alcobaça that Pedro had designed, which lay, according to his wishes, opposite his own —so that on Judgment Day the lovers would ascend to heaven facing one another.

The graceful twin-tiered **cloister** was added in the 14th and 16th centuries. The Kings Hall, just to the left of the main entrance, is lined with a series of 18th-century azulejos illustrating the building of the monastery. *Admission: 300$00. Open daily 9–5.*

While you're in Alcobaça, you may want to visit the interesting **Wine Museum,** in an old winery on N8 heading north at the edge of town, to see wine-making implements and presses. *Highway N8. Admission: 100$00. Open Mon.–Sat. 9–12:30 and 2–5:30.*

Stay on N8 for the next 18 kilometers (11 miles) to the town of **⑥ Batalha.** The monastery church of **Santa Maria da Vitoria** (Saint Mary of Victory) was built to commemorate a decisive Portuguese victory over the Spanish on August 14, 1385, in the battle of Aljubarrota. In this battle the Portuguese king, John of Avis, who had been crowned only seven days earlier, took on and routed a superior Spanish force. In so doing he maintained independence for Portugal, which was to last until 1580, when the crown finally passed into Spanish hands.

The monastery, a masterly combination of Gothic and Manueline styles, was built from 1388 to 1533. Some 15 architects were involved in the project, but the principal architect was Alfonso Domingues, whose portrait, carved in stone, graces the wall in the chapter house. In the great hall lie the remains of two unknown Portuguese soldiers who died in World War I, one in France, the other in Africa. The tomb in the center of the Founder's Chapel, beneath the star-shaped, vaulted ceiling, is that of John of Avis, lying hand- in-hand with his English queen, Philippa of Lancaster. The tombs along the south and west walls are those of the couple's children, including Henry the Navigator. Perhaps the finest part of the entire project is the Unfinished Chapels, seven chapels radiating off an octagonal rotunda, started by Dom Duarte in 1435, and left roofless owing to lack of funds. Note the intricately filigreed detail of the main doorway. *Admission to the cloister: 400$00. Open daily 9–5.*

The heroic statue of the mounted figure in the forecourt is that of Nuno Álvares Pereira, who, along with John of Avis, led the Portuguese army at Aljubarrota. There is a small battlefield museum 5 kilometers (3 miles) south on N8. *Admission: 100$00. Open Tues.–Fri. 10–12, weekends 10–12 and 2–5.*

**⑥ Leiria,** 11 kilometers (7 miles) north of Batalha on N1, is a pleasant, modern, industrial town at the confluence of the Rios Liz and Lena. The region is known for its handicrafts, particularly the fine hand-blown glassware from Marinha Grande. Interesting highlights of Leiria are the hilltop castle and, beneath it, the old town quarter and the cathedral. The castle, built in 1135 by Prince Afonso Henriques (later Portugal's first king), was an important link in the chain of defenses along the southern border of what was at the time the Kingdom of Portugal. When the Moors were driven from the region, the castle lost its strategic significance and lay dormant until the early 14th century, at which time it was restored and modified and became the favorite residence of King Dinis and his queen, Isabel of Aragon. With these modifications the castle became more of a palace than a fortress and remains one of the loveliest structures of its kind in Portugal. Within the perimeter walls you'll encounter the ruins of a Gothic church, the castle keep, and—built into the section of the fortifications overlooking the town—the Royal Palace. Lined by eight arches, the balcony of the palace affords a lovely view of the town. *Admission: 120$00. Open daily 9–6:30.*

## Tour 6: The Ribatejo

**⑥ If** you want to see a bullfight in Portugal, **Vila Franca de Xira** is the place to do it. The town is 30 kilometers (18 miles) north of Lisbon via the A1 motorway. The best time to visit Vila Franca de Xira is during the first week in July for the *Festa do Colete Encarnado* (Festival of the Red Waistcoat). Had Hemingway and his buddies taken a wrong train and wound up in Vila Franca de Xira some 60 years ago, perhaps Pamplona would have remained an unsung, grimy industrial town, and the world would have flocked instead to the Ribatejo each July for one of Portugal's greatest parties. The downtown streets are cordoned off, and the bulls are let loose as would-be bullfighters try their luck at dodging the charging beasts. At night the streets are alive with *fado* and flamenco dancing. The running of the bulls also takes place during the Autumn Fair held in early October. The bullring, one of Portugal's finest, contains a small museum with a collection of bullfighting memorabilia. For more information call the tourist office (tel. 063/33219). *Admission: 200$00. Open Tues.-Sun. 10–12:30 and 2–6; closed Mon. and holidays.*

The Portuguese bullfight —known as the *courada*—is quite different from any version of this ancient spectacle you might have seen in Mexico or Spain. In Portugal the bull's principal opponent is not a sword-carrying matador but a *cavaleiro*—a horseman elegantly attired as an 18th-century nobleman with plumed hat and embroidered coat. Displaying finely tuned equestrian skills he provokes the bull and, just inches away from the animal's padded horns, manages to deftly place a colorfully festooned *bandarilha* (dart) in a designated part of the bull's back. With each pass of an ever shorter bandarilha, the danger to horse and rider increases—in spite of the bull's blunted horns. At the proper moment, when the bull is sufficiently fatigued, the final dart is placed, and with a flourish the cavaleiro exits the arena. (Following a decree by the Marquis of Pombal in the 18th century, bulls are not killed in Portuguese rings.) The stage is now set for the *pega*, an audacious display of bravery with burlesque overtones. A file of eight men—the *forcados*—dressed in bright-crimson vests and green stocking caps parades into the arena and, hands on hips, confronts the tired but still-enraged bull. When the bull charges, the leader meets him head-on with a running leap and literally seizes the bull by the horns. The other men rush in and by grabbing the bull's tail, try to force the animal to the ground. At times this can be quite an amusing sight, though there is the ever-present element of danger, and forcados have been killed during the pega. At the end of the spectacle, a few cows are led in to lure the bull from the ring. If he has shown exceptional bravery, the bull will be spared for stud purposes; otherwise, he will be slaughtered for the meat. Bullfights are held from Easter to October. Call the tourist office (tel. 063/33219) for more information.

There are two routes to Santarém. The more interesting follows the
**64** east bank of the Rio Tejo and takes you through the **Leziria,** the marshy plain along the river, and across rich pasturelands with stud farms. From Vila Franca de Xira, cross the bridge, and follow N118 north. As you drive through the town of **Benavente** and surrounding countryside, look for *campinos* (farm hands) in the fields working
**65** the bulls and horses. The road runs through **Almeirim,** where you may visit a working stud farm and a winery at the **Quinta da Alorna.** From Almeirim head back across the river to Santarém.

**66** Present-day **Santarém,** perched high above the Tejo, is an important farming and livestock center. Some historians believe that its beginnings date to as early as 1200 BC and the age of Ulysses. Its strategic location led several kings to choose it as their residence, and the *Cortes* (Parliament) frequently met here.

To get the feel of the town, walk up to the **Portas do Sol,** a lovely park within the ancient walls. From this vantage point you can look down on a sweeping bend in the Rio Tejo and beyond to the rich farmlands stretching into the neighboring Alentejo. Thanks to its royal connections, Santarém is more richly endowed with treasures and monuments than other towns of its size. The Portuguese refer to it as their "Gothic Capital." Of particular interest are the 17th-century **Seminary Church,** built on the ruins of a royal palace, and the azulejo-bedecked **Marvila Church.**

Inside the **Archaeological Museum** you'll find the finely sculpted tomb of Duarte de Meneses, which, according to legend, contains a single tooth, all that remained of the nobleman after his brutal murder by the Moors in Africa. The museum is on Rua Figueiredo Leal, directly across from the bell tower known as the Torre das Cabaças. *Admission free. Open Tues.– Sun. 9:30–1 and 2–3; closed Mon. and holidays.*

**Time Out**    **Xantarin** (Travessa da Misericórdia 6), one of the region's most popular bars, was once a Roman cistern. Today you may snack and sip your drinks under the original ceiling with Roman arches.

Also in Santarém, on the Largo Pedro Alvares Cabral, is the **Graça Church,** which contains the gravestone of Pedro Cabral, the discoverer of Brazil. There is a tomb of the explorer in Belmonte, the town of his birth, too, but no one is really sure just what is in which tomb! Of note in this 14th-century Gothic church is the delicate rose window whose setting was carved from a single slab of stone. *Largo Pedro Alvares Cabral.*

**67**   Cross the Rio Tejo again and take N368 to nearby **Alpiarça,** where you'll have the chance to see how a wealthy country gentleman lived at the beginning of this century. The **Casa dos Patudos,** now a museum, was the estate of Jose Relvas, a diplomat and gentleman farmer. The unusual three-story manor house with its zebra-striped spire is surrounded by gardens and vineyards. An impressive assemblage of furnishings, including Portugal's foremost collection of Arraiolos carpets, is contained in the museum. *Admission: 250$00. Open Wed.–Sun. and holidays 10– 12 and 2–5; contact Alpiarça town hall for other opening hours.*

**68**   From Alpiarça continue north on N118/N243 through the horsebreeding center of **Golegã.** During the first two weeks of November, this is the site of the colorful **National Horse Fair,** the most important event of its kind in the country. Another 10 kilometers (6 miles) **69**   north on N243 will bring you to the fortified town of **Torres Novas.** The crenellated, 14th-century hilltop castle encloses a delightful garden. At the foot of the castle stands a caricature statue of Dom Sancho I created by João Cutiliero, a prominent contemporary sculptor.

**70**   Some 20 kilometers (12 miles) northwest on N357, across the scrubcovered limestone hills of the Serra de Aire, lies **Fátima,** an important Roman Catholic pilgrimage site. (Ironically, this great Christian shrine is a village named after the daughter of Mohammed, the prophet of Islam!) If you visit this sleepy little Portuguese town in between pilgrimages, it will be difficult to imagine the thousands of the faithful who come from all corners of the world to make this religious affirmation, cramming the roads, squares, parks, and virtually every square foot of space. Many of the pilgrims go the last miles on their knees.

When Pope John Paul II visited in 1991, it was estimated that more than one million people flocked to Fátima. Where there are so many people, there are bound to be opportunists. That Fátima is no exception is attested to by the presence of such places as the "Virgin Mary Souvenir Shop" and the "Pope John Paul II Snack Bar."

It all began on May 13, 1917, when three young shepherds—Lúcia dos Santos and her cousins Francisco and Jacinta—reported having seen the Virgin Mary in a field at Cova de Iria, near the village. The Virgin promised to return on the 13th of each month for the next five months, and amid much controversy and skepticism, each time accompanied by increasingly larger crowds, the three children reported successive apparitions. This was during a period of anticlerical sentiment in Portugal, and after the sixth apparition, in October, the children were arrested and interrogated. But they insisted that the Virgin did speak to them and had told them three secrets. Two of these, revealed by Lúcia in 1941, were interpreted to foretell the coming of World War II and the spread of communism and atheism. The third secret is still held by the Vatican. In 1930, in a Pastoral Letter, the Bishop of Leiria declared the apparitions worthy of belief, thus approving the "Cult of Fátima." On the 13th of each month, and especially in May and October, the faithful flock here to witness the passing of the statue of the Virgin through the throngs, to participate in candlelight processions, and to take part in solemn masses.

At the head of the huge esplanade is a large, neoclassical basilica (built in the late 1920s) flanked on either side by a semicircular peristyle.

Other pilgrimage sites include the cottages in the nearby hamlet of Aljustrel, where the children were born, and the **Chapel of Apparitions,** built on the spot where the appearances of the Virgin Mary are said to have taken place. There is a **Wax Museum** in the center of town with tableaux representing the story. *Admission: 600$00. Open daily 9–5.*

The hills to the south and west of Fátima are honeycombed with limestone caves, the largest such caverns in Portugal. Within about a 25-kilometer (15-mile) radius of Fátima, there are four sets of these chambers that are equipped with artificial lighting and elevators; here visitors can see the subterranean world of limestone formations, underground rivers and lakes, and multicolored stalagmites and stalactites. They are: **São Mamede Caves, Mira de Aire Caves, Alvados Caves,** and **Santo António Caves.** The tourist office can assist you with further details. *Admission: 450$00. Open Oct.–Mar., daily 9–6; Apr.–June and Sept., daily 9–8; July–Aug., daily 9–9.*

**❼** From Fátima take N113 east to **Tomar,** a town laid out on both sides of the Rio Nabão, with the new and old parts linked by a graceful, arched stone bridge. The river flows through a lovely park with weeping willows and an old wooden waterwheel.

Atop a hill rising from the old town is **The Convent of Christ,** a remarkable architectural achievement. You can drive to the top of the hill or hike for about 20 minutes along a path through the trees; at the top there are wonderful views from the castle walls. You enter through a formal garden lined with azulejo-covered benches. This was the headquarters of the order of Knights Templar, from 1160 until the order was forced to disband in 1314. Identified by their white tunics emblazoned with a crimson cross, the Templars were at the forefront of the Christian armies in the Crusades and during the years of struggle against the Moors. King Dinis in 1334 resurrected the order in Portugal under the banner of the Knights of Christ and re-established Tomar as its headquarters. In the early 15th century, under the leadership of Prince Henry the Navigator (who for a time resided in the castle), the order flourished. The caravels of the era of discovery sailed under the order's crimson cross.

When they constructed the original fortifications in 1160, the Templars drew heavily upon their experiences with the Moslems during the Crusades. The buildings within the battlements are made up of a series of cloisters formed around the **Templar's Rotunda**—the complex's showpiece. This two-story, octagonal church, constructed in the Byzantine style, is patterned after the Church of the Holy Sepulchre in Jerusalem and is part of the original 12th-century construction. The paintings and wooden statues are 16th-century Portuguese. To see what the Manueline style is all about, stroll through the nave with its many examples of the twisted ropes, seaweed, and nautical themes, which typify the style, and be sure to look at the **Chapter House Window,** probably the most photographed one in Europe. Its lichen-encrusted sculpture manifests the Manueline style and evokes the feeling and spirit of the great age of discovery. *Admission: 300$00. Open daily, Oct.–Mar. 9:15–12:30 and 2–5; Apr.–Sept. 9:15–6.*

Back in the old town walk along the narrow, flower-lined streets, particularly Rua Dr. Joaquim Jacinto, where in the heart of the old Jewish quarter you'll find the **Sinogoga de Tomar** (Synagogue of Tomar), a much more modest religious building. Built in the mid-15th century, this is the oldest Jewish house of worship in Portugal. Inside is a small museum with exhibits chronicling the Jewish presence in the country. The once-sizable Jewish population was considerably reduced when in 1496 Dom Manuel issued an edict that ordered the Jews either to leave the country or convert to Christianity. Many, who became known as *Marranos,* converted but secretly practiced their original religion. *Rua Dr. Joaquim Jacinto. Admission free; donations accepted. Open Thurs.–Tues. 9:30–12:30 and 2–5:30.*

To leave Tomar head south on N210 for 7 kilometers (4 miles) to **72** N358–2, the turnoff for **Castelo de Bode.** Follow this road across the dam. The huge lake that fans out north from the dam on the Rio Zêzere is a popular water-sports area. For information regarding boat excursions on the lake, inquire at the Hotel dos Templários in Tomar or at the dock by the Pousada de São Pedro (*see* Dining and Lodging, *below*).

Take the N358–2 south along the Zêzere to where it joins the Tejo. **73** For a close look at **Almourol Castle,** a storybook edifice sitting on a craggy island downstream in the middle of the river, turn right and take the mile-long dirt road leading down to the water. The riverbank in this area is practically deserted, making it a wonderful picnic spot. (In summer you can take a boat to the island.) The setting could hardly be more romantic: an ancient castle with crenellated walls and a lofty tower sits on a greenery-covered rock in the middle of a gently flowing river. The stuff of poetry and legends, Almourol was the setting for Francisco de Morais's epic *Palmeirim of England.*

**Time Out** On N3 just west of the castle is a good lunch stop, **Restaurante Almourol,** in a lovely old house with gardens, orange trees, and a terrace overlooking the castle.

Back on N3 head east to **Constância,** a peaceful hamlet where the Zêzere joins the Rio Tejo. The town is best known as the place where Camões was exiled in 1548, the unfortunate result of his romantic involvement with Catarina de Ataide, the "Natercia" of his poems and a lady-in-waiting to Queen Catarina. There is a bronze statue of the bard in a reflective pose at the riverbank.

**74** Farther along the Rio Tejo on a hill is the strategically situated town of **Abrantes.** During the 16th century, when the Rio Tejo was naviga-ble all the way to the sea, Abrantes flourished and became one of the country's most populous and prosperous towns. With the coming of the railroad and the development of better roads, the town's com-mercial importance waned. The main attraction here is the castle (built in the 16th century). Walk up through the maze of narrow, flower-lined streets to the ruins of the ancient fortress. Much of the castle is in disrepair, but with a bit of imagination you can conjure visions of what an impressive structure this must have been. The at-tractive garden that's been planted between the twin fortifications makes a wonderful place to watch the sunset: The play of light upon the river and the lengthening shadows along the olive groves pro-vide an inspiring setting for an evening picnic.

**75** Northeast of Abrantes on N244–3 some 12 kilometers (7 miles) is **Sardoal,** an island of white houses with red-tiled roofs in a sea of wooded hills. It's an enchanting place of narrow streets paved with pebbles from nearby streams, modest, yellow- trimmed houses, and flowers everywhere—hanging from windows and from balconies and lining the winding streets and alleys. In such a spot you might expect art to flourish, and in fact the 17th-century **Parish Church** contains a collection of fine 16th-century paintings by the "Master of Sardoal," an unknown painter whose works have been found in oth-er parts of the country and whose influence on other artists has been noted.

**76** Continue on N244–3 and follow it through the pine-covered hills to Chão de Codes, then take N244 south toward Gavião. As you come down from the hills toward the Rio Tejo, you'll see a cone-shaped hill (looking as if its top has been sliced off) with a fairy-tale castle planted on top. This is the fortress of **Belver,** built in the last years of the 12th century by the Knights Hospitallers under the command of King Sancho I. In 1194 this region was threatened by the Moorish forces who controlled the lands south of the Rio Tejo, except for Évora. The expected attack never took place, and the present struc-ture is little changed from its original design. The walls of the keep, which stands in the center of the courtyard, are some 12 feet thick, and on the ground floor is a great cistern of unknown depth. Accord-ing to local lore, an orange dropped into the well will later appear bobbing down the Rio Tejo.

## What to See and Do with Children

**Lucena Karting,** a go-cart track in Évora, provides an outlet for pent-up youthful energy. *N114 to Montemor-o-Novo, tel. 066/ 734990. Admission: 400$00–6,000$00, depending on vehicle and length of rental time. Open Tues.–Sun. 10–8; closed Mon.*

Young aviation enthusiasts will enjoy seeing old planes at the **Museu do Ar** (Aviation Museum), in Alverca, at the airport. *Tel. 01/958-2782. Admission: 100$00. Open Tues.–Sun. 10–8.*

**Beja Aquatica,** a waterslide park in Beja, will occupy young water rats for a good part of the day. *On N260, toward Serpa, tel. 084/*

*329755. Admission: 1,600$00 (full day), 1,200$00 (half day) adult; 1000$00 (full day), 900$00 (half day) children under 12. Open daily 10–8.*

**Peniche Sportagua,** a large water-park complex with a separate slide area and adults' and children's swimming pools, also has a restaurant, cafeteria, and disco. *Av. Monsehnor M. Basto, R. Sonsa, tel. 062/789125. Admission: 1,700$00 (full day), 1,200$00 (half day) adult; 1,200$00 (full day), 1000$00 (half day) children under 12.*

The **boat trip** from Peniche to the Berlenga Islands is great fun for kids as well as adults. *See* Tour 5.

Children will love exploring the **caves** near Fátima. *See* Tour 6.

Of the many castles in the region, **Marvão** (*see* Tour 3), **Óbidos** (*see* Tour 5), and **Monsaraz** (*see* Tour 3) are the most fun for kids to scamper about.

## Off the Beaten Track

The **Parque Natural das Serras de Aire e Candeeiros** is a sparsely populated rural region that straddles the boundary between the Estremadura and the Ribatejo and is roughly midway between Lisbon and Coimbra. Within its 75,000 acres of scrublands and moors, you'll find small settlements, little changed in hundreds of years, where farmers barely eke out a living. In this rocky landscape stones are the main building material for houses, windmills, and the miles of walls used to mark boundary lines. In the village of Minde, you can see women weaving the rough patchwork rugs for which this region is well known.

# Shopping

## Crystal and Glass

**Marinha Grande,** just west of Leiria, is the center for the production of Stephens Lead Crystal. The Stephens Brothers Factory School (Bairro Benta, tel. 044/568680), where much of the glass is still produced by hand, may be visited. The school is open weekdays 9–12 and 2–5. **Alcobaça** is another center for quality crystal and hand-blown glass.

## Pottery and Ceramics

The brightly colored hand-painted plates, bowls, and figurines from the upper Alentejo are popular throughout Portugal. You'll find the best selection of this distinctive type of folk art in and around **Estremoz,** where the terra-cotta jugs and bowls are adorned with chips of marble from local quarries. Saturday morning the Rossío is chock-full of vendors displaying their wares. **Redondo** and the village of **San Pedro do Corval,** near Reguengos, are also good sources of this type of pottery.

An entirely different type of ceramics is produced in **Caldas da Rainha,** a large ceramics-manufacturing center. Its characteristic cabbage-leaf and vegetable-shaped pieces are famous throughout the country. To visit a ceramics factory and showroom contact: **SECLA** (Rua S. João de Deus, tel. 062/842151) and **Armando Baiana** (Rua Casais da Ribeira 37, tel. 062/ 24355). South of Batalha (on N8) there are a number of roadside shops with good selections of hand-painted ceramics in classical patterns. In **Alcobaça** try the **Casa Lisboa,** across from the monastery.

## Rugs

The village of **Arraiolos,** near Évora, is famous for its hand-embroidered wool rugs, and the main street is lined with showrooms and workshops. Some of the best selections can be found at **Calantica** (Rua Alexandre Herculano 20, tel. 066/42356) and **Condestavel** (Rua Bombeiros Voluntarios 7, tel. 066/42219), a large shop with branches in Évora and Lisbon.

## Sweaters

The beachfront promenade in **Nazaré** is lined with shops selling the traditional cable-stitch Portuguese fishermen's sweaters. The best are made of pure wool rather than acrylic blends. You'll also find a wide selection of wool plaid shirts and caps. It pays to shop around, as prices vary widely and bargaining is the order of the day.

# Sports and the Outdoors

## Participant Sports

Golf  The one golf course in the region is located at the beach at **Praia de Porto Nova** (Hotel Praia do Porto Nova, 2560 Torres Vedras, tel. 061/984157) and is part of the Hotel Golf Mar. The par 67, nine-hole course designed by Frank Pennink is 5,259 yards long. Reserve greens in advance, even if you're a hotel guest.

Horseback Riding  **Sela Real** (Caldas da Rainha, tel. 062/842096) offers a riding school as well as excursions in Vale da Couto. Contact **Centro Hipico de Caldas da Rainha** (tel. 062/35851) for information.

In Évora contact **Centro Hipico de Évora** (tel. 066/21376). In Montemor-o-Novo contact **Cavalgada** (*see below*) for Alentejo trail rides. For riding along the beach near Sines, contact **Centro Equestre de Santo Andre** (Monte V. Cima, Santo Andre, tel. 069/71235). Half-day escorted trail rides in small groups for all levels of riders through the Alentejo farmlands are available from **Cavalgada,** (Apt. 68, 7050 Montemor-o-Novo, tel. 066/82071). Half-day rides are 3,500$00 and full-day rides cost 6,500$00; two-day weekend rides are also offered. The price of 18,000$00 includes one night's accommodation in a B&B along the way. Reservations are advised. Because most tourists are not familiar with the terrain it is difficult to arrange unescorted rides. Hourly rates for groups of as many as five persons are about 1,500$00 per person. Riding lessons cost 1,200$00 per half-hour.

Water Sports  Most of the larger towns and many smaller ones have modern municipal swimming pools, so even in the middle of the dry Alentejo, you'll never be very far from a refreshing dip.

The Óbidos Lagoon at Foz do Arelho is popular with **sailboarders,** and Windsurfers can be rented at the beach. The cost for just the rig is about 1,500$00 per hour; rental and lessons cost about 3,000$00 per hour.

**Surfers,** on the other hand, prefer beaches at Peniche, Ericeira, and along the rugged Alentejo coast.

The clear waters and bizarre rock formations off the Berlenga Islands are frequented by **scuba divers;** spearfishing with scuba gear is prohibited. Boats may be rented at the harbor in Peniche.

Fishermen like these waters, too. The most commonly caught fish in this area are sea bass, bream, and red mullet. A fishing license is not necessary.

## Beaches

From Odeceixe in the south, where the Alentejo and Algarve join, to the northern end of the Estremadura just south of Figuiera da Foz, there's an almost-continuous, 241-kilometer (150-mile) stretch of sandy beach. There are beaches to meet just about every need. If you like quiet, uncrowded areas with fine, soft sand and clear waters, your best bet is on the Alentejo coast. Even in July and August, when most of Europe's beaches are packed elbow to elbow, you can find solitude by heading west on almost any of the unmarked tracks along the coast. The following signposted beaches, all south of Lisbon, are seldom crowded: **Carvalhal, Zambujeira, Almograve,** and **Fontainhas.**

Beaches in the region that fly a blue banner, indicating they've met European Union standards for safety and hygiene, are in: **Pedrogão, São Pedro de Moel Foz do Arelho, Baleal, Consolação, Porto Dinheiro, Santa Cruz,** and **Porto Covo.**

Some of the more popular beaches (but not necessarily with blue flags) where you will find the customary range of facilities, hotels, restaurants, and equipment are in: **Nazaré, Peniche, Foz do Arelho, Ericeira,** and **Milfontes.**

# Dining and Lodging

**Dining**  In the Alentejo, a region known as the country's granary, bread is a major ingredient in the cuisine. It's the basis of a popular dish known as *açorda,* a thick, stick-to-the-ribs bread porridge to which various ingredients such as fish, meat, eggs, or shellfish are added. *Açorda de marisco,* a tasty combination of bread, eggs, seasonings, and a hearty portion of assorted shellfish, is one of the more popular varieties. Another version, *açorda da Alentejana,* is a clear broth with olive oil, slices of bread, garlic, and a poached egg floating on the surface. Pork from the Alentejo is the best in the country and often is combined with clams, onions, and tomatoes in the classic dish *carne de porco Alentejana.* The cheese is excellent, particularly the tangy sheep's cheese from the Serpa region. Elvas, near the Spanish border, is known for its tasty sugar plums. Alentejo wines—especially those from around Borba and Reguengos—are regular prizewinners at national tasting contests.

In Ribatejo and Estremadura restaurants, the culinary emphasis is on fish, including the ubiquitous *bacalhau* (dried salt cod) and *caldeirada* (a hearty fish stew). The seaside resorts of Ericeira, Nazaré, and Peniche are famous for fresh lobster and other seafood. In Santarém and other spots along the Rio Tejo, a bread soup made with *savel,* a shadlike fish from the river, is popular, as are *enguias* (eels) prepared in a variety of ways. Roast lamb and kid are also widely enjoyed. Portuguese nuns have the reputation of making wonderful sweets, and the abundance of convents in the region has added many tasty and colorful sounding dishes—such as *queijinhos do ceu* (little cheeses from heaven)—to local dessert menus. The straw-color white wines from the Ribatejo district of Bucelas rank with the country's finest.

Between mid-June and mid-September reservations are advised at upscale restaurants. However, most of the establishments we list are moderate or inexpensive, they don't accept reservations, and they have informal dining rooms where it's quite acceptable to share a table with other diners. Dress at all but the most luxurious restaurants is casual; any exceptions to the dress code or reservation policy are noted in the reviews.

Highly recommended restaurants are indicated by a star ★.

| Category | Cost* |
|----------|-------|
| $$$$ | over 5,000$00 |
| $$$ | 3,500$00–5,000$00 |
| $$ | 2,500$00–3,500$00 |
| $ | under 2,500$00 |

*per person for 3-course meal, including service and tax but excluding drinks*

**Lodging** The vast, primarily agricultural Alentejo and the Ribatejo are lacking in first-class hotels; the best accommodations in this region are the government-run inns called *pousadas*. Two of the finest in the country are in the Alentejo, one in the ancient convent in Évora and the other in the castle at Estremoz. The pousadas are small, some with as few as six rooms, so reserving well in advance is essential. There are also a number of high-quality, government-approved private guest houses in the region. Look for signs reading TURISMO RURAL or TURISMO DE HABITAÇÃO. Several of these are included in our listings. For information about additional guest houses, contact: **Promoções e Idéias Turísticas** (PIT: Rua Fredrico Arouca, 72, 2750 Cascais, tel. 01/484–4207, fax 01/484–2901). The more densely populated Estremadura is better equipped with quality lodgings, especially along the coast. In summer, you will need reservations. Most establishments offer substantial off-season discounts.

Highly recommended lodgings are indicated by a star ★.

| Category | Cost* |
|----------|-------|
| $$$$ | over 15,000$00 |
| $$$ | 12,000$00–15,000$00 |
| $$ | 8,000$00–12,000$00 |
| $ | under 8,000$00 |

*Unless noted otherwise, all prices are for a standard double room with bath in high season, including tax, service, and breakfast.*

**Abrantes**
*Dining*
**Cristina.** In a town where good restaurants are scarce, this attractively decorated, rustic, family-run place on N3, 5 kilometers (3 miles) west of Abrantes, is worth the drive. Ask the restaurant's namesake, Cristina Mota, to tell you the daily special and hope it's *bacalhau com natas* (dried cod baked in a casserole with cream and potatoes), one of her most popular creations. *Rio de Moinhos, tel. 041/98177. MC, V. Closed Mon.* $

Dining and **Hotel Turismo.** This hotel is perched in such a spectacular location,
Lodging on a hill high above the Rio Tejo, that it's a shame the architect didn't
create a more pleasing exterior design than this nondescript, pink-
stucco eyesore. But inside is a different story, with an inviting, club-
by lounge featuring a fireplace and comfy leather chairs. Guest
rooms are on the small side but are comfortably furnished, and many
of the newer rooms have terraces with wonderful vistas. The dining
room—surrounded with picture windows—affords inspiring views,
and is an excellent place to sample the delicious *palha de Abrantes*
(straw of Abrantes), a tasty local dessert specialty that consists of
thick egg and almond paste topped with yellow threadlike wisps
made of eggs and sugar. *Largo de Santo António, 2200, tel. 041/
21261, fax 041/25218. 34 rooms. Facilities: restaurant, bar, pool,
tennis, parking. AE, DC, MC, V. $$$*

Alcácer do Sal **O Brazão.** Don't be put off by the run-down exterior of this no-frills
Dining restaurant: It's the favorite eating place of local businesspeople.
The open kitchen allows you to peek in and see for yourself what
looks good. Sample the *ensopa da garoupa* (fish stew), a typical dish
from this part of the country. *Largo Prof. Francisco Gentil, tel. 065/
62576. No credit cards. Closed Sun. $–$$*

Dining and **Pousada do Vale do Gaio.** Located 27 kilometers (16 miles) east of
Lodging Alcácer do Sal and 8 kilometers (5 miles) from Torrão in a secluded
wooded area overlooking a man-made lake, this small, rustic lodge
was built to house the engineers who constructed the nearby dam.
In 1977 it was converted into a pousada and has become a favorite
spot for hunters and fishermen. The rooms are utilitarian but comfortable and look out over the lake, and a surprising variety of excellent local dishes come out of the tiny restaurant. This is a good place
to get away from it all. *Pousada do Vale do Gaio, 7595 Torrão, tel.
065/669610, no fax. 7 rooms. Facilities: restaurant, bar, water
sports and fishing in lake, parking. AE, DC, MC, V. $$*

Alcobaça **Trindade.** An unpretentious, popular restaurant, Trindade is con-
Dining sidered one of the town's best. The intimate dining room, lined with
old photos of local scenes, reveals some of Alcobaça's history. Try
the house specialty, açorda de marisco, and for dessert the home-
made pastry. *Praça D. Afonso Henriques 22, tel. 062/42397. MC, V.
$*

Lodging **Casa da Padeira.** In this family establishment Senhora Ventura
★ cooks and keeps house while son Miguel manages the place. Guests
mingle freely with the hosts of this delightful country inn, 5 kilome-
ters (3 miles) outside of Alcobaça on N8, where comfortable living
and sitting rooms are shared with the proprietors as well as other
visitors. The bedrooms are large, and each is furnished with period
reproductions and covered with dainty flowered wallpaper. Break-
fast features hot, fresh, out-of-the-oven homemade bread, and mom
will cook you a wonderful dinner upon request. *Aljubarrota, 2460,
tel./fax 062/508272. 8 rooms, 2 apartments. Facilities: bar, pool, bil-
liards, minigolf, parking. MC, V. $$*

Alvito **Pousada do Castelo de Alvito.** This newly opened pousada is within
Dining and the walls of a 15th-century fortress at the edge of the village. The
Lodging essential architectural elements of a castle, including crenelated
battlements and massive round towers, have been retained, and
there is a large garden and courtyard. The cozy restaurant serves a
variety of Alentejo specialties, including an excellent *caldeirada de
bacalhau* (codfish stew). *Castelo de Alvito, 7920, tel. 084/48383. 20
rooms. Facilities: bar, restaurant, pool, chapel, parking. AE, DC,
MC, V. $$$$*

# So, you're getting away from it all.

## Just make sure you can get back.

### AT&T Access Numbers
Dial the number of the country you're in to reach AT&T.

| | | | | | |
|---|---|---|---|---|---|
| *AUSTRIA††† | 022-903-011 | *GREECE | 00-800-1311 | NORWAY | 800-190-11 |
| *BELGIUM | 078-11-0010 | *HUNGARY | 00◇-800-01111 | POLAND†◆² | 0◇010-480-0111 |
| BULGARIA | 00-1800-0010 | *ICELAND | 999-001 | PORTUGAL† | 05017-1-288 |
| CANADA | 1-800-575-2222 | IRELAND | 1-800-550-000 | ROMANIA | 01-800-4288 |
| CROATIA‡◆ | 99-38-0011 | ISRAEL | 177-100-2727 | *RUSSIA† (MOSCOW) | 155-5042 |
| *CYPRUS | 080-90010 | *ITALY | 172-1011 | SLOVAKIA | 00-420-00101 |
| CZECH REPUBLIC | 00-420-00101 | KENYA† | 0800-10 | S. AFRICA | 0-800-99-0123 |
| *DENMARK | 8001-0010 | *LIECHTENSTEIN | 155-00-11 | SPAIN• | 900-99-00-11 |
| *EGYPT¹ (CAIRO) | 510-0200 | LITHUANIA◆ | 8◇196 | *SWEDEN | 020-795-611 |
| *FINLAND | 9800-100-10 | LUXEMBOURG | 0-800-0111 | *SWITZERLAND | 155-00-11 |
| FRANCE | 19◇-0011 | F.Y.R. MACEDONIA | 99-800-4288 | *TURKEY | 00-800-12277 |
| *GAMBIA | 00111 | *MALTA | 0800-890-110 | UKRAINE† | 8◇100-11 |
| GERMANY | 0130-0010 | *NETHERLANDS | 06-022-9111 | UK | 0500-89-0011 |

Countries in bold face permit country-to-country calling in addition to calls to the U.S. **World Connect**ˢᴹ prices consist of **USADirect**® rates plus an additional charge based on the country you are calling. Collect calling available to the U.S. only. *Public phones require deposit of coin or phone card. ◇Await second dial tone. †May not be available from every phone. †††Public phones require local coin payment through the call duration. ◆Not available from public phones. • Calling available to most European countries. ¹Dial "02" first, outside Cairo. ²Dial 010-480-0111 from major Warsaw hotels. ©1994 AT&T.

Here's a travel tip that will make it easy to call back to the States. Dial the access number for the country you're visiting and connect right to AT&T. It's the quick way to get English-speaking AT&T operators and can minimize hotel telephone surcharges.

If all the countries you're visiting aren't listed above, call **1 800 241-5555** for a free wallet card with all AT&T access numbers. Easy international calling from AT&T. **TrueWorld Connections.**

AT&T

# American Express offers Travelers Cheques built for two.

Cheques *for Two*[SM] from American Express are the Travelers Cheques that allow either of you to use them because both of you have signed them. And only one of you needs to be present to purchase them.

Cheques *for Two* are accepted anywhere regular American Express Travelers Cheques are, which is just about everywhere. So stop by your bank, AAA* or any American Express Travel Service Office and ask for Cheques *for Two*.

**Batalha**
*Dining and Lodging*
★

**Pousada do Mestre Afonso Domingues.** This newly refurbished pousada named for the architect who designed the famous Batalha Monastery offers 20th-century comfort in a modern, two-story, white-stucco building, just steps away from the historic monument. The good-size upstairs rooms with patterned wallpaper are furnished in 17th- and 18th-century style, and several look out on the monastery. The first-floor restaurant, with its polished calçada floor and wood ceiling, faces the monastery. The menu includes several types of bacalhau, and there's an extensive wine list. *Pousada do Mestre Afonso Domingues, 2440, tel. 044/ 96260, fax 044/96247. 20 rooms, 1 suite. Facilities: restaurant, bar, parking. AE, DC, MC, V. $$$$*

*Lodging*

**Quinta do Fidalgo.** This historic two-story manor house adjacent to the monastery features a homey ambience: Guests gather and chat in the spacious living room or outside on the large terrace and in the pleasant garden. The rooms are comfortably and traditionally furnished. Reservations in summer are advised. *Quinta do Fidalgo, 2440, tel. 044/96114, fax 044/96114. 5 rooms. Facilities: bar, parking. No credit cards. $$*

**Beja**
*Dining*

**Gatus.** In a quiet alley close to the convent, the Gatus is a small, intimate establishment with a marble floor and wood paneling and is one of the best choices in this restaurant-poor town. The *ensopado de borrego* (lamb stew) or *bife Gatus* (braised beef with mushrooms and cream) are recommended. *Rua João Conforte 16–18, tel. 084/25418. MC, V. Closed Mon. $*

*Dining and Lodging*

**Pousada do Convento de São Francisco.** This newly opened pousada fulfills a longstanding need for first-rate accommodations in the Beja region. Although little remains of the original 13th-century convent, the conversion has been accomplished in a tasteful manner and the guest rooms are comfortably furnished. The pousada has an excellent restaurant and spacious gardens, and its ancient chapel has been largely preserved and incorporated into the complex. *Pousada do Convento de São Francisco 7800. tel. 01/848–1221, fax 01/805846. 37 rooms. facilities: bar, restaurant, pool, tennis, chapel, parking. AE, DC, MC, V. $$$$*

*Lodging*

**Cristina.** This comfortable pensão occupies a modern, five-story building, conveniently located on one of the main shopping streets. Light and airy rooms have been recently decorated but are a bit sterile. *Rua de Mértola 71, 7800, tel. 084/323035, fax 084/329874. 28 rooms, 3 suites. Facilities: bar. AE, DC, MC, V. $*

**Caldas da Rainha**
*Dining*
★

**Adega do Borlão.** Tucked away on a quiet back street near the courthouse and decorated as an old winery with wine barrels and farm implements, the Adega has become popular with the young professionals in the area who come here to relax and enjoy a good meal. The open kitchen enables you to watch your food being prepared, and the bread is baked fresh each day in a brick oven. If it's in season, try the *javali* (wild boar), a house special from the strictly Portuguese menu. *Rua Eng. Cancela de Abreu 11, tel. 062/842690. Reservations advised. MC, V. Closed Sun. $$*

*Dining and Lodging*

**Hotel Malhoa.** Most business travelers to the area choose this modern, eight-story hotel conveniently placed near the town center. The rooms are comfortable, but there aren't many details to indicate that you're in Portugal. *Rua António Sergio 31, 2500, tel. 062/842180, fax 062/842621. 111 rooms, 2 suites. Facilities: restaurant, bar, pool, sauna, disco, bingo, garage. AE, DC, MC, V. $$*

*Lodging* **Quinta da Foz.** This large, two-story manor house dating from the
★ 16th century is beautifully situated amidst lawns and trees at the
edge of the Óbidos Lagoon, some 15-minutes' walk to the beach. This
can be a quiet base from which to explore Caldas da Rainha, only 9
kilometers (5½ miles) away, or other towns in the region. The bedrooms are large and comfortably furnished with lots of flowers
about. *Largo do Arraial, 2500, tel. 062/ 979369. 5 rooms. Facilities:
tennis, horseback riding, parking. No credit cards. $$$*

**Castelo de** **O Cantinho Particular.** This tiny place on a side street near the town
**Vide** square engages the help of all the family members—Mom cooks
*Dining* while Dad and Junior take care of the customers. The dining room is
old but clean, and the basic Portuguese fare is simple and tasty.
Your best bet is to ask Senhor Bernardo what he recommends. *Rua
Miguel Bombarda 9, tel. 045/91151. No credit cards. $*

*Dining and* **Sol e Serra.** This modern, three-story, Mediterranean-style hotel
*Lodging* sitting at the edge of town is just a five-minute walk to the castle and
Juderia. Large rooms have balconies looking over the park, and the
bar and spacious lounge that overlooks the pool is the town's most
popular gathering place. The tastefully decorated restaurant with
wooden beams is considered Castelo de Vide's best eatery and is one
of the few places in Portugal where you can get a kosher menu.
*Estrada de São Vincente, 7320, tel. 045/91301, fax 045/91667. 51
rooms. Facilities: restaurant, bar, parking. AE, DC, MC, V. $$$*

**Constância** **Quinta de Santa Barbara.** If you're looking for a place to immerse
*Dining and* yourself for a while in the peace and quiet of the Portuguese coun-
*Lodging* tryside, look no farther. The Quinta, located about 3 kilometers (2
★ miles) east of Constância, has several sprawling buildings (a few of
which date back to the 16th century) and occupies some 45 acres of
farmland and cork and olive groves overlooking the Rio Tejo. This
country inn, opened in 1988, achieves a wonderful blend of old-world
charm and modern convenience. Each of the eight spacious rooms in
the main house is individually furnished with 18th-century Portuguese reproductions and has a modern tiled bathroom. The small
restaurant with a barrel-vault ceiling and stone walls specializes in
local dishes prepared from old recipes (many of the ingredients are
from the Quinta's own organic gardens). *Quinta de Santa Barbara,
2250, tel. 049/99214. 8 rooms. Facilities: restaurant, bar, tennis,
pool, horseback riding, parking. No credit cards. $$*

**Elvas** **Pousada de Santa Luzia.** Opened in 1942, this was Portugal's first
*Dining and* pousada, and its convenient location—just 12 kilometers (7 miles)
*Lodging* from one of the major border crossings between Spain and Portu-
★ gal—was no accident. The two-story, Moorish-style building has
been remodeled several times, most recently in 1994. All bedrooms
on the second floor are good-size and cheerfully decorated with
hand-painted Alentejo furniture and bright floral fabrics. The mod-
ern tiled bathrooms are small but adequate. The large restaurant
has arched windows overlooking an attractive garden and is a favor-
ite with Elvas residents. One of the most popular dishes is *bacalhau
dourado* (cod fish sautéed with eggs, potatoes, and onions). Reserve
a room in advance of your visit. *Pousada de Santa Luzia, 7350, tel.
068/622194, fax 068/622127. 15 rooms, 1 suite. Facilities: restau-
rant, bar, parking. AE, DC, MC, V. $$$$*

**Ericeira** **Hotel de Turismo.** Strangely reminiscent of a New York state
*Dining and* Catskills Mountain resort hotel transplanted to the seashore, the
*Lodging* Turismo is a sprawling, self-contained, low-rise—a classic old Por-
★ tuguese beach hotel. The dramatic location at the edge of the break-
ers adds to the distinctive feel of the place. Public rooms are

decorated with a delightful variety of colored tiles, and flowers and plants seem to be everywhere. Most of the spacious guest rooms have balconies with sea views. When you dine, choose your setting: The large restaurant is lined with picture windows looking out on the water, or you can be served on the seaside terrace. The international menu emphasizes seafood, and the quality is good. *Hotel de Turismo da Ericeira, 2655, tel. 061/864045, fax 061/63146. 165 rooms. Facilities: restaurant, bar, tennis, 3 pools, beach, disco, parking. AE, DC, MC, V. $$$*

**Pedro O Pescador.** If you prefer your hotels on a small scale, then you'll like this intimate, pastel blue, family-run hotel within walking distance of the beach. Cheerful rooms have planked floors and are decorated with flowered Alentejo furniture. The small, modern restaurant is frequented mostly by hotel guests. *Rua Dr. Eduardo Burnay 22, 2655, tel. 061/62504, fax 061/864302. 25 rooms. Facilities: restaurant, bar. AE, DC, MC, V. $$*

**Estremoz** **Adega do Isaias.** Hidden away on a narrow side street a few minutes'
**Dining** walk from the town square, this is the best place in town for hearty,
★ no-nonsense roasts and grilled meats. The front part of the former wine cellar is a rough-looking bar; walk through to the dining area—a sloping, cement-floored cave that's lined with huge terracotta wine jugs. During your meal you sit on benches at planked tables; expect the service to be casual, at best, but the food is great and the place, popular with the locals, is always jammed. *Rua do Almeida, 21, tel. 068/ 22318. No credit cards. Closed Sun. $*

**Dining and** **Pousada da Rainha Santa Isabel.** Occupying a hilltop castle steeped
**Lodging** in history, this pousada is the most luxurious in the country. The
★ sumptuous lobby and other public rooms display literally tons of gleaming Estremoz marble and are decorated with 15th-century tapestries, Arraiolos rugs, and original paintings. The generous-size bedrooms are furnished with 17th- and 18th-century reproductions, and some of the rooms have elaborate four-poster beds. Just to sit in the baronial dining hall is a treat, and the food and service—in tune with the decor—are fit for a queen. Reservations are advised. *Pousada da Rainha Santa Isabel, 7100, tel. 068/22618, fax 068/23982. 20 rooms, 3 suites. Facilities: restaurant, bar, parking. AE, DC, MC, V. $$$$*

**Lodging** **Monte Dos Pensamentos.** This comfortable old country manor house
★ surrounded by olive and orange trees is just 2 kilometers (1¼ miles) from Estremoz. The living room and large bedrooms are cluttered with enough painted plates, dolls, and antiques to stock a good-size museum. The mood is casual and relaxed, and guests typically sit around the fire and share the cozy sitting room. *Estrada Estacão Ameixial, 7100, tel. 068/22375, fax 068/284290. 7rooms. Facilities: bar, pool, parking. No credit cards. $$*

**Évora** **Fialho.** Amor and Gabriel Fialho are the third generation of Fialhos
**Dining** to operate this popular, traditional restaurant, one of Évora's best.
★ The beamed ceiling and painted plates on the walls lend a rustic ambience to what is quite a sophisticated kitchen. You might start with a selection of appetizers that includes an excellent *salada de polvo* (marinated octopus salad), and as a main course try *coelho de convent a cartuxa* (roasted rabbit with potatoes and carrots, according to a recipe from a nearby monastery). A wide selection of Alentejo wines is offered. *Travessa das Mascarenhas 16, tel. 066/23079. Reservations advised. AE, DC, MC, V. Closed Mon. $$$*

★ **A Choupana.** Popular with the locals, this is a pleasant restaurant just off the main square. In one of its two rooms, there are a few tables and a counter with stools, and in the other there's a small, pan-

eled dining area. Service is friendly, and the food is good. Try
açorda de marisco. *Rua dos Mercadores 20, tel. 066/24427. DC, MC,
V. Closed Sun. $$*

*Dining and* **Pousada dos Lóios.** This pousada, in the historic 15th-century mon-
*Lodging* astery opposite the Roman Temple of Diana, rates among the most
★ luxurious in the chain. Except for the small size of the rooms, which
were the former monks' cells, and the need for anyone over 5 foot 2 to
duck when entering, there's no trace of monastic austerity here.
The opulent period furnishings compensate for the slightly cramped
quarters, while the elegant lounges and public rooms deserve a visit
even if you don't plan to spend the night. Superbly prepared
Alentejo specialties are served in the restaurant in the former clois-
ter, a marvel of Manueline ceilings and columns. *Largo Conde de
Vila Flor, 7000, tel. 066/ 24051, fax 066/27248. 31 rooms, 1 suite. Fa-
cilities: restaurant, bar, pool. AE, DC, MC, V. $$$$*

**Évora Hotel.** This pleasant, modern establishment opened in 1992 on
the outskirts of town on the road toward Montemor–o–Novo, a wel-
come addition to Évora. The public areas are light and spacious as is
the dining room, which presents a delicious buffet with regional spe-
cialties. Rooms are generous in size and all have small balconies.
*Quinta do Cruzeiro. Estrada Nacional 114, 7001. tel. 066/734800,
fax 066/734806. 114 rooms. Facilities: restaurant, bar, pool, tennis,
sauna, fitness room, parking. AE, DC, MC, V. $$$*

*Lodging* **O Eborense.** In a historic building with a delightful arched gallery in
the heart of the old town, this comfortable, family-run guest house
provides quiet, old-fashioned hospitality. The rooms, while small,
are comfortably furnished, as is the TV lounge. *Largo da Misericórdia 1, 7000, tel. 066/22031. 24 rooms, 1 suite. Facilities: bar. No
credit cards. $$*

**Riviera.** This cozy, three-story old manor house is well situated be-
tween Giraldo Square and the Roman Temple. The small, cheerful
entry is decorated with colorful azulejos, and the rooms are covered
with flowered wallpaper. Furnishings are in the traditional, painted
Alentejo style. *Rua 5 de Outubro 49, 7000, tel. 066/23304, fax 066/
20467. 22 rooms. Facilities: lounge. AE, DC, MC, V. $$*

*Fátima* **Tia Alice.** Considered the best restaurant in the area, Tia Alice,
*Dining* which means "Aunt Alice," is concealed in an inconspicuous old
★ house with French windows, across from the parish church, near
the Sanctuary at Cova de Iria. A flight of wooden stairs inside leads
to a small, intimate dining area with a wood-beam ceiling and stone
walls. Try the *borrego assado* (roast lamb). *Rua do Adro, tel. 049/
531737. Reservations advised. MC, V. No dinner Sun., closed Mon.
and July. $$*

**Retiro dos Caçadores.** A big brick fireplace, wood paneling, and
stone walls set the mood in this cozy hunter's lodge, where the food
is simple, but portions are hearty and the quality good. This is the
best place in town for fresh game, especially *coelho con arroz* (rabbit
with rice) and *perdiz* (partridge). *Lombo Egua, tel. 049/531323.
MC, V. Closed Thurs. $*

*Lodging* **Hotel de Fátima.** This modern, four-story building— part of the
Best Western chain—is close to the Sanctuary. With its spacious
lobby, green-marble floors and wood-paneled walls (it was remod-
eled in 1993), it is generally considered to be Fátima's top hotel. *Rua
João Paulo II, 2496, tel. 049/533351, fax 049/532691. 126 rooms, 7
suites. Facilities: restaurant, bar, garage, parking. AE, DC, MC,
V. $$*

**Casa Beato Nuno.** This large pink-stucco inn, in a quiet setting just a
few minutes' walk from the Sanctuary, is run by the Carmelites but

is open to visitors of all denominations. The austere rooms are clean and comfortable. *Av. Beato Nuno, 51, 2496, tel. 049/532199, fax 049/ 532757. 132 rooms. Facilities: restaurant, parking. DC, MC, V. $*

**Leiria**
**Dining**
★

**O Casarão.** Five kilometers (3 miles) south of Leiria in Azoia, at the Nazaré turnoff, O Casarão occupies a large rustic house surrounded by gardens. Chef José Rodrigues supervises the outstanding kitchen staff while his wife, Clarissa, presides over the dining room. The service and presentation are flawless without being pretentious, and the extensive menu includes several ancient recipes from nearby monasteries. One of the best dishes is *bacalhau Tibarna* (thick cod filets baked in a casserole with olive oil, corn bread, and potatoes). Be sure to leave room for the *bolo pinão* (pinenut cake). The comprehensive wine list displays the labels of 120 different wines. *Cruzamento de Azoia, tel. 044/871080. AE, DC, MC, V. Closed Mon. $$*

**Lodging**

**Eurosol.** A pair of modern, "medium-rise" hotels, the Eurosol and Eurosol Jardim, occupy a hilltop that's about 15 minutes' walk from the town center. These hotels are popular stops for businessmen; the recently remodeled lobbies and bedrooms are spacious and smartly furnished; and the eighth-floor restaurant is ringed with picture windows that give bird's-eye views of the town. *Rua Dom JoséAlves Correia da Silva, 2400, tel. 044/812201, fax 044/811205. 128 rooms, 7 suites. Facilities: restaurant, bar, pool, fitness room, garage. AE, DC, MC, V. $$*

**Liz.** Conveniently situated in the town center across from the park, the Liz is a cozy old hotel with creaking floors and a lived- in feel. The large lounge with its fireplace can be particularly homey. Clean and comfortable bedrooms offer plain furnishings. *Largo Alex, Herculano 10, 2400, tel. 044/31017, fax 044/ 25099. 41 rooms. Facilities: bar. AE, DC, MC, V. $*

**Lourinhã**
**Lodging**

**Golf Mar.** This hotel's idyllic location—on a rise overlooking a broad, sandy beach—is the main reason you'd choose to stay here: The high rise's huge, concrete-block facade is hardly alluring, and the interior lacks inspiration. But if you're a golfer looking for a course, this is your only option in the region. *Praia do Porto Novo, 2560 Torres Vedras, tel. 061/984157, fax 061/ 984261. 267 rooms, 9 suites. Facilities: restaurant, bar, 9-hole golf course, tennis, horseback riding, indoor and outdoor pools, disco, billiards, parking, AE, DC, MC, V. $$$$*

**Estalagem Areia Branca.** This is a small, modern hotel with a favored cliff-top location, about 10 minutes by foot from a lovely sandy beach. The furnishings are not much more than serviceable, and the place could use an injection of charm (save for the fantastic views from some of the rooms). The restaurant looks out over the ocean and serves mostly seafood, including fresh shellfish taken from a large tank. *Praia da Areia Branca, 2530, tel. 061/412491, fax 061/ 413143. 34 rooms. Facilities: restaurant, bar, pool, parking. AE, DC, MC, V. $$*

**Areia Branca Youth Hostel.** This large, full-facility hostel on the beach provides 112 beds in multi-bedded single-sex rooms and two rooms for families, a lounge, bike rentals, and three meals a day. *Areia Branca beach, 2530, tel. 061/422127. $*

**Marvão**
**Dining and**
**Lodging**
★

**Pousada de Santa Maria.** In 1976 several old houses within the city walls were joined together to create the Pousada de Santa Maria and in 1992 the inn was enlarged and remodeled. The rooms are decorated with traditional Alentejo furnishings and the restaurant serves some of the best food in the village. Try some of the local favorites such as *migas a Alentejana com carne de porco* (marinated

pork with a bread and sausage stuffing). *Pousada de Santa Maria, 7330, tel. 045/ 93201, fax 045/93440. 27 rooms. Facilities: restaurant (reservations advised in summer), bar. AE, DC, MC, V. $$$$*
**Dom Dinis.** This comfortable country inn at the foot of the castle occupies a restored 200-year-old house with massive stone window and door frames. Bedrooms, which have fantastic cliffside views, are furnished with light pine furniture. In the adjacent building is the restaurant, where you sit at planked-wood tables while enjoying good hearty regional fare. *Rua Dr. Matos Magalháes 7330, tel. 045/ 93236. 15 rooms, 8 with bath. Facilities: restaurant, bar. AE, DC, MC, V. $*

**Monsaraz**
**Dining**
★
**Casa do Forno.** The labor of love of two ambitious women (Gloria and Mariana), Casa do Forno is an upscale restaurant in a picturesque fortified village. At the entrance is a huge, rounded oven with an iron door, hence the name O Forno—Portuguese for "oven." Picture windows line the dining room and offer a spectacular view over the rolling plains. The Alentejan menu appropriately features roasts, and one special dish worth trying is the *borrego Convento Orado* (roast lamb from an ancient recipe obtained at the nearby monastery). *Travessa da Sanabrosa, tel. 066/55190. Reservations advised in summer. MC, V. Closed Tues. $$*

**Lodging**
**Horta da Moura.** This self-contained mini-resort 15 kilometers (9 miles) east of Reguengos de Monsaraz, on a well-signed dirt road, is set on a working farm between the walled city and the Ria Guadiana. The main house, whose white-stucco facade is highlighted with blue trim and an arched portico, is typical of Alentejo-style architecture. Inside, vaulted brick ceilings with wood beams and traditional furnishings make the atmosphere comfortable. The outlying buildings include stables, a riding school, a crafts room, a winery, and a recreation center with a large fireplace. The helpful staff eagerly arranges walking, horseback-riding, and cycling trips along the nearby Ria Guadiana, as well as four-wheel-drive and canoe excursions. Hunting and fishing trips can also be arranged. *Horta da Moura, Apt. 64, 7200 Reguengos de Monsaraz, tel. 066/55206, fax 066/ 55241. 4 rooms, 7 suites, 1 apartment. Facilities: pool, tennis, horseback riding, bicycling, snooker, fishing, hunting. AE, DC, MC, V. $$$$*
**Casa Nuno.** This small, rustic guest house occupies a restored old white house on the main street of the walled town. Clean rooms with modern furnishings offer fantastic views over the valley, and the sunsets alone are worth the price of a room. Casa Nuno is a perfect little romantic hideaway in an ancient village. *Rua do Castelo 6, 7200, tel. 066/55146. 8 rooms. Facilities: parking. AE, DC, MC, V. $*

**Nazaré**
**Dining**
**Arte Xavega.** Set on a hill overlooking the town, this is by far Nazaré's classiest restaurant. Gardens and plants help to establish the comfortable blend of elegance and intimacy that owner Antonio Figueira has achieved for Arte Xavega. The international menu emphasizes local seafood specialties, including *arroz de marisco*. *Ladeira Sitio-Meia Laranja, tel. 062/552136. AE, DC, MC, V. $$$*

**Dining and**
**Lodging**
**Ribamar.** This family-run restaurant and boardinghouse on the main drag across from the beach couldn't hope for a more convenient location, though sometimes in summer it's noisy. Bedrooms are small, but all are clean and well-kept; ask for one that faces the sea. The restaurant, decorated like a country tavern, has large windows overlooking the beach; seafood is the main attraction, particularly the caldeirada. *Rua Gomes Freire 9, 2450, tel. 062/551158. 23 rooms. Facilities: restaurant (reservations advised in summer), bar. AE, DC, MC, V. $$*

*Lodging* **Hotel Praia.** In spite of its popularity, Nazaré lacks a really first-rate hotel, but the 25-year-old, six-story Praia comes closest to filling the bill. The hotel is comfortable and clean and was remodeled in 1993. *Av. Vieira Guimaraes 39, 2450, tel. 062/561423, fax 062/561436. 40 rooms. Facilities: garage. AE, DC, MC, V. $$*

**Óbidos** **Alcaide.** From the upstairs dining room of this rustic tavern on the
*Dining* main street, patrons can enjoy a lovely view of the old town. The Alcaide is often jammed with hungry sightseers, especially from May through October; this is not a quiet, romantic hideaway. The food, however, is always carefully prepared, and the service is attentive. Try the *coelho a Alcaide* (grilled rabbit with potatoes). *Rua Direita between main gate and castle, tel. 062/959220. AE, DC, MC, V. Closed Mon. $$*

*Dining and* **Pousada do Castelo.** If you've ever fantasized about living in luxury
*Lodging* within a medieval castle, this is a wonderful place to fulfill that wish.
★ Pousada do Castelo occupies parts of the castle that in 1282 King Dinis gave to his young bride, Isabel. Except for the electric lights and the relatively modern plumbing, the style of the Middle Ages prevails throughout, from the guest rooms to the beautifully tiled lounge and dining room. Room 2, in one of the massive stone towers, is especially evocative of ancient times; other rooms are uniquely furnished with 16th- and 17th-century reproductions. The food and service are worthy of royalty, and there's a curtained alcove where you can dine in privacy and still enjoy a splendid view of the castle walls and valley below. Try the *cabrito assado* (roast kid). *Pousada do Castelo, 2510, tel. 062/ 959105, fax 062/959148. 6 rooms, 3 suites. Facilities: restaurant, bar, parking. AE, DC, MC, V. $$$$*

**Albergaría Josefa d'Óbidos.** Built into the hillside at the main gate, this attractive, flower-bedecked country inn is the next best thing to Pousada do Castelo. The rooms are outfitted with comfortable 18th-century reproductions, including massive wood furniture that enhances the old-country-inn feeling, even though the place was built in 1983. The Albergería has several reproductions of Josefa d'Óbidos's works hanging in the bar; and a large, rustic restaurant with an open brick grill serves a variety of regional specialties. Try the *arroz de tamboril* (monkfish with rice) or one of the many preparations of bacalhau. The ambience of the otherwise- charming dining room is sometimes disturbed by the presence of large tour groups. *Rua D. João de Ornelas, 2510, tel. 062/ 959228, fax 062/959533. 40 rooms, 2 suites. Facilities: restaurant, bar, disco. AE, DC, MC, V. $$*

**Peniche** **O Canhoto.** Unlike many of the expensive touristy restaurants along
*Dining* the harbor, O Canhoto puts less emphasis on the trappings and more on the simple but tasty food. This is a typical, no-frills Portuguese fish restaurant—set on a narrow side street—where you're almost always assured a good meal, especially if you ask for the *peixe do dia* (fish of the day). *Rua Tenente Valadim, 23, tel. 062/784512. No credit cards. $*

*Lodging* **Praia Norte.** This modern three-story hotel on the outskirts of town offers reasonable rates. Most rooms are generous in size and overlook the hotel's large pool. Guest quarters are light and simply furnished but lack charm. The large water park adjacent to the hotel is a nice feature for families with children. *Av. Monsenhor Basto, 2520, tel. 062/781166, fax 062/781165. 97 rooms, 3 suites. Facilities: restaurant, bar, pool, parking. AE, DC, MC, V. $$*

**Portalegre** **O Abrigo.** This is a small, very "local" restaurant, on a quiet street
*Dining* around the corner from the cathedral. The small, cork- lined dining

room, presided over by owners Adriano and Pedro, is entered through a snack bar—indication that this is a modestly run establishment. One of the best dishes on the menu is the açorda de marisco, served steaming hot in a terra-cotta bowl. *Rua de Elvas 74, tel. 045/22778. MC, V. Closed Tues. $*

**Dining and Lodging** **Dom João III.** This is a modern multistoried hotel across from the city park. Although the lobby and hallways are somewhat institutional, the rooms are more pleasant: Many have balconies overlooking the park. The large, top-floor restaurant, a favorite with local businessmen, is ringed with picture windows looking over the town. An international menu offers regional specialties. *Av. da Liberdade, 7300, tel. 045/21192, fax 045/24444. 58 rooms, 2 suites. Facilities: restaurant, bar, pool. AE, DC, MC, V. $$$*

**Santa Clara** **Pousada de Santa Clara.** Its remote hidden setting, overlooking the
**Dining and** Santa Clara dam and a huge lake, and its proximity to the Algarve
**Lodging** (an hour's drive from the crowded beaches) make this pousada a
★ great retreat. At press time, however, the hotel was closed for extensive remodeling. By April 1995 it should be open. *Enatur, Pousadas de Portugal, Av. Santa Joana a Princesa 10, 1700 Lisbon, tel. 01/8481221, fax 01/805846. 32 rooms. AE, DC, MC, V. $$$*

**Santarém** **Portas do Sol.** A small restaurant in the town's most scenic location,
**Dining** the Portas do Sol is surrounded by flowers and trees in the gardens of the same name. This is a good place to combine a pleasant lunch on the brick-walled terrace with a walk around the gardens. Good regional dishes are offered here: Try the *bacalhau a bras* (cod slivers with scrambled eggs and onions). *Jardim das Portas do Sol, tel. 043/ 29520. AE, DC, MC, V. $$*

**Lodging** **Quinta de Vale de Lobos.** This is a delightful two-story, 19th-century farmhouse on N3, 6 kilometers (4 miles) from Santarém, among trees, ponds, and gardens. Guests enjoy lounging in the large comfortable living rooms and strolling in the adjacent woods. The generously sized bedrooms and apartments are comfortably furnished. *Azoia de Baixo, 2000, tel. 043/429264, fax 043/429313. 4 rooms, 2 apartments. Facilities: pool, access to 600-acre hunting estate, parking. No credit cards. $$$*
**Vitória.** On a quiet street in a residential apartment building, Vitória provides a relaxing stopover. The owner of this eponymous family-run lodging, Senhora Vitória, will make you feel right at home. The old section is a bit drab, so try for a room in the new wing. *Rua Visconde 2, 2000, tel. 043/ 22573. 25 rooms. Facilities: limited parking. MC, V. $$*
**Alfageme.** This new, unpretentious establishment helps to fill out the otherwise sparse Santarém hotel scene. The rooms are comfortable but for a new hotel somewhat uninspiring in their decor. *Ave. Bernardo Santareno, 38, 2000, tel. 043/370870, fax 043/370850. 67 rooms. Facilities: bar, restaurant, parking. MC, V. $*

**Santiago do** **O Retiro.** The joint efforts of an Austrian and his Portuguese wife
**Cacém** have turned this Alentejo cottage in the heart of town into a cozy
**Dining** international restaurant. Farm implements adorning the walls help
★ set a "down-home" tone in this friendly but professional restaurant, which also serves good solid Portuguese fare. *Rua Machado dos Santos 8, tel. 069/22659. Reservations advised in summer. MC, V. Closed Sun. $$*

**Dining and** **Pousada de Santiago.** Sitting atop a small rise at the end of town is
**Lodging** this rose-colored, ivy-clad manor house surrounded by mature trees
★ and gardens. One of the first pousadas created, the Santiago has had time to cultivate comfort: Over the years its guest and public rooms

have been extensively remodeled so that visitors feel almost as if they're staying in a private house. Some rooms have views of the castle; all units are furnished with decorative Alentejan pieces. As for the restaurant, the intimate dining room has a wood-beamed ceiling and a tiled fireplace, and you'll be served good-quality local favorites such as *carne de porco Alentejana* (pork and clams). In summer the terrace opens up for meals under the stars. *Pousada de Santiago, 7540, tel., fax. 069/22459. 8 rooms. Facilities: restaurant, bar, pool, parking, AE, DC, MC, V. $$*

★ **Quinta da Ortiga.** This lovely old country estate, just 5 kilometers (3 miles) from Santiago do Cacém, sits amid 10 acres of trees and farmland. Its interior decor— wood-panel ceilings and Arraiolos carpets—can best be described as "luxury rustic." The ambience is reminiscent of a comfortable rural villa, and the intimate restaurant, which serves the cuisine of the region, is more like an old-style family dining room than a commercial establishment. Try this inn— managed by Enatur, the government organization that also handles the pousadas—for a quiet, comfortable base from which to enjoy the Alentejo's beaches. *Apartado 67, 7540, tel. 069/22871, fax 069/ 22073. 12 rooms. Facilities: restaurant, bar, chapel, pool, horseback riding, parking. AE, DC, MC, V. 7-night stay with ½-board required July–Sept. $$*

**Serpa** **Pousada de São Gens.** Perched on a hill next to the Chapel of Guada-
*Dining and* lupe, overlooking the white houses and fortifications of Serpa, this
*Lodging* modern, white-domed, Moorish-style pousada offers a relaxed and
★ informal lodging option. The Arabic influence continues as you walk through the green-tiled entrance to the lobby with its many arches and vaulted ceilings. Each of the rooms has a small terrace, and bright, cheery fabrics nicely offset the white walls and ceilings. The restaurant has a small, brick-floored dining room with an open fireplace, and in summer guests may dine on the terrace looking over the pool and the plains. Tasty local specialties include *poejada de bacalhau* (dried cod fried with bread and seasoned with pennyroyal). *Pousada de São Gens, 7830, tel. 084/53724, fax 084/53337. 16 rooms, 2 suites. Facilities: restaurant, bar, pool, parking. AE, DC, MC, V. $$$$*

**Terena** **Casa de Terena.** A few years ago Susanna Bianchi and her partner,
*Dining and* Arnaldo Aboim, gave up successful careers in Lisbon to buy and re-
*Lodging* store a dilapidated 18th-century town house in this out-of-the-way
★ village. Now a charming inn, Casa de Terena offers six comfortably furnished bedrooms featuring period reproductions. In the morning guests dine in what was once the stable, but is now a delightful breakfast room. Across the street the rustic Migas Restaurant— named after the family dog—serves simple but tasty traditional fare. *Rua Direita 45, 7250 Alandroal, tel. 068/45132, fax 068/45155. 5 rooms, 1 suite. Facilities: restaurant, bar, parking. DC, MC, V. $$*

**Tomar** **A Bela Vista.** The date on the polished *calçada* (pavement with small
*Dining* black stones on a white background) reads "1922," which was when
★ the Sousa family opened this attractive little restaurant next to the old arched bridge. For summer dining there's a small, rustic terrace with views of the river and the Convent of Christ. Carrying on the family tradition, son Eugenio Sousa presides over the kitchen, which turns out great quantities of hearty regional fare. Try one of the house specialties such as cabrito assado or *dobrada com feijao* (tripe with beans), and wash it down with a robust local red wine. *Marquês de Pombal 68, tel. 049/312870. No credit cards. Closed Tues. $$*

*Dining and Lodging* ★ **Hotel dos Templários.** A large, modern hotel set in a tranquil park along the Rio Nabão, the Templários offers a number of rooms in a completely new wing and many units with views of the Convent of Christ. The big, airy dining room has picture windows facing the park and serves interesting regional dishes. With its spacious grounds and several swimming pools, the hotel makes a good base from which to visit the area's many attractions. *Largo Candido dos Reis 1, 2300, tel. 049/321730, fax 049/322191. 176 rooms. Facilities: restaurant, bar, indoor and outdoor pools, tennis, barbershop, beauty parlor, parking. AE, DC, MC, V. $$$*

★ **Pousada de São Pedro.** Originally built in 1946 to house engineers building the dam on the Rio Zezere, this pousada, which sits on a wooded hill and overlooks the man-made lake has recently undergone extensive remodeling. The pousada's location 18 kilometers (11 miles) from Tomar, makes a good place from which to explore nearby villages. The restaurant, in a lovely setting, features high quality regional fare. *Pousada de São Pedro, Castelo de Bode, 2300, tel. 049/382274, fax 049/381176. 25 rooms. Facilities: restaurant, water sports, parking. AE, DC, MC, V. $$$*

**Torres Novas** *Dining* ★ **A Tavolá.** This simple, friendly, family-run neighborhood restaurant, presided over by Francisco and Isabel Vieira, emphasizes regional dishes, and their *cabrito assado no forno* (roast kid filled with bacon, sausage, and olives) garnered first prize at a regional gastronomic fair. Since it's only about a 10-minute walk from the castle, A Tavolá makes a good dining spot after seeing the sights. *Av. Dr. Manuel de Figueiredo 12, tel. 049/ 23983. MC, V. Closed Sat. $$*

*Dining and Lodging* **Hotel dos Cavaleiros.** Conveniently located facing the main square, this modern three-story hotel blends in well with the surrounding 18th-century buildings. Rooms are moderately sized and have plain, light-wood furnishings; ask for one with a terrace on the third floor. In spite of its sterile, coffee-shop appearance, the restaurant serves generous portions of well-prepared traditional dishes. Try the *espetada mista* (grilled pork, squid, and shrimp on a spit). *Praça 5 de Outubro, 2350, tel. 049/ 811951, fax 049/812052. 57 rooms, 3 suites. Facilities: restaurant (closed Sun.), bar. AE, DC, MC, V. $$*

**Vila Franca de Xira** *Dining* ★ **Redondel.** This restaurant inside the walls of the famous bullring sees a lot of action and is considered Vila Franca's top eatery. There are high-vaulted brick ceilings and, in keeping with the theme, the dining room is adorned with bullfight posters and memorabilia. On the menu are regional dishes including *açorda de saval* (bread porridge with fish from the Rio Tejo). *Arcadas da Praça de Touros, tel. 063/22973. Reservations required on bullfight and festival days. AE, DC, MC, V. Closed Mon. $$*

**Marisqueira Fartazana.** In this spotlessly clean local fish restaurant, the accent is on good, simple food rather than decor, and the specialty is shellfish of all kinds. Try the arroz de marisco, a good filling dish. *Rua Almirante Cândido Reis 131, tel. 063/32943. No credit cards. Closed Mon. $*

*Dining and Lodging* **Flora.** For simple but well-maintained budget accommodations, try this modern, four-story hotel conveniently located in the center of town. The small, homey restaurant provides good food at reasonable prices. *Rua Noel Perdigão 12, 2600, tel. 063/ 271272, fax 63/26538. 19 rooms with bath. Facilities: restaurant, bar, limited parking. MC, V. $*

*Lodging* **Quinta do Alto.** Once you drive through the massive iron gates of this hotel, you may have a hard time leaving. Situated on 50 choice acres of orchards, gardens, and vineyards in the hills high above the Rio

Tejo, just 30 minutes from the Lisbon airport, the Quinta do Alto— once the exclusive summer residence of a prominent Portuguese family—has been recently opened for paying guests. The feeling here is more that of visiting a wealthy friend or relative than of being a lodger. Each of the 10 large bedrooms is comfortably furnished and has a luxurious bathroom; half the units provide terraces and views of the countryside overlooking the Rio Tejo. Red brick adorns the vaulted ceilings, and the tile floors are enhanced with Arraiolos carpets. The price includes use of all the facilities and transportation to and from the airport. *Quinta do Alta, 2600, tel. 063/26850, fax 063/26027. 10 rooms. Facilities: bar, disco, snacks, pool, tennis, squash, fitness room, sauna, kennels, parking. AE, DC, MC, V. $$$$*

★ **Lezíria Parque Hotel.** This four-story, modern hotel-and-apartment complex offers the first new accommodations to be built in Vila Franca de Xira in many years. Conveniently situated off the main Lisbon–Oporto road, the hotel provides a comfortable base from which to explore the bull- and cattle-breeding region across the Rio Tejo. The rooms are small and plainly furnished; there's a pleasant coffee shop on the ground floor. *Estrada Nacional 1, Povos, 2600, tel. 063/26670, fax 063/26990. 71 rooms. Facilities: parking. AE, DC, MC, V. $$*

**Vila Nova de Milfontes** **O Quebra Mar.** If you're looking for fresh grilled fish and a fantastic view of the estuary and sand dunes, there's no better place in town *Dining* than this simple beach bar-restaurant. *End of Beach rd., tel. 083/99263. No credit cards. $*

*Dining and Lodging* **Castelo de Milfontes.** This 16th-century castle was built on ancient foundations, for it was believed that the spirits there would ward off ★ marauding Algerian pirates. In recent times owner and hostess Dona Margarida de Castro e Almeida has lovingly transformed this ivy-covered edifice into a comfortable guest house. Nearly everything you would expect a castle to have is still intact: battlements, a drawbridge, moat, and a suit of armor. The rooms are comfortably furnished and offer inspiring views over the dunes and estuary. There is no public restaurant, but the hotel provides meals for guests in a lovely, intimate, family-style dining area lined with tiles. Full board is required. *Castelo de Milfontes, 7645, tel. 083/96108. 7 rooms. Facilities: bar. $$*

# 6 The Algarve

*By Jules Brown*

The Algarve, Portugal's southernmost coastal region, is the most favored destination of foreign visitors to the country. It's a well-known holiday center with clean, sandy beaches and excellent sports facilities, coupled with an equable climate and dining and lodging choices to suit all budgets. Many Europeans fly here directly and rarely stray more than a few kilometers from their resorts. Even for those visitors based in Lisbon, the Algarve is an easy 300-kilometer (183-mile) drive south, and it provides an interesting contrast to the rest of the country.

Along with the region's popularity has come progress, and during the past two decades, the Algarve has been heavily developed, with parts of the once pristine, 240-kilometer (146-mile) coastline now seriously overbuilt. In certain areas apartment complexes, hotels, discos, and bars sprout from every bay and cliff top.

Just 60 years ago, though, the Algarve was rarely visited by tourists, and for centuries before that it remained isolated from the rest of Europe. Phoenicians, Romans, and Visigoths established fishing and trading communities here, but it wasn't until the arrival of the Moors in the 8th century that the region became an important strategic settlement. The Moorish capital of El Gharb (the land beyond), established at the inland town of Silves (in those days called Chelb), had direct access to the sea and at its peak was a grand city with a population of more than 30,000. Although Silves fell to the Christians in 1189, the Moors weren't completely out of the region until the middle of the 13th century, leaving from their 500-year rule many tangible reminders: the Arabic place names; the white, cube-like houses in the coastal fishing villages; the popular fruits and sweets of the region; and the physical features of many of the people.

In the 15th century Prince Henry the Navigator established a town and a pioneering navigational school at Sagres, where the principles were developed that would enable Portuguese mariners of the 16th century to explore much of the world. After this flurry of activity, though, the Algarve once again settled into obscurity.

The region, a mere 40 kilometers (25 miles) long, is bordered in the north by the Serra de Monchique (Monchique Mountains) and the Serra de Caldeirão (Caldeirão Mountains) and in the east by the Rio Guadiana, a river that isolated the Algarve from contact with neighboring Spain. Over the centuries the region's geography has enabled the inhabitants to keep to themselves, and the area has many natural advantages: Being in the southern part of Portugal and protected by hills makes the Algarve much warmer than any other place in the country; the vegetation is far more luxuriant; the land, originally irrigated by the Moors, supports a profusion of fruits, nuts, and vegetables; and the fishing industry has always flourished.

Despite the development the region still makes a fine coastal vacation spot: There are small fishing villages and secluded beaches (particularly in the west) that so far have escaped attention; an abundance of extraordinary rock formations and idyllic grottoes, also in the west; and (to the east) a series of isolated sand-bar islands and sweeping beaches that balance the crowded excesses of the middle. Even where tourist development is at its heaviest, new construction means landscaped villa and apartment complexes of local materials, which not only fit in well with the surroundings, but keep money circulating within the community. But the Algarve is often seen at its best by visitors who are prepared to abandon the popular beaches for a drive inland. Here, rural Portugal still survives in hill villages, market towns, and agricultural landscapes which, though only a few miles from the coast, seem a world away in attitude.

Year-round the Algarve's weather is welcoming: Winters are mild, and spring is positively delightful, with blossoms covering the hillsides. Summer is, of course, high season, when lodgings are at a premium, prices at their highest, and crowds at their thickest. But you'll also find warm seas, piercing blue skies, and golden sands at the foot of glowing, ocher-red cliffs.

**Warning**  The Algarve is one of Europe's most popular sites for holiday or retirement homes. If you didn't know that before you arrived, you'll soon get the picture in towns such as Albufeira and Praia da Rocha, where an entire industry exists to persuade visitors to tour apartment developments and proposed sites, in hopes that they'll sign on the dotted line. You may be approached by agents offering all sorts of inducements (such as free gifts and meals and drinks) to encourage you to visit time-share properties and villa complexes. Even if you do agree to go on a tour—*never* sign anything, regardless of the promises made.

# Essential Information

## Important Addresses and Numbers

**Tourist Information**  Albufeira (Rua 5 de Outubro, tel. 089/512144), **Armação de Pêra** (Av. Marginal, tel. 082/312145), **Faro** (Airport, tel. 089/818582; Rua da Misericórdia 8–12, tel. 089/803604), **Lagos** (Largo Marquês de Pombal, tel. 082/763031), **Loulé** (Edifício do Castelo, tel. 089/63900), **Monte Gordo** (Av. Marginal, tel. 081/44495), **Olhão** (Largo da Lagoa, tel. 089/713936), **Portimão** (Largo 1 de Dezembro, tel. 082/23695), **Praia da Rocha** (Av. Tomás Cabreira, tel. 082/22290), **Quarteira** (Av. Infante de Sagres, tel. 082/312217), **Sagres** (Promontório de Sagres, tel. 082/64125), **Silves** (Rua 25 de Abril, tel. 082/442255), **Tavira** (Praça da República, tel. 081/22511), **Vila Real de Santo António** (Praça Marquês de Pombal, tel. 081/44495; Frontier Tourist Post, tel. 081/43272).

**Consulates**  **American** and **Canadian** citizens must contact their consulates in Lisbon (*see* Important Addresses and Numbers in Chapter 3). However, there is a **British** consular office in the Algarve: at Portimão (Largo Francisco A. Mauricio 7, tel. 082/417800).

**Emergencies**  If you need medical help, dial **115,** the national emergency number. Each Algarve region has a **health center** for primary medical treatment (the local tourist offices will supply addresses and telephone numbers).

*Hospitals*  **Lagos** (Rua do Castelo dos Governadores, tel. 082/763034); **Faro** (Rua Leão Pinedo, tel. 089/22011); **Portimão** (tel. 082/803411).

*Police*  **Lagos** (Rua General Alberto Silveira, tel. 082/762930); **Faro** (Rua Serpa Pinto, tel. 089/822022).

*Late-Night Pharmacies*  Each town in the Algarve has at least one pharmacy that stays open late; check with the local tourist office for current schedules.

**Travel Agencies**  There are travel agencies on practically every corner in every town in the Algarve. Reliable ones include: **Abreu** (Av. da República 124, Faro, tel. 089/805335; Rua Infante Dom Henrique 83, Portimão, tel. 082/416151), one of the largest and oldest in the country; **Marcus & Harting** (Rua Conselheiro Bivar 69, Faro, tel. 089/24034; Rua Caetano Feu 2, Praia da Rocha, tel. 082/416202; and Areias de São João,

Albufeira, tel. 089/512825); **Star** (agents for American Express: Rua Conselheiro Bivar 36, Faro, tel. 089/805525, and Rua J. Biker 26A, Portimão, tel. 082/416063); **Viagens Rawes** (Rua Conselheiro Bivar 72–78, Faro, tel. 089/803195; Rua da Hortinha 34C, Portimão, tel. 082/23092); **Wagon-Lits** (Rua do Pé da Cruz 14, Faro, tel. 089/ 805403).

## Arriving and Departing by Plane

**Airport and Airlines** International and domestic airlines use **Faro Airport** (tel. 089/ 818281; flight information on 089/818982), which is 6 kilometers (3½ miles) west of the town. Considerably expanded in 1989, the airport now accommodates frequent flights from various European cities, and TAP has regular daily service from Lisbon and Oporto. Flying time from Lisbon is 45 minutes; from Oporto, 90 minutes. At the airport you'll find car rental agencies and a tourist office. (The staff can assist you in finding a hotel room in town.)

**Between the Airport and Faro** It's easiest to take a taxi from the terminal building to the center of Faro. It should cost about 1,000$00, but ask the price in advance. Buses 14 and 16 make the same journey hourly, 8AM–9PM (until 11PM July–mid-Sept.); buy tickets on board (140$00).

## Arriving and Departing by Car, Train, Bus, and Ferry

**By Car** To reach the Algarve from Lisbon, cross the Rio Tejo bridge and take the toll road to Setúbal. Beyond here, the main IP1 highway runs via Alcacer-do-Sal, Grandola, and Ourique, eventually joining N125, the main east–west thoroughfare. To reach Portimão, Lagos, and the western Algarve, turn right; go straight to reach Albufeira; and turn left for Faro and the eastern Algarve. The drive from Lisbon to Faro, Lagos, or Albufeira takes about four hours, longer in the summer weekend and holiday traffic.

Visitors driving from Spain can now cross a new suspension bridge over the Rio Guadiana, from Ayamonte to Vila Real de Santo António. The border is open year-round 7AM–11PM; from July through September and at Easter and Christmas it's open 24 hours.

**By Train** There are regular daily departures to the Algarve from Barreiro station, 10 kilometers (6 miles) south of Lisbon (*see* Essential Information in Chapter 3, Lisbon). The route runs through Setúbal to the rail junction of Tunes (3 hours from Barreiro): Trains continue from Tunes on to Albufeira (another 10 minutes), Faro (another 40 minutes), and all stations east to Vila Real de Santo António (another 2 hours). For the western route to Silves (20 minutes) and Lagos (1 hour), you must change trains at Tunes.

**By Bus** Various companies run daily express buses between Lisbon and Portimão (4 hours 30 minutes), Lagos (5 hours 30 minutes), Faro (5 hours 30 minutes), Tavira (5 hours), and Vila Real de Santo António (5 hours 30 minutes). Generally this is more comfortable than traveling by train, and some of the luxury coaches have a toilet, TV, and food service. Any travel agency in Lisbon can reserve a seat for you; in summer, book at least 24 hours in advance.

Four buses a day run from the Spanish town of Ayamonte to Vila Real de Santo António. The 3:15PM bus connects in Vila Real de Santo António with buses that go on to Faro and Lagos.

**By Ferry** The car/passenger ferry that runs between Ayamonte in Spain and Vila Real de Santo António is an alternative to driving over the new suspension bridge. In season ferries run April through October, daily 8AM–1PM with departures every 30 minutes; November–March, daily 9AM–9PM, with hourly departures. The journey takes 15 minutes and costs 130$00 per person, 800$00 per car.

## Getting Around

Public transportation in general is fairly good although sometimes infrequent on Sundays and holidays. Regardless, this region is one of the few in Portugal where having a car isn't essential (though, of course, it would make you more flexible).

**By Car** The east–west N125 extends 165 kilometers (100 miles) from the Spanish border to Vila do Bispo, in the far west of the Algarve. It runs parallel to the coast but slightly inland, with clearly signed turnoffs to the beach towns.New, faster stretches of highway are under construction everywhere, and roadwork and diversions add to the traffic that's normally to be expected near the busy resorts. In places the driving can be very slow indeed. In inland areas, minor country roads are not always well maintained.

*Car Rentals* Most of the major international firms have offices at Faro Airport, and many have branches elsewhere in the Algarve, too. Try **Auto Jardim** (Albufeira: Av. da Liberdade, tel. 089/589715; Faro: airport, tel. 089/818433); **Avis** (Albufeira: Rua da Igreja Nova 13, tel. 089/52678; Faro: airport, tel. 089/818538; Lagos: Largo das Portas de Portugal 11, tel. 082/63691; Praia da Rocha: Hotel Algarve, Av. Tomás Cabreira, tel. 082/415029; Quarteira: Centro Comercial Abertura Mar, tel. 089/314519); **Budget Rent-a-Car** (Faro: airport, tel. 089/818888, and Hotel Eva, Av. da República 1, tel. 089/803491; Albufeira: Cerro Grande, tel. 089/514997; Praia da Rocha: Av. Cabreira, tel. 082/415370); **Europcar** (Albufeira: Rua Dr. Diogo Leote 6. tel. 089/512444; Faro: airport, tel. 089/818777 or 089/818726, and Av. da República 2, tel. 089/823778; Monte Gordo: Praça Luis de Camões, Loja D, tel. 081/41747; Praia da Rocha: Av. Tomás Cabreira, tel. 082/415465); **Hertz** (Faro: Rua 1 de Maio, tel. 089/824877).

**By Train** The railroad connects Lagos in the west with Vila Real de Santo António in the east—running close to N125. Several trains a day run the entire scenic route, which takes three to four hours; tickets are very reasonably priced, and the trip is pleasant. Some of the faster trains don't stop at every station, and some of the stations are several kilometers from the towns they serve, though there is usually a connecting bus. The main train stations usually have someone who speaks some English, but it's easiest to get information at the tourist offices. At the Faro and Lagos offices, timetables are posted.

**By Bus** The main form of public transportation in the Algarve is bus, and every town and village has its own terminal. The major terminals are at Lagos (Rossío São João, tel. 082/762944), Faro (Av. da República, tel. 089/803792), Portimão (Largo do Dique, tel. 082/23211), Albufeira (Av. da Liberdade, tel. 089/514301), and Vila Real de Santo António (Av. da República, tel. 081/43195). Most ticket offices have someone who speaks at least a little English. The booklet *Guia Horário* (150$00, available at main terminals) lists every bus service, with timetables and information in English.

Some local services are infrequent or don't run on Sunday. Tickets are relatively inexpensive, though a bus ride always costs more than the comparable train journey.

**Guided Tours**

**Orientation** In summer, various companies regularly run similarly priced guided tours from Faro, Quarteira, Vilamoura, Albufeira, Portimão, and Lagos (*see* Travel Agencies, *above*). Ask for recommendations from your hotel reception staff or the local tourist office representatives.

**Special Interest** A unique tour for the Algarve is a Jeep "safari," which involves traveling to fascinating inland villages on minor, rural roads; lunch is usually included in the price. One company that operates such a tour is **Miltours** (Rua Veríssimo de Almeida 14, Faro, tel. 089/802030).

**Coastal Excursions** Many companies and individual fishermen along the Algarve coast hire out boats for excursions. These range from one-hour tours of local grottos and rock formations to full-day excursions that usually involve a stop at a beach for a barbecue lunch. Main centers for coastal excursions are Albufeira, Vilamoura, Portimão, Tavira, Lagos, Sagres, Vila Real, and Armação de Pêra. Consult the tourist offices in these towns for details, or simply wander down to the local harbor, where the prices and times of the next cruise will be posted.

# Exploring the Algarve

## Orientation

The Algarve may be the simplest region in Portugal to explore, since the one main road—the N125—and the train line connect towns and villages along the entire coast. Towns are close together, and it's possible to see all of the Algarve in a week's time, at a fairly relaxed pace. But even if you spend several days at one of the resorts, you should make an effort to see both the eastern and western ends of the Algarve and an inland town or two, for each has a very distinct character.

The first tour begins in Faro—the Algarve's capital—and goes to various nearby beaches and inland towns. The second tour moves east to the border town of Vila Real de Santo António, from which you may cross into Spain. The third suggested route covers the area from Faro west to Portimão, the most built-up part of the coast, bursting with attractions. The final tour begins in Lagos, the main town of the western Algarve, and continues west to Cabo São Vicente.

### Highlights for First-Time Visitors

Albufeira (*see* Tour 3)
Cabo São Vicente (*see* Tour 4)
Cidade Velha, Faro (*see* Tour 1)
Fortaleza de Sagres (*see* Tour 4)
Igreja de Santo António, Lagos (*see* Tour 4)
Olhão's beaches (*see* Tour 1)
Portimão's harbor (*see* Tour 3)
Serra de Monchique (*see* Tour 3)
Silves (*see* Tour 3)
Tavira (*see* Tour 2)

## Tour 1: Faro and its Environs

*Numbers in the margin correspond to points of interest on the Algarve and Faro maps.*

**1** **Faro,** the provincial capital of the Algarve, is a prosperous city with around 30,000 residents. Many people fly in and pass straight through on their way to beaches east and west, but Faro has an attractive harbor and old town that are worthy of at least one night's stay, and the town makes a fine base for touring the region.

Founded by the Moors, Faro was taken by Afonso III in 1249, at the end of the Arab domination. Much of its architectural value was lost in the late 16th century, when it was sacked by the English under the Earl of Essex. It was further damaged by two 18th-century earthquakes (the last was the one in 1755 that also destroyed Lisbon), although remnants of the medieval walls and some historic buildings can still be seen in the delightful Cidade Velha (Old Town).

**2** You enter the old town through the 18th-century gate, the **Arco da Vila,** which stands in front of the central **Jardim Manuel Bivar** (Manuel Bivar Garden)—note the white marble statue of Saint Thomas Aquinas in a niche at the top.

**3** Take the narrow, cobbled Rua do Município up to the Largo da Sé, a grand square bordered by orange trees and whitewashed palace buildings. The squat, mostly Renaissance-style **Sé,** at the top of the road, retains a Gothic tower but is mostly of interest for its stunning interior of decorated 17th- and 18th-century *azulejos* (tiles). Another highlight, on one side of the nave, is the red Chinoiserie organ, from 1751. *Largo da Sé. Admission free. Open weekdays 10–noon, Sat. at 5PM for services, Sun. 8AM–1 for services.*

**4** Southeast of the cathedral, in Praça Afonso III, you'll come to the 16thcentury Convent of Nossa Senhora da Assunção, which has been converted to house the **Museu Municipal** (Municipal Museum). The conversion makes fine use of the convent's beautiful two-story cloister. The best displays are the archaeological collections: These include fascinating Roman remains from local settlements predating Moorish Faro as well as Roman statues from the excavations at Milreu (*see below*). *Praça Afonso III 14, tel. 089/822402. Admission: 120$00. Open Mon.–Sat. 9:30–noon and 2–5.*

**5** The quiet streets and squares of the old town, with balconies and tilework that decorate even the most unappealing facade, are perfect for strolling through. Other than this there's nothing to do in Old Town unless you can gain entry to one of the churches. Many of them are locked, but you may want to ask the tourist office about seeing the **Igreja de São Francisco** (Church of Saint Francis), east of the Municipal Museum, whose plain facade gives no hint of the richness of its baroque interior. Inside are glorious 18th-century blue-and-white azulejos and a chapel adorned with giltwork. *Largo de São Francisco. Admission free.*

**6 7** Walk back past the Cathedral and through the town gate to the water. The *porto,* or harbor, flanked by Faro's main square, the **Praça Dom Francisco Gomes,** and the Manuel Bivar Gardens, is one of the prettiest places in town. You can sit here at an outdoor café, and watch the boats go about their business.

**8** Continue around the harbor, and on the dockside past the Hotel Eva you'll find the **Museu Maritimo** (Maritime Museum), where models of local fishing craft are displayed alongside real boats of war and

181

# The Algarve

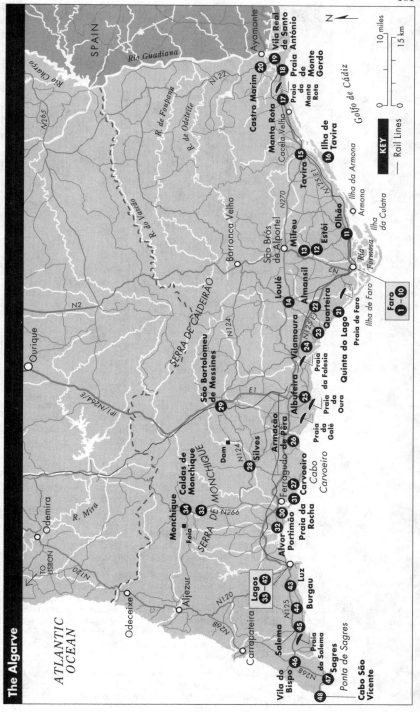

182

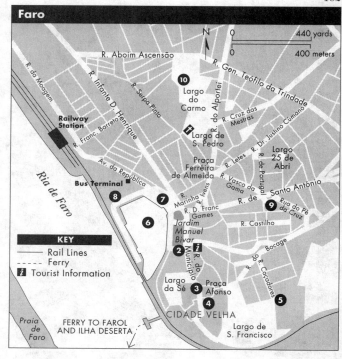

Arco da Vila, **2**

Igreja do
Carmo, **10**

Igreja de São
Francisco, **5**

Museu
Etnografico
Regional, **9**

Museu
Maritimo, **8**

Museu
Municipal, **4**

Porto, **6**

Praca Dom
Francisco
Gomes, **7**

Sé, **3**

exploration. *Rua Comunidade Luisada, tel. 089/822001. Admission: 120$00. Open Mon.–Sat. 10–11 and 2:30–4:30.*

**Time Out**  The **Café Alianca** (Rua Francisco Gomes 7–11) is an old-style coffeehouse situated halfway around the harbor between Rua Francisco Gomes and Rua Marinha. Inside you'll find a timeworn ambience, and outside a sidewalk café facing the water.

East of the harbor, in the pedestrian shopping streets around Rua de Santo António, you'll find much of what makes Faro tick as a tourist town: dozens of bars, restaurants, shops, and sidewalk hawkers selling souvenirs and snacks. Spare some time for culture, too, in the nearby **Museu Etnografico Regional**, just off Rua de Santo António. This gallery sheds light on the local fishing industry by way of various models and diagrams, and displays crafts and the reconstructions of typical house interiors. *Rua do Pé da Cruz, tel. 089/27610. Admission: 120$00. Open weekdays 9:30–noon and 2–6.*

Ten minutes' walk northwest across the city center, you'll come to the Baroque **Igreja do Carmo** (Carmo Church), which is flanked by twin bell towers and looks very out of place amid the modern buildings surrounding it. The real interest is inside: a door to the right of the altar leads to the **Capela dos Ossos** (Chapel of the Bones), whose walls are covered in skulls and bones taken from nearby monks' graves—an eerie sight, to say the least! *Largo do Carmo. Admission 50$00. Open Mon.–Sat. 10–1 and 3–5.*

After touring the city, most visitors are keen to head for the local beaches, and the nearest one, though it's thick with crowds, is on the **Ilha de Faro,** a sandbar island 5 kilometers (3 miles) southwest of

town. You can reach the long, sandy beach—the Praia de Faro—by
road; Bus 16 leaves hourly (8AM–10PM) from a stop opposite the bus
terminal for the 25-minute ride. Or, you can take a ferry from the jetty
below Cidade Velho to Farol on Culatra Island (*see below*) or to Ilha
Deserta (June–Sept. 3 ferries daily; fare 1,000$00 round-trip).

**⑪** Leaving Faro, take the N125 east 8 kilometers (5 miles) to the small
18th-century port town of **Olhão,** on the Ria Formosa (River Formosa). (Regular trains and buses also come here from Faro.) During
the Napoleonic Wars, Olhão's inhabitants defied the French block-
ade on trade with Britain and profited greatly from smuggling,
building their North African–style, cube-shaped whitewashed
houses with the proceeds. Local fishermen reputedly sailed to Brazil in 1808 to inform the exiled Dom João VI that the French had de-
parted from Portugal—for which service, undertaken without
navigational aids, Olhão was granted a town charter.

Though modern construction has destroyed a great deal of its former charm, Olhão's fishing port is still colorful, and its intricate old
town quarter has retained some of its earlier attraction. For a view
over Olhão, visit the 17th-century **parish church** (south end of Av. da
República, open Tues.–Sun. 9–noon and 2–5), from whose bell tower you can look down upon the narrow streets and cubical houses.
One of the Algarve's best food **markets** (Mon.–Sat. 7–2) is held in the
buildings on the riverfront in the town gardens. Feast your eyes
upon the shellfish for which Olhão is renowned: Mussels, in particular, are a local specialty.

To get to the local beaches, take a ferry from the jetty east of the
town gardens. (If the kiosk is closed, you can buy tickets on board.)
The sandy islands of **Armona** and **Culatra** lie to the east and are
reached in 15 and 40 minutes, respectively. Armona is the best, with
some fine, isolated stretches of sand, holiday villas, and café–bars;
Culatra supports several ramshackle fishing communities, although
at the southern village of **Farol** (meaning lighthouse), you'll find
agreeable beaches. This entire section of coastline, including the islands and river inlets, has been declared a nature reserve, because a
great number of migratory birds flock to the area on their way south
for the winter. *Ferries run hourly in July and Aug., 3 or 4 times a
day the rest of the year. Schedule available at tourist office. Round-
trip fare:160$00 Armona, 200$00 Culatra.*

**⑫** About 9 kilometers (6 miles) north of Faro, a road branches east
from the N2 to the village of **Estói** (which you can also visit by bus).
Here the 18th-century **Palácio do Visconde de Estói** (Palace of the
Counts of Estói) is closed to the public, but visitors can stroll around
the formal gardens. *Admission: free. Open Tues.–Sat. 9–12:30 and
2–5:30.*

**⑬** Ten minutes' walk west of the village brings you to the extensive Roman ruins at **Milreu,** first excavated in 1876. The settlement was
once known as Roman Ossonoba, and the remains date from the second to the sixth centuries; they include a temple (later converted
into a Christian basilica) and mosaic fragments that adorn some of
the third-century baths. You will have seen some of the more porta-
ble remains in the gardens of the Palace of the Counts; others are in
Faro's Municipal Museum. *Admission free. Open Tues.–Sun. 10–
12:30 and 2–5.*

Seven kilometers (4 miles) farther north on the N2 is the village of
**São Brás de Alportel,** which boasts one of the Algarve's two
*pousadas* (inns). Turn west off N2, and take N270 13 kilometers (8
**⑭** miles) to **Loulé,** a little market town in the hills. Once a Moorish

stronghold, the town has preserved the ruins of its medieval **Castelo** (Castle), which houses the historical museum and archives, as well as the tourist office. Nearby is the restored 13th-century **Igreja Matriz** (Parish Church), which is decorated with handsome tiles and wood carvings and has an unusual wrought-iron pulpit. *Castle and museum: Largo Dom Pedro I, no phone. Admission free. Open daily 9–12:30 and 2:30–5; Igreja Matriz: Largo Pr. C. da Silva. Open Mon.–Sat. 9–noon and 2–5:30.*

Loulé is known for its crafts. The tiny, cobbled streets with white-washed houses that run between the castle and the church are lined with workshops where lace, leather, and copper goods are manufactured. It's fascinating to wander this area, watch the craftspeople at work, and explore the nooks and crannies of the old town. Note the many houses with sculpted plasterwork on the white chimneys, a typical Algarve sight. The rest of Loulé, which is more developed, is overwhelmed by the main boulevard and modern buildings, but there's a pleasant municipal park at the top of town.

Return to Faro on N125-4, which runs southeast and after 8 kilometers (5 miles) joins N125. (It's a 17-kilometer/10-mile trip to Loulé by direct bus from Faro, which makes an easy half-day tour.)

## Tour 2: The Eastern Algarve

Take N125 east from Faro for 30 kilometers (18 miles) to reach ⑮ **Tavira,** often called the prettiest town in the Algarve. At the mouth of the Rio Gilão, it is immediately endearing, with its old streets and pastel-colored houses strung along both sides of the quiet river. Of the two low bridges that span the river, the one adjacent to the arcaded Praça da República is of Roman origin, though it was rebuilt in the 17th century. Many of Tavira's white 18th-century houses retain their original doorways and coats-of-arms; others have peculiar, four-sided roofs. From the battlemented walls of the central **Castelo** (Admission free. Open weekdays 8–5:30, weekends 10–7), reached by a stepped street from Rua da Liberdade, you can look down over Tavira's many church spires and across the river delta to the sea.

If it's open, take a look inside the adjacent church of **Santa Maria do Castelo,** which was built upon the site of a Moorish mosque in the 13th century. Although almost all of it was destroyed by the 1755 earthquake, the church retains its original Gothic doorway. Tavira's other major church, located just west of the main square, is the nearby **Igreja da Misericórdia** (open daily 10–noon and 2–5), a beautiful Renaissance building with a portal dating from 1541.

Tavira is a tuna-fishing port, and you'll find it full of local color—especially if you walk along the riverfront gardens, past the vibrant covered market, to the harbor. The market always has an array of fresh fish, while farther up the quayside the picturesque tangle of fishing boats and nets makes a good snapshot.

**Time Out** You should be sure to sample the *atum* (fresh tuna) while you're in Tavira. Fresh tuna steaks, often grilled and served with onions, are on the menus of restaurants all over town at remarkably low prices. For no-frills dining at its best, with the local fishermen, walk past the market to the line of little basic café-restaurants facing the fishing boats.

⑯ On the nearby **Ilha de Tavira,** a long, offshore sandbar, there are good beaches served regularly by ferries that leave from a jetty 2 kilometers (1¼ miles) east of Tavira. In summer, a bus (marked Quatro Águas) shuttles from the center of town to the jetty. *Ferries run daily May–mid-Oct.; on the half-hour July–Aug., hourly at other times. Fare: 130$00 round-trip.*

There are more good beaches east of Tavira: A particularly nice one, which also has an offshore sandbar, is at the tiny, undeveloped village of **Cacela Velha,** 10 kilometers (6 miles) away. A few miles farther, where the sandbars merge with the shore, is the excellent **㉗ Manta Rota** beach. Unfortunately, those long, unbroken beaches make ideal terrain for heavy touristic development.

㉘ Six kilometers (4 miles) east of Manta Rota on N125, pine woods and orchards break up the flat landscape around the large resort of **Praia de Monte Gordo,** which lies just 4 kilometers (2½ miles) from the Spanish border. A town of brightly colored houses and extensive tourist facilities, Monte Gordo features plenty of hotels and restaurants, as well as a casino, nightclubs, and discos. The long, flat stretch of beach is very popular, and visitors enjoy the highest average seawater temperature in the country. Be careful, though: The beach is steeply sloped, and swimmers quickly find themselves in deep water.

㉙ **Vila Real de Santo António,** is the last stop before Spain. The original town was destroyed by a tidal wave in the 17th century and was not rebuilt until the late 18th century, when the Marquês de Pombal constructed a new, gridded town. Consequently, Vila Real, which took only five months to complete, is a showpiece of 18th-century town planning. Like most border towns, it's a lively place, with plenty of bars and restaurants and some traffic-free central streets that encourage evening strolling. For all that, however, there's very little to see.

You might want to take an hour or so to visit the **Museu de Manuel Cabanas,** on the main square, which contains some paintings, engravings, and local ethnographical items. *Praça Marquês de Pombal, no phone. Admission free. Open Tues.–Sun. 11–1 and 2–7.*

The new suspension bridge to Spain is open for traffic, and ferries still cross the river to the Spanish town of Ayamonte.

A short excursion 5 kilometers (3 miles) north on N122 takes you through low hills and parallels the course of the Rio Guadiana to **㉚ Castro Marim.** This was the first headquarters of the monastic Order of Christ, founded in the 14th century after the dissolution of the Knights Templar. The town has the remains of what was once a massive castle, built by Afonso III, which was unfortunately laid to waste by the 1755 earthquake. The views from here are grand, and the surroundings have been turned into a nature reserve; there are paths through the nearby river marshes.

## Tour 3: The Central Algarve

The central Algarve, between Faro and Portimão, sees the heaviest concentration of tourist development: Although some of the resorts are household names in Europe, in between built-up areas you can still discover quiet bays, amazing rock formations, and exclusive, secluded hotels and villas. With a car it's easy to travel the few kilometers inland that make all the difference: Minor roads lead into the hills, to towns that have resisted the changes wrought upon the developed coast.

About 10 kilometers (6 miles) northwest of Faro on N125 you'll see minor roads branching off south to the luxury resort villages of **Quinta do Lago** and **Vale do Lobo,** the latter one of the Algarve's earliest resorts. Both have superb facilities—from golf to sailboarding—and the tennis center at Vale do Lobo is among the best in Europe.

Just off N125, 13 kilometers (8 miles) from Faro, you'll come to the town of **Almansil** with its chapel of **São Lourenço** (St. Lawrence), built in 1730. Notable are the chapel's blue-and-white azulejo panels and its intricate gilt work. The cottages next to the church have been transformed into an art gallery that exhibits contemporary Portuguese works and holds occasional classical music concerts.

Turn off N125 southwest onto N396, which in about 6 kilometers (4 miles) will bring you to **Quarteira,** a bustling high-rise resort that was once a quiet fishing village. There was always an excellent beach, but now there are also golf courses and tennis courts. The remains of a Roman villa have been unearthed in the area. The adjacent town of **Vilamoura** (4 kilometers/2½ miles west), with no historic pedigree whatever, is another highly developed resort: It has an impressively large marina, several golf courses, a major tennis center and other sports facilities, as well as luxury hotels and a casino.

Several beaches west of Vilamoura—Falesia, Olhos d'Agua, and Praia da Oura—fall within the ambit of **Albufeira,** which lies 4 kilometers (2½ miles) south of the main road. Brash Albufeira, a favorite with British holidaymakers, has mushroomed from an attractive fishing village into the Algarve's largest and busiest resort. The town beach with its interesting rock formations, caves, and grottoes, attracts thousands of visitors daily (it's reached by tunnel from the main street, Rua 5 de Outubro). The noisy center, around Largo Eng. Duarte Pacheco, is dominated by cafés, bars, restaurants, discos, and souvenir shops.

Despite the crowds, Albufeira has much to commend it, and a lunchtime stop at one of the cafés in the old town may be worth your while. One of the last Algarve towns to hold out against the Christian army in the 13th century, Albufeira still has a distinctly Moorish flavor that's apparent in the steep, narrow streets and hundreds of whitewashed houses snuggled on the slopes of nearby hills. There are scant remains of a Moorish castle on the heights above town—under the Arabs the town was called Al-Buhera (castle on the sea)—and the bustling fish market and old harbor retain some interest, too.

On most summer days, the town beach is so crowded that it may be hard to enjoy: If you want more space, you'll have to move farther afield. Possibilities include the beautiful beaches of São Rafael and Praia da Galé, though there's been much recent development here, too. They're just 4 kilometers (2½ miles) west on local roads. The coves and rocks are very attractive, but don't expect them to be deserted.

The bustling resort of **Armação de Pêra,** 14 kilometers (8½ miles) west of Albufeira, has the largest beach in the Algarve, a wide, sandy stretch with a pretty promenade. Local boats take sightseers on cruises to the caves and grottoes along the shore, past the Praia Senhora da Rocha (the Beach of Our Lady of the Rocks) to the west, named after the Romanesque chapel above the beach.

Return to N125—and at **Porches,** 16 kilometers (10 miles) farther, you can stop at a variety of roadside shops that sell handmade pottery. Five kilometers (3 miles) farther west is **Lagoa,** a market town known for its wine, *vinho Lagoa;* the red is particularly good. It's possible to tour the winery here, but you must ask the tourist office in Portimão to help you arrange for the visit.

㉗ The local beach is 5 kilometers (3 miles) south, at **Carvoeiro,** whose picturesque harbor will merit the diversion. Like many small-scale fishing villages in the region, Carvoeiro is beginning to show the strain of recent development.

Return to Lagoa and take N124-1 north 7 kilometers (4 miles) to ㉘ **Silves,** on the Rio Arade. Here you can see the rural side of the Algarve: It's not unusual to be stuck for miles behind tractors or donkey carts, and you may have to be bold when you pass. But while you're exercising your patience, note the surrounding fields planted with orange groves and nut—particularly almond—trees.

Once the Moorish capital of the Algarve, Silves is one of the region's most intriguing inland towns. Rich and prosperous in medieval times, it remained in Arab hands until 1249, though not without attempts by Christian forces to take it. In 1189, following a siege led by Sancho I, the city was sacked by Crusaders, who subsequently put thousands of Moors to the sword. Silves finally lost its importance after its almost complete destruction by the 1755 earthquake. Today it's an enjoyable excursion from the coast, as trains and buses make the 20-kilometer (12-mile) trip north from Portimão.

The Moors built an early fortress in Silves, which survived untouched until the Christian sieges. The remains that you see today, from the 12th-century sandstone **fortress,** with its impressive parapets, were restored in 1835 and still dominate the upper part of town. You can walk around the walls for expansive views over Silves and the surrounding hills. The rest of the castle is a mere shell, its interior a modern garden watched over by a statue of Sancho I. *Admission free. Open daily 9–1 and 2:30–5:30.*

Immediately below the fortress stands the 12th- to 13th-century **Santa Maria da Sé** (Cathedral of Saint Mary), built on the site of a Moorish mosque, which saw service as the Cathedral of the Algarve until the 16th century. The 1755 earthquake and indifferent restoration have left it rather plain inside, but its exterior gargoyles and tower still are interesting to see. *Admission free; donations accepted. Open June–Sept., daily 8:30–1 and 2:30–6; Oct.–May, until 5:30.*

Silves's excellent **Museu Arqueologia** is a few minutes' walk below the cathedral, off Rua da Sé. Although the labels are in Portuguese, the items on display still give interesting insights into the history of the area. A primary attraction is an Arab water cistern, preserved in situ, with a 10-meter- (30-foot-) deep well—which is among the best Arab remains in town. *Rua das Portas de Loulé, tel. 082/ 444832. Admission: 300$00. Open Mon.–Sat. 10–12:30 and 2–6.*

**Time Out** From the archaeological museum, walk back to the Praça do Município and then downhill to the foot of town where, close to the medieval bridge, you'll come to the **produce market.** It's open Monday through Saturday, and is at its liveliest during the morning. If you arrive at lunchtime, you can have a delicious meal of spicy grilled chicken or fish from the outdoor barbecue of one of the simple restaurants facing the river.

Take N124 northeast for 12 kilometers (7 miles) for a pleasant excursion to the scenic **Barragem de Arade,** a man-made dam set in the hills, where there's a restaurant, a picnic area, and boat rentals. Another 8 kilometers (5 miles) farther the road passes through the attractive countryside village, **São Bartolomeu de Messines,** whose parish church dates from the late 14th century and has interior columns of spiraling, rope-like stonework. You can take a coffee break in the village before retracing your steps through Silves to N125.

Once back on the main road, continue for another 9 kilometers (5½ miles) to **Portimão,** the most important fishing port in the Algarve. Even before the Romans arrived, there was a settlement here, at the mouth of the Rio Arade. Devastated in the 1755 earthquake, the town was revived by the fish-canning industry in the 19th century. Modern Portimão sprawls with concrete high-rise buildings but remains a cheerful, busy place: Tourists from nearby resorts come here especially to shop. The colorful fishing boats now unload their catch at a modern terminal across the river, but you can still sample charcoal-grilled sardines—a local specialty—at open-air restaurants along the harbor.

**Time Out**  Lunch outdoors at Portimão's **harborside** is a must. You sit at one of many inexpensive eateries eating the excellent grilled sardines, chewy fresh bread, a simple salad, and local red wine, while around you the air is thick with barbecue smoke and the tang of the sea.

Across the bridge, in the former fishing hamlet of **Ferragudo,** are the ruins of the 16th-century castle of São João, built to defend Portimão from the marauding English, Dutch, and Spanish. Although it has not yet gone the tourist route of nearby Praia da Rocha (*see below*), Ferragudo is fast becoming developed around its attractive beach to the south, where there are restaurants and bars and you can rent sailboards.

**Praia da Rocha,** 3 kilometers (2 miles) south of Portimão, was one of the first resorts in the Algarve to undergo a transformation for the mass market, and it's now dominated by high-rise apartments and hotels. It nevertheless has an excellent beach, made all the more interesting by a series of huge colored rocks worn into strange shapes by the wind and sea. There's also the 16th-century **Santa Catarina,** a defensive castle that has been partially restored and contains an open-air café. Regular buses run throughout the day between Portimão and Praia da Rocha.

Other beaches stretch to the west, toward the handsome old port of **Alvor,** whose central narrow streets and whitewashed houses are increasingly being encroached upon by villa and hotel development. The crowds are attracted to Alvor's huge beach which, while not one of the region's best, does usually have space to spare.

While you're in the central Algarve, you should drive (there are buses, too) north from Portimão on route N124, which becomes N266, into the green hills of the **Serra de Monchique,** where the cool breezes will revive you after the summertime heat of the coast. After 18 kilometers (11 miles) you'll reach the beautifully sited spa of **Caldas de Monchique,** whose natural therapeutic waters have been in use since Roman times. A revival in popularity in the 19th century left the town with an attractive set of period houses and municipal buildings, including a casino, which is now a handicrafts market. These somewhat make up for the unappealing modern spa buildings.

The N266 climbs another 6 kilometers (4 miles) to the market town of **Monchique,** also known for its handicrafts, particularly the carving and woodworking. From here, take N266-3 west a short way to the highest point of the mountain range, the peak at **Foia** (902 meters), where there's a café and superb views over the western Algarve.

Having taken in the views, you can return to Portimão, where the N125 will take you either east back to Faro, or west and on to Lagos.

## Tour 4: Lagos and the Western Algarve

*Numbers in the margin correspond to points of interest on the Lagos and the Algarve maps.*

From the bustling holiday town of Lagos, the rest of the western Algarve is easily accessible. This is the most unspoiled part of the region, with some genuinely isolated beaches and bays along a wind-buffeted route that reaches to the southwest Cape of Saint Vincent.

**㉟** **Lagos**—an attractive, busy fishing port with some beautiful cove beaches nearby—draws a mixed international crowd. Here, you feel, is a town whose inhabitants follow a way of life that goes beyond simply catering to tourists, although there is no shortage of attractions for visitors. The main pedestrian streets leading off the central **㊱** **Praça Gil Eanes** are lined with shops, restaurants, cafés, and bars— all of which do a roaring business in summer.

The town has a venerable history, with sights to prove it. Lagos's deep-water harbor and wide bay have made it a natural choice for various groups of settlers, starting with the Carthaginians, who founded the town around 400 BC. Under the Moors Lagos was a center for trade between Portugal and Africa, and even after the town fell to the Christians in 1241, trade continued and was greatly expanded under the rule of Prince Henry the Navigator, who used Lagos as his base. The town later became capital of the Algarve, a role it lost in 1756 after the great earthquake had reduced much of the city to rubble. Nonetheless, some interesting buildings remain, as does the circuit of defensive walls, built between the 14th and 16th centuries over older, Moorish bastions. Some of the best-preserved parts of the walls can be seen from near the Praça da República, at the southwest end of Avenida dos Descobrimentos.

**㊲** In the 15th century, an African slave market was held under the arches of the old **Casa da Alfandega** (Customs House), at the back of the Praça da República.

**㊳** Across the square stands the **Igreja da Santa Maria** (Church of Saint Mary), from whose Manueline windows the king Dom Sebastião is said to have addressed his troops before setting off on his crusade of 1578. The crusade was a failure, and the king and his men died in Morocco at Alcácer-Quibir; Dom Sebastião is remembered by a much-maligned modernistic statue that stands in Praça Gil Eanes. *Praça da República. Admission free. Open daily 10–1 and 2–5.*

**㊴** A short walk away, up Rua Henriques Correira Silva, is Lagos's most extraordinary building, the early 18th-century Baroque **Igreja de Santo António** (Church of Saint Anthony), off Rua General Alberto Silveira. The decoration inside is a magnificent riot of gilt extravagance made possible by the import of gold from Brazil. Dozens of cherubs and angels clamber over the walls, among fancifully carved woodwork and azulejos. Alongside the church is the **Museu Municipal** (Municipal Museum), housing an amusing jumble of exhibits, including mosaics, archaeological and ethnological items, and an early town charter from 1504—all arranged haphazardly. *Rua*

Casa da
Alfandega, **37**

Igreja da Santa
Maria, **38**

Igreja da Santo
António, **39**

Ponta da
Bandeira, **40**

Ponta da
Piedade, **42**

Praça Gil
Eanes, **36**

Praia de Dona
Ana, **41**

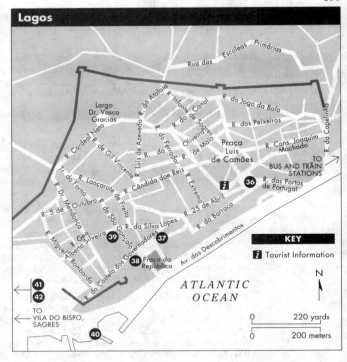

*Henriques Correira Silva, tel. 082/762301. Admission to church
and museum: 200$00. Open Tues.–Sat. 9:30–12:30 and 2–1.*

The largest beach near town and one of the best centers for water
sports is the 4-kilometer (2½-mile) stretch of Meia Praia to the
northeast. Buses leave for here from the riverfront Avenida dos
Descobrimentos, and in summer there's ferry service from **Ponta da
Bandeira,** close to the 17th-century fort that defended the entrance
to the harbor in bygone days. From inside the fort you can look out
onto decent ocean views. *Av. dos Descobrimentos. Admission:
200$00. Open Tues.–Sat. 10–1 and 2–6, Sun 10–1.*

All the other good beaches are south of town and can be reached on
the main road (an extension of Avenida dos Descobrimentos) running past the fort. You could drive to the prettiest one—**Praia de
Dona Ana**—by following the signs for the Hotel Golfinho (*see* Dining
and Lodging, *below*), but the 30-minute walk along the cliff top is
also very enjoyable. If you choose to hoof it, pass the fort, turn left
at the fire station, and follow the footpaths, which go all the way to
the most southerly point, **Ponta da Piedade,** and its lighthouse.
Along the way are several delightful cove beaches with fascinating
rock formations and some beach-cafés. An interesting perspective is
a view of the rocks and caves from the water: Fishing boats near the
Ponta da Bandeira advertise cruises; check for departure times at
the boards on the quayside.

Lagos is the western terminus of the railway that runs from Vila
Real de Santo António. To go farther west it's convenient to have a
car, though new highway construction slows traffic considerably in
places. There's good bus service from Lagos to all the destinations

on this tour, but you may have to walk from N125 to the more isolated beaches.

(43) Six kilometers (4 miles) west along the N125 is the resort town of **Luz,** whose beautiful beach is 3 kilometers (2 miles) south of the highway, down a signposted minor road. Most visitors stay in fairly new villa or apartment complexes, which have excellent watersports facilities. Despite the modern nature of the development, Luz is an attractive place. The tourist office in Lagos can advise about accommodations.

(44) **Burgau,** a few kilometers farther west, is similarly developed, while retaining something of its erstwhile village character. It has a main square and narrow streets, and is very popular with British tourists. After another 5 kilometers (3 miles) you'll come to the turnoff
(45) for **Salema,** with a lovely, 600-meter-long beach at the foot of surrounding green hills. New development is fast changing the face of this pretty place, until recently a simple fishing village, but Salema is still one of the most relaxed of local towns.

(46) The N125 highway ends its run 8 kilometers (5 miles) farther west, at the small inland town of **Vila do Bispo,** a quiet place whose church—right in the center—is covered inside with 18th-century azulejos. Once you've seen this, and stopped for a coffee at one of the cafés on the central square, you'll be ready to take N268 south through the rugged terrain that appears as you approach the windy
(47) headland at **Sagres.** In the 15th century, on this harsh, barren moorland, Prince Henry the Navigator established the famous school of navigation where he trained his captains before they set out on their voyages of discovery.

In the 19th century the village of Sagres was rebuilt over earthquake ruins and today has little of note apart from a series of fine, sweeping beaches. Mainly a young crowd vacations here, and apartments and villas are growing steadily in number, with the expansion threatening to overwhelm the little square and fishing harbor.

You'll see the road that leads from the village to the tunnel-like entrance of the **Fortaleza de Sagres** (Sagres Fortress), an enormous run of defensive walls that sit high above the crashing ocean. On foot from the village, it's about a 15-minute walk, and the views are spectacular. The fortress was rebuilt in the 17th century and contains buildings often claimed to be Prince Henry's house and school (now used as the tourist office), though it's more likely that Henry built his school at Cabo São Vicente (*see below*). But this doesn't detract from the powerful atmosphere at the fortress: Certainly the **Venta da Rosa** (Wind Compass, or compass rose) dates from Prince Henry's period: this large circular construction made of stone and packed earth is set in the courtyard just inside the fortress. It was only uncovered this century, though it is of the same age as the partially ruined and forlorn Graça chapel, which stands near the tourist office.

(48) Even more breathtaking than the views from the fortress are the sights from **Cabo São Vicente** (Cape of Saint Vincent), 6 kilometers (4 miles) west, at the end of the flat coastal road. At this point—the southwest tip of the European continent, justly called *O Fim do Mundo,* "the end of the world"—the landmass juts starkly into the rough waters of the Atlantic. Legends attach themselves easily to this desolate place, which the Romans once considered sacred. It takes its modern name from the martyr Saint Vincent, whose relics were brought here in the 8th century; it is said that they were transported to Lisbon 400 years later in a boat piloted by ravens.

Most historians agree it was here that Henry built his house and school and that Vasco da Gama, Ferdinand Magellan, and other great explorers learned their craft 500 years ago. The ancient buildings were long ago destroyed by pirates and earthquakes—and the only structure that remains is a splendidly isolated **lighthouse,** the grounds of which are open to the public. The beacon is said to have the strongest reflectors in Europe—they cast a beam 96 kilometers (59 miles) out to sea. And the views are remarkable: Turquoise water whips across the base of the rust-color cliffs below; the fortress is visible to the east; and beyond lies the immense Atlantic.

On your return from the cape to Sagres you can stop halfway at **Belixe** for a drink or a bite at one of the café-bars, and if you're not staying overnight at the Pousada do Infante (*see* Dining and Lodging, *below*), you can return on N125 to Lagos.

## What to See and Do with Children

The Algarve has several aquatic theme parks, where you'll find huge water slides, rapids, surf pools, other water-based amusements, and restaurants and snack bars. The main ones include **The Big One,** at Alcantarilha (tel. 082/322827), **Atlantic Park,** near Quarteira (tel. 089/397–8282), and **Slide & Splash,** near Portimão (tel. 082/341685). **Zoo Marine,** a park with rides, swimming pools, gardens, a cinema, and dolphin and sea lion shows, is at Guia near Albufeira (tel 089/561104). Other attractions: the splendid castle at **Silves** (*see* Tour 3); a **boat trip** to the caves and grottoes at Lagos (*see* Tour 4) or at Armação de Pêra (*see* Tour 3); the dramatic fort at **Sagres** and **Cabo São Vicente** (*see* Tour 4).

## Off the Beaten Track

The following loop tour inland along beautiful drives puts you in open countryside, which, while not exactly uncharted territory, will show you a side of the Algarve that most visitors never see.

Take N122 north from just outside Vila Real de Santo António. It climbs into low hills and parallels the course of the Rio Guadiana as it passes through **Castro Marim** (*see* Tour 2). After 37 kilometers (22½ miles), take N122-1 northeast to the border town of Alcoutim, a quiet little village with a ruined castle. Return to N122 and continue west along the N124, a 65-kilometer (40-mile) route with especially fine views, until it joins N2, 14 kilometers (8½ miles) north of São Brás de Alportel.

# Shopping

In every Algarve town you'll be able to find a selection of local crafts and souvenirs in centrally located shops or at the markets and country fairs. In summer, all the main tourist resorts have a lot of casual sidewalk stalls, where you can buy items such as jewelry, handicrafts, art, and clothes.

Probably the best place to shop is in Portimão, where many visitors enjoy spending at least half a day. The main shopping street is **Rua do Comércio,** while **Rua de Santa Isabel** specializes in crafts, leather goods, ceramics, crystal, and fashion. The enormous **Prisunic Shopping Center** (open daily 10 AM–10 PM), has 150 shops and restaurants under one roof. It's on the N124 (toward Praia da Rocha) at the junction with Avenida Miguel Bombarda.

Albufeira also boasts a **Prisunic Shopping Center** (open daily 10 AM–10 PM), a complex with more than 60 shops on the bypass road above town. In Faro the best shopping area is the pedestrian **Rua do Santo António** and the surrounding streets, where you'll find local handicrafts, ceramics, and leather goods.

## Markets and Country Fairs

All the main towns and villages have regular **food markets,** usually held daily from 8–2. Among the best are those in Olhão, Tavira, Lagos, and Silves. Larger weekly and monthly markets where a wider variety of produce and goods is sold are held in Albufeira on the first and third Tuesdays of the month; in Loulé every Saturday; in Lagos on the first Saturday of the month; in Portimão on the first Monday; in Quarteira on the second Wednesday; in Sagres on the first Friday; and in Silves on the third Monday. Ask the local tourist office for up-to-the-minute details and directions on how to get there.

Every town of any consequence in the Algarve also holds an annual **country fair,** where alongside the market stalls you'll find crafts and entertainment. The dates vary from year to year, so check with local tourist offices.

## Specialty Stores

Ceramics   The **Olaria Pottery** (on the main N125), directly opposite the turn-off for Porches, produces fine traditional and originally designed tiles and tableware. In Portimão there's a branch of the well-known **Vista Alegre** (Rua de Santa Isabel 21), a showroom displaying high-quality, hand-painted porcelain, and also **O Aquario III** (Rua Direita, Loja 10), which sells ceramics, porcelain, and crystal. Albufeira has **Infante Dom Henrique House** (Rua Cândido dos Reis 30), whose stock includes porcelain dishes and baskets and handmade Portuguese earthenware with 17th-century motifs.

Clothing   Reasonably priced hand-knitted sweaters are sold in stores all over the Algarve, and some of the best bargains are at roadside stalls like those outside the fortress at Sagres. For other clothing, you'd do best to visit Portimão's shopping streets, one of the shopping centers, like Prisunic, or one of the regular markets.

Crafts and   For handmade copper items and other metal crafts, visit Portimão's
Antiques    **O Aquario II** (Rua Vasco da Gama 41). Small woven sisal baskets make good souvenirs and are available nearly everywhere. You'll sometimes see women sitting in the doorways of their houses as they weave. Loulé supports several craft workshops (closed Sundays) in the streets of its old town, particularly along **Rua 9 de Abril.** Also, the 19th-century casino in the spa town of Caldas de Monchiqueis now a **handicrafts market** (closed Sundays), selling an excellent range of pottery, clothes, lace, jewelry, and silk. On N125 between Porches and Alcantarilha, **Artisans Village** offers wine tastings and a variety of goods—from ceramics to candles and cork.

Lagos has several good antiques shops. **Casa do Papagaio** (25 Rua 25 de Abril) is more like a messy museum, with its dusty antiques and bric-a-brac piled high in every corner. It's great for browsing even if you don't buy.

Leather Goods   There are branches of the Parisian shoe store **Charles Jourdan** in Portimão (Rua de Santa Isabel 26) and in Albufeira (Edifício Tural, Av. de 25 Abril). For other leather goods, including bags and purses, visit **Gaby's** in Portimão (Rua Direita 5 and Praça Visconde Bívar 15), which sells high-quality items.

# Sports and the Outdoors

### Fishing

Individuals and charter companies offer organized fishing trips from various ports along the Algarve coast. Check the boards on quaysides for prices and departure times, or consult local tourist offices. The best fishing grounds are considered to be the waters off Sagres and Carrapateira (on the Algarve's west coast), and local fishermen recommend October through January as the most fruitful (fishful?) months. You're likely to catch gray mullet, sea bass, moray eels, scabbard fish, and bluefish. **Turinfo** (Praça da República, Sagres, tel. 082/64520) can organize fishing trips around the Sagres peninsula.

### Golf

The Algarve has some of Europe's best golf courses, designed by the likes of Henry Cotton, Frank Pennink, and William Cotton. It's a year-round game here, and most of the courses have a clubhouse with bar and restaurant, practice grounds, and equipment rentals. Contact the **Quinta do Lago Golf Club** (Almansil, tel. 089/396002 or 089/394529), a 36-hole course on the superb Quinta do Lago estate, where the Portuguese Open Championship is held in October; the **Vale do Lobo Golf Club** (Vale do Lobo, tel. 089/394444), with three 9-hole courses; the **Vilamoura Golf Club** (Vilamoura I, tel. 089/313652; Vilamoura II, tel. 089/315562; Vilamoura III, tel. 089/380722 or 089/380724), which has three different courses: two with 18 holes and one with 27; the 18-hole **Parque da Floresta** (Budens, 16 km/9.7 mi west of Lagos, near Salema, tel. 082/65333); or the **Palmares Golf Club** (Monte Palmares, Meia Praia, Lagos, tel. 082/762953 or 082/762961), whose 18 holes overlook Lagos Bay.

Several other courses are currently under construction (ask at local tourist offices for information and a copy of "Sportugal," a brochure that gives details of all Algarve courses). One that was recently finished is the 9-hole **Pine Cliffs Golf and Country Club** (Almansil, tel. 089/501787), a few miles west of Vilamoura. This Martin Hawtree course is magnificently sited, just back from some impressive, scenic cliffs.

At the many hotels with golf facilities, greens fees are included in the room rate. The newest facilities are available to guests at the Sheraton Algarve Hotel, at Pine Cliffs Golf and Country Club. Guests staying at the Hotel Dona Filipe in Vale do Lobo have free use of the **San Lorenzo Golf Club** (Almansil, tel. 089/396522) and a 20% discount at the Vale do Lobo Golf Club. Guests at Alvor's Golfe da Penina may use the hotel's own course, the **Penina Golf Club** (Montes de Alvor, tel. 082/415415).

### Horseback Riding

Equestrian centers in the region include: **Quinta dos Amigos** (Almansil, tel. 089/39436); **Centro Hipico de Vilamoura** (Vilamoura, tel. 089/313033); **Quinta do Paraíso Alto** (Bensafrim, a few miles north of Lagos, tel. 082/67263); and **Paradise Inn** (Almansil, Quinta do Lago road, tel. 089/396864).

## Sailing

**Vilamoura Marina** (8125 Quarteira, tel. 089/312023 or 089/302925), is an enormous, self-contained marina complex with apartments, shops, hotels, sporting and leisure facilities, and 1,000 berths. There are also anchorage and harbor facilities at: Faro, Lagos, Olhão, Portimão, Sagres, and Vila Real. The tourist office will provide details.

Sailboats can be rented at the marinas in Vilamoura (tel. 089/313933), Vale do Lobo (tel. 089/394444), and Torralta, Alvor (tel. 082/20462). If you'd like someone else to do the work, book a cruise on the *Condor de Vilamoura* (tel. 089/314070), which sails out of Vilamoura Marina twice a day toward Albufeira. A 3-hour cruise costs 4,000$00; 7 hours, including lunch, costs 8,000$00.

## Tennis

Tennis can be played at every resort, and many hotels and villa complexes have their own courts. Vale do Lobo boasts the famous **Roger Taylor Tennis Center** (tel. 089/394311), one of Europe's best, with 12 all-weather courts, a clubhouse, sauna, pool, and restaurant. Other centers include the **Carvoeiro Tennis Club** (tel. 082/357847), with 10 courts; the **Vilamoura Tennis Center** (tel. 089/380088), with four courts; and the **Luz Bay Ocean Club** (tel. 082/789472), with three courts. The **Burgau Sports Centre** (tel. 082/69350), on the Lagos–Sagres road, has tennis and squash courts, plus table tennis and a pool.

## Water Sports

Snorkeling and scuba diving are possible at several places along the coast, and can be excellent in the western Algarve, where certified, experienced divers can explore the many caves and rock formations. The **Sea Sports Center** (Av. dos Pescadores, Loja 4, tel. 082/789538) at Praia da Luz rents all the necessary equipment and organizes dives.

Windsurfing equipment is available throughout the Algarve, and you can also rent from stands on the beaches at Meia Praia (Lagos), Quarteira, Vale do Lobo, Albufeira, Armação de Pêra, Ferragudo, Burgau, and the Luz Bay Club. Waterskiing is less widely practiced, although it's possible to arrange it at the **Sea Sports Center** and at several of those same beaches.

## Beaches

The glory of the Algarve is its beaches, which are generally clear and impressive, some of the finest in the country. There are hundreds from which to choose on the long stretch of coast, some of which are described in the tours above. Most beaches (especially those in the main resorts) have snack bars and showers, and many have watersports equipment for rent. Remember that although it's possible to wade out for a swim from most Algarve beaches, you should heed local warnings about currents and steeply sloping seabeds.

The best cove beaches are at **Lagos** (*see* Tour 4). Other interesting beaches are those with enormous rock formations such as the ones at **Albufeira** and **Praia da Rocha** (*see* Tour 3). If you require more breathing space, particularly if traveling with young children, try the strands near **Olhão** (*see* Tour 1) and **Tavira** (*see* Tour 2); these and the beaches near Sagres (*see* Tour 4) are less populated than those at major resorts.

# Dining and Lodging

**Dining**  Algarvian cooking is of very high quality, and menus usually feature local seafood that's worthy of the cooking. Take, for example, that most unusual of regional appetizers, *espadarte fumada* (smoked swordfish), which is sliced thin, served with a salad, and best appreciated if accompanied by a dry white wine. Most restaurants serve their own version of *sopa de peixe* (fish soup) and a variety of succulent shellfish: *perceves* (barnacles), *santola* (crab), and *gambas* (shrimp). Main courses often depend on what has been landed that day, but there's generally a choice of *roballo* (sea bass), *pargo* (bream), atum, and espadarte. Perhaps the most famous Algarvian dish is the *cataplana*, a stew of clams, pork, onions, tomatoes, and wine, which takes its name from the lidded utensil used to steam the dish. You will generally have to wait for the dish to be specially prepared, but once you've tasted it, you won't mind waiting again and again.

In rural areas inland, game highlights most menus, with many meat dishes served *o forno* (oven-roasted). Specialties include *cabrito* (kid), *leitão* (suckling pig), and *codorniz* (quail), as well as *ensopado de borrego* (lamb stew).

You don't need to dine in a proper restaurant to taste the Algarve's best. At simple beach cafés and harbor stalls the unmistakable smell of *sardinhas assadas* (charcoal-grilled sardines) permeates the air—a tempting lunch served with fresh bread and smooth red wine. Alfresco dining is possible all year, and in any season you're assured a wonderful array of fresh fruit—the Algarve is particularly known for its oranges and figs.

For dessert there are rich egg, sugar, and almond custards that reflect the Moorish influence, including *doces de amendoa* (marzipan cakes in the shape of animals, birds, and flowers); *bolos de Dom Rodrigo* (almond sweets with egg-and-sugar filling); *bolo Algarvio* (cake made of sugar, almonds, eggs, and cinnamon); and *morgado de figos do Algarve* (fig and almond paste).

Unless otherwise noted, casual dress is acceptable, and reservations are not needed off-season. In summer, you'll need reservations at many of the best restaurants, but in the larger resorts there are dozens of places that serve good food of comparable price and quality.

Restaurant ratings correspond to Lisbon's dining chart, in Chapter 3. Highly recommended restaurants are indicated by a star ★.

**Lodging**  The Algarve has some of Portugal's best hotels, whose leisure and sports facilities are second to none. There are busy beachside hotels in large resorts and secluded retreats in luxuriant country estates. In summer, advance reservations at most places are esssential.

Apartment and villa complexes with luxurious amenities are popular in the Algarve. Some properties—built on the most beautiful parts of the coast—are fancy indeed. They may be a good distance from major towns, but most have bars, restaurants, shops, and other facilities.

Budget lodgings are also available. In most towns and resorts, travelers will be approached by people offering very reasonably priced *quartos* (rooms) in private houses, which are almost always clean and cheerful, if small and with shared bathrooms. You can expect to pay 4,000$00 for a double. Don't ever book a room without seeing it first since it may be farther from the town center than you have been led to believe.

Traveling off-peak in the Algarve is recommended, since the weather from October to April is still good and most hotels reduce their rates by up to 50%. It's worthwhile to check in every instance whether a discount applies.

Hotel ratings correspond to Lisbon's lodging chart, in Chapter 3. Highly recommended hotels are indicated by a star ★.

**Albufeira**
*Dining*
★
**A Ruina.** This big, multilevel rustic restaurant on the beach is the place to go for charcoal-grilled seafood, especially the fresh sardines or tuna steak (the day's catch comes from the nearby fish market). Start with a shellfish salad and choose your main course from the display. You may sit outdoors, on the beach, or inside in one of two simple but attractively furnished dining rooms. There's a top-floor bar and a roof terrace, too. *Cais Herculano, Praia dos Pescadores, tel. 089/512094. No credit cards. $$–$$$*

★ **Cabaz da Praia.** You'll have spectacular views of the beach from the cliff-side terrace of this long-established restaurant, named "beach basket" in Portuguese, and converted from an old fisherman's cottage. There's fine French-Portuguese cooking here—fish soup, grilled fish served imaginatively, and chicken with seafood. Desserts are traditional Algarvian sweets. Try the soufflé, perhaps the restaurant's most popular dish. *Praça Miguel Bombarda 7, tel. 089/512137. Reservations recommended. AE, MC, V. Closed Sat. lunch and Thurs. $$–$$$.*

*Dining and*
*Lodging*
★
**Estalagem Vila Joya.** This is one of the most luxurious inns and restaurants in the Algarve, situated above the Praia da Galé, just 4 kilometers (2½ miles) west of town. The 14 spacious, Moorish-style rooms and three opulent suites are superbly appointed. Internal arches create a delightful sense of space, and the exquisite bathrooms are adorned with rich mosaic tiling. The inn has direct access to the beach, a heated pool, and excellent à la carte lunches. At night you'll choose from the mostly French menu and dine in a candlelighted setting. *Praia da Galé, tel. 089/591839, fax 089/591201. 14 rooms and 3 suites with bath. Facilities: restaurant ($$$$; reservations and jacket and tie required), bar, pool, putting green. AE, DC. $$$$*

**Hotel Montechoro.** This modern development in the village of Montechoro, 3½ kilometers (2 miles) north of town, is ideal for those who like to be cocooned in the privacy of their own resort complex. Among the health facilities are two pools, tennis and squash courts, and a sauna. Guest rooms are furnished in up-to-the-minute style and look out over the surrounding countryside. Your every wish can be fulfilled here even if you never go off the property: There are four separate bars, the Montechoro Restaurant, and the rooftop Amendoeiras Grill, from which you can get stupendous views. *Av. Dr. Francisco Sá Carneiro, tel. 089/589423, fax 089/589947. 362 rooms with bath. Facilities: restaurant ($$$$), grill, 4 bars, 2 pools, sauna, gym, tennis and squash courts, billiards, shops, garden, parking. AE, DC, MC, V. $$$*

*Lodging* **Sheraton Algarve.** This new luxury hotel, in a spectacular cliff-top location overlooking the sea, has access to some of the Algarve's finest beaches. The architecture and decoration blend Moorish features with modern elements—the spacious reception area incorporates arches and Oriental designs, and the guest rooms mix traditional tiling with up-to-the-minute appointments. Service is superb. The hotel is 8 kilometers (5 miles) from town, and guests like to spend their time at the excellent private beach (to which you descend in a glass elevator), where there's a bar and a small restaurant. They can also use without charge the facilities of the associated Pine Cliffs Golf and Country Club. *Praia da Falésia, 8200 Albufeira, tel. 089/501999, fax 089/501950. 215 rooms with bath. Facilities: restaurant, bar, 9-hole golf course, indoor and outdoor pools, gym, sauna, tennis, parking. AE, DC, MC, V. $$$–$$$$*

**Hotel Cerro Alagoa.** This modern hotel on the hill above town provides the most comfortable of Albufeira's central lodgings. The smart, well-equipped guest rooms have private balconies; be sure to ask for one with a sea view instead of facing the road. The Cerro Alagoa is popular with Europeans, who like to relax around the pleasant pool and garden. It's a 10-minute walk to the center of Albufeira, which makes the hotel a good base for exploring the town. A courtesy bus runs guests to nearby beaches. *Via Rápida, Apt. 2155, tel. 089/588261, fax 089/588262. 310 rooms with bath. Facilities: restaurant, bar, live entertainment, outdoor pool, fitness center, shop, garage. AE, DC, MC, V. $$$*

**Alvor**
*Dining and*
*Lodging*
★

**Golfe da Penina.** This impressive golf hotel on 360 well-maintained, secluded acres between Portimão and Lagos has elegant public rooms and attentive service. It was one of the first luxury hotels in the Algarve and is now a member of the Forte Grand chain; recent renovations are keeping up the hotel's high standards. Most of the smartly furnished guest rooms have balconies; those in back, with the best views, face the Monchique Mountains. The superlative golf course was designed by Henry Cotton, and hotel guests pay no greens fees. A bus shuttles you (in five minutes) to and from the hotel beach, which has a restaurant and water-sports facilities. A supervised children's village has its own pool, zoo, and restaurant. The Grill Room serves excellent Portuguese dishes, and the Harlequin restaurant specializes in Italian fare. *Montes de Alvor, Penina, 8502 Portimão, tel. 082/415415, fax 082/415000. 192 rooms with bath. Facilities: restaurant ($$$$; reservations required), grill, bar, 18-hole golf course and two 9-hole courses, tennis courts, horseback riding, Olympic-size pool, windsurfing, sailing, children's pool, sauna, private beach, shops, small private airport, parking. AE, DC, MC, V. $$$–$$$$.*

*Lodging*

**Hotel Alvor Praia.** This comfortable, split-level luxury hotel is set on low cliffs overlooking the beach and the bay. The rooms in the rear face the Monchique Mountains, and those on the sea have spacious balconies. The dining room has picture windows overlooking the coast, and there's a deck where you can enjoy alfresco lunches. An elevator (or an easy walk) will take you down to the pleasant sand beach below the hotel. Guests of this hotel get a 30% discount at nearby golf courses. *Praia dos Tres Irmãos, 8500 Portimão, tel. 082/458900, fax 082/458999. 241 rooms and suites with bath. Facilities: restaurant, bar, pool, sauna, gardens, mini-golf, tennis courts, boating, shops, garage. AE, DC, MC, V. $$$*

**Aparthotel Torralta.** With good-size rooms, fully equipped kitchens, and daily maid service, this large apartment complex near the beach is a very good value all around, particularly out of season. Some of the leisure facilities are appealing to children, making this an excellent choice for families. *Praia de Alvor, 8500 Portimão, tel. 082/459211, fax 082/459171. 655 units. Facilities: restaurant, disco, bar,*

2 pools, horseback riding, boating, golf, tennis courts, billiard room, supermarket, parking. AE, DC, MC, V. $$

**Armação de Pêra**
*Dining*

**A Santola.** This delightful restaurant, with windows that look out to the beach, is considered the best in town for everything it offers, but the seafood is especially good—the restaurant's name means "crab." Try the excellent cataplana, a real Algarve specialty chock-full of everything delicious. *Largo da Fortaleza, tel. 082/312332. Reservations recommended. MC, V. Closed Sun.* $$

*Lodging*

**Hotel Garbe.** The bar, lounge, and restaurant—all with terraces that provide unhindered views of the sea—maximize the superb location of this squat, white hotel that looms over the western edge of the beach. It sits on top of a low cliff and is built on several levels, with a flight of steps to the beach below. Rooms are modern and smartly furnished, the public rooms are bright and attractive, and the bar has a fine sea view. *Av. Marginal, tel. 082/312194, fax 082/312087. 140 rooms with bath. Facilities: restaurant, coffee shop, bar, pool, garage. AE, DC, MC, V.* $$$

**Hotel Viking.** About ½ mile west of town, the Viking stands near the coast, not far from a good, sandy beach. Its swimming pools (one for children), tennis courts, and bars are situated between the main building and the cliff top. You may bargain with the town's fishermen for a sail around the impressive local grottoes. *Praia Nossa Senhora da Rocha, tel.082/314870, fax 082/314852. 184 rooms with bath. Facilities: restaurant, bar, disco, 2 pools, tennis courts, boating, shops, garage. AE, DC, MC, V.* $$$

**Caldas de Monchique**
*Dining and Lodging*

**Albergaria do Lageado.** This charming little inn right in the center of the spa town has rather small guest rooms, though they are attractively furnished and some overlook the lush gardens. There's no great wealth of facilities—in fact, just a cozy lounge and an outdoor pool—but the simplicity is in keeping with the quiet nature of the town. The tiled dining room serves good Portuguese cooking, and there's a terrace for summer dining. You can park in the little square just down the hill. *Caldas de Monchique, 8550 Monchique, tel. 082/92616. 19 rooms with bath. Facilities: lounge, dining room ($), pool, gardens. No credit cards. Closed Nov.–Apr.* $

**Faro**
*Dining*
★

**Cidade Velha.** Located in an 18th-century house beside the cathedral and within the walls of the Old Town, this small, intimate restaurant is easy to reach and serves excellent international cuisine. Many of the imaginative dishes utilize classic Portuguese ingredients: Try the pie made with *bacalhau* (dried codfish) or the rich house specialty—filet of pork stuffed with dates and walnuts and cooked in port. *Rua Domingos Guieiro 19, tel. 089/27145. Reservations recommended. MC, V. June–Sept. dinner only; closed Sat. lunch and Sun.* $$$

**Adega Nova.** This atmospheric *adega* (wine cellar) offers excellently prepared traditional Portuguese dishes indown-to-earth surroundings that foster the lively atmosphere. Drinks are served at the tile-covered bar, and you sit at long wooden tables and benches for dinner. The restaurant is close to the train station, in an otherwise dreary area. *Rua Francisco Barreto 24, tel. 089/813433. No credit cards.* $$

**Dois Irmãos.** In business since 1925, this pretty and centrally located large restaurant (one of several on the square) specializes in cataplana, as evidenced by the utensils hanging from the wood-beamed ceiling. Almost any of the other seafood dishes are worth trying, too, but save room for the homemade *pudim caseiro* (crème caramel). Choose your wine from one of the hundreds of bottles that line the upper walls. *Largo do Terreiro do Bispo 14–15, tel. 089/ 823337. MC, V. $$*

**Sol e Jardim.** This restaurant offers dining with a difference—at outdoor tables in a covered "garden" setting. The decor consists of cooking utensils, farm equipment, flags, and other objects hanging from the ceiling. The good-natured staff serves traditional Portuguese dishes: the clams are good and so are the grilled meats and fish. The restaurant is next door to (and associated with) the Dois Irmãos, so it's guaranteed to be a good value. *Praça Ferreira de Almeida 22–23, tel. 089/823337. MC, V. $$*

*Lodging*
★ **Hotel Eva.** This well-appointed hotel on the main square has the best location in Faro, giving guests unique views of the yacht-filled harbor, the sea, and the old town. The public rooms are comfortably furnished; there's a bar with evening entertainment; and the novel rooftop pool and top-floor restaurant add further ambience. The guest rooms are modern and just adequately furnished, though the best are enhanced by spacious balconies with vast views. There's also a courtesy bus to the town beach on nearby Faro Island. *Av. da República 1, tel. 089/803354, fax 089/802304. 150 rooms with bath. Facilities: restaurant, bar, disco, pool. AE, DC, MC, V. $$$*

★ **Casa de Lumena.** This graceful 150-year-old mansion has been tastefully converted into a small hotel, and some rooms overlook the pretty square. Each guest room has a character of its own, and its unique furnishings reflect the care that the English owners have taken in their restoration. The courtyard's "Grapevine" bar is an especially pleasant place for a drink. The hotel is near the central Rua de Santo António, just a five-minute walk from the harbor. *Praça Alexandre Herculano 27, tel. 089/801990, fax 089/804019. 12 rooms with bath. Facilities: restaurant, bar. AE, DC, MC, V. $*

**Hotel Faro.** The functional but friendly Faro is decidedly second-best to the Eva, but as the only other harbor-front hotel in town, it's still a remarkably good value. The rooms are of reasonable size, if rather anonymous in character, and the ones in the front offer water views (but you must ask for them). Other amenities include a rooftop terrace and a darkly lighted bar with picture windows. *Praça D. Francisco Gomes 2, tel. 089/803276, fax 089/803546. 52 rooms with bath. Facilities: restaurant, bar, terrace. AE, DC, MC, V. $*

**Lagos**
*Dining*
**Alpendre.** One of the oldest and best restaurants in the Algarve, Alpendre is renowned for its French-style meat dishes and local fish and shellfish specials. On a side street just off the Praça Luis de Camões, the comfortable restaurant has a relaxed interior that includes a wood-beam ceiling and walls adorned with porcelain plates. The service is leisurely and the food excellent. Finish your meal with one of their famous crepes, cooked and flambéed at your table. *Rua António Barbosa Viana 17, tel. 082/762705. Reservations recommended. AE, MC, V. $$$*

★ **Dom Sebastião.** Portuguese cooking, charcoal-grilled fish specials, and unobtrusive service are the attractions at this cheerful restaurant on Lagos's main pedestrian street. You can dine inside at elegant, candlelighted tables that sit upon a cobblestone floor, or outside on the sidewalk terrace. While you ponder the menu, you'll be served an impressive array of appetizers (included in the cover charge). You may wish to start your meal with smoked swordfish and follow it with grilled tuna or the cataplana—all extremely good. *Rua 25 de Abril 20, tel. 082/762795. Reservations recommended. AE, DC, MC, V. Closed Sun. Oct.–May. $$$*

**Mirante.** Perched on the cliff above the beautiful Praia de Dona Ana and just to the south of the town center, this restaurant shouts its fishermen's credentials loudly: A cork ceiling, ropes, and nets decorate the narrow interior. Mirante makes an excellent lunch stop, or a place for an early dinner in summer when the views over the sea are lovely. Try the splendid tuna steak stewed with onions and, for dessert, the filling homemade cream tart. The staff is very friendly and efficient. *Praia de Dona Ana, tel. 082/762713. Reservations recommended for dinner. MC, V. $$*

**O Galeão.** This restaurant, tucked away in a back street, is a popular local choice—so much so that you'll wait in line unless you've made a reservation. There's a bustling, informal atmosphere here, and the food is first-rate, particularly the steaks—for once, fish isn't the main event, though it, too, is well cooked. A reasonably priced wine list encourages you to sample some more unusual regional choices; ask for advice if you're unsure. *Rua da Laranjeira 1, tel. 082/763909. Reservations recommended. MC, V. $$*

**Piri-Piri.** This small, low-key restaurant, done in understated pastel colors, is on one of the main tourist streets and offers an inexpensive but extensive menu. The long list of Portuguese dishes includes a variety of market-fresh fish, but the house specialty is the tasty *piri-piri* (spicy) pork and chicken that give the restaurant its name. *Rua Afonso d'Almeida 10, tel. 082/763803. MC, V. $*

Lodging
★

**Hotel de Lagos.** This state-of-the-art hotel is attractively laid out at the eastern edge of the Old Town, within easy walking distance of the center. The rooms are strung across several levels, and the uniquely designed building includes gardens, tasteful lounges, and patios. Guest rooms are large and elegantly appointed, with attractive tiling everywhere, even on lamps and tabletops. They look out over the pool or across the river to the coast. A regularly scheduled courtesy bus shuttles guests to the Meia Praia beach, where the hotel has some outstanding club facilities. Guests also get reduced greens fees at nearby golf courses. *Rua Nova da Aldeia, tel. 082/ 769967, fax 082/769920. 317 rooms with bath. Facilities: restaurant, bar, 2 pools, children's pool, shops, beach club, tennis courts, golf, parking. AE, DC, MC, V. $$$*

**Hotel Golfinho.** On the cliffs above a pretty cove beach, this hotel maximizes its location with balconies, which give lovely views of the sea and inland reaches. The Golfinho is large and modern, but its guest rooms are done in traditional Portuguese style, with attractive wood and leather furniture. It's geared toward tour groups, and the amenities tend to be practical—there's a ground-floor coffee shop and terrace, where many guests congregate. The hotel is just under a mile from the town center, and a courtesy bus shuttles people back and forth all day. Cliff-top paths lead from the Golfinho to beautiful cove beaches nearby. *Praia de Dona Ana, tel. 082/769900, fax 082/769999. 262 rooms with bath. Facilities: restaurant, bar, coffee shop, pool, disco, bowling alley, shops, garage. AE, DC, MC, V. $$$*

**Pensão Mar Azul.** Its choice central location makes this simple, budget-priced *pensão* (pension) a terrific value, although rooms that face the pedestrian thoroughfare can be noisy in high season. Nonetheless, the sparely furnished quarters—some with a terrace—are more than adequate, and there's a comfortable community lounge. *Rua 25 de Abril 13–1. tel, 082/769749 or 082/769143, fax 082/769960. 18 rooms, 17 with bath. No credit cards. $*

Monchique
Dining
★

**Teresinha.** The interior decor of this modest restaurant is simple, but real atmosphere can be found on the outdoor terrace, which overlooks a lovely valley and the coastline. Located just west of Monchique, Teresinha offers good country cooking and a particularly tasty local ham as well as chicken specials, done on the outdoor grill. *Estrada da Foia, tel. 082/92392. MC, V. Closed Mon. $*

Dining and
Lodging

**Estalagem Abrigo da Montanha.** This pleasant, rustic inn—in the heart of the Serra de Monchique—is noted for its magnolia trees, camellia-filled garden and panoramic views. A leisurely lunch in the restaurant, where dependable regional dishes are prepared, always makes for an enjoyable afternoon. If you want to stay longer to take in the scenery, be sure to reserve in advance one of the six welcoming rooms (all with views). *Corto Pereiro, Estrada da Foia, 8550 Monchique, tel. 082/92131, fax 082/93660. 6 rooms with bath. Facilities: restaurant ($$), bar, garden, parking. AE, DC, MC, V. $–$$*

Monte Gordo
Dining

**Mota.** This large, lively, unpretentious restaurant that has been around for more than 30 years is on the sands of the Praia de Monte Gordo near the Vasco da Gama hotel, a bit west of Vila Real de Santo António. During the day you can drop in for a snack or salad if you don't want a full meal. You sit on the large covered terrace facing the ocean, and in the evening you're served seafood, grills, and regional dishes, while live music accompanies your meal. *Praia de Monte Gordo, tel. 081/42650. No credit cards. $*

Lodging

**Alcazar.** The unusual exterior and interior design makes this hotel one of the most striking in Monte Gordo. The white balconies contrast with the redbrick facade, while inside the sinuous arches and low, molded ceilings recall a cave's interior or an Arab tent. The guest rooms have their own terraces and window boxes. Alcazar has a pleasant atmosphere, a very accommodating staff, and a convenient location two blocks off the beach. *Rua de Ceuta 9, tel. 081/ 512184, fax 081/512242. 95 rooms with bath. Facilities: restaurant, snack bar, bar, pool, disco, shops. AE, DC, MC, V. $$*

**Vasco da Gama.** This long, low-lying hotel, occupying one of the prime beach sites in town, has a red roof with two typical Algarvian chimneys. It's well-equipped for water sports and has many other amenities. Families, especially, make good use of the extensive stretch of sandy beach and the children's pool and play area; everyone likes the capable and friendly staff. All the rooms have terraces, and the ones with a sea view are worth their extra cost. *Av. Infante Dom Henrique, tel. 081/511321, fax 081/511622. 200 rooms with bath. Facilities: restaurant, bar, pool, children's pool, tennis courts, mini-golf, billiards, bowling, water sports, disco, parking. AE, DC, MC, V. $$*

Olhos d'Agua
Dining

**La Cigale.** This restaurant, 9 kilometers (5 miles) east of Albufeira, is renowned among locals and its many repeat customers for excellent French and Portuguese cooking. It's right on the beach, and the terrace is the most sought-after place to sit, though you'll have to reserve in advance. *Olhas d'Agua, tel. 089/501637. Reservations recommended. DC, MC, V. Closed Dec.–Feb., dinner only Mar.– May. $$$*

Portimão
Dining

**A Lanterna.** This well-run restaurant, on the main road just over the bridge on the Ferragudo side, serves exceptional, rich fish soup and smoked swordfish, both genuine Algarvian treats. Other seafood specialties are worthy too. *Parchal, tel. 082/23948. Reservations recommended. MC, V. Closed Sun. $$*

**A Vela.** This pleasant restaurant on one of Portimão's back streets has a serene, welcoming ambience. The cool, shaded dining area is decorated in Moorish fashion with white-and-blue tiles, and the spacious open kitchen produces a varied selection of tasty Portuguese and international specialties. The accommodating staff adds to the enjoyment of dining here. *Rua Dr. Manuel de Almeida 97, tel. 082/ 414016. Reservations recommended in summer. AE, DC, MC, V. Closed Sun. $$*

**Flor da Sardinha.** This is one of several open-air eateries next to the bridge, by the fishing harbor. Fresh sardines are superbly grilled on stoves at the quayside and served to the crowds sitting in informal rows at plastic tables and chairs. A plateful of these delicious fish, with fries and a bottle of the local red wine, is one of Portugal's best treats—at giveaway prices. *Cais da Lota, tel. 082/24862. No credit cards.* $

**Portimão**
*Lodging*

Rather than staying in Portimão, most visitors choose one of the excellent local beach resorts in Alvor, *above*, or Praia da Rocha, *below*, which lets them visit Portimão as a day trip. If you prefer to stay in town, the local tourist office can help you find accommodation at one of the hotels or pensões (which are of reasonable quality).

**Praia da Luz**
*Lodging*

**Luz Bay Club.** You may rent these well-appointed two- three- or four-bedroom self-service villas (with daily maid service) for short or long stays, but you must reserve well in advance. One of the best (and earliest) complexes in the Algarve, the Luz Bay Club blends well with the old village surroundings, yet still provides a high level of comfort in its carefully decorated units. They are all near the beach, where the water-sports facilities are excellent. The club is off the main road on the way from Lagos to Sagres, and there are several restaurants and bars nearby. Though there's plenty to do, you'll need a car to explore the area. *Rua Direita 101, tel. 082/789640, fax 082/789641. 131 villas with bath and kitchen. Facilities: 2 restaurants, 3 pools, tennis courts, water sports, gardens, playground, squash court, game room, sauna. V.* $$$

**Praia da Rocha**
*Dining*

**Fortaleza de Santa Catarina.** The 16th-century fortress of Santa Catarina, on the esplanade, has been converted into a bar, restaurant, and *salão de cha* (tearoom) complex. Come for a moderately priced full meal (the food is good, and there are picture windows that look out to the beach) or simply afternoon tea or a snack. Either way, the fort makes an atmospheric stop. *Av. Tomás Cabreira, tel. 082/22066. No credit cards.* $$

**Safari.** Set on a cliff above the beach, this lively Portuguese restaurant has a distinctly African flavor. Seafood and delicious Angolan recipes are the best choices: Try the chicken curry or one of the charcoal grills, and enjoy your meal on the terrace. *Rua António Feu, tel. 082/415540. Reservations recommended. AE, DC, MC, V.* $$

*Lodging*

**Algarve.** This modern luxury hotel—the best in Praia da Rocha—is perched atop a cliff with marvelous sea views, and it even has a disco set into the rocks! Many of the public rooms are brightly decorated in Moorish style, and the spacious guest rooms have tile floors and balconies facing the water. Among the numerous facilities are two saltwater pools and a beach bar. The staff at all levels is most helpful, and there's 24-hour room service. *Av. Tomás Cabreira, tel. 082/415001, fax 082/415999. 220 rooms with bath. Facilities: restaurant, bar, disco, 2 pools, tennis courts, health center, mini-golf, boating, water sports, garden, shops, parking. AE, DC, MC, V.* $$$–$$$$

★ **Bela Vista.** This small, tastefully decorated beachfront hotel was built at the turn of the century as a private house in Moorish style. Its remarkable furnishings—including magnificent azulejos, a wonderful staircase, and a large open fireplace—make this one of the most delightful accommodations in the Algarve. The guest rooms that face the sea are more expensive than the others but are worth the extra escudos. Early reservations are essential. *Av. Tomás Cabreira, tel. 082/24055, fax 082/415369. 14 rooms with bath. Facilities: restaurant, bar. AE, DC, MC, V.* $$$

**Sagres**
*Dining and*
*Lodging*
★

**Pousada do Infante.** Beautifully poised on the cliffs across the bay from the fortress, this modern pousada (1960) is a delightful two-story country house. There are relatively few facilities here, but the inn does have one attraction that really matters—the glorious view of the sea and the craggy rock cliffs. The public rooms have Moorish embellishments and are very comfortable, particularly the bar/terrace, a perfect place to watch the sun set. Guest rooms feel homey, and little touches around the property—such as the minarets and arches alongside the pool—make this place unique. The light, airy restaurant is a charming place for lunch or dinner, a well-respected spot that serves locally caught fish. The service is accomplished and the dessert selection particularly noteworthy—after-dinner coffee is served on the terrace. *8650 Sagres, tel. 082/64222, fax 082/64225. 39 rooms with bath. Facilities: restaurant ($$$), bar, pool, tennis court, parking. AE, DC, MC, V. $$$*

★ **Fortaleza do Belixe.** Two kilometers (1¼ miles) past Sagres on the coastal road to Cabo São Vicente, the remnants of an isolated clifftop fortress have been converted into the Fortaleza do Belixe. The restaurant and very small hotel is an annex of the Pousada do Infante (*see above*). Although it is similar—the furnishings are smart and the rooms comfortable—the room rates here are a considerably better value. This is also an excellent spot for a meal, with good food served in the strikingly decorated dining room. *8650 Sagres, tel. 082/64124. 4 rooms with bath. Facilities: restaurant ($$$), bar, parking. AE, DC, MC, V. $$*

**Santa**
**Bárbara de**
**Nexe**
*Dining and*
*Lodging*
★

**Hotel La Reserve.** Tucked in the hills a few miles inland from Faro, this intimate member of the Relais & Chateaux chain delivers luxury, seclusion, and comfort. The air-conditioned suites (with a Moorish flavor) have private terraces or balconies, and lush plantings set off the low white buildings. In a six-acre park, the hotel's rural atmosphere is conducive to total relaxation, but you can work up an appetite at the tennis courts or pool and then satisfy it in the formal restaurant (tel. 089/90234). Elegant cuisine with a French accent (dinner only) is the fare, with game dishes as specialties, and there's a complimentary Continental breakfast. Advance reservations are required for both the hotel and restaurant. *Santa Bárbara de Nexe, 8000 Faro, tel. 089/90474, fax 089/90402. 20 suites. Facilities: restaurant ($$$$; closed Tues.), bar, garden, tennis courts, pool, garage. Closed Nov. No credit cards. $$$–$$$$*

**São Brás de**
**Alportel**
*Dining and*
*Lodging*

**Pousada de São Brás.** This is one of the region's only pousadas, a delightful 1940s hotel set in low hills. Rooms are comfortably furnished, and there's a rustic restaurant serving good regional dishes and other Portuguese specialties. The major attractions are the peaceful surroundings and the splendid views of the hills that can be seen from the terrace. *Estrada de Lisboa, 8150 São Brás de Alportel, tel. and fax 082/842305. 29 rooms with bath. Facilities: restaurant ($$$), bar, pool, parking. AE, DC, MC, V. $$*

**Silves**
*Dining*

**Rui Marisqueira.** The food is the main event here, as the functional decor doesn't offer much in the way of atmosphere. The fish and shellfish are a remarkably good value, which is one reason the crowds from the coast come up into the hills to dine. Grilled sea bream and bass are usually offered, and there's locally caught game—wild boar, rabbit, and partridge—in season. *South side of the river, at Albergaria Rui Marisqueira, tel. 082/443106. Reservations recommended in summer. MC, V. Closed Tues. $$*

**Churrasqueira Valdemar.** At this inexpensive grill room on the riverfront behind the market, whole chickens are barbecued outside over charcoal. Eat under the stone arches, and enjoy your *piri-piri* chicken with salad, fries, and local wine. *Facing the river, behind the market. No phone. No credit cards.* $

**Tavira**
*Dining*

**Restaurante Imperial.** This is the best restaurant on the riverfront, —behind the riverside gardens—and it's well known for its fish and shellfish, including clams, tuna (the local catch) and a tasty mixed fried-fish plate. Desserts are not a strong point. There's seating on the sidewalk in summer. The waiters are good at their job but a little aloof—after 40 years of service, the Imperial doesn't have to try hard to attract customers. *Rua José Pires Padinha 22–24, tel. 081/ 22306. Closed Wed. in winter. MC, V.* $$

*Lodging*

**Residencial Princesa do Gilão.** Across the river from the main square, this gleaming white small hotel stands on the quayside, offering fine views of the fishing harbor and castle walls. All the rooms are modern and compact, with tile floors, but you should try for one that faces the front and has a balcony. The landings and reception areas sparkle with cool marble and Portuguese tiles. *Rua Borda de Água de Aguiar 10–12, tel. 081/325171 or 081/22665. 22 rooms with bath. Continental breakfast. No credit cards.* $

**Vale do Lobo**
*Dining and Lodging*
★

**Dona Filipa.** This is one of the most luxurious hotels in the Algarve, with a lavish and striking interior, superb service, and pleasant air-conditioned rooms with balconies (most of which overlook the sea). It's on extensive, beautifully landscaped grounds near the beach west of Faro. The hotel has its own tennis courts, and is very close to the famous Roger Taylor Tennis School. Also, greens fees for the fine 18-hole golf course nearby are included in the room rate. The hotel's chic restaurant offers an excellent international menu and an impressive wine list. *Vale do Lobo, 8136 Almansil, tel. 089/ 394141, fax 089/394288. 147 rooms with bath. Facilities: restaurant, grill, bar, disco, gardens, pool, tennis courts, golf, shops, parking. AE, DC, MC, V.* $$$$

**Vilamoura**
*Dining and Lodging*

**Vilamoura Marinotel.** One of the Algarve's newest accommodations, the luxurious Marinotel overlooks Vilamoura's stupendous marina. The guest rooms come equipped with the most up-to-the-minute hardware, including VCRs, and the facilities are wide-ranging. Many people think the Marinotel is the best place to eat in town: The extra-smart grill overlooking the boats serves fish and has live music, while the restaurant that faces the hotel gardens specializes in Spanish and Portuguese food. *Vilamoura 8125, Quarteira, tel. 089/ 389988, fax 089/389869. 399 rooms with bath. Facilities: restaurant ($$$), grill, bar, gardens, pool, children's pool, tennis, boating, terrace, shops, parking. AE, DC, MC, V.* $$$

*Lodging*

**Hotel Dom Pedro Golf.** Part of a highly successful vacation complex, the Dom Pedro is the best of the three hotels operated here by the Dom Pedro Hotel Group. It's close to the casino, not far from the splendid beach, and five minutes from the marina. Each bright room is attractively furnished and has its own balcony facing the sea. *Vilamoura, 8125 Quarteira, tel. 089/315482. 263 rooms with bath. Facilities: restaurant, bar, 2 pools, children's pool, shops, tennis courts, golf, parking. AE, DC, MC, V.* $$$

**Vila Real de Santo António**
*Dining*

**Caves do Guadiana.** Located in a large, old-fashioned building facing the fishing docks and the river estuary, this accommodating restaurant is popular for its well-prepared seafood and Portuguese specialties. Stop for lunch on the way to or from the Spanish border crossing. *Av. da República 90, tel. 081/44498. DC, MC. Closed Thurs.* $

# The Arts and Nightlife

## The Arts

Most of the towns in the Algarve have annual festivals lasting several days, and locals and tourists alike join in on the parades and celebrations. Nearly every town and village also features religious celebrations during Easter week and on Saint John's Eve (June 23–24).

The **Algarve Regional Tourist Board** (Av. 5 de Outubro, 8000 Faro, tel. 089/800400) produces a monthly calendar of events, which you may pick up at local tourist offices and hotels. The Tourist Board also provides information on venues and ticket prices for the annual **Algarve Music Festival,** a series of concerts and recitals throughout May and June, sponsored by the Gulbenkian Foundation.

**Faro**     Mid-July sees the **Festa e Feira da Senhora do Carmo** (Festival and Fair of Our Lady of Carmen), a religious procession followed by an agricultural fair. In October the **Feira de Santa Iria** (Fair of Santa Iria) is another happy excuse for traditional celebrations held over several days.

**Loulé**     An annual **street carnival**—or Mardi Gras—is held every February and is an enjoyable local affair with a procession of floats, mask competitions, dancing, and more. On the second Sunday after Easter, Loulé hosts the **Romaria da Senhora da Piedade,** a pilgrimage and procession to the local shrine of Monte da Piedade. There are also flower-decked celebrations here on May 1, enlivened further by performances of traditional song and dance.

**Monchique**     The **Feira de Outubro** (October Fair), held at the end of the month, gathers together crafts, goods, and produce from villages throughout the Serra de Monchique. It's one of the best of the Algarve's annual fairs.

**Portimão**     Every August the town's "sardine festival" celebrates that most Portuguese of fish and, of course, is an excuse to eat them at the open-air stalls and cafés.

**Praia da Rocha**     In the first week of September a **folklore festival** is held at various venues around the resort. Each evening traditional song and dance is performed by special folkloric groups.

**Silves**     In July, Silves hosts a thoroughly enjoyable **Beer Festival** on the castle grounds, where apart from being able to sample all the different kinds of Portuguese beer, visitors may watch folk dances and listen to traditional and orchestral music.

## Nightlife

There are more bars, discos, and clubs in the Algarve than anywhere else in Portugal. In the major resorts new places open and close with alarming speed or suddenly attract a different clientele, so it's not guaranteed that spots listed here will still be the trendiest when you visit; but they are representative of the range of nightlife available. If you prefer a quieter evening, the Algarve's open-air cafés are perfect for a drink and people-watching, and sometimes a traveling musician will stroll by. Many hotels also put on performances of fado and other traditional music.

To gamble, head for one of the Algarve's three casinos: at **Alvor** (tel. 082/23141), **Vilamoura** (tel. 089/302996), and **Monte Gordo** (tel. 081/42224). (Remember to take your passport.)

**Albufeira**  Albufeira tries hard to maintain its reputation as the Algarve's number-one nightspot. Many bars and discos here have promotional nights that are enormously popular with the young, with free or reduced-price drinks and admission. Of the discos **Kiss** (Montechoro) and **Silvia's** and **Club 7½** (both on Rua São Gonçalo de Lagos) are still very lively and stay open nightly until 4 AM. Rua São Gonçalo de Lagos also boasts several other bars that guarantee a lively crowd. The **Classic Bar** at No. 10 is a good late-night haunt. For a less energetic evening, there's **Sir Harry's Bar,** on the Largo Eng. Duarte Pacheco, an English-style pub with an interesting clientele of different nationalities. It's open daily 10 AM–3AM.

**Faro**  Faro's central pedestrian streets are filled at night with throngs of café-goers, while Rua do Prior, in particular, is known for its wide selection of late-closing, stylish bars. **Kingburger** (No. 40) and **Bar Chaplin** (No. 37) are current favorites. For a disco, visit either trendy **Megahertz** (Rua do Prior 38), which stays open until 4AM, or the more mainstream **Sheherazade** (at the Hotel Eva, Av. da República 1). The Hotel Eva puts on traditional music and fado at least once a week in summer as well.

**Lagos**  A good bar in Lagos is **Mullens** (Rua Cândido dos Reis 86), whose enthusiastic staff makes things swing until 2 AM; full meals are served here, too. **Shots in the Dark** (Rua 1 de Maio 16) is a raucous rock bar; the **Zanzibar** (Rua 25 de Abril 93) is a little more refined, though its music is still brutally loud at times. For late-night dancing, **Phoenix** (Rua 5 de Outubro 11) plays disco and pop until 4 AM.

**Sagres**  Sagres is a well-known haunt of young travelers, who stay the summer for the laid-back beach scene. Consequently, there are several music-bars near the village square. **A Rosa dos Ventos,** in the square, and **The Last Chance Saloon,** on the road down to Praia da Mareta, are both loud, lively, and open late.

# 7 Coimbra and the Beiras

**By Dennis
Jaffe**

It's not far from one point in the Beiras to any other. In fact, you can drive from the Atlantic shore to the lonely fortified towns along the Spanish border in the time it takes many residents of Los Angeles or London to commute to work; it's only 160 kilometers (100 miles). But within this small area you will encounter tremendous diversity.

To the east Portugal's highest mountains, the Serra da Estrela, rise to a height of nearly 6,600 feet and provide a playground of alpine meadows, wooded hills, and clear, rushing streams. High in the granite reaches of the Serra, a tiny trickle of an icy stream begins its tortuous journey to the sea. This is the Mondego, praised in song and poetry as the most Portuguese of all rivers. The longest river entirely within Portugal and the lifeblood of the Beiras, it provides vital irrigation to fruit orchards and farms as it flows through the heart of the province. Coimbra, the country's first capital and home to one of Europe's earliest universities, rises above its banks. Closer to the sea, under the imposing walls of Montemor Castle, the river widens to nurture rice fields before finally merging with the Atlantic at the popular beach resort of Figueira da Foz.

In the mountains and along the border with Spain, life is difficult. The winters are cold and harsh and the summers broiling hot. Crops do not flourish here, and many of the villages have lost their ablest workers to the factories of France and Germany. In this part of the country, where the climate is most severe and tourists are still somewhat of a curiosity, you will find perhaps the warmest welcome.

The coastal region presents a much gentler face. The long, sandy beaches and sun-baked dunes are some of the most inviting you will find in all of Europe. The great lagoon at Aveiro, with its colorful kelp boats, is unique. A bit farther inland are the lush forests of Buçaco and the sedate spa resorts of Curia and Luso.

Historically, this region has played an important role in Portugal's development. The Romans built roads, established settlements, and, in 27 BC, incorporated into their vast empire the remote province known as Lusitania, which encompassed most of what is now central Portugal, including the Beiras. They left many traces of their presence in the region, including the well-known and well-preserved ruins at Conímbriga, near Coimbra.

Next came the Moors, who swept through the territory in the early 8th century and played a leading role for several hundred years. Many of the region's elaborate castles and extensive fortifications show a strong Moorish influence. The fortified towns stretching along the Spanish frontier have been the scene of many fierce battles, from the seesaw struggle against the Moors (known as the wars of Christian reconquest) to battles with the Spanish, as the fledgling Portuguese nation fought the invaders from neighboring Castile.

The Beiras also played a part in Portugal's golden age of discovery. In 1500 Pedro Álvares Cabral, a nobleman from the town of Belmonte on the eastern flank of the Serra da Estrela, led the first expedition to come upon what is now Brazil. Much of the wealth garnered during this period, when tiny Portugal controlled so much of the world's trade, financed the great architectural and artistic achievements of the Portuguese Renaissance. Throughout the region there are fine examples of the Manueline style, the uniquely Portuguese art form that reflects the nation's nautical heritage. The cathedrals at Guarda and Viseu, the Monastery of Santa Cruz at Coimbra, and the Convent of Jesus in Aveiro are especially noteworthy.

During the Peninsular War, between Napoleon's armies and Wellington's British and Portuguese forces in the early 19th century, a decisive battle was fought in the tranquil forest of Buçaco. Later in the same century, this area witnessed a much more peaceful invasion, as people from all corners of Europe came to take the waters at such well-known spas as Luso, Curia, and Caramulo. Around the turn of the century, when the now tourist-packed Algarve was merely a remote backwater, Figueira da Foz was coming into its own as an international beach resort.

# Essential Information

## Important Addresses and Numbers

**Tourist Information**
The regional tourist offices for **Coimbra** and the surrounding area are the **Região de Turismo do Centro** (Largo da Portagem, 3000 Coimbra, tel. 039/33028; Edificio Marisol, Av. 25 de Abril, 3080 Figueira da Foz, tel. 033/22610). Within this region there are local tourist offices in: **Arganil** (Praça Simões Dias, tel. 035/22859), **Buarcos** (Largo Tomas de Aquino, tel. 033/25019), **Condeixa** (Edificio da Câmara, tel. 039/941114), **Curia** (Praça Dr. Luís Navega, tel. 031/ 512248), **Figueiro dos Vinhos** (Av. Padre Diogo Vasconcelos, tel. 036/52178), **Lousa** (Edificio da Câmara, tel. 039/991502), **Lus o/Buçaco** (Rua Emidio Navarro, Luso, tel. 031/93133), **Mira** (Edificio da Câmara, tel. 031/451506), **Montemor-O-Velho** (Praça da República, tel. 039/68187), and **Penacova** (Miradouro do Terreiro, tel. 039/477115).

For information about **Aveiro** and the **Rota da Luz** region, consult the **Região de Turismo da Rota da Luz** (Rua Joâo Mendonça 8, 3800 Aveiro, tel. 034/23680). The principal local tourist offices in this region are in: **Águeda** (Estrada Nacional 1, tel. 034/ 601412), **Costa Nova** (Praia da Costa Nova, at the beach, tel. 034/369560, open June–Sept.), **Ilhavo** (Av. Mario Sacramento), **Ovar** (Edificio da Câmara, Praça da República, tel. 056/572215), and **Torreira** (Av. Hintze Ribeiro, tel. 034/48250).

The regional tourist office for the **Dão-Lafões** area is the **Região de Turismo de Dão-Lafões** (Av. Gulbenkian, 3500 Viseu, tel. 032/ 422014). Local tourist offices are in: **Caramulo** (Estrada Principal do Caramulo, tel. 032/861437), **Nelas** (Largo Prof. Veiga Simão, tel. 032/944384), and **São Pedro do Sul** (Largo dos Correios, tel. 032/ 711320).

The **Serra da Estrela** district is represented by the **Região de Turismo da Serra da Estrela** (Praça do Município 1, 6200 Covilhã, tel. 075/322170). There are local tourist offices in: **Belmonte** (Praça Pedro Álvares Cabral, tel. 075/911488), **Castelo Branco** (Alameda da Liberdade, tel. 072/21002), **Fundão** (Av. da Liberdade, tel. 075/ 52770), **Gouveia** (Av. 1 de Maio, tel. 038/42185), **Guarda** (Praça Luis Camões, tel. 071/222251), **Manteigas** (Rua Dr. Gaspar de Carvalho, tel. 075/981129), **Oliveira do Hospital** (Praça do Município, tel. 038/ 52522), **Penamacor** (Praça 25 de Abril, tel. 077/314316), and **Seia** (Praça do Mercado, tel. 038/922272).

**Emergencies**
The national emergency number is 115. **Hospitals** with emergency rooms (*urgências*) are in Castelo Branco (Hospital Distrital de Castelo Branco, Av. Pedro A. Cabral, tel. 072/322133), Coimbra (Hospital da Universidade Coimbra, Praça Prof. Mota Pinto, tel. 039/ 403939), Figueira da Foz (Hospital Distrital da Figueira da Foz,

Gala, tel. 033/31033), and Guarda (Rua Dr. Francisco Prazeres, tel. 071/222133).

*Late-Night* Pharmacies in all sizable towns operate a rotating system for stay-
*Pharmacies* ing open after normal closing hours, including weekends and holidays. Consult a local newspaper or the notice posted on the door of
every pharmacy.

**Mail** The central post office in Coimbra, **CTT Estação Central** (Av.
Fernão de Magalhães 223), is adjacent to the train station and is the
center for poste restante (general delivery). Most other towns have
just one central post office, where poste restante is received.

**Travel Agency** In Coimbra, a useful agency is **Abreu** (Rua da Sota 2, tel. 039/ 27011).

### Arriving and Departing by Plane

Although there are some international flights into Oporto (to the
north), Lisbon is the preferred choice for the international air traveler. It's 160 kilometers (99 miles) northeast from the Lisbon airport
to Coimbra via the newly completed A 1 highway.

### Arriving and Departing by Car, Train, and Bus

**By Car** Although you can zip from Lisbon to Coimbra on the A 1 *auto-
estrada* (tollway) in less than two hours or drive from Oporto to
Coimbra in under an hour, smaller roads provide a much richer and
more varied travel experience. The eastern part of the Beiras is
readily accessible from Spain. It's 90 kilometers (56 miles) on N620
from Salamanca and 320 kilometers (199 miles) from Madrid to the
border crossing at Vilar Formoso.

**By Train** Coimbra, Guarda, Mangualde, Ovar, and Aveiro are on the main
Lisbon/Oporto–Paris line. Two trains arrive from Paris and two depart daily. There is also regular train service linking the principal
cities in the Beiras with Madrid, Lisbon, and Oporto. In summer a
daily car-train operates between Paris and Lisbon. There are two
train stations in Coimbra: **Coimbra A** (Estação Nova), located along
the Rio Mondego, a five-minute walk from the center of town (for domestic routes), and **Coimbra B** (Estação Velha), 5 kilometers (3
miles) west (for international trains). There are frequent bus and
rail links between stations. For information call 039/27263. Schedules for all trains are posted at both stations.

**By Bus** The **Rodoviária Nacional** (RN) provides comfortable motor- coach
service between Lisbon, Oporto, and Coimbra. RN stations in Coim-
bra (Av. Fernão de Magalhães, tel. 039/27081), Castelo Branco
(Rodrigo Rebelo 3, tel. 072/323301), and Covilhã(Largo das Forcas
Armadas, tel. 075/24914) all have international as well as domestic
service. International **Euroline** motor coaches link Coimbra with
London, Paris, Amsterdam, and Frankfurt. For information call
Euroline in Lisbon (tel. 01/ 547300), or contact a travel agent.

### Getting Around

**By Car** The Beiras, with their many remote villages, are particularly well
suited to exploration by car. Distances between major points are
short, there are no intimidating major cities to negotiate, and, except for the coastal strip in July and August, traffic is light. Roads in
general are quite good and destinations well-marked; however,
parking is a problem in most towns.

Although it is possible to whiz through the region in a few hours on the Lisbon–Oporto highway or the newly completed IP5 that links Aveiro with Vilar Formoso at the Spanish frontier, resist the temptation. The heart and soul of the Beiras are to be found along the many kilometers of those squiggly yellow and white lines lacing the road map of Portugal. The best map for motorists, both for scale and ease of reading, is Michelin map number 437 (Portugal-Madeira), available at bookstores throughout Portugal and in the United States from Michelin Travel Publications (1 Parkway S, Greenville, SC 29615, tel. 803/458–6330).

In addition to the numerous car-rental agencies in Lisbon, there are Hertz and Avis offices in Coimbra (Hertz, Av. Fernão de Magalhães 133, tel. 039/37491; Avis, Coimbra A, Làrgo das Ameias, tel. 039/34786) and Viseu (Hertz, Rua da Paz 21, tel. 032/421846; Avis, Hotel Grão Vasco, Rua Gaspar Barreiros, tel. 032/25750).

**By Train**  Although the major destinations in this chapter are linked by rail, service to most towns, with the exception of Coimbra, is infrequent. The equipment on the Beira line, which connects Lisbon with Guarda and the Serra da Estrela, has recently been upgraded.

Using Coimbra as a hub, there are three main rail lines serving the Beiras. Line 110 goes northeast to Luso, Viseu, Mangualde, Celorico da Beira, and Guarda. Line 100 extends south through the Ribatejo to intersect with line 130, which runs from Lisbon northeast through the Beira Baixa towns of Castelo Branco and Fundão, to Covilhã, the gateway to the Serra da Estrela. Going north from Coimbra, line 100 services Curia, Aveiro, and Ovar and continues north to Oporto and Braga. Schedules are posted at all train stations.

**By Bus**  If you choose not to drive, an extensive bus network provides the next best way of getting around. Vehicles of various vintages can take you to almost any destination, and unlike train stations, which are often some distance from the town center, bus depots are centrally located. Rural buses, often packed with people going to and from regional markets, provide a wonderful microcosm of Portuguese life. Regional and local bus schedules are posted at the terminals. Information may also be obtained at local tourist offices.

## Guided Tours

**Orientation**  There are very few regularly scheduled guided tours originating in the Beiras. **RN Tours** (Rua da Sofia 102, 3000 Coimbra, tel. 039/22849) offers a half-day tour of Coimbra on Wednesday and Sunday during summer. **Mivitur** (Av. do Ramalhâo, 3220 Miranda do Corvo, tel. 039/52304) has an all-day tour of the Rio Mondego region on Tuesday and Thursday, mid-June–mid- September. There are also one- to seven-day tours that leave from Lisbon and Oporto and cover the Beiras. For further information contact a travel agency or, in Lisbon, **RN Tours** (Av. Fontes Pereira de Melo 14–12, tel. 01/577523) or **Tip Tours** (Av. Costa Pinto 91–A, Cascais, tel. 01/483–3821).

**By Boat**  From mid-June to mid-September, excursion boats cruise the Ria de Aveiro, the vast, 45-kilometer (28-mile) hydralike delta of the Rio Vouga. Boats leave daily at 10 AM from the main canal just in front of the tourist office in Aveira and return at 5 PM. Tickets are 1,750$00. There's a small bar on board, and a stop is made along the way for lunch.

**Horseback**  With advance notice, horseback tours of the countryside around Aveiro can be arranged with the **Escola Equestre de Aveiro** (Eques-

trian School of Aveiro, Quinta Chão Agra, Vilarinho, tel. 034/
912108). The school is about 6 kilometers (3½ miles) north of Aveiro
on N109.

# Exploring Coimbra and the Beiras

## Orientation

The Beiras region encompasses the provinces of the Beira Lit oral
(Coastal Beira), the Beira Baixa (Lower Beira), and the Beira Alta
(Upper Beira), which together make up roughly one quarter of continental Portugal's landmass. This part of Portugal is on the verge of
being discovered, but it still contains some of the last remaining areas in Europe unscathed by mass tourism.

The first tour visits Portugal's first capital, the ancient university
town of Coimbra. Our second tour covers the western part of the region: the seaside resort of Figueira da Foz and the canals and lagoons in and around Aveiro; moves inland to Viseu, with its
wonderful parks and historic old quarter; follows the spa trail, visiting the mountain resort of Caramulo and the Belle Epoque spas of
Luso and Curia; and passes through the dense forest of Buçaco before heading back toward Coimbra along the Mondego. The third
tour travels east into the Serra da Estrela and to the chain of ancient
fortified towns along the Spanish border.

## Highlights for First-Time Visitors

Centum Cellas (*see* Tour 3)
Palace Hotel Buçaco (*see* Tour 2)
Palácio des Condes de Anadia, Mangualde (*see* Tour 2)
Ria Aveiro (*see* Tour 2)
Roman ruins, Conimbriga (*see* Tour 2)
Sé and Largo da Sé, Viseu (*see* Tour 2)
Sé Velha, Coimbra (*see* Tour 1)
University, Coimbra (*see* Tour 1)
Walled city, Sortelha (*see* Tour 3)

## Tour 1: Coimbra

*Numbers in the margin correspond to points of interest on the
Beiras and Coimbra maps.*

❶ The exact origins of **Coimbra** lie deeply buried in prehistoric times.
However, from its emergence as the Roman settlement of Aeminium
to the present, this city on the banks of the Rio Mondego has played
an influential and often crucial role in the country's development. In
Roman times, it was an important way station, the midway point on
the road connecting Lisbon with Braga to the north. Several of
today's main thoroughfares are built on top of this ancient road. The
open-air café on the Praça do Comércio is actually on the site of a
Roman circus.

The year 711 marked the beginning of a centuries-long period of
Moorish domination, which, except for one hiatus, lasted until the
final reconquest by Christian forces in 1064. At that time, Coimbra
became the capital of a vast territory extending north to the Rio
Douro and encompassing much of what are now the Beiras. By the

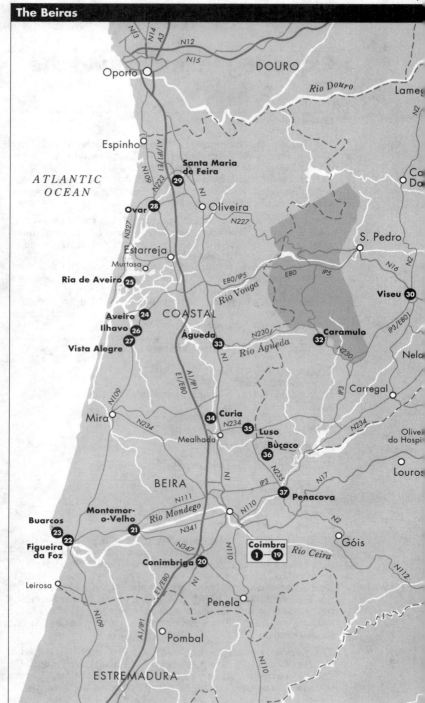

214

The Beiras

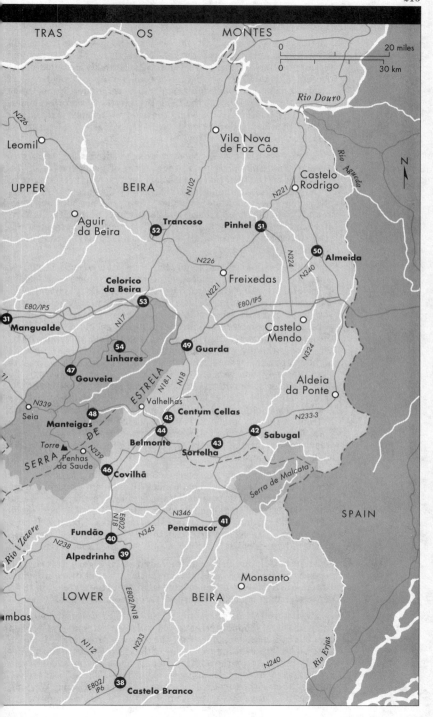

12th and 13th centuries, it had become the capital of the young Portuguese nation.

Coimbra is best known for its university—though it was first established in Lisbon by King Dinis I in 1290 and transferred back and forth between Coimbra and Lisbon, it was finally installed on its present site in 1537. Since then the university has been one of Europe's major learning centers and important in the life of both the city and the nation. During the 1960s the university was a focal point for much of the unrest preceding the 1974 revolution. Many of the current political leaders were educated there, as was Dr. António Salazar, who was dictator from 1932 until 1968.

Coimbra, essentially a college town, is best visited when school is in session. The students, even in today's era of jeans and T- shirts, proudly wear the traditional black capes and adorn their briefcases with colored ribbons denoting which faculty they attend (for example, red for law, yellow for medicine). Their presence adds much color and life to the streets, bars, and restaurants of the city. In May, after final exams, students, with great exuberance, burn their colored ribbons in a ceremony called Queima das Fitas (Burning of the Ribbons). It's quite a party.

To devotees of *fado*, that uniquely Portuguese art of musical expression, Coimbra has a very special significance. It is here on the banks of the Mondego that the second great style of fado was born. With the exception of a few bars where it is performed mostly for tourists, you won't find fado "shows" in Coimbra; here, it is more a form of personal expression than an entertainment medium. Wandering through the narrow, steep passageways of the old university quarter, you are likely to hear plaintive sounds drifting through the night air, perhaps from a student serenading his love. In contrast to the brasher Lisbon version, the Coimbra fado, performed only by men, is softer and gentler. Musical accompaniment is played on the traditional heart-shape, 12-string guitar, and tradition dictates that one does not applaud. During the Queima das Fitas, the square in front of the old cathedral is full of people listening in silence to fado. During the student demonstrations of the 1960s, this music was used as a form of protest in much the same manner as the folk song was in America.

Coimbra's romantic side is reserved for those willing to devote a bit more time than that required for quick hit-and-run visits to the obligatory sights. Sit in the cafés and student restaurants, watch young lovers walking hand in hand through parks, and stroll through the gardens of the Quinta das Lágrimas (House of Tears), where more than six centuries ago the ill- fated Inês de Castro was murdered (*see* Alcobaça in Chapter 5, Évora and Central Portugal).

**❷** The tour of Coimbra begins at the **Largo da Portagem,** the triangular plaza at the foot of the Ponte Santa Clara. The statue of Joaquim António de Aguiar with pen in hand represents the signing, in 1833, of a decree banning religious orders throughout Portugal.

A few hundred yards up the busy Rua Ferreira Borges, one of the city's principal shopping streets, you will see a tall, graceful, arched opening in a massive stone wall: the **Arco de Almedina** (Almedina Gate). The 12th-century arch is one of the last vestiges of the medieval city walls. Above the arch is a Renaissance carving of the virgin and child and an early Portuguese coat of arms. The adjacent tower houses the city's historical archives and the **Sino de Correr** (Warning Bell) used from medieval times until 1870 to signal the populace to return to the safety of the city walls. The tower is also used as an art gallery.

Go through the gate into the old city and head up the hill along one of Coimbra's most famous streets, **Rua Quebra Costas** (Street of the Broken Backs). Try carrying a heavy load of groceries up this steep street, and you will see where the name came from! Quebra Costas is the main pedestrian link between the Baixa (Lower Town) and the **Sé Velha** (Old Cathedral). The cathedral was designed and constructed in the 12th century by the French master builders Robert and Bernard. Made of massive granite blocks and crowned by a ring of battlements, the cathedral looks more like a fortress than a house of worship. (Engaged in an ongoing struggle with the Moors, the Portuguese, who were building and reconstructing castles for defensive purposes throughout the country, often incorporated fortifications in their churches.) The harsh exterior is softened somewhat by graceful 16th-century Renaissance doorways. The somber interior has several interesting features, including a gilded wood altarpiece, a late-15th-century example of the Flamboyant Gothic style by the Flemish masters Olivier of Ghent and Jean d'Ypres. The walls of the Chapel of the Holy Sacrament are lined with the touching, lifelike sculptures of Jean de Rouen, whose life-size Christ figure is flanked by finely detailed representations of the apostles and evangelists. The cloisters, built in the 13th century, are distinguished by a well-executed series of transitional Gothic arches. *Largo da Sé Velha, tel. 039/25273. Admission: cathedral free; cloisters: 100$00. Open daily 10–12:30 and 2–6.*

**Time Out**   The cathedral square is ringed with cafés and restaurants. **Café Sé Velha** (Rua da Joaquim António Aguiar 136), decorated with azulejo panels depicting local scenes, is one of the most inviting; you can sit outside in summer.

Continue uphill from the Largo da Sé Velha along Rua Borges Carneiro, the narrow street to the left of the cathedral, and you'll come to the **Museu Machado de Castro** (Machado de Castro Museum). The building, itself a work of art, was constructed in the 12th century to house the prelates of Coimbra; it was extensively modified 400 years later and was converted to a museum in 1912. It contains one of Portugal's finest collections of sculpture, including work by Jean de Rouen and Master Pero and an intriguing little statue of a mounted medieval knight. The Bishop's Chapel, adorned with 18th-century azulejos and silks, is a highlight of the upstairs galleries, which also contain a diverse selection of Portuguese paintings and furniture. Be sure to take in the view from the terrace of the Renaissance loggia. As you exit the museum, note the large 18th-century azulejo panel depicting Jeronimo translating the bible. *Largo Dr. José Rodrigues, tel. 039/23727. Admission: 500$00, Sun. morning free. Open Tues.–Sun. 10–5.*

As you leave the building, you'll see two churches. The first, on your left, with the Romanesque facade, is the 12th-century São Salvador Church, currently closed to the public. Across the street and to the right is the **Sé Nova** (New Cathedral). This 17th-century Jesuit church was, as were many such churches of the day, patterned after the Baroque church of Il Gesù in Rome. *Admission free. Open daily 9:30–12:30 and 2–5:30.*

Leaving the cathedral, follow the Rua São Pedro through the university to the Praça Porta Férrea, at the end of which is the **Porta Férrea**

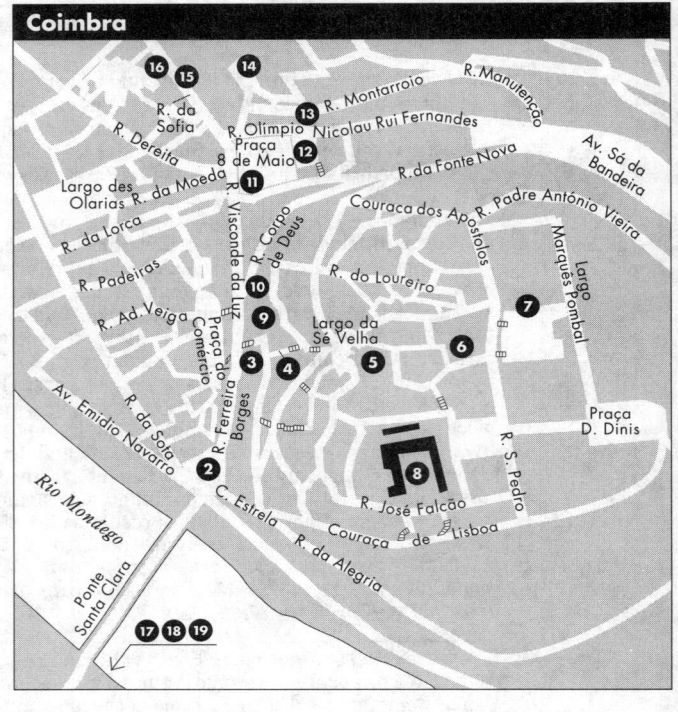

itself. Built in 1634 as a triumphal arch, it is adorned with the figures of the kings Dinis and João III. *Open daily 9:30–12:30 and 2–5.*

**8** Walk through the gate, and you're in the principal courtyard of the **Velha Universidade** (Old University), steeped in centuries-old tradition.

Although there are modern dormitories and apartments available, many of the 20,000 students, some because of tradition and some for economic reasons, choose to live in one of approximately 30 old, ramshackle *repúblicas* (student republics) scattered around the university quarter. Groups of students live together (coed since the revolution) in these old houses, with the bare minimum in creature comforts, sharing costs and chores; the one indulgence they allow themselves is a cook. Traditionally to the left on the political spectrum, the repúblicas were a hotbed of anti-Salazar activity during the years of the dictatorship. The República Bota-Abaixo (Rua São Salvador 6), near the Machado de Castro Museum, is a typical example of this Portuguese-style cooperative. The repúblicas are not really tourist attractions, nor are they open to the public, but if you can get an invitation, don't pass up the opportunity for a glimpse of Portuguese student life.

The statue in the center of the courtyard is of Dom João III; it was during his reign that the university moved permanently to Coimbra. Walk to the far end of the courtyard for a view of the Mondego and across it to the Convento de Santa Clara-a-Nova. The double stairway rising from the courtyard leads to the graceful colonnade framing the **Via Latina** (Latin Way), the scene of colorful student processions at graduation time. Amid much pomp and ceremony, doctoral degrees are presented in the **Sala dos Capelos** (Ceremonial Hall) which is capped with a fine paneled ceiling and lined with a series of portraits of the kings of Portugal. *Admission: 250$00. Open daily 10–12 and 2–5.*

The 18th-century clock-and-bell tower rising above the courtyard is one of Coimbra's most famous landmarks. The bell, used to summon students to class and, in centuries past, to signal a dusk-to-dawn curfew, is derisively called the *cabra* (goat). In the southwest corner of the courtyard is a building with four huge columns framing a set of massive wooden doors. It contains one of the world's most beautiful libraries, the **Biblioteca Joanina.** Constructed in the early 18th century, the library contains three dazzling book-lined halls and has one of the loveliest Baroque interiors in the country. The large painting in the center is of Dom João V, the monarch responsible for the library's construction. *Admission: 250$00. Open Mon.–Sat. 10–12 and 2–5.*

Leave the courtyard and return to the lower town via the Rua do Norte. Along the way you will pass the **Casa dos Melos,** an elegant, 16th-century building now housing the School of Pharmacy.

Return to the old cathedral, and follow the Rua Coutinhos to the **9** **Palácio de Sobre Ribas** (Palace above the Riverbanks). A tower in the ancient walls, it was converted into a private residence in the 16th century. The exterior of the building is graced by several Manueline doorways and windows. A short distance along the same street is **10** another converted tower, the **Torre de Anto** (Tower of Anto), now a regional handicrafts center. Anto is the nickname of the Portuguese poet Antònio Nobre, who lived in the tower during the 19th century. *Rua Sobre Ribas. Handicrafts center: Open weekdays 9–12:30 and 2–5:30.*

Continue down the hill and through the Almedina Gate to the Rua Ferreira Borges. Across the street and down a short flight of steps is the **Praça do Comércio,** one of the lower town's most attractive and active plazas. A variety of fashionable shops occupy the 17th- and 18th-century town houses lining the square. In the corners of the Comércio, street vendors sell everything from combs to carpets. In Roman times this was the site of the circus. Currently closed to the public, the Church of Sant'Iago, in the northeast corner, is a small, late-13th-century stone structure with finely carved Romanesque columns. At the opposite corner is the Church of São Bartolomeu. Dating back to 957, it is one of the oldest churches in the city. Destroyed several times, it was rebuilt in its present form in 1756. The interior is of no special interest.

Leave the Comércio along the Rua Eduardo Coelho. Lined on both sides with shoe shops, this was once known as the Street of the Shoemakers. At the Rua do Corvo turn right, and continue until you emerge onto a bustling elongated plaza, Praça 8 de Maio. Your eyes **11** will be drawn to the magnificent **Igreja e Mosteiro de Santa Cruz** (Church and Monastery of Santa Cruz), one of the country's richest in history and culture. The stark 12th-century stone facade is greatly enhanced by the Renaissance entrance, added as part of an extensive renovation in 1507. Unfortunately, much of the fine detail has been damaged by corrosion. Inside you will see the delicate features of the Renaissance altar carved in 1521 by Nicolas Chanterene. The high altar is flanked on either side by the intricately detailed tombs of the first two kings of Portugal, Dom Afonso Henriques and his son, Dom Sancho I. In the sacristy there are several notable examples of 16th-century Portuguese painting. The lower portions of the interior walls are lined with azulejos depicting various religious motifs. From the sacristry a door opens to the **Casa do Capitulo** (Silent Cloister); this double-tier Manueline cloister contains scenes from *The Passion of Christ*, attributed to Nicolas Chanterene. *Praça 8 de Maio, tel. 039/ 22941. Admission: church free; cloister: 200$00. Open daily 9– noon and 2–6.*

**Time Out** Even if you aren't hungry or thirsty, take the time to stop at the **Café Santa Cruz,** one of the most popular and unusual watering holes north of Lisbon. Until its conversion to more pedestrian uses in 1927, this was an auxiliary chapel for the Santa Cruz Monastery. Now its high-vaulted Manueline ceiling, stained-glass windows, and wood paneling provide a wonderful setting in which to indulge a favorite Portuguese pastime: sitting in a café with a strong, murky *bica* (Portugal's answer to espresso) and a brandy, reading the day's newspaper. In summer there are tables outside. *Praça 8 de Maio. Closed Sun.*

Turn right at the northeast corner of the Praça 8 de Maio onto the broad Rua Olímpio Fernandes. Continue past the public library to a small park with an odd assortment of domed, rose-color turrets
**12** grouped around a fountain. This is part of the **Jardim de Manga** (Manga Garden). Once belonging to the cloisters of the Santa Cruz Monastery, the garden was designed by Jean de Rouen in the 16th century. The fountain symbolizes the fountain of life and the eight pools radiating from it, the rivers of paradise. The impressive fountain on the other side of the Rua Olímpio Fernandes is known as the
**13** **Fonte dos Judeus** (Jewish Fountain), which dates to 1725 and marks one of the boundaries of the old Jewish quarter. A few steps past the fountain, back toward the Praça 8 de Maio, is a small alley, Rua Pe-
**14** dro da Rocha, which leads into the notorious **Patio da Inquisição** (Patio of the Inquisition). This once-feared site is now home to the local Red Cross.

Stay to your right after leaving the Patio, and you'll reach a broad, one-way street branching off from the Praça 8 de Maio. This is the
**15** renowned **Rua da Sofia.** Developed in the 16th century, the rua is famous for its many fine religious monuments, including the Carmo, Graça, São Pedro, and Santa Justa churches. To preserve the architectural integrity of the neighborhood, the entire street has been classified as a national monument.

**16** The **Palácio da Justiça** (Hall of Justice), on the Rua da Sofia, just around the corner from the new Tivoli Coimbra Hotel, occupies a stately, 16th-century building that was once the College of St. Thomas. To the left of the main entrance is a large azulejo panel showing the goddess of justice watched over by a Knight Templar. The three panels in front read "Work," "Justice," and "Order." Gracing the interior is a two-tier cloister, decorated with azulejo panels depicting historical themes associated with Coimbra. *Rua da Sofia. Admission free. Open weekdays 9–12:30 and 2–5:30.*

To return to the starting point at the Portagem, follow the Praça 8 de Maio to the shop-lined Rua Visconde da Luz and the Rua Ferreira Borges.

**Time Out** Why not succumb to the temptation of the pastry-filled windows of the inviting cafés along the Rua Ferreira Borges? The **Café Nicola** (No. 35) is a good choice for sampling *arrufada*, Coimbra's most notable contribution to the great pastries of the world. This curved confection is said to represent the tortuous course of the Rio Mondego.

From the Portagem, cross the bridge over the Mondego, turn left on the Rua António Augusto Gonçalves, and left again down the Rua de Baixo. There you will see a stark Gothic structure with a single ⑰ pointed tower—the **Convento de Santa Clara-a-Velha** (Old Santa Clara Convent). Although the convent is steeped in history, there isn't much left to see of the original 13th-century building, since the periodic flooding of the Mondego has taken its toll. At one time both Inês de Castro and Queen Isabel, the patron saint of Coimbra, were interred here.

Continue along the Rua António Augusto Gonçalves for about 15 ⑱ minutes to reach the **Quinta das Lágrimas** (House of Tears), where Dom Pedro and Inês de Castro lived with their children. It was here, as the legend goes, on a black January night in 1355, that Inês was killed by agents of Dom Pedro's father, Afonso IV. The 19th-century manor house on the grounds is closed to the public, but you can wander around the gardens and pause at the celebrated **Fonte dos Amores** (Fountain of the Lovers). *Admission free. Open daily 9–7.*

⑲ The **Convento de Santa Clara-a-Nova** (New Santa Clara Convent) stands on a hill overlooking the city. On foot it's about a 20-minute climb after crossing the river. The term "new" is relative; it was built nearly 300 years ago to escape the periodic flooding that beset the old convent, which was abandoned in 1677. The new building was consecrated in 1696, and the body of Queen Isabel was relocated. The original painted stone tomb may be seen at the end of the lower chancel, and the 17th-century tomb, a fine example of the silver craftsmanship of the time, is in the main chancel. The church also contains an impressive statue of Isabel in nun's garb, carved from a single 10-foot-high block of limestone. During the Peninsular War, the French general Massena used the convent as a hospital for 300 troops wounded during the battle of Buçaco. The carefully hidden convent treasures escaped the desecration inflicted on so many Portuguese monuments during this period. Don't leave Santa Clara without a relaxing stroll through the enormous cloisters. *Admission. 50$00 Open daily 9–12:30 and 2–5:30.*

## Tour 2: The Western Beiras

⑳ **Conimbriga,** in a bucolic setting 16 kilometers (10 miles) southwest of Coimbra, is one of the Iberian Peninsula's most important archaeological sites. It began as a small settlement in Celtic or possibly pre-Celtic times. In 27 BC, during his second Iberian visit, the emperor Augustus established the Roman province called Lusitania. It was in this period that, as the Portuguese historian Jorge Alarção said, "Conimbriga was transformed by the Romans from a village where people just existed into a city worth visiting." You enter via a brick reception pavilion with pools and gardens surrounding a museum. Exhibits chronicle the development of the site from its Iron Age origins, through its heyday as a prosperous Roman town, to its decline following the 5th-century barbarian conquests. The museum is best appreciated after visiting the excavations.

At the site's entrance is a portion of the original Roman road that connected Olissipo (as Lisbon was then known) and the northern town of Braga. If you look closely, you can make out ridges worn into the stone by cart wheels. The uncovered area represents just a small portion of the Roman city, but within this area are some wonderful mosaic floors. The 3rd-century House of the Fountains has a large, macabre mosaic depicting Perseus offering the head of Medusa to a

monster from the deep, an example of the amazing Roman craftsmanship of the period.

Across the way is the **Casa do Cantaber** (House of Cantaber), named
for a nobleman whose family was captured by invading barbarians in
465. A tour of the house reveals the comfortable lifestyle of Roman
nobility at the time. Private baths included a *tepidarium* (hot pool)
and *frigidarium* (cold pool). Remnants of the under-floor central
heating system are also visible. Fresh water was carried 3 kilometers (2 miles) by aqueduct from Alcabideque; parts of the original
aqueduct can still be seen. There is daily bus service between
Conimbriga and Coimbra. *Condeixa-a-Velha, tel. 039/941177. Admission: ruins and museum: June–Sept. 400$00, Oct.–May
300$00; ruins only: Mon., 150$00. Open: ruins: daily 9–1 and 2–6,
until 8 during summer; museum: Tues.–Sun. 10–12:30 and 2–5,
until 6 during summer; closed holidays.*

For the most scenic route, return to Coimbra, and from there take
N341, which runs along the south bank of the Mondego to
㉑ **Montemor-o-Velho.** Occupying a strategic hilltop position overlooking the fertile Mondego basin between Coimbra and Figueira da
Foz, Montemor figures prominently in the history and legends of the
region. One popular story tells how the castle's besieged defenders
cut the throats of their own families to spare them a cruel death at
the hands of the Moorish invaders; many died before the attackers
were repulsed. The following day the escaping Moors were pursued
and thoroughly defeated. Legend has it that all those slaughtered at
Montemor were resurrected but forever carried a red mark on their
necks as a reminder of the battle.

The castle walls and tower, which command the hill and fertile plains
below, are largely intact, although little remains inside the impressive ramparts to suggest that this noble family's home once garri-
soned 5,000 troops. Archaeological evidence indicates that the hill
has been fortified for more than 2,000 years. Although Montemor
Castle played an important role in the long-standing conflict between the Christians and Moors, changing hands many times, the
structure seen today is primarily of 14th-century origin. The two
churches on the hill are also part of the castle complex. The Church
of Santa Maria de Alcaçova dates back to the 11th century and contains some well-preserved Manueline additions.

Here again are threads of the story of Inês de Castro, for in January
of 1355, Dom Afonso IV, meeting in the castle with his advisers,
made the decision to murder her. In 1811, during the Napoleonic invasions, the castle was badly damaged. *Admission free. Open
Tues.–Sun. 10–12:30 and 2–5.*

㉒ There are various theories as to the origin of the name **Figueira da
Foz.** The consensus around the fishing harbor at this popular seaside
resort favors the literal translation: the fig tree at the mouth of the
river. The belief is that when this was just a small settlement, ocean-
going fishermen and traders from up the river would arrange to
meet at the big fig tree to conduct their business. Although today
there are no fig trees to be seen at this busy fishing port, the name
has stuck.

Shortly before the turn of the century, with the improvement of
road and rail access, Figueira, with its long, sandy beach and mild
climate, developed into a popular seaside resort. Today, although
the beach is little changed, a broad four-lane divided boulevard runs
along its length. The town side is lined with the usual melange of

apartments, hotels, and restaurants, but, fortunately, the beachfront has been spared from development.

One of the things to do here or in any Portuguese fishing town is to go down to the docks early in the morning to watch the *lota* (the auctioning of the day's catch). Although this colorful spectacle is closed to the public, if you are lucky perhaps the customs police will look the other way.

One of the more curious sights in the town is the 18th-century **Casa do Paço,** the interior of which is decorated with about 7,000 Delft tiles. These traditional Dutch tiles were salvaged from a shipwreck at the mouth of the harbor. *Largo Prof. Vitor Guerra 4, around corner from main post office. Admission free. Open weekdays 9:30–12:30 and 2–5.*

The triangular 17th-century **Fortaleza da Santa Catarina** (Santa Catarina Fortress), adjacent to the beachfront tennis courts, was occupied by the French during the early days of the Peninsular War.

**Time Out** | There are a number of brightly painted wooden-shack restaurants sitting directly on the beach. These are wonderful places for fresh grilled fish or just a cold drink. **A Platforma** is one of the best.

**Palácio Sotto Mayor,** a luxurious, elegantly furnished, French-style manor house, was constructed as part of the wave of development in the late 19th and early 20th centuries that made Figueira da Foz a world-class resort. Long in the hands of one of Portugal's leading families, the palace now belongs to the owners of the casino (*see* The Arts and Nightlife, *below*). Local gossip has it that it was "donated" as payment for gambling debts. Its collection includes paintings and fine furnishings. *Rua Joaquím Sotto Mayor, tel. 033/22121. Admission: 100$00. Open weekends 2–6.*

㉓ Just north of Figueira, **Buarcos,** with a fine sandy beach, has managed to retain some of the character of a Portuguese fishing village in spite of a heavy influx of tourists. Here colorfully painted boats are still pulled up onto the beach, and fishermen sit around mending nets. From Buarcos take a trip to the Cape Mondego lighthouse for a wonderful, uncluttered view of the coastline. Then continue climbing through a wooded area to the little village of Boa Viagem (Good Journey); from here you can trace the course of the Rio Mondego as it flows into the sea. Now head north, following the narrow road running along the dunes to Aveiro.

㉔ To refer to **Aveiro** as the Venice of Portugal, as is sometimes done, does not make for a good comparison. Yes, there are a few canals running through its center, and the swan-necked *moliceiros* (kelp boats) do remotely resemble Venetian gondolas, but that's the extent of the similarity. Aveiro's mood is not the drama and splendor of Venice but rather a quiet confidence and dignity.

Like Venice, though, Aveiro is first and foremost a water city. Its
㉕ traditions are closely tied to the sea and to the **Ria de Aveiro,** the vast, shallow lagoon that formed in 1575 when a violent storm caused shifting sand to block the flow of the Rio Vouga into the ocean. This unique combination of fresh and salt water, narrow waterways, and tiny islands is bordered by salt marshes and lush pine forests, and the ocean side is lined with lovely sandy beaches. The tranquil ria is the realm of the moliceiros, the graceful, colorfully painted craft that glide along the shallow waterways harvesting seaweed. A boat tour through the ria is a must (*see* Guided Tours in Es-

sential Information, *above*), and, if you have a car, a drive through the ria's back roads is also recommended.

With the loss of its seaport, Aveiro, once a major center for boats working the Newfoundland codfish banks, suffered a prolonged decline. It was only in 1808, when a breakwater was built of stones from the old city fortifications, that a passage to the sea was reestablished and the town once again flourished. Deep-sea fishing was reinstituted, new industries were established, and the city took on the prosperous air it maintains today.

Aveiro is great for walking, because most of the industry and the new university are on the periphery, and places of interest in the old town are easily accessible on foot. In many parts of town, the sidewalks and squares are paved with *calçada* (traditional Portuguese hand-laid pavement) in intricate nautical patterns.

The most attractive buildings date back to the latter half of the 15th century. In 1472 the princess Joana, daughter of King Afonso V, retired, against her father's wishes, to the **Mosteiro de Jesus** (Convent of Jesus), where she spent the last 18 years of her life. This royal presence gave impetus to the city's economic and cultural development. The convent, which now houses the **Museu de Aveiro** (Aveiro Museum), was established by papal bull in 1461. The late-18th-century facade is not particularly interesting, but the interior of the church, completed in the early 18th century, is a masterpiece of Baroque art. The elaborately gilded wood carvings and ornate ceiling, done by António Gomes and José Correia from Oporto, are among the finest in Portugal. Scenes depicting the life of Joana, who was canonized in 1693, can be seen on azulejo panels, and Joana's tomb is in the lower choir. The multicolor inlaid marble sarcophagus is supported at each corner by delicately carved angels. The museum contains an assortment of sculpture, coaches and carriages, artifacts, and paintings, including a particularly fine 15th-century portrait of the Princess Joana by Nuno Gonçalves. *Rua Santa Joana Princesa. Admission: museum: 300$00. Open Tues.–Sun. 10–12:30 and 2–5.*

The austere stone structure across from the convent is the Aveiro Cathedral, more commonly known as the Church of São Domingos. The interior of the church has no definitive architectural style but does contain some fine azulejos.

**Time Out** | The **Sonatura,** overlooking the central canal, offers a rare opportunity to have a vegetarian snack or meal. Service is cafeteria-style inside a health-food store. To your right, as you leave the restaurant, note the modern tile relief showing kelp gatherers at work. *Praça Humberto Delgada, Rua Clube dos Galitos 6. Closed Sun.*

The Praça da República has two interesting buildings: the graceful, three-story Town Hall, with a pointed bell tower, and the 18th-century Misericórdia Church, whose imposing Baroque portal is set against a background of blue-and-white azulejos.

Also of interest in Aveiro is the headquarters of the port captain, an attractive, two-story building perched on arches in the middle of the central canal. The best place for viewing the brightly decorated fishing boats is along the Canal de São Roque. To the west are huge, glistening mounds of white salt, recovered by evaporation from the lagoon. At the northeast edge of the city, the train station displays some lovely azulejo panels depicting traditions and customs of the region.

**26** **Ilhavo,** 4 kilometers (2½ miles) south of Aveiro, is a small town of attractive, tiled manor houses. The **Museu do Mar** (Museum of the Sea), situated in a drab, concrete building next to a fish- processing plant, documents the region's close relationship with the sea and has a collection of local pottery and Vista Alegre china. *Rua Vasco da Gama, tel. 034/321797. Admission: 200$00. Open Wed.–Sat. 9– 12:30 and 2–5:30, Sun. and Tues. 2–5:30.*

**27** Continue south from Ilhavo for 2 kilometers (1¼ miles) to **Vista Alegre,** where Portugal's finest china is produced. The business was started in 1824 as a sort of commune, with housing furnished for workers from all parts of the country. Training was provided by French master craftsmen, and the clay came from the nearby town of Ovar. The large, tree-filled square is bordered by the factory, a china museum, a gift shop, and a small 17th-century chapel with the delicately carved tomb of the chapel's founder. *Fabrica Vista Alegre, tel. 034/322365. Admission free. Museum and gift shop open weekdays 9–12:30 and 2–5:30.*

**28** Back in Aveiro head north on N109 to Estarreja; then turn west and follow N109-5 through quiet farmlands. After crossing the bridge over the ria, continue north on N327 to **Ovar.** Situated at the northern end of the ria, Ovar provides a convenient jumping-off point for visiting the string of beaches along the narrow northern peninsula. This small town with its many tiled houses is a veritable showcase of azulejos. The courthouse, built in the 1960s, is adorned with some unusually beautiful multicolor tile panels, and the exterior of the late-17th-century Parish Church is completely covered with blue-and-white azulejos. The small **Museu Regional de Ovar,** in an old house in the town center, also exhibits many tiles and local handicrafts. *Rua Heliodoro Slagado, tel. 056/52822. Admission: 200$00. Open Sat.–Thurs. 10–noon and 2–4 except holidays.*

**29** Drive 10 kilometers (6 miles) on N223 from Ovar to **Santa Maria de Feira,** and you will be rewarded with the lovely fairy-tale Castle of Vila da Feira. The four square towers are crowned with a series of cone-shaped turrets in a display of Gothic architecture more common in Germany or Austria than Portugal. Although the original walls date back to the 11th century, the present structure is the result of modifications made 400 years later. From atop the tower you can make out the sprawling outlines of the Aveiro Ria. *Admission: 300$00. Open Tues.–Sun. 9–12:30 and 2–6.*

**30** After visiting the castle, it's a scenic but twisting, bone-jarring 70-kilometer (43½-mile) drive on N227 across the Serra da Gralheira mountains to **Viseu.** (The new IP1 and IP5 highways offer a smoother, faster, but much less interesting alternative.) A thriving provincial capital situated in one of Portugal's prime wine-growing districts, the Dão region, Viseu has managed to preserve the ambience of a country town in spite of its obvious prosperity. The newer part of town is comfortably laid out. Parks and wide boulevards radiate from a central traffic circle but, unlike many Portuguese towns, through traffic does not have to go into its center.

A good place to start a visit is the tree-lined **Praça da República,** also known as the Rossío This pleasant square is framed at one end by a massive azulejo mural depicting scenes of country life. The heroic figure in bronze, standing sword in hand, is Prince Henry the Navigator, the first duke of Viseu. The stately building across from the tile mural is the **Câmara Municipal** (Town Hall). Walk inside to admire the colorful Aveiro tiles and fine woodwork, and be sure to see the courtyard. Just to the south of the square, a graceful stairway leads to the 18th-century, baroque **A Igreja dos Terceiros de São Francisco** (Church of the Terceiros de São Francisco). Behind the church is a large, wooded park with paths and ponds, offering an ideal respite from the summer heat.

From the Rossío walk up the hill past a garden with a bronze figure of a mother and child to the Moorish-style mansion on the hill. This is the **A Casa-Museu de Almeida Moreira** (Almeida Moreira Museum). Almeida Moreira, the first director of the Grão Vasco Museum, bequeathed his house and a diverse collection of paintings, furniture, and ceramics to the city. The house alone is worth the admission price. *Rua Soar Cima, tel. 032/ 23769. Admission: 150$00. Open Tues.–Sun. 10–12:30 and 2–5 except holidays.*

Continue along the Largo Pintor Gata into the old town, and you will emerge onto the **Largo da Sé.** Bounded by three imposing edifices— the cathedral, the palace housing the Grão Vasco Museum, and the Misericórdia Church—this is one of the most impressive squares in Portugal.

The **Sé Catedral** (Cathedral), a massive stone structure with twin bell towers, lends a solemn air to the large plaza. Construction was started in the 13th century and continued on and off until the 18th century. The interior is marked by a mixture of Gothic and Manueline elements. Massive Gothic pillars support a network of twisted, knotted forms that reach across the high, vaulted roof. The dazzling gilded Baroque high altar contrasts with the otherwise somber stone interior. To the right of the Mannerist main portal is a double-tiered cloister. The lower level was constructed in the 16th century in the style of the Italian Renaissance. The harsh lines of the upper level (added 200 years later) appear awkward in contrast to the graceful Italianate arches below. The walls of the lower level are adorned with a series of excellent azulejo panels depicting various religious motifs. A well-preserved, transitional, Gothic-style doorway connects the cloister with the cathedral. *Admission free. Open daily 9:30–12:30 and 2–5:30.*

Directly adjacent to the cathedral is the former 16th-century Bishop's Palace, which now houses the **Museu de Grão Vasco.** The second-floor galleries are devoted to the display of the works of the great 16th-century Portuguese painter Vasco Fernandes (Grão Vasco) and his Viseu school. *Adro de Sé, tel. 032/26249. Admission: 300$00, weekends free. Open Tues.–Sun. 10–12:30 and 2–5 except holidays.*

Directly opposite the cathedral stands the white, rococo **Misericórdia Church,** whose soft, graceful lines contrast sharply with the harsh, gray lines of the cathedral. *Admission free. Open daily 9:30– 12:30 and 2–5:30.*

Return to the lower town by way of the **Praça de Dom Duarte,** one of those rare places where just the right combination of rough stone pavement, splendid old houses, wrought-iron balconies, and views of an ancient cathedral come together to produce a magical effect. Try to be here at night, when the romance of the setting is further enhanced by the soft glow of the streetlights.

At the edge of town on the road toward Aveiro is a statue of a warrior standing on a rock. This is a monument to Viriáto, the leader of the Lusitanian resistance to the Roman invasion in the 2nd century BC. Some historians believe that this was the site of his encampment.

**31** The market town of **Mangualde** is 13 kilometers (8 miles) southeast of Viseu on N16. The principal attraction is the **Palácio des Condes**

**de Anadia** (Palace of the Counts of Anadia). The two- story, 17th-century, rococo manor house is one of the best from this era in the region. The walls are decorated with 18th- century Coimbra azulejos, and the interior contains period furniture and paintings from the 17th to the 19th century. *Admission: 400$00. Open Oct.–Aug., Tues.–Sun. 9–noon and 2–6.*

Driving through the heart of the Dão region from Mangualde to Caramulo, you will see many vineyards, some carefully terraced. The wines pressed from these grapes are some of Portugal's finest.

㉜ In the early part of this century, when tuberculosis was rife, people came to **Caramulo** for the beneficial effects of the fresh mountain air. Tuberculosis is no longer a problem, but Caramulo has not lost its appeal. People still come to enjoy the heather-clad, wooded slopes and to walk through the lovely parks and gardens. Mineral water bottled at the nearby spring is popular throughout the country.

The town has an unusual museum, the **Museu de Arte do Caramulo** (Caramulo Art Museum), founded and supported by Abel Lacerda, a local doctor. The varied collection, consisting solely of donations, includes jewels, ceramics, and a fine assortment of paintings, representing such diverse artists as Salvador Dali, Picasso, and Grão Vasco. Next door is the **Museu do Automóvel,** whose collection of perfectly restored antique cars includes such rare items as a 1902 Darracq. Also on exhibit are vintage bicycles and motorcycles. *Tel. 032/86270. Admission: both museums 350$00. Open Tues.–Sun. 10–12:30 and 2–6.*

**Caramulinho** and **Cabeça da Neve,** two nearby observation points, offer spectacular vistas. Take Avenida Abel de Lacerda west from town until it runs into N230–3. After 3 kilometers (2 miles) on N230–3, you come to a trail leading to Caramulinho. It's about a 30-minute climb to the top. Here at the tip of the Serra do Caramulo mountains, at an elevation of 3,500 feet, you can look out across a vast panorama taking in the coastal plain to the west and the Serra da Estrela to the southeast. On the drive back, take the turnoff marked Cabeço da Neve. From there you have a bird's-eye view of the Mondego basin.

㉝ As you continue west on N230, the road snakes down the mountain following the course of the Rio Águeda as it flows into the great Aveiro lagoon. The industrial town of **Águeda** is a center for the production of paper products. With the exception of the parish church, the town has little of interest.

㉞ Head south on N1 to **Curia,** a small but popular spa in the heart of the Bairrada region, an area noted for its fine wines and roast suckling pig. The waters of the spa, with their high calcium and magnesium sulphate content, are said to help in the treatment of kidney disorders. Curia offers a quiet retreat of shaded parks, a small lake, and grand Belle Epoque hotels just a half-hour's drive from the clamor of the summer beach scene. In fact, any of the three resorts in this area, Curia, Luso, or Buçaco, makes a good, quiet base for visiting the beaches and other attractions of the region. Coimbra, Aveiro, Figueira da Foz, the Serra do Caramulo, and Viseu are all within an hour's drive.

㉟ **Luso,** another charming town built around "the taking of the waters," is located on the main Lisbon–Paris train line. It sits in a little valley at the foot of the Buçaco forest and attracts visitors from all over the world. Like Curia, it has an attractive park with a lake, elegant hotels, and medicinal waters. The Luso water emerges at a warm 27°C (81°F) from the *Fonte de São João*, a fountain in the center of town. Slightly radioactive and with a low sodium and high silica content, the water is said to be effective in the treatment of a wide range of kidney and rheumatic disorders.

In the early 17th century, the head of the Order of Barefoot Carmelites, searching for a suitable location on which to found a monastery, came upon an area of dense virgin forest. Having rejected an offer to settle in Sintra because there were too many distractions, he chose instead the tranquil forest of **Buçaco.** A site for the monastery was selected halfway up the hill on the greenest slope, and by 1630 the simple stone structure was occupied. To preserve their world of isolation and silence, the monks built a wall enclosing the forest. Their only link with the outside world was through one door facing toward Coimbra, which one of them watched over. The Coimbra Gate, still in use today, is the most decorative of the eight gates constructed since that time.

So concerned were the Carmelites for the well-being of their forest that they obtained a papal bull in 1643 calling for the excommunication of anyone caught cutting down even a single tree. They planted many trees, including a number of exotic varieties, and the forest flourished. Attracted by the calm and tranquility of the forest, individual monks would leave the monastery to be alone with God and nature. They built simple hermitages, where they would stay, without human companionship, for several months at a time. You can still see vestiges of these hermitages as you walk through the forest.

In 1810 this serenity was shattered by a fierce battle in which the Napoleonic armies under Massena were repulsed by Wellington's British and Portuguese troops. An obelisk marks the site of the Battle of Buçaco, a turning point in the French invasion of the Iberian peninsula. Nearby is the small **Museu da Guerra Peninsular** (Peninsular War Museum), with uniforms, weapons, and various memorabilia from the battle. *Admission: 100$00. Open June 15–Sept. 15, Tues.–Sun. 9–5:30; Sept. 16–June 14, Tues.–Sun. 10–4.*

A decree in 1834 banned religious orders throughout Portugal, and the monks were forced to leave the monastery. In the early years of this century, much of the original structure was torn down to construct what was to be a royal hunting lodge. The commission was given to the Italian architect Luigi Manini, and the project grew and grew. The opulent, multiturreted, pseudo-Manueline extravaganza that is now the **Palace Hotel Buçaco** was the result (*see* Dining and Lodging, *below*). With the exception of one brief vacation and a dubious romantic fling involving the 20-year-old Manuel II, Portugal's last king, this "simple hunting lodge" was never used by the royal family. The hotel prospered, and in the years between the two world wars it became one of Europe's most fashionable vacation addresses. Tales told in the local villages have it that during World War II, when neutral Portugal was a hotbed of espionage activity, Nazi agents ensconced in the hotel's tower rooms beamed radio signals to submarines off the coast. Today the hotel is still going strong, somewhat of a dinosaur among the sleek new breed of glass-and-steel hostelries. Many come to Buçaco just to view this unusual structure, to stroll the shaded paths that wind through the forest, and to climb the hill past the Stations of the Cross to the **Alta Cruz** (High Cross), their efforts rewarded by the spectacular view extending all the way to the sea.

From Buçaco take N235 through the wooded countryside along the foot of the Serra do Buçaco to **Penacova,** a delightful little town perched on a hill at the junction of three low mountain ranges. There are panoramic views wherever you look and wonderful opportunities for hiking. Several paths lead over the hills to the Monastery of Lorvão or through the vineyards and fields down to the Mondego. The attractive parish church in the town square was built in 1620.

Two kilometers (1¼ miles) south of Penacova on N110 toward Coimbra takes you to the turnoff for the monastery in Lorvão. In a delightful setting among the hills above the Mondego, it is patterned after the massive Baroque edifice at Mafra. Archaeological evidence places the existence of a monastery here as far back as the 6th century, but the present church is principally an 18th-century construction. It has a fine carved choir and the intricate silver tombs of Teresa and Sancha, daughters of Dom Sancho I. A large part of the original monastery has been taken over by a psychiatric hospital, but it is possible to visit the church, choir, and sacristry. There is also a small museum next door. *Admission free. Open daily 10–5.*

From Lorvão it's a pleasant 22-kilometer (14-mile) drive along the Mondego back to Coimbra.

## Tour 3: The Serra da Estrela and Fortified Towns

The third tour covers a part of Portugal seldom visited by foreign tourists. The rugged mountains of the Serra da Estrela and sparse vegetation of the stone-strewn high plateau along the border with Spain present a sharp contrast to the sandy beaches, lush valleys, and densely forested mountains along the coast. As you drive east, the red tile roofs and brightly trimmed, white stucco houses are replaced by stone and slate construction, reflecting the harsher, more somber environment.

**38** The start of the tour is **Castelo Branco,** a modern town of wide boulevards, parks, and gardens and the provincial capital of Beira Baixa. Lying at the confluence of three major roads, the N112 from Coimbra; the N118, which runs along the Tejo; and the N18, which connects Guarda in the North with the Alentejo, it is easily accessible from all parts of the country.

Start with a stroll through the **Jardim do Antigo Paço Episcopal** (Gardens of the former Episcopal Palace). These 18th-century gardens are planted with rows of hedges cut in all sorts of bizarre shapes and contain a most unusual assemblage of sculpture. Bordering one of the park's five small lakes are a path and stairway lined on both sides with granite statues of the Apostles, the Evangelists, and the kings of Portugal. The long-standing Portuguese disdain for the Spanish is graphically demonstrated here; the kings who ruled when Portugal was under Spanish domination are carved to a noticeably smaller scale than the "true" Portuguese rulers. Unfortunately, many statues were damaged by Napoleon's troops when the city was ransacked in 1807. *Admission: 150$00. Open daily 9–6.*

Adjacent to the gardens is the old Episcopal Palace, which houses a small regional museum, the **Tavares Proença National Museum.** In addition to the usual Roman artifacts and odd pieces of furniture, the collection contains some fine examples of *bordado,* the embroidery for which Castelo Branco is so well known. Adjacent to the museum is a workshop where embroidered bedspreads are made and sold. *Rua Bartolomeu da Costa, tel. 072/24277. Admission: 250$00, Sun. free. Open daily 10–12:30 and 2–5:30 except holidays.*

Leave the park, and wander through the old town past the curious clock tower to the Praça Luis de Camões, the town's best-preserved medieval square. The building with the arched stone stairway is the 16th-century town hall. At the top of the hill are the ruins of the 12th-century Templar's Castle. Not much remains of the series of walls and towers that once surrounded the town. Adjoining the castle is the flower-covered **Miradouro de São Gens** (Terrace of São Gens), which provides a fine view of the town and surrounding countryside.

**Time Out** For a refreshing pause, drop into the **Cervejeria Bohemia** (Av. 1 de Maio, near tourist office), an inviting snack bar–restaurant with a long, marble-top bar.

Travel north from Castelo Branco on N18. As you cross the broad plains dotted with olive trees, you can see the Serra da Estrela
**39** mountains in the distance. **Alpedrinha,** a village known for its fine fountains, also has well-preserved remnants of the Roman road that connected this fertile agricultural region with the Spanish town of
**40** Merida. From here N18 climbs to **Fundão,** the principal market town for the area's many orchards. The pears and cherries grown here are the best in Portugal. The 18th-century parish church is noted for its azulejos and decorative ceiling. Fundão is also a convenient gateway to the fortified towns along the Spanish border.

Head east on N345 to the intersection with N346. Then take N346 to
**41** **Penamacor.** Dominated by the ruins of an ancient cas tle that guarded the northern approaches to the Rio Tejo, Penamacor was a key link in the chain of strategically placed fortified towns. Many of the newer stucco houses that you see on the outskirts of the towns in this region were built by Portuguese emigrants with money earned working in France and Germany. Head up the hill to the **castle.** In the wake of the 11th- and 12th-century campaigns to reconquer this region from the Moors, Penamacor lay in ruins; it was Dom Sancho I who, in 1180, ordered the reconstruction of the fortifications. Although you can still find traces from that period, much of what you now see, including the solitary watchtower, dates from the early 16th century. The tower, which has no entrance, was used as an observation post and has a direct line of sight with the fortifications at Monsanto to the south and Sortelha to the north. *If castle is closed, ask for key at tourist office.*

Also of interest are the 16th-century Misericórdia Church, distinguished by a fine Manueline entrance, and a rare octagonal pillory in front of the old town hall. The town has a small but interesting **Regional Museum,** housed in a building that was a political prison until the 1974 revolution. One of the original cells has been kept intact, and among the other exhibits is the only complete Roman crematorium on the Iberian Peninsula. *Admission free. Open daily 9–12:30 and 2–5:30.*

Follow N233 north for 35 kilometers (22 miles) across the high pla-
**42** teau to **Sabugal.** This harsh, rocky country is a tough place to make a living. Traditionally, many inhabitants of these towns supplemented their meager farming incomes by smuggling contraband across the nearby border with Spain. The region was greatly affected by the wave of emigration to northern Europe between 1950 and 1970; a half-million Portuguese went to France alone. As a consequence many villages are populated primarily by senior citizens.

The main attraction in Sabugal is the 13th-century **Sabugal Castle,** which sits majestically atop a grassy knoll and is noted for its unusual pentagonal tower. Some historians maintain that the five sides represent the five shields of the Portuguese national coat of arms. Climb the stone stairs in the courtyard, and walk around the battlements. The castle overlooks the Rio Côa, an important tributary of the Douro. *Admission free. Open Mon.–Sat. 10–5. If castle is closed, ask for key at tourist office.*

**43** If you only have time to visit one fortified town, then **Sortelha** should be it. From the moment you walk through its massive ancient stone walls, you feel like you are experiencing a time warp. Except for a few TV antennas, there is little else to evoke the 20th century. The streets are not littered with souvenir stands, nor is there a fast-food outlet in sight. Stone houses are built into the rocky terrain and arranged within the walls roughly in the shape of an amphitheater.

**Time Out** The **Bar Dom Sancho I,** in the main square, occupies the lower level of a carefully restored stone house. A "hobby project" of a local mining engineer, it is a pleasant place to pause for drinks and snacks. Upstairs you can purchase locally made handicrafts.

Perched above the village are the ruins of a small but imposing **castle.** The present configuration dates back mainly to a late- 12th-century reconstruction, done on Moorish foundations; additional alterations were made in the 16th century. Note the Manueline coat of arms at the entrance. Wear sturdy shoes so that you can walk along the walls (it's possible to circle the entire village this way). As you walk along, there are views of Spain to the east and of the Serra da Estrela to the west. The three holes in the balcony projecting over the main entrance were used to pour boiling oil on intruders. Just to the right of the north gate are two linear indentations in the stone wall. One is exactly a meter in length, and the shorter of the two is a *covada* (66 centimeters). Traveling cloth merchants used these in medieval times to ensure an honest measure.

**44** From Sortelha take N18–3 west and N345 north to **Belmonte.** As you approach the town, three distinct objects, which say a lot about Belmonte, catch your eye. The first two, the ancient castle and the church, represent the town's historic past, while the third structure, an ugly water tower, symbolizes the new industry of the town, now a major clothing manufacturing center. Historically, Belmonte's importance can be traced back to Roman times, when it was an important outpost on the road between Merida, the Lusitanian capital, and Guarda. Elements of this road may still be seen.

Ask a Portuguese, or better yet any Brazilian, what Belmonte is best known for, and the answer will undoubtedly be Pedro Álvares Cabral. In 1500 this native son "discovered" Brazil and in doing so contributed to making Portugal one of the richest and most powerful nations of that era. The monument to Cabral in the town center is an important stop for Brazilians visiting Portugal.

Head up through the old town to the **castle.** Only the tower and battlements remain intact from what once was a mighty complex of fortifications and dwellings. As you enter the castle, note the scale-model replica of the caravel that carried Cabral to Brazil. On one of the side walls is a coat of arms with two goats, the emblem of the Cabral family. (As mentioned above, "cabra" means goat in Portuguese.) The graceful Manueline window incorporated into the heavy fortifications seems misplaced. *Admission: 200$00. Open Mon.–Sat. 10–12:30 and 2–5:30.*

As you leave the castle, you will see a cluster of old houses to your right. This was the *juderia* (the old Jewish quarter). Belmonte had (and, in fact, still has) one of the largest Jewish communities in Portugal. Many present-day residents are descendants of the *Morranos*, the Jews who were forced to convert to Christianity during the Inquisition.

Adjacent to the castle is the 12th-century stone **Igreja de São Tiago** (Church of Saint James), which contains fragments of original 12th-century frescoes and a fine pietà carved from a single block of granite. The tomb of Pedro Cabral is also in this church. Actually there are two Pedro Cabral tombs in Portugal, the result of a bizarre dispute with Santarem, where Cabral died. Both towns claim ownership of the explorer's mortal remains, and no one seems to know just who or what is in either tomb. *Admission free. Open daily 10–6. If closed, ask at tourist office.*

Just outside Belmonte, on a dirt track leading off the N18 toward Guarda, is a strange archaeological find, **Centum Cellas.** This massive, solitary tower constructed of granite blocks is thought to be of Roman origin, and some archaeologists believe it's part of a much larger complex. Excavations of the surrounding area are planned.

Although its origins go back to Roman times, there is little in present-day **Covilhã** of historic significance. Built into the foothills of the Serra da Estrela, the mostly modern town is closely linked to sheep raising. Its tangy *queijo da Serra,* a ewe's-milk cheese, is popular throughout the country, and the town is Portugal's most important wool-producing center. However, most visitors come to Covilhã because it is a convenient gateway to the Serra da Estrela (*see* National Parks in Sports and the Outdoors, *below*).

Nestled into the western side of the Mondego valley, **Gouveia,** a quiet town of parks and gardens, is another popular base from which to explore the Serra da Estrela. The exterior of the Baroque parish church is covered with blue and white tiles. Across the street a series of well-executed azulejos depicting the Stations of the Cross lines the inside walls of the small, dimly lit chapel. The **Museu Abel Manta,** in an 18th-century manor house, displays the paintings of this local, 20th-century artist. *Admission free. Open Tues.–Sun. 10–noon and 2–5.*

Gouveia is the principal center for the famous Serra da Estrela dogs, beautiful sheepdogs known for their loyalty and courage. In earlier days, when marauding wolf packs were an ever-present menace, the dogs wore metal collars with long spikes to protect their throats. You can visit **Montes Herminios Kennels,** one of the major breeding kennels in the Vale do Rossim on N232 between Gouveia and Manteigas. *Solar do Cão da Serra, Estrada da Serra, tel. 038/42426.*

Follow N232 as it winds its way to **Manteigas,** a pleasant spa town at the foot of the Zêzere valley and another popular base for visiting the park. From Manteigas continue east on N232, passing a lovely 12th-century church in **Valhelas,** and turn northeast onto N18-1. The road then climbs to **Guarda,** which, at about 3,300 feet, is Portugal's highest city. Guarda is aptly referred to by the four Fs: *forte, feia, fria, e farta* (strong, ugly, cold, and wealthy). A somber conglomeration of austere granite buildings set in a harsh, uncompromising environment, it is no charming mountain hamlet. The winters are cold and gloomy, often cutting into the short springtime.

From pre-Roman times, Guarda has been a strategic bastion on the northeastern flank of the Serra da Estrela, protecting the approaches from Castile. The town is thought to have been a military base for Julius Caesar. Following the fall of the Roman Empire, the Visigoths and later the Moors gained control. Guarda was liberated in the late 12th century by Christian forces and, along with a number of towns in the region, enlarged and fortified by Dom Sancho I.

The castle tower, perched on a small knoll above the cathedral, and a few segments of wall are all that remain of these extensive fortifications. From atop the ruins there is an impressive view across the rock-strewn countryside toward the Castilian plains. Walk down the hill to the fortresslike **Sé** (Cathedral). Although construction started in 1390, it was not completed until 1540. As a consequence, the imposing Gothic building also shows Renaissance and Manueline influences. Although built on a smaller and less majestic scale, the cathedral shows similarities to the great monastery at Batalha. Inside, a magnificent, four-tier relief contains more than 100 carved figures. The work is attributed to the 16th-century sculptor Jean de Rouen.

Leave the cathedral by the side door, and you are in the Praça Luis de Camões, a square lined with some fine 16th- and 18th- century houses. The statue is of Dom Sancho I. The **Regional Museum,** in a stately, early 17th-century palace adjacent to the 18th-century Misericórdia Church, is worth a visit. *Rua Alves Rocadas, tel. 071/ 23460. Admission: 300$00, Sun. free. Open Tues.–Sun. 10–12:30 and 2–5:30.*

From Guarda take either N16 or IP5 east to N324/N340 north. Enclosed within a star-shaped perimeter of massive stone walls, moats, and earthen bulwarks lies the quiet little town of **Almeida.** Less than 10 kilometers (6 miles) from the Spanish border, the town has been the scene of much fighting over the centuries. This is a place for walking, for clambering along the walls and bulwarks, and for giving your imagination free rein, perhaps to conjure up ghosts of battles past.

Travel north on N332 to **Castelo Rodrigo,** an old fortified town that is now mostly deserted; here turn south on N221, crossing the Serra da Marofa and a desolate, rocky moonscape to **Pinhel.** The town, which sits atop a hill in the Marofa range, was a key bastion during the 17th-century wars of restoration. The most striking remnants from that period are the two solitary towers rising above the town. On one of the towers, below the balcony facing the town, you can make out the graceful form of a Manueline window.

**Trancoso,** to the west of Pinhel, is best approached along the scenic but tortuous N226. Portions of the well-preserved castle walls and towers date to the 9th century. The town reached its pinnacle in 1282, when King Dinis chose this as the site for his marriage to Isabel of Aragon. Above one of the gates, the **Porta do Carvalho,** you can make out the figure of a knight. This was a local lad who, during one of the many battles with the Spanish, left the safety of the castle walls to capture the Spanish flag. He was caught, but before being spirited away, he was able to defiantly hurl the flag over the wall.

**Celorico da Beira,** 18 kilometers (11 miles) south, is a major producer of Serra cheese and the site of one of Europe's largest cheese markets, held every other Friday. The cheese is made from the best-quality ewe's milk, using traditional methods. Cheese production takes place between December and March. Celorico also has the requisite **fortress,** and a large portion of the castle walls and an impressive tower have remained intact. *Key to castle can be obtained at town hall (open Mon.–Sat. 10– 12:30 and 2–5).*

**54** Continue southwest on N17 from Celorico for 12 kilometers (7 miles), and take the turnoff to the left to **Linhares.** The road climbs to a rocky outcrop on the northeastern shoulder of the Serra da Estrela. At an elevation of 2,625 feet, a good place for a lookout, stand the fortifications of Linhares. Much of the outer walls and two square, crenellated towers from the time of King Dinis remain intact. Encircled by the walls is a small, quiet village of stone houses, a church, and a few shops. There's a 16th-century pillory in front of the church.

## What to See and Do with Children

At Coimbra's **Portugal dos Pequenitos** (Portugal of the Little Ones), children will have great fun poking around the models of Portugal's most important buildings, built to the scale of a five- year-old child. Then they can compare them with what they have seen firsthand. *Admission: 350$00, 100$00 children under 11. Open daily 9–5:30, until 7 in summer. Closed Easter, Christmas, and November 1.*

A day at the beach is a treat for children of all ages. The beaches at Figueira da Foz, Tocha, Mira, and Furadouro (Ovar) are particularly well-suited to children; they all have lifeguards and have met the European Union standards for safety and hygiene. (*See* Beaches in Sports and the Outdoors, *below.*)

Places of interest to children in the Western Beiras (*see* Tour 2, *above*) include the city parks in Aveiro and Viseu, which have playgrounds; the antique-car museum in Caramulo; and the Museum of the Sea in Ilhavo. Watching the unloading of the big ships in Aveiro and Figueira da Foz can be fun for the whole family, as is the morning fish auction (officially off-limits) at any of the harbors. The Curia Palace hotel, with its old water-powered mill, antique cars, and animals of all kinds, is a wonderful place to stay with children (*see* Dining and Lodging, *below*).

The many castles along the third tour provide wonderful opportunities for children to let their fantasies run wild. The ruins at Almeida, Sortelha, and Belmonte are particularly suitable for scrambling and scampering about. In addition, the miles of hiking trails in the Serra da Estrela are enough to absorb the energy of even the most restless of children (*see* National Parks in Sports and the Outdoors, *below*).

## Off the Beaten Track

Relief from Coimbra's oppressive summer heat can be found in the shade and greenery of the **Jardim Botânico** (Botanical Gardens), adjacent to the university, and in the city's fine parks. **O Choupal,** near the railroad bridge, is a lovely wooded area along the river at the west end of the city. **Parque de Santa Cruz** (Santa Cruz Park), at the Praça da República, offers a pleasant mixture of luxuriant vegetation, ornate fountains, and meandering walking paths.

# Shopping

The Beiras are rich in artisans' traditions. Surprisingly, even today much of what is made is only available within a limited geographic area. For example, the intricate, hand-carved **willow toothpicks** of Penacova are rarely found outside this little town on the Mondego.

The **ceramics** produced in and around Coimbra, mostly blue- and-white reproductions of delicate 17th- and 18th-century patterns, are among the loveliest in the country. A good selection may be found at **Bazar de Louças** (Rua das Padeiras 44, Coimbra, across from the Hotel Oslo).

The region around Aveiro produces Portugal's finest **china,** including the well-known Vista Alegre brand. There is a retail outlet with a good selection of this fine-quality bone china at the factory just outside of Ilhavo (*see* Tour 2, *above*). In Aveiro the **Armazéms de Aveiro** (Rua Conselheiro Luís de Magalhães 1) sells the leading Portuguese brands, including Vista Alegre, Quinta Nova, and Artebus, and they will ship your purchases.

In Viseu, a walk along the Rua Direita in the old town can be rewarding. The narrow street is lined with shops displaying lo cally made **wood carvings, pottery,** and **wrought iron.**

Tradition in Castelo Branco dictates that a new bride make an **embroidered bedspread** for her wedding night. This custom is still followed, and these delicately patterned, hand-embroidered linen and silk spreads are among the finest examples of Portuguese handicrafts. There is a display-and-sales room next to the regional museum (*see* Tour 3, *above*).

In the Serra da Estrela the famous **Serra cheese** and **presunto** (cured ham) are available in most towns, along with hand-carved, wooden kitchen implements and wicker baskets.

# Sports and the Outdoors

## Participant Sports

**Biking** You can rent bikes and mopeds in Figueira da Foz at **AFGA Travel Agency** (Av. Miguel Bombarda 79). In Aveiro bicycles can be rented in summer in front of the tourist office.

**Fishing** There is excellent trout fishing in the rivers and lakes of the Serra da Estrela and in the Rio Vouga. The coastal strip known as the Beira Litoral is full of beaches and rocky outcroppings where you can try your luck with a variety of fish, including bass, bream, and sole. Check with the local tourist offices for information about obtaining permits. No permit is required for ocean fishing.

**Hiking** The Serra da Estrela National Park has a number of well- marked hiking trails. For a detailed booklet and maps, contact the regional tourist office in Covilhã (*see* Tourist Information in Essential Information, *above*).

**Horseback Riding** There is a well-equipped riding center near Aveiro: **Escola Equestre de Aveiro** (Quinta Chãs Agra, Vilarinho, tel. 034/ 912108).

**Water Sports** The Quiaios Lakes near Figueira da Foz are well-suited for windsurfing and sailing. The bay at Buarcos is also a popular windsurfing location. Windsurfers can be rented at most of the popular beach resorts. Board surfers often find 10- to 12-foot waves at Quiaios Beach (just north of Cape Mondego) and good surf at Furadouro and Torreira beaches (near Aveiro). In sum mer there are kayak trips down the Mondego from Penacova to Coimbra. Information can be obtained from the Penacova tourist office (*see* Tourist Information in Essential Information, *above*).

## Beaches

If you haven't already discovered that Portugal's beaches are some of the best in Europe, then you should during the course of Tour 2. There is a virtually continuous stretch of good sandy beach along the entire Beira Litoral from Praia de Leirosa in the south to Praia de Espinho in the north. One word of caution: If your only exposure to Portuguese beaches has been the Algarve's south coast, be careful at west-coast beaches, which tend to have heavier surf and stronger undertows. If you see a red or yellow flag, do not go swimming. The water temperature on the west coast is usually a few degrees cooler than it is on the south coast.

You can take your choice of beach types. There are fully equipped resorts, such as Figueira da Foz and Buarcos, or, if you prefer sand dunes and solitude, you can lay your mat down at any one of the more northern beaches. Just point your car down one of the unmarked roads between Praia de Mira and Costa Nova and head west.

## National Parks

The **Serra da Estrela** is Portugal's largest national park. Until the end of the 19th century, this mountainous region was little known except by shepherds and local hunters. The first scientific expedition to the Serra was in 1881. Since that time it has developed into one of the country's most popular recreation areas. In summer the high, craggy peaks, alpine meadows, and rushing streams become the domain of hikers, climbers, and trout fishermen. The lower and middle elevations are heavily wooded with large stands of deciduous oak, sweet chestnut, and pine. Above the tree line, at about 4,900 feet, is a rocky, subalpine world of scrub vegetation and boggy meadows, which in late spring are transformed into a vivid, multicolored carpet of wildflowers. The Serra da Estrela is home to many species of animals, the largest of which include wild boar, badger, and, in the more remote areas, the occasional wolf.

This is a hiker's paradise, amply supplied with well-marked trails. A comprehensive trail guide is available at tourist offices in the region, and, although it's in Portuguese, the maps, elevation charts, and pictures are useful. There are several official campsites within the park, but if you are discreet about it, you can pitch a small tent just about anywhere without being bothered. The Zêzere, which cuts through one of Europe's deepest glacial valleys, is excellent for trout fishing. There is also good fishing in the Comprida and Loriga lakes. If you prefer to take in the scenery from the comfort of your car, the roads through the Serra da Estrela, although hair-raising at times, are well-maintained and offer many inspiring vistas. The drive between Covilhã and Seia on N339, the highest road in the country, affords a breathtaking view of the Zêzere valley. Along the way you will pass a small fountain marking the source of the Rio Mondego.

With the coming of winter and the first snows, the area becomes a winter playground, offering many Portuguese their only exposure to winter sports. Although there are two ski lifts at **Torre,** the highest point in continental Portugal with an elevation of 6,539 feet, the conditions and facilities are not on a par with ski resorts in the rest of Europe.

One of Portugal's newest national parks, the **Serra da Malcata,** is virtually unknown to foreign tourists. The 50,000-acre area along the Spanish border between Penamacor and Sabugal was created primarily to protect the natural habitat of the Iberian lynx, which was threatened with extinction. This is not a place of rugged beauty and spectacular vistas like you would find in Yosemite or even in the Serra da Estrela; it is a quiet region of heavily wooded, low mountains with few traces of human habitation. In addition to the lynxes, the park shelters wildcats, wild boars, wolves, and foxes.

# Dining and Lodging

**Dining** The cuisine found in this region reflects the geographical diversity of the Beiras. Along the coast, as would be expected, the accent is on fresh fish. At almost any of the ubiquitous beach- bar/restaurants, you can't go wrong by ordering the grilled *peixe do dia* (fish of the day). In most cases it will have been caught hours before and will be prepared outside on a charcoal grill. You will usually be served the whole fish along with boiled potatoes and a simple salad. Wash it down with a chilled white Dão wine, and you have a tasty, healthy, and relatively inexpensive meal. In Figueira da Foz and also in the Aveiro region, *enguia* (eels), *lampreia* (lamprey), and *caldeirada*, a fish stew that is a distant cousin of the French bouillabaisse, are popular.

Moving inland, although fish is readily available, the emphasis shifts to meat dishes. The Bairrada region, between Coimbra and Aveiro, and in particular the town of Mealhada are well known for *leitâo assado* (roast suckling pig). In Coimbra the dish to try is *chanfana;* this is traditionally made with tender young kid braised in red wine and roasted in an earthenware casserole. In the mountains, *truta* (fresh trout) pan-fried with bacon and onions, is often served, as is *javali* (wild boar). *Bacalhau* (salt cod) is found in one form or another on just about every menu in the region. *Bacalhau a brás* (slivers of cod fried in olive oil with eggs, onions, and sometimes potatoes) is one of many popular salt-cod dishes.

The Beiras contain two of Portugal's most notable wine districts: Bairrada and Dão. Particularly good years for these wines are 1983 and 1985; if you see a 1983 Porta dos Cavaleiros Reserva *tinto* (red) on a wine list, grab it. The full-bodied Dão will go wonderfully with your chanfana or leitâo assado.

This region is also justly famous for its contribution to the country's dessert menus, although many of these pastry delights, such as the arrufada of Coimbra, are rarely found far from home. The tangy sheep's cheese of the Serra da Estrela is popular throughout the country.

With the exception of some luxury hotel dining rooms, restaurants are casual in dress and atmosphere. The emphasis is generally more on the food than on the trappings. Good restaurants are found throughout the region, and in many towns hotel dining rooms are popular places to eat. With the exception of pizza, ethnic food is virtually nonexistent outside of Lisbon and the Algarve. Reservations are not necessary unless noted otherwise.

Restaurant ratings correspond to Évora and Central Portugal's dining chart in Chapter 5. Highly recommended restaurants are indicated by a star ★.

**Lodging** Until recently, the visitor to the Beiras in search of high-quality accommodations was almost solely dependent on the government-run chain of pousadas and a few venerable old luxury hotels, such as the Palace Hotel Buçaco. During the past few years, especially near the coast, a number of new hotels and inns have been built, and, to keep up with the competition, many existing facilities have been refurbished. However, accommodations in the eastern portions of the Beiras are still limited. If you plan to travel during the busy summer months, study the maps and lodging recommendations, and make advance reservations to avoid disappointment. There are seven pousadas within the Beiras, which can be used as bases to explore the entire region. (These pousadas are small; the one at Caramulo has just six rooms.) In addition, there are several government-approved private manor houses that take guests. Most establishments offer substantial off-season discounts. (High season varies by hotel but generally runs July 1–September 15.)

Hotel ratings correspond to Évora and Central Portugal's lodging chart in Chapter 5. Highly recommended hotels are indicated by a star ★.

**Águeda**
*Dining and*
*Lodging*
★

**Palácio.** There are few good reasons to come to the industrial town of Águeda. This converted early 17th-century manor house, just off the N1 toward Coimbra, is one of them. Completely rebuilt to the highest standards and first opened as a hotel in 1990, the Palácio has that rare blend of old-world charm and elegance with modern convenience. The generous-size bedrooms are furnished with excellent 15th- and 16th-century French reproductions. The reception area, lounges, and reading room tastefully combine elements ranging from Baroque to Italian Romantic. The 5 acres of ponds and gardens are a delight for strolling. There is even a private chapel. The intimate restaurant overlooking the gardens puts a strong emphasis on such regional dishes as leitão assado. The house specialty is *bacalhau a palácio* (cod filets baked with cheese, onions, mayonnaise, and potatoes). The Palácio has become a favorite with the Lisbon film-and-TV set. *Quinta da Borralha, 3750, tel. 034/601977, fax 034/601976. 41 rooms, 7 suites. Facilities: restaurant, bar, pool, tennis court, parking. AE, DC, MC, V. $$$$*

**Pousada de Santo António.** Conveniently located outside Águeda in Serem, near the junction of the new IP1 and IP5 highways, this comfortable, three-story, pink-stucco country house is based on a concept of Raul Lino, one of the country's foremost architects. A tranquil retreat with good access to the region's attractions, it is 48 kilometers (30 miles) to Coimbra and 19 kilometers (12 miles) to Aveiro. The pousada sits atop a knoll surrounded by trees and looks over the Rio Vouga valley. Although it was built in 1942 and was one of the first in the pousada chain, it has been recently remodeled, and the 12 wood-floor bedrooms are comfortably furnished in traditional style. The circular dining room has large windows facing the valley, and the walls are trimmed with azulejos. There is a small terrace for outside dining and a bar with a brick fireplace. The restaurant does well with regional dishes. One tasty specialty that you probably won't find at your favorite restaurant back home is *ensopada da enguias* (a delicate stew made with eels from the Aveiro Ria). *Serem, 3750 Águeda, tel. 034/ 523230, fax 034/523192. 12 rooms. Facilities: restaurant, bar, pool, tennis court, parking. AE, DC, MC, V. $$$$*

**Almeida**
*Dining and*
*Lodging*
★

**Pousada Senhora das Neves.** Portuguese architect Cristiano Moreira has mastered the difficult task of integrating this modern hotel into historic fortress walls. The bedrooms as well as the public rooms are spacious and light, and there are large terraces that look out across the high tablelands into Spain. You can sip your afternoon glass of chilled white port and imagine Wellington's troops facing Napoleon's armies on this very spot. The restaurant, divided into two inviting plank-floor dining rooms, serves a wide variety of regional dishes, including *sopa de peixe do rio Côa* (a rich, tomato-based soup made with fish from the nearby Rio Côa). The extensive wine list offers more than 60 selections. *6350, tel. 071/54283, fax 071/54320. 20 rooms, 1 suite. Facilities: restaurant, bar, parking. AE, DC, MC, V. $$$$*

**A Muralha.** This modern *residencial* (inn that was once a private residence), just outside the fortifications, is the creation of two ex-schoolteachers, Manuel and Eliza Dias. He has traded teaching English for running the 24-room residencial, and Eliza gave up her geography courses to oversee the small restaurant. The rooms are clean and simply furnished. Cork floors in the bedrooms and cork paneling in the hallways contribute to a homey atmosphere. The restaurant's specialties include roast suckling pig and curried shrimp. *Bairro de São Pedro, 6350, tel. 071/54357. 24 rooms. Facilities: restaurant, bar, parking. MC, V. $*

**Aveiro**
**Dining**
★

**A Nossa Casa.** Located on a quiet street a few blocks from the town center, this small, unassuming, family-operated restaurant produces some of the best meals in town. The dining room is lined with wine bottles, and the tables are separated by wooden dividers. The favorite dish of proprietor Manuel Facteira is *parrilhada de peixes e mariscos no churrasco* (a generous assortment of grilled fish and shellfish served on a large platter around a special sauce made from ground shellfish). *Rua do Gravito 10, tel. 034/29236. DC, MC, V. Closed weekends. $$*

**O Mercantel.** This restaurant is the brainchild of Sr. Costa da Lota, who, after 13 years of working at the nearby fish market, decided to try his hand at the other side of the business. He has done quite well. In 1990 O Mercantel took first prize in the national gastronomic fair in Santarem. Specialties include fresh fish, fish stew, and *arroz de marisco* (shellfish with rice). *Rua António dos Santos Le 16, tel. 034/28057. AE, DC, MC, V. Closed Mon. $$*

**Dining and**
**Lodging**
★

**Pousada da Ria** Built on the edge of the lagoon, this light and airy two-story inn is filled with and surrounded by plants and flowers. The entry is a tasteful blend of wood and tile with a loft sitting area. Ten of the 16 cheerfully furnished rooms have large picture windows and look out over the water; you can stand on your balcony and watch the colorfully painted  moliceiros glide by. Midway down the narrow, pine-covered peninsula separating the lagoon from the sea, the pousada is in a great location for exploring. It's about 30 minutes by car to Aveiro. The restaurant has an open, spacious feeling and a lovely view. There is also a terrace for outside dining during the summer. The tasty *ensopada de cabrito* (kid stew) is recommended. *3870 Murtosa, tel. 034/48332, fax 034/48333. 16 rooms, 3 suites. Facilities: restaurant, bar, pool, tennis court. AE, DC, MC, V. $$$$*

**Imperial.** If you like an efficient, business-oriented, modern hotel in the heart of a city, then the Imperial is for you. The rooms are comfortable but lack charm. Some rooms on the upper floors have views and small balconies. The restaurant is luxurious without being ostentatious and is popular with the business community. Specials include *enguias fritas* (fried eels) and *bacalhau com natas* (cod with cream). The breakfast buffet is the best in town. *Rua Dr. Nascimento Leitão, 3800, tel. 034/ 22141, fax 034/24148. 100 rooms, 8 suites. Facilities: restaurant, 2 bars, solarium. AE, DC, MC, V. $$$*

**Lodging**
★

**Arcada.** The location, at the foot of the bridge over the central canal, couldn't be more convenient. This is a comfortable, family-owned Portuguese classic. The 50-year-old, arched, red-tile-roofed, four-story building is well kept up. Room size is adequate, and the furnishings vary from blond 1950s to traditional Portuguese. The lounge and bar are reminiscent of a gentleman's club slightly past its prime. *Rua Viana do Castelo 4, 3800, tel. 034/23001, fax 034/21886. 49 rooms, 1 suite. Facilities: bar, breakfast room. AE, DC, MC, V. $$*

**Belmonte**
*Dining and Lodging*

**Belsol.** Pleasant and modest, the hotel is conveniently situated in a quiet spot off N18 between Castelo Branco and Guarda. Rooms are large, and a number have balconies with views of the Zêzere. Owner João Pinheiro is representative of a new breed of enterprising young Portuguese businesspeople looking to provide quality and service. The downstairs restaurant, although simple in decor, offers excellent food and is a favorite with local businesspeople. Try the fresh trout from the local rivers. *Quinta do Rio, 6250, tel. 075/912206, fax 075/912315. 44 rooms. Facilities: restaurant, bar, swimming pool, solarium, playground, parking. MC, V. $*

**Buçaco**
*Dining and Lodging*
★

**Palace Hotel Buçaco.** They just don't make them like this anymore. This is one of the few remaining great old hotels in the world. Staying at the Palace, even if just for one night, is an experience to be remembered. Yes, there is an elevator, but who can resist the temptation to walk up the grand, red-carpeted stairway, its walls lined with heroic azulejo panels, and past the suit of armor with the electric lights for eyes—a refreshing bit of kitsch in the midst of so much splendor? A former royal hunting lodge set in a historic 250-acre forest, the hotel is a hodgepodge of architectural styles, ranging from Gothic to neo-Manueline to early Walt Disney. It's worth ordering a meal in the dining room just to sit at the finely laid table and take in the ornate, carved-wood ceiling, inlaid hardwood floors, and massive, arched Manueline windows. In keeping with the decor, Chef Manuel Lorenço turns out some masterpieces of his own. The hotel also has its own winery: The fine Buçaco wines laid down in the cellars, which contain some 200,000 bottles, are only available here. *3050 Mealhada, tel. 031/930101, fax 031/930509. 53 rooms, 6 suites. Facilities: restaurant, bar, parking. AE, DC, MC, V. $$$$*

**Caramulo**
*Dining and Lodging*
★

**Pousada de São Jeronimo.** One of the smallest pousadas, with just six rooms, this one is located in the Serra do Caramulo between Viseu and Coimbra, and, reminiscent of an alpine chalet, sits alone on a hill 1 kilometer (⅔ mile) from the spa resort of Caramulo. The reception area has lovely Arraiolos carpets hung on a knotty pine wall. Rooms are small but adequate, each with a modern marble bathroom and small balcony with a table and chairs. Views are spectacular. The lounge, restaurant, and bar are divided by a see-through wood partition, and there is an inviting open fireplace. The cozy dining room's picture windows frame a mountain panorama extending to the Serra da Estrela. The fare is country style, with *chanfana de borrego* (roast lamb with red wine) one of the favorites. The pool, cabana bar, and a badminton court are in a private wooded park across from the main building. *3475, tel. 032/861291. 6 rooms. Facilities: restaurant, bar, pool, badminton, parking. AE, DC, MC, V. $$*

**Castelo Branco**
*Dining*
★

**Praça Velha.** Set in a historic stone building on a lovely square (the plaque outside reads 1685), this is by far the best restaurant in town. Of the two dining rooms, the older section with the beamed ceiling and stone floors is preferred. One intriguing specialty is *bife na pedra* (grilled beefsteak served on a hot slab of marble). *Largo Luis Camões 17, tel. 072/286330. Reservations advised. AE, DC, MC, V. $$*

*Lodging* **Rainha Dona Amelia.** Castelo Branco's first new hotel to be opened in decades, the Dona Amelia is housed in a graceful, modern five-story building conveniently placed in the center of the city. The "no frills" rooms are pleasant, functional, and airy. *Rua de Santiago, 15, 6000, tel. 072/326315, fax 072/326390. 64 rooms. Facilities: bar, restaurant, parking. AE, MC, V. $$*

**Arraina.** Although this modern *residencial* is conveniently located and offers small but clean rooms, it is strictly a one-nighter. *Av. 1 de Maio 16, tel. 072/21634, fax 072/331884. 31 rooms. Facilities: bar. MC, V. $*

**Celorico da** **Mira Serra.** This modern, four-story hotel is conveniently located
**Beira** just off IP5. Owner Fernando Batista was formerly the manager of a
*Dining and* five-star luxury hotel in the Algarve before striking out on his own.
*Lodging* The rooms are comfortable and furnished in traditional style; some have a small balcony. The restaurant serves the best food in the area. Try the *bacalhau a brás* (slivers of dried cod fried with eggs and onions). *6360, tel. 071/ 72604, fax 071/741382. 42 rooms. Facilities: restaurant, bar, garage. AE, DC, MC, V. $$*

**Coimbra** **Dom Pedro.** The entrance, next to a car dealer, is hardly impressive,
*Dining* but inside it's a different story. The tasteful blend of arches, tile,
★ and wood creates just the right atmosphere in which to enjoy some of Coimbra's best food. The service is efficient without being stuffy. The *chanfana* is excellent, as is the *açorda de mariscos* (a sort of bread porridge mixed with eggs and mounds of fresh shellfish). There is an extensive list of Portuguese wines. The restaurant is just a few steps along the riverfront from the tourist office. *Av. Emidio Navarro 58, tel. 039/29108. DC, MC, V. $$*

**Democratia.** The best that can be said about the decor is that it is functional, although the recently added rustic *adega* (like a wine cellar) adds a touch of old Portugal. The students and locals who frequent this popular old establishment are here for the food and not the atmosphere. The fare is simple and inexpensive. A tasty *caldo verde* (potato soup with shredded cabbage and sausage) and some fresh grilled fish make a typical meal. *Travess da Rua Nova 7, tel. 039/23784. MC, V. Closed Sun. $*

**Kanimambo.** This pleasant, small, no-frills restaurant on a side street off the Praça Comércio offers pleasant service and occasional live music. Try their special dessert: *doce da casa* (a layered vanilla and chocolate pudding with cream). *Rua das Azeiteiras 65–69, tel. 039/27115. No credit cards. $*

★ **Zé Manel.** It's just a hole-in-the-wall in a back alley. The open kitchen is a jumble of pots and pans, and the walls are plastered with an odd assortment of yellowing paper announcements. Simple wooden tables and chairs constitute the decor, but the food is great and cheap. If you can get in, don't pass this one up. It's a favorite with students and hasn't yet succumbed to the tourist trade. There is an amazing choice of dishes for such a small place. They make a wonderful *sopa da pedra* (a rich vegetable soup served with hot stones in the pot to keep it warm). *Beco do Forno 10/2, tel. 039/23790. No reservations. No credit cards. $*

*Dining and* **Astoria.** Occupying a prominent downtown location facing the
*Lodging* Mondego, the domed, triangular Astoria (owned by the people who
★ own the Buçaco Palace) has been a Coimbra landmark since its construction in 1927. In spite of a recent face-lift, the 1920s ambience has been largely maintained, although the aluminum windows around the balconies seem out of step. If you like your hotels with old-world charm and tradition and almost state-of-the-art comforts, then you will like this veteran. Ask for a room facing the river. The

wood-paneled L'Amphitryon Restaurant is one of the city's finest in both ambience and quality, and Buçaco wines are served here. *Av. Emidio Navarro 21, 3000, tel. 039/22055, fax 039/ 22057. 64 rooms. Facilities: restaurant, bar. AE, DC, MC, V. $$$*

★ **Pousada de Santa Cristina.** This newly opened pousada 15 kilometers south of Coimbra in the delightful town of Condeixa-a-Nova makes an ideal base for visiting the city, and it's one kilometer from the Roman ruins at Conimbriga. The pousada occupies a converted palace with spacious, comfortably furnished bedrooms and one of the area's best traditional restaurants. *3150 Condeixa-a-Nova, tel. 039/ 941286. 45 rooms. Facilities: restaurant, bar, pool, tennis, parking. AE, DC, MC,V. $$$*

★ **Tivoli.** This four-star addition to the Coimbra hotel scene, opened in 1990, is currently the best address in town. It's sleek, efficient, well located, and outfitted with all of the latest gadgets. The only thing lacking is that certain sense of place that the other great hotels in the Tivoli chain have achieved: Once in your comfortable room, you could be anywhere. The Porta Férrea restaurant serves excellent food, both international and regional, in a subdued setting. *Rua João Machado 4–5, 3000, tel. 039/26934. 90 rooms, 10 suites. Facilities: restaurant, bar, health club, pool, garage. AE, DC, MC, V. $$$*

*Lodging* **Dona Inês.** The best of several recently constructed three-star facilities, this modern glass and marble hotel, conveniently located on the banks of the Mondego, is just a few minutes' walk from Coimbra's main commercial district. Although simply furnished, the rooms are light and airy. *Rua Abel Dias Urbano, 12, 3000, tel. 039/25791, fax 039/25611. 72 rooms, 2 suites. Facilities: restaurant, bar, tennis court, garage. AE, DC, MC, V. $$*

**Coimbra Youth Hostel.** The hostel occupies a large house near the Santa Cruz Park. Breakfast is available. *Rua Henriques Seco 12–14, 3000, tel. 039/22955. 80 beds in multibed rooms, 2 family rooms. Facilities: members' kitchen. $*

**Larbelo.** A quiet, family-run residencial in an old, green-tiled building, it has a good central location facing the Largo da Portagem, adjacent to the tourist office. The 17 upstairs rooms have high, ornate ceilings, and some have views to the river. Room 209 has the best view. Only breakfast is served. *Largo da Portagem 33, 3000, tel. 039/ 29092. 17 rooms (9 with bath and toilet, 8 with shower). No credit cards. $*

**Covilhã** **Hotel Serra da Estrela.** Originally built in the early part of this cen-
*Dining and* tury as a tuberculosis sanitorium, the hotel was recently completely
*Lodging* renovated. Rooms are large, and those in the front have good views looking down into the valley. At an elevation of 3,936 feet and 12 kilometers (7½ miles) from Covilhã, the hotel provides an excellent base for a few days in the mountains. The restaurant is light and spacious, with lots of glass and wood. *Penhas da Saude, 6203 Covilhã, tel. 075/ 313809, fax 075/323789. 38 rooms. Facilities: restaurant, snack bar, bar, tennis courts, parking. AE, DC, MC, V. $$*

**Hotel Turismo.** This attractive modern hotel, conveniently situated at the eastern edge of town, is the first new hotel to be built in Covilhã in several decades. The decor is simple but pleasant and functional. Among the local specialties served in the rooftop panoramic restaurant is fresh trout from nearby mountain streams. *Acesso a Variante, Quinta da Olivosa, 6200. tel. 075/324545, fax 075/324630. 60 rooms. Facilities: bar, restaurant, health club, sauna, squash, disco, parking, AE, DC, MC, V. $$*

**Solneve.** In the town center, Solneve was the prime hotel in Covilhã since its opening some 50 years ago. It's now starting to fray a bit around the edges, and has been eclipsed by the newly opened Hotel

Turismo. The restaurant, in spite of a decor reminiscent of a high-school cafeteria, offers a nice variety of tasty regional dishes, including *truta a solneve* (fresh trout grilled with cured ham and onions). *Rua Visconde da Coriscada 126, 6200, tel.075/323001, fax 075/323001. 32 rooms, 6 suites. Facilities: restaurant, bar. MC, V. $*

*Lodging* **Penas da Saude Youth Hostel.** The hostel is in a large, rustic mountaintop building. Meals are available. *Penas da Saude, 6200 Covilhã, tel. 075/25375. 163 beds in multibed rooms. Facilities: bar, members' kitchen, library, recreation room. $*

**Curia** **Pedro dos Leitões.** Of the several suckling pig specialty restaurants
*Dining* clustered on the EN1 from Coimbra to Oporto, "Suckling Pig Pete"
★ is the most popular. A meal here is one of those traditional things that you do when you visit Portugal. You eat sardines by the old bridge in Portimão, and you have suckling pig at Pedro's in Mealhada. The size of the parking lot is a dead giveaway that this is no intimate little bistro. In the busy summer season, Pete's spitted pigs pop out of the huge ovens at an amazing rate. In spite of the volume, quality is maintained. *EN1, Sernadelo, Mealheado, tel. 031/ 22062. MC, V. Closed Mon. $$*

*Dining and* **Curia Palace.** The approach down a long, tree-lined drive past formal
*Lodging* gardens is like the beginning of an old movie. In fact, parts of *The*
★ *Buster Keaton Story* were filmed here. Enter the spacious, polished, marble-floored reception area, and you will be transported back to the Europe of the 1920s. The four-story hotel is the centerpiece of 15 acres of gardens, vineyards, a deer park, an aviary, orchards, and a duck pond, all of which support the hotel kitchen. A meticulously restored 18th-century water mill grinds wheat and corn for the bakery. There are also a winery, a distillery, and a chapel on the premises. The swimming pool is 60 feet by 107 feet, one of the largest in Portugal. For car buffs there is a small collection of antique autos. Bedrooms are large, with high ceilings and modern bathrooms, and the spacious corridors all have names (the Avenue of the Roses, for example). Room 255 is one of the larger rooms and has a fine view of the gardens. The dining room is light and airy, the enormous height of the ceiling broken somewhat by an encircling mezzanine. The cuisine, prepared from garden-fresh ingredients, is excellent. *3780 Anadia, tel. 031/512131, fax 031/ 515531. 114 rooms. Facilities: restaurant, bar, pool, miniature golf, 2 tennis courts, billiards, playground, boarding kennels, horseback riding, parking. AE, DC, MC, V. Closed Nov.– Mar. $$$$*

★ **Grande Hotel de Curia.** The task of taking a grand old 1890s spa hotel and bringing it up to 1990s standards is not an easy one, but the Belver Hotel Group did just that. And it was not merely a cosmetic face-lift. New polished-marble floors, dark mahogany furniture and paneling, elegant bathroom fixtures, and fine carpets and draperies are some of the more visible changes. The hotel also has its own fully equipped, state-of-the-art health center with a full-time medical staff. Various exercise and diet programs are available. The restaurant, with wood-plank floors and soft draperies, exudes a subdued elegance. The menu is primarily international with a few regional specialties. *3780 Anadia, tel. 031/515720, fax 031/515317. 78 rooms, 6 suites. Facilities: restaurant, bar, library, indoor and outdoor pools, tennis, gym, whirlpool, sauna, Turkish bath, massage, parking. AE, DC, MC, V. $$$$*

*Lodging* **Quinta de São Lourenço.** This delightful 18th-century country manor house surrounded by vineyards and pine groves is in the tiny village of São Lourenço do Bairro, 3 kilometers (2 miles) from Curia. The house has six comfortable-size bedrooms with wood floors, period furniture, and modern bathrooms. There is also a small apartment. Meals can be arranged upon request. *São Lourenço do Bairro, 3780 Anadia, tel. 031/528168, fax 031/528594. 6 rooms, 1 apartment. Facilities: bar, library, card room, billiards. $$*

**Figueira da Foz Dining**

**Covil do Caçador.** An open kitchen and a dining room with a vaulted, beamed ceiling cluttered with hanging strings of corn, garlic, and other herbs and vegetables give this restaurant a comfortable country feeling. It's across the river from downtown at the foot of the bridge and looks out over the bay. Chef José Olivio does a fine job with a varied menu. Try the *arroz de tamboril* (cubes of monkfish mixed with rice and seasonings). *Morraceira, tel. 033/31507. AE, DC, MC, V. $$*

**Teimoso.** Located in Buarcos, about 2 kilometers (1¼ miles) from Figueira da Foz, this seaside restaurant with large picture windows has become a local institution. Although the menu choices are varied, seafood is what put this place on the map. Shellfish comes fresh from the restaurant's huge saltwater tanks. *Estrada do Cabo Mondego, Buarcos, tel. 033/32785. MC, V. Closed Wed. $$*

★ **O Peleiro.** In the quiet village of Paião, 10 kilometers (6 miles) from Figueira, this popular restaurant was once a tannery, and that's what the name means. Owner Henrique has achieved a tranquil ambience through the use of wood and tile. The menu is heavy on regional specialties. The *sopa da pedra* (stone soup), a thick vegetable soup with sausage, beans, and potatoes served in a tureen with hot stones, is a must. Grilled pork or veal on a spit is excellent, and there's a good wine selection. *Paião, tel. 033/940120. Closed May 1–15, Sept. 1–15, and Sun. MC, V. $*

**Dining and Lodging**

**Grande.** This five-story, 1950s-vintage hotel enjoys a favored location overlooking the broad, sandy beach. Public and guest rooms are spacious and airy, and seafront rooms have a small balcony. A large swimming pool has a view of the beach. The hotel is popular with tour groups. The restaurant is a large, rather sterile room with picture windows, and the menu is international with regional specialties. Although this dowager of a hotel is beginning to show her age, she is still the top choice directly in town. *Av.25 de Abril, 3080, tel. 033/22539, fax 033/22420. 91 rooms. Facilities: restaurant, piano bar, pool. AE, DC, MC, V. $$$$*

**Clube Vale de Leão.** This self-contained cluster of Mediterranean-style, semidetached villas is unobtrusively nestled in the hills high above Buarcos. Rooms and apartments are small but comfortable, and the views over the bay are magnificent. The restaurant, a bit garish in decor, does a good job with both international and regional dishes. *Vais-Buarcos, 3080, tel. 033/ 33057, fax 033/32571. 6 rooms, 17 studios, 1 apartment. Facilities: restaurant, piano bar, tearoom, movies, pool, tennis, squash, gym, sauna, massage, parking. AE, DC, MC, V. $$$*

**Lodging**

**Aparthotel Atlantico.** In this high-rise tower at the beach the rooms have apartments with kitchenettes. The rooms are small but adequate, with plain, functional furnishings. Some apartments have a wonderful sea view. *Av. 25 de Abril, 3080, tel. 033/ 24045, fax 033/22420. 70 apartments. Facilities: bar, pool. AE, DC, MC, V. $$*

★ **International.** A comfortable, small hotel on a quiet street just a five-minute walk from the beach, the classic stone building was built in 1914 and completely remodeled in 1989, retaining the original ambience. *Rua da Liberdade 32, 3080, tel. 033/ 22051, fax 033/22420. 50 rooms. Facilities: bar, breakfast room, pool. AE, DC, MC, V. $$*

**Pensão Esplanada.** This turn-of-the-century corner house is across from the beach. The floors creak and the rooms have seen better days, but it's clean and well-maintained. Ask for a room with a sea view. *Rua Engenheiro Silva 86, 3080, tel. 033/ 22115. 19 rooms, 10 with bath. No credit cards. $*

**Fundão**
*Dining*

**O Casarão.** This quiet neighborhood restaurant's three small dining areas have beamed ceilings and are divided by brick pillars. Owner José Pereira proudly proclaims that he serves the best food in Fundão, and in this restaurant-poor town he is probably right. Try the Oporto-style tripe. *Rua José Germano da Cunha 2/4, tel. 075/ 52844. No credit cards. $*

**Dining and**
*Lodging*

**Estalagem da Neve.** A small, cozy, Victorian-style inn on the road from Castelo Branco, it has small but comfortably furnished rooms. The restaurant, with its beamed ceiling and tiled walls, provides an inviting setting in which to enjoy a fine Portuguese meal. Try the trout or roast kid. *Calçada de São Sebastião, 6230, tel. 075/52215, fax 075/53816. 22 rooms, 6 with bath. Facilities: restaurant, bar, pool, parking. MC, V. $*

**Gouveia**
*Dining*

**O Foral.** Located on the ground floor of the Hotel Gouvia, this comfortable restaurant is the eatery of choice among the town's civic and business community. Service is attentive, and the kitchen is noted for its roast kid. *Av. 1 de Maio, tel. 038/491010. AE, DC, MC, V. $*

★ **O Julio.** Thanks to the talents of chef and owner Julio, this simple, unassuming restaurant was chosen to represent the Serra da Estrela region at the 1992 tourist fair in Lisbon. Julio recommends the *vitela estufada na maneira antiga* (veal stew). *Travessa do Loureiro 1, tel. 038/42142. No credit cards. Closed Tues. $*

*Lodging*

**Hotel Gouvia.** A small, modern hotel on one of the main approaches to the Serra da Estrela, it offers comfortable rooms furnished in traditional style. Several have small balconies. *Av. 1 de Maio, 6290, tel. 038/42890. 27 rooms, 4 suites. Facilities: restaurant, bar, pool, tennis, parking. AE, DC, MC, V. $*

**Guarda**
*Dining*

**Belo Horizonte.** Guarda is not noted for its good restaurants, but the Belo Horizonte, a modest establishment in the old quarter, is one of the few exceptions. It features hardy regional fare and a different type of bacalhau daily. *Largo de São Vicente 2, tel. 071/211454. MC, V. Closed Sat. $*

**Dining and**
*Lodging*

★ **Hotel Turismo.** Since it opened in 1940 in a stately, country-style manor house, the Turismo has been Guarda's leading hotel. Extensively remodeled in 1988, it has maintained its position, albeit in a town with little competition. The extensive use of wood and leather in the bar and lounges lends a comfortable, clubby atmosphere to the place. Bedrooms are adequate in size and furnished in traditional style. The restaurant serves the best food in town in a quiet, refined atmosphere. *Av. Cor. Orlindo de Calvalho, 6300, tel. 071/ 223366, fax 071/223399. 100 rooms, 2 suites. Facilities: restaurant, bar, pool, garage. AE, DC, MC, V. $$$*

**Filipe.** Across the street from the Misericórdia Church, this newly redecorated, family-run residencial offers plain but comfortable rooms and a personal touch not found at the more-formal Hotel Turismo. Owner Americo Alexis has traveled the world and will be happy to pass the time of day in just about any language. The upstairs restaurant, the domain of Senhora Alexis, is a good place to enjoy *camarões piri-piri* (giant prawns with hot-pepper sauce). *Rua Vasco da Gama 9, 6300, tel. 071/212658, fax 071/221402. 41 rooms. Facilities: restaurant, bar. AE, DC, MC, V. Restaurant closed Nov.–Jan. $$*

**Luso** **O Cesteiro.** Situated at the western edge of town just past the Luso
*Dining* bottling plant, this popular local restaurant has been recently remodeled. The fare is simple and includes several types of cod, roast
kid, and fresh fish. *Rua Dr. Lucio Abranches, tel. 031/939360. MC,
V. $*

*Dining and* **Grande Hotel das Termas.** The hotel is a large, yellow-stucco complex
*Lodging* in a park at the center of town. The buildings, constructed in 1945,
are an architectural zero, but the recently remodeled interior is attractive. Rooms are large and airy, with modern tiled bathrooms;
some bedrooms have terraces overlooking the Olympic-size pool.
The hotel is adjacent to the renowned Luso Spa, which offers a wide
range of therapeutic programs. If you are looking for a hotel where
you can settle in and really make use of the facilities, either this or
the Palace in nearby Curia are ideal. The restaurant offers a good
selection of international and regional foods in a pleasant environment overlooking the pool. *Luso-3050 Mealhada, tel. 031/930450,
fax 031/930350. 173 rooms. Facilities: restaurant, bar, disco, solarium, indoor and outdoor pools, tennis, miniature golf, sauna, parking. AE, DC, MC, V. $$$$*

*Lodging* **Vila Duparchy.** As you pass through the old gate and go up the long,
★ curved, tree-lined driveway, you'll soon realize that this is no ordinary hotel. The two-story stucco house was built in the late 19th century. In 1988 Maria and Oscar Santos, the current resident owners,
opened it as a guest house. Upstairs there are just six rooms; each
has a fireplace, modern bath, and individually selected period furnishings. On the ground floor are three comfortable sitting rooms,
which guests share with the Santos. The spacious grounds are full of
trees and flowers, and there is a small swimming pool. Breakfast is
included, and other meals, which are far superior to the local restaurant fare, are prepared on request. *Luso-3050 Mealhada, tel. 031/
939120, fax 031/930307. 6 rooms. Facilities: pool. AE, MC, V. $$$*
★ **Pensão Alegre.** On a hill overlooking the park, this 19th-century
manor house has been receiving guests since 1931. The present own-
er, Manuel Alegre, took over the pension from his father. Filled
with colorful tiles and rich wood, it exudes charm. If you're after Old
World ambience and hospitality at bargain prices, look no farther.
There are 20 rooms, all with high ceilings and plank floors. Ask for
number 103; it has a large terrace. Home-cooked meals are available
on request. *3050, tel. 031/930256. 20 rooms. Facilities: parking.
MC, V. $*

**Mangualde** **Quinta Magarenha.** This large, attractive, French-style manor
*Dining* house has been a great success for owner José Oliveira. There is a
comfortable lounge with plush sofas and tiled walls. The single large
dining room has an attractive wooden ceiling and tile floors. The at-
mosphere is gregarious, with rows of long tables, and the food is
Portuguese, with an emphasis on fish. The *lombino de pescada* (fil-
lets of whiting with a sauce made from ground shellfish) is recom-
mended. *Exit Viseu-leste from IP5, Caçador, tel. 032/479106. MC,
V. $$*

*Dining and* **Senhora do Castelo.** A large, four-story complex that shares a hilltop
*Lodging* park with the church of the same name, the 10-year-old hotel is conveniently located adjacent to the new IP5 highway but far enough
away to avoid the noise. The buildings are pseudo-Mediterranean.
Many of the rooms have small balconies; those facing south have the
best view. The restaurant and public rooms, while spacious and
cheerful, lack character. However, the views, especially from the
terrace restaurant, are spectacular. Of the two indoor restaurants,
the Grill Restaurant has a warmer atmosphere. Try the *bacalhau*

*espiritual* (the translation is "spiritual codfish"); what you get on your plate is a tasty combination of dried, salted cod baked with potatoes, onions, and tomatoes. *3531, tel. 032/611608, fax 032/ 623877. 85 rooms, 3 suites. Facilities: restaurants, bar with live music, indoor and outdoor pools, sauna, 2 tennis courts. AE, DC, MC, V. $$$*

**Manteigas**
*Dining and Lodging*
★

**Pousada de São Lourenço.** The pousada is 13 kilometers (8 miles) from Manteigas in the heart of the Serra da Estrela at an elevation of 4,231 feet. This newly remodeled granite mountain lodge is a favorite stopover for Portuguese and foreign visitors. The ample use of wood and brick in the rooms and a cozy fireplace in the lounge contribute to the high-country ambience. Ask for room 207; it has a loft for sleeping and one of the best views. If you are just driving through, stop for lunch at the restaurant, and try the unusual but delicious *bacalhau a lagareiro* (baked cod with corn bread, olive oil, and potatoes). *6260, tel. 075/ 982450, fax 075/982453. 21 rooms, 1 suite. Facilities: restaurant, bar, parking. AE, DC, MC, V. $$$$*

**Oliveira do Hospital**
*Dining and Lodging*
★

**Pousada de Santa Barbara.** Located in the pines high on the western flank of the Serra da Estrela, this mountainside pousada offers a restful and cool respite from the summer heat. Many of the rooms have balconies supported by massive stone columns. The restaurant features a variety of tasty local dishes. *Povoa das Quartas, 3400, tel. 038/59551, fax 038/59645. 16 rooms. Facilities: restaurant, bar, pool, tennis court, parking. AE, DC, MC, V. $$$$*

**Penacova**
*Dining*

**O Panorâmico.** This small, family-run restaurant is an ideal spot to stop for lunch while driving through this lovely countryside. It's easy to see where the name came from: There is a wonderful panoramic view looking down on the Rio Mondego as it snakes its way along to Coimbra. Maria da Graça, the proprietress, suggests the house specialty, *lampreia a mode de Penacova* (lampreys cooked with rice). *Largo Alberto Leitão, tel. 039/477333. MC, V. $*

**Penamacor**
*Dining and Lodging*
★

**Vila Rica.** If you like to "collect" quaint country inns, this is a place to add to your collection. The 19th-century converted farmhouse is surrounded by trees and gardens and is adjacent to a popular hunting area. Not just by coincidence, the excellent restaurant serves many game dishes, including rabbit, quail, and wild boar. The 10 large bedrooms are simply but comfortably furnished. *6090, tel. 077/ 94311, fax 077/94321. 10 rooms. Facilities: restaurant, bar, private chapel, parking. $*

**Seia**
*Dining*
★

**Cabana do Pastor.** A cozy mountain restaurant with a fireplace and panoramic views, this is a good place to partake of the locally made cheese, queijo da Serra, and presunto. *Behind souvenir shop on N339 toward Torre, tel. 038/ 22073. AE, DC, MC, V. $*

*Lodging*
★

**Albergaria Senhora do Espinheiro.** This newly built mountain inn is next to the Cabana do Pastor restaurant. Both are the labors of love of Antonio Mora, a big, gentle, bear of a man who will enhance your stay or meal. The use of wood and tile throughout gives the inn a warm feeling. The rooms are small and furnished in pine. Ask for one at the back, where the views are best. *N339, 6270, tel. 038/22073 24 rooms. Facilities: bar, parking. AE, DC, MC, V. $*

**Sortelha**
*Dining*
★

**Albaroque.** This is the sort of place that interior designers are always trying to create with imitation wood beams and plastic rocks. The Albaroque, the town's only real restaurant, occupies an ancient stone building. You walk up some rickety wood stairs to a cozy, stone-wall dining area with massive wood beams overhead. Owner Raul Clara has done more than create an atmosphere; he also manages to turn out some wonderful food in this inviting restaurant.

Specialties include wild boar and venison in season as well as a first rate *caldeirada de borrego* (lamb stew). *Tel. 071/68129. No credit cards.* $

**Lodging** Although this medieval town has no hotels or pensions, several ancient stone houses have been converted into tourist accommodations. These are comfortable but not luxurious. They do have running water and bathrooms and offer an unusual opportunity to actually live in a medieval Portuguese village.

**Casa Arabe.** *Sortelha, 6320 Sabugal, tel. 071/68276 or 01/269– 0149. 1 apartment, sleeps 4. Facilities: parking. No credit cards.* $
**Casa do Vento que Soa.** *Sortelha, 6320 Sabugal, tel. 071/68182. 2 rooms. Facilities: parking. No credit cards.* $

**Viseu** **A Veranda da Sé.** After 37 years of running a restaurant in Rio de
**Dining** Janeiro, João Correira became homesick for his native Portugal.
★ Now back in the town of his birth, he is doing what he does best: running a restaurant. In an ancient stone building that was once a warehouse, he has created a cozy Portuguese bistro. There is a small loft for dining, and the original stone walls and floor remain. The menu is Portuguese with an accent on grilled meats. On Sunday, João, saluting his days in Brazil, serves *feijoada do Brasil* (a tasty stewlike dish of beans, sausage, and meat). *Rua Augusto Hilario 55, tel. 032/ 421135. AE, DC, MC, V. Closed Tues.* $$
**O Fontelo.** This is a storefront grill restaurant specializing in chicken, which tastes as good as it looks in the window. *Av. Alfonso da Melo 45, tel. 032/424221. No credit cards. Closed Sat.* $

**Dining and** **Grão Vasco.** For many years the Grão Vasco has been Viseu's leading
**Lodging** hotel, and, recently remodeled, it still retains that distinction. Its
★ location in a wooded park just a few steps from the main square is ideal, offering the convenience of the city and the quiet of the countryside. Many of the rooms have balconies looking out on the oval pool. The restaurant, which serves a wide variety of principally Portuguese dishes, is one of the best in town. If it's in season, try the javali. *Rua Gaspar Barreiros, 3500, tel. 032/423511, fax 032/ 27047.110 rooms. Facilities: restaurant, bar, pool, parking. AE, DC, MC, V.* $$$
**Monte Belo.** This modern hotel, newly built in a quiet residential neighborhood just a few minutes' walk from the center of town, is a welcome addition to the hotel scene. *Urbanização Quinta do Bosque. tel. 032/415444, fax 032/415400. Facilities: restaurant, bar, pool, health club, tennis, parking. AE, DC, MC, V.* $$
★ **Hotel Maná.** Owner and manager Nelson Campos has done a fine job of putting together just the right combination of tasteful decor and modern comfort to make this small hotel on the outskirts of Viseu one of the best of its kind in the region. Ask for a room on the third floor with a balcony facing the Serra da Estrela. The restaurant provides surprisingly good food and service. If you've acquired a taste for bacalhau, try their version of the tasty *bacalhau a Zé do Pipo* (a wonderful combination of baked, breaded cod with mayonnaise, pimentos, onions, and potatoes). *N16, Via Caçador, 3500, tel. 032/ 479243, fax 032/478744. 60 rooms. Facilities: restaurant, bar, pool, parking. AE, DC, MC, V.* $$

**Lodging** **Bela Vista.** This comfortable residential on a quiet street about a mile from the center of town has rooms that are small but comfortable. *Rua Alexandre Herculano 510, 3500, tel. 032/426026. 44 rooms. Facilities: parking. No credit cards.* $

**Campgrounds** As might be expected, the greatest concentration of campgrounds is along the coast. There are also well-equipped campgrounds in Coimbra, Viseu, Guarda, Castelo Branco, and the Serra da Estrela. Camping fees in Portugal are considerably less than in most of the rest of Europe. Two people with a camper can plan to pay 1,000$00–1,500$00 per night, electrical hookup included. Many campgrounds also rent inexpensive cabins. Here are a few recommendations.

*Aveiro* **Camping Costa Nova.** It's right at the beach, less than 10 kilometers (6 miles) from Aveiro. There's a bus to town, and stores and restaurants are nearby.

*Castelo Branco* **Camping Castelo Branco.** This is a level, partly shaded municipal site on N18, 1½ kilometers (1 mile) north of the town center. There is a bus to town.

*Coimbra* **Camping Municipal Coimbra.** This city-run facility is adjacent to the sports stadium and the municipal swimming pool. There is a bus to town.

*Covilhã/ Serra da Estrela* **Camping Pião.** On a wooded hillside on EN339, 5 kilometers (3 miles) from Covilhã, this is a good base for visiting the Serra da Estrela. *Closed Nov.–Apr.*

*Figueira da Foz* **Camping Municipal Figueira da Foz.** This large site is in a pine grove 1½ kilometers (1 mile) from town and beach. A bus, playground, and tennis are available.

*Guarda* **Camping Orbitur.** The campground is in a pleasant, parklike setting at the northwest edge of town. There is a bus to Guarda center and a swimming pool.

*Ovar* **Parque de Campismo Furadouro.** In a wooded site at the beach, this is a good base for exploring the Aveiro lagoon. Tennis and outdoor movies are available.

*Viseu* **Parque do Fontelo.** In a wooded park just north of N16 at the east end of town, the campground makes for difficult maneuvering for large campers. There is a bus to town.

# The Arts and Nightlife

## The Arts

In the Beiras, people are respectful of their traditions and folklore, and just about every town and village celebrates some sort of festival or fair. In many cases dates vary from year to year. Check with local tourist offices for details.

*Aveiro* The large regional **Feira do Marco** held in the month of March has been celebrated for more than 500 years, with folk music and dancing on weekends.

*Coimbra* In addition to the **Quiema das Fitas** (*see* Tour 1, *above*), the **Festas da Rainha Santa** (Festival of the Queen Saint) is held during even years in early July. It's marked by colorful processions and fireworks along the Mondego.

*Figueira da Foz* Every year during the last week in June, the **Festas de São João** (Festival of Saint John) features dancing around huge bonfires until dawn. The exhausted dancers then plunge into the sea for the ancient ritual of the "holy bath."

*Gouvia* The **Festa do Senhor do Calvário** (Festival of Our Lord of Calvary), during the first week in August, starts on a Sunday with a colorful procession. Other events include a handicrafts fair, games, and a sheepdog competition.

**Viseu** Held from mid-August through mid-September, the **Feira de São Mateus** (Fair of Saint Matthew) is like a giant county fair, where agricultural products and handicrafts are exhibited. There is also folk music and dancing.

## Nightlife

With the exception of the casino at Figueira da Foz, this region is not known for its nightlife. In most of the larger towns, you can find theaters showing recent English-language films in the original version.

**Figueira da Foz** The casino is part of an entertainment complex that, although small by Las Vegas standards, is pretty big stuff for this part of the world. Built in 1886, the gambling room, with its frescoed ceilings and chandeliers, provides a subdued atmosphere in which to try your luck at a variety of games, including blackjack, American and Continental roulette, and an old European game played with three dice, known simply as the French table. Within the same building, there is also a large Belle Epoque show room featuring a Vegas-type revue. *Av. Bernado Lopes, tel. 033/22041. Gambling room: admission: 1,500$00; minimum age 18 (bring your passport); open daily 3PM–3AM. Show room: minimum admission: Fri.–Sat. 3,000$00, Sun.–Thurs. 2,000$00; shows 10 PM and 1 AM. Reservations advised July–Sept. No jeans or T- shirts.*

# 8 Oporto and the North

*By Jules Brown*

*Updated by Dennis Jaffe*

The city of Oporto (Porto in Portuguese) is famous the world over for the wine that bears its name—port—but the rest of the North is undiscovered country for most visitors to Portugal. Intrepid travelers may visit the valley of the Rio Douro (River of Gold) or cross the bare uplands of the far northeastern Trás-os-Montes (Beyond the Mountains). Some towns, like Chaves (Keys), bear curious names and complicated histories. Festivals such as the Holy Week parade at Braga (complete with a torchlit procession through dark, old-town streets) evoke an earlier time. The North can be beautiful, as it is in the deep, rural heartland of the Minho, the coastal province north of Oporto; it can also be hostile, as in the Terra Fria (Cold Land), the remote, rugged parts of the northern Trás-os-Montes. From here come the mysterious, prehistoric *porcas* (stone pigs), reminders of early tribes who scratched a living from the cold earth.

The remote corners of northern Portugal seem far away in Oporto, a trading center since pre-Roman times and still a vibrant, cosmopolitan city. Oporto makes a fine contrast to Lisbon. The Moors never had the same strong foothold here that they did farther south, and the city remained largely unaffected by the great earthquake of 1755; as a result, Oporto shows off a Baroque finery lacking in the capital. Its grandiose granite buildings were financed by the trade that made the city wealthy: Wine from the upper valley of the Rio Douro was transported to Oporto and from there exported. Visitors may follow that trail today, by boat or by the beautiful Douro Line train route along the river.

Though it's not immediately apparent, northern Portugal *is* a popular holiday destination—with the Portuguese. The Minho, which takes its name from the river forming Portugal's northern border with Spain, is bounded by the Atlantic in the west and cut by the long, peaceful Lima and Cávado rivers. The Minho coast is advertised as the Costa Verde (Green Coast), a sweeping stretch of beaches and fishing villages. Some locations have been appropriated as resorts by the Portuguese, but there are still plenty of places where you can find solitary dunes or splash in the brisk Atlantic away from crowds. Inland you can lose yourself in ancient villages with country markets and fairs that have hardly changed for hundreds of years. You'll also see that little of the green countryside is wasted. Vines are trained on poles and in trees high above cultivated fields, forming a natural canopy, for this is *vinho verde* (green wine) country. (The Costa Verde is named for its lush, green landscape, and vinho verde is so called because it is drunk young; it also has a slightly greenish cast.) This refreshing wine, which comes only from the Minho region, is a true taste of the North, one to which you'll quickly become accustomed as you sit, glass in hand, by a river or the coast and reflect upon the day's events.

To the northeast there's adventure at hand, in the winding mountain roads and remote towns and villages of the Trás-os-Montes region. After centuries of isolation, the area is being accessed by new roads, but there's still great excitement in the rattling trans-mountain train ride from Oporto to Bragança, in the far northeastern corner of the country. The imposing, medieval castle towers and fortress walls of this frontier region are a great attraction, but—unusual in such a small country— it's often the journey itself that's the greatest prize: traveling past voluminous man-made lakes, through forested valleys rich in wildlife, across bare crags and moorlands, and finally down to coarse, stone villages where TV aerials sit oddly in almost medieval surroundings.

It's best to visit the North in summer, when Oporto and the Costa Verde have a generally warm climate, but be prepared for drizzling rain at any time. Temperatures in the North are a good few degrees cooler than in the south. Inland, and especially in the northeastern mountains, traveling in winter can be cold, hard going.

# Essential Information

## Important Addresses and Numbers

**Tourist Information**
There are two tourist offices in **Oporto:** one just east of Avenida dos Aliados (Praça Dom João I 43, tel. 02/317514) and one to the west of the town hall, at the top of Avenida dos Aliados (Rua Clube dos Fenianos 25, tel. 02/312740). Both will provide maps of the city, information about tours, and help in finding accommodations.

There are local tourist offices providing similar services in the following towns: **Amarante** (Rua Cândido dos Reis, 4600, tel. 055/432259), **Arcos de Valdevez** (Av. da Marginal, 4970, tel. 058/ 66001), **Barcelos** (Torre de Menagem, Largo da Porta Nova, 4750, tel. 053/811882), **Braga** (Av. da Liberdade 1, 4700, tel. 053/22550), **Bragança** (Av. Cidade de Zamora, 5300, tel. 073/ 22273), **Caminha** (Rua Ricardo Joaquim Sousa, 4910, tel. 058/ 921952), **Chaves** (Rua de Santo António 213, 5400, tel. 076/ 21029), **Espinho** (Angulo das Ruas 6 e 23, tel. 02/720911), **Esposende** (Rua 1 de Dezembro, 4740, tel. 053/961354), **Gerês** (Av. Manuel Ferreira da Costa, 4700, tel. 053/391133), **Guimarães** (Av. Resistentes ao Fascismo 83, 4800, tel. 053/412450), **Lamego** (Av. Visconde Guedes Teixeira, 5100, tel. 054/62005), **Monção** (Largo do Loreto, 4950, tel. 051/652757), **Ponte da Barca** (Largo da Misericórdia, 4980, tel. 058/42899), **Ponte de Lima** (Praça da República, 4990, tel. 058/942335), **Póvoa de Varzim** (Av. Mouzinho de Albuquerque 166, tel. 052/614609), **Valença do Minho** (Av. de Espanha, 4930, tel. 051/23374), **Viana do Castelo** (Rua do Hospital Velho, 4900, tel. 058/822620), **Vila do Conde** (Rua 25 de Abril, 4480, tel. 052/642700), **Vila Nova de Cerveira** (Rua Dr. A. Duro, 4920, tel. 051/795787), **Vila Nova de Gaia** (Rua General Torres, 1141, 4400, tel. 02/303653), **Vila Praia de Âncora** (Av. Ramos Pereira, 4915, tel. 058/911384), **Vila Real** (Av. Carvalho Araújo 94, 5000, tel. 059/322819).

**Consulates**
In Oporto: **United Kingdom** (Av. da Boavista 3072, tel. 02/6184789). There isn't a U.S. or Canadian consulate in the North.

**Emergencies**
The general emergency number is 115. In Oporto specific services include: **The Red Cross** (tel. 02/6006353), **Hospitals** (Hospital de Santa Maria, Rua de Camões, tel. 02/550–4844; Hospital Geral de Santo António, Largo Professor Abel Salazar, tel. 02/200–5241; Hospital de São João, Alameda Professor Hernâni Monteiro, tel. 02/527151), **Police** (Rua Augusto Rosa, tel. 02/ 200–6821), **Fire** (tel. 02/524121).

**Late-Night Pharmacies**
Pharmacies take turns staying open late. Schedules and addresses are posted on the door of each pharmacy, and listings of late-night services are carried in the local press.

**Travel Agencies**
Travel agencies are the best places to obtain tickets and travel information without difficulty. In Oporto, many are found around the central Avenida dos Aliados. Reliable ones include: **Star,** agents for American Express (Av. dos Aliados 202, Oporto, tel. 02/200–3637; Av. Dom Afonso Henriques 638, Guimarães, tel. 053/515750); **Viagens Rawes** (Largo Ferreira Lapa 34, Oporto, tel. 02/666148); **Wasteels–Expresso** (Rua Pinto Bessa 29, Oporto, tel. 02/570589).

**Mail and Telephones** The main post office in Oporto is in Praça General Humberto Delgado (tel. 02/208–0251). It is open weekdays 8 AM–10 PM, Saturday 8–8. General-delivery mail (mark it Poste Restante) is received here, and telephones are available for international calls.

## Arriving and Departing by Plane

**Airports and Airlines** Oporto's **Sá Carneiro Airport** (tel. 02/941–3141) is 13 kilometers (8 miles) north of the city and is the gateway to all of northern Portugal. There is direct service from European and South American cities but not from the United States. TAP runs regular flights from Lisbon. The airport has car-rental agencies and money-exchange facilities. In addition, there are regional airports handling domestic flights in Bragança (tel. 073/22075) and Chaves (tel. 076/21995). For regional service, contact the airline LAR Transregional at the Oporto airport.

**Between the Airport and Downtown** Buses 56 and 87 run from the airport to downtown Oporto and cost 150$00. It takes up to an hour, depending on the traffic, to reach the stop at Cordoaria, the area behind the Clérigos Tower. Taxis are available, too, outside the terminal; fare will run 1,500$00–2,000$00.

## Arriving and Departing by Car, Train, and Bus

**By Car** Oporto is a key destination for travelers driving to the North, since all of the region's major roads fan out from the city. It takes about 3½ hours from Lisbon on the fast highway. From Spain, the closest border crossing is at Tuy/Valença do Minho; from there it's 125 kilometers (77½ miles) south to Oporto on the N13. Other border crossings are to the east, at various points in the Trás-os-Montes region. Chaves, Bragança, or Miranda do Douro are your first stops; from each you face a long and winding drive across the country to Oporto.

**By Train** Most trains into Oporto (including those from Lisbon) arrive at **Estação de Campanhã** (Campanhã, tel. 02/565645), just east of the city center. From here, you take a five-minute connecting ride to the central **Estação de São Bento** (Praça Almeida Garrett, tel. 02/200–1054); connecting trains run regularly. When leaving Oporto, be sure to leave plenty of time from São Bento Station to make your connection. For the express service to and from Lisbon, it's necessary to reserve your seat at least a day in advance.

A few trains, those from Guimarães and from the coast immediately north of the city, use the **Estação da Trindade** (Rua Alferes Malheiro, tel. 02/200–5224), which is a few minutes' walk from downtown Oporto, behind the town hall at the top of Avenida dos Aliados.

From Spain, the Vigo–Oporto through-train uses the Tu y/Valença border crossing and runs south down the Costa Verde to Oporto via Viana do Castelo. These trains usually stop at the Campanhã and São Bento stations, but some only stop at Campanhã, and you'll have to change for São Bento.

**By Bus** There are several bus terminals in Oporto. The main areas where buses arrive and depart are at Praça Filipa de Lencastre (close to Av. dos Aliados) and in the streets behind São Bento Station (particularly Rua de Alexandre Herculano and Av. de Rodrigues de Freitas). For information on buses to Lisbon, contact **Caima**, (Rua das Carmelitas 32, tel. 02/318668). The journey to or from Lisbon takes about five hours, and you should reserve seats at least a day in advance in summer.

## Getting Around

**On Foot**   You'll be able to walk around most of central Oporto, although be prepared for the hills, which can prove tiring in the summer heat. The city is very congested, so leave your car at your hotel while sightseeing in the city. Central parking is difficult to find, and much of the downtown area (in particular, the riverside and the winding streets of the old town below the cathedral) is not accessible to cars.

**By Car**   Outside Oporto a car is the most convenient way to get around, but be prepared for lengthy journeys, particularly in the northeast, where roads can be tortuous. Many roads have been improved in recent years—the fast N15 highway between Oporto and Bragança has been completed, and there are quick routes from Oporto to towns both north and south, as well as to Braga in the northeast—but, given the nature of Portuguese terrain, some journeys will never be anything but slow. Examples are the routes Bragança–Chaves–Braga (N103), Vila Real–Chaves (N2), and Bragança–Mirando do Douro (N218). It's best simply to accept the roads' limitations, slow down, and appreciate the scenery.

Off the beaten track, particularly in the northeast, always check with local tourist offices to make sure that the routes you wish to follow are navigable. Road work and winter landslides can cause detours and delays. In isolated regions, take special care at night, because many roads are unlit and unpaved.

*Car Rentals*   All the major companies are represented at Oporto's airport, and some have offices at the larger hotels. Other addresses include: **Avis** (Rua Guedes de Azevedo 125, Oporto, tel. 02/ 315947; Braga train station, Rua Gabriel P. Castro 28, tel. 053/ 72520; Rua do Gontim 35, Viana do Castelo, tel. 058/823994), **Europcar** (Rua de Santa Catarina 1158, Oporto, tel. 02/318398; Campanhã Station, Oporto, tel. 02/ 580723), **Hertz** (Rua de Santa Catarina 899, Oporto, tel. 02/312387; Rua Gabrial P. Castro 28, Braga, tel. 053/616744; Av. Conde da Carreira, Viana do Castelo, tel. 058/822250). In other towns consult the tourist office for the best deals with local companies.

**By Taxi**   In Oporto there is a taxi stand in Praça da Liberdade, or you may phone for a cab (tel. 02/528061, 02/482691, or 02/676093). Make sure that the driver switches on the meter. Note that taxis add a surcharge for crossing the Ponte Dom Luis I to Vila Nova de Gaia, the suburb known for its port wine.

**By Bus and Tram**   Oporto has a decent public transportation system, consisting of *carris* (buses) and *elétricos* (trams). The tourist office provides a city map with all the main routes and numbers. Main stops are at Praça da Liberdade, Praça de Dom João I, and Cordoaria, behind the Clérigos Tower. A useful bus route is No. 78, which runs from Praça da Liberdade, past the Soares dos Reis museum and the Palácio de Cristal gardens, along the main Avenida da Boavista, to the Museum of Modern Art. The tram system is of less use to visitors, though Trams 1 and 18 make a pleasant run along the river to the beach at Foz.

Ticket prices vary according to the distance traveled, but most trips through the downtown area cost 150$00. The driver will tell you how much to pay when you get on. If you're going to make considerable use of public transportation, purchase a block of 20 tickets

(1,400$00) or a four-day (1,400$00) or seven- day (1,800$00) *Passe Turístico*. All are available at kiosks at the main bus stops.

Outside the city system there's a confusion of bus companies in the North, with several providing service between the same destinations. Generally, however, companies use one central station in each town. Major terminals are found at Oporto, Braga, Guimarães, Vila Real, and Chaves. The best source of information about departures is the local tourist office, since bus station personnel invariably speak no English. However, most bus stations do offer timetables for main routes, which you should be able to decipher with the aid of a dictionary.

The main company operating in Trás-os-Montes is **Cabanelas,** whose terminal in Oporto is at Rua da Alegria (tel. 02/200– 2870). Bus trips in this region are slow and, on some of the minor routes, uncomfortable. One useful tip is to take the bus rather than the train between the neighboring towns of Guimarães and Braga (*see* Tour 3 *below*). It's only 22 kilometers (14 miles) on the road, but the circuitous train ride involves two changes.

**By Train**  All the region's train routes originate in Oporto; from here some of the finest lines in the country stretch out into the river valleys and mountain ranges of the northeast. Even if you've rented a car, try to take a day trip on at least one of the beautiful lines that traverse the region, because the countryside is often best seen from a rattling train window. The **Douro Line** runs from Oporto's São Bento Station east to Pocinho via Livração, Peso da Régua, and Tua (a four-hour journey). Three narrow-gauge lines branch off from it: the **Tâmega Line,** linking Livração with beautiful Amarante (25 minutes); the **Corgo Line,** from Peso da Régua to Vila Real (one hour); and the **Tua Line,** from Tua to Mirandel a/Bragança (two hours/four hours). The trains on these lines generally have just one class of car and stop at every station. Journeys are slow but rewarding. (Tickets are reasonably priced.) Recently there have been service cuts on the minor lines, and some route sections have been closed altogether. The lines mentioned above should still be operational, but for reservations and current schedules contact São Bento Station (tel. 02/2002722) or the tourist office in Oporto.

Trains on main route north along the Costa Verde, depart approximately hourly from both São Bento and Campanhãstations and run through Barcelos and Viana do Castelo, as far as Valença do Minho. Branch lines connect with Braga and Guimarães.

**By Boat**  Cruises on the Rio Douro are offered by various companies based in Oporto. These range from short trips taking in Oporto's bridges and the local fishing villages to one- and two- day cruises that include meals and accommodations. Expect to pay around 1,500$00 for one-to two-hour cruises, most of which depart several times daily from the Cais da Ribeira, at the foot of Oporto's old town (*see* Tour 1, *below*). The longer cruises usually depart weekly and often involve taking a train from São Bento Station that connects with a boat farther down the Douro. The cost for these is 11,000$00–30,000$00 per person. The cruise company with the best reputation is **Endouro** (Rua da Reboleira 49, Oporto, tel. 02/324236, fax 02/ 317260). More information can be obtained from the tourist office in Oporto.

## Guided Tours

**Orientation**  In Oporto, consult a tourist office or travel agency (*see* Important Addresses and Numbers, in Essential Information *above*) for the latest information on bus tours of the city. Usually these last half a day and take in all the principal sights, including a visit to the port-wine lodges (where the vintage is stored) at Vila Nova de Gaia. Short river cruises from Oporto are also a pleasant way to orient yourself (*see* By Boat in Getting Around, *above*).

For tours farther afield, **RN Tours** (Rua Sá da Bandeira 629, Oporto, tel. 02/2001109) operates half- and full-day coach tours throughout the region, to destinations as diverse as the Douro valley, the Costa Verde, and Peneda-Gerês National Park. Consider, too, the longer cruises operated by Endouro (*see* By Boat in Getting Around, *above*), which cover the towns of the Douro valley.

**Special Interest**    All the port-wine lodges at Vila Nova de Gaia offer free tours of the production process as well as wine tastings. (*See* Tour 1, *below*.)

# Exploring Oporto and the North

## Orientation

Oporto is just 3½ hours north of Lisbon by highway or express train, so even a short trip to Portugal can include a night or two here. Tour 1 takes in the most interesting sights and monuments in Oporto and allows time for a visit to the famous port-wine lodges. Tour 2 explores Oporto's environs, including the local beaches and the lovely scenery of the Rio Douro valley. The third tour encompasses the Minho's two most intriguing historic towns, Guimarães and Braga, and also includes a visit to the country's biggest weekly market at Barcelos. Tour 4 continues from here, covering the beautiful Costa Verde coastline and the peaceful inland towns and villages along the rivers Lima and Minho. The final tour strikes off into the remote northeastern Trás-os-Montes, where a long circuit takes in the fascinating towns of Bragança and Chaves before cutting back to the area covered in Tour 3.

Following all the tours in this chapter would be a major undertaking, requiring at least two weeks on top of your time in Oporto, perhaps longer if you have to rely on public transportation. But in a week you could see the best parts of the coast and Minho province or travel widely in Trás-os-Montes. With just a few days for exploration, you could follow Tours 2 and 3, which cover varied towns and landscapes easily accessible from Oporto. Visitors coming from Spain to Trás-os-Montes would be advised to undertake Tour 5 before moving on to Oporto and the rest of the North.

## Highlights for First-Time Visitors

Amarante (*see* Tour 2)
Baroque staircase and shrine of Bom Jesus, Braga (*see* Tour 3)
Cais da Ribeira district, Oporto (*see* Tour 1)
Chaves (*see* Tour 5)
Citadel, Bragança (*see* Tour 5)
Guimarães (*see* Tour 3)
Ponte de Lima (*see* Tour 4)
Port-wine tasting at Vila Nova de Gaia, Oporto (*see* Tour 1)
Solar de Mateus, Vila Real (*see* Tour 5)
Thursday market, Barcelos (*see* Tour 3)
Viana do Castelo (*see* Tour 4)

View from the Torre dos Clérigos, Oporto (*see* Tour 1)

## Tour 1: Oporto

*Numbers in the margin correspond to points of interest on the North and Oporto maps.*

❶ Industrious **Oporto**—Portugal's second city, with a population of half a million—considers itself the capital of the North and, more contentiously, the economic center of the country. Locals support this claim by quoting a typically down-to-earth maxim: "Coimbra sings, Braga prays, Lisbon shows off, and Oporto works." Certainly wherever you look there's evidence of a city in rude financial health. Massive new business developments on the outskirts give way to a fashionable commercial area in the heart of town; shops and restaurants bustle with high-spending locals; and the city's buildings, churches, and monuments— both old and new—impress with their solid construction. There's poverty here, of course, in the ragged old-town areas near the river; parts are positively medieval. But in the shopping centers, the stately Stock Exchange building, and the affluent port-wine industry, Oporto oozes confidence. Hard work, one feels, is the city's biggest asset.

This emphasis on worth rather than beauty means that Oporto is not a graceful city. Significant sights are few, and aesthetically pleasing monuments are rare. Visitors may find their first impression disappointing, although the city's glorious location—on a steep hillside above the Rio Douro—does much to compensate. The river has influenced the city's development since pre-Roman times, when the town of Cale on the left bank prospered sufficiently to support a trading port, called Portus, on the site of today's city. Under the Romans this twin town of Portus-Cale became a thriving commercial center, and it continued to be successful despite the later ravages of Moorish occupation and Christian reconquest. Significantly, given the outward-looking nature of its inhabitants, Henry the Navigator—the great explorer king—was born here at the end of the 14th century.

The importance of the river trade to the city is reflected in its current name, whose use began in early medieval times. Oporto, from the Portuguese *O Porto*, means simply "the port," and over the centuries the city has traded widely in fish, salt, and wine. As the result of an agreement with England in 1703, the region's most notable product—wine, made from the grapes of the Douro's vineyards—found a new market and was shipped out of the city in ever-increasing quantities. The port-wine trade is still big business, based just over the river from the city in the suburb of Vila Nova de Gaia (site of the Roman town of Cale).

Having reached the city center (often a slow business because of the traffic), you'll do best to tour Oporto on foot, taking buses or taxis to ❷ the few outlying attractions. Start at the **Avenida dos Aliados,** an imposing, sloping boulevard that lies at the commercial heart of the city and points toward the river. Providing some welcome open space in Oporto's busy center, it is planted with bright flower beds and lined with grand buildings, including the broad **Câmara Municipal** (Town Hall), which stands at the top of the avenue. The roof of this early 20th-century palace-like building sprouts a tall bell tower, and inside an impressive Portuguese wall tapestry is displayed. At the other end of the avenue, **Praça da Liberdade** is the hub from which downtown Oporto radiates. Two statues adorn the square: a cast of Dom Pedro IV sitting on a horse and an unusual, modern stat-

**The North**

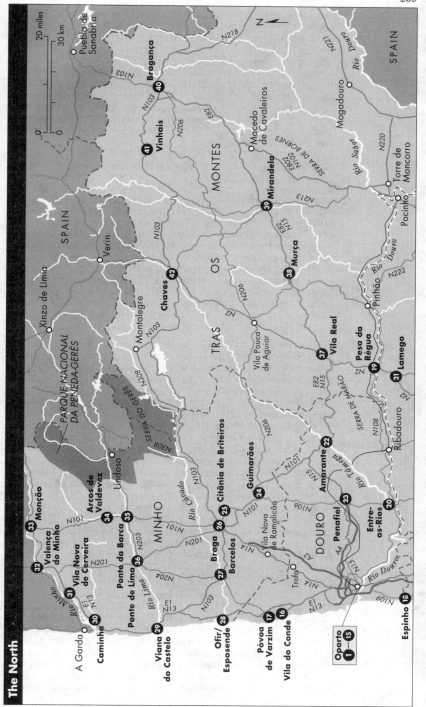

ue of the great 19th-century Portuguese poet and novelist Almeida Garrett. *Town hall: Praça General Humberto Delgado, tel. 02/200–9871. Admission free. Open weekdays 9:30–noon and 2–5.*

**Time Out** The city has several fine old-style coffeehouses, which, like those in Lisbon, feature turn-of-the-century decor. The large **Café Imperial**, on the eastern side of Praça da Liberdade, is a good place to watch the busy traffic and shoppers; there are tables inside and out. Around the corner, the similarly decorated **A Brasileira** (Rua Sá da Bandeira 61, closed Sun.) has brisker service. For just a drink or snack, pay first at the cash desk and present your receipt at the busy bar. Both are inexpensive.

Rua dos Clérigos leads smartly uphill to the west from Praça da Liberdade, culminating in an odd oval-shaped church, whose tower is an immediately recognizable finger on the Oporto skyline. The ❸ **Torre dos Clérigos** (Clérigos Tower), designed by Italian architect Nicolau Nasoni and begun in 1754, consists of six stories that leap to a height of 249 feet, making it one of the tallest towers in the country. There are 225 steep stone steps to the belfry at the top, and the very considerable effort required to climb them is rewarded by stunning views of the old town, the river, and beyond to the mouth of the Douro. The **Igreja dos Clérigos**, also built by Nasoni, predates the tower and is an elaborate example of Italianate Baroque architecture. *Rua dos Clérigos, tel. 02/200–1729. Tower: Admission: 100$00. Open Thurs.–Tues. 10–noon and 2–5, Sun. to 5:30. Church: Admission free. Open Mon.–Sat. 7:30–9, 10– noon, 2–5, and 6–7:30; Sun. 10–1.*

Back at Praça da Liberdade, use the pedestrian underpass to cross ❹ to the **Estação de São Bento,** Oporto's most central railroad station, whose main hall is decorated with enormous azulejos depicting the history of Portuguese transportation. From the steps of the station ❺ you can look across to the granite **Sé** (Cathedral), situated on a sweeping terrace and perched over the old town, which is a few minutes' walk to the south. Originally constructed in the 12th century by the parents of Afonso Henriques (the first king of Portugal), the cathedral has been rebuilt twice: first in the late 13th century and again in the 18th century, when the architect of the Clérigos Tower, Nasoni, was among those commissioned to work on its expansion. Despite these renovations, it remains a severe, fortress-like structure, and, as such, is an uncompromising statement of the city's medieval wealth and power. Sheer size apart, the cathedral's interior is unusually disappointing, and only when you enter the two-story, 14th-century cloister does the building come to life. Decorated with gleaming azulejos, a staircase added by Nasoni leads to the second level and into a magnificent, richly furnished chapter house, from which there are fine views of the old town through narrow windows. *Terreiro da Sé, tel. 02/314837. Admission: cathedral free; cloister: 150$00. Open daily 9–12:30 and 2:30–5.*

Nasoni also designed the **Archbishop's Palace,** behind the cathedral, although since it was converted to public offices, visitors can see no farther than the impressive 60-meter-long facade. However, you may visit the elegant interior of another 18th- century building at- ❻ tributed to Nasoni, the **Casa Museu de Guerra Junqueiro** (Guerra Junqueiro House and Museum). It lies on Rua de Dom Hugo, a narrow street that curves around the eastern side of the cathedral. This white mansion was home to the poet Guerra Junqueiro (1850–1923) and is a quiet retreat. However, the short tour of his enviable collection of furniture, sculpture, paintings, and silver is less than en-

# Oporto

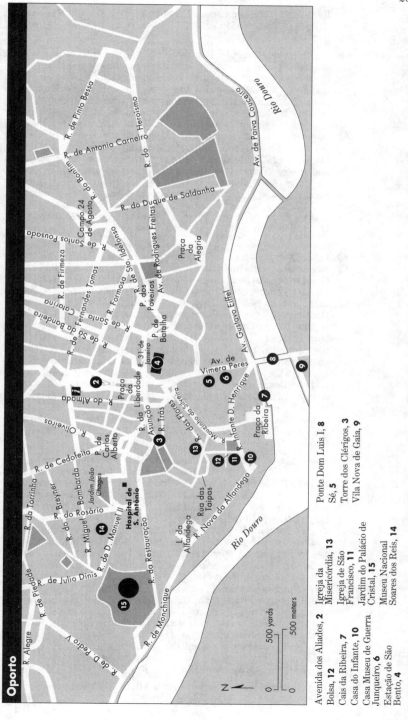

N
0    500 yards
0    500 meters

Avenida dos Aliados, **2**
Bolsa, **12**
Cais da Ribeira, **7**
Casa do Infante, **10**
Casa Museu de Guerra
Junqueiro, **6**
Estação de São
Bento, **4**

Igreja da
Misericórdia, **13**
Igreja de São
Francisco, **11**
Jardim do Palácio de
Cristal, **15**
Museu Nacional
Soares dos Reis, **14**

Ponte Dom Luís I, **8**
Sé, **5**
Torre dos Clérigos, **3**
Vila Nova de Gaia, **9**

lightening if you don't speak Portuguese. *Rua de Dom Hugo 32, tel. 02/313644. Admission: 150$00. Open Tues.–Sat. 11– 12:30 and 2:30–6.*

Continue southwest on Rua de Dom Hugo and then head down, by way of the steep steps that cut through surviving sections of the medieval city walls, into a web of tangled alleys, leaning buildings, and down-at-the-heel street markets. This decaying neighborhood has missed out on the city's economic progress, and there's much poverty here, however colorful the timeworn buildings with their long rows of balconies may appear. Whichever route you follow, the **❼** stepped alleys all eventually emerge at the riverfront **Cais da Ribeira,** the quayside of the fascinating Ribeira district. Here there's a small daily market and a string of excellent fish restaurants and *tascas* (taverns) built into the street-level arcade of the old buildings (*see* Dining and Lodging, *below*). In the Praça da Ribeira, people sit and chat around the odd, modern, cube-like sculpture, while farther on, steps lead up to a raised walkway, backed by tall houses, that runs above the river. There are good views from here of the port-wine lodges at Vila Nova de Gaia.

From the quayside there's access to the lower level of the two- tier **❽ Ponte Dom Luis I,** the middle bridge across the Douro. This bridge **❾** was built in 1886 and leads directly to the suburb of **Vila Nova de Gaia,** which has been the headquarters of the port-wine trade since the late 17th century. Import bans on French wine had led British merchants to look for alternative sources, and by the 18th century the British had established companies and a regulatory association at Oporto to control the quality of the wine they were importing from Portugal. The wine was transported from vineyards on the up-per Rio Douro to port-wine "lodges" (warehouses) at Vila Nova de Gaia, where it was allowed to mature before being shipped out of the country. Very little has changed in the relationship between Oporto and the Douro since those days, as wine is still transported to the city, matured in the warehouses, and bottled. However, instead of traveling down the river on traditional *barcos rabelos* (flat-bottomed boats), the wine is now carried by truck. A couple of the boats are moored at the quayside on the Vila Nova de Gaia side, as a re-minder of bygone days.

There are more than 25 companies with **port-wine lodges** in Vila Nova de Gaia (many still foreign-owned), from such well-known names as Sandeman, Croft, and Cockburn to less-well-known Portu-guese firms, such as Ramos Pinto and Borges. All are signposted within a few minutes' walk of each other, and their names are dis-played in huge white letters across their roofs. Each company offers guided tours of the premises and the fascinating port-wine making and bottling process—tours that always end with a tasting of one or two wines and an opportunity to buy bottles from the company store. Tours begin regularly, usually when enough visitors are as-sembled. Even without taking a tour, you'll find the back streets of this suburb entertaining; they are filled with trucks loading and un-loading in narrow alleys and offer glimpses of huge vats and techni-cal equipment inside warehouses. The tourist office at Vila Nova de Gaia (*see* Important Addresses and Numbers in Essential Informa-tion, *above*) offers a small map of the main port-wine lodges and can advise you on hours of the smaller operations. At the larger lodges: *Admission free. Open June–Sept., weekdays 9–12:30 and 2–7, Sat. 9– 12:30; Oct.–May, weekdays 9–12:30 and 2–5.*

Vila Nova de Gaia isn't solely devoted to the port-wine trade. Com-bine a tour of the wine lodges with a visit to the **Casa Museu de**

**Teixeira Lopes,** the home of the sculptor António Teixeira Lopes (1866–1942), who was born in town. It contains some excellent sculpture as well as a varied collection of paintings by Teixeira Lopes's contemporaries. A selection of books, coins, and ceramics is also interesting. *Rua Teixeira Lopes 32, tel. 02/301224. Admission free. Open Oct.–May, Tues.–Sat. 9:30–12:30 and 2–5:30; June–Sept., Tues.–Sat. 9:30–12:30 and 2–5:30, Sun. 1–7.*

You can cross back to the city using the narrow footway on the upper level of the Ponte Dom Luís I, which puts you on Avenida de Vimara Peres, close to the cathedral. But at 200 feet above the river and with traffic thundering past, this is not a crossing for those with faint hearts or for those who have tasted of the port not wisely but too well.

To continue the city tour, retrace your path to the Cais da Ribeira. Away from the water, Rua do Infante Dom Henrique, which used to be known as Rua dos Ingleses (English Street), contains shipping offices and warehouses. Where it meets Rua de São João stands the granite **Feitoria Inglesa** (Factory House of the British Association), built at the end of the 18th century as the headquarters of the Port Wine Shippers' Association. It retains an impressive interior, but ❿ the general public is not admitted. Farther west is the **Casa do Infante** (House of the Prince), a foursquare, restored mansion said to be the birthplace of Oporto's most famous son, Prince Henry the Navigator (born in 1394). The building now holds part of the city archives and is open to the public for temporary exhibitions. *Rua do Infante, tel. 02/316025.*

Follow Rua do Infante Dom Henrique to the square of the same name, which is marked by a statue of Prince Henry. Here the late ⓫ 14th-century **Igreja de São Francisco** (Church of Saint Francis) appears to be an unremarkable Gothic building on the outside but reveals its astounding interior to inquisitive visitors. The profusion of gilded carving was added in the mid-18th century and swarms over every inch of the building— up the pillars, over the altar, and across the ceiling. An adjacent museum houses valuable furnishings from the Franciscan monastery that once stood here. *Rua do Infante Dom Henrique, tel. 02/200–6493. Admission: 500$00. Open Tues.– Sat. 9–12 and 2–5, July–Aug. 9–5.*

Behind the church, facing the square, Oporto's 19th-century, neo- ⓬ classical **Bolsa** (Stock Exchange) takes up much of the site of the old Franciscan monastery. Guided tours (the only way to see the interior) stroll around the huge, showy edifice, much of it in questionable taste. The Arab-style ballroom, in particular, has critics as numerous as the glowing adjectives with which the guides describe it. *Rua Ferreira Borges, tel. 02/ 200–4497. Guided tours: 500$00; May– Sept., Mon.–Sat. 9–5, every 15–20 min.; Oct.–Apr., weekdays 9– noon and 2–5:30, every 30 min.*

North of the stock exchange, at Largo de São Domingos, Rua das Flores—a street known for its silversmiths and striking wrought-iron balconies—leads back toward São Bento Station. On the left is ⓭ the **Igreja da Misericórdia** (Church of the Misericórdia), which dates from the 16th century but was largely remodeled two centuries later by Nicolau Nasoni. Call at the adjacent offices, and you will be shown the *Fons Vitae* (Fountain of Life), considered one of the country's finest paintings. It is an anonymous Renaissance work of brilliant colors, showing the founder of the church, Dom Manuel I, his queen, and their eight children kneeling before a crucified

Christ. *Tel. 02/200– 0941. Admission free. Open weekdays 10–noon and 2–5.*

Retrace your steps to Largo de São Domingos and follow Rua de Belmonte west, admiring the graceful, balconied houses en route. Take Rua das Taipas north, until you reach the **Jardim João Chagas** (João Chagas Gardens), where the **Palácio da Justiça** (Palace of Justice) towers on your left. Facing the corner of the gardens is the large, 18th-century **Hospital de Santo António** and a little farther west is the **Museu Nacional Soares dos Reis,** in a former royal palace. The building was the headquarters, during the Peninsular War, of Napoleon's Marshal Soult, who in 1809 was forced to flee before the rapid advance of the British expeditionary force. The museum is closed for repairs; ask at the tourist office when it's scheduled to re-open. It is named after the 19th-century Portuguese sculptor whose works are contained within, and its large art collection includes several Portuguese primitive works of the 16th century as well as superb collections of silver, ceramics, glassware, and costumes. *Rua de Dom Manuel II, tel. 02/200–7110. Admission: 200$00, free on Sun. Open Tues.–Sun. 10–noon and 2–5.*

Continue west on Rua de Dom Manuel II to the **Jardim do Palacio de Cristal** (Crystal Palace Gardens), named for a 19th-century palace that once stood here but that was replaced in the 1950s by an enormous domed pavilion used for sports and exhibitions. Follow Rua de Entre Quintas on the far side of the gardens to reach the **Quinta da Macierinha.** This is a charming 19th-century country house containing the so-called **Museu Romântico** (Romantic Museum), featuring period furniture and decoration. The ground floor of the Quinta is of special interest, for here the **Solar do Vinho do Porto** (Port Wine Institute) offers relaxed tastings of port wine, in much the same fashion as its counterpart in Lisbon; however, Oporto's Solar has a much friendlier reputation, and, in addition, the wine has only had to travel across the river before being served! Tasting prices vary but start at 100$00 per glass. This is a fine place to end your tour of the city, and, when it's time to return downtown, either catch Bus 78 (which runs along Rua de Dom Manuel II, past the Soares dos Reis Museum, to Praça da Liberdade) or jump into a taxi. *Rua de Entre Quintas 220. Museum: Tel. 02/691131; open Tues.–Sat. 10–noon and 2–5, Sun. 2–5:30. Solar: Tel. 02/697793; open weekdays 11 AM–11 PM, Sat. 5–11:30.*

## Tour 2: Environs of Oporto—The Coast and the Rio Douro

Both north and south of Oporto are beach resorts much favored by locals. To the north there are beaches in nearby Foz do Douro, and Matosinhos, but they are unattractive places, much influenced by the industrial port of Leixoes. It's better to drive as far as **Vila do Conde,** 27 kilometers (17 miles), which has a long sweep of fine sand and an interesting fishing port, ship-building industry, and medieval quarter. The town is further distinguished by the huge **Convento de Santa Clara** (Convent of St. Clara), overwhelming the north bank of the Rio Ave on which the town is situated. The convent was founded in the 14th century by Dom Afonso Sanches and his wife, Dona Teresa Martins, and it retains its original cloister and the beautiful tombs of its founders. The **Igreja Matriz** (Parish Church), in the center of town near the market, is also worth seeing. Completed in the 16th century, it features a superb Gothic portal. If you're looking for souvenirs, Vila do Conde is the center of a flourishing lace industry, and the tourist office will direct you to a lace-making school in the town center that welcomes visitors. *Convent open Mon.–Sat. 9–noon and 2–5.*

**⓱ Póvoa de Varzim,** four kilometers (2½ miles) north, also has a long beach, but the town has little of Vila do Conde's charm. It is, instead, a major resort, with high-rise hotels used mostly by Portuguese on vacation. The recently refurbished casino (open daily 3 PM–3 AM) on the waterfront attracts much attention. Entertainment includes nightly floor shows; to gamble, take along your passport.

**⓲** South of Oporto, frequent trains and route N109 run past a string of quiet family beaches to **Espinho,** 18 kilometers (11 miles) from the city. Built on a grid pattern, it has become an increasingly fashionable resort over the years, with a casino of its own, a full range of other leisure facilities, and good shopping. The long, sandy beach is very popular in summer, but you can find some space by walking through the pinewoods to less developed areas to the south. The Oporto Golf Club, founded in 1890 by members of the Port Wine Shippers' Association, is just 2 kilometers (1¼ miles) south of Espinho (*see* Sports and the Outdoors, *below*).

The beaches are pleasant, but a more interesting attraction is the **Rio Douro,** which makes its presence felt throughout Oporto and its surroundings. Visitors can see the beauty of the river and the local countryside by train, car, or boat (*see* Getting Around in Essential Information, *above*).

**⓳** Even if you are traveling by car, it's worth considering at least a day trip using the Douro Line train. The main route runs 40 kilometers (25 miles) inland from Oporto to join the Douro at Ribadouro and follows the north bank of the river as far as **Peso da Régua,** a 2½-hour journey. This small river port is in the heart of port- wine country, and through it passes all the wine from the vineyards of the Upper Douro valley on its way to Oporto. Local wine lodges offer tours of their cellars, which make a nice contrast to the large-scale operations in Vila Nova de Gaia. From Peso da Régua the train continues east to the end of the line at Pocinho, providing a glorious 70-kilometer (43½-mile) ride that hugs the Rio Douro all the way. Unfortunately, service to the Spanish border has been discontinued. The Tâmega Line branches off the main line and runs northeast up the Rio Tâmega tributary to Arco de Baulhe, past Amarante (*see below*). Service on both routes is currently under review, since they're used less and less by locals, who prefer the fast inland roads gradually extending from Oporto.

**⓴** Drivers can get some of the same sense of rural splendor by following the minor N108 east from Oporto along the north bank of the river to Peso da Régua. It makes for a grand, if slow, journey that you can continue all the way to the Spanish border. One of the most striking sights in the valley is the point at which the Douro and the Tâmega join, at **Entre-os-Rios,** 40 kilometers (25 miles) southeast of Oporto.

**㉑** At Peso da Régua you have a choice of routes. It's 25 kilometers (15½ miles) north along the scenic N2 to Vila Real, the town marking the start of the tour of Trás-os-Montes (*see* Tour 5, *below*). Alternatively, cross the Rio Douro and follow the equally scenic N2 south for 13 kilometers (8 miles) to **Lamego.** A prosperous wine-producing town, Lamego is rich in Baroque churches and mansions, though none is so impressive as the town's most famous monument—the 18th-century pilgrimage church and shrine of **Nossa Senhora dos Remedios.** It stands on a hill to the west of the town center, and a marvelous granite staircase leads up the hillside to the church. The steps and terraces are decorated with azulejos, small chapels, and statues. During the annual pilgrimage on September 8, many penitents climb the steps on their knees, just as they do at the shrine of Bom Jesus near Braga (*see* Tour 3, *below*). Rest at the top under the chestnut trees, and enjoy the view over the town to the distant mountains.

Return to the Douro and Peso da Régua, and take the N108 west back to Mesão Frio. Then take the N101, which climbs northwest out of the Douro valley and across the Serra do Marão (Marão Hills) before descending to join the N15/E82. Forty kilometers (25 miles) from Peso da Régua is the small, agreeable town of **Amarante,** situated on both sides of the Ria Tâmega. It's also possible to reach Amarante on the Tâmega Line, with a change at Livração.

**②②**

Amarante itself is charming, if ever a town deserved the adjective, and it's the one place in Oporto's environs that really demands an overnight stop. Its halves are joined by a narrow 18th-century bridge, sitting above the river's tree-shaded banks. Although the river is polluted (which precludes swimming), it's beautiful to look at. Rowboats and pedal boats are for hire at several points along the riverside paths.

**Time Out**    Along Rua 31 de Janeiro, the narrow main road leading to the bridge, several small cafés and restaurants have terraces overlooking the river. Enjoy a drink, a snack, or a meal as you soak up the views.

On the north side of the river, across the bridge from the main part of town, is the imposing, 16th-century **Convento de São Gonçalo** (Convent of Saint Gonçalo). The effigy of the saint, on the left of the altar, is reputed to guarantee marriage to anyone who touches it. Not surprisingly, his features have almost been worn away over the years, as desperate suitors try one last time for success. *Praça da República. Admission free. Open daily 9–noon and 2–5.*

Adjacent to the church are the cloisters and associated buildings of the convent, now housing the tourist office and the **Museu Municipal Amadeo de Sousa,** a small but intelligent collection of modern art revolving around the largely abstract paintings of Cardoso, who was born in the area. In 1906 Cardoso moved to Paris and shared a studio with Modigliani, but he returned to Portugal in 1914 and died four years later at the early age of 31. The museum also hosts exhibitions of other artists' work, and there's some intriguing modern sculpture displayed in the attractive courtyard. *Alameda Teixeira de Pascoais, tel. 055/432663. Admission free. Open Tues.–Sun. 10–12:30 and 2–5:30.*

Beyond the museum is the riverside site of the local **market,** held every Wednesday, which is perhaps the best day to be in Amarante. Until lunchtime this entire area is alive with activity, and the usually peaceful town is disturbed by manic traffic racing along the main street and over the bridge.

From Amarante the fast, new N15 highway runs 36 kilometers (22 miles) east to Vila Real, which marks the start of Tour 5 (*see below*). But to complete this tour, follow the road west, back toward Oporto. About halfway the highway passes just north of the town of **Penafiel,** which is also accessible from the Douro Line train. The surrounding valleys are terraced with vineyards, not of the heavy port variety but of the slightly sparkling vinho verde (green wine). Other than some fading granite mansions, there's little in the town itself to see, but do stop for a glass of this always-refreshing local wine.

**②③**

Many of the small villages in the land between Penafiel and the Tâmega and Douro rivers have lovely Romanesque churches. The closest is a little way off the main road, at **Paço de Sousa,** just to the southwest of Penafiel and 2 kilometers (1¼miles) south of the train station at Cete. Here the 12th-century church is part of the Convento de São Salvador and contains the tomb of Egas Moniz, who was adviser to Afonso Henriques, the first king of all Portugal. Back on the highway you're just 40 kilometers (25 miles) from Oporto.

## Tour 3: Guimarães, Braga, and Barcelos

Guimarães and Braga are of sufficient historic interest to warrant at least a day spent in each. Both make easy day trips from Oporto by road or rail, although they can be seen in a more relaxed fashion on a driving tour of the southern part of Minho province, which also takes in the market town of Barcelos. The tour below begins in Guimarães, but remember that you should visit Barcelos on market day, Thursday; you may have to revise your tour accordingly.

**24** **Guimarães,** 51 kilometers (32 miles) northeast of Oporto, is the birthplace of Afonso Henriques. Born in 1110, within 20 years he was being referred to as king of *Portucale* (the united Portuguese lands between the Minho and Douro rivers) and had made Guimarães his capital. From this first "Portuguese" capital, Afonso Henriques drove south, taking Lisbon back from the Moors in 1147. Today Guimarães is a provincial town proud of its past, and this is evident in a series of delightful medieval buildings and streets. In the narrow, cobbled thoroughfares of the old town, small bars open onto the sidewalk; balconied, pastel-colored houses overhang little squares; and flowers brighten every windowsill.

It's best to start at the **Castelo** (Castle) at the top of the town, which is, after all, where the story began. It was built (or at least reconstructed from earlier remains) by Henry of Burgundy; his son, Afonso Henriques, was born within its great battlements and flanking towers. Standing high on a solid rock base above the town, the castle has been superbly preserved. A path leads down from the walls to the tiny Romanesque **Igreja de São Miguel de Castelo,** the plain chapel where it's believed that Afonso Henriques was baptized. *Rua D. Teresa de Noronha. Castle: Open Tues.–Sun. 9:30– 12:30 and 2–5; Church: Open irregular hours.*

Below the chapel is the **Paço dos Duques** (Palace of the Dukes), a much-maligned, renovated 15th-century palace belonging to the dukes of Bragança. Critics claim that the restoration during the Salazar regime, which turned the building into an official state residence, damaged it irrevocably. Certainly the palace's brick chimneys and turrets bear little relation to the original structure, which was an atmospheric ruin for many years, but you can judge for yourself on a guided tour of the interior. The collections inside contain much of interest, from tapestries and furniture to porcelain and paintings. Guided tours can be booked at the main desk. *Tel. 053/ 412273. Admission: 350$00, June–Sept.; 200$00 Oct.–May. Open daily 10– 12:30 and 2–5.*

Walk down Rua de Santa Maria into the peaceful old town, and the centuries roll away with every step: You'll see granite archways, wooden balconies, iron grilles, and paving stones underfoot. In Largo da Oliveira, a delightful square enclosed by buildings, stands the **Colegiada de Nossa Senhora da Oliveira** (Church of Our Lady of the Olive Branch). It was founded in the 10th century to commemorate one of Guimarães's most enduring legends. Wamba, elected king of the Visigoths in the 7th century, refused the honor and thrust his olive-branch stick into the earth, declaring that only if his stick were to blossom would he accept the crown—whereupon the stick promptly sprouted foliage. In the square in front of the church, an odd 14th-century Gothic canopy sheltering a cross marks the alleged spot.

The adjacent convent buildings, surrounding the Romanesque cloister, house the **Museu Alberto Sampaio,** a beautifully displayed collection of religious art. The cloister itself holds medieval statuary, sarcophagi, and various coats-of-arms, but the interior rooms provide the highlight: a 14th-century silver triptych of the Nativity, full of animation and power. This is said to have been captured from the King of Castile at the crucial Battle of Aljubarrota and presented to the victorious Dom João I, whose tunic, worn at the battle, is preserved in a glass case nearby. *Largo da Oliveira, tel. 053/412465. Admission: 250$00. Open Tues.–Sun. 10–12:30 and 2–5.*

**Time Out** | An inexpensive café in Largo da Oliveira, **A Medieval** has seats outside in the square. Relax over coffee and a cake. *Closed Sun.*

The old-town streets peter out at the Almeida da Liberdade, a swath of gardens at the southern end of Guimarães, whose benches and cafés are often full. Here the **Igreja de São Francisco** (Church of Saint Francis) is worth seeing. Its chancel is decorated with 18th-century azulejos depicting the life of the saint. The church also boasts a fine Renaissance cloister. *Largo de São Francisco, tel. 053/412228. Open daily 9–noon and 3–6.*

Follow the gardens as they curve west and north, and at the top of the adjacent Largo do Toural is Guimarães's other museum, the excellent **Museu Martins Sarmento.** It, too, is contained within the cloister and buildings of a church, the **Igreja de São Domingos.** The museum has rich finds from the Celtic settlement of Citânia de Briteiros (*see below*), as well as Lusitanian and Roman stone sarcophagi, a strange miniature bronze chariot, various weapons, and elaborate ornaments. Two finds stand out: the decorative, carved stone slabs known as the **Pedras Formosas** (beautiful stones), one of which was found at a funerary monument at Briteiros, and the huge, prehistoric, granite *Colossus of Pedralva*, a figure of brutal power, thought to have been used in ancient fertility rites. *Rua de Paio Galvão, tel. 053/415969. Admission: 300$00. Open Tues.–Sun. 10–noon and 2–5.*

Go north from Guimarães toward Braga on the N101, and after 8 kilometers (5 miles) turn right at Caldas das Taipas (Caldelas on some ❷❺ maps). This leads to **Citânia de Briteiros,** the fascinating remains of a Celtic *citânia* (hill settlement). It dates back to around 300 BC and was probably not abandoned until AD 300, making it one of the last Celtic strongholds against the Romans in Portugal. The walls and foundations of 150 huts and a meeting house have been excavated (two of the huts have been reconstructed to show their original size), and paths are clearly marked between them. Parts of a channeled water system also survive. The site was excavated in the late 19th century by Dr. Martins Sarmento, who gave his name to the museum in Guimarães (*see above*), where most of the finds from Briteiros were transferred. If you intend to visit the site, don't miss the museum. *Site open daily 9–6.*

❷❻ **Braga,** fifteen kilometers (9 miles) north, is one of the outstanding surprises of northern Portugal. Its attractive city center is a delight to negotiate, featuring many fine buildings whose Baroque facades front on small squares and pedestrian streets. A city of ancient origin, Braga prospered under the 6th-century Visigoths when it became an important bishopric, marking the start of the religious authority it maintains today. Braga's later archbishops often wielded greater power than the Portuguese kings themselves. During the city's golden age, in the 16th century, Braga was beautified with churches, palaces, and fountains, many of which were subsequently altered (some say ruined) in the 18th century.

The city feels like the country's religious capital. Shops selling religious artifacts line the streets around the cathedral, and Braga hosts the most impressive of Portugal's Easter celebrations. It also has a conservative reputation, since it was at Braga that the military coup began that brought Salazar to power. However, Braga seems increasingly dynamic, both in its local economy and artistic life, and the city of 65,000 is growing fast. The preserved city center is now surrounded by noisy streets and apartment blocks, and traffic congestion is assuming legendary proportions.

The center of the old town is marked by the huge **Sé**, originally Romanesque in character but now an impressive blend of styles. The delicate Renaissance stone tracery on the roof is particularly eye-catching. Enter from the main Rua do Souto through the 18th-century cloister; the cathedral interior is on your left, and there are various interesting chapels. Steps by the entrance to the cathedral lead to the Museu de Arte Sacra, which has a fascinating collection of religious art and artifacts, including a 14th-century crystal cross set in bronze. From the magnificent *coro alto* (upper choir), which you cross as part of the treasury tour, there are views of the great Baroque double organ. Across the cloister, you'll see the **Capela dos Reis** (Kings' Chapel), a 14th-century chapel containing the tombs of Afonso Henriques's parents, Henry of Burgundy and his wife, Teresa. *Tel. 053/23317. Admission: cathedral free; treasury: 250$00. Open daily 8:30–12:30 and 2:30–6:30.*

Across narrow Rua do Souto from the cathedral is Largo do Paço. It is flanked by the impressive, well-proportioned **Paço dos Arcebispos** (Archbishop's Palace), which overlooks an attractive, castellated fountain. Parts of the building date from the 14th century. Today it's occupied by faculties from the city's university and functions as the public library, which is among the most impressive in the country, containing more than 300,000 volumes.

The pedestrian Rua Diogo de Sousa leads down from the cathedral and Archbishop's Palace to one of the city's former gateways, the 18th-century **Arco do Porta Nova.** Pass through here and turn right for the **Palácio dos Biscainhos** (Biscainhos Palace), a Baroque mansion typical of many in the city. The elegant rooms are furnished in 18th-century style and display silver and porcelain collections. Interestingly, the ground floor of the palace is stone flagged, which allowed carriages to run through the interior to the stables beyond. At the back of the palace is a formal garden with decorative tiles. *Rua dos Biscainhos, tel. 053/27645. Admission: 300$00. Open Tues.– Sun. 10–noon and 2–5:30.*

Walk back past the gateway to the area beyond the Igreja de São Sebastião (Church of Saint Sebastian). Here you'll find the **Zona Arqueologica** (Archaeological Zone), which contains the excavations of an old Roman city known as *Bracara Augusta*. (The site isn't usually open to the public.) To the east, the Roman city stretched as far as the large Largo de São Tiago, where an imposing building contains the **Museu Pio XII e Medina** (Pio XII Museum). It contains two collections, one of religious works and the other of paintings and sculpture, though perhaps the most interesting elements of the museum are the few architectural and archaeological fragments gathered from local sites and churches. *Largo de São Tiago, tel. 053/ 23370. Admission: 250$00. Open Tues.–Sun. 10–12:30 and 3–6.*

From Largo de São Tiago, Rua do Anjo leads back toward the city center, eventually emerging at **Praça da República,** the square at the head of Braga's elongated central gardens. The west side of the square is arcaded, while behind it stands the dominating 14th-century tower, the **Torre de Menagem,** currently being restored.

**Time Out**   There are two inexpensive cafés in the arcade at Praça da República, either of which makes a pleasant stop. **Café Astoria** is the most elegant, with mahogany-paneled walls, mirrors, marble tables, and a molded ceiling. **Café Vianna** has been in business since 1871 and serves a wider variety of snacks. It's also a good place for breakfast and offers views of the fountain and gardens. *Both cafés open 8 AM– 11 PM.*

Many people visit Braga specifically to see the pilgrimage center of **Bom Jesus do Monte,** a 400-meter-high, densely wooded hill, 5 kilometers (3 miles) east of the city. Here, a stone staircase, started in 1723, climbs up to an 18th-century sanctuary-church, whose terrace commands wonderful views. But it's the stairway itself—a marvel of Baroque art—that is the most extraordinary attraction. Many pilgrims climb up on their knees. Fountains placed at various resting places represent the five senses and the virtues, and small chapels display a series of tableaux, with life-size figures illustrating the Stations of the Cross. If you don't want to climb up the staircase (which would be a pity!), you can take the funicular or drive up the winding road. There are restaurants, refreshment stands, and even a couple of hotels beside the sanctuary at the top. On weekends the area is popular with local families, who come here to picnic. Buses run every half hour from the center of Braga. *Funicular: 50$00.*

From Braga you can follow the N103 due west to the small market **27** town of **Barcelos,** 20 kilometers (12 miles) away. Attractively situated on the banks of the Rio Cávado, Barcelos is the center of a flourishing handicrafts industry, particularly ceramics and wooden toys and models. It pays to come here if you plan to carry home a host of souvenirs. Unquestionably, the best time to visit is during the famous weekly **Feira de Barcelos** (Barcelos Market), a vast affair—the largest in the country— held every Thursday in the central Campo da República starting very early in the morning. Stalls appear overnight, and on market day the square resembles a small city, with rows of covered stalls selling mounds of vegetables, fruits, fresh bread and cakes, clothes, shoes, ceramics, leather, kitchen equipment, and almost anything else you can think of. At times, when the early mist rises off the ground and the cries of the vendors echo across the square, it seems almost medieval. This is the place to buy traditional Barcelos ceramics (brown pottery with yellow and white decoration) as well as more workaday earthenware, baskets, rugs, and figurines. From the Campo da República, Rua Dom António Barroso leads down through the old town toward the river. On the left, the former medieval town tower now houses the tourist office and the excellent **Centro Artesanato** (Artesan's Center), which brings together some of the best local handicrafts at very reasonable prices. Ceramic dishes and bowls, often signed with the artist's name, are a good buy. Figurines, too, are popular, though none approach the individuality of those made by the late Rosa Ramalho, a local potter whose work first made famous the ceramics of Barcelos. *Largo de Porta Nova, tel. 053/811882. Open Mon.– Sat. 9–5:30.*

The river, crossed by a medieval bridge, is the most attractive part of town, shaded by overhanging trees and bordered by municipal gardens. High above the river stands the ruin of the medieval Paço dos Condes (Palace of the Counts), whose grounds constitute the **Museu Arqueologico** (Archaeological Museum). Among the empty sarcophagi and stone crosses is the 14th-century crucifix known as the *Cruzeiro do Senhor do Galo* (Cross of the Gentleman of the Cock). According to a local legend, after sentencing an innocent man to death, a judge prepared to dine on a roast fowl. When the condemned man said, "I'll be hanged if that cock doesn't crow," it flew from the table. The Barcelos cock is on sale in pottery form throughout the town; indeed, it's become almost a national symbol. *Admission free. Open daily 10–noon and 2–6.*

Barcelos is just 54 kilometers (33½ miles) north of Oporto, to which it's connected by train. The quickest way back to Oporto by car is to follow the minor N205 southwest until you reach the N13, just north of Póvoa da Varzim. However, it's also enjoyable to stop overnight in Barcelos and, after the market, to move on to Viana do Castelo, which is covered in the next tour.

## Tour 4: Costa Verde and the Minho and Lima Rivers

The coastline of Minho province, north of Oporto, is known as the **Costa Verde** (Green Coast), a largely unspoiled stretch of small towns and sandy beaches that runs all the way to the border with Spain. The weather in this northwestern region of Portugal is more inclement than elsewhere, a fact hinted at in its very name: The Costa Verde is green because it sees a disproportionate amount of rain. Summers can be cool, and swimming in the Atlantic is bracing at best. But visitors will find much of interest in a tour of the little-known region. Days spent at the coast can be alternated with trips inland to medieval towns along the lush Ria Lima, or through the historic border settlements along the Rio Minho. Most coastal towns are easily accessible by train from Oporto, and regular buses connect with the most interesting inland destinations. By car, a leisurely tour of the major points of interest could occupy three or four days.

**28** Driving north on the N13, the first beach worth noting in the Minho is at **Ofir,** on the south bank of the Rio Cávado estuary, 46 kilometers (29 miles) from Oporto. The sweeping white sands, dunes, pinewoods, and water sports have made this a popular resort in recent years. On the opposite bank of the river, **Esposende,** which also has a beach, retains elements of the small fishing village it once was. If you travel by train, you won't get to see either place, since the line runs inland at this point, passing through Barcelos (*see* Tour 3, *above*).

**29** The train rejoins the coast at **Viana do Castelo,** 25 kilometers (15½ miles) farther north. An enjoyable resort at the mouth of the Ria Lima, it has been a prosperous trading center since it received its town charter in 1258. While you shouldn't miss the excellent local beach, Praia do Cabedelo (reached by ferry from the riverside at the end of the main street), there's plenty in town to occupy an inveterate stroller. Ask at the tourist office for their English-language brochure, which includes a walking tour of the town.

Many of Viana's finest buildings date from the 16th and 17th centuries, the period of its greatest prosperity, and the town's best face is presented in the old streets and squares that radiate from the charming Praça da República. The most striking building here is the **Misericórdia,** a 16th-century almshouse whose two upper stories are supported, unusually, by tall caryatids (carved, draped female figures). The stone fountain, also Renaissance in style, harmonizes perfectly with the surrounding buildings, which include the restored town hall and its lofty arcades.

Cross the main avenue, and take a 10-minute walk west to the **Museu Municipal** (Municipal Museum), housed in one of Viana's most impressive mansions. The early 18th-century interior has been carefully preserved, and the collection of 17th-century ceramics and ornate period furniture shows how wealthy many of Viana's merchants were. A little way beyond the museum are the great ramparts of the **Castelo de São Tiago da Barra,** the 16th-century fortification that added the words "do Castelo" to the town's name and protected Viana against attack from pirates eager to share in its wealth. Outside the walls Viana holds a large market every Friday. *Museum: Largo de São Domingos, tel. 058/24223. Admission: 200$00. Open Tues.–Sun. 10–noon and 2–5.*

An *elevador* (funicular railway) behind the train station climbs to the modern basilica of **Santa Luzia,** a white, domed building overlooking the town from its wooded heights. The views from the steps of the basilica are magnificent, and a staircase to the side (marked *Zimbório*) allows access to the very top of the dome for some extraordinary coastal views. Be warned that this steep climb, up a very narrow staircase to a little viewing platform, is for the agile only. *Estrada de Santa Luzia. Funicular: Cost: 60$00; operates 10–7, every 30 min. Basilica: Open 10–noon and 2–6. Admission to dome: 50$00.*

Leaving Viana, both the train and the road (N13) continue north, following the coast, and pass a succession of small villages with delightful beaches. There are good stretches of sand at the local resorts of **Vila Praia de Âncora** and **Moledo,** but if you keep your eyes open, you'll find some side roads that lead to fairly isolated beaches.

**③** At **Caminha** you reach the Rio Minho, which forms the border with Spain. The fortified town hall on the main square once was part of Caminha's defenses. There's a 16th-century clock tower in the square, too, while the nearby **Igreja Matriz** (Parish Church) dates from a century earlier, when Caminha was an important trading port. The rich interior of the church and the surviving mansions in the surrounding streets are reminders of the town's former wealth, but by the 17th century Caminha had lost much of its business to flourishing Viana do Castelo.

**③** **Vila Nova de Cerveira,** 12 kilometers (7½ miles) farther up the river, has a medieval castle that has been converted into the luxurious, government-run Pousada de Dom Dinis (*see* Dining and Lodging, *below*). A minor ferry crossing connects to the Spanish town of Goian,
**③** but it's **Valença do Minho,** another 15 kilometers (9 miles) northeast, that is the major crossing point, with road-and-rail service to Spain. The old town of Valença is enclosed by perfectly preserved walls, which face the similarly defended Spanish town of Tuy. Strolling along the river and ramparts is very pleasant—even more so in the evening, when the day-trippers from Spain have retreated to their own side of the river. As at Vila Nova de Cerveira, Valença's fortifications contain a pousada, from which there are fine river views.

③③ Beyond Valença, the N101 leads east 16 kilometers (10 miles) to the riverside town of **Monção.** Once again, this is a fortified border settlement with a long history of skirmishes with the Spanish. In town there are the remains of a 14th-century castle, which withstood a desperate siege in 1368, when a local woman baked some small cakes with the last of the flour and sent them to the Spaniards with the message that there was plenty more where that came from. The bluff worked, the Spanish retreated, and the little cakes are still on sale in town in honor of the event. There is a spa to the east of Monção, which attracts some tourists, but the town is generally peaceful. If you stop, try a glass of the local vinho verde, a noteworthy wine available in several bars.

South of Monção the N101 traverses glorious rural countryside before descending to the valley of the Rio Vez, a tributary of the Lima.
③④ **Arcos de Valdevez,** 35 kilometers (22 miles) south of Monção, makes a nice stop. It is a typically serene little river town, where you can rent rowboats for a closer look at the surroundings.

Five kilometers (3 miles) farther south you arrive at the **Rio Lima** itself, one of the most beautiful rivers in the country. It was known to the Romans as the River of Oblivion, because its blissful beauty was said to make travelers forget their home. You may not fall into the same reverie as the Romans, but two towns along the river do make very enjoyable stops. You'll pass both if you continue south to the N203 and travel west back toward Viana do Castelo.

③⑤ At the old town of **Ponte da Barca,** the *ponte* in question is a beautiful, 10-arched bridge, built in the 15th century. At the junction of four main roads, the small town has been an important market center for centuries, and the Tuesday market here is well worth catching. On other days you can spend time quite happily walking along the riverbank.

③⑥ **Ponte de Lima,** eighteen kilometers (11 miles) down the road, is as delightful a town as you're likely to come across in the region. The graceful bridge here is of Roman origin, long and low, and open only to foot traffic; drivers cross a new concrete bridge at the edge of town. The square tower near the old bridge still stands guard over the town, while beyond, in the narrow streets, there are several fine 16th-century mansions and a busy market. Walking around town, you'll return again and again to the river, which is the real highlight of a visit. A wide beach usually displays lines of drying laundry, and a riverside avenue lined with plane trees leads down to the Renaissance church of São António. The twice-monthly Monday market, held on the riverbank, is the oldest in Portugal, dating back to 1125. On market days and during the New Fairs festival in mid-September, also held since the 12th century, you'll see the town at its effervescent best.

**Time Out** The main square by the old bridge in Ponte de Lima has a central fountain and benches and is ringed by little cafés. It's a perfect place to stop for a leisurely drink.

From Ponte de Lima you have your choice of routes. To the west lies Viana do Castelo (23 kilometers [14 miles]), Valença do Minho is to the north (38 kilometers [24 miles]), and Braga is to the south (33 kilometers [20½ miles]). Buses run to all these places from the town's bus station, by the market. To the east is Ponte da Barca, and 30 kilometers (19 miles) beyond that is the village of Lindoso, a point of entry for the Peneda-Gerês National Park (*see* National Park, below).

## Tour 5: Trás-os-Montes

The remote and beautiful region of Trás-os-Montes, in Portugal's extreme northeast, attracts very few foreign visitors. The name means "Beyond the Mountains," and though new roads have made it easier to reach in recent years, exploring the region still requires a certain sense of adventure. Great distances separate the fascinating towns, and twisting roads can drive you to the point of distraction. Medieval villages exist in a landscape that alternates between splendor and harshness, and the population, thinned by emigration, retains rural customs that have all but disappeared elsewhere. Having a car is obviously the easiest way to tour the region, but driving exclusively would mean missing out on some of the finest train journeys in the country. The trip from Oporto to Bragança provides an excellent opportunity to see the changing landscape, but it is slow going. Trains stop at every village, and the entire journey, a distance of 280 kilometers (174 miles), takes eight to nine hours.

**37** **Vila Real** is the first sizable town in the province you'll come to if traveling inland from Oporto. By train you'll need to change at Peso da Régua (*see* Tour 2, *above*) to the Corgo branch line, which ends at Vila Real. The capital of Trás-os-Montes, it is superbly situated between two mountain ranges and boasts the only significant industry in the northeast—along with which have come modern suburbs and a traffic-choked center. Still, Vila Real retains a pleasant, small-town air. Although there's no great wealth of sights, it's worth stopping in town to stroll down the attractive central avenue, which ends at a rocky promontory poking out over the gushing Rio Corgo below. A path around the church at the head of the promontory provides views of stepped terraces and green slopes. At the southern end of the avenue, a few narrow streets are filled with 17th- and 18th-century houses, their entrances decorated with coats of arms. The finest Baroque work in town is the **Capel dos Clérigos,** also called the Capela Nova (New Chapel). This is a curious fan-shape building set between two heavy columns. *Between Rua 31 de Janeiro and Rua Direita. Admission free. Open daily 10–noon and 2–6.*

An exceptional Baroque mansion built in the mid-18th century, the **Solar de Mateus** is 4 kilometers (2½ miles) east of town. Its U-shape facade with high, decorated finials at each corner (which adorns the Mateus Rosé wine label) is recognized worldwide. The building is believed to have been designed by Nasoni (architect of Oporto's Clérigos Tower), and, typically, the huge portal is approached by a double staircase. Set back to one side is the chapel, with an even more extravagant facade. The elegant interior is open to the public, as are the formal gardens, which are enhanced by a cypress tunnel, with trees trained to shade the path. *N322, Sabrosa Road, Mateus, tel. 059/323121. Admission: 450$00. Open for guided tours daily 9–1 and 2–6.*

The **Sogrape** winery, just before the mansion, offers tours of its premises. At the end of the tour, you'll have an opportunity to taste the wine and perhaps purchase a bottle. *Circuito Internacional, tel. 059/323074. Admission free. Open weekdays 10– noon and 2–5.*

The main road northeast of Vila Real (the N15) has recently been straightened for much of its length. You'll drive through exceptionally fine, high countryside; rolling, arable land continues as far as
**38** **Murça,** 40 kilometers (25 miles) away. Here you'll see the largest of the Iron Age *porcas* (stone pigs), which are found all over the region. This particular granite boar stands on a plinth in the town's central square and is presumed to be a fertility symbol.

㊴ Thirty-one kilometers (19 miles) farther northeast is **Mirandela,** midway between Vila Real and Bragança and the point at which the train route meets the road. Train travelers from Vila Real will have to return to the main line at Peso da Régua and then change at Tua, to the east, to reach Mirandela. The train runs through superb country, following the course of the Rio Tua, a tributary of the Douro. Mirandela, an attractive town, has a medieval bridge with 17 arches, but its grandest monument is the 17th-century **Palácio dos Tavoras** (Tavora Palace), right in the center of town. Its great facade has elaborate pediments and Baroque ornaments. Once the residence of the prominent Tavora family, it's now used as the town hall.

Beyond Mirandela the road passes through groves of poplars and willows before climbing into the Serra de Nogueira (Nogueira

㊵ Mountains). Eventually the great castle at **Bragança** appears in the distance. This ancient town in the very northeastern corner of Portugal has been inhabited since Celtic times (from about 600 BC). The town lent its name to the noble family of Bragança (or Braganza), whose most famous member, Catherine, married Charles II of England. Descendants of the family ruled Portugal until 1910; their tombs are contained within the church of São Vicente de Fora in Lisbon (*see* Chapter 3). Unfortunately, the approaches to Bragança have been spoiled by many ugly new buildings, since improved roads have encouraged development.

Above the modern town rises the magnificent, 12th-century **Castelo** (Castle) and a ring of battlemented walls that surrounds a perfectly preserved medieval village—one of the most thrilling sights in Trás-os-Montes. This citadel developed as the medieval community drew close to its castle for protection, and within the walls you'll find the **Domus Municipalis** (City Hall), a rare Romanesque civic building dating from the 12th century. If it's closed, the key can be obtained from one of the local cottages, as can the key to the 18th-century **Igreja de Santa Maria** (Church of Saint Mary), which has a superb painted ceiling. Another prehistoric granite boar stands below the castle tower, this one with a medieval stone pillory sprouting from its back. The tower itself, the **Torre de Menagem,** now contains a military museum that's well worth visiting. *Castle and walls always open. Tower and museum: tel. 073/22378; open daily 10–noon and 2–5.*

On your way back down to town, along this route, you'll pass the Renaissance **Igreja de São Bento,** with a fine Mudejar (Moorish-style) vaulted ceiling and a recently regilded retable. The church may or may not be open. Farther along, however, you can be assured of entry to the excellent **Museu do Abade de Baçal,** housed in Bragança's former bishop's palace. The exhibits were collected by a local priest, the Abade de Baçal, who died in 1947, and include more prehistoric pigs, ancient tombstones, some nice furniture, local costumes, fine silver, coins, and paintings—anything that caught the priest's eye. *Museum: Rua do Consilheiro Abílio Beca 27, tel. 073/ 23242. Admission: 150$00. Open Tues.–Sun. 10–12:30 and 2–5.*

Once you've seen the castle and nearby buildings, you've seen almost everything Bragança has to offer. The central cathedral is unusually small and disappointing, but the modern town center is attractive in its way, with a wide central avenue and several cafés that open onto the sidewalk in summer. You'll easily exhaust all the local sights in under a day, but it's worth staying overnight for the views of the castle from the pousada on the outskirts of town (*see* Dining and Lodging, *below*).

The N103 runs west from Bragança toward Chaves. One of the most spectacular roads in the country, it winds through bleak uplands, with the mountains of Spain to the north and the distant mass of the Serra da Estrela (Estrela Mountains) to the south. After 31 kilometers (19 miles), you'll arrive at **Vinhais,** which provides a welcome break. Its most notable sight is the great Baroque facade of the former **Convento de São Francisco** (Convent of St. Francis). Continue west on N103, and shortly before reaching Chaves, you'll see the ruins of the 13th-century **Castelo do Monforte** (Monforte Castle), built upon the site of an earlier Roman fort, a remote outpost of the great empire.

**Chaves,** 96 kilometers (59½ miles) west of Bragança, was known to the Romans as Aquae Flaviae (Flavian's Waters), in honor of the emperor Flavian. They established a military base here and popularized the town's thermal springs, which are still in use today. The impressive, 16-arch Roman bridge across the Rio Tâmega, at the southern end of town, dates from the first century AD and displays two original Roman milestones. Today Chaves is characterized most by a series of fortifications built during late-medieval times, when the city was prone to attack from all quarters. The town lies only 12 kilometers (7½miles) from the Spanish border. Its name means "keys"; whoever controlled Chaves held the keys to the north of the country.

Of the three surviving defensive structures, the most obvious landmark is the great, blunt fortress overlooking the river, the 14th-century **Torre de Menagem.** As at Bragança, this now houses a military museum, and its grounds offer views of the town. The tower is surrounded by narrow, winding streets filled with elegant houses, most of which have lovely ironwork balconies on their top floors. In Praça de Camões, the main square below the tower, the late 17th-century **Igreja da Misericórdia** is lined with huge panels of blue- and white azulejos that depict scenes from the New Testament. Adjacent to this, the **Museu da Região Flaviense** is thoroughly recommended; it contains an indiscriminate hodgepodge of local archaeological finds and relics that tell the town's history. *Tower: Largo da Câmara Municipal de Chaves, tel. 076/21965; open daily 9–noon and 2–5. Museum: open Tues.–Fri. 9:30–12:30 and 2–5, weekends 2–4:30.*

The spa buildings are contained within the **Parque Termal** (Thermal Park), below the tower and close to the river. Local legend has it that the hot water here was cast up from the entrails of the underworld, which is exactly what a mouthful tastes like, so be warned. *Largo das Termas, tel. 076/21446. Open Apr.–Oct., daily 9–5.*

At Chaves you have a choice of routes. The N2, south to Vila Real, is a glorious road down the Corgo valley. It used to be accessible by train, but that part of the Corgo branch line has been closed, leaving only the short section to the south of Vila Real (*see above*). Alternatively, you may continue west along the N103; after 35 kilometers (22 miles) you come to an enormous system of lakes and hydroelectric dams along the Rio Cávado. At this point it's possible to make a short side trip to see the ruined castle at **Montalegre,** which is visible from miles around. Take a right turn onto the N308, and drive for 12 kilometers (7½ miles). The views are worth the detour.

Back on the N103, you'll follow along the edge of the great lake system, skirting drowned valleys in an endless series of long loops. Allow plenty of time, because you're sure to want to stop often to take in the incredible views. To the north is the Peneda-Gerês National

Park; there are occasional access points along the road (*see* National Park, *below*). Finally, after passing the village of Cerdeirinhas, the road runs for 30 kilometers (19 miles) through rocky heights and down tree-clad slopes to reach Braga, where you are firmly in Minho province and back in civilization.

## What to See and Do with Children

In the north of Portugal, away from Oporto and the Costa Verde, hotels are comfortable enough, but they generally don't offer such distractions as pools and game rooms, and the distances, especially in Trás-os-Montes, require long hours in a car or on a train.

In Oporto (*see* Tour 1, *above*), children will enjoy the climb to and view from the **Torre dos Clérigos.** Have lunch in the **Cais da Ribeira district,** where you can watch the river as you eat, and then walk across the exciting **Ponte Dom Luís I bridge.** Children are usually welcome on the tours of **Vila Nova de Gaia's** port-wine lodges, which show off their huge warehouses and all sorts of interesting machinery.

The **beaches** of the Atlantic and the many northern rivers provide some great entertainment (*see* Beaches, *below*, and Tours 2 and 4, *above*). In addition to swimming, children can enjoy boating at several river towns. During the summer Amarante (*see* Tour 2, *above*) has rowboats and pedal boats for rent along a particularly beautiful stretch of river.

In a border region dotted with ancient defenses, there are plenty of **castles** to visit, some of them so complete as to provide a virtual medieval playground. The best include those at Guimarães (*see* Tour 3, *above*), Monção (*see* Tour 4, *above*), and Bragança and Chaves (*see* Tour 5, *above*). Don't miss the region's two vast ornamental staircases, good for clambering up, at the pilgrimage sights of Lamego (*see* Tour 2, *above*) and Bom Jesus do Monte (*see* Tour 3, *above*).

The busy **markets** of the Minho are fascinating, and children will love the noises and smells of a genuine local affair. All sell food, toys, and games, in addition to handicrafts and clothes. The best is the weekly market at Barcelos, but there are smaller ones at Viana do Castelo, Ponte de Lima, and Ponte da Barca (*see* Shopping, *below*).

## Off the Beaten Track

In the west of Oporto, beyond the range of the walking tour, is the **Museu Nacional de Arte Moderna** (Museum of Modern Art), run by the Gulbenkian Foundation, which administers a similar collection in Lisbon. The museum occupies the Serralves mansion, set on impressive grounds, and displays the work of a representative selection of modern Portuguese painters, sculptors, and designers. Exhibitions change constantly, and the museum closes for two weeks at a time for rehanging. Check with the tourist office for the latest information. You can take either a taxi or Bus 78, which takes 30 minutes from the town center and passes the Palácio de Cristal. *Rua de Serralves 977, tel. 02/680057. Admission: 250$00. Open Tues.–Sun. 2–8.*

Also take time to visit the **Igreja de São Martinho da Cedofeita** (Church of Saint Martin), north of the city center, near the main Av. da Boavista. It was rebuilt in the 12th century from the remains of a mid-6th-century church erected by the Suevi king Theodomir. Suevi was an early tribe, originally from Germany, that settled in northern Portugal. Some claim this is one of the oldest Christian buildings in Europe, but because of the rebuilding, points of architectural interest are few. *Cedofeita* means "built quickly," and it's assumed that the church was erected in a hurry to house the relics of Saint Martin. *Rua de Anibal Cunha, tel. 02/200–0635. Admission free. Open daily 10–noon and 2–5.*

Trás-os-Montes (*see* Tour 5, *above*) is remote to begin with, but the minor roads south of Bragança are even more isolated. The N218 leads southeast through high cultivated country to **Miranda do Douro** on the Spanish border, a winding, 84-kilometer (52-mile) journey that takes the better part of two hours. Miranda do Douro is a small town with a Renaissance cathedral and cobbled streets. It has an excellent pousada, where you can stop before crossing into Spain: Zamora is due east. Back in Portugal the N221 shadows the frontier for the 50-kilometer (31-mile) drive southwest to **Mogadouro,** formerly a border stronghold and now a market town with a 13th-century tower. Continue south for 46 kilometers (29 miles), and you'll reach the oddly named town **Freixo de Espada à Cinta** (Ash Tree of the Girded Sword), which retains a tall defensive tower and a fine parish church. Or turn off the N221 14 kilometers (9 miles) before Freixo, and take the N220 to **Torre de Moncorvo,** which surrounds an enormous church with a high, solid tower. Just to the north you can pick up the main N102, which eventually joins the N15, running between Vila Real and Bragança. Alternatively, you could wander westward through the network of minor roads that flank the Rio Douro until you reach Peso da Régua.

# Shopping

The North is an excellent region in which to shop for souvenirs, with a wide range of crafts available in many towns and villages. Oporto, of course, has the best selection of shops, but don't miss the smaller towns of the Minho, which often specialize in particular handicrafts. The region's weekly and monthly markets are also famous throughout Portugal, for here you can buy some of the best local crafts at very reasonable prices. The main post office in Oporto can help you send gifts overseas.

### Barcelos

The great Thursday **market** at Barcelos is the place to purchase ceramics, glazed figurines (including the famous Barcelos cock), basketry, and wooden toys. There's also a handicrafts center in the old town tower, which houses the tourist office. (*See* Tour 3, *above*.)

### Braga and Guimarães

In Braga, many shops in the pedestrian streets around the cathedral sell **religious artifacts,** from candles to statues. The town's weekly market is on Tuesday. Guimarães, nearby, is a center for the local **linen** industry. The linen is hand-spun and handwoven, then embroidered, all to impressive effect; it is available in local shops. Here the weekly market is on Friday.

### Oporto

New **shopping centers** are a feature of Oporto's burgeoning commercial life. One of the best, with lots of shops on several floors, is the

**Centro Comercial de Brasileira** (Av. da Boavista), in the city's northwest, or try **Centro Comercial Dallas** (Av. da Boavista 1588).

Excellent shopping can also be found in the downtown streets off the central Praça da Liberdade—particularly on Rua 31 de Janeiro, Rua dos Clérigos, Rua de Santa Catarina, Rua Sá da Bandeira, and Rua das Flores. Traditionally, Rua das Flores has been the street for **silversmiths. Pedro A. Baptista** (Rua das Flores 235) deals in antique and modern silver. **Gold-plated filigree** is also a regional specialty, and examples are numerous along the same street and along Rua de Santa Catarina. Rua 31 de Janeiro and nearby streets are the center of the **shoe** trade, and many shops make made-to-measure shoes upon request. For a general **handicrafts** emporium, try **Artesanato dos Clérigos** (Rua da Assunção 33, next to the Clérigos Tower). The **Artesanato Centro Regional de Artes Tradicionais** (Center for Traditional Arts), at Rua da Reboleira 37, in the Cais da Ribeira district, sells an excellent selection of regional arts and crafts. For a good general **market**, visit the **Bolhão** market, off Rua Sá da Bandeira (closed Sun.). There's a daily **flea market** in the streets below the cathedral, particularly lively on Calçada Vandoma.

You'll see **port** on sale throughout the city. First taste the wine at either the Solar do Vinho do Porto or the lodges at Vila Nova de Gaia (*see* Tour 1, *above*). You may want to buy a bottle of the more unusual white port, drunk chilled as an aperitif, as it's not commonly sold in the United States or Britain.

### Trás-os-Montes

Both Chaves and Bragança have locally made **ceramics.** Also in Bragança, there's a good **crafts** shop within the walls of the citadel. In Vila Real you can purchase some of the world-famous, slightly sparkling **wine** from the winery close to the Solar de Mateus (*see* Tour 5, *above*).

### Viana do Castelo

Viana is regarded as the folk capital of the region and specializes in producing traditional **embroidered costumes,** which are worn at its most important festivals. These make colorful souvenirs, though the town also sells less elaborate **crafts,** including ceramics, lace, and jewelry. The large Friday market is a good place to shop, and the tourist office also displays a nice selection.

### Vila do Conde and Póvoa de Varzim

Vila do Conde is known for its **lace** and has supported a lace-making school since the beginning of the century. The town also produces excellent hand-knit and embroidered **sweaters,** which are on sale here and in neighboring Póvoa de Varzim. An international handicrafts exhibition takes place in Vila do Conde every year, usually at the end of July.

# Sports and the Outdoors

### Participant Sports

**Canoeing** There's canoeing on the Rio Cávado near Braga. Contact the **Clube Nautico de Prado** (Prado, tel. 053/921101).

**Fishing**   Inland, especially in the northeast, fishing is a traditional leisure activity. The best freshwater fishing is in the Lima and Minho rivers, where trout can be caught. Local tourist offices can assist with fishing licenses, or contact Direção Geral dos Desportos (tel. 02/666227) in Oporto.

**Golf**   There are two golf clubs at resorts south of Oporto. The 18-hole **Oporto Golf Club** (Pedreira-Silvalde, tel. 02/722008) is 2 kilometers (1¼ miles) south of Espinho; the **Miramar Golf Club** (Praia de Miramar, tel. 02/762–2067) has nine holes and is a few kilometers farther north.

**Swimming**   Swimming pools are not standard in northern hotels, other than along the Costa Verde and in the largest of the region's other hotels. If you want to stay at a hotel with a pool, check the facilities in Dining and Lodging, *below*, and book accordingly. There are public pools in Barcelos, Braga, Bragança, Chaves, Oporto, Viana do Castelo, and Vila Real.

## Spectator Sport

**Soccer**   As in Lisbon, the main sporting obsession in Oporto is soccer, and the city has one of the country's best teams, **FC Oporto,** which rivals Lisbon's Benfica for domestic fame and fortune. Matches are played September through May at the Antas Stadium (Av. de Fernão de Magalhães, tel. 02/410–5844) in the east of the city; Buses 6, 78, and 88 run past it. The other team in the region to watch is **Guimarães,** a small soccer club that has enjoyed unexpected success in recent years.

## Beaches

Swimming in the Atlantic can be very cold, even at the height of summer, and beaches along the Costa Verde are notoriously windswept. More pleasant is river swimming in the small towns along the Lima and Minho rivers, though you should take local advice about currents and pollution before plunging in. Ponte de Lima has a particularly nice wide, sandy beach.

Espinho, south of Oporto, and the main Costa Verde resorts to the north (Póvoa de Varzim and Ofir) are the best places for watersports enthusiasts. Equipment rental is usually available at the beaches, or inquire at local tourist offices. (For details on particular ocean beaches, *see* Tours 2 and 4, *above;* for river beaches, *see* Tour 4, *above.*)

## National Park

Northeast of Braga, the 172,900-acre **Parque Nacional da Peneda-Gerês** (Peneda-Gerês National Park) was created in 1970 to preserve the diverse flora and fauna that exist in the region. Even just a short trip to the main towns and villages contained within the park shows you wild stretches of land framed by mountains, great woods and lakes, and the peaceful beauty of a region allowed to live a traditional, unmolested life.

Bordered to the north by the frontier with Spain, the park is divided into two sections: a northern area encompassing the **Serra da Peneda** (Peneda Mountains), and a southern area around the **Serra do Gerês** (Gerês Mountains). Access is free, and accommodations are concentrated mostly in the attractive spa town of **Caldas do Gerês,** in the southern section. It's a two- hour drive from Braga; turn off the N103 just after Cerdeirinhas, along the N304. (There are buses, too.) To see the northern part of the park, it's best to come from Melgaço, a small town on the Rio Minho, 25 kilometers (15½ miles) east of Monção. From Melgaço, it's 27 kilometers (17 miles) on the N202 to the village of Castro Laboreiro, at the northernmost point of the park. There's just one small hotel—and lots of fine, long-distance hiking. The central region of the park is accessible from Ponte da Barca, from which the N203 leads to Lindoso, or from Arcos de Valdevez, from which the minor N202 leads to the little village of Soajo. Both offer basic accommodations and superb hiking.

General information about the park is available at tourist offices in Oporto, Braga, and Caldas do Gerês. There's also a park information center at Caldas do Gerês, which can provide a walking map and more specific hints and help.

# Dining and Lodging

**Dining**  This chapter covers various regions, each with its own cuisine. The cooking in Oporto is rich and heavy. It is typified by the city's favorite dish, *tripas á moda do Porto* (Oporto tripe), which is made with beans, chicken, sausage, vegetables, and spices to make a heavy concoction suitable for winter. So fond are the locals of tripe that elsewhere in Portugal they're known as *tripeiros* (tripe-eaters)—a nickname earned when the city was under siege during the Napoleonic Wars and tripe was the only meat available. However, tripe doesn't dominate the menu in Oporto, and dishes tend to resemble those served in the Minho region. *Caldo verde* (literally "green soup") is ubiquitous; it's made of potato and shredded kale (cabbage) in a broth and is usually served with a slice or two of *chouriço* sausage. Fresh fish is found all the way up the coast, and every town has a local recipe for *bacalhau* (dried cod); in the Minho it's often cooked with potatoes, onions, and eggs. *Lampreias* (lampreys), oily, eel-like fish, are found in Minho rivers from February to April and are a particular specialty of Monção. Pork is the meat most often seen on menus, appearing in inventive stews and sausages, though *cabrito* (kid) is popular, too, served roasted.

In the mountains there is little fish and shellfish to offer, except for the wonderful *truta* (trout), available at any town or village close to a river. Trás-os-Montes menus are enlivened by hearty meat stews, which usually include various parts of the pig you may wish had been left out (turning up an ear or a trotter is common!). Sausages are a better bet, particularly *alheira* or chouriço, the spicy, smoked variety. The other smoked specialty of the region is *presunto de Chaves*, a delicious smoked ham from Chaves.

The wine available throughout the North is of very high quality. The Minho region is home to vinho verde, a light, slightly sparkling red or white wine that is drunk young. The taste is refreshing, both fruity and acid. Both reds and whites are served chilled (most people prefer the white), and vinho verde goes exceptionally well with fish and shellfish. Port is, of course, the most famous of the local wines (ask for *vinho do Porto*). Try a chilled white port as an aperitif. Other good regions for wine include the area around Chaves, particularly at Valpaços, which produces some excellent reds.

On the whole, restaurants in Oporto and the North offer extremely good value. Aside from a very few restaurants (noted below) dress throughout the region is informal, and reservations are usually unnecessary; often, they do not accept credit cards.

Restaurant ratings in Oporto correspond to Lisbon's dining chart, in Chapter 3; prices elsewhere correspond to the dining chart in Chapter 5, Évora and Central Portugal. Highly recommended restaurants are indicated by a star ★.

**Lodging** Most of the lodgings in the Minho and Trás-os-Montes are very reasonably priced compared to their counterparts elsewhere in the country—perhaps a reflection of the previous lack of attention paid by tourists to these regions. In Oporto, however, matters are much the same as in Lisbon, and, if at all possible, you should reserve a room well in advance to avoid disappointment. The North also hosts some of the country's most famous festivals and markets, at which times the sources of available lodging quickly dry up. For these dates (*see* The Arts and Nightlife, *below*), book rooms well in advance.

The **Turismo de Habitação** (Manor House Tourism) system allows visitors to spend time at a variety of private historic manor houses and country farms scattered throughout the Minho. Most of these converted 17th- and 18th-century buildings are found in the lovely rural areas around Ponte de Lima. You will also find manor house accommodations near Barcelos, Caminha, Guimarães, Monção, and Viana do Castelo. Reservations have to be made in advance through *Turihab* (Praça da República, 4990 Ponte de Lima, tel. 058/943327 or 058/942729, fax 058/941864), and bookings are for a minimum stay of three nights at each house. The cost includes bed and breakfast, although some manor houses will also arrange other meals on request. Full addresses and descriptions of the houses in the system are available from Turihab, and there is some information in the Ponte de Lima entry (*see below*).

Hotel ratings in Oporto correspond to Lisbon's lodging chart, in Chapter 3, and those in other towns correspond to the lodging chart in Chapter 5, Évora and Central Portugal. Highly recommended lodgings are indicated by a star ★.

**Amarante** **Zé da Calçada.** Situated on the town's narrow main street, this res-
***Dining*** taurant specializes in regional food, including a traditional baked bacalhau dish that takes the restaurant's name. Sweets and wines are local, too. A very elegant reception area leads into a comfortable dining room decorated in homey fashion; there's a fireplace, too, and a terrace that provides admirable riverside views. If you're taken with the decor, there are a few similarly turned-out, inexpensive rooms available. *Rua 31 de Janeiro, tel. 055/422023. Reservations advised. MC, V. $$$*

**Restaurante Estoril.** This simple, family-run restaurant makes a good lunch stop. It features river views from its windows and summer terrace and serves up plenty of good-value, standard Portuguese dishes. There's a short local wine list, and service is cheerful and friendly. The English-speaking owner also has some inexpensive rooms available on the other side of the river. *Rua 31 de Janeiro 49, tel. 055/431291. No credit cards. $*

***Dining and*** **Pousada de São Gonçalo.** The small, modern São Gonçalo pousada
***Lodging*** lies 16 kilometers (10 miles) east of Amarante on the road to Vila Real. Located in the Serra do Marão at an altitude of nearly 3,000 feet, it offers wonderful views. The rugged terrain outside is matched by rustic decor within, and the pousada has lovely wood furniture, a large fireplace, and tile floors. Having worked up an ap-

petite in the hills, you can count on the restaurant to satisfy you with good, hearty, regional cooking. *Curva do Lancete, Ansiães, 4600 Amarante, tel. 055/461113, fax 055/461353. 15 rooms with bath. Facilities: restaurant, bar, parking. AE, DC, MC, V. $*

**Lodging** **Hotel Navarras.** A new three-star hotel (according to the Portuguese rating system), the Navarras is part of a modern shopping complex in the center of Amarante, a five-minute walk from the river. Decor throughout is smart and up-to-date, though unexceptional, and service is competent. Given the local river pollution, which prevents swimming, perhaps the greatest attraction is the hotel's covered pool. *Rua António Carneiro, 4600, tel. 055/431036, fax 055/432991. 61 rooms with bath. Facilities: restaurant, bar, pool, shops, garage. AE. $*

**Hotel Silva.** This modest, friendly hotel lies on the road past the convent. Rooms in the back have French windows opening on a long balcony with splendid views of the river and adjacent gardens; there's also a pretty terrace for calm contemplation of the river. The interior has seen better days, though the simply furnished rooms remain comfortable, and bathrooms are functional. Breakfast is the only meal served, taken outside on the terrace in summer. *Rua Cândido dos Reis 53, 4600, tel. 055/ 423110. 21 rooms, 7 with bath. Facilities: riverside terrace. No credit cards. $*

**Barcelos** **Pensão Bagoeira.** The Bagoeira is a genuine and friendly old inn on
**Dining and** the edge of the main square, perfect for a night's rest before an early
**Lodging** visit to the Thursday market. The few large, bright rooms are indi-
★ vidually furnished, with some nice old pieces, and there's a spotless bathroom down the hall. Downstairs, the excellent country restaurant does a fast and furious business on market day, as the vendors call in for a bowl of warming soup. Dishes are prepared in full view on a huge range, with all the spluttering flames and hisses that entails. Decor is rustic to the point of parody, with a wood ceiling, great metal chandeliers, and fresh flowers at every turn. Specialties include homemade corn bread, good vegetable soup, and any number of meat and fish grills, including tasty cod steaks. *Av. Dr. Sidonio Pais 495, 4750, tel. 053/811236. 6 rooms share bath. Facilities: restaurant, bar. Restaurant reservations advised for Thurs. lunch; room reservations advised, especially for Wed. night. No credit cards. $*

**Braga** **A Ceia.** One of the city's best finds, A Ceia is a truly local haunt,
**Dining** with crowds of regulars digging into vast helpings of authentic Por-
★ tuguese food. As the restaurant fills up, service becomes frenetic, but it's always friendly and lively. Try the spit-roasted chicken platter, and save room for one of the homemade desserts; the almond cake is good. There's a short list of reasonably priced local wines. If you haven't reserved a table and don't want to wait in line, it's possible to eat diner-style at the long bar. *Rua do Raio, tel. 053/23932. Reservations advised after 8 PM Fri. and Sat. No credit cards. Closed Mon. $$*

**Restaurante Inácio.** Just outside the 18th-century town gate, the Arco da Porta Nova, this appealing restaurant emphasizes locally inspired dishes. Bacalhau is a favorite, and there's usually roasted cabrito, too. The house wine is just fine, or try one of the other local wines that appear on the decent wine list. Service in the stone-clad interior is brisk and efficient. *Campo das Hortas 4, tel. 053/513235. Reservations advised. AE, DC, MC, V. Closed Mon. $$*

**Lodging** **Hotel de Turismo.** Braga is not well endowed with hotels, and the Turismo is among the best of a rather poor selection. It's a smart high-rise on a main road, just a few minutes away from the old town. Everything is uncompromisingly modern, from the soaring lobby to the spacious rooms, whose balconies provide views of the downtown traffic. There's a comfortable bar, a good restaurant, and the bonus of a rooftop pool. *Praceta João XXI, Av. da Liberdade, 4700, tel. 053/612200, fax 053/ 612211. 132 rooms with bath. Facilities: restaurant, bar, pool, parking. AE, DC, MC, V. $$*

**Residencial Inácio Filho.** This central, old-town guest house, a two-minute walk from the cathedral, is a wonderful bargain. A friendly private home, the well-cared-for building is decorated with antiques and bric-a-brac: Bellows, old typewriters, and porcelain lie side by side on the polished wooden floors and staircase. The few, simple rooms are spotless, if rather bare. There are no facilities, but many cafés and restaurants are within easy walking distance. Be sure to reserve in advance for a summer visit. *Rua Francisco Sanches 42–2, 4700, tel. 053/23849. 8 rooms, 6 with bath. No credit cards. $*

**Bragança**
**Dining**

**La Em Casa.** This low-key but attractive, rustic town-center restaurant lies between the castle and the cathedral. It serves regional Portuguese food with—unusual this far inland—a decent menu of fish and shellfish. These are expensive, though. A more moderately priced meal can be had by picking from the extensive selection of meat dishes, and there's a particularly reasonable tourist menu available, too. *Rua Marquês de Pombal, tel. 073/22111. Reservations advised. AE, DC, MC, V. Closed Mon. $$–$$$*

**Dining and**
**Lodging**
★

**Pousada de São Bartolomeu.** Bragança's pousada is located on a hill just to the west of the town center and offers terrific views of the citadel. It's a modern building, though very comfortable; its bar and lounge feature an open fireplace and wooden furnishings. Guest rooms are rustically decorated and have scenic balconies. The pousada is a few kilometers from the town and its restaurants, but it doesn't matter, since the formal dining room is the best in Bragança. It serves fine regional mountain cooking, including good stews and game. The pousada will be closed for remodeling during the first half of 1995. *Estrada do Turismo, 5300, tel. 073/331493, fax 073/ 23453. 16 rooms with bath. Facilities: restaurant, bar, tennis court, parking. AE, DC, MC, V. $*

**Chaves**
**Dining**

**O Pote.** A little way out of town on the Bragança road, this family-run restaurant has no pretensions. It serves tasty Portuguese food to an enthusiastic local clientele. Ask about the daily specials, or order what everybody else is eating. To reach the restaurant, cross the bridge from the town center and drive for 1 kilometer (⅔ mile). The restaurant is on the right, and parking is available. *Estrada da Fronteira, tel. 076/21226. No credit cards. Closed Mon. $*

**Dining and**
**Lodging**

**Trajano.** The basement restaurant of the Hotel Trajano is a good place to try the presunto; for which the town is famous. *Truta a Transmontana* (river trout) is another good choice, served with boiled potatoes and salad. There's a reasonably priced selection of local wines to accompany your meal, which is served promptly on monogrammed plates. Such touches, and the very attentive service, more than make up for the rather subdued basement surroundings. The good service continues upstairs, where the hotel's pleasant guest rooms are decorated in Portuguese country style. *Travessa Cândido dos Reis, 5400, tel. 076/332415, fax 076/25722. 39 rooms with bath. Facilities: restaurant, bar. MC, V. $*

**Lodging**

**Hotel Aquae Flaviae.** Although it bears the ancient Roman name for Chaves, this is a brand-new, gleaming hotel, adjacent to the Parque

Termal and a cannon shot away from the town's fortified tower. It's well-equipped, and rooms are spacious and attractively decorated. The facade has an art deco touch—it looks more like an enormous movie house than a hotel—and the interior impresses with its smooth lines and polished surfaces. *Praça do Brasil, 5400, tel. 076/ 26711, fax 076/26497. 170 rooms with bath. Facilities: restaurant, bar, piano bar, garden, pool, shops, garage. AE, DC, MC, V. $$$*

**Guimarães**
*Dining and Lodging*
★

**Pousada de Santa Marinha.** Guimarães has two pousadas: This one, overlooking the town from the Penha National Park to the northwest, is one of the finest in the country. It occupies a beautifully converted 12th-century monastery, which was originally founded by the wife of Dom Afonso Henriques to honor the patron saint of pregnant women. The history contained within the building is almost tangible: Some of the attractive guest rooms used to be monks' cells; antiques from Lisbon's Ajuda Palace brighten the public rooms; and the great stone dining room (serving regional and Continental dishes) was once the monastery kitchen. *Estrada de Penha, 4800, tel. 053/514453, fax 053/514459. 51 rooms with bath. Facilities: restaurant, bar, garden, parking. AE, DC, MC, V. $$$*

**Pousada da Nossa Senhora da Oliveira.** An elegant mansion, this pousada was fashioned when various adjacent 16th- and 17th-century town houses in the center of Guimarães were remodeled. Antique reproductions throughout provide old-style atmosphere, and the service, too, is straight from the old school— courteous and efficient. Guest rooms are not particularly large, but there's compensation at hand in the superb restaurant, whose windows overlook the lovely Largo da Oliveira. A large fireplace catches the eye, and the menu features a wide range of regional Minho dishes. Even if you don't stay here, this would make a fine place for lunch while sightseeing. *Rua de Santa Maria, 4800, tel. 053/514157, fax 053/514204. 16 rooms with bath. Facilities: restaurant, bar, parking. Restaurant reservations advised. AE, DC, MC, V. $$*

**Oporto**
*Dining*
★

**O Escondidinho.** High-quality food from the Douro region, as well as a range of French-influenced dishes, is served here. Steak is prepared no less than six ways, and the sole is always good. The surroundings are engaging; the restaurant's on a central shopping street, and a tiled entrance announces its country-house decor. *Rua dos Passos Manuel 144, tel. 02/2001079. Reservations advised. AE, DC, MC, V. Closed Sun. $$$*

**Portucale.** On the top of the modern building that houses the hotel Albergaria Miradouro, the Portucale is known equally for the excellence of its food and the city-wide views from its windows. Dishes are rich, making imaginative use of local ingredients, such as tripe and game, and mountain-style cabrito is sometimes served. There's a pleasing attention to detail, typified by expert service. *Rua da Alegria 598, tel. 02/570717. Reservations required. Jacket and tie advised. AE, DC, MC, V. $$$*

★ **Casa Filha da Mãe Preta.** One of the best choices at the riverside Cais da Ribeira, this restaurant is part of the parade of tall buildings facing the river. The lovely first-floor dining room is decorated with azulejos. Reserve ahead, or arrive early enough, and you can eat by the arched windows and look across to the port-wine suburb of Vila Nova de Gaia. There's a reasonable tourist menu, and—as at every restaurant down here—any of the fish specialties is worth trying. Many dishes, including grilled sardines, come with an ample serving of rice and beans. *Cais da Ribeira 39–40, tel. 02/315515. Reservations advised for window tables. AE, DC, MC, V. Closed Sun. $$*

**Taverna do Bebobos.** A stone tavern in business since 1876, the gloomily authentic Bebobos has survived the century's floods (water levels are marked on the wall outside) to offer modern- day diners the atmosphere of a crumbling, rustic interior. There's a very pleasant upstairs dining room with views of the river. Specialties are mostly fish, though there are some meat dishes on the menu, too. Choose local wine; it comes from a cask balanced on the bar. *Cais da Ribeira 24–25, tel. 02/313565. Reservations advised. No credit cards. Closed Sun. $$*

**Tripeiro.** This is just the place to try tripe, which is nearly always on the menu in one form or another. In case you don't appreciate Oporto's favorite food, the spacious restaurant is also good for most meat dishes, and there are several bacalhau specialties, too. Along with the typically Portuguese food comes typically Portuguese decor: wooden ceiling beams, whitewashed walls, and potted plants throughout. *Rua de Passos Manuel 195, tel. 02/200–5886. AE, DC, MC, V. Closed Sun. $$*

**Majestic Café.** One of Oporto's grand old coffeehouses, the art deco Majestic doubles as a reasonably priced grill-restaurant. Sit amid the sculpted wood, carved nymphs, and mirrors, and choose from a fair list of steaks, burgers, and omelets, or just take coffee and cake. Service is brisk (and occasionally brusque), but you'll have plenty of opportunity to observe the bustling local crowd, both inside and outside on the busy pedestrian shopping street. *Rua de Santa Catarina 112, tel. 02/23387. No credit cards. Closed Sun. $*

**O Castico da Sé.** Above a bar on a steep old-town street close to the cathedral, this tiny upstairs dining room does a roaring lunchtime trade. Make a stab at the indecipherable handwritten menu, and you'll be rewarded with huge portions of grilled and stewed meat and fish, which come with salad and vegetables. The clientele is mostly local business people, who know a bargain when they see one. The stone walls, beams, and lanterns provide atmosphere, while the fine food is dispensed with little ceremony. Be prepared to wait in line at lunchtime. *Rua da Bainharia 18, no phone. No credit cards. $*

**Pedro dos Frangos.** In an area full of budget restaurants, the popular Pedro dos Frangos stands out for the quality of its barbecued chicken, which grills temptingly in the window. If you're in a hurry, sit at the bar, though it's more comfortable upstairs in the plain dining room, where ordering a *meia frango* gets you a sublime half-chicken and fries. *Rua do Bonjardim 219–223, tel. 02/200–8522. No credit cards. Closed Tues. $*

*Lodging* **Infante de Sagres.** This, Oporto's first luxury hotel built after World
★ War II, is named after the city's most famous son, Prince Henry the Navigator, and does indeed provide formal, princely service. Visiting royalty have been happy to stay here for years, and you'll be pleased by its very central location, close to Avenida dos Aliados. Public rooms are very impressively turned out, in a style closer to the 1890s than the 1990s, with a lot of carved wood. Guest rooms have less character, though all are supremely comfortable and have good marble bathrooms. *Praça D. Filipa de Lencastre 62, 4000, tel. 02/200–8101, fax 02/ 314937. 83 rooms with bath. Facilities: restaurant, bar, garden, solarium. AE, DC, MC, V. $$$$*

**Dom Henrique.** The Dom Henrique attracts business travelers who want a central base; its elegant rooms and amenities are spread throughout the 22 floors of an octagonal downtown tower. The spacious guest rooms are extremely well-appointed, and many have superb city views—as do the main restaurant and bar. While perhaps not the place for a leisurely vacation, the hotel is ideal if you require more than just the basic comforts. *Rua Guedesa Azevedo 179, 4000,* *tel. 02/200–5755, fax 02/ 201–9451. 112 rooms with bath. Facilities: restaurant, grill, bar, shops. AE, DC, MC, V. $$$*

★ **Tivoli Porto Atlântico.** This small hotel lies west of the city center, off Avenida da Boavista, in a residential suburb near the Museum of Modern Art. Part of the Lisbon-based Tivoli group, it's a quiet, relaxed base from which to tour the city and the surrounding area. The comfortable interior is unobtrusively modern. Guest rooms share a terrace and provide every little service, down to a shoe-shine kit; bathrooms are marble-clad and luxurious. Other facilities are good, including two pools (one indoor, one outdoor). A fine buffet breakfast is the only meal served, but there's an excellent French-style restaurant, the Foco, associated with and adjacent to the hotel. *Rua Afonso Lopes Vieira 66, 4100, tel. 02/694941, fax 02/ 667452. 58 rooms with bath. Facilities: restaurant, bar, 2 pools, shops, parking. AE, DC, MC, V. $$$*

**Grande Hotel do Porto.** Once Oporto's finest hotel, the Grande offers a touch of old-fashioned style at reasonable prices. It's on the city's best shopping street, and visitors are immediately impressed with its turn-of-the-century public rooms and restaurant and its efficient staff. Guest rooms were remodeled in 1993 and furnished with such mod-cons as air conditioning and satellite TV, but the hotel's ambience has been preserved. *Rua de Santa Catarina 197, 4000, tel. 02/ 200–8176, fax 02/311061. 100 rooms with bath. Facilities: restaurant, bar, parking. AE, DC, MC, V. $$*

**Hotel Peninsular.** Centrally located between São Bento Station and Praça da Liberdade, this popular small hotel has a grand tiled entrance hall, spick-and-span rooms with TV, and a modern—if slightly cheerless—bar. *Rua Sá da Bandeira 21, 4000, tel. 02/200–3012, fax 02/384984. 57 rooms with bath. Facilities: bar. AE, MC, V. $*

**Pensão Estoril.** The Estoril has been renovated in recent years and now offers compact but smart rooms at reasonable rates. It's in a quiet location near the city center and has a terrace and small garden, a bar, and parking nearby. Ask for a room with a balcony. *Rua de Cedofeita 193, 4000, tel. 02/200–2751, fax 02/208–2468. 17 rooms with bath. Facilities: bar, terrace, garden. No credit cards. $*

**Ponte de Lima**
*Dining*
**Restaurante Encanada.** Close to the old town and market, the Encanada is adjacent to the tree-lined avenue along the riverfront. A terrace provides river views. The menu is limited, but you can count on good local cooking, with dishes that depend on what's available at the market. Homemade fish cakes, with rice and salad, make a tasty, light lunch. *Praça Municipal, tel. 058/ 941189. MC, V. Closed Thurs. $$*

*Lodging*
**Turismo de Habitação.** The Ponte de Lima region is well-known for its Manor House Tourism program; the organizing body, Turihab, has its central reservations office in town (*see* the Lodging introduction, *above*). There are 26 properties in the area, mostly concentrated on the north bank of the Rio Lima. All have a limited number of rooms and have to be booked through Turihab. Ask about the early 18th-century **Paço de Calheiros,** which has lovely gardens; the 17th-century **Casa de Pomarchão** (closed Dec.–Jan.); the **Moinho de Estorãos,** a converted water mill by an old Roman bridge (open May–Sept.); and the 18th-century manor house **Casa do Outeiro.** All these are 1 kilometer–7 kilometers (⅝ mile–4 miles) from Ponte de Lima. *Facilities: usually minimal; houses may have communal lounge, bar, pool or local swimming facilities, fishing, gardens; lunch and dinner may be available on request. No credit cards. $–$$*

**Viana do Castelo**
*Dining*

**Os Tres Arcos.** This locally renowned seafood restaurant, facing the town gardens and river, is always a good bet. Sole, trout, and eel are especially recommended, and while the selection of shellfish changes according to the season, what there is sits temptingly in the window. You can eat at the bar or, more expensively, in the arched interior (the name means "The Three Arches"). *Largo João Tomás da Costa 25, tel. 058/24014. MC, V. Closed Mon. $$*

**Os Tres Potes.** The cellarlike dining room, converted from a 16th-century bakery, gets very busy in summer as people crowd in to eat to the accompaniment of the weekend folksinging and dancing sessions. Sitting at tables under stone arches or on the open-air terrace, you can choose from a fine range of regional dishes: Start with the *aperitivos regionais* (a selection of ham, spicy sausage, cheese, and olives), and move on to the house-style bacalhau. There's a good wine list, too. *Beco dos Fornos 7, off Praça da República, tel. 058/23432. Reservations required for Fri. and Sat. dinner; advised other times. MC, V. $$*

*Lodging*
★

**Hotel Santa Luzia.** Majestically situated on a wooded, rocky outcrop behind the basilica, the government-owned Santa Luzia overlooks the town and coast. A large white country mansion, it was recently renovated in sumptuous 1930s style, and the grand public rooms are a delight, as are the private gardens and terrace. There's an outdoor pool, too. Guest rooms are spacious and well-equipped, and some have a beautiful view of the sea. For location and solitude, the Santa Luzia can't be beat, but note that it's 4 kilometers (2½ miles) from the center of Viana. *Monte de Santa Luzia, 4900, tel. 058/828889 or 058/828890, fax 058/828892. 55 rooms with bath. Facilities: restaurant, bar, garden, pool, tennis courts, parking. AE, DC, MC, V. $$$*

**Vila Nova de Cerveira**
*Dining and Lodging*

**Pousada de Dom Dinis.** The pousada in Vila Nova de Cerveira makes a superb first- or last-night stop in Portugal, just 13 kilometers (8 miles) from the Spanish border at Valença. Opened in 1982, it was built inside the town's 14th-century fortified castle walls, which face the Rio Minho. Ancient, mottled buildings within the ramparts now house the guest rooms, which have been enhanced by lovely reproductions of traditional Minho furniture. Some rooms have private patios. The modern restaurant features local Minho dishes, including the popular river fish. In season, lamprey is a particular favorite. *Praça da Liberdade, 4920, tel. 051/795601, fax 051/795604. 29 rooms with bath. Facilities: restaurant, bar. AE, DC, MC, V. $$$*

**Vila Real**
*Dining*

**O Aldeão.** A popular local restaurant, the Aldeão piles its plates high with Portuguese specialties, which include a full range of meat grills. The steak comes garnished with a bit of everything and satisfies even the largest of appetites. Service is friendly, the surroundings straightforward, and the prices unbeatable for this quality and quantity of food. *Rua Dom Pedro de Castro 70, tel. 059/24794. MC, V. $*

*Lodging*

**Miracorgo.** This hotel is a rather unattractive modern block in the center of town, but its exterior can be forgiven once you've secured a room that faces the valley, with views of the dramatic stepped terraces of the Rio Corgo below. The handsome reception area, bright guest rooms, and good service add to the hotel's attractions. *Av. 1 de Maio 76–78, 5000, tel. 059/25001. 76 rooms with bath. Facilities: bar, indoor pool, health club, shops, garage. AE, DC, MC, V. $$*

# The Arts and Nightlife

## The Arts

Outside Oporto there's little in the way of concerts and artistic events to appeal to visitors, but the annual festivals of northern Portugal are vibrant and colorful affairs, perhaps more so than in any other region. Many date back hundreds of years, and the local populations display an infectious enthusiasm for the celebrations that most visitors will find hard to resist. If at all possible, try to have your trip coincide with at least one of the events noted below.

**The Minho**  At Easter, **Braga** has the country's most impressive **Semana Santa** (Holy Week) festivities—including eerie torchlit processions of hooded participants—which reach their climax on Good Friday. In June, as part of the city's **Festas de São João** (Feast of Saint John) celebration, there's a costumed procession of King David and the Shepherds and a traditional fair.

In **Guimarães,** the first week in July marks the **Festas de São Torcato,** when there's a fair and procession to the nearby village of São Torcato. The biggest celebration is the following month: The first Sunday in August sees the **Festas Gualterianas** (Festival of Saint Walter), a boisterous festival and fair that dates back to the 15th century. **Barcelos** hosts the colorful **Festas das Cruzes** (Festival of the Cross) in the first week of May, when the town is lit up by bright lights and the river illuminated by a grand fireworks display.

The most spectacular Minho festival is the **Romaria de Nossa Senhora da Agonia** (Procession and Fair of Our Lady of Sorrows), held in **Viana do Castelo** in August (over the weekend closest to the 20th) and attracting thousands of pilgrims. In addition to religious parades, there are floats, fireworks displays, traditional dancing, and music. At **Esposende** and **Ponte da Barca,** the **Festas de São Bartolomeu do Mar** (Festivals of Saint Bartholomew of the Sea) fall in the same month, August, as does **Caminha's Festas de Santa Rita de Cassia** (Festival of Saint Rita of Cassia), which features the usual processions, dancing, and fireworks. In mid-June, **Monção** celebrates the **Festa do Corpo de Deus** (Festival of Corpus Christi), which includes a symbolic battle between good and evil.

Inland, **Ponte de Lima's** highly enjoyable **Feiras Novas** (New Fair), dating back to the 12th century, is held in mid-September. It includes an enjoyable fair, a religious procession, fireworks, music, and various traditional entertainments.

**Oporto and the Douro**  **Oporto** is the place to find the more traditional arts. For concerts and recitals consult the tourist office, whose staff will advise you of events worth attending. Noted as a center for modern art, Oporto enjoys regular exhibitions at the Museum of Modern Art (*see* Off the Beaten Track, *above*), as well as at a variety of galleries, some of which are on the main Avenida da Boavista. Films in Oporto are shown in their original language; check local newspapers for current listings.

The region also has its share of festivals. Oporto's major celebration is the **Festas de São João** held on June 23–24 every year. The whole city erupts with bonfires and barbecues, and people gather to eat the traditional roast kid, washing it down with vinho verde. The local population roams the streets all night, hitting passersby on the head with, among other things, leeks and plastic hammers. There are similar, but less extensive, revels at **Vila do Conde** at the same time.

On the first weekend in June, **Amarante** hosts the **Festa de São Gonçalo** (Festival of Saint Gonçalo), when the saint is commemorated by the baking of phallus-shaped cakes, which are exchanged between unmarried men and women. Other celebrations include a fair, folk dancing, and traditional singing. The town's art museum also hosts regular exhibitions of modern art.

The pilgrimage to the shrine at **Lamego** is the centerpiece of the **Festas de Nossa Senhora dos Remedios** (Festival of Our Lady of Cures). The main religious procession, in which many pilgrims climb the staircase on their knees, is on September 8, but the festivities start at the end of August and include concerts, dancing, parades, a fair, and torchlit processions.

**Trás-os-Montes**   **Vila Real**, like many towns, has festivals in June for the "popular saints," Anthony and Peter, with fairs, music, and fireworks. **Chaves** hosts the **Feira dos Santos** at the beginning of November. It is a winter fair that emphasizes the region's rural character and attracts people from miles around. **Mirandela** holds the **Festa de São Tiago** (Festival of Saint James) at the end of July; it includes traditional dancing, games, and fireworks over the river. In August, **Bragança** celebrates its annual festival in similar style.

## Nightlife

Outside Oporto, nightlife in the region is fairly restricted. The liveliest places, with numerous bars and discos, are Braga and the coastal Minho resorts, including Viana do Castelo.

**Amarante**   Every Saturday night from July through September, the gardens of the **Casa da Calçada,** near the bridge in town, host a festival with traditional music and dancing. It starts at 8 PM, and the entrance price includes as much barbecued and buffet food as you can eat.

**Braga**   Braga has a surprisingly active nightlife for such a conservative, religious city. Its central café-bars, such as **Café Vianna** and **Café Astoria,** both in the arcaded Praça da República, are good places for a drink and are lively at any time of the day or night. **O Nosso Café** (Av. da Liberdade) is a popular bar with a late-night disco. Along the same avenue, Braga's youth also converge upon the notorious disco under the **Hotel Turismo** (Praceta João XXI). Others frequent the less trendy but enjoyable **Salsa** (Rua de Diu), a little farther down the avenue.

**Oporto**   The nicest places for an evening drink are the old-style cafés: either the **Brasileira** (Rua Sá da Bandeira 61), the **Majestic** (Rua de Santa Catarina 112), or the **Imperial** (Praça da Liberdade), all of which are open daily until around 10 PM. For a restful glass of port, the best place is the **Solar do Vinho do Porto** (Jardim do Palácio do Cristal), which is open until midnight every day except Sunday (*see* Tour 1, *above*). Livelier is **Postigo do Carvão** (Rua Fonte Taurina 26), a former warehouse in the Ribeira district converted into a fashionable bar. The **Mal Cozinhado** (Rua do Outeirinho 13, tel. 02/381319; closed Sun.) is a lively restaurant hosting traditional music and dancing, including *fado* (traditional folk music), during the summer.

Oporto has a number of good discos—for the very young and fashionable—west of the city center in the new commercial developments. In the *Centro Comercial Brasileira* (Av. da Boavista), try **Griffon's** and **Swing,** which are open until 4 AM. For a more sophisticated evening's entertainment, there are two casinos within reach of Oporto, at Espinho to the south and Póvoa de Varzim to the north (*see* Tour 2, *above*). Both are open daily throughout the year 3 PM–3 AM and feature dining, dancing, and cabaret in addition to the gaming tables. Foreign visitors must take their passports.

**Viana do Castelo** The center of Viana do Castelo is lively in the summer, and several bars and cafés cater to the mostly Portuguese tourists. The young crowd hangs out at the **Ministerio** (Rua do Tourinho 41), a fun bar with loud music. On the town beach, Praia da Cabedelo, the **Luziamar** bar and disco are popular.

# 9  Madeira

By Deborah
Luhrman

Born in the
United States,
Deborah
Luhrman
was an
award-winning
television
producer in
Los Angeles
before moving
to Madrid,
where she
writes on
business, on
food and
wine, and on
Portugal.

Madeira is a mountainous, subtropical island blanketed with colorful flowers and overflowing with waterfalls. It's warmed by Atlantic currents in winter (making swimming possible on sunny days), and cooled by trade winds in summer. Located 900 kilometers (560 miles) southwest of Lisbon, Madeira has roughly the same latitude as Casablanca. In the middle of the island is a backbone of high, rocky peaks and the crater of a now-extinct volcano. Steep-sided green ravines fan out from the center like the spokes of a wheel. Although Madeira is only 57 kilometers (35 miles) long and 22 kilometers (13 miles) wide, the distances seem much greater, as the roads climb and descend precipitously from one ravine to the next. Grouped with Madeira are: tiny Porto Santo, about 50 kilometers (30 miles) northeast, which has a popular sandy beach and only 5,000 inhabitants; the Ilhas Desertas, a chain of waterless and unpopulated islands 20 kilometers (12 miles) southeast of Madeira; and the Ilhas Selvagens, much farther south, near the Canary Islands, and also uninhabited.

Madeira was discovered and claimed for Portugal in 1419 by explorer João Gonçalves Zarco, whose statue you can see at the main intersection in Funchal, the capital. Because the uninhabited island was at that time covered with a nearly impenetrable forest, Zarco named it Madeira, which means "wood" in Portuguese. The colony gradually became populated, and in the 15th and 16th centuries grew rich from sugar plantations. After alternative sources of sugar were developed in the New World, Madeira's wine industry sustained the island's growth, and later, banana plantations prospered. More recently, tourism—which now accounts for 20% of the economy—has become big business.

Madeira displays an unmistakable air of British colonialism that dates to the 1650s and the marriage of Portuguese princess Catherine of Bragança to England's King Charles II. Charles gave Madeira an exclusive franchise to sell wine to England and all its colonies, and he granted Madeirans the same free-trade rights as English captains. The wine sales created a business boom on the island and that prosperity lured many British families to live in Funchal.

Today the British still flock to Madeira, although nowadays most visitors arrive with large tour groups; it's also a popular holiday destination for Germans and Scandinavians. And though the island has lots of sports and entertainment, it's best loved by a reserved crowd that likes to wander through gardens and sip afternoon tea. Young people seeking an action-packed vacation may be unfulfilled in Madeira. Traditionally Madeira has been a winter resort, but that has begun to change—even though the best (and most crowded) time to visit is still during Christmas week, when every tree in Funchal is decorated with lights and the main boulevard becomes an open-air folk "museum." Traditional pastimes, from making bread and pressing sugarcane to weaving and basketry, are demonstrated throughout the week. On New Year's Eve, cruise ships from all over the world pull into the harbor for an incomparable fireworks display from the hilltops surrounding Funchal. In April the Flower Festival capitalizes on Madeira's best natural resource; and in September there's the Fiesta Nossa Senhora do Monte, which commemorates the patron saint of the island.

# Essential Information

## Important Addresses and Numbers

**Tourist Information** The busy tourist office of **Madeira** (Av. Arriaga 18, Funchal, tel. 91/229057 or 91/225658; open weekdays 9–8 and weekends 9–6) dispenses maps, brochures, and up-to-date information on the constantly changing bus schedules. On the island of **Porto Santo,** a tiny tourist office (Av. Henrique Vieira de Castro, Vila Baleira, tel. 91/98-23-61) with a helpful staff attends to visitors weekdays 9–5:30 and weekends and holidays 10–12:30.

**Consulates** **United States** (Av. Luís Camões, Block D, Apt. B, Funchal, tel. 91/743808), **Great Britain** (Av. Zarco 2, 4th Floor, Funchal, tel. 91/221221).

**Emergencies** In the event of an emergency in Madeira you can dial the nationwide number **115,** or in Funchal call the **police** (tel. 91/222022), **fire department** (tel. 91/222122), or for **medical emergencies** the **Red Cross** (tel. 91/741115).

*Late-Night Pharmacies* Pharmacies are open at night and on Sunday according to a rotating schedule. Dial **166** for information.

## Arriving and Departing by Plane

**Airport and Airlines** There is no longer any regularly scheduled passenger-boat service to Madeira, so visitors must arrive by plane at the **Aeroporto Santa Catarina** (tel. 91/524941 or 91/524972), situated east of Funchal in Santa Cruz and about 35 minutes away by car. (Numerous charter flights link Funchal with most northern European capitals.) The island is also served by **TAP Air Portugal** (Av. Comunidades Madeirenses 8–10, Funchal, tel. 91/239200; Aeroporto Santa Catarina, tel. 91/524362), which makes six flights daily from Lisbon (one hour, 45 minutes) and at least four trips daily from London (four hours), and **Gibraltar Airways** (Av. Zarco 2, tel. 91/29113) has also begun nonstop service between London and Funchal, several times a week. A local charter carrier called **Air Columbus** (Aeroporto Santa Catarina, tel. 91/524001) and its Canadian affiliate **Ultra Mar Charter Corporation** (347 College St., Suite 205, Toronto, Ont. M5T 1S5, tel. 416/921–9191, fax 416/921–3443) offer flights twice a month along the Toronto–Montréal–Azores–Funchal route.

**Between Madeira and Porto Santo** *By Plane* The interisland flight to Porto Santo from Madeira provides spectacular low-altitude views of Machico and São Lorenço peninsula. **TAP** shuttles an 18-seat Dornier turboprop plane on the 15-minute flight between the islands four times daily. Tickets cost 12,000$00 round-trip, and children 2–12 pay half-fare. Reservations should be made in advance, especially for July and August.

*By Boat* The *Independência,* a sleek, 244-passenger catamaran, plies between Funchal and Porto Santo twice-daily June through September, and once a day (except Tuesday) October through May, weather permitting. The boat sails from the Funchal harbor at 8 AM for the 1½-hour voyage and heads back from Porto Santo at 5, making this a popular day trip. A round-trip ticket costs 6,800$00; children 4–12 pay half-fare. Tickets may be purchased in advance at the Funchal marina (tel. 91/227020), which is open weekdays 9–12:30 and 2–5:30 and Saturday 9–12:30, or at the dock before the boat departs. For sailings on summer weekends, it's a good idea to buy tickets in advance.

## Getting Around

**By Car** The best way to explore Madeira is by car. Although it's a small island, the terrain is steep, so bear in mind that driving can be torturously slow. For example, the drive from Funchal to Porto Moniz on the western end is only 156 kilometers (93 miles) round-trip but takes all day, as the roads twist and turn up the mountains and along terraced ravines.

Porto Santo roads are easier to handle, but the 10-kilometer-long (6-mile-long) island is so small that most visitors get around on foot or by taxi.

*Car Rentals* Most major agencies have rental offices at the Madeira airport and in Funchal, including **Hertz** (R. Ivens 12, tel. 91/226026), **Avis** (Largo António Nobre 164, tel. 91/763495 or 91/764546), **Budget** (Hotel Duas Torres, Estrada Monumental, tel. 91/765619), and **Europcar** (Aeroporto Santa Catarina, tel. 91/524633).

Car rentals on Porto Santo are handled by **Moinho** (Hotel Praia Dourada, Rua Estevádo D'Alencastre, tel. 91/982403 or 91/982780).

**By Bus** Madeira has two extensive bus systems that are frequently used by visitors and islanders. Yellow buses serve Funchal and its surrounding neighborhoods: Buses 1 and 3 run west from the city, and make stops along Estrada Monumental, where most of the hotels are located. Beige-and-red buses fan out to other points on the island. Both systems leave from an outdoor terminal at the end of Avenida do Mar, near the old town. Generally several buses a day travel to each village on the island, but schedules change constantly, so inquire at your hotel or the tourist office for departure times.

## Guided Tours

*Orientation* Travel agencies specializing in island tours abound in Funchal. Visits usually include multilingual motor-coach tours to Cabo Girādo, the inland peaks, Porto Moniz, the village of Santana; and meals or snacks in typical island restaurants. The best operators are **InterVisa** (Av. Arriaga 30, 3rd floor, tel. 91/22-83-44 or 91/25642), and **Orion** (Rua de João Gago, 2–A, tel. 91/228576).

*Special Interest* **Viva Travel** (tel. 91/922661 or 91/221751) offers a different hiking tour through the mountains every day. Levels of difficulty vary and each excursion includes something extra, such as a peek at local weavers or a stop at a hidden cave for wine tasting. **Blandy** (reservations at: Adegas de São Francisco, Av. Arriaga 28, tel. 91/220121) runs full-day excursions for wine lovers on Friday, visiting vineyards on the north side of the island, as well as the village of Santana and the Madeira Wine Lodge for extensive tastings.

In summer there are afternoon boat excursions up and down the coast from Funchal on the 130-passenger *Pirata Azul* (*Blue Pirate*). Tickets cost 3,500$00 and are available in advance at the marina boat office (tel. 91/232258 or 91/232258). Ask at the tourist office for schedules.

# Exploring Madeira

## Orientation

Madeira is a small island that receives about 300,000 tourists per year, so its attractions are heavily visited and easily accessible. The following exploring tours cover the capital city of Funchal, its environs, the western end of Madeira, the mountains, and the neighboring island of Porto Santo. Each tour begins in Funchal and can be completed in one day, although visitors who have more time may want to divide their sightseeing into smaller portions. For example, a drive to Câmara de Lobos or Ribeira Brava (Tour 3) would make a satisfying excursion from Funchal (Tour 1) for lunch and the afternoon. Be sure to allow plenty of time when driving around the island. Destinations often appear close on the map but take a long time to reach, due to winding mountain roads and slow-moving trucks.

## Highlights for First-Time Visitors

Beach at Porto Santo (*see* Tour 5)
Botanical Gardens (*see* Tour 2)
Flower and Fruit Market (*see* Tour 1)
Levada walk (*see* Tour 4)
Madeira Wine Tour (*see* Tour 1)
Pico de Arieiro and Pico Riuvo (*see* Tour 4)
Sled ride from Monte (*see* Tour 2)
Waterfalls on the road to Porto Moniz (*see* Tour 3)

## Tour 1: Funchal

*Numbers in the margin correspond to points of interest on the Madeira and Funchal maps.*

When the first colonists arrived in Madeira in July 1419, the valley they were about to settle was a mass of bright yellow fennel, or *funchal* in Portuguese. Today the bucolic fields are gone, and the city of ❶ **Funchal** is the bustling business and political center of the island. Although a number of historic buildings can be toured, the best way to get to know Funchal is to observe the activities at the waterfront, market, and city squares, daily haunts of the islanders.

❷ Our exploring tour starts at **Parque Santa Catarina,** which overlooks the harbor and Avenida Arriaga, the main street of Funchal. In spring the street is ablaze with the bright purple blossoms of the jacaranda trees that line both sides; flowers bloom in the park year-round. At the top of the gardens is a pink mansion called **Quinta Vigia,** the residence of the president of Madeira. In the center of the park rests the tiny **Capela de Santa Catarina** (Santa Catarina Chapel), built by Zarco in 1425 and one of the oldest buildings on the island.

❸ From here, descend to the **docka** (dock), where the big container ships—mostly from northern Europe—unload. Luxury cruise ships also moor here for day visits to the island. Walk east on Avenida Comunidades Madeirenses (commonly known as Avenida do Mar), the seafront boulevard. Across the street from the yacht harbor ❹ you'll pass **Palácio de São Lourenço** (St. Lawrence Palace), built in the 17th century as Madeira's first fortress and still used as a military headquarters. One more block east will bring you to the ❺ **parlamento** (parliament), which is housed in the restored 16th-cen-
❻ tury **Antigua Alfândega** (Old Customs House). From here deputies govern the island, which is part of Portugal but enjoys greater autonomy than other mainland provinces.

❼ At the traffic circle head up Rua Profetas to the **Mercado dos Lavradores** (Workers' Market). Orchids, bird-of-paradise flowers, anthuriums, and other less-exotic blooms are sold in the center patio

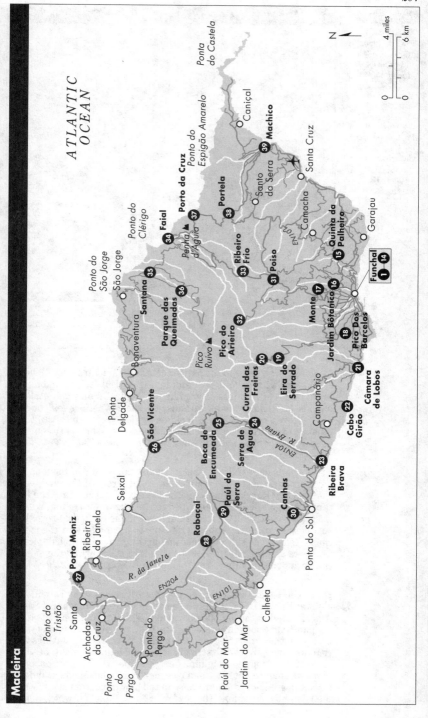

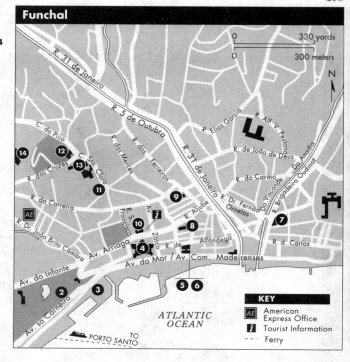

by women who dress in the native costume of Madeira—a full, home-spun skirt with yellow, red, and black vertical stripes and an em-broidered white blouse. Pyramids of tropical fruits and stalks of bananas are sold at produce stands, and the downstairs seafood mar-ket features rows of fierce-looking *espada* (soft whitefish); huge bulging eyes are caused by the change in pressure between their deep-water habitat and the sea level. *Open Sat.–Thurs. 7–2, Fri. 7 AM–8 PM.*

Cross the bridge and walk back toward the center of town on Rua Dr. Fernão Ornelas, the main commercial street of Funchal, which changes into Rua do Aljube and then to Avenida Arriaga at the 15th-century **Sé** (cathedral). Renowned for its mozarabic ceiling, with in-tricate geometric designs of inlaid ivory, the cathedral reveals an Arabic influence throughout. Be sure to have a look at the carved choir-stalls in the side entrance and in the chancel, which depict the prophets and the apostles, and the antique tilework at the side en-trance and in the belfry. *Av. Arriaga, no phone. Open daily 9–1 and 3–6.*

From the square in front, go north on Rua João Tavira and turn right at Rua do Bispo to the **Museu de Arte Sacra** (Museum of Sacred Art), located in the old bishop's house. The museum contains Flem-ish paintings, polychrome wood statues, and other religious treas-ures gathered from the island's churches. Most of the paintings were commissioned by the first merchants of Madeira, many of whom came from Brugge, Belgium. For example, the *Adoration of the Magi* was painted in 1518 for a rich merchant from Machico and paid for not in gold but in sugar. You can tell how important sugar was to the island by examining the coat of arms of Funchal, which depicts five loaves of sugar in the shape of a cross. *Rua do Bispo 21, tel. 91/ 228900. Admission: 200$00. Open Tues.–Sat. 10–1:30 and 2:30– 6:00, Sun. 10–1.*

**Time Out**  A good place to stop for coffee, afternoon tea, or a light lunch is **O Patio** (Rua da Carreira 43), a cool, tiled open-air patio. At the same address you can find Livraria Inglesa, Funchal's only English-language bookstore, where magazines, novels, and books about Portugal are sold.

🔟 Back on Avenida Arriaga be sure to tour the **São Francisco Adega du Vinho** (wine lodge), where you can see a demonstration of how the barrels are made, visit cellars where the wine is stored, and hear tales about Madeira wine. The wineries, however, are outside town and are closed to visitors. One legend has it that when the blood-thirsty duke of Clarence in 1478 was sentenced to death for plotting against his brother King Edward IV, he was given his choice of execution methods. He decided to be drowned in a "butt of malmsey," a barrel of the drink! There is plenty of time for tasting at the end of the visit. *Av. Arriaga 28, tel. 91/220121. Admission: 500$00. Tours weekdays 9–1 and 2:30–6:30, Sat. 10–2.*

⓫ Next head uphill and north three blocks on Rua São Francisco and Calçado Santa Clara. Naturalists will want to stop in at the **Museu Municipal** (City Museum) for its displays of animals found on Madeira and in its seas—including a ferocious collection of stuffed sharks. Attached is a small aquarium, where you may watch the graceful movements of an octopus and view a family of sea turtles. *Rua Mouraria 31, tel 91/229761. Admission: 65$00. Open Tues.–Fri. 10–6, weekends noon–6.*

⓬ Continue to climb Calçada Santa Clara to **Quinta das Cruzes**, a museum housed in a gracious mansion that was once the home of Zarco. The building itself is impressive, as is the collection of antique furniture inside: Of special interest are the *palanquins*—lounge chairs that were once used to carry the grand ladies of colonial Madeira around town. Outside the Quinta is a botanical garden filled with stone columns and tombstones. *Calçada do Pico 1, tel. 91/741382. Admission: 100$00. Open Tues.–Sun. 10–12:30.*

As you leave the gate, follow the wall of the Quinta to the front for a great view of Funchal. The big pink building downhill is the
⓭ **Convento de Santa Clara** (Santa Clara Convent), where Zarco is buried. Inside the church, walls are lined with ceramic tiles, giving the
⓮ sanctuary an Arabic look. You can also see the old walls of the **Fort do Pico** (Fort of the Peak), which was built in the late 1500s to protect the settlement against pirate attacks. One of the worst raids on Funchal was made in the 16th century by the pirating nobleman Bertrand de Montluc, who sacked the churches and stole barrels of Madeira. He resold the wine to his noble friends and unwittingly helped spread the reputation of the island's drink.

## Tour 2: The Funchal Environs

Although buses stop at most attractions on this tour, exploring is much easier if you drive: You won't have to return to Funchal after each sight, and you'll be able to stop at the lookouts to enjoy spectacular views along the way.

Head out of Funchal on EN101, the road to the airport. At the fork
⓯ take a left on to EN102 and follow signs toward Camacha. **Quinta da Palheiro,** also known as the Blandy Gardens, is on the right, 5 kilo-

meters (3 miles) outside the city. Here you may stroll the 30-acre estate owned by the Blandy wine family. Garden enthusiasts come here for the famous collection of camelliatrees that bloom between December and April and for the formal gardens with flowering perennials. Unfortunately, visitors are not invited to tour the big white house, in which the family lives. *Follow signs to Camacha. Admission: 450$00. Open weekdays 9:30–12:30.*

**⑯** Even more impressive is the **Jardim Botânico** (Botanical Garden), which you can reach by backtracking toward Funchal and turning uphill on Caminho do Meio. The garden, with wonderful views of the town, was opened by the government in 1960 on the grounds of the old plantation Quinta do Bom Sucesso and includes well-labeled subtropical plants from Asia, Africa, South America, and Australia; anthurium, bird-of-paradise plants, and a large cactus collection are just some examples. Be sure not to miss the petrified trunk of an ancient heather tree that was found near Curral das Freiras: It's been dated 10 million years old. A house on the grounds serves as a simple natural-history museum. *Caminho do Meio. tel. 91/226035 Admission: 300$00 adults, 100$00 children. Open daily 10–6.*

**⑰** Go back to Funchal and turn up Rua 31 de Janeiro to get to the village of **Monte** (6 kilometers/4 miles), home of one of Madeira's oddest attractions: the snowless sled ride. Before taking the plunge, stop at the white-stucco church **Nossa Senhora do Monte** (Our Lady of the Mountain). The tiny statue above the altar was found by a shepherdess in the nearby town of Terreira da Luta in the 15th century and has become the patron saint of Madeira. The small church also contains the tomb of Emperor Charles I of Austria, the last Habsburg monarch, who died here from tuberculosis in 1922 after being sent to the beneficial climate of Madeira.

**Time Out** If you need refreshment before you take part in the traditional sled ride back to Funchal, stop at the **Bar Catanha**, just uphill from the church. While sipping your beer, notice the old photos of sleds and drivers. Not much has changed over the years.

You'll recognize the sled drivers because they'll be lined up on the street where the church is and adorned in white pants, a white shirt, and goatskin boots soled with rubber tires. The sleds look like big wicker baskets on wood runners and have flowered cushions for passengers to sit on. Running alongside the sleds are two drivers, who control the vehicle with ropes as it careens over the slippery cobblestones for the 20-minute ride back to Funchal. The sled's runners are greased with lard, but if the basket starts going too fast the drivers jump on the back to slow it down; if it stalls, they push and pull until it gets going again. The life span of the sleds is only about two years, since they were first created to carry only supplies from Monte to Funchal; later, passenger sleighs were developed that could haul as many as 10 people at a time and required six drivers. Nowadays people generally take the bus or a taxi to Monte, and the sled ride back down is purely a joyride. If you've driven to Monte, however, and want to take the sled down, a taxi or bus from Funchal can bring you back up to your car.

Next, head west out of Funchal on Rua Dr. João Brito Câmara, which turns into the new highway, and go 6 kilometers (3½ miles) to
**⑱** a *miradouro* (lookout) at **Pico Dos Barcelos;** this is a fine spot from which to take pictures of the city. Continue on EN–105 and then EN–107, and follow signs to the village of Curral das Freiras. At
**⑲** **Eira do Serrado,** 16 kilometers (9½ miles) from town, park the car

and walk to the viewpoint that looks over the Grande Curral—the crater of a long-extinct volcano in the center of the island. From here Pico Riuvo and the craggy summits of central Madeira look like a granite city shimmering in the sunlight or shrouded in mist. Island legend says the peaks are the castle fortress of a virgin princess, who can be seen sleeping peacefully in the *rocha da cara* (rock face). It's said that she wanted to live in the sky like the clouds and the moon, and was so unhappy at being earthbound that her father—the volcano god—caused an earthquake that pushed the rocky cliffs high into the sky so she could live near the heavens.

**㉑** Back on the road you'll pass through a series of switchbacks and two tunnels leading down to the village of **Curral das Freiras** (Nuns' Shelter). The sisters of the Convent of Santa Clara took refuge here from bands of marauding pirates. Nearly the geographic center of Madeira, the valley sits in the middle of a circle of extinct volcanoes that long ago pushed the island up from the bottom of the sea.

## Tour 3: Western Madeira

The tour of the western part of Madeira includes the greenest and lushest part of the island: In some places you can see a dozen waterfalls spilling into a cool pine forest. The route follows the dramatic north coast, where a narrow highway clings to the cliff face, and passes under and through several more waterfalls. You can't avoid getting your car wet as you drive through the cascades.

**㉑** Begin this tour by heading west from Funchal along the coast on EN–101. You'll drive past banana plantations en route to **Câmara de Lobos,** 20 kilometers (12 miles) from the city. This impoverished fishing village was made famous by Winston Churchill, who, during a visit to Madeira in the 1950s, painted pictures of the multicolored boats and the fishermen's tiny homes. The boats are still here, pulled up onto the rocky beach during the day. You will also see women doing the wash in public fountains and bare-bellied children running riot in the narrow streets. A crumbling promenade, which protrudes from the main plaza, offers views west to Cabo Girão.

Back on the tour the uphill road reveals houses of all sizes, all of whose grounds are landscaped with flowers. It's easy to see why Madeira is called "a floating garden in the Atlantic." Ten-foot-tall poinsettias, scarlet hibiscus, bougainvillea, rhododendron, aloe, geraniums, hydrangeas, roses, sunflowers, and bird-of-paradise plants thrive in this subtropical climate, where flowers bloom year-round.

**㉒** Continue west to **Cabo Girão.** At 1,900 feet, it's one of the highest sea cliffs in the world. From here you can see ribbons of terraces carved out of even the steepest slopes and farmers daringly cultivating grapes or garden vegetables. Neither machines nor animals are used on Madeiran farms because the plots are so small and difficult to reach. Not long ago, farmers blew into conch shells as a means of communication with neighbors across the deep ravines.

**㉓** The route skirts eucalyptus and pine forests as you travel toward the town of **Ribeira Brava,** a pleasant village with a pebbly beach and a seafront fruit market, one of the sunniest spots on the island. At the town, turn right on EN–104, where the road snakes through a sheer-sided canyon. In every direction you can see high waterfalls tumbling down canyon walls and into a pine forest. Straight ahead **㉔** there are cloud-shrouded peaks. At **Serra de Agua,** 7 kilometers (4 miles) away you may notice a stone *pousada* (a state-run inn) sur-

rounded by moss-green rocks, ferns, and more waterfalls. The road
㉕ continues to climb 41 kilometers (25 miles) until it reaches the **Boca
de Encumeada** (Mouth of the Heights), where there are good views
of the north coast. Many hiking trails begin here. (*See* Hiking in
Sports and the Outdoors, *below.*)

㉖ At the town of **São Vicente,** the road joins the one-lane north-coast
highway that is chiseled out of the cliff face and is said to be one of
the most expensive road projects, per mile, ever undertaken. At the
beginning of the century, workers in baskets were suspended by
rope so they could carve out ledges and tunnels along the planned
route. Proceed with caution and make sure to sound your horn when
going around blind curves. Large tour buses constantly use this narrow road; if you happen to meet a coach, you may be forced to back up
to a turnout.

As you wind west along the coast there are a number of waterfalls
ahead: At one point the road passes behind a falls, and there's another delightful falls cascading right onto the road so you have to drive
through it. Stop at one of the viewpoints and notice the windbreaks,
made of thick mats of purple heather, that protect the terraced vineyards.

㉗ **Porto Moniz,** with its natural pools formed by ancient lava, is the
destination of nearly all visitors to this part of the island, 16 kilometers (11 miles) from São Vicente. Even though the town is such a
popular place, there's not much to do except splash around the pools
(no changing facilities), eat, and sunbathe: It's getting here that's
fun. Several large restaurants are situated along the coast and cater
to tourists.

As you drive along the winding uphill road to the viewpoint at **Santa,**
be sure to look back and see the patterns made by the heather windbreaks in the village of Porto Moniz. At the fork, turn left on EN204,
a road that crosses through Madeira's widest valley and provides a
unique perspective of both sides of the island. If you have time, take
㉘ a short detour to **Rabaçal,** a water wonderland. Madeirans love to
come here in summer to picnic alongside the cascades and quiet
pools.

㉙ Past Rabaçal the road heads into a moorland called **Paúl da Serra,**
where sheep graze and seagulls spiral above the marshes. This is the
closest thing to flatland in Madeira, and it looks strangely out of
㉚ place. Turn right on EN208, and follow signs to the town of **Canhas.**
The twisting road passes more terraced farms and houses outshone
by their bright flowering gardens and in 20 kilometers (12 miles)
joins the southern coastal road EN–101 that returns you to Funchal.

---

## Tour 4: Central Peaks and the Village of Santana

The barren high peaks of central Madeira offer spectacular views of
the island and ample opportunity for hiking. Included in this tour is
the much-photographed village of Santana with its thatch-roof, A-
frame houses.

Head out of Funchal on Rua 31 da Janeiro, which turns into EN–103
as it passes the village of Monte. The road twists and climbs through
eucalyptus groves and pine forests before it reaches a crossroads at
㉛ the town at the pass of **Poiso,** where you should turn left and follow
signs to Pico do Arieiro. This stretch travels over a barren plain
above the tree line: Watch for errant sheep and goats wandering
across the pavement on their way to graze stubbly gorse and bil-
berry.

③ **Pico do Arieiro,** at 5,963 feet, is Madeira's third-highest mountain; stop in the parking lot of the pousada and make the short climb to the lookout, where you can scan the rocky central peaks. There are views of the clouds below, and to the southeast is the Curral das Freiras crater. Look in the other direction, and try to spot the huge **Penha d'Aguia,** (Eagle Rock), that stretches up like a monolith on the north coast. The trail from the lookout that crosses the narrow ridge leads to Pico Ruivo (6,104 feet), the highest point on the island (*see* Hiking in Sports and the Outdoors, *below*). Winter days can be chilly at these heights, so there is usually an inviting fire blazing in the bar of the strategically placed pousada here.

③ Head back to Poiso and continue the scenic drive north to **Ribeiro Frio.** The landscape grows more lush on this side of the island, and the road is full of waterfalls that splash the passing cars. At Ribeiro Frio there's a **trout hatchery,** the starting point for an interesting 40-minute *levada* walk to the lookout of Balcões (*see* Hiking in Sports and the Outdoors, *below*). *Levadas* are a network of irrigation canals that crisscross the island and often flow through tunnels, bringing valuable water from the mountains to the tiny terraced farms. Some levadas were hand-chiseled in stone hundreds of years ago; they're still being built today, with the aid of modern machinery.

**Time Out**  If you need some refreshment after your hike, stop at **Victor's,** in Ribeiro Frio. Inside the rustic wood-and-glass building is a welcoming fireplace, and you can get a beer or afternoon tea and the best *bolo de mel* (spice cake) on the island.

③ Continue north on EN–103 and follow signs to **Faial;** expect the road to descend in a series of switchbacks into a deep ravine. The tiny A-frame huts that dot the terraces along the steep sides are used as barns for cows, which are never allowed to graze freely on Madeira. The prohibition was made, first, because there is not enough land for the animals to graze, and, second, because the animals could easily fall off a ledge.

③ At Faial turn left toward **Santana,** a village famous for its A-frame, thatch-roof cottages painted in bright colors. Most of these are upscale versions of traditional Madeiran homes. Sadly, this style has been replaced elsewhere on the island by nondescript concrete-
③ block houses. A road from Santana leads to **Parque das Queimadas,** where you can stop to picnic or pick up another hiking trail that approaches Pico Ruivo from a different angle.

③ Backtrack to Faial on EN–103, and from there continue east to **Porto da Cruz,** on the road that skirts the back of the landmark **Penha D'Aguia rock,** whose sheer cliffs tower over the village. Positioned in a fertile valley filled with tiny farms and gardens, the town is as pretty as any on Madeira, with its little bay and cliffs.

③ Climb again on EN–101 to **Portela,** where the view looks south over the gentler valley of Machico. From here it's an easy drive through banana plantations and sugarcane fields and into the village of
③ **Machico.**

Local folklore says the bay of Machico was discovered in 1346 by two English lovers, Robert Machin and Anne d'Arfet, who set sail from Bristol for France to escape Anne's disapproving parents. The couple's boat was thrown off course by a storm and was wrecked in this bay. After becoming ill, Anne died a few days later, and Robert then died of a broken heart. But their crew, according to legend, escaped on a raft, and news of the island made its way back to the court of the Portuguese king, who sent Zarco to investigate. When the explorer arrived he found a wood cross with the lovers' sad story, and he named the place in memory of Machin.

Explore the village church, and wander through the fishermen's quarter. From the seafront you can capture clear views of the **Ponta São Lourenço peninsula,** which sticks out into the ocean to the east. From here you can head back past the airport at Santa Cruz and return to Funchal on EN–101.

## Tour 5: Porto Santo

Beachcombers will love **Porto Santo,** some 50 kilometers (30 miles) northeast of Madeira. The tiny island is very dry and measures only 11 kilometers (6½ miles) by 6 kilometers (3½ miles), and its wide, sandy beach runs along the entire south coast—perfect for long walks in the surf. The rest of the island has little to offer, however, and remains refreshingly underdeveloped. It once supported many farms, but a severe drought in the 1970s killed the vineyards and drove most farmers out of business. Fields now lie barren, and residents have either moved away or switched to tourism-related jobs.

Porto Santo's main village, **Vila Baleira,** is a sleepy town with cobblestone streets and whitewashed buildings. A flower-filled park extends from the center to a fishing pier that is flanked on both sides by endless beach. The park contains an idealized statue of Christopher Columbus, the most important personage in Porto Santo's history. Columbus married Isabela Moniz, daughter of Bartolomeu Perestrelo, the first governor of the island. This was before Columbus was famous, when he sailed for Portuguese merchants and simply dreamed of a shortcut to the Indies. The young couple never lived on the island, but they spent some time in Funchal.

The **Casa de Cristóvão Colombo** (Columbus Museum and Home) is in the old governor's house. Inside, lithographs illustrate the life of Columbus, and there are copies of 15 portraits of the discoverer, which prove that nobody really knows what he looked like. Ask to see the restored kitchen and bedroom in the upper part of the house. *Rua Cristóvão Colombo 12. Admission free. Open weekdays 10–12 and 2–5:30.*

Traveling counterclockwise around the island you should stop first at the scenic **Portela** viewpoint, which overlooks the harbor, the town, and the long ribbon of beach. Move on to **Serra de Foca,** where a dirt track passes old salt flats before winding down to a rocky beach popular with divers. As you continue around the island you may have to dodge goats grazing along the edges of the road.

Along the road is **Pico do Castelo,** a favorite picnic spot named in memory of the castle that once stood here to protect the town from pirates. All that remains, however, is one of the castle's four cannons. The young pine trees covering the slopes were planted by the government to help retain moisture; they're a special variety that will never grow taller than 9 feet, so the views will not be lost. From here it's an easy walk to **Pico do Facho** (1,552 feet), the highest point on the island.

A little more than 2 kilometers (1¼ miles) farther is the **Fonte da Areia** (Spring in the Sand), a spring that flows out of a sandstone cliff. Women used to come here to do their washing, but they don't now, since the water is piped into town. As you head to the southern tip of the island you'll pass several windmills in disrepair, which were once used for grinding wheat.

The next sight—**Pico dos Flores,** another lookout—is worth a trip down the bumpy dirt roads. From here you can enjoy long-distance views of Madeira and the rocky, uninhabited islet south of Porto Santo called Ilhéu de Baixo. Back on the road that runs along the beach, encroaching development becomes apparent: A handful of high-rise apartment blocks is a sign. Since there is no longer any agriculture, islanders seem anxious to sell their property. But it could be that Porto Santo's remote location will help protect it from uncontrolled growth.

### What to See and Do with Children

Younger visitors to Madeira will be enthralled by the **sled rides** down cobblestone streets from Monte (*see* Tour 2, *above*) to Funchal.

There is also an exotic-bird park just downhill from the Botanical Gardens called **Jardim dos Loiros,** where kids and their parents can see colorful tropical species from Asia, Africa, South America, and Australia. *Quinta Bom Sucesso, Funchal, tel. 91/26035. Admission: 300$00 adults, 100$00 children 6–14. Open daily 8–6.*

An imaginative playground with wood climbing equipment at the gardens of **Quinta Magnolia** is perfect for taking a break from the sightseeing circuit. *Rua Dr. Pita, Funchal, tel. 91/764598. Admission free. Open daily 9–dusk.*

# Shopping

Not many visitors to Madeira escape without purchasing some of the local products. In addition to wine (*see* Tour 1, *above*), island merchants specialize in embroidered table linens, needlepoint, basketry, and tropical flowers.

### Basketry

The wickerwork industry of Madeira is centered in the village of Camacha, where there's a large cooperative shop on the main square that sells every imaginable type of basket as well as some wicker furniture. Most of the work is done at home, and on many rural roads it's common to see men carrying huge bundles of willow branches to be used for basketry. *Open daily 10–8:30.*

### Embroidery

Thousands of local women spend their days stitching intricate flowered patterns on organdy, Irish linen, cambric, and French silks. Their handiwork decorates tablecloths, place mats, and napkins, all of which are expensive and highly prized by northern Europeans. When buying embroidery, make sure it has a lead seal attached to certify that it was made on the island and not imported from elsewhere. One of the most popular shops is **Patricio & Gouveia** (Rua do Visconde de Anadia 33, tel. 91/22928), where you can visit the upstairs factory and see the white-uniformed employees stencil patterns and check production; the actual embroidery is done by an army of women in their homes. Some of the most beautiful work can be found at the **Casa do Turista** (José S. Ribeiro 2, tel. 91/24907), near the Funchal marina.

**Needlepoint**

Needlepoint and tapestry-making were introduced to Madeira in the early part of this century by a German family. You can visit their factory, **Kiekeben Tapestries** (Rua da Carreira 194, tel. 91/22073), and buy pieces at their shop, **Bazar Maria Kiekeben** (Av. do Infante 2, tel. 91/27857), which also has a branch in Tampa, Florida.

**Flowers**

Tropical flowers, such as orchids and birds of paradise, are available boxed for shipping home from any florist. Flower stands in the market and behind the church in Funchal also sell bouquets wrapped to withstand an airplane ride home. The **Quinta Boa Visita** (Rua L. F. Albuquerque, tel. 91/220468) grows orchids and will pack them for shipping Mon.–Sat., 9–5:30.

# Sports and the Outdoors

**Fishing**

Madeira and Porto Santo are meccas for those hoping to reel in huge blue marlin, yellowfin tuna, albacore, swordfish, and dorado. The European marlin record (1,212 pounds) was set here. Fishing excursions can be arranged at the Funchal harbor through **Turipesca** (tel. 91/231063 or 91/742468) and in Porto Santo through **The Dive Center** (Rua J. G. Zarco 5, tel. 91/982162) or **Anguilla** (tel. 91/983573).

**Golf**

Golf enthusiasts have managed to carve two courses from Madeira's hillsides. The oldest club is the 27-hole **Campo de Golfe da Madeira** (Hwy. EN–102, tel. 91/552345 or 91/552356) near the airport in Santo da Serra. Somewhat closer to Funchal is the new **Palheiro Golf** (São Gonçalo, tel. 91/792116), operated by a consortium of five-star hotels. It is at the edge of the Blandy Gardens and boasts 18 holes.

**Hiking**

Walking is a favorite outdoor activity in Madeira, and you can do it among the mountain peaks or alongside the levadas (*see* Tour 3 in Exploring Madeira, *above*). The tourist office sells a book called *Landscapes of Madeira,* listing 45 hikes of varying length and difficulty. The most popular hike on the island is an 8-kilometer (5-mile) trek that departs from behind the pousada at **Pico de Arieiro** and winds along a ridge top to Pico Ruivo. The four-hour hike is of medium difficulty and provides great views of the entire island.

An easy excursion that will give you a taste of Madeira footpaths begins just north of the trout hatchery, in **Ribeiro Frio.** Follow signs to Balcões: The route includes 2 kilometers (1¼ miles) of mossy forest along the path of an old levada. From the viewpoint at Balcões the jagged peaks of central Madeira tower behind you, and there are views of villages along the north coast. The round-trip hike should take about 40 minutes.

## Horseback Riding

Horses were once a common means of transportation on Madeira, but now they're used only for pleasure. Horse rentals are available through the **Riding Club of Choupana** (reservations at Hotel Estrelicia, tel. 91/792582), in Madeira, and the **Quinta dos Profetas** (tel. 91/983165) in Porto Santo.

## Scuba Diving

Madeira is too far north for colorful tropical fish, but divers enjoy the clear, still seas of summer and report lots of interesting marine life and coral formations. A diving center at the **Carlton Hotel** (Largo António Nobre, tel. 91/934611) rents scuba gear, as does **Scorpio Divers** (Rua Gorgulho, 91/762023) at the Lido swimming complex. **The Dive Center** (Rua J. G. Zarco 5, tel. 91/982162) organizes underwater excursions and boat trips in Porto Santo.

## Swimming

Although Madeira has no sandy beaches, sea swimming is possible from access points at three hotels: the **Carlton** (*see* Lodging, *below*), the **Savoy** (Rua Imperatriz Dona Amelia 108, tel. 91/25301), and **Reid's** (*see* Lodging, *below*). Also available are two public swimming pools and sea access, slightly west of Funchal, at the **Lido Swimming Complex** (Rua Gorgulho; 170$00 adults, 50$00 children 11–17; open summer, daily 9–7, and winter, daily 9–6) and **Quinta Magnolia** (Rua Dr. Pita, tel. 91/764598, 135$00 adults, 55$00 children). The onetime British Country Club, now a public park, with beautiful views of Funchal, is open daily 9–4 and includes acres of gardens and lawns, as well as a jogging-and-fitness course and tennis courts available by reservation.

In **Porto Moniz** cement pools have been built around the rocky coastline for delightful summer wading.

When Madeirans want a sandy beach they head for **Porto Santo** (*see* Tour 5, *above*). The idyllic, undeveloped strand of soft, golden sand is 9 kilometers (5½ miles) long, and although it may get crowded close to town in summer, there are always empty stretches and quiet sand dunes. The warm ocean currents make swimming possible on sunny winter days.

# Dining and Lodging

**Dining**   There are a number of restaurants on Madeira that specialize in island cuisine, and most typical meals revolve around a deep-sea fish known as espada (in Madeira this is a soft whitefish that's like scabbard or cutlass fish; on mainland Portugal it means "swordfish"). It's served everywhere and prepared dozens of ways, from poached à la Provençal to fried with bananas. Seafood gourmets will also want to try the Portuguese version of bouillabaisse, called *caldeirada de peixes variados*, a slowly simmered combination of fish, shellfish, potatoes, onions, and olive oil. The other popular fish plate is *bifede atum*, a hearty tuna steak. Those with adventurous tastes should search out *polvo com vinagre*—a tangy octopus salad.

A favorite meal of tourists and locals alike is *espetada*, a beef shish kebab seasoned with bay leaves and butter. Traditionally it was a party dish prepared in the country over open fires, and the meat was skewered on laurel branches. Nowadays, the delicacy is served on iron skewers and is hung vertically from special stands placed in the center of each table so the kebabs are shared by all diners. Also worth trying is *milho frito* (fried cubes of savory corn pudding), a side dish native to Madeira, and a round flat bread made with sweet potatoes called *bolo de caco*.

Typically, dessert menus include bananas, papaya, *anona* (custard apples); and *maracujá* (passion fruit). Those with a sweet tooth will also enjoy bolo de mel, a spicy Christmas cake made with molasses and served with a glass of Madeira.

Madeira's wines have been enjoyed for more than 500 years and they graced the tables of Napoleon, the Russian czars, and even George Washington. It is a fortified wine served as an aperitif or with dessert, depending on its sweetness. Unlike other wines, Madeira is heated to produce its distinctive mellow flavor—a process that supposedly developed after thirsty sailors sampled the Madeira that had been shipped through equatorial heat. They discovered that it actually tasted better that way. There are four varieties of Madeira. From driest to sweetest, they are: sercial, verdelho, boal, and malmsey. For a tasty nonalcoholic drink, try *Brisa maracujá*, a sparkling passion-fruit drink.

Funchal has a variety of dining places and two restaurant rows: One is in the Old Town on Largo do Corpo Santo, and the other is between the Carlton and Casino Park hotels, on Rua Imperatriz Dona Amelia. Eating out in Funchal is a fairly formal activity, especially in hotel restaurants, where men are expected to wear suits, and reservations are always required. Village restaurants in other parts of the island are informal and generally serve huge plates of fish and vegetables at bargain prices.

Restaurant ratings correspond to Lisbon's dining chart, in Chapter 3. Highly recommended restaurants are indicated by a star ★.

**Lodging** Nearly all visitors to Madeira stay in Funchal, where a strip of hotels begins at the casino and extends westward along the sea for miles. As a general rule, the hotels closest to the casino are most expensive.

Madeiran hotels cater to package-tour operators, who offer better prices and reserve huge blocks of rooms during peak holiday-travel periods. This may be one place where do-it-yourself travelers are better off going through an agency. Christmas and New Year's is the busiest season to visit Madeira, and reservations must be made far in advance. Summer can also be crowded, especially during August, when the Portuguese take vacations.

Highly recommended lodgings are indicated by a star ★.

| Category | Cost* |
| --- | --- |
| $$$$ | over 25,000$00 |
| $$$ | 18,000$00–25,000$00 |
| $$ | 12,000$00–18,000$00 |
| $ | under 12,000$00 |

**All prices are for a standard double room for two, including tax, except during Christmas week, when rates are substantially higher.*

**Câmara de Lobos**
*Dining*

**Santo António.** To try Madeira's most authentic and delicious espetada, seek out this unassuming restaurant in the hills above Câmara de Lobos in the hamlet of Estreito near the new Funchal–Ribeira Brava highway. The big dining room is plain, with a linoleum floor and paper tablecloths, but it is cheered by the sight and smells of rows of espetadas being grilled over an open hearth. The small menu also features the typical bolo do caco bread with garlic butter. *Estreito, tel. 91/945439. Reservations advised at lunchtime, no reservations accepted on weekends. Dress: casual. MC, V. $$*

**Coral Bar.** Ignore the pleasant tables on the plaza and head upstairs to the simple rooftop terrace, where you can look out over Madeira's most famous fishing village and beyond to the spectacular cliffs of Cabo Girão. The day's catch is unloaded about a block away and served here in big earthenware bowls. Try the *peixe mista* (mixed seafood) in spicy tomato-and-mushroom sauce or the espada with fried bananas. *Largo República 2, tel. 91/942469. No reservations. Dress: casual. AE, DC, MC, V. $*

**Funchal**
*Dining*

**Les Faunes.** Named for the series of Picasso lithographs that adorns the walls, Les Faunes is the reincarnation of the famous Reid's Grill, which for decades was the epitome of Madeira dining. In 1991 Reid's Hotel (*see* Lodging, *below*) refurbished its crowning jewel with a sophisticated blue-gray decor and placed tables on two tiers so all diners can enjoy the stunning view of Funchal at night. A pianist plays romantic background music during your meal. The nouvelle menu changes daily, but expect to find such dishes as artichoke custard with sweet red-pepper sauce, carpaccio of sea bass with caviar, duck breast baked with peaches, and hot passion-fruit souffle. *Reid's Hotel, Estrada Monumental 139, tel. 91/763001. Reservations required. Jacket and tie required. AE, DC, MC, V. No lunch. $$$$*

**Casa Dos Reis.** A favorite with regular visitors to Madeira, the Casa dos Reis serves high-quality international food in a dining room reminiscent of Grandma's house. Lobster crepes, sole in lemon mustard sauce and medallions of veal sautéed in Armagnac are all among the accomplished chef's repertoire. *Rua Penha de França 6, tel. 91/225182. Reservations advised. Jacket advised. AE, DC, MC, V. $$$*

**Casa Madeirense.** Wedged into a restored house next to Reid's hotel, this restaurant has been lavishly decorated with Portuguese tile, handpainted murals, and a bar that resembles one of the thatch-roof houses of Santana. The menu leans heavily toward fresh seafood and regional dishes, which the chef likes to dress up with tropical fruits and flambé presentations. *Estrada Monumental 153, tel. 91/766700. Reservations advised. Jacket advised. AE, DC, MC, V. Closed Mon. $$$*

★ **O Celeiro.** The farmhouse decor provides a dignified atmosphere for the traditional Portuguese home cooking served at O Celeiro. A favorite for business lunches, the dining room fills up at night with a mix of tourists and local families celebrating special occasions. Among the most popular items on the menu are the Algarve-style *cataplanas*, seafood stews served in special copper-lidded pots. *Rua dos Aranhas 22, tel. 91/230622, Reservations advised. Dress: informal. MC, V. $$–$$$*

★ **Solar do F.** The emphasis here is on high-quality Portuguese dishes in an upscale atmosphere with impeccable service. Choose your dining area: a stone chamber that looks like a wine cellar, or an elegant French-provincial dining room. The restaurant, one block uphill from the Madeira Carlton hotel, is perched at the edge of an overgrown ravine, and in good weather tables are placed outside in the garden. Try the avocados stuffed with shrimp or the espada served Madeiran style, with mushrooms in a spicy tomato sauce. *Av. Luís*

*Camões 19, tel. 91/220212. Reservations advised. Jacket and tie advised. AE, DC, MC, V. $$–$$$*

★ **A Seta.** It's tacky, and the parking area is crammed with tour buses, but this hilltop restaurant situated high above Funchal serves some of the best espetada on the island. You'll share long narrow tables with other diners, while high-energy waiters dodge in and out among folk dancers and fado singers. The meat is cooked over a charcoal fire in the dining-room fireplace, then the skewers are suspended from ingenious wrought-iron hooks at each table. It's a messy meal but lots of fun. *Estrada do Livramento 80, tel. 91/743643. Reservations advised. Jacket advised. AE, DC, MC, V. Closed Wed. $$*

**Carochinha.** Amber Victorian lamps, candlelight, and lace tablecloths create the romantic atmosphere of this English-style restaurant beside the municipal gardens in the center of town. Salads are available at lunch, as well as traditional British fare such as roast beef and Yorkshire pudding. Evening diners usually go for specialties with French accents, such as duck in orange sauce and coq au vin. Afternoon tea is served weekdays 3:30–5:30. *Rua São Francisco 2A, tel. 91/223695. Reservations advised for dinner. Jacket advised. AE, DC, MC, V. Closed Sun. $$*

**Gavina's.** Beyond the Lido swimming complex, at the edge of the sea, is this unadorned seafood house with a long tradition of providing Funchal with the freshest fish and shellfish. The grim concrete exterior may be off-putting, but once inside you can choose your dinner from the seafood tank then settle down in front of long picture windows that look out over the waves. Free transportation to and from most hotels is provided on request. *Rua do Gorgulho (Praia), tel. 91/62918. No reservations. Dress: casual. AE, DC, MC, V. $$*

**Golfinho.** Owner Virgilio Gavina, a former championship swimmer and water-skier, has a passion for the sea, and it shows in his old town restaurant. Resembling the inside of a submarine, but with a beautifully polished wood interior, the dining area displays an eclectic collection of old scuba gear and brass ship-fittings. Gavina owns a fleet of three fishing boats and goes fishing whenever possible to bring his customers a wide selection of fresh seafood. In addition to the ubiquitous espada, there are usually three or four varieties of fish on the menu, often *dourada* (sea bass), red mullet, and turbot. Meat dishes are also served, including a tasty espetada. Don't miss the house special, *espadarte* (an appetizer of smoked swordfish). *Largo do Corpo Santo 21, tel. 91/226774. No reservations. Jacket advised. AE, DC, MC, V. Closed Sun. $$*

**Le Jardin.** Dine in the glass-enclosed sidewalk café or in the plant-filled dining room decorated with wrought-iron furniture. This old town restaurant is a favorite with Scandinavian visitors, who appreciate the international cuisine cooked table-side and served with panache. Pepper steak is popular, as are the bananas flambé. *Rua Don Carlos, tel. 91/222864. Reservations advised. Dress: casual. AE, MC, V. $$*

**Combatentes.** This large plain dining room behind the municipal gardens is where Funchal's businesspeople go for inexpensive daily lunch specials. You can get big portions of simple Madeiran cooking such as espada, tuna, chicken, and grilled pork chops. Dinner is also served. *Rua Ivens 1, tel. 91/221388. No reservations. Dress: casual. MC, V. $*

**Xaramba.** When young Madeirans want a break from seafood they usually head for this lively pizza place tucked behind the church in the old section of town. Individual-size pies are prepared behind a long bar as hungry customers watch. The ovens stay hot until 3 AM, and the tiny restaurant fills up late at night, so come early or be prepared to wait for a table. *Rua Portão São Tiago 11, tel. 91/229785. No reservations. Dress: casual. No credit cards. No lunch. $*

*Lodging* **Madeira Carlton.** A top-notch staff adds warmth to this 18-story beachfront high-rise 10 minutes on foot from central Funchal. Many of the guests are repeat visitors who have come here every season since the hotel opened, in 1971, and are still attracted by the friendly service and a range of sports facilities. The Carlton has a bustling lobby furnished in '70s-modern style and large bedrooms with terraces that provide sweeping views of the ocean or mountains. Ask for a room on one of the renovated floors, where carpets, draperies, and spreads are coordinated in an airy pastel color scheme and baths have been refurbished with Portuguese tile. *Largo António Nobre, 9000, tel. 91/231031, fax 91/223377. 374 rooms with bath. Facilities: 4 restaurants, 3 bars, disco, 2 saltwater pools, children's pool, tennis court, miniature golf, sailboarding, scuba-diving school, hairdresser, satellite TV. AE, DC, MC, V. $$$$*

★ **Reid's.** It's a marvelously old-fashioned and decadently luxurious hotel, with corridors that smell of furniture wax, bathwater that comes out tinted blue (from water softeners), and a bellhop who plays a chime to announce dinner each evening. For more than 100 years Reid's has been an exclusive British resort, where aristocrats and business tycoons get away from it all. Situated on a rocky point a 15-minute walk from the center of town, the hotel is surrounded by 10 acres of flowering gardens. Rooms are large, with wainscoting and pastel bargello bedspreads, and all have wide balconies with sea views. Baths include towel warmers. Cruise-ship visitors to Funchal and those staying in other hotels often stop by for afternoon tea on the terrace or a nightcap in the bar. Formal wear is advised in the dining room. *Estrada Monumental 139, 9000, tel. 91/763001, fax 91/764499. 173 rooms with bath. Facilities: 2 restaurants, bar, 2 saltwater pools, 2 tennis courts, sailboarding, waterskiing, sauna, massage. AE, MC, V. $$$$*

**Casino Park.** Part of the casino complex designed by Oscar Niemeyer, the architect of Brasilia (capital of Brazil), this hotel is a rather drab gray concrete building that sits next to what looks like a nuclear reactor but is actually the casino. Inside, the public rooms are much more pleasant and are flooded with natural light from floor-to-ceiling windows that overlook the gardens and sea. A bright orange-and-beige color scheme pervades the guest rooms. The hotel has convention facilities. *Quinta da Vigia, 9000, tel. 91/233111, fax 91/232076. 400 rooms with bath. Facilities: 2 restaurants, 2 bars, coffee shop, saltwater pool, tennis court, fitness center, sauna, Jacuzzi, satellite TV. AE, DC, MC, V. $$$*

**Eden Mar.** This seven-story inn up the street from the Lido swimming complex is one of the newest hotels to capitalize on the package-tour trade. It's a favorite with families, who settle in for long stays and appreciate the kitchenettes in each unit. The lobby is white marble, but the rest of the hotel has a homey floral-print decor. All rooms have sea views. *Rua do Gorgulho 2, 9000, tel. 91/762221, fax 91/761966. 68 two-room suites and 37 studios, all with kitchenette and bath. Facilities: restaurant, coffee shop, bar, saltwater pool, gym, sauna, squash court. AE, MC, V. $$$*

★ **Quinta do Bela Vista.** Formerly the mansion of the rich Doctor Roberto Monteiro, this hotel provides elegance and hospitality that will make you feel like you're visiting a well-to-do family friend. The Quinta, which opened in 1991, is located in the hills above Funchal and offers only four guest rooms in the original home; the downstairs has been converted into an elegant restaurant. The other rooms are arranged in two new buildings, constructed in the same gracious colonial style as the main house. All guest quarters are classically decorated with mahogany furniture, four-poster beds, and French doors that open onto the gardens. *Caminho do Avista Navios 4, 9000, tel. 91/764144, fax 91/765090. 72 rooms with bath. Facilities: restaurant, bar, pool, tennis court, gym, sauna, Jacuzzi. AE, DC, MC, V. $$$.*

**Quinta da Penha França.** Located in an unbeatable area—just above Funchal harbor—this is the place for those who prefer their resorts casual rather than glitzy. The homey, four-story white house with green shutters is surrounded by gardens and a sunny pool. Every room is slightly different, and the furnishings border on the antique. *Rua da Penha França 2, 9000, tel. 91/229087, fax 91/229261. 41 rooms with bath. Facilities: swimming pool. AE, MC, V. $$*

**Estrelicia.** Named for Madeira's exotic bird-of-paradise flower, the Estrelicia is topmost of three high-rise towers built uphill from the hotel strip. Perhaps because of its somewhat inconvenient location, the hotel is an especially good value. This Best Western accommodation has a lively waterfall in its lobby and gold bedspreads and brown leather chairs in its large, carpeted guest rooms. *Caminho Velho da Ajuda, 9000, tel. 91/765131, fax 91/761044. 148 rooms with bath. Facilities: restaurant, 2 bars, disco, saltwater pool, children's pool, tennis court, hairdresser. AE, MC, V. $*

**Hotel Madeira.** This hotel on a quiet street in central Funchal has a pleasant marble lobby and tiny rooftop pool. Rooms are basic but carpeted, and each has a balcony—some overlook the municipal gardens. *Rua Ivens 21, 9009, tel. 91/230071. 53 rooms with bath. Facilities: restaurant, bar, pool. AE, MC, V. $*

**Pico Do Arieiro**
*Dining and Lodging*

**Pousada do Arieiro.** Designed for visitors who would rather hike than sunbathe, this state-owned inn is located among Madeira's rocky peaks, high above the tree line. The exterior of the white-stucco building is bleak, but inside you'll find cozy rooms with chintz curtains and bedspreads. The dining room has spectacular views of the island and serves traditional island cooking, including good soups and espada. In winter there is usually a welcoming fire blazing in the bar. *Mailing address: Apart. 478, 9006 Funchal, tel. 91/230131, fax 91/228611. 21 rooms with bath. Facilities: restaurant. AE, MC, V. $$*

**Porto Moniz**
*Dining*

**Restaurant Orca.** This is the place to go for espada caught fresh and prepared in every way imaginable. Try it fried with orange, banana, kiwi, or passion fruit. All meals come with big servings of vegetables and rice and are served in the large, fern-filled dining room with long picture windows that overlook the rocky swimming area at the far end of Madeira. *By rocks at end of rd., tel. 91/852359. No reservations. Dress: casual. AE, MC, V. $*

**Porto Santo**
*Dining*

**Gazela.** Not far from the Campo de Cima airport, this large, modern dinner house is where islanders go for Sunday lunch or to celebrate special occasions. The menu is basic Madeiran—espada, espetada, and a delicious seafood soup. *Campo de Cima, tel. 91/984425. Reservations advised on summer weekends. Dress: casual. MC, V. $$*

**Arsénios.** Red-and-white-check tablecloths are your clue that this is the place for pizza, spaghetti, and lasagna. Portuguese specialties are also served in a rustic, comfortable dining room. *Av. Dr. Manuel Pestana Jr., tel. 91/982348. No reservations. Dress: casual. AE, MC, V. $*

**Baiana.** A covered patio serves as a combination sidewalk café and town meeting-place, as just about everybody seems to wander by in the morning for a cup of coffee. Baiana also serves sandwiches, *feijoada* (bean stew), and *carne vinho e alho* (pork marinated in wine and garlic). *Rua Dr. Nuno S. Teixeira, tel. 91/984649. No reservations. Dress: casual. No credit cards. Closes at 5. $*

**Pôr do Sol.** At the far end of the beach, near Ponta da Calheta, an island housewife makes sandwiches and fries burgers and fresh seafood in a primitive kitchen. The dining room is gleaming white and spotless, and there's a wide terrace at the beach's edge. This place has tables on the terrace and has the feel of a beach-picnic take-out restaurant but is not. *Ponta da Calheta, tel. 91/984380. No reservations. Dress: casual. No credit cards. $*

**Teodorico.** In this farmhouse restaurant, authentic espetada is the one and only dish available. It can be accompanied by carafes of the dry red wine that's produced on the island and served here. In warm weather you can eat outdoors at tables and chairs made from tree stumps; indoors you'll sit in a tiny tiled dining room with four tables and a wood-burning oven at one end. *Sera de Fora, tel. 91/982257. Reservations necessary. Dress: casual. No credit cards. No lunch. $*

*Lodging*
★
**Hotel Porto Santo.** On the beach about a 15-minute walk from town, this hotel—a member of the Forte chain—is a beachcomber's dream come true. Aside from the seemingly endless stretches of golden sand, there's a country-club atmosphere, numerous sports activities, and a library-lounge that resembles a comfortable living room. Rooms overlook the countryside instead of the beach and are heavily booked throughout August, but during spring and fall you may have the place to yourself. *Porto Santo, 9400, tel. 91/982381, fax 91/982611. 102 rooms with bath. Facilities: restaurant, bar, saltwater pool, tennis court, sailboarding, bicycle rentals, ping-pong, darts, minigolf. AE, MC, V. $$*

**Praia Dourada.** This comfortable white-stucco hotel in the middle of the village is a five-minute walk from the beach and is popular with budget-minded German and Portuguese travelers. Inside, the corridors are dark, but the carpeted rooms are bright, and there's a small pool with a sun deck. *Rua D. Estevão D'Alencastre, 9400, tel. 91/982315, fax 91/982468. 180 rooms with bath. Facilities: saltwater pool. AE, MC, V. $*

**Torre Praia Suite Hotel.** Right on the beach, a 5-minute walk from the center of town, this simple 2-story hotel was built around an old watch tower that now houses the restaurant. All rooms come with kitchenettes, and the hotel has all the amenities you really need for a relaxing holiday in the sun. *Rua Goulart Medeires, 9400, tel. 91/985292, fax 91/982487. 65 suites. Facilities: swimming pool, restaurant, coffee shop, bar, discothèque. $*

**Ribeira Brava**
*Dining*
**Agua Mar.** This restaurant, with sun umbrellas and bright blue tablecloths, has a popular beachfront setting and is frequented on the weekend by large families who drive out from Funchal to lunch here. Just about all the classic Portuguese specialties are served; the house favorite is the fresh fish and *peixe com arroz* (seafood rice). *Tel. 91/951148. No reservations. Dress: casual. MC, V. $$*

**Ribeiro Frio**
*Dining*
**Victor's Bar.** This rustic, pinewood-and-glass restaurant a few steps from the trout hatchery in the central Madeiran mountains makes the best of the local product. Trout soup, smoked trout, and grilled trout are served, and in the background is the sound of a rushing river that passes by outside the dining room. *Tel. 91/782898. No reservations. Dress: casual. No credit cards. $$*

**Santana**
*Dining*
**Quinta do Ferão.** Set amidst a newly planted vineyard with sweeping views of the sea, this restaurant opened in 1994 and has quickly become the premier draw of the north coast. Funchal residents are helicoptered here for Sunday lunches, and a hotel wing is planned for 1995. The dining room is vast and decorated with arrangements

of dried flowers and fruit. Food is a cut above the typical island fare, featuring such dishes as steak in pastry with roquefort sauce, lamb chops in thyme and honey, and prawns on a spit with avocado sauce. Local north-coast wines are served. *Achado do Gramacho, tel. 91/ 572132. Reservations advised Sunday lunch. Dress: casual. AE, DC, V, MC. $$–$$$*

**Serra de Agua**  **Pousada dos Vinháticos.** This tiny stone lodge perched on the edge of
*Dining and*  a pine forest provides accommodations for nature lovers, most of
*Lodging*  whom swear this is the most beautiful part of Madeira. Although Vinháticos is state-operated, the friendly staff gives it the feel of a private house. The interior features wood paneling and exposed stone. Madeira specialties espetada and carne vinho e alho are featured in the restaurant. *Hwy. EN–104 between Brava and Encumeada Pass, 9350, tel. 91/952344, fax 91/952148. 12 rooms with bath. Facilities: restaurant. AE, MC, V. $$*

# The Arts and Nightlife

## The Arts

**Festivals**  Madeira proudly makes the most of its folkloric traditions. No matter when you visit, there's a good chance you will see folk dances performed at a restaurant or hotel. Costumed dancers whirl to the music of a small guitarlike instrument called a *machête*, the forerunner of the ukelele. Musicians also shake a colorful pole decorated with tiny folk-dancer dolls that jangle like a tambourine. Special occasions include the weekend before Lent, when **Carnival** is celebrated throughout Funchal with processions and costume parades; the **Flower Festival**, in the last week of April, which brightens the downtown with a flower carpet, a parade, and lots of music; August 14 and 15, when the **Festival of Nossa Senhora do Monte,** the patron saint of Madeira, attracts pilgrims from all corners of the island; the last week of September, when the **Wine Harvest Festival** takes place, with plenty of singing, dancing, and wine tasting; and **New Year's Eve,** with demonstrations of traditional crafts, bands of strolling dancers and singers, thousands of lights, and spectacular fireworks launched from the hillsides surrounding Funchal.

**Theater**  The **Teatro Municipal Baltazar Diaz** (Av. Arriaga, tel. 91/220416), in Funchal, offers occasional concerts and plays. The local newspaper carries listings, but the easiest way to find out the schedule is to check posters outside the theater. Tickets can be purchased at the box office.

## Nightlife

Evening entertainment in Funchal is sedate and centers around the big hotels, which offer Las Vegas–style floor shows and bands for cheek-to-cheek dancing.

**Bars**  If you're looking to meet someone or simply to have a quiet chat against a backdrop of live jazz, the current "in" spot is the terrace-bar **Salsa Latina** (Rua Imperatriz D. Amélia 101, tel. 91/225182). For a more unusual evening's entertainment try the Japanese-style **Karaokki Bar** (Hotel do Mar, Estrada Monumental, tel. 91/761001), where would-be singing stars from the audience have a chance to show their stuff.

**Cabaret** Young entertainers perform nightly dinner shows at the **Madeira Carlton Hotel** (Largo António Nobre, tel. 91/231031) and the **Casino Park Hotel** (Quinta da Vigia, tel. 91/233111).

**Casino** Gamblers will want to try their luck in the **Casino da Madeira** (Av. do Infante, tel. 91/231121), which opens nightly at 8 and is housed in a modern building that resembles a roulette wheel.

**Discos** Funchal's elegant younger set gravitates to **Baccará** (Av. do Infante, tel. 91/231121), a postmodern disco beneath the casino, or **Vespas** (Av. Sá Carneiro 7, tel. 91/234800) a warehouse-style disco next to the docks. The over-30 crowd sometimes prefers the huge **O Farol** (Largo António Nobre, tel. 91/231031) at the Madeira Carlton Hotel, where hits from the '70s and '80s are mixed in with contemporary disco tunes.

**Fado** A steady stream of tourists fills the tables of Funchal's fado club, **Marcelino Pão y Vinho** (Travessa da Torre 22–A, tel. 91/230834). In the center of the old town, the club attracts aficionados as well as the just plain curious, who come to hear Portugal's soulful national music played each night from 9:30 until about 2AM.

# Portuguese Vocabulary

If you have reading knowledge of Spanish and/or French, you will find Portuguese easy to read. Portuguese pronunciation, however, can be somewhat tricky. Despite obvious similarities in Spanish and Portuguese spelling and syntax, the Portuguese sounds are a far cry—almost literally so—from their ostensible Spanish equivalents. Some of the main peculiarities of Portuguese phonetics are the following.

*Nasalized vowels:* if you have some idea of French pronunciation, these shouldn't give you too much trouble. The closest approach is that of the French *accent du Midi*, as spoken by people in Marseille and Provence, or perhaps an American Midwest twang will help. Try pronouncing *"an," "am," "en," "em," "in," "om," "un,"* etc., with a sustained *"ng"* sound (e.g. *"bom"-"bong,"* etc.).

Another aspect of Portuguese phonetics is the vowels and diphthongs written with the tilde: *ã, ão, ães*. The Portuguese word for *"wool," "lã,"* sounds roughly like the French word *"lin,"* with the *"-in"* resembling the *"an"* in the English word *"any,"* but nasalized. The suffix *"-tion"* on such English words as "information" becomes in Portuguese spelling *"ção,"* pronounced *"-sa-on,"* with the *"-on"* nasalized: *"Informação,"* for example. These words form their plurals by changing the suffix to *çoes*, which sounds like *"-son-ech"* (the *"ch"* here resembling a cross between the English *"sh"* and the German *"ch": hence "informações"*).

The cedilla occurring under the *"c"* serves exactly the same purpose as in French: it transforms the *"c"* into an *"ss"* sound in front of the three so-called "hard" vowels ("a," "o," and "u"): e.g., *graça, Açores, açúcar*. The letter *"c"* occurring without a cedilla in front of these three vowels automatically has the sound of "k": *pico, mercado, curto*. The letter "c" followed by "e" or "i" is always "ss," and hence needs no cedilla: *nacional, Graciosa, Terceira*.

The letter "j" sounds like the "s" in the English word "pleasure." So does "g" except when the latter is followed by one of the "hard" vowels: hence, *generoso, gigantesco, Jerónimo, azulejos, Jorge*, etc.

The spelling *"nh"* is rendered like the *"ny"* in *"canyon"*: cf. *"senhora."*

The spelling *"lh"* is somewhere in between the *"l"* and the *"y"* sounds in *"million"*: cf. *"Batalha."*

In the matter of syllabic stress, Portuguese obeys the two basic Spanish principles: (1) in words ending in a vowel, or in "n" or "s" the tonic accent falls on the next-to-the-last syllable: *fado, mercado, azulejos;* (2) in words ending in consonants other than "n" or "s," the stress falls on the last syllable: *favor, nacional*. Words in which the syllabic stress does not conform to the two above rules must be written with an acute accent to indicate the proper pronunciation: *sábado, república, politécnico*.

## Numbers

| | |
|---|---|
| 1 | um, uma |
| 2 | dois, duas |
| 3 | três |

| | |
|---|---|
| 4 | quatro |
| 5 | cinco |
| 6 | seis |
| 7 | sete |
| 8 | oito |
| 9 | nove |
| 10 | dez |
| 11 | onze |
| 12 | doze |
| 13 | treze |
| 14 | catorze |
| 15 | quinze |
| 16 | dezaseis |
| 17 | dezasete |
| 18 | dezoito |
| 19 | dezanove |
| 20 | vinte |
| 21 | vinte e um |
| 22 | vinte e dois |
| 30 | trinta |
| 40 | quarenta |
| 50 | cinquenta |
| 60 | sessenta |
| 70 | setenta |
| 80 | oitenta |
| 90 | noventa |
| 100 | cem |
| 110 | cento e dez |
| 200 | duzentos |
| 1,000 | mil |
| 1,500 | mil e quinhentos |

## Days of the Week

| | |
|---|---|
| Monday | Segunda-feira |
| Tuesday | Terça-feira |
| Wednesday | Quarta-feira |
| Thursday | Quinta-feira |
| Friday | Sexta-feira |
| Saturday | Sábado |
| Sunday | Domingo |

## Months

| | |
|---|---|
| January | Janeiro |
| February | Fevereiro |
| March | Março |
| April | Abril |
| May | Maio |
| June | Junho |
| July | Julho |
| August | Agosto |
| September | Setembro |
| October | Outubro |
| November | Novembro |
| December | Dezembro |

## Useful Phrases

| | |
|---|---|
| Do you speak English? | Fala Inglês? |
| Yes | Sim |
| No | Não |
| Please | Por favor |
| Thank you | Obrigado |
| Thank you very much | Muito obrigado |
| Excuse me, sorry | Com licença, desculpe |
| I'm sorry | Desculpe-me |
| Good morning or good day | Bom dia |
| Good afternoon | Boa tarde |
| Good evening or good night | Boa noite |
| Goodbye | Adeus |
| How are you? | Como está? |
| How do you say in Portuguese? | Como se diz em Português? |
| Tourist Office | Turismo |
| Fine | Optimo |
| Very good | Muito bem (muito bom) |
| It's all right | Está bem |
| Good luck | Felicidades (boa sorte) |
| Hello | Olá |
| Come back soon | Até breve |
| Where is the hotel? | Onde é o hotel? |
| How much does this cost? | Quanto custa? |
| How do you feel? | Como se sente? |
| How goes it? | Que tal? |
| Pleased to meet you | Muito prazer em o (a) conhecer |
| The pleasure is mine | O prazer é meu |
| I have the pleasure of introducing Mr., Miss, Mrs., or Ms. . . . | Tenho o prazer de lhe apresentar o senhor, a senhora . . . |
| I like it very much | Gosto muito |
| I don't like it | Não gosto |
| Many thanks | Muito obrigado |
| Don't mention it | De nada |
| Pardon me | Desculpe-me (Perdão) |
| Are you ready? | Está pronto? |
| I am ready | Estou pronto |
| Welcome | Seja benvindo |
| I am very sorry | Desculpe (Lastimo muito) |
| What time is it? | Que horas são? |
| I am glad to see you | Muito prazer em o (a) ver |
| I don't understand | Não entendo |
| Please speak slowly | Fale lentamente por favor |
| I understand (or) It is clear | Compreendo (or) Está claro |

| Whenever you please | Quando quizer |
|---|---|
| Please wait | Faça favor de esperar |
| Toilet | Casa de banho |
| I will be a little late | Chegarei um pouco atrasado |
| I don't know | Não sei |
| Is this seat free? | Está vago este lugar? |
| Would you please direct me to . . . ? | Por favor indique-me . . . ? |
| Where is the station, museum . . . ? | Onde é a estação, museu . . . ? |
| I am American, British | Eu sou Americano, Inglês |
| It's very kind of you | É muito amavel |
| Please sit down | Por favor sente-se |

## Sundries

| cigar, cigarette | charuto, cigarro |
|---|---|
| matches | fosforos |
| dictionary | dicionário |
| key | chave |
| razor blades | laminas de barbear |
| shaving cream | creme de barbear |
| soap | sobonete |
| map | mapa |
| tampons | tampões |
| sanitary pads | pensos higiénicos |
| newspaper | jornal |
| magazine | revista |
| telephone | telefone |
| envelopes | envelopes |
| writing paper | papel de carta |
| airmail writing paper | papel de carta de avião |
| post card | postal |
| stamps | selos |

## Merchants

| bakery | padaria |
|---|---|
| bookshop | livraria |
| butcher's | talho |
| delicatessen | charutaria |
| dry cleaner's | limpeza a seco |
| grocery | mercearia |
| hairdresser, barber | cabeleireiro, barbeiro |
| laundry | lavandaria |
| shoemaker | sapateiro |
| supermarket | supermercado |

## Emergencies/Medical

| ill, sick | doente |
|---|---|
| I am ill | estou doente |

| | |
|---|---|
| I have a fever | Tenho febre |
| My wife/husband/ child is ill | Minha mulher/marido/criança está doente |
| doctor | doutor/médico |
| nurse | enfermeira/o |
| prescription | receita |
| pharmacist/chemist | farmacia |
| Please fetch/call a doctor | Por favor, chame o doutor/medico |
| accident | acidente |
| road accident | acidente na estrada |
| Where is the nearest hospital? | Onde é o hospital mais proximo? |
| Where is the American/British Hospital? | Onde é o hospital Americano/Britanico? |
| dentist | dentista |
| X-ray | Raios-X |
| aspirin | aspirina |
| pain-killer | analgésico |
| bandage | ligadura |
| ointment for bites/stings | pomada para picadas |
| cough mixture | xarope para a tosse |
| laxative | laxativo |
| thermometer | termómetro |

## On the Move

| | |
|---|---|
| plane | avião |
| train | comboio |
| boat | barco |
| taxi | taxi |
| car | carro/automovel |
| bus | autocarro |
| seat | assento/lugar |
| reservation | reserva |
| smoking/no-smoking compartment | compartimento para fumadores/não fumadores |
| rail station | estação caminho de ferro |
| subway station | estação do Metropolitano |
| airport | aeroporto |
| harbor | estação maŕtima |
| town terminal | estação/terminal |
| shuttle bus/train | autocarro/comboio com ligação constante |
| sleeper | cama |
| couchette | beliche |
| porter | bagageiro |
| baggage/luggage | bagagem |
| baggage trolley | carrinho de bagagem |
| single ticket | bilhete de ida |
| return ticket | bilhete de ida e volta |
| first class | primeira classe |
| second class | segunda classe |
| When does the train leave? | A que horas sai o comboio? |
| What time does the train arrive at . . . ? | A que horas chega o comboio a . . . ? |

| | |
|---|---|
| When does the first/last train leave? | Quando parte o primeiro/ último comboio? |

## Hotels

| | |
|---|---|
| room | quarto |
| bed | cama |
| bathroom | casa de banho |
| bathtub | banheira |
| shower | duche |
| toilet/Men/Women | toilete/Homens/Senhoras |
| toilet paper | papel higiénico |
| pillow | almofada |
| blanket | cobertor |
| chambermaid | criada/empregada de quarto |
| breakfast | pequeno almoço |
| lunch | almoço |
| dinner | jantar |
| Do you have a single/double/ twin-bedded room? | Tem um quarto individual/ duplo/com duas camas? |
| I'd like a quiet room | Eu gostave de um quarto sossegado |
| I'd like some pillows/blankets | Gostava de mais almofadas/ cobertores |
| What time is breakfast? | A que horas é o pequeno almoço? |
| Is it served in the room? | Éi servido no quarto? |
| Come in! | Entre! |
| Are there any messages for me? | Há algum recado para mim? |
| Would you please call me a taxi? | Por favor chama-me um taxi? |
| Please take our bags to our room | Por favor leve as nossas malas para o nosso quarto |

## Dining Out

| | |
|---|---|
| menu | ementa |
| fixed-price menu | preço fixo |
| wine list | carta de vinhos |
| house wine | vinho da casa |
| waiter | criado/empregado |
| Waiter! | Faz favor! |
| bill/check | conta |

## Food/Beverages

| | |
|---|---|
| coffee | café |
| tea | chá |
| milk | leite |
| water | água |
| wine (white/red/green) | vinho (branco/tinto/verde) |
| beer | cerveja |
| fruit | fruta |

| | |
|---|---|
| apple | maça |
| peach | péssego |
| orange | laranja |
| banana | banana |
| pineapple | abacaxi |
| grapes | uvas |
| pear | pera |
| eggs | ovos |
| fish | peixe |
| seafood/shellfish | marisco |
| chicken (roasted) | frango (assado) |
| steak | filé/bife |
| suckling pig | leitão |
| sausage | chouriço |
| salad | ensalada |
| lettuce | alfâce |
| tomato | tomate |
| olives | azeitonas |
| bread | pão |
| butter | manteiga |
| cheese | queijo |
| dessert | sobremesa |
| egg custard | flan |
| cake | bolo |
| tart | tarta |
| ice cream | gelado |
| salt | sal |
| pepper | pimenta |

# Index

# Personal Itinerary

**Departure** *Date*

*Time*

**Transportation**

**Arrival** *Date*      *Time*

**Departure** *Date*      *Time*

**Transportation**

**Accommodations**

**Arrival** *Date*      *Time*

**Departure** *Date*      *Time*

**Transportation**

**Accommodations**

**Arrival** *Date*      *Time*

**Departure** *Date*      *Time*

**Transportation**

**Accommodations**

*Personal Itinerary*

**Arrival** *Date*                *Time*

**Departure** *Date*                *Time*

**Transportation**

**Accommodations**

**Arrival** *Date*                *Time*

**Departure** *Date*                *Time*

**Transportation**

**Accommodations**

**Arrival** *Date*                *Time*

**Departure** *Date*                *Time*

**Transportation**

**Accommodations**

**Arrival** *Date*                *Time*

**Departure** *Date*                *Time*

**Transportation**

**Accommodations**

# The only guide to explore a Disney World® you've never seen before:

# The one for grown-ups.

0-679-02490-5 $14.00 ($18.50 Can)

This is the only guide written specifically for the millions of adults who visit Walt Disney World® each year <u>without</u> kids. Upscale, sophisticated, packed full of facts and maps, *Walt Disney World® for Adults* provides up-to-date information on hotels, restaurants, sports facilities, and health clubs, as well as unique itineraries for adults. With *Walt Disney World® for Adults* in hand, you'll get the most out of one of the world's most fascinating, most complex playgrounds.

At bookstores everywhere, or call **1-800-533-6478**.

# Fodor's Travel Guides

*Available at bookstores everywhere, or call 1–800–533–6478, 24 hours a day.*

## U.S. Guides

Alaska

Arizona

Boston

California

Cape Cod, Martha's Vineyard, Nantucket

The Carolinas & the Georgia Coast

Chicago

Colorado

Florida

Hawaii

Las Vegas, Reno, Tahoe

Los Angeles

Maine, Vermont, New Hampshire

Maui

Miami & the Keys

New England

New Orleans

New York City

Pacific North Coast

Philadelphia & the Pennsylvania Dutch Country

The Rockies

San Diego

San Francisco

Santa Fe, Taos, Albuquerque

Seattle & Vancouver

The South

The U.S. & British Virgin Islands

USA

The Upper Great Lakes Region

Virginia & Maryland

Waikiki

Walt Disney World and the Orlando Area

Washington, D.C.

## Foreign Guides

Acapulco, Ixtapa, Zihuatanejo

Australia & New Zealand

Austria

The Bahamas

Baja & Mexico's Pacific Coast Resorts

Barbados

Berlin

Bermuda

Brittany & Normandy

Budapest

Canada

Cancún, Cozumel, Yucatán Peninsula

Caribbean

China

Costa Rica, Belize, Guatemala

The Czech Republic & Slovakia

Eastern Europe

Egypt

Euro Disney

Europe

Florence, Tuscany & Umbria

France

Germany

Great Britain

Greece

Hong Kong

India

Ireland

Israel

Italy

Japan

Kenya & Tanzania

Korea

London

Madrid & Barcelona

Mexico

Montréal & Québec City

Morocco

Moscow & St. Petersburg

The Netherlands, Belgium & Luxembourg

New Zealand

Norway

Nova Scotia, Prince Edward Island & New Brunswick

Paris

Portugal

Provence & the Riviera

Rome

Russia & the Baltic Countries

Scandinavia

Scotland

Singapore

South America

Southeast Asia

Spain

Sweden

Switzerland

Thailand

Tokyo

Toronto

Turkey

Vienna & the Danube Valley

## Special Series

**Fodor's Affordables**

Caribbean

Europe

Florida

France

Germany

Great Britain

Italy

London

Paris

**Fodor's Bed &
Breakfast and
Country Inns Guides**

America's Best B&Bs

California

Canada's Great
Country Inns

Cottages, B&Bs and
Country Inns of
England and Wales

Mid-Atlantic Region

New England

The Pacific
Northwest

The South

The Southwest

The Upper Great
Lakes Region

**The Berkeley Guides**

California

Central America

Eastern Europe

Europe

France

Germany & Austria

Great Britain &
Ireland

Italy

London

Mexico

Pacific Northwest &
Alaska

Paris

San Francisco

**Fodor's Exploring
Guides**

Australia

Boston &
New England

Britain

California

The Caribbean

Florence & Tuscany

Florida

France

Germany

Ireland

Italy

London

Mexico

New York City

Paris

Prague

Rome

Scotland

Singapore & Malaysia

Spain

Thailand

Turkey

**Fodor's Flashmaps**

Boston

New York

Washington, D.C.

**Fodor's Pocket Guides**

Acapulco

Bahamas

Barbados

Jamaica

London

New York City

Paris

Puerto Rico

San Francisco

Washington, D.C.

**Fodor's Sports**

Cycling

Golf Digest's Best
Places to Play

Hiking

The Insider's Guide
to the Best Canadian
Skiing

Running

Sailing

Skiing in the USA &
Canada

USA Today's Complete
Four Sports Stadium
Guide

**Fodor's Three-In-Ones
(guidebook, language
cassette, and phrase
book)**

France

Germany

Italy

Mexico

Spain

**Fodor's
Special-Interest
Guides**

Complete Guide to
America's National
Parks

Condé Nast Traveler
Caribbean Resort and
Cruise Ship Finder

Cruises and Ports
of Call

Euro Disney

France by Train

Halliday's New
England Food
Explorer

Healthy Escapes

Italy by Train

London Companion

Shadow Traffic's New
York Shortcuts and
Traffic Tips

Sunday in New York

Sunday in San
Francisco

Touring Europe

Touring USA:
Eastern Edition

Walt Disney World and
the Orlando Area

Walt Disney World
for Adults

**Fodor's Vacation
Planners**

Great American
Learning Vacations

Great American
Sports & Adventure
Vacations

Great American
Vacations

Great American
Vacations for Travelers
with Disabilities

National Parks and
Seashores of the East

National Parks
of the West

**The Wall Street
Journal Guides to
Business Travel**

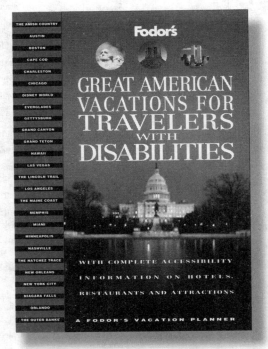